Contemporary Music *under the* Spotlight

BY DAVID W. CLOUD

WHAT YOU WILL FIND IN THIS BOOK

A definition of Contemporary Christian Music
The history of Christian rock music
What kind of music should be used in churches
The spiteful anti-fundamentalist attitude which permeates CCM
The intimate connection between end-time apostasy and CCM
Southern gospel yesterday and today
How CCM musicians love secular rock music
The ecumenicalism of Contemporary Christian Music
The close association of CCM with Roman Catholicism
The intimate connection between CCM and the Charismatic Movement
An encyclopedia of 200 CCM musicians, containing profiles of their lives and ministries, church affiliations, philosophies, ecumenical associations, music, etc.
Documentation proving that CCM is owned largely by secular corporations
Lyrics to CCM songs illustrating the vagueness and heresy of their message
CCM arguments answered (must use rock music to win young people, music is neutral, people are getting saved, God doesn't look on the outward appearance, Luther used tavern music, God created all music, Christians are not to judge, etc.)
Careful documentation of every fact presented
How to keep Contemporary Christian Music out of churches
Where Christians should draw the line with music

Contemporary Christian Music Under the Spotlight
Cloud, David W., 1949-

Copyright © 1998 by David W. Cloud

ISBN 1-58318-057-5

This material cannot be posted on BBS or Internet Web Sites

Published by
Way of Life Literature
P.O. Box 610368, Port Huron, MI 48061
866-295-4143 (toll free) • fbns@wayoflife.org (e-mail)
http://www.wayoflife.org (web site)

Canada:
Bethel Baptist Church, 4212 Campbell St. N., London, Ont. N6P 1A6
• 519-652-2619 (voice)• 519-652-0056 (fax) • info@bethelbaptist.ca (e-mail)

Printed in Canada by
Bethel Baptist Print Ministry

CONTENTS

INTRODUCTION   5

End times apostasy   6
The importance of music   9
Worshipping God in music is a Christian obligation   9
CCM is one of the most dangerous things facing Bible-believing churches   10
How does worldly music enter the churches?   11

PART I: The Characteristics & Error of Contemporary Christian Music   15

The Definition of Contemporary Christian Music   16
Characteristic #1: CCM can be identified by its unscriptural philosophy   19
Characteristic #2: CCM can be identified by its sensual rhythms   29
Characteristic #3: CCM can be identified by its ecumenism   37
Characteristic #4: CCM an be identified by its charismatic associations   61
Characteristic #5: CCM can be identified by its weak, unscriptural message   72
Characteristic #6: CCM can be identified by its worldliness   128

PART II: ANSWERS TO COMMONLY ASKED QUESTIONS   149

1. Isn't music neutral?   150
2. Isn't the sincerity of the musicians the important thing?   150
3. Isn't some of CCM acceptable? Do you condemn all of it?   151
4. What about the miracles which some CCM artists witness?   153
5. Why does traditional church music seem dull?   154
6. Can you prove a connection between rock music and African paganism?   155
7. Didn't Luther use tavern music?   160
8. Isn't the issue of music just a matter of different tastes?   162
9. Doesn't the Bible encourage us to use cymbals and loud instruments?   162
10. What is wrong with "soft rock"?   162
11. If Christian rock is demonic, why would the Devil sing about God?   164
12. Didn't God create all music?   164
13. Christians are not supposed to judge, are they?   165
14. Isn't love is more important than doctrine and standards of living?   165
15. Since God looks on the heart, why be concerned about appearance?   168
16. Isn't Christianity all about grace?   169
17. Shouldn't we use rock music to reach young people?   169
18. Making rules about music, etc., is Pharisaical legalism, isn't it?   170
19. Don't 1 Corinthians 6:12 teach that the Christian has liberty?   170
20. Doesn't the Bible encourage dancing?   172
21. Why do you say that the Charismatic movement is unscriptural?   174
22. Aren't you are hindering the ministries of CCM musicians?   174

23. What about all the young people who are being saved through CCM? 176

PART III: THE CHURCH AND ITS MUSIC   **190**

How does worldly music enter the churches? 191
Why is the music portion of many church services so lifeless? 191
How to keep Contemporary Christian Music out of the churches. 196

PART IV: DIRECTORY OF CONTEMPORARY CHRISTIAN MUSICIANS   **202**

PART V: SOUTHERN GOSPEL   **444**

PART VI: CCW MUSIC AT HOME IN LAUGHING REVIVAL   **462**

PART VII: RESOURCES AND BIBLIOGRAPHY   **468**

Helpful resources on music 469
Bibliography on Christian music 482

INTRODUCTION

My experiences with rock music

When I was converted in 1973 from a hippie lifestyle, one of the first things the Lord dealt with me about was my music. Growing up, I loved all sorts of music. I played first chair first clarinet during much of my junior and senior high school years. I took private music lessons, won first place ribbons at music competitions both for solos and as a participant in ensembles, was selected to attend a special summer music program at the University of South Florida between my 10th and 11th grades, and had an opportunity to join a symphony orchestra. I am not saying I am a music expert, but I do have a background in it.

I also immersed myself in rock music for many years before I was saved. In fact, I grew up with rock music. Born in 1949, I was alive when Elvis, Little Richard, Chuck Berry, Jerry Lee Lewis and others cooked up rock & roll in the '50s out of the ingredients of rhythm & blues, country-western, and Southern gospel and black spirituals. I wasn't old enough to know a lot about what was going on with music in the 50s, but I do remember listening to rockabilly music at the home of an elementary-school friend. We were fascinated by the new beat. Fifties rock was still popular at dances when I was in junior and senior high school. I began my teen years in 1962 and by the time I obtained my learners driving permit in 1963 the Beatles were roaring into popularity; and when I got my regular drivers license in 1965 the Rolling Stones megahit "Satisfaction" was blasting from radios, enflaming the passions of young people across the land. The year I graduated from high school, Jimi Hendrix was asking "Are You Experienced?" (referring to psychedelic drug usage) and the Doors were singing "Light My Fire." I journeyed through '60s rock and part way through '70s rock before I was saved. When I was drafted into the Army two years after high school, the Woodstock movie was sweeping the land. During the year and a half I spent in Vietnam, I was stationed at Tan Son Nhut Airbase outside of Saigon. I was a clerk in a military police unit attached to MACV headquarters, the control center for the South Vietnam U.S. military operation. We lived at the R&R out processing center, and the unit's job was to keep drugs from leaving the country on soldiers bound for R&R and in personnel containers being shipped to the States. We had access to every conceivable luxury, an Olympic-sized swimming pool, tennis courts, racket ball, gym, movie theater, night clubs, photo processing labs, you name it. I even had frequent use of a jeep for trips to Saigon. One of the facilities I used extensively was the reel to reel recording rooms. The Army had a massive library of music, and soldiers who lived at or visited MACV could record as much as they wanted. I spent countless hours there recording rock music. I also utilized the PX system to purchase a sophisticated stereo system.

By the time I was discharged from the Army I was all set to stock my first hippie apartment in Hollywood, Florida, with wall to wall rock music. My hippie heaven didn't last long, though. My buddies and I were buying and selling drugs, and two of us were arrested for illegal possession of controlled substances and public disturbance. Though I got off lightly, I lived in constant fear of being caught again and going to jail for a longer time. I began to drift around. On one trip I hitchhiked all the way to northern California and back to central Florida. On that trip I met some young people from India who introduced me to reincarnation and the Self Realization Fellowship Society. I began to practice meditation and study eastern religion, and I excitedly made another trip to California to visit the headquarters of the Self Realization Fellowship Society in Los Angeles. On the way there I won roughly $70 in a slot machine in Las Vegas and I thought it was an answer to my prayers!

Everything I was doing and thinking was supported by rock music—drugs, eastern religion, restlessness, rebellion against parents and government, spiteful attitude toward law enforcement, licentious living, long hair, communism (I obtain Mao's *Red Book* and other communist propaganda during my stay in Vietnam and was very sympathetic to that wicked philosophy). Rock music never encouraged me to be an obedient, submissive, God-honoring person. It taught me, rather, that I was "born to be wild," born to follow my natural impulses, born to live without rules. It taught me that if it feels good, it can't be wrong. After I was saved I understood that rock music is intimately connected to everything that is evil and rebellious and antichrist, that rock music perfectly fits the biblical definition of the worldliness which the Christian is not to love: the lust of the flesh, lust of the eyes, and pride of life (1 John 2:15-17). The first book I wrote, the first year I was saved, was titled *Mom and Dad Sleep While the Children Rock in Satan's Cradle*, a warning about the dangers of rock music (not currently in print, though I plan to publish an updated edition in 1999, the Lord willing).

Twenty-five years later I am more convinced than ever that secular rock music is spiritually destructive and that "Christian rock" is a misnomer. Rock music is not a proper medium for singing the praises of a holy God.

End of the age characterized by apostasy

The Bible prophesies that the end of the church age will be characterized by widespread apostasy and rebellion. Apostasy means to turn from the apostolic New Testament faith to follow man-made traditions and demonic fables. The Bible does not predict worldwide revival preceding the coming of Christ, but massive error and confusion among those who profess to know Christ. Note the following warnings:

> "And as he sat upon the mount of Olives, the disciples came unto him privately, saying, Tell us, when shall these things be? and what shall be the sign of thy coming, and of the end of the world? And Jesus answered and said unto them, Take heed that no man deceive you. For many shall come in my name, saying, I am Christ; and shall deceive many. ... And many false prophets shall rise, and shall deceive many. ... For there shall arise false Christs, and false prophets, and shall show great signs and wonders; insomuch that, if it were possible, they shall deceive the very elect" (Matthew 24:3-5,11,24).

> "For the mystery of iniquity doth already work: only he who now letteth will let, until he be taken out of the way. And then shall that Wicked be revealed, whom the Lord shall consume with the spirit of his mouth, and shall destroy with the brightness of his coming: Even him, whose coming is after the working of Satan with all power and signs and lying wonders" (2 Thessalonians 2:7-9).

> "Now the Spirit speaketh expressly, that in the latter times some shall depart from the faith, giving heed to seducing spirits, and doctrines of Devils" (1 Timothy 4:1).

> "This know also, that in the last days perilous times shall come. ... Having a form of godliness, but denying the power thereof: from such turn away. ... But evil men and seducers shall wax worse and worse, deceiving, and being deceived" (2 Timothy 3:1,5,13).

> "For the time will come when they will not endure sound doctrine; but after their own lusts shall they heap to themselves teachers, having itching ears; And they shall turn away their ears from the truth, and shall be turned unto fables" (2 Timothy 4:3-4).

> "Little children, it is the last time: and as ye have heard that antichrist shall come, even now are there many antichrists; whereby we know that it is the last time" (1 John 2:18).

We see the fulfillment of these prophecies in the doctrinal and spiritual confusion which abounds in modern-day Christianity. For the most part, Contemporary Christian Music ignores these prophecies and refuses to warn of or separate from false teaching and apostasy. In fact, Contemporary Christian Music is one of the most effective tools in the Devil's workshop for building the end times apostate "church." CCM is drawing together Christians of every stripe, regardless of whether or not their gospel and doctrine is sound. CCM promotes the ecumenical non-judgmental philosophy. I am convinced that Contemporary Christian Music is a fulfillment of 2 Timothy 4:3-4. Those who follow it turn their ears from sound Bible doctrine and from New Testament Christianity to ecumenical fables.

Further, the prophecies that expose the end-time apostasy often mention the sensuality of false teachers.

> "But there were false prophets also among the people, even as there shall be false teachers among you, who privily shall bring in damnable heresies, even denying the Lord that bought them, and bring upon themselves swift destruction. And many shall follow their pernicious ways; by reason of whom the way of truth shall be evil spoken of. ... But chiefly them that WALK AFTER THE FLESH IN THE LUST OF UNCLEANNESS, and despise government. Presumptuous are they, selfwilled, they are not afraid to speak evil of dignities. ... HAVING EYES FULL OF ADULTERY, and that cannot cease from sin; beguiling unstable souls: an heart they have exercised with covetous practices; cursed children. ... For when they speak great swelling words of vanity, THEY ALLURE THROUGH THE LUSTS OF THE FLESH, through much wantonness, those that were clean escaped from them who live in error. WHILE THEY PROMISE THEM LIBERTY, THEY THEMSELVES ARE THE SERVANTS OF CORRUPTION: for of whom a man is overcome, of the same is he brought in bondage" (2 Peter 2:1,2,10,14,18,19).

> "Beloved, when I gave all diligence to write unto you of the common salvation, it was needful for me to write unto you, and exhort you that ye should earnestly contend for the faith which was once delivered unto the saints. For there are certain men crept in unawares, who were before of old ordained to this condemnation, ungodly men, TURNING THE GRACE OF OUR GOD INTO LASCIVIOUSNESS, and denying the only Lord God, and our Lord Jesus Christ. ... These be they who separate themselves, SENSUAL, having not the Spirit" (Jude 3,4,19).

Notice that the false teachers turn the grace of God into lasciviousness. As we shall see, this is precisely what many CCM musicians do. They claim that the grace of God is freedom to listen to any kind of music they please, regardless of how licentious it is; to dress in any fashion they please, regardless of how immodest or worldly it is. They argue that grace gives them liberty to go to wicked rock concerts and to play music to entertain the bar or night club crowd, to have a shallow or nonexistent relationship with the church, etc. They confuse grace with license, which is precisely the earmark of the false teachers described in Jude. Peter adds that false teachers will "allure through the lusts of the flesh." Again, this is precisely what many Christian rockers and CCM supporters do. They say, "Come on over here; we won't tell you how to live; we won't put any guilt trips on you; you can dress as you please and listen to whatever music you please; you can come to church or not come to church; you can cuss a little or drink a little; you can watch R-rated movies and ogle at MTV; we don't have any rules. God gives you liberty; He wants you to have fun."

Beware, friends; this worldly philosophy, which lies at the heart of Contemporary Christian Music, is exposed in the Word of God as the mark of apostasy.

Music is one of the most important influences in the Christian life and in the churches. Music can feed the flesh or the Spirit. It can promote carnality or spirituality. The idea that music is a neutral force and that any music can be used to glorify God and serve His purposes is one of the key philosophies of the end times apostasy. It is unscriptural and foolish to the highest degree. We answer the charge of the neutrality of music in Point One of the "Characteristics of Contemporary Christian Music." Here we will state simply that it is absolutely crucial that a church's music be genuinely spiritual and that it perfectly match the all-important message which is being communicated.

Worshipping God in music is a Christian obligation, and God's Word has much to say about it.

> "Speaking to yourselves in psalms and hymns and spiritual songs, singing and making melody in your heart to the Lord" (Eph. 5:19).
>
> "Let the word of Christ dwell in you richly in all wisdom; teaching and admonishing one another in psalms and hymns and spiritual songs, singing with grace in your hearts to the Lord" (Col. 3:16).
>
> "Is any among you afflicted? let him pray. Is any merry? let him sing psalms" (James 5:13).
>
> "Serve the LORD with gladness: come before his presence with singing" (Psalm 100:2).

The Bible is literally filled with references to singing and music. It is mentioned more than 550 times, in 44 of the 66 books of the Bible. The term "music" (and associated terms "musical," "musician," etc.) appears 75 times in the Bible. The term "song" appears 98 times. "Sing" (singing, singer, etc.) appears 196 times. It is obvious that God loves worshipful and joyful singing which is done in accordance with His Word. A large portion of the Bible is composed of spiritual songs! The organized music ministry was an important part of the Old Testament worship system.

> "And he set the Levites in the house of the LORD with cymbals, with psalteries, and with harps, according to the commandment of David, and of Gad the king's seer, and Nathan the prophet: for so was the commandment of the LORD by his prophets. And the Levites stood with the instruments of David, and the priests with the trumpets. And Hezekiah commanded to offer the burnt offering upon the altar. And when the burnt offering began, the song of the LORD began also with the trumpets, and with the instruments ordained by

David king of Israel. And all the congregation worshipped, and the singers sang, and the trumpeters sounded: and all this continued until the burnt offering was finished" (2 Chronicles 29:25-28; see also 1 Chronicles 15:16-22; 1 Chronicles 25; etc.).

God's people have always sang His praises. The angels <u>sang</u> at creation (Job 38:7). Israel <u>sang</u> at the Red Sea (Ex. 15). Israel <u>sang</u> when the water came from the rock (Num. 21:16,17). Israel <u>sang</u> when God overthrew the Canaanites by the hand of Barak and Deborah (Judges 5). Israel <u>sang</u> when Saul and David defeated the Philistines (1 Sam. 18:6). Israel <u>sang</u> when the ark was brought to Jerusalem (1 Chron. 15:27,28). Israel <u>sang</u> in the Tabernacle and in Solomon's Temple (1 Chron. 6:31-32). Solomon <u>sang</u> 1,005 songs (1 Kings 4:32). Israel <u>sang</u> at the rebuilding of the temple (Ezra 3:11). Israel <u>sang</u> at the rededication of the walls of Jerusalem (Neh. 12). Mary <u>sang</u> at the birth of Christ (Luke 1:46-55). Jesus <u>sang</u> with the disciples at the Last Supper (Mk. 14:26). Paul and Barnabas <u>sang</u> in prison (Acts 16:25). The elders and saints <u>sing</u> God's praises around the throne in Heaven (Rev. 5:8,9). Those who overcome the Antichrist will <u>sing</u> in Heaven (Rev. 15:2,3). The 144,000 will <u>sing</u> in Heaven (Rev. 14:1-3). Those martyred by the antichrist will <u>sing</u> in Heaven (Rev. 15:1-3). God's people will <u>sing</u> when Christ establishes His kingdom (Isaiah 26:1).

It is plain that the matter of music is not something God takes lightly, and it is not something His people should take lightly.

I am convinced that CCM is one of the most dangerous things facing fundamental Baptist and other Bible-believing churches. It is one of the most effective Trojan horses of the ecumenical movement. Consider the following statement which was made almost 20 years ago by a discerning preacher:

> "Now there is a new form that modernism and apostasy has taken to creep surreptitiously into our churches and destroy their Scriptural testimony. THIS TIME IT DOES NOT COME IN THE FORM OF PREACHING OR TEACHING, BUT RATHER IN THE CARNAL PRODUCTION OF THE MUSICAL PROGRAM FROM MANY CHURCH PLATFORMS. Much of the singing heard today by choirs and specials on the average church platform is what is known as contemporary or as soft rock and is often backed with the sound of canned music that could be produced by the average dance or disco band at the corner honky-tonk. The sad truth is that most of this new contemporary, soft rock, offbeat style of music was conceived in hell, hatched among the charismatic crowd, and printed in their publishing houses. Good fundamental Baptists and others that refuse the teachings of the charismatic crowd concerning tongues, signs, miracles, and so forth are now singing their music in our churches and preparing our people for the world, the flesh and the Devil. It is THE NEW TROJAN HORSE MOVE OF MODERNISM TO DEADEN OUR CHURCHES TO SPIRITUAL TRUTH" (Victor Sears, BBF leader, *Baptist Bible Tribune*,

1981).

Consider a similar warning from another Baptist leader:

> "PERHAPS NOTHING PRECIPITATES A SLIDE TOWARD NEW EVANGELICALISM MORE THAN THE INTRODUCTION OF CONTEMPORARY CHRISTIAN MUSIC. Pastors of large churches inform us that we cannot hope to attract the masses with the old, outdated church music. We must change our style so as to catch the attention of the godless. Services are often created to minimize discomfort for the unbeliever so that he or she begins to accept Christianity as an affirming influence. People ought to leave church feeling good about themselves, it is said, instead of being called to self-examination, sincere repentance, and faith toward God. One of the chief ways of making a church more 'contemporary' is to introduce contemporary music, of which there is a great abundance available. THIS INEVITABLY LEADS TOWARD A GRADUAL SLIDE IN OTHER AREAS AS WELL UNTIL THE ENTIRE CHURCH IS INFILTRATED BY IDEAS AND PROGRAMS ALIEN TO THE ORIGINAL POSITION OF THE CHURCH" (Ernest Pickering, *The Tragedy of Compromise: The Origin and Impact of the New Evangelicalism*, Bob Jones University Press, 1994).

Churches that neglect the subject of music do so to their spiritual detriment. Through background tapes and private listening, Contemporary Christian Music is flooding into fundamental Bible-believing churches.

HOW DOES WORLDLY MUSIC ENTER THE CHURCHES?

Pastor Vic Sears, as previously quoted, calls CCM "the new Trojan Horse move of modernism" and warns that it prepares people for the world, the flesh, and the Devil. Dr. Ernest Pickering warns that the introduction of CCM "leads toward a gradual slide in other areas." Note four of the ways this new music is entering fundamentalist congregations:

1. Through desensitization. The average church member today is inundated with rock music and has been inundated all or most of his or her life. Since the 1950s, rock has permeated Western society. Rock music is incorporated into practically every radio and television broadcast and every Hollywood movie. It blares from loudspeakers at businesses as diverse as clothing stores and gas stations. Rock music is in the malls and the restaurants. Rock music is an integral part of practically every professional sporting event. People become so desensitized to rock that they don't even recognize that the "Christian" music they are listening to is rock music. Preachers need to warn of the dangers of rock music frequently, but it is not uncommon for pulpits today to be almost silent on the subject.

2. Through private listening. Contemporary Christian Music is pervasive in Christian circles today. Even in churches which do not support CCM, many of the members listen to this music in their daily lives. I have found that it is not uncommon for members of fundamental Bible-believing churches to listen to Petra, Carman, the Gaithers, Keith Green, Steven Curtis Chapman, John Michael Talbot, Michael Card, and many other CCM groups. Most Christian book stores simply do not carry spiritual music, and it is not easy for church members to obtain good music. Unless a church continually educates and warns its people, sets the right example in the lives of its leaders and workers, and makes good music available, CCM will make steady inroads into the congregation. As more and more people listen to Contemporary Christian Music in their private lives, there is increasing pressure to bring the jazzy music right into the services.

3. Through the specials. Contemporary Christian Music is entering into fundamental Baptist and other fundamentalist Bible-believing churches through the specials. *First, this happens when there is a poor choice of music on the part of those performing the special.* It is not uncommon to find church members singing popular CCM songs as specials in churches which otherwise stand against CCM. I have witnessed this on several occasions as I have traveled on preaching trips. *CCM is also entering the churches through background tapes used in many churches during the specials.* These tapes frequently use snare drums and an electric bass guitar to produce a rock background. It is not uncommon that the music on the tapes is performed by professional musicians who are not even professing Christians or by the same ecumenical-charismatic crowd which produces the popular Contemporary Christian Music. One of the largest distributors of background tapes is Soundtraks, based in Oklahoma City. On May 31, 2001, I talked with Don, who works in the production department at Soundtraks, and he plainly told me:
"We don't have any spiritual standards for the musicians. Some are out of Nashville. They don't have to go to any church. We just use good musicians. The same musicians are used for Southern Gospel and Contemporary."

4. Through contemporary Southern gospel. Another way Contemporary Christian Music is entering into Bible-believing churches is through some of the Southern gospel, with its boogie-woogie rhythms and entertainment-orientation. Consider the following warning:

> "I am a musician who has studied his Bible for the sake of personal purification for years. I do not speak out of ignorance. We must recognize the fact that the style can be the same, even if the instruments are different. Just because a church may not employ strumming guitars, a trap set, and a thumping bass, doesn't mean that our let's-get-with-it-Suzie 'Stepping on the Clouds,

We'll See Jesus,' tear up the piano, boogie-woogie Gospel is any better" (Ron Spencer).

Much of Southern gospel has always been too akin to boogie-woogie. (This is by no means the case with all of Southern gospel, and we praise the Lord for all Christian music, Southern or otherwise, which rejects worldly rhythms, which has scriptural lyrics, and which seeks solely to glorify Jesus Christ and edify the saints.) The late Bruce Lackey, who was the Dean of Tennessee Temple Bible School in the 1970s, played the piano professionally in bars before he was saved. He often warned that much of the Southern gospel music would be at home in these licentious environments because the rhythm is the same. Boogie-woogie is boogie-woogie, regardless of the words which accompany it. It was arose from the same sleazy side of 1920s and 1930s Negro juke joint culture as rhythm & blues. It is sensual dance music and is not fitting for the Gospel of Jesus Christ. Music which fits the bar scene is not fit to glorify a holy God. Further, Southern gospel has deteriorated rapidly in recent decades and has become increasingly akin to secular rock music. The beat has gotten heavier. The popular Southern gospel groups have gotten more worldly. The Gaithers and The Imperials are prime examples. They have adopted the music and the fashions of the world. Some of the men in these groups have grown their hair long like a woman's and they have used hard rock music. They have also become increasingly ecumenical. I attended the National Quartet Convention in 1999 with press credentials, and the main evening shows were little more than rock concerts. I observed that most of the 12,000 or so attendees were middle-aged or older and were dressed rather conservatively and modestly. Fifteen years ago, many of the people in this crowd would not have enjoyed the music they heard at the NQC. What has happened? They have allowed worldly contemporary Southern gospel musicians to lead them, little by little, into a love affair with sensual music.

Many church members who would never listen to Petra or dc Talk or Audio Adrenaline, do listen to the Gaithers and The Imperials. (See the entry the chapter on "Southern Gospel" in the 'Directory of Contemporary Christian Musicians" at the back of this book for more on this.)

"If any music has been guilty by association, it is rock music. It would be impossible to make a complete list, but here are a few of the 'associates' of rock: drug addicts, revolutionaries, rioters, Satan worshippers, drop-outs, draft-dodgers, homosexuals and other sex deviates, rebels, juvenile criminals, black Panthers and White Panthers, motorcycle gangs, blasphemers, suicides, heathenism, voodooism, phallixism, Communism in the United States (communist Russia outlawed rock music around 1960), paganism, lesbianism, immorality, demonology, promiscuity, free love, free sex, disobedience (civil and uncivil), sodomy, venereal disease, discotheques, brothels, orgies of all kinds, night clubs, dives, strip joints, filthy musicals such as 'Hair' and 'Uncle Meat'; and on and on the list could go almost indefinitely"
(Dr. Frank Garlock, *The Big Beat*, pp. 12-13).

PART I
THE CHARACTERISTICS AND ERROR OF CONTEMPORARY CHRISTIAN MUSIC

THE CHARACTERISTICS OF CONTEMPORARY CHRISTIAN MUSIC

Let me say at the outset that when I say I am opposed to Contemporary Christian Music, I am not saying I am opposed to *new* music. There is a wide variety of new Christian music that I love, and I have included a list of suggested sources for such music at the end of this book. What I am opposed to is not new music, but worldly, sensual, heretical music.

Let me also say at that I do not believe all musicians involved with the CCM industry can be lumped together in the same spiritual boat. Some are born again; some are not. Some are sincerely seeking to do everything to the glory of Jesus Christ; some are not. Some even protest the commercialism and sensuality and widespread hypocrisy of the CCM industry as a whole. The Lord alone can judge the hearts of men and women, and it is before Him alone that the child of God will stand to give account for his earthly life. On the other hand, He has given us the task of proving all things (1 Thessalonians 5:21), of watching out for false teachers (Matthew 7:15; 24:11,24), of guarding against unsound doctrine (1 Timothy 1:3), of earnestly contending for the faith once delivered to the saints (Jude 3). We can't judge men's hearts, but we can certainly judge doctrine and practice, and that is precisely what we will do in the following pages in regard to Contemporary Christian Music.

Let me also be quick to testify that I don't think of myself as better than the CCM musicians I have analyzed in this report. I am just a sinner saved by grace. I am under no delusions of spiritual grandeur. I know exactly what I am spiritually: a zero with the rim rubbed out! Apart from the grace of Jesus Christ, I am and I have nothing before God. I am not trying to preach myself; I am preaching the Word of God.

> "Preach the word; be instant in season, out of season; reprove, rebuke, exhort with all longsuffering and doctrine" (2 Timothy 4:2).
>
> "These things speak, and exhort, and rebuke with all authority. Let no man despise thee" (Titus 2:15).

Contemporary Christian Music is *mostly* rock, but it covers every style of music. Like rock music, Contemporary Christian Music is not easy to define. There is soft rock, hard rock, folk rock, mood rock, country rock, blues rock, acid rock, punk rock, 50s rock, 90s rock. There is reggae, rap, ska, industrial, and metal—but it is all rock. The same is true for Contemporary Christian Music. It is 95% rock music, but it comes in a wide variety of rock styles. In the Mardel Christian book stores in Oklahoma City, for example, the large music sections are divided into at least nine categories:

Contemporary (which itself covers every type of worldly music, from bee bop to jazz to Latin American rumbas to big band), Praise-Worship (which likewise covers a wide range of rock styles), Rap, Country, Alternative, Hard, Techno-Drive (the latter three categories cover a wide range of cutting-edge harsh rock styles, including punk, metal, ska, retro, industrial, etc.), **Southern gospel**, and black Gospel (the latter two categories also incorporate a wide variety of heavy beat music). (Ska is defined by *CCM Magazine* as "the bouncy, horn-driven, reggae-on-caffeine music—first played by Jamaicans in the early '60s.")

Not every CCM song or musician will fit every detail of the following definition, but having listened to hundreds of CCM songs in researching this book and having read magazine articles and interviews for many years, I am convinced that the following definition of CCM is an accurate picture of the whole. Exceptions do not overthrow the rule.

Let me also note that **Contemporary Worship Music (CWM)** should be considered a unique division within Contemporary Christian Music. CWM is not completely separate from CCM, in that many of the same musicians are involved in CWM as are involved in other segments of CCM, and CWM is published by some of the same secular corporations as other segments of CCM, and CWM incorporates a wide range of rock rhythms as do other segments of CCM. The significant difference is in the lyrics to CWM, which are more Scriptural than those we find generally in the concert-chart driven segments of CCM. Consider, for example, the words to "How Majestic Is Your Name" by Michael W. Smith:

> "O Lord, our Lord, how majestic is Your name in all the earth/ O Lord, our Lord, how majestic is your name in all the earth/ O Lord, we praise Your name/ O Lord, we magnify Your name/ Prince of Peace, mighty God/ O Lord God Almighty."

It is not uncommon within Christian Worship Music for the lyrics to be composed entirely or almost entirely of Scripture. Certainly we have nothing to say against singing Scripture or singing Scripture-based songs. **The four-fold problem we have with much of CWM is as follows:** (1) Undependable modern versions are frequently followed. (2) Rock rhythms are incorporated, with a heavy bass line, etc. This is not always the case. There are folk styles and country-western and other non-rock styles used for CWM; but generally speaking, CWM is established upon a rock music foundation. (3) There is also the problem of repetition, which the Lord Jesus Christ condemned. "But when ye pray, use not vain repetitions, as the heathen do: for they think that they shall be heard for their much speaking" (Matthew 6:7). I have attended dozens of contemporary church worship services for the purposes of analysis, and repetition is definitely an integral part of it. (4) CWM is intimately connected with the unscriptural and very dangerous charismatic-ecumenical movement.

CWM is only a small part of the Contemporary Christian Music whole. The following analysis of CCM looks at it as a whole.

CHARACTERISTIC #1 — CONTEMPORARY CHRISTIAN MUSIC CAN BE IDENTIFIED BY ITS UNSCRIPTURAL PHILOSOPHY

Contemporary Christian Music is built upon the premise that music itself is a neutral force and that only a song's words determine its morality. CCM therefore incorporates the full spectrum of modern rock/folk/jazz/country music, believing that any style of music is acceptable to carry the Christian message and to glorify Jesus Christ. The theme of the Gospel Music Association's weeklong convention in 2001 was "Music Without Walls." The following is the *Christian Rocker's Creed* as it was published in the popular *CCM Magazine*:

> "We hold these truths to be self-evident, that all music was created equal, that no instrument or style of music is in itself evil—that the diversity of musical expression which flows forth from man is but one evidence of the boundless creativity of our Heavenly Father" (*CCM Magazine*, November 1988, p. 12).

Note the following statements from the CCM crowd:

> "There is no such thing as 'gospel music.' Every style and form of music can become gospel, whether it's jazz, pop, rock 'n' roll, or rap" (Don Butler, Gospel Music Association, *Inhouse Music*, March/April 1991, p. 27).

> "There's no such thing as Christian music. That's because all kinds of music are capable of expressing Christian thought. It's not the music that's Christian, it's the lyrics" (John Styll, "What Makes Music Christian," *CCM Magazine*, June 1991, p. 22; reprinted from the April 1987 issue; Styll [1952-] is the Founder and Executive Editor of *CCM Magazine* and President of the Gospel Music Association).

> "I believe music, in itself, is a neutral force" (Keith Green, *Can God Use Rock Music?*).

> "Music per se ... can be considered morally neutral—it is neither sinful nor holy. Its morality is determined by the use to which it is put" (David Scheer, *PG: A Parental Guide to Rock*, p. 167).

> "We take the music of the street and apply Christian lyrics to it" (Billy Ray Hearn, owner of Sparrow Records and creator of ABC's Myrrh label, cited by Ric Llewellyn, "Christian Rock," *Foundation*, Vol. VI, Issue 2, 1985, p. 16).

"We need to know rock 'n' roll. We need to know the gentleness of a folk tune. We need to know the majesty of Handel's Messiah. We need to know the awesome reverence of the Gregorian chant" (John Michael Talbot, *CCM Magazine*, July 1998, p. 28).

"We're like Billy Graham with guitars, basically ... rock and roll is neutral. It depends on the spirit" (Michael Bloodgood, *Duluth News Tribune*, October 9, 1987, p. 1C).

"Music is not good or evil because of the formation of the notes or the structure of the beat. Music is good because the heart of the person playing it is innocently and sincerely giving praise to our God" (Mylon LeFevre, cited by Jeff Godwin, *What's Wrong with Christian Rock?*, p. 122).

"...music is just music. It's the message that's important" (Mylon LeFevre, *Seattle Post-Intelligencer*, Seattle, Washington, Oct. 11, 1984).

"God is the King of Soul; He's the King of all rhythm" (Phil Driscoll, cited by Tim Fisher, *Battle for Christian Music*, p. 82).

"There's no such thing as Christian music. Music is generic" (Chris Christian, cited by Kit Frieden, "Christian Music Guru Says There's 'No Such Thing,'" *The Patriot*, Harrisburg, Penn., Nov. 29, 1986).

"God gave rock and roll to you/ Put it in the soul of every one/ If you love the sound/ Then don't forget the source" ("God Gave Rock and Roll," Petra).

"All music was His to begin with and He'll use any medium necessary to convey this message" (Editorial in the Christian rock magazine *Take a Stand*, July 1987).

"... rock 'n' roll doesn't have a conscience of its own. It was the people who were playing it" (Randy Stonehill, cited by Chris Willman, "Randy Stonehill: Turning Twenty," *CCM Magazine*, August 1990).

"The problem, essentially, is there is no such thing as 'Christian music.' There is only music and what it's about. ... Every genre, every style, every media needs to be claimed—or reclaimed—to glorify God" (Chris Well, *7Ball*, July-August 1998, p. 66; Well is Editor in Chief of *7Ball*, a bimonthly publication which reports on alternative rock Christian music, such as metal, punk, rap, and ska).

"We believe all music comes from God, and that liberates us to express ourselves in a wider range of artistic expression than some others" (Bebe Winans, *CCM Magazine*, Feb. 1989, p. 21).

> "There is nothing un- or anti-Christian about any kind of music" (Best, *Music Through the Eyes of Faith*, p. 52; Best is dean of the conservatory of music at Wheaton College).
>
> "Using WHAT IS NEUTRAL in a society as a vehicle for the gospel is not only acceptable; it is sound missionary strategy" (Steve Miller, *The Contemporary Christian Music Debate*, p. 49).
>
> "I believe that music, particularly instrumental music, is absolutely void of moral qualities for either good or evil" (Dana Key, *Don't Stop the Music*).
>
> "Other than Heavy Metal and vulgar lyrics, it's all a matter of taste and has nothing to do with Christianity" (Jerry Falwell, speaking at Word of Life, New York, 1980s).

Even the CCM musicians who do not perform hard rock music hold this strange philosophy about the neutrality of music. Speaking at Word of Life in New York in the 1980s, Jerry Falwell said: "Other than Heavy Metal and vulgar lyrics, it's all a matter of taste and has nothing to do with Christianity." During a concert tour in New England in 1986, Bill Gaither admitted that he had changed his musical styles due to the influence of the "world's culture." He said he believed there was a place for Christian rock, and he expressed his philosophy of music in these words: "God speaks through all different kinds of art forms and musical styles and musical forms" and the "format itself is not necessarily spiritual or non-spiritual" (Gaither, *F.B.F. News Bulletin*, Fundamental Baptist Fellowship, March-April 1986, p. 3). Southern Baptist pastor Rick Warren, influential author of *The Purpose Driven Church*, has this same philosophy: "I reject the idea that music styles can be judged as either 'good' or 'bad' music. Churches need to admit that no particular style of music is 'sacred'" (*The Purpose Driven Church*, p. 281).

IS MUSIC A NEUTRAL FORCE?

The following are the reasons why we reject the idea that music is neutral and communicates no message in and of itself:

1. Ask common sense. Common sense tells us that music is not neutral, that all music is not the same. Such an idea is strictly contrary to our experiences in life. There is sensual music and spiritual music, music for partying and music for worship, music for marching and music for dancing, music for romance and music for warfare. The notes and components of music are neutral, but when these are arranged into a pattern, that piece of music no longer is neutral but becomes a voice, a language. "Just as vowels and consonants can become blasphemy and pen and paper in the hand of an artist can become pornography, so notes and rhythm, in the hands of a composer or artist, can become sensual" (Frank Garlock, *Music in the Balance*, p. 100).

This truth is seen in the alphabet. Individual letters of the alphabet are "neutral," in that, standing alone, they do not communicate a message; but as soon as those letters are combined to form words and sentences, a message is communicated and those letters so formed are no longer neutral. Take the letter "E," for example. It can spell hatE or it can spell lovE; it can spell jEsus or it can spell dEvil. Likewise, musical components are neutral as long as they remain by themselves, but as soon as they are arranged into a piece of music, that piece of music communicates a message which can be sensual or spiritual, godly or satanic. The idea that music is neutral is contrary to common sense and observation.

2. Ask knowledgeable men from centuries past. Knowledgeable men of all ages, even secular men, have recognized the power of music for good or evil. In fact, the strange idea that music is neutral is only a few years old.

Plato, B.C. 428-348, "Musical training is a more potent instrument than any other, because rhythm and harmony find their way into the inward places of the soul" (Plato, Fourth Book of the *Republic*).

Aristotle, B.C. 384-322, "Music directly represents the passions or states of the soul—gentleness, anger, courage, temperance ... If a person habitually listens to the kind of music that rouses ignoble passions, his whole character will be shaped to an ignoble form. In short, if one listens to the wrong kind of music he will become the wrong kind of person; but conversely, if he listens to the right kind of music he will tend to become the right kind of person" (Aristotle, Republic, Politics, 8, 1340, quoted in Donald J. Grout, *A History of Western Music*, 1980, p. 8).

Boethius, A.D. 480-524, Greek philosopher and statesman — "Music is part of our human nature, it has the power either to improve or debase our character" (Boethius, *De Institutione Musica*, cited in Paul Hindemith, *A Composer's World*, Cambridge, 1952, p. 7).

John Calvin, A.D. 1509-1564 — "We know by experience that music has a secret and almost incredible power to move hearts" (John Calvin, *Works*, Vol. VI).

Martin Luther, A.D. 1483-1546 — "For whether you wish to comfort the sad, to terrify the happy, to encourage the despairing, to humble the proud, to calm the passionate, or to appease those full of hate—and who could number all these masters of the human heart, namely, the emotions, inclinations, and affections that impel men to evil or good?—what more effective means than music could you find?" (Martin Luther, quoted from Friedrich Blume, *Protestant Church Music*, p. 10).

3. Ask professionally trained musicians. Max Schoen, 1940 — "Music is the most powerful stimulus known among the perceptive senses. The medical, psychiatric and other evidence for the non-neutrality of music is so overwhelming that it frankly amazes me that anyone should seriously say otherwise" (Dr. Max Schoen, *The Psychology of Music*, 1940).

Howard Hanson, 1942 — "Music is a curiously subtle art with innumerable, varying emotional connotations. It is made up of many ingredients and, according to the proportions of these components, it can be soothing or invigorating, ennobling or vulgarizing, philosophical or orgiastic. It has powers for evil as well as for good" (Dr. Howard Hanson, American composer, conductor, and teacher, Director of the Eastman School of Music at the University of Rochester, *American Journal of Psychiatry*, Vol. 99, p. 317; the quotation is from an address entitled "A Musician's Point of View Toward Emotional Expression," delivered by Dr. Hanson at the 98th annual meeting of the American Psychiatric Association).

Dimitri Tiomkin, 1965 — "The fact that music can both excite and incite has been known from time immemorial. … Now in our popular music, at least, we seem to be reverting to savagery … and youngsters who listen constantly to this sort of sound are thrust into turmoil. They are no longer relaxed, normal kids" (*Los Angeles Herald-Examiner*, Aug. 8, 1965; Dr. Tiomkin is a famous composer and conductor).

William J. Shafer, 1972 — "Rock is communication without words, regardless of what ideology is inserted into the music" (Dr. William J. Shafer, *Rock Music,* 1972).

Richard M. Taylor, 1973 — "We cannot change the basic effect of certain kinds of rhythm and beat simply by attaching to them a few religious or semi-religious words. The beat will still get through to the blood of the participants and the listeners. Words are timid things. Decibels and beat are bold things, which can so easily bury the words under an avalanche of sound. … There are music forms, whether secular or sacred, which create moods of pensiveness, of idealism, of awareness of beauty, of aspiration, and of holy joyousness. There are other forms of music which create moods of recklessness and sensual excitement. Surely it doesn't take much judgment to know which forms are most appropriate for religious functions" (Dr. Richard M. Taylor, *The Disciplined Lifestyle*, 1973, pp. 86, 87).

Steven Halpern, 1978 — "Words are incidental at best, or monotonous and moronic as usual. But the points is, that they don't matter. What you dance to is the beat, the bass and drums. And with this mix and volume, not only is the beat sensed, but literally felt, as this aspect of the rhythm section takes precedence over melody and harmony" (Dr. Steven Halpern, *Tuning the Human Instrument*, 1978, p. 14).

Leonard Seidel, 1980 — "There is a certain type of music around which demons feel very uncomfortable. Check the other side of the coin. There is a type of music under which evil spirits find it quite easy to progress with their work and influence" (Leonard Seidel, concert pianist, lecturer, *God's New Song*, 1980, p. 9).

Simon Frith, 1981 — "Most rock records make their impact musically rather than lyrically. The words, if they are noticed at all, are absorbed after the music has made its mark" (Simon Frith, sociology professor at University of Warwick in England, *Sound Effects,* 1981, p. 14).

Eddy Manson, 1983 — "Music is a two-edged sword. It's really a powerful drug. Music can poison you, lift your spirits or make you sick without knowing why" (Eddy Manson, Oscar-winning film composer, quoted by David Chagall, *Family Weekly*, Jan. 30, 1983, pp. 12-15).

Mike Coyle, 1983 — "Since music is an emotional language, and since some emotions are wrong for the child of God, then some music is wrong for the Christian" (Mike Coyle, former world-class professional French horn virtuoso, "Music: Is There an Absolute?" *Baptist Bulletin*, April 1983, p. 10).

Adam Knieste, 1983 — "Music is a two-edged sword. It's really a powerful drug. Music can poison you, lift your spirits, or make you sick without knowing why. Whereas mellow tones can relax you, loud grinding music can cause blood pressure to rise, leading to headaches and an anxious feeling" (*Family Weekly*, January 30, 1983; Dr. Knieste is a musicologist who studies the effects of music on human behavior).

David Tame, 1984 — "Music is a form of language ... music is more than a language. It is the language of languages. ... Like human nature itself, music cannot possibly be neutral in its spiritual direction" (David Tame, musical researcher, *The Secret Power of Music*, 1984, pp. 151, 187).

Carol Merle-Fishman and Shelley Katsh, 1985 — "Music is a form of non-verbal communication" (Carol Merle-Fishman and Shelley Katsh, music therapists and instructors at New York University, *The Music Within You*, 1985, p. 206).

Gilbert Rouget, 1985 — "...what we need to remember is that music has a physical impact upon the listener and that it produces a sensorial modification in his awareness of being. This physical impact, of course, is what pop music is consciously striving for" (Gilbert Rouget, *Music and Trance*, 1985, p. 120).

Leonard Bernstein, 1990 — "Music is something terribly special ... it doesn't have to pass through the censor of the brain before it can reach the heart ... An F-sharp doesn't have to be considered in the mind; it is a direct hit, and, therefore, all the more powerful" (Leonard Bernstein, cited in Katrine Ames, "An Affair to Remember," *Newsweek*, Oct. 29, 1990, p. 79).

Tim Fisher, 1992 — "Music is not neutral. It has the capability of communicating imbalance and sensuality, and it can confuse the spiritual effectiveness of the message. Therefore, I as a Christian must draw a line. Any music that cannot appropriately communicate the message is unfit to use to worship the Lord" (Tim Fisher, musician, teacher, *The Battle for Christian Music,* 1992, p. 56).

Robert Shaw, 1998 — "I believe all the arts are moral. I can't see how any of the arts can be neutral" (Kurt Woetzel, "Is Music Neutral? An Interview with Robert Shaw," distinguished choral music director, *FrontLine,* September-October 1998, p. 11).

Philip Merriam — "There is probably no other cultural activity which is so all-pervasive and which reaches into, shapes and often controls so much of human behavior" (Philip Merriam, *The Anthropology of Music*).

4. Ask the movie maker. Music paints a picture, creates a mood. The television/movie industry understands this and they spend millions upon millions of dollars annually to create just the right musical effect for each scene. Tension and danger calls for tense music. Romance calls for romantic music. The musical score must precisely match the script. How foolish, then, for CCM musicians to claim that the rhythms of a song do not have to match the words because the rhythms are "neutral." There is no such thing.

5. Ask the advertiser. Businesses understand that music is not a neutral force. They know that certain kinds music can increase sales while other kinds of music can actually reduce sales. The Muzak Corporation, which distributes music for businesses, describes their philosophy of music: "The Science of Stimulus Progression — employs THE INHERENT POWER OF MUSIC IN A CONTROLLED PATTERN TO ACHIEVE PRE-DETERMINED PSYCHOLOGICAL AND PHYSIOLOGICAL EFFECTS ON PEOPLE. Leading companies and commercial establishments now employ the Muzak concept to improve environment, attitudes and performance" (Muzak ad). Muzak knows that music is not neutral, because certain kinds of music produce certain kinds of responses in the hearers, and other kinds of music produce entirely different responses.

6. Ask the tavern owner. Why does the owner of a tavern or a night club choose a certain kind of music? Because that type of music creates the right atmosphere to promote the fleshly activities of that establishment. If a tavern owner attempted to play traditional hymns, he would create an entirely different atmosphere which would not be conducive for the type of recreation his patrons are engaged in. Every tavern owner knows that music is not neutral.

7. Ask the band or orchestra director. A band or orchestra director understands the power of music to move people in different ways, and he carefully selects the type of music desired to create whatever mood or effect is required by the situation. I played first clarinet in a large school band for six years and had an opportunity to join a symphony orchestra. Music was never randomly selected. If our high school band was rallying the crowd for a football game, we did not play a waltz or a lullaby!

8. Ask the rock band. The rock band strives to create a certain reaction in its hearers, and it uses exactly the type of music required to produce that reaction. Rock star Jimi Hendrix understood this: "Atmospheres are going to come through music, because the music is a spiritual thing of its own. ... You can hypnotize people ... and when you get them at their weakest point you can preach into the subconscious what you want to say" (*Life*, Oct. 3, 1969, p. 74). Hendrix was right. "Atmospheres" do come through music. Consider the godly atmosphere of peace and blessing and conviction which comes through truly spiritual church music, and contrast this with the atmosphere which comes through rock music. Rock star Frank Zappa of the Mothers of Invention said: "Rock music is sex. The big beat matches the body's rhythms" (*Life*, June 28, 1968). Rock star Ted Nugent says, "Rock is the total celebration of the physical" (*Rolling Stone*, Aug. 25, 1977, pp. 11-13). Gene Simmons of the rock group KISS agrees: "That's what rock is all about—sex with a 100 megaton bomb, the beat!" (*Entertainment Tonight*, ABC, Dec. 10, 1987). Debbie Harry of the rock band Blondie says amen to this: "Rock 'n' roll is all sex. One hundred percent *sex*" (cited by Steve Peters, *The Truth about Rock*, p. 30). John Oates of the rock duo Hall & Oates says, "Rock 'n' roll is 99% sex" (*Circus*, Jan. 31, 1976). Rock drummer King Coffey observes: "...the whole idea of rock 'n' roll is to offend your parents" (*The Truth about Rock*, p. 30). Lita Ford of heavy metal group The Runaways says, "Listen, rock 'n' roll AIN'T CHURCH. It's nasty business" (*Los Angeles Times*, August 7, 1988). Malcolm McLaren, punk rock manager, describes rock music as "pagan and primitive, and very jungle, and that's how it should be!" (*Rock*, August 1983). *Time* magazine notes: "In a sense all rock is revolutionary. By its very beat and sound it has always implicitly rejected restraints and has celebrated freedom and sexuality" (*Time*, Jan. 3, 1969). Allan Bloom observes: "... rock music has one appeal only, a barbaric appeal to sexual desire—not love, not eros, but sexual desire undeveloped and untutored" (*The Closing of the American Mind*, New York: Simon and Schuster, 1987, p. 73). *Rolling Stone* magazine says that "...rock and roll is more than just music; it is the energy center of the new culture and your revolution" (cited by John Blanchard, *Pop Goes the Gospel*, p. 12). Michael Ross, in his treatise on rock music, observes that the music of licentious rock groups like the Rolling Stones "REFLECTS THEIR WAY OF LIVING" (*Rock Beyond Woodstock*, p. 13).

Concert pianist and musical researcher Leonard Seidel wisely notes: "Rock and roll's corrupt degenerate lifestyle is fueled by the language of *a certain kind of music*" (Leonard Seidel, *Face the Music*).

9. Ask the rock music lover. If music is a neutral thing in and of itself, it would be a simple matter for a rock music lover to give it up. That is not the case, though! "Any 'Christian' rock star/fan who thinks music is neutral should face up to one simple fact: nobody gets hooked on neutral music. Why don't you do a little experiment? Spend the next 30 days without listening to or playing ANY rock music. Try it, C-Rock fans. You'll quickly find yourself going through withdrawal. Rock music is a drug! Don't believe it? Go 30 days without it" (Jeff Godwin, *What's Wrong with Christian Rock?*, p. 38). The same cannot be said for many other types of music. This is irrefutable evidence that all music is not the same.

10. Ask the Bible. The Bible plainly states that music is not neutral. Christians are instructed to use *a certain kind* of music to worship God and to build up the Christian life.

> "Speaking to yourselves in psalms and hymns and spiritual songs, singing and making melody in your heart to the Lord" (Ephesians 5:19).
>
> "Let the word of Christ dwell in you richly in all wisdom; teaching and admonishing one another in psalms and hymns and spiritual songs, singing with grace in your hearts to the Lord" (Colossians 3:16).

Psalms, hymns, and spiritual songs do not describe the world's music. God's Word is reminding us that there is a music which is fitting to the Christian life and there is a music which is not, and it is the Christian's task in every generation to glorify God *only* with the type of music which is fitting for that exalted task. The music is to be spiritual as opposed to carnal.

The philosophy that music is neutral and that apart from the words it has no influence or voice of its own is the Devil's lie, and this false philosophy is being used to build the ecumenical end-times apostate religion.

The fact that music IS NOT neutral is a loud warning to Christians that we must be very careful about what type of music we listen to and what type of music we allow in our homes and churches. Some music encourages the flesh, while some music encourages the spiritual. Some is demonic and some is Spirit-inspired. When I was saved in the summer of 1973, I loved rock music and I continued to listen to it for the first few weeks. I was excited when I heard about "Christian rock," because I thought it would allow me to please the Lord while retaining the type of music I loved. One day I was riding along in my car with the radio tuned to a rock station, and I was praying earnestly about my new walk with the Lord. I was telling the Lord that I wanted Him to take complete control of me, that I wanted Him to receive glory from my life. I believe the Lord spoke to my heart and told me to turn off the rock music and to put it out of my life. I reached over and turned off the radio and I have never again tuned my radio to a rock station for listening pleasure. I dedicated my radio and tape players to the Lord and determined that I would not use them for carnal rock music. It took awhile for me to learn to enjoy spiritual music, because my musical taste was corrupted by many years of complete devotion to rock music, but I praise the Lord that He dealt with me about music and that He gave me the wisdom to know that music is not a neutral thing.

CHARACTERISTIC #2 — CONTEMPORARY CHRISTIAN MUSIC CAN BE IDENTIFIED BY ITS SENSUAL RHYTHM.

Rhythm itself is not wrong unless it is misused. Rhythm is a necessary part of music. It keeps the music moving, but it should not dominate. Contrast "Onward Christian Soldiers" with a rock song. Both have rhythm, but the rhythm in most rock songs absolutely dominates and overwhelms the musical piece, whereas the rhythm in "Onward Christian Soldiers" simply complements the lyrical message.

Dr. Frank Garlock contrasts the rhythm section of an orchestra with that of a rock band:

> "How much rhythm is too much rhythm, as thought of from a numerical perspective? The typical symphony, such as the Boston Symphony Orchestra or the Chicago Symphony Orchestra, includes approximately one hundred musicians. Three to four of them are responsible for the rhythm as they play the percussion instruments like the timpani, bass and snare drums, cymbals, triangle, bells, and several other rhythmic devices. Since the percussion instruments do not perform much of the time, it can be concluded that LESS THAN FOUR PERCENT OF THE ORCHESTRA IS RESPONSIBLE FOR THE BASIC RHYTHM. It might be argued that all of the instruments play some part of the rhythm, but this only makes the analogy between rhythm and the pulse stronger. All parts of our bodies are affected by the pulse, but it is the pulse itself which gives the body its basic rhythm. In addition to this, it must be remembered that just as the spirit, mind, and body are interrelated, so are the melody, harmony, and rhythm. One cannot exist without the other two.
>
> "The conventional secular or Christian rock group has a slightly different blend. Typically there are four basic instruments: the rhythm guitar, a bass guitar, an array of drums, and the lead guitar. Although the guitar is not usually considered a rhythm instrument, as used by a rock group it definitely is. All four instruments can be classified as belonging to the rhythm family. The only one which offers the 'melody' on occasion is the lead guitar. At best, the sound which comes from THE TYPICAL ROCK GROUP IS SEVENTY-FIVE PERCENT RHYTHM" (Frank Garlock, *Music in the Balance*, pp. 67,68).

Changing the rhythm of a song changes its message. The song "Sweet Hour of Prayer" is traditionally set to music which matches its message. The music is contemplative, restful, gentle, convicting. It creates a mood of prayerfulness. If the same words were sung to the music of a Sousa march or a Beatles tune the piece would immediately lose at least some of its original message, even if the words remained the same.

Christian rock is an absolute contradiction. The music paints one picture, the words another. *Time* magazine, in a 1985 article on Christian rock music, called it "new lyrics for the Devil's music" (*Time*, March 11, 1985, p. 60). Even the world recognizes that there is a contradiction between the music and the words. The words speak of obedience and humility and holiness; the music, of rebellion and pride and sensuality. Rock music was created to produce sensuality and rebellion and license; it cannot possibly be used to paint pictures of godliness and obedience and reverence; it is a music used effectively to worship the Devil in many cultures; it cannot possibly be acceptable to a holy God. Instead of writing music to match the words, the CCM musician synthesizes the world's music and the Bible's message. It is unholy confusion.

The late CCM artist Rich Mullins opened most of his concerts with "Hallelujah" sung in Beach Boys style. That is confusion.

The CCM group Digital Interference has a song titled "Omnipotent" on their "God Rules" album. This song speaks of God's omnipotence but it is "complimented by dirty electronic hard rock" (*HM magazine*, May-June 1998). Note that even the Christian rock defender admits that rock music itself is "dirty." What great confusion it is to use dirty music to communicate a holy message.

Carman's "Mission 3:16" album contains a heavy bee bop, finger snapping rendition of John 3:16. This is confusion. The words are communicating the love of God in Jesus Christ, while the music is communicating sensual dance moods.

The Gaithers have a song titled "Singin' with the Saints" which is a boogie-woogie version of "He Keeps Me Singing." This is confusion.

The rhythm of the song must match the lyrics of the song and communicate exactly the same message.

The right use of rhythm is a matter of balance: spirit, soul, body. God's Word plainly tells us what is to have the priority. The Christian is to focus on the spiritual above the physical.

> "Therefore take no thought, saying, What shall we eat? or, What shall we drink? or, Wherewithal shall we be clothed? (For after all these things do the Gentiles seek:) for your heavenly Father knoweth that ye have need of all these things. But seek ye first the kingdom of God, and his righteousness; and all these things shall be added unto you" (Matt. 6:31-33).
>
> "For bodily exercise profiteth little: but godliness is profitable unto all things, having promise of the life that now is, and of that which is to come" (1 Timothy 4:8).

Even more, the physical is to be subjected to the spiritual. The child of God is in the midst of a war. In fact, that war is not only without; it is within his very mind and body. He has an old nature and a new. There is the flesh and there is the indwelling Spirit. There is the old man and the new. To be spiritually victorious the child of God must starve the old and feed the new. He is to die to the flesh and live unto God.

> "The light of the body is the eye: if therefore thine eye be single, thy whole body shall be full of light. But if thine eye be evil, thy whole body shall be full of darkness. If therefore the light that is in thee be darkness, how great is that darkness! No man can serve two masters: for either he will hate the one, and love the other; or else he will hold to the one, and despise the other. Ye cannot serve God and mammon" (Matt. 6:22-24).

> "For if ye live after the flesh, ye shall die: but if ye through the Spirit do mortify the deeds of the body, ye shall live. For as many as are led by the Spirit of God, they are the sons of God" (Romans 8:13,14).

> "The night is far spent, the day is at hand: let us therefore cast off the works of darkness, and let us put on the armour of light. Let us walk honestly, as in the day; not in rioting and drunkenness, not in chambering and wantonness, not in strife and envying. But put ye on the Lord Jesus Christ, and make not provision for the flesh, to fulfil the lusts thereof" (Romans 13:12-14).

> "This I say then, Walk in the Spirit, and ye shall not fulfil the lust of the flesh" (Galatians 5:16).

> "And they that are Christ's have crucified the flesh with the affections and lusts" (Galatians 5:24).

> "That ye put off concerning the former conversation the old man, which is corrupt according to the deceitful lusts; And be renewed in the spirit of your mind; And that ye put on the new man, which after God is created in righteousness and true holiness" (Ephesians 4:22-24).

It is absolutely impossible to serve the flesh with the music of a song while serving the spiritual mind with the words. These are enmity one with the other. The Contemporary Christian Music scene feeds the old man its beloved rock music while attempting to feed the new man lyrically. It is confusion.

> "If the body and physical things are a priority in one's life, that person is sensual. If the rhythm is the primary dominating part of any piece of music, then that music is sensual" (Frank Garlock).

THE MUSICAL TEST

The following is a simple test to determine whether or not the rhythm or the music itself is proper for a certain song:

1. Where does the music fit?

"Worldly music can be identified by its sound. A reasonably accurate picture can be gained simply from listening to the sound. The noise emanating from a bar or nightclub causes a variety of images to flood the mind. The mind forms images, consciously or unconsciously, of the activities taking place from each sound source. What kind of picture does the world get in its mind as it passes your church when the windows or doors are open? What images are brought to the listeners' consciousness as they hear the sound of the music from your home or car? Is it different from the music heard Saturday night as they may have walked a mall or downtown sidewalk? Do they hear an immediate contrast which tells them this is Christian music? IF THEY ARE TIRED OF THE NOISE WHICH THE WORLD OFFERS AND SEEK MUSIC WHICH FEEDS THE SPIRIT, DOES YOUR CHURCH MUSIC ATTRACT THEM OR DOES IT HAVE THE SAME QUALITIES AND SOUND AS THE WORLD'S?" (Frank Garlock).

When Moses and Aaron descended from Mt. Sinai and heard the music which the people were using for their immoral idolatry, they recognized from afar that something was seriously wrong. Joshua thought the music was the noise of war. Obviously it was very clamorous and very loud! There were screams and shouts. That is a perfect description of modern rock music. Moses recognized that it was not warfare, but was riotous, fleshly music.

> "And when Joshua heard the noise of the people as they shouted, he said unto Moses, There is a noise of war in the camp. And he said, It is not the voice of them that shout for mastery, neither is it the voice of them that cry for being overcome: but the noise of them that sing do I hear. And it came to pass, as soon as he came nigh unto the camp, that he saw the calf, and the dancing: and Moses' anger waxed hot, and he cast the tables out of his hands, and brake them beneath the mount" (Exodus 32:17-19).

If a music fits a tavern, it does not fit the house of God. If it fits an idolatrous, demonic orgy, it does not fit the praises of the Lord Jesus Christ.

2. What does it make people want to do?

If a piece of music makes people want to dance in a sexual manner, it is dance music, and sensual dance music does not glorify God; it stimulates the flesh. If a song is about prayer, the music should make me want to pray. If a song is about God's holiness, the music should exalt holiness.

3. What mood does it create?

The portrait painted by the musical rhythms must match the message of the lyrics. If one is singing about the grace of God and the sacrifice of Christ, the music should not paint a depressing mood. It should be uplifting, encouraging, strengthening, edifying. If one is singing about the peace of God, the music should not be discordant or tense. If one is singing about the holiness and majesty of God, the music should not be romantic or sensual. If a piece of music puts people into a depressed, introspective, blue mood, it is soulish and is fit for a bar but is not music which can be used to edify the saints.

Christian music should not speak confusion but peace (1 Cor. 14:33).
Christian music should not speak discord but harmony (1 Cor. 14:40).
Christian music should not speak harshness but gentleness (2 Timothy 2:24).
Christian music should not speak worldliness but holiness (1 Peter 1:15).
Christian music should not speak rebellion but submission to authority (James 4:7; 1 Peter 2:13).
Christian music should not speak pride but humility (1 Peter 5:5).
Christian music should not speak sensuality but spirituality (1 Peter 2:5).
Christian music should not ask questions but should answer questions (1 John 5:20).
Christian music should not speak entertainment but edification (1 Corinthians 14:26).

Creating a Soft, Non-Offensive Sound

Even Contemporary Christian Music which has a soft, gentle rhythm can be dangerous. The following important warning is from *Confronting Contemporary Christian Music* by Dr. H.T. Spence:

> "In 1973 a Neo-Evangelical movement swept across America called 'Key '73.' Many of the evangelical denominations, including the Pentecostals, joined this movement, believing it would be the strongest evangelistic thrust to date in our country. An extensive invitation was sent out for new music to be written that promoted the message of 'Key '73' with several stipulations: the words *righteousness*, *judgment*, *holiness*, *repentance*, and several other biblical terms were not allowed to be used, and THE LYRICS WERE TO BE OF A POSITIVE NATURE. There was an intentional effort made to write NON-OFFENSIVE songs. A number of these were produced that year through this evangelical effort, strengthening the move away from biblical, doctrinal standards in the music.

"By 1972, Bill Gaither, a member of the Nazarene Church who started his pubic music career in Southern gospel, was experimenting with a disco form of music, and because of the reaction from the more moderate element of the evangelical spectrum, he started the Bill Gaither Vocal Band in order to further his music in the strong contemporary vein. It has only been in the last few years that he has returned to his Southern gospel roots and conventional style, especially in his reminiscing Gospel-sing videos. He is the man who promulgated the 'praise' music which was at its height during the mid 1980s and early 1990s. ITS INFLUENCE IS NOW AFFECTING THE BORDERS OF THE FUNDAMENTALISTS' MUSIC WITH THE CHARISMATIC SOUND IN A NUMBER OF CHORUSES SUNG IN THE CHURCHES AND YOUTH CAMPS. No, we are not against praise, but such an emphasis with certain types of music can be a ploy to make us leave off taking a stand against the apostasy of our time. Gaither's song 'Get All Excited' was written to pull the people away from speaking against anything that would cause division among 'God's people,' specifically doctrine and biblical concepts of separation. It truly intimidates the child of God in taking a stand in his church that is drifting away from the Word of God. The Charismatic leaders are regularly reminding us that the Book of Psalms is truly a hymnbook dedicated to praise. But we must carefully read this precious book: praise is often in the context of battle themes, imprecatory prayers, overcoming those who are against God, and instruction of godly living in opposition to carnal living. THE BATTLE THEME IN PRESENT DAY FUNDAMENTALIST MUSIC COMPOSITIONS IS CONSPICUOUSLY ABSENT. The term *apostasy* is never mentioned. The melodies and arrangements are progressively lacking strength and literally CREATING THE 'SOFT SOUND' IN CHURCH MUSIC.

"One of the characteristics that should be upon the hearts of Fundamentalist music leaders is the hope for balance in the repertoire. When the 'easy listening' and the 'soft sound' flow steadily from the pens of the music composers, the music will definitely produce soft and weak Christians. We were told back in 1969 that the 'music is the message,' not just the lyrics. MUCH OF THIS SOFT AND PRETTY SOUND IS COMING FROM FEMALE ARRANGERS TEACHING IN OUR CHRISTIAN COLLEGES AND UNIVERSITIES. God made the feminine gender soft and pretty. And her tendency in history has been to write from that perspective. A few women in the past have written lyrics with strength and fewer have written melodies with strength. In this age when love and softness on apostasy have practically become the perfume of the modern Church, our dear Fundamentalist ladies who are part of the music ministry must be careful that they do not contribute to this 'falling away' with their published, weak arrangements of once strong hymns. SUCH MUSIC ENCOURAGES PASSIVITY ON THE BATTLEFIELD. WE ARE IN DESPERATE NEED OF STRONG MELODIES BEARING ALONG STRONG LYRICS, FEEDING STRENGTH TO THE WARRIORS FOR CHRIST" (Dr. H.T. Spence, *Confronting Contemporary Christian Music*, pp. 142-143).

What about the Children's Music?

For some strange reason, many churches and families who take a stand against Contemporary Christian Music in general allow their children to be subjected to music with a heavy beat or worldly syncopation or incredibly shallow, even unscriptural lyrics. Not only is this inconsistent, it is dangerous for the spiritual well-being of the child. If children are weaned on a diet of "Nashville" syncopation it is only reasonable to assume they will desire even heavier types of such music as they grow older. Also, if children are weaned on music with shallow, even unscriptural lyrics, how will they ever discern between truth and error in music?

Note the following very important comments by men who have studied the effects of music:

> "If you raise your child on seemingly innocent but worldly jingle sounding music they will have a definite thirst for the CCM sound when they become a teenager. You won't be able to say, Oh, now that you're older let me teach you what good music is all about. It will be too late. You need to give them a standard of excellence and spirituality from their earliest years" (David G. Parker, *Music in Our Contemporary Christian Culture*. 1997).

> "If we teach our children only choruses and do not give equal weight to the strong, meaty hymns of the Faith, we may be spiritually damaging their generation. To intimidate these hymns of the Faith by saying 'they are too deep and way over the heads of our young people' is to say we have a better way of producing a Christian than our forefathers had. Children of earlier days had their spiritual teeth cut on those hymns, and such music became the bedrock for building mature, godly lives. Such weakness reminds me of a sixteen-year-old young man whom I saw in a church service one Sunday morning bringing a 'cartoon' Bible which had been published by the Jimmy Swaggart ministries. When I casually asked him about it, he said this was the only Bible he understood. And yet, he was born in a Christian home and attended church all of his life. Cartoon scripts used as a method for telling Bible stories may have a place from time to time with a child, but it can never take the place of the Bible itself. If it does, it will plant in the child's mind, 'My parents have their Bible and I have my own.' No, the Bible was given by God for all ages; it is the one book for all generations. Even so, we never want chorus singing to take the place of hymn singing, for the child will unconsciously think the hymns are more for the adults. This may be a growing problem with the concept of 'Children's Church' on Sunday morning: it splits up the family in worship before God, and tends to imply to the child that they are too young for the worship in the sanctuary" (Dr. H.T. Spence, *Confronting Contemporary Christian Music*, p. 144).

The key to the problem of children's music is the parents and the youth leaders. We must be praying and thinking about the music our children listen to. All too often we don't give serious thought to these matters. There are many questions we should be asking ourselves: Is the rhythm contemporary-sounding? Will it create in the children an appetite for worldly music? Are the lyrics scriptural? Are the lyrics honoring to a holy God? Are they teaching the children to be serious about the things of God? Is this music edifying the children spiritually, or is it merely entertaining them? The Bible says we are to use music to teach and admonish (Col. 3:16).

CHARACTERISTIC #3—CONTEMPORARY CHRISTIAN MUSIC CAN BE IDENTIFIED BY ITS ECUMENISM.

Contemporary Christian Music is ecumenical music. In fact, Contemporary Christian Music is one of the glues holding together the end-times ecumenical movement.

In his book *Making Musical Choices*, Richard Peck makes the following important observation about modern church music.

> "Aside from its commercialism and its increasing resemblance to the world, contemporary Christian music is becoming a religious melting pot. Some in the community admit that they are not believers. And while this is still an exception, CCM IS PROUD OF ITS ECUMENICAL AND CHARISMATIC SPIRIT. THIS ECUMENISM EXTENDS OPEN ARMS TOWARD APOSTATE PROTESTANT DENOMINATIONS AND THE ROMAN CATHOLIC CHURCH" (*Making Musical Choices*, Bob Jones University, 1986, p. 86).

Not one NOT ONE CCM musician that I know of stands *against* ecumenism and stands boldly *for* the Word of God, the New Testament church, the whole counsel of Bible doctrine, ecclesiastical separation, personal separation from the world, etc.

Consider the doctrine of biblical separation. The Bible solemnly warns God's people to avoid those who teach false doctrine.

> "Now I beseech you, brethren, mark them which cause divisions and offences contrary to the doctrine which ye have learned; and AVOID THEM" (Romans 16:17).

> "Be not deceived: evil communications corrupt good manners" (1 Cor. 15:33).

> "Be ye not unequally yoked together with unbelievers: for what fellowship hath righteousness with unrighteousness? and what communion hath light with darkness? And what concord hath Christ with Belial? or what part hath he that believeth with an infidel? And what agreement hath the temple of God with idols? for ye are the temple of the living God; as God hath said, I will dwell in them, and walk in them; and I will be their God, and they shall be my people. WHEREFORE COME OUT FROM AMONG THEM, AND BE YE SEPARATE, saith the Lord, and touch not the unclean thing; and I will receive you, And will be a Father unto you, and ye shall be my sons and daughters, saith the Lord Almighty" (2 Corinthians 6:14-18).

> "But I fear, lest by any means, as the serpent beguiled Eve through his subtlety, so your minds should be corrupted from the simplicity that is in Christ. For if he that cometh preacheth another Jesus, whom we have not preached,

or if ye receive another spirit, which ye have not received, or another gospel, which ye have not accepted, YE MIGHT WELL BEAR WITH HIM" (2 Corinthians 11:3-4). [Paul rebuked the Corinthian believers for their carnal tolerance of error and for their refusal to deal plainly with false teachers.]

"Now we command you, brethren, in the name of our Lord Jesus Christ, that ye WITHDRAW YOURSELVES from every brother that walketh disorderly, and not after the tradition which he received of us" (2 Thessalonians 3:6).

"Perverse disputings of men of corrupt minds, and destitute of the truth, supposing that gain is godliness: from such WITHDRAW THYSELF" (1 Timothy 6:5).

"But SHUN PROFANE AND VAIN BABBLINGS: for they will increase unto more ungodliness. And their word will eat as doth a canker: of whom is Hymenaeus and Philetus" (2 Timothy 2:16,17).

"If a man therefore PURGE HIMSELF FROM THESE, he shall be a vessel unto honour, sanctified, and meet for the master's use, and prepared unto every good work" (2 Timothy 2:21).

"Alexander the coppersmith did me much evil: the Lord reward him according to his works: Of whom BE THOU WARE also; for he hath greatly withstood our words" (2 Timothy 4:14-15).

"Having a form of godliness, but denying the power thereof: FROM SUCH TURN AWAY" (2 Timothy 3:5).

"Be not carried about with divers and strange doctrines. For it is a good thing that the heart be established with grace; not with meats, which have not profited them that have been occupied therein. We have an altar, whereof they have no right to eat which serve the tabernacle. For the bodies of those beasts, whose blood is brought into the sanctuary by the high priest for sin, are burned without the camp. Wherefore Jesus also, that he might sanctify the people with his own blood, suffered without the gate. LET US GO FORTH THEREFORE UNTO HIM WITHOUT THE CAMP, bearing his reproach" (Hebrews 13:9-13).

"Look to yourselves, that we lose not those things which we have wrought, but that we receive a full reward. Whosoever transgresseth, and abideth not in the doctrine of Christ, hath not God. He that abideth in the doctrine of Christ, he hath both the Father and the Son. If there come any unto you, and bring not this doctrine, RECEIVE HIM NOT INTO YOUR HOUSE, NEITHER BID HIM GOD SPEED: For he that biddeth him God speed is partaker of his evil deeds" (2 John 8-11).

> "I know thy works, and thy labour, and thy patience, and how THOU CANST NOT BEAR THEM WHICH ARE EVIL: and THOU HAST TRIED THEM which say they are apostles, and are not, and hast found them liars" (Revelation 2:2).

> "And I heard another voice from heaven, saying, COME OUT OF HER, MY PEOPLE, that ye be not partakers of her sins, and that ye receive not of her plagues" (Revelation 18:4).

I do not know of one CCM artist who takes these verses seriously by attempting to separate from and warn plainly of doctrinal error and of those who are committed to heresy.

The CCM scene is riddled with doctrinal confusion. Key terms which permeate the CCM scene are "anointed," "the body," "united," "John 17," "tolerance," "non-critical love," "judge not," "no finger pointing," etc. These are terms which identify the philosophy of the end-times ecumenical movement which is described in such passages as the following:

> "Preach the word; be instant in season, out of season; reprove, rebuke, exhort with all longsuffering and doctrine. For the time will come when they will not endure sound doctrine; but after their own lusts shall they heap to themselves teachers, having itching ears; And they shall turn away their ears from the truth, and shall be turned unto fables" (2 Timothy 4:2-4).

The end-times apostasy is characterized by a rejection of strong biblical absolutes and reproof and doctrine and by teachers who pamper instead of preach, who generalize instead of being specific, who are positive rather than negative, who build self esteem rather than call for repentance. The modern ecumenical movement, of which Contemporary Christian Music is an integral part, perfectly fulfills this dire prophecy.

Contemporary Christian Music is at home in the most ecumenical of contexts. The same music will be perfectly at home in a Roman Catholic retreat or a World Council of Churches conference or a charismatic Laughing Revival.

CCM is the music of ecumenical evangelism, as epitomized by Billy Graham and Luis Palau crusades. The following is a description of Billy Graham's 1997 crusade in San Antonio, Texas.

> "More than 700 San Antonio churches representing over 50 denominations have joined together for the Graham crusade, which hopes to attract South Texas youth with big-name Christian rock acts [Amy Grant, dc Talk, Charlie Daniels Band, Michael W. Smith, Steve Green, and Jaci Velasquez] and a Saturday service just for kids" (*Houston Chronicle*, April 2, 1997).

CCM was the music of the massive "Key '73" evangelistic program which was promoted by Billy Graham and many other key Christian leaders. The program brought together Baptists, Methodists, Episcopalians, Presbyterians, Lutherans, Pentecostals, Charismatics, and Roman Catholics. To create such a broad ecumenical unity requires that doctrinal issues be ignored. The message must be limited when the fellowship is enlarged. This ecumenical philosophy controlled the type of music which was used:

> "An extensive invitation was sent out for new music to be written that promoted the message of 'Key '73' with several stipulations: the words *righteousness, judgment, holiness, repentance*, and several other biblical terms were not allowed to be used, and THE LYRICS WERE TO BE OF A POSITIVE NATURE. There was an intentional effort made to write NON-OFFENSIVE songs" (H.T. Spence, *Confronting Contemporary Christian Music*, p. 142).

Contemporary Christian Music was also the music of the largest ecumenical charismatic conference of the 1980s. This was New Orleans '87, held in July 1987. I attended with press credentials. After four days of "renewal" choruses and Christian rock, it was obvious to me that CCM was the preferred music of the roughly 40,000 ecumenical-charismatics in attendance. Approximately 40 different denominations and groups came together under one roof, including Episcopalian, Church of Christ, United Methodist, American Baptist, Evangelical Lutheran Church in America, Presbyterian Church USA, and dozens of others. Fifty percent of those in attendance were 20,000 Roman Catholics. Roman Catholic priest Tom Forrest delivered the closing message and brought the mixed multitude to their feet when he called for unity. "We must reach the world," he cried, "and we must reach it the only way we can reach it; we must reach it TOGETHER!" At those words the crowd became ecstatic, leaping to their feet, shouting, stomping, speaking in tongues, dancing. This same priest spoke at a conference I attended in Indianapolis in 1990 and said he is thankful for Purgatory because he knows that he will not go to Heaven except through that means. Obviously he does not believe in the once-for-all sufficiency of Christ's atonement. At the book sales area in New Orleans one could purchase Rosary beads and Madonna's to assist in one's prayers to Mary. A Catholic mass was held every morning during the conference. The music that held all of this confusion together was CCM. Youth Explosion '87 was held at the same time, and 5,000 young people were bombarded with a steady diet of unscriptural teaching, ecumenism, testimonies by sports stars and entertainment figures, and ROCK music.

CCM is perfectly at home in the midst of such apostate ecumenical confusion.

The intimate charismatic connection within Contemporary Christian Music guarantees that it will be ecumenical. For example the Full Gospel Business Men's Fellowship International, in its earlier days, popularized a song which proclaimed, "I don't care what church you belong to." That was dropped and replaced with a Catholic song, "We Are One in the Spirit," which proclaims, "We are one in the Spirit, we are one in the Lord .... and we pray that all unity may one day be restored..." (Michael Harper, *Three Sisters: A Provocative Look at Evangelicals, Charismatics, & Catholic Charismatics and Their Relationship to One Another*, Wheaton: Tyndale House Publishers, 1979, pp. 28,29). When the Roman Catholic Church sings about Christian unity, of course, it is singing about non-Catholics being united with Rome!

The 1996 CCM hit "Gather at the River" promotes the ecumenical theme:

> "Sometimes we don't see eye to eye/ WE DON'T AGREE; WE DON'T KNOW WHY/ BUT JESUS PRAYED THAT WE'D BE ONE/ For the sake of God's own Son/ CAN WE PUT AWAY OUR DIFFERENCES/ LAY DOWN OUR PRIDE/ It's time we start turning the tide" (Joel Lindsey and Regie Hamm, "Gather at the River," *20 Contemporary Christian Hits*, Vol. 2, Benson Music Group, 1996).

This song is built upon the false ecumenical interpretation of John 17:21, which claims that the unity for which Christ prayed is an ecumenical unity of professing Christians which disregards biblical doctrine. The context of John 17 destroys this myth. In John 17 the Lord plainly emphasizes that the unity He desires is one based on salvation and Truth. It is not a unity of true Christians with false. It is not a unity which ignores doctrinal differences for the sake of an enlarged fellowship. (1) The unity of John 17 is a God-created unity (John 17:11). There is nothing in Christ's prayer to indicate that men are to do something to create the unity for which He prayed. John 17 *is a prayer addressed to God the Father, not to men*. It is not something man needs to do; it is something God has already done. The prayer was answered almost 2,000 years ago. It is a *spiritual reality* which was created by God among genuine believers who are committed to the Scriptures, not a *possibility* which must be organized by man. (2) The unity of John 17 is a unity in truth (vv. 17,19,6,8,14). Christ emphasized that He was praying for those who love and obey the Word of God. This is certainly not a prayer which envisions the modern ecumenical crowd which downplays and ignores the Word of God for the sake of a broad, lowest-common-denominator unity.

Note, too, that this ecumenical CCM song pretends that the doctrinal divisions between Christians are the result of pride ("lay down our pride") and ignorance ("we don't agree; we don't know why"). This conveniently overlooks the Bible's commands about defending the faith and separating from error. Christians who take these commands seriously refuse to be ecumenical, not because they are proud or ignorant, but because they desire to please the Lord. This ecumenical song slanders Bible-believing Christians who practice biblical separation.

CCM's influence toward ecumenism is well stated by a man who at one time preached against it—**Bob Larson**.

> "Have you ever seen a bunch of young people (be they Lutheran, Presbyterian, or Baptist, charismatic or evangelical) setting aside their religious idiosyncrasies to jump and shout when Petra walks on stage?... The shared experience will send them back to their own churches less theologically exclusive. From that moment on, they are 'not of this world' with all of its petty ecclesiastical divisions." (Bob Larson, *Contemporary Christian Music Magazine*, December 1985).

This statement by Larson is extremely sad. There was a time when he preached against Christian rock, yet he refused to separate from charismatics and others who were walking a path of disobedience and error. He held meetings under charismatic and ecumenical sponsorship, as well as the sponsorship of other groups and churches which were not scriptural. Now we see the fruit of this disobedience and reckless disregard for biblical separation. Has God not warned that evil communications corrupt good manners?

Again, God is proven true. Men set aside God's commands for separation to their own spiritual detriment. Once Larson preached against Christian rock; now he is ensnared by it and promotes the Devil's grand worldwide ecumenical schemes. (Not only has Larson abandoned his former position on music, but he divorced the wife of his youth and married another woman.)

Larry Norman is called the father of Christian rock music. His attitude toward churches and denominations is typical of a large percentage of CCM musicians. Norman is non-denominational, in fact, almost anti-denominational. When asked the simple question by *Buzz* magazine about what church he attended, he became very defensive and absolutely refused to answer, except to say that "I think it's unimportant" and "I just don't like the question." He also said, "I'm non-denominational in my thinking." He also implied that he believes it is an "obsessive compulsion" to meet at regular weekly times for church.

Clay Crosse, one of the top 30 CCM artists of 1998, reveals his ecumenical philosophy in the song "Saving the World" —

> "So many preachers/ So many churches and denominations/ Got their opinions and their documents/ And statements and beliefs/ and sometimes there's a miscommunication/ And we complicate the truth/ And convolute the story/ But as far as I recall/ I do believe it all comes down to a man dying on a cross/ Saving the world/ Rising from the dead/ Doing what he said he would do/ Loving everyone."

While it is true that some denominational divisions have complicated the truth and there is some miscommunication between professing Christians, Crosse leaves his listeners with the false and dangerous impression that doctrine and statements of faith are unimportant and unnecessary, that all that is important is the central fact of Christ's death and resurrection and an ill-defined universal love. The words to this song reflect the ecumenical philosophy of organizations such as Promise Keepers and March for Jesus. We must put aside doctrinal disputes and have unity among all who "love Jesus." This ecumenical philosophy lightly passes over the Bible's warnings about false teachers. It ignores the Bible's prophecies of worldwide apostasy. It fails to address Paul's warning that there are false christs and false gospels. If the only thing that is truly important before God is the central fact of the Gospel, why does the Bible contain so much else? Timothy was instructed to keep the Word of God "without spot" (1 Timothy 6:13-14). This refers to keeping the smallest detail.

Phil Driscoll, who is frequently voted by readers of *CCM Magazine* as one of the most popular CCM musicians, holds the ecumenical philosophy: "In the November 23, 1987, *Today's Banner*, Driscoll said: 'I have felt in my heart for a long time that music was the power that God would use to transcend every denomination, every barrier that has kept God's people apart.' Driscoll's *Make Us One* was the theme song for the April 1988 Washington For Jesus charismatic rally. Yet he is featured in concert at Jerry Falwell's Liberty University!" (*Calvary Contender*, January 1, 1989).

John Fischer is a CCM performer and writer and a regular columnist for *CCM Magazine*. His unscriptural philosophy is evident from the following statement:

> "I'd love to see the labels fall off. I'd love to not have to call things Christian or secular anymore. ... I'd rather we weren't so trapped in dogma, so busy confirming what we already know, so eager to hear what we already agree with, that we miss another point of view that might just happen to come from God. I'd love to see Christians less concerned about getting the words right and more concerned about the heart" (John Fischer, *CCM Magazine*, March 1990, p. 52).

This is completely contrary to the teaching of the Word of God. Fischer wants Christians to stop being trapped in dogma, but what is dogma? It is doctrine or teaching, and doctrine is precisely why God gave His Word. The Bible is for doctrine (2 Timothy 3:16-17). Timothy was instructed to stand fast in the doctrine he had been taught by the Apostle and to impart that exact same doctrine to others. "'And the things that thou hast heard of me among many witnesses, THE SAME commit thou to faithful men, who shall be able to teach others also" (2 Timothy 2:2). Timothy was to allow NO OTHER DOCTRINE to be taught (1 Timothy 1:3). The faith once delivered to the saints is to be defended by every generation of Christians (Jude 3). This means God's people are to know the sound doctrine of the Word of God and they are to fight for it against anything that is contrary to it. Doctrine is a basis of separation (Romans 16:17). It is impossible to stand for sound doctrine without being deeply concerned about "getting the words right." Doctrine is given to us in words, and it is promoted and defended by words, and if those words are not right the doctrine is not right. Fischer wants less concern for doctrinal truth and more concern for the heart. The attitude and motives of the heart are very important before God, but the heart is not the standard for truth; it is too undependable. The heart of man is deceitful above all things and desperately wicked (Jeremiah 17:9).

Steve Green is a popular CCM musician who has sung at ecumenical forums such as the Religious Broadcasters Association annual convention, Moody Bible Institute's Founders Week, Billy Graham crusades, and Promise Keepers rallies. He has performed at a half dozen Promise Keepers meetings since 1993. At the Promise Keepers Atlanta Clergy Conference in 1996, Green sang, "Let the Walls Come Down," referring to PK's goal of breaking down of walls between denominations. Several Catholic priests were present at that conference, and Dr. Ralph Colas, who attended the event, described it in these words: "The big beat, contemporary music brought the ministers to their feet...." Steve Green belted out repeatedly "Let the Walls Come Down." The 40,000 clergy shouted, whistled, clapped, and cheered as they worked to a higher and higher pitch of emotion. Dr. Colas said: "While there may be some good things said at a PK conference, this meeting included compromise, ecumenism, apostasy, Jesuit casuistry (end justifies the means), and hyper-emotionalism, along with a theology based on relationships rather than Biblical truth."

The Imperials are also very ecumenical. In 1992, for example, they conducted concerts at the First Assembly of God in Virginia Beach, Virginia, and at the Lancaster Bible College the same month. They frequently appear on Trinity Broadcasting Network. On August 21, 1998, they appeared at Focus on the Family in Colorado Springs, Colorado.

The Gaithers are very ecumenical and have a close, non-critical relationship with the Pentecostal-Charismatic movement. They provided the music one evening at Indianapolis '90, a large ecumenical charismatic gathering I attended with press credentials. One-half of the 25,000 participants were Roman Catholics and the other half represented roughly 40 different denominations. A Catholic mass was held each morning during this conference, and a Catholic priest brought the closing message. The Gaithers were at home in this unscriptural gathering and entertained the mixed multitude with their jazzy music.

The Gaithers frequently perform and record songs which present an ecumenical philosophy. "Songs that Answer Questions" from their *Back Home in Indiana* album has the following lyrics:

> "Don't want to spend my life a preachin' sermons/ that give answers to the questions no one's asking anywhere/ When there's so much pain and hurting/ there's no time to be searching/ for the needles in the haystacks that aren't there/ I wanna spend my time a wearin' myself out for Jesus/ with the news a cure's been found to heal our land/ Stead of making lists, inventing creeds/ that aren't concerned with people's needs/ I'll show 'em how to touch the nail scarred hand/ Don't wanna spend my time prayin' prayers/ Bombarding heaven with requests to rain down fire on saints who care [unclear]/ In our methods we may differ, but if Christ the Lord we live for/ May we not forget the enemy is OUT THERE."

This song contains half-truths and subtle errors, which are more dangerous than plain and obvious errors. While it is true that God's people are to be concerned about suffering and are to be showing people how to "touch the nail scarred hand," it is not true that preaching is to be limited merely to answering questions people have. The preacher is instructed to preach the whole counsel of God and the whole Word of God (Acts 20:27; 2 Tim. 3:16-17; 4:1-2). The Bible warns that it is apostate people who will desire teachers who teach merely what they want to hear, what they feel a need for (2 Timothy 4:3-4). This sounds very much like what the Gaithers are singing about. It is also not true that "a cure's been found to heal our land." The cure provided by the Gospel is the cure for personal salvation, not national salvation. The Apostles did not try to "heal the land," they preached the Gospel and discipled believers. It is also not true that it is wrong to "make lists" or "invent creeds" that aren't concerned with people's needs. The lists and creeds mentioned in this song refer to doctrinal studies and statements of faith. Doctrinal studies must, first of all, faithfully represent Bible truth, regardless of whether or not it meets "people's needs." Sound Bible doctrine does meet man's deepest needs, of course, but that does not mean that Bible doctrine meets the *felt needs* of unsaved or carnal people. The unsaved or carnal man does not feel he has a need to be told he is a sinner or that he is has no righteousness before God or that he is to repent or that he is to die to self or that he is to separate from the world or that there is an eternal hell, etc., but sound Bible doctrine tells him all of these things. The unsaved crowd does not believe it needs any of the Bible, really! This song encourages the hearers to despise doctrinal studies and research and teaching and statements of faith, which is the attitude typically found in the ecumenical movement. It is also not true that the divisions among Christians are merely about differing methods or that differing methods are not important. Take baptism, for example. Some denominations "baptize" infants. That is their "method." Some baptize only those who have trusted Jesus Christ as their Savior. Some sprinkle; others immerse. These are differing methods, but they are not insignificant and cannot be ignored. It is also not true that the "enemy" is limited to things outside of the churches. The Bible warns of false teachers, false christs, false spirits, false gospels, deluding spirits, doctrines of devils—all of which will be found within churches and among professing Christians. It is also not true that fundamentalists are praying for fire to fall on those with whom they disagree doctrinally. That is a nonsensical, actually a vicious, slander. The unscriptural and very dangerous message of this song is put across by the effective means of pleasant country-rock music and by the use of repetition.

Another ecumenical Gaither song is "Jesus Built This Church on Love" from their *Back Home in Indiana* album. The lead on the song is performed by Candy "Hemphill" Christmas, who travels with the Gaithers. The song is sung at many of the Gaither concerts. It is done in the style of a mid-tempo jazzy black spiritual with heavy drums and bass guitar.

> "Do you ever just get to wonderin'/ 'bout the way things are today?/ So many on board this gospel ship/ Trying to row in a different way/ If we'd all pull together/ Like a family me and you/ We'd come a lot closer to doin'/ what the Lord called us to do.
>
> Chorus: "Jesus built this church on love/ and that's what it's all about/ Trying to get everybody saved/ not to keep anybody out..."

This song implies that the divisions within Christianity are largely if not entirely man-made and unnecessary, that if professing Christians would merely "pull together" and exercise love the divisions would be healed. It is a feel-good sentiment, a nice fairy tale which has wide appeal, but it is unreasonable and unscriptural. The Lord Jesus Christ and the Apostles warned repeatedly that false teachers would lead many astray, that there would be false christs, false spirits, false gospels, false churches, doctrines of devils (Matt. 7:15-23; 24:3-5,11,24; Acts 20:28-30; 2 Cor. 1:1-4; Galatians 1; 1 Tim. 4:1; 2 Tim. 3:13; 4:3-4; 2 Pet. 2; 1 John 4:1; Jude; etc.). The book of Revelation predicts a one-world end-time harlot Christian religion (Rev. 17). Those who preach an ecumenical unity rarely even mention these Bible warnings and never focus on them. They do not tell us where these false christs, false gospels, false spirits, false teachers, and false churches are in Christianity today. They imply, rather, that the denominational divisions are largely unnecessary and petty which could be overcome by a little ecumenical love. There are many problems among Christians which can be healed through love, but it simply is not true that love will heal the major divisions within Christianity. The differences between denominations involve serious doctrinal issues which cannot be ignored and which cannot be solved through sentimental songs. This Gaither song also says the churches are "not to keep anybody out." That is openly contrary to the Bible's command to separate from error and to exercise church discipline (Rom. 16:17; 1 Corinthians 5; 2 Cor. 6:14-18; 1 Tim. 6:3-5; 2 Tim. 2:16-21; 3:5; 2 John 8-11; Rev. 18:4).

Another ecumenical Gaither song is "Loving God, Living Each Other" from the album by that name.

> "They pushed back from the table/ To listen to his words/ His secret plan before he had to go/ It's not complicated/ Don't need a lot of rules/ This is all you need to know/ We tend to make it harder/ Build steeples out of stone/ Fill books with explanations of the way/ But if we'd stop and listen/ And break a little bread/ We would hear the Master say/ It's Loving God, loving each other/ Making music with my friends/ Loving God, loving each other/ And the story never ends."

The song contains more half truths and subtle errors. Love is a very important part of the Christian life, but true Christian love is obeying God's Word (John 14:23; 1 John 5:3). To say that we "don't need a lot of rules" ignores the fact that the New Testament is literally filled with commandments! To say that we don't need to "fill books with explanations of the way" ignores the fact that the Bible instructs us to "Study to show thyself approved unto God, a workman that needeth not to be ashamed, rightly dividing the word of truth" (2 Tim. 2:15). It ignores the fact that the Bible is given for "doctrine" (teaching) (2 Tim. 3:16) and that preachers are instructed to teach other men (2 Tim. 2:2), that older women are instructed to teach younger women (Titus 2:3-5), etc. Bible teaching certainly involves "filling books with explanations of the way." That is precisely what the Apostles did in the Epistles. The Bible itself contains 66 books with explanations of the way! This Gaither song presents a sentimental, ecumenical approach to the Christian life and ministry which is simplistic and appealing to a modern crowd but which is patently contrary to the Scriptures. The unscriptural message of this song is put across by the very effective means of pleasant country-rock music and by the use of repetition.

Darlene Zschech, worship director at Hills Christian Life Centre in Australia, has published many popular worship albums under the title of Hillsong Music Australia. She makes the following comment about the album "You Shine" —
"There is a new sound and a new song being proclaimed across the earth. **It's the sound of a unified church**, coming together, in one voice to magnify our magnificent Lord" (from the album cover). She gives no warning about the fact that many churches are apostate.

The founder of the Resurrection Band, **Glenn Kaiser**, describes the group's ecumenical philosophy:

> "Jesus prayed that all of His followers 'may be one' (John 17:20-23). ... Ninety-nine percent of all true Christians believe in the same basic Bible doc-

> trines. But when hairs are split ... so are we—one from another. ... Over the years, I have had the pleasure of meeting true Christians in nearly every kind of denominational (large and small) and inter- or nondenominational church" (Kaiser, *The Responsibility of the Christian Musician*, pp. 53-55).

Kaiser misrepresents Christ's prayer in John 17. The Lord Jesus was not asking Christians to build ecumenical unity. He was praying to God the Father to create supernatural unity among those who are born again. That prayer was answered. Those who are born again are members of the same family. Christ certainly did not pray that His people will ignore false doctrine and sin for the purpose of creating a man-made unity. That would be contrary to the teaching of many other passages. Timothy, for example, was instructed not to allow ANY OTHER DOCTRINE (1 Timothy 1:3). That is an extremely narrow view of doctrinal soundness. Such an attitude toward doctrine will not allow a Christian to be ecumenical, because he cannot ignore false doctrine.

Kaiser's idea that 99% of "true" Christians believe the same basic doctrines is simply not accurate. The largest group of professing Christians are Roman Catholics—roughly one billion strong. Roman Catholicism teaches all sorts of unscriptural doctrines, such as the mass as a re-sacrifice of Christ, baptism as regeneration, the pope as the holy father, Mary as the Queen the Heaven, the priests as representatives of Christ, the sacraments as means of salvation, and purgatory as the means of purification. Perhaps Kaiser and the Resurrection Band do not consider Roman Catholics true Christians. If so, why did he not warn about Catholic doctrine in his book and why does he not warn of the following CCM musicians who are themselves Catholic or of those who treat Romanists as if they are true Christians? Another large group of professing Christians are members of various Protestant denominations, such as Lutheran and Episcopalian. Both of these teach a form of infant baptism and baptismal regeneration. This one heresy alone would require that we mark and avoid them in obedience to Romans 16:17. Another large group are Pentecostals, many of whom have perverted the doctrine of the Holy Spirit and denied the doctrine of eternal security. These are doctrinal errors which cannot be ignored for the sake of ecumenism.

As could be expected by those who study the ecumenical movement, **THERE IS A STRONG CONNECTION BETWEEN CCM AND THE ROMAN CATHOLIC CHURCH.**

The very popular **John Michael Talbot** is a Roman Catholic who prays to Mary and believes in tongues speaking, dreams, and other forms of extra-biblical revelation. He became a lay "brother" in the order of Secular Franciscans in 1979 and lives in Little Portion Hermitage in Eureka Springs, Arkansas. This is the home of the Brothers and Sisters of Charity, "an integrated monastic community of families, celibates and singles" founded by Talbot. It is formally recognized by the Catholic Church as a "Public

Association of the Faithful." In his book *Simplicity,* Talbot stated: "Personally, I have found praying the Rosary to be one of the most powerful tools I possess in obtaining simple, childlike meditation on the life of Jesus Christ." The Rosary is largely a prayer to Mary as the Queen of Heaven. In 1984 Talbot said: "I am also feeling the presence of Mary becoming important in my life. ... I feel that she really does love me and intercedes to God on my behalf" (*Contemporary Christian Music Magazine,* November 1984, p. 47).

Talbot says: "Music is an extension of my life. When I became a Christian, my music became Christian music. When I became Catholic, my music became Catholic music" (B. Cole Bennett, "John Michael Talbot: An Encounter with the Counter-Culture," *Shout!* magazine, February 1996).

Talbot's albums were the first by a Catholic artist to be accepted by both Protestant and Catholic listeners. "In 1988, *Billboard Magazine* reported that Talbot out-ranked all other male Christian artists in total career albums sold. After more than three million sales with Sparrow Records, making him Sparrow's all-time best-selling recording artist, John Michael Talbot started a new record label in 1992 called Troubadour for the Lord" ("John Michael Talbot," Talbot's web site).

In an article entitled "Our Fathers, and Our Divided Family," in the Catholic charismatic magazine *New Covenant,* Talbot called for Christian unity on the basis of the Roman Catholic papacy:

> "A Roman Catholic, I respect other Christians. We are especially close to those who value apostolic tradition as well as Scripture. But even in this we face further debates that are obstacles to complete Christian unity. THIS IS WHY THE CATECHISM OF THE CATHOLIC CHURCH INSISTS THAT SCRIPTURE, TRADITION AND MAGISTERIUM ARE NECESSARY FOR A FULLY UNIFIED PEOPLE. WE ROMAN CATHOLICS FIND THIS IN THE POPE AS BISHOP OF ROME, TOGETHER WITH THE BISHOPS OF THE CHURCHES IN FULL COMMUNION WITH ROME. This has theologically freed us to develop the greatest mystical and functional unity in Christendom. It has also given us an authority that enables us to enter into interfaith and ecumenical dialogue without defensiveness. ... May we all hear these ancient truths and experience real conversion of heart" (emphasis added) (John Talbot, "Our Fathers, and Our Divided Family," *New Covenant,* September 1997, p. 21).

Talbot says Catholic tradition and the papacy are equal in authority with the Scripture. He says the fullest expression of true Christian unity can be found only in fellowship with the pope of Rome. He prays that his readers will hear this message and experience conversion to Rome. What could be more unscriptural? The Apostle Paul said anyone, even an angel from heaven, who preaches a false gospel is cursed of God (Galatians 1).

The Roman Catholic popes, with their sacramental gospel and blasphemous claims and titles, have been under this curse from their unscriptural origin. Nowhere does the New Testament say the Apostles passed on their authority at death. The true Apostles were given miracle-working signs to authenticate their calling (2 Cor. 12:12). Nowhere does the New Testament establish a pope over all of the churches, and nowhere do we see Peter acting or living as a pope. We don't need the so-called "church fathers" to explain to us the rule of faith and practice; God has given us an infallible and sufficient rule in the Scriptures (1 Timothy 3:16,17) which were completed by the Apostles and which were sealed with a solemn seal in Revelation 22:18,19.

There is room, though, for Talbot's apostate theology in the doctrinally confused world of Contemporary Christian Music. He is considered a brother in Christ and is welcomed with open arms, even in the face of God's commands that we mark and avoid those who promote doctrine contrary to that taught by the Apostles (Romans 16:17-18). This is one of the many reasons why we refuse to have anything to do with CCM and its rebellious musicians and worldly musical styles. The Devil is using the ecumenical thrust of CCM to break down the walls between truth and error toward the completion of the one-world apostate "church." Referring to the mixed crowds who attended his concerts in Catholic churches, Talbot said that he delights to see Protestants who never would have darkened the doorstep of a Catholic church come to one of his concerts. "All of a sudden they say, 'Hey, I feel very much at home here. That doesn't mean necessarily I want to be a Roman Catholic, but I feel very much at home worshipping God with other people who are not that different from me'" (John Talbot, quoted in "Interfaith Album Strikes Sour Note," Peter Smith, Religious News Service, Dec. 8, 1996).

There is room, though, for Talbot's apostate theology in the doctrinally confused world of Contemporary Christian Music. He is considered a brother in Christ and is welcomed with open arms, in the face of God's commands that we mark and avoid those who promote doctrine contrary to that taught by the Apostles (Romans 16:17-18). This is one of the many reasons why we refuse to have anything to do with CCM and its rebellious musicians and worldly musical styles. The Devil is using the ecumenical thrust of CCM to break down the wall between truth and error toward the completion of the one-world apostate "church." Referring to the mixed crowds who attend his concerts in Catholic churches, Talbot said that he delights to see Protestants who never would have darkened the doorstep of a Catholic church come to one of his concerts. "All of a sudden they say, 'Hey, I feel very much at home here. That doesn't mean necessarily I want to be a Roman Catholic, but I feel very much at home worshipping God with other people who are not that different from me'" (John Talbot, quoted in "Interfaith Album Strikes Sour Note," Peter Smith, Religious News Service, Dec. 8, 1996). Surveys show that 60 percent of Talbot's listeners are non-Catholic.

In 1996 Talbot produced an album jointly with fellow CCM performer **Michael Card** (who claims to be an evangelical). They also embarked on a concert tour which included concerts in eight cities, "with the audience mix estimated at 50 percent Catholic and 50 percent Protestant" (*Charisma*, December 1996, p. 29). In March 1996 they performed together for the largest gathering of Catholics in America at the Los Angeles Religious Education Congress. Roughly 20,000 "clergy and laity" attended this congress. Both men also spoke at the formation retreat for the Catholic Musicians Association. Talbot is the president of this new association.

On their album Talbot and Card sing:

> "There is one faith/ One hope and one baptism/ One God and Father of all/ There is one church, one body, one life in the spirit/ Now given so freely for all."

What one faith, baptism, and church? The Roman Catholic faith is not the Bible faith. It's infant baptism certainly is not biblical baptism. The Roman church is not the New Testament church found in Scripture. Consider what the Vatican II Council said about purgatory:

> "The doctrine of purgatory clearly demonstrates that even when the guilt of sin has been taken away, punishment for it or the consequences of it may remain to be expiated or cleansed. They often are. In fact, in purgatory the souls of those who died in the charity of God and truly repentant, but who had not made satisfaction with adequate penance for their sins and omissions are cleansed after death with punishments designed to purge away their debt" (Vatican II documents, Apostolic Constitution on the Revision of Indulgences, 3).

Purgatory means to cleanse or purify. It is a plain and open denial of the perfect sufficiency of the atonement of the Lord Jesus Christ to take away all sin. The Bible says, "For by one offering he hath perfected for ever them that are sanctified" (Heb. 10:14). Rome has a faith, a baptism, and a church, but it is not the one we read about in the Holy Scriptures. Why, then, would Michael Card pretend that he and John Talbot are singing about the same thing? If Card believes Talbot's faith is the one true faith, why does he not become a Roman Catholic?

Of this ecumenical venture with Talbot, Card testified: "Doing this project has enabled us to become real friends. And along the way, THE DENOMINATIONAL LINES HAVE BECOME REALLY MEANINGLESS TO ME, AND TO JOHN, TOO" (*CCM Magazine*, July 1996). It is painfully obvious that doctrinal truth means nothing to these CCM performers. If Talbot really took his Catholic doctrine seriously, he would not yoke together with those who deny that doctrine, and if Card really took his evangelical doctrine seriously he would not yoke together with a man who denies that doctrine. If the Pope is truly the Vicar of Christ and the head of all Christians, it would be wicked to deny it; but if the Catholic papacy is nothing but a man-made tradition, it is wicked to believe it. If Mary is truly the immaculate ever-virgin Queen of Heaven, it would be wicked to deny it; but if the Catholic Mary is a demonic idol, it is wicked to believe it. If the Catholic priesthood really is ordained by God, it would be wicked to deny it; but if it has no authority from God and is merely a tradition of man, it is wicked to accept it. There is no middle ground here. There can be no fellowship between those who hold doctrines this diverse. The Bible says those who teach doctrine contrary to that which the Apostles delivered are to be marked and avoided (Romans 16:17). The Bible wisely asks: "Can two walk together, except they be agreed?" (Amos 3:3).

In 1996, Talbot was instrumental in forming the **Catholic Musicians Association** to encourage Catholic musicians and to help them find a place in the more mainstream Contemporary Christian Music world. Talbot's friend Michael Card performed at the formation meeting for the new Association. Joining Talbot at the founding meeting in April 1996 were Tony Melendez, Dana, Susan Stein (an executive of Catholic-owned Heartbeat Records), Paulette McCoy (Oregon Catholic Press), Catholic church officials and professionals involved in marketing and publicity (Steve Rabey, "Association Formed to Support Catholic Music," *CCM Update*, May 27, 1996). At the meeting Stein said she "would like Protestants and Catholics to set aside what are basically petty differences" and she urged evangelicals "to be a bit less judgmental and a bit more open to understanding" (Ibid.). You can be sure that Stein's advice will be taken by the ecumenically-minded CCM crowd.

The most prolific musician with Heartbeat Records is **Dana**. She performed for Pope John Paul II at World Youth Day in 1993, and has an album titled "The Rosary" which is about praying to Mary as the Queen of Heaven. Dana's album "We Are One Body" is a call for ecumenical unity.

Other Catholic musicians who move within Contemporary Christian Music circles are **Kathy Troccoli, Tom Booth, Sarah Hart, Danny Langdon, and Sheryl Crow**. The *National Catholic Register* mentioned all of these in an article in the March 8-14, 1998, issue, stating that they are using their music to "evangelize" evangelical young people into the Catholic faith.

Kathy Troccoli has been nominated five times as the Gospel Music Association female vocalist of the year. Her 1995 album, *Sounds of Heaven*, spawned five No. 1 singles. She is a national spokesperson for Chuck Colson's Prison Fellowship. In an interview with *CCM Magazine* in 1997 she said: "But I'd been very judgmental toward the Catholic church for years, and I've recently been able to go back to it without having a chip on my shoulder. I now have a much greater capacity for—as the album says—*Love and Mercy*." Troccoli preaches an ecumenical, non-judgmental, anti-fundamentalist philosophy:

> "To me it's very simple: if the world doesn't see God's love in us and our love for each other, they're never going to want what we have. Our dogma and legalism strangle the love of Christ right out of us" (*CCM Magazine*, June 1997).

This sounds good to many ears, and there is no doubt about the importance of Christian love; but it is impossible to obey the Bible without being deeply concerned about doctrine ("dogma") and obedience to the details of God's Word ("legalism"). Jude 3 explains that God has given one faith to His people and that faith, as recorded in the New Testament Scriptures, is to be preserved and fought for until Jesus returns. It is absolutely impossible to obey Jude 3 and be ecumenical and non-judgmental at the same time. The chief thing which divides denominations is doctrine.

Troccoli's 1997 album, *Love One Another*, has an ecumenical theme: "Christians from all denominations demonstrating their common love for Christ and each other" (Dave Urbanski, "Chatty Kathy," *CCM Magazine*, June 1997). The recording of the title song involved 40 CCM artists: Amy Grant, Gary Chapman, Clay Crosse, Sandi Patty, Michael W. Smith, Carman, Tony Vincent, Jonathan Pierce, Mark Lowry, Phillips, Craig and Dean, Aaron and Jeoffrey, Jaci Velasquez, Lisa Bevill, Scott Krippayne, Sarah Masen, Babbie Mason, Sara Jahn, Carolyn Arends, Vestal Goodman, Paul Vann, Billy and Sarah Gaines, Tim Taber, Sarah Hart, Peter Penrose, Janet Paschal, Beverly Crawford, Phil Joel of the Newsboys, Kevin Smith of dc Talk, Tai Anderson of Third Day, plus the members of Out of the Grey, Beyond the Blue, 4 HIM, Christafari, and Audio Adrenaline. Like most CCM songs, this one is owned by a secular corporation. It is copyrighted 1996 by Sony/ATV Songs, Tree Publishing, Pants Down Music, and Radioquest Music Publishing. The song talks about tearing down the walls of denominational division.

> "Look around the world today/ There is anger there is hate/ And I know that it grieves His heart/ When His people stand apart/ Cause we're the only Jesus they will see/ Love one another, and live as one in His name/ Love one another we can tear down walls by His grace" ("Love One Another").

The broad range of participants who joined Kathy Troccoli in recording "Love One Another" demonstrates the ecumenical agenda of Contemporary Christian Music. The song witnessed Catholics, Pentecostals, Baptists, etc., yoked together to call for Christian unity. The New Testament repeatedly warns of widespread apostasy among those who claim to be Christians, yet the ecumenical movement ignores apostasy and calls for almost unqualified unity among professing Christians. While there is little doubt that God is grieved by some of the divisions among Bible-believing Christians, it is not true that the heart of God is grieved by all divisions within Christianity, because there are divisions He Himself has commanded. He has commanded that His people separate from those who follow doctrinal error.

In 1988 the Catholic Daughter's of St. Paul formed **Krystal Records**. The first release was the album "No Greater Love" by Dana. One of the songs is "Totus Tuus," which means "Totally Yours" and which is Pope John Paul II's motto. The words, which are embroidered on his papal robes, refer to his dedication to Mary. Some have falsely claimed that the motto refers to the pope's dedication to Jesus Christ, but in his own book, *Crossing the Threshold of Hope* (Alfred A. Knopf, 1994), John Paul II testifies that *Totus Tuus* describes his devotion to Mary.

Phil Keaggy made a commitment to Christ in an Assemblies of God church in 1970, but he has not rejected Roman Catholicism. Note the following statement from a 1995 interview:

> "... the Gospel is preached in many Catholic churches, and the truth is known there. ... Over the years, I've been a part of many nondenominational churches and denominational churches, but I have even a higher regard and respect for my Catholic upbringing, because I believe it planted the seeds of faith in me. And I read books that give me a greater understanding of the Catholic faith today. I'm not a practicing Catholic, but I believe that I'm a true believer who responds to the truth that is there. Because it's ancient tradition; it goes way back. I think Martin Luther had some great ideas, and showed us that we're saved by grace through faith, but he was a Catholic when he posted all that up! ... I have great fellowship with my Catholic brethren today. I have some dear friends across the country that I've made. That's a whole other subject; but I think when the Lord looks at his Bride, he doesn't see the walls that we use to divide ourselves from each other. He sees one body, and that body is comprised of his children, those who he bought and paid for with his blood ... I love the liturgy; I think liturgy with the Spirit is one of the most powerful ways of communicating the life of God to us" (Phil Keaggy, cited by Tom Loredo, "Phil Keaggy in His Own Words," *Way Back Home*, December 1995).

It is true that Catholicism can plant seeds of faith in God which can sometimes be watered by the Gospel, but to say that Catholic churches preach the Gospel is completely untrue. Any Catholic church which preaches the true Gospel that salvation has nothing whatsoever to do with works or sacraments is preaching contrary to what Roman Catholicism teaches in its official proclamations. The Catholic Church plainly states that salvation is by grace PLUS works and sacraments. Not only does the Catholic Church deny the Gospel of the grace of Christ by its formal declarations, but in many other ways, as well. The all-sufficiency of Christ's once-for-all atonement is denied by the

Catholic Mass, which alleges to be a continual re-offering of Christ's sacrifice. The all-sufficiency of Jesus Christ is also denied by the Catholic priesthood, which alleges to stand between the believer and Christ. The all-sufficiency of Christ is further denied by the Catholic sainthood, which alleges to mediate between men and God. Keaggy says he loves the Catholic liturgy, but it is contrary to the Bible. There is no mass in the Bible. The Lord's Supper is not a sacrifice or a priestly ritual, it is a simple memorial meal (1 Corinthians 11). In fact, there are no sacraments in the New Testament Scriptures. Sacraments are supposed to be channels of grace, but the ordinances of the New Testament churches are not channels of grace but are symbols and reminders only.

When Keaggy says that God does not see differences between churches and denominations, he is discounting the importance of sound doctrine. The Lord Jesus Christ warned that there would be many false teachers who would lead many astray from the truth (Matt. 7:15). He warned that as His return draws nearer, the false teachers would increase (Matt. 24:11,24). The Apostles likewise warned of a great apostasy or turning away from the true New Testament faith, of the rise of many false teachers, of the creation of false churches (1 Timothy 4; 2 Timothy 3-4; 2 Peter 2; 1 John 2,4; Jude; Revelation 17). If God sees all denominations as a part of His one body, where are the false teachers? Where are the false churches? Where is the spirit of antichrist?

In an joint interview with *Religious Broadcasting*, Keaggy further emphasized his ecumenical philosophy and his view that Roman Catholicism is a legitimate expression of Christianity:

> "I think also the unity that is so necessary in the body of Christ is important. I admire Charles Colson. He got a lot of flack for writing the book, *The Body*, and being associated with Catholics. I was raised Catholic and my mother's influence was powerful in my life. I came to the Lord when she passed away. She sowed the seeds in my life for me to become a believer. There are divisive voices out there. People who thrive on disunity are the ones [to whom] you've got to say, 'I'm not going to contend with this, I'm not going to argue, I'm just going to go about my business'" ("Saran E. Smitha and Christine Pryor, "Integrity Times Two: Michael Card and Phil Keaggy," *Religious Broadcasting*, National Religious Broadcasters, July-August 1995).

The Christian life would be much simpler if one could follow Keaggy's advice and not get involved in contentions about doctrine and Christian living, but faithfulness to the Word of God does not allow it. God requires that His people "earnestly contend for the faith once delivered to the saints" (Jude 3) and reprove the unfruitful works of darkness (Ephesians 5:11). The Apostle Paul, looking back over his life, said that he had fought a good fight (2 Timothy 4:7) and instructed Timothy to fight the good fight of faith (1 Timothy 6:12). There is doctrinal fighting to be done. Most of Paul's epistles contain warnings about false doctrine. In his Pastoral Epistles, Paul warned of false teachers and compromisers BY NAME 10 times (1 Tim. 1:20; 2 Tim. 1:15; 2:17; 3:8; 4:10,14). Obedience to such commands does not allow me to follow Keaggy's New Evangelical advice.

Keaggy's unscriptural ecumenical philosophy is perfectly at home, though, in the world of Contemporary Christian Music.

Michael W. Smith performed at the Catholic-sponsored World Youth Day in Denver, Colorado, in 1993. Smith and guitarist-songwriter **Billy Sprague** performed with Catholic Kathy Troccoli at a concert in November 1985 in Tampa, Florida. The concert was sponsored by Youth for Christ and the First Assembly of God of Clearwater, Florida (*St. Petersburg Times*, Florida, Religious Section, Nov. 9, 1985, p. 3).

Smith and **Amy Grant** are among the CCM artists who have had interviews published in the Roman Catholic youth magazine *YOU* (*The Fundamentalist Digest*, May-June 1992). Kathy Troccoli was the backup singer for Amy Grant before she began her own recording career in 1982. In 1994 the Catholic St. John's University gave its highest award, the Pax Christi, to Grant (*Houston Chronicle*, May 7, 1994). Pax Christi is the radical International Catholic Peace Movement .

Margaret Becker claims to have had a religious experience which has made her more appreciative of her Roman Catholicism. In a 1994 interview she said she began mixing faith with her music and gained a greater appreciation for her own faith, Catholicism. "Now, I'm taking that knowledge with me back to the church of my youth. Becker declared: "The familiar prayers and practices are very rich and touch me in a different, more intimate way" (*The Fundamentalist Digest*, May-June 1994). She is ecumenical and moves in a wide range of denominational forums. For example, she was scheduled to appear at the First Assembly of God in Warrenton, Virginia, in September 1993. That same month she was featured in a "Margaret Becker Youth Fest" at a large Baptist Bible Fellowship church, Riverdale Baptist Church, Riverdale, Maryland. She was scheduled to appear at a Church of Christ in Converse, Indiana, in March 1994.

Rich Mullins died in an automobile accident in 1997. At the time of his death it was reported that he was taking the final steps to enter the Roman Catholic Church. He was attending mass at least weekly, and the night before he died, Mullins talked on the phone with priest Matt McGinness to corroborate that he was ready to say his first confession and be confirmed. McGinness describes the conversation as follows:

> "There was a sense of urgency. He [Mullins] told me, 'This may sound strange, but I HAVE to receive the body and blood of Christ.' I told him, 'That

doesn't sound strange at all. That sounds wonderful.' Rich finally sounded like he was at peace with his decision" (Terry Mattingly, "Rich Mullins—Enigmatic, Restless, Catholic," www.gospel.com.net/tmattingly/col.05.06.98.html).

Some have contradicted McGinness's report and have stated that Mullins was not actually going to join the Catholic Church, that he was only very interested in it. When asked if Rich converted to Catholicism, Dave Mullins, Rich's brother, made the following statement: "That's a topic of great many differing opinions. I can't say for sure. I don't think so. I know that he was very interested in the Catholic church, he was very interested in things that they could say about God that his upbringing and religious background had but he was that way with every group and so I think that he was very interested and he felt they had a better handle on some things than others but I don't see it happening. I know there's a Father in Wichita who said he was coming there and he was taking his vows and definitely doing it and I heard from others who talked to him the day before he died and he said, 'No, I'm not going to do it. There are things I can't go along with.' And from what I know of my brother even if he would've done it he wouldn't have lasted there" ("For Such a Time as This: An Interview with Dave Mullins," http://www.kidbrothers.net/interviews/dave/bro.html).

Rich Mullins' music reflected both his ecumenism and his latent Catholicism. The last project he completed, *Canticle of the Plains,* was based on the life and legend of the Catholic St. Francis of Assisi. The song "Creed" on Mullins' *Songs* album contains the words: "I believe in the Holy Spirit/ One Holy Church, the communion of Saints." This, of course, is from the so-called Apostles Creed, but Mullins sings the words in a Catholic context. On the booklet accompanying the CD the lyrics to this song are superimposed on a photo of a Catholic Madonna. The lyrics to the song "Alright ok uhhuh amen" are also superimposed on a picture of a Catholic Madonna holding a Rosary. The Rosary is a prayer to Mary as the Queen of Heaven.

Consider another song:

> "Faith without works baby/ It just ain't happenin'/ One is your left hand/ One is your right/ It'll take two strong arms/ To hold on tight" (Rich Mullins, "Screen Door").

This song presents the false gospel of Roman Catholicism and of every cult. One of the marks of false Christianity is to confuse faith and works, to somehow mix faith and works together for salvation. While it is true that faith without works is dead and that true saving faith produces works, it is not true that faith and works are the two strong arms by which we hold on tight to God and salvation (Ephesians 2:8-10), yet that is exactly the heresy what this song teaches. The Bible warns that grace and works cannot be mixed: "And if by grace, then is it no more of works: otherwise grace is no more grace. But if it be of works, then is it no more grace: otherwise work is no more work" (Romans 11:6).

The very popular **Sandi Patty** moves freely in ecumenical circles. She has entertained audiences as diverse as Billy Graham crusades, Jerry Falwell meetings, Southern Baptist Convention annual conferences, and Pope John Paul II masses (she performed at a papal mass in Los Angeles in September 1987).

Sheila Walsh frequently "performs" in charismatic-ecumenical settings. Together with roughly 20,000 Roman Catholics, she participated in the North American Congress on the Holy Spirit & World Evangelization in New Orleans in 1987.

When Pope John Paul II visited the United States in January 1999, many well-known Contemporary Christian musicians joined hands with hundreds of thousands of Catholics to welcome him. Featured at a Catholic youth rally connected with the Pope's visit, were **dc Talk**, **Audio Adrenaline**, **Rebecca St. James**, **Jennifer Knapp**, **The W's**, and **the Supertones** (*CCM Magazine*, April 1999, p. 12). According to Music and Entertainment News, **Jars of Clay** was also scheduled to appear, though other reports did not mention them (Music and Entertainment News, http://www.theenews.com/news/slug-12599_dctalk-pope.html). Knapp said she was excited about joining the Pope to "build on the unity of faith" (*CCM Magazine*, op. cit.). dc Talk's Kevin Max praised the Catholic youth for coming out to hear the Pope, describing John Paul II as "someone with something of substance to say" (Ibid.). A large group of nuns and Dominican priests "danced with abandon" at the Supertones rock music. Each attendee received a rosary with instructions about how to pray to Mary. This event portrays how Contemporary Christian Music is helping create the End Times, One-World Apostate "church."

The **Vineyard churches**, founded by the late **John Wimber**, have had a wide influence with their praise music. Wimber himself, who was the manager of the secular group The Righteous Brothers before his conversion, wrote many popular songs, and many of the Vineyard churches are noted for their influential music groups. The Vineyard is very ecumenical. Wimber frequently spoke on the same platform with Roman Catholic priests and apparently saw no serious problem with their doctrine. In 1986 Wimber joined Catholic priest Tom Forrest and Anglican Michael Harper at the European Festival of Faith, an ecumenical meeting in Birmingham, England. The Festival leaders and the 8,000 participants sent the pope of Rome a message: "We are ready to join you in the united evangelism of Europe" (*Australian Beacon*, March 1988).

Wimber was a featured speaker at the North American Congress on the Holy Spirit & World Evangelization in Indianapolis, August 1990. In that forum he joined hands with roughly 12,000 Roman Catholics, including countless priests and nuns. A Catholic mass was held every morning of the convention. I was present at this conference with press credentials and heard Wimber speak.

In October 1991, the Wimber conference in Sydney, Australia, featured Catholic priests Tom Forrest and Raniero Cantalamessa, as well as Catholic layman Kevin Ranaghan. Tom Forrest spoke at Indianapolis '90 and said he praises God for purgatory. Cantalamessa is the papal preacher at the Vatican. Ranaghan claims that the Roman Catholic Church alone contains the fullness of God and truth and that the pope is the infallible head of all churches. In spite of their blasphemous heresies, these men were featured by Wimber as Spirit-filled men of God.

In his church planting seminar Wimber said there is nothing scripturally wrong with the Catholic practice of seeking healing through relics: "In the Catholic church for over a 1,200 year period people were healed as a result of touching the relics of the saints. We Protestants have difficulty with that ... but we healers shouldn't, because there's nothing theologically out of line with that" (John Wimber, *Church Planting Seminar*).

Wimber was not only open to Roman Catholic doctrine but actively encouraged the reunification of Protestants with the church of Rome. "During the Vineyard pastors' conference, he went so far as to 'apologize' to the Catholic church on behalf of all Protestants ... He stated that 'the pope, who by the way is very responsive to the charismatic movement, and is himself a born-again evangelical, is preaching the Gospel as clear as anyone in the world today'" (Pastor John Goodwin, *Testing the Fruit of the Vineyard,* San Jose, Calif., citing John Wimber's *Church Planting Seminar*, audio tapes, 5 volumes, unedited, 1981).

In an article in the June 2001 issue of *CCM Magazine*, Contemporary Christian musicians are quoted praising Mother Teresa. **Mark Lowry**, who sings with the Gaither Quartet, praised Mother Teresa and Princess Diana. "Diana and Mother Teresa were using their influence for good. One from a palace and the other from poverty. That's what we all should do" (Gregory Rumburg and April Hefner, "The Princess and the Nun," *CCM Magazine*, June 2001). **Ray Boltz**, who met Mother Teresa in 1996, is also quoted in the article. He said: "Mother Teresa was an example to us. When she started this ministry, she was a teacher. She felt God calling her to minister to the poor. At that time, for a woman to tell her superiors she was called to ministry—that was really out of the ordinary. I am impressed she did not go along with status quo, but followed the call of God. That is refreshing and different and part of why she stands out" (Ibid.). Neither Lowry nor Boltz had a word of warning about Mother Teresa's false gospel that has caused multitudes to die with a false hope.

Contemporary Christian Music is ecumenical music, and for this reason alone it would be deeply suspect. Churches which do not allow ecumenical speakers and do not participate in ecumenical meetings and organizations are not wise to allow the ecumenical music to pervade the congregation. "Be not deceived: evil communications corrupt good manners" (1 Corinthians 15:33). "A little leaven leaveneth the whole lump" (Galatians 5:9).

CHARACTERISTIC #4 — CONTEMPORARY CHRISTIAN MUSIC CAN BE IDENTIFIED BY ITS CHARISMATIC ASSOCIATIONS

The third major characteristic of Contemporary Christian Music is its Pentecostal-Charismatic association. One observant writer called CCM "Commercial Charismatic Music" (Jerry Huffman, *Calvary Contender*, June 1, 1996).

The danger of allowing charismatic music into fundamental churches is spelled out by musician/teacher Tim Fisher:

> "There are many CCM performers who do not believe the Bible, yet we allow them to sing in the homes of our people on a daily basis without warning. If you would not allow a charismatic preacher in your pulpit, why let one sing to your people? I am not trying to portray all charismatics as unsaved, but we certainly do not want them as our teachers. To keep doctrine pure, we must separate from those who teach false doctrine and never give them an audience in our churches" (Tim Fisher, *The Battle for Christian Music*, p. 122).

Today's Contemporary Christian Music world traces its heritage back to the Jesus Movement of the 1970s. "Jesus" became popular among many within the rebellious hippie movement, yet in too many cases it was not a "Jesus" who called them out of the world but a "Jesus" who did not care if men continued to look like women, if women continued to dress immodestly, if young people continued to love the evil rock music they had enjoyed before "conversion." They wanted "Jesus" but they did not want to be very different from the world. There were pastors who were willing to cater to this attitude. Maranatha Music, which has popularized charismatic music throughout a wide range of churches, began as an outreach of Calvary Chapel of Costa Mesa, California. *CCM Magazine* describes Calvary Chapel as "a Mecca for long-haired Jesus people." Resurrection Band began as an outreach of Chicago's Jesus People USA.

When I was saved in 1973 from a hippie lifestyle, I knew that God wanted me to separate from the old ways, and when I saw in the Scripture that God was not pleased even with something as seemingly insignificant as my long hair, I cut it in order to please Him. The Jesus Movement did not have this attitude of submission to the details of God's Word. The insubordinate attitude on the part of the Christian rockers is admitted in an article in *CCM Magazine* which traces the history of Contemporary Christian Music:

> "If these new believers wound up in traditional churches, they were often taught that God wanted them to cut their hair, lengthen their skirts and turn a deaf ear to the Devil's music. But those who became part of the Jesus

Movement, a burgeoning Christian counter-culture, believed that God could redeem and use their music just the same as He had done with them" (Steve Rabey, "Age to Age," *CCM Magazine*, July 1998, p. 20).

Some of the early Christian rockers were Mylon LeFevre, Larry Norman, Phil Keaggy, Don Francisco, Michael and Stormie Omartian, Randy Matthews, Keith Green, and groups such as Petra, Resurrection Band, Love Song, and the Second Chapter of Acts. Most have Charismatic-Pentecostal roots, as do the majority of current CCM writers/performers.

"In the early 1970s, many churches adopted a new worship style. The February 1994 *Charisma* says: 'They traded in their hymns for praise songs accompanied by guitars, drums, clapping and even dancing.' It said, 'Today, praise music has entered the mainstream. Songs that were only sung in charismatic churches a few years ago are now heard throughout mainline and non-charismatic churches.' Southern Baptists and traditional evangelicals such as the Christian and Missionary Alliance are adopting charismatic worship styles, too. A March for Jesus coordinator says: 'Through praise and worship, we're seeing all denominations—Methodists, Baptists, Catholics, charismatics come together to proclaim the most important points of the gospel'" (*Calvary Contender*, Feb. 15, 1994).

The following are just a few examples of the Pentecostal-Charismatic connection in Contemporary Christian Music.

As noted already, the **2nd Chapter of Acts** was one of the early Jesus movement groups. They put Christian lyrics to soft rock music. The group was composed of three siblings: Annie, Nelly, and Matthew Ward. The group's manager and producer, Buck Herring, is Annie's husband. Herring is also the producer for CCM artists Barry McGuire, Phil Keaggy, Terry Talbot, Mike Deasy, Michael and Stormie Omartian, among others. The members of 2nd Chapter of Acts began attending Jack Hayford's Foursquare Pentecostal church in the early 1970s and were discipled by him. Hayford's denomination was founded by the divorced female Pentecostal preacher, Aimee Semple McPherson. The 2nd Chapter of Acts readily admitted that they are guided by prophetic "words" from the Lord. Consider this testimony by Annie: "Some years, He'd tell us, 'You are going to be planted. You will be harvesting in three years, but this year you are going to plant.' Another year He'd say, 'This year you are going to be ushering people into the presence of the Holy Spirit,' or 'This year is going to be a year of deliverance'" (Ibid.). They recorded their *Hymns* album because of "words" which were delivered to them three times by different individuals who approached them and said: "I believe God has a word for you—that you should do a hymns album." As they were recording this album Buck claims that "The Lord spoke to my heart and said, "I have chosen you to breathe life back into these songs for your generation.'"

I don't believe the Christ-honoring hymns ever ran out of life, and I reject the idea that they need new life breathed into them by wedding them to jazzed up music. I do agree that all too often the song services in Bible-believing churches are unnecessarily boring, but that is not usually the fault of the songs. Rather it is the fault of the leaders and congregation and the half-hearted manner with which the song service is approached. I address this at the end of the book in the section "Why Is the Music Part of Our Church Services Frequently So Lifeless?"

The 2nd Chapter of Acts taught the false latter rain theology that Christ's return will be preceded by a worldwide miracle evangelistic revival. "The Word of God says that we are to wait for the former and the latter rain, that in the last days God is going to pour out His Spirit. There is coming an outpouring of His Spirit and an ingathering that will make the 'Jesus Movement' of the early '70s pale by comparison. We can see that beginning to happen already. It's gonna rain!" (Buck Herring, Ibid.).

4 HIM is composed of four male singers: Andy Chrisman, Marty Magehee, Kirk Sullivan, and Mark Harris. Their song "Great Awakening" from their 1998 "Obvious" album, demonstrates their Pentecostal theology:

> "I believe there's a mighty power/ I believe it's a latter rain/ I believe there's a move of God calling us all higher/ Oh I believe these are the days of the great awakening/ More than our hearts can contain/ It is an overflow of God's amazing grace/ Coming to reconcile a world that's lost its way/ Oh, all consuming fire come purify us once again."

Another song on that album is titled "Signs and Wonders."

> "You light the dark/ You are the truth in love/ So we just need to trust the signs and wonders of the heart. ... You sent love to live in us, so we just need to trust the signs and wonders of the heart."

Nowhere in the New Testament are we told to trust "the signs and wonders of the heart." This is an unscriptural experiential approach to Christianity (as opposed to trusting the Bible explicitly rather than looking within oneself for signs) which has produced confusion and shipwreck in its path.

Pat Boone is a member of Jack Hayford's Foursquare Pentecostal Church.

Carman is extremely popular, even in fundamental Baptist circles, but he is a charismatic-ecumenist and his unscriptural Pentecostal theology permeates his music. In his song "Satan, Bite the Dust," Carman claims that he has "been sent with a warrant from the body of Christ" to arrest the Devil and to run every unclean spirit out of town. He claims to have the authority to cast out "depression, strife, disease and fear." In this strange song Carman asserts, "Satan, you coward, you molester of souls, I command you to appear." The Apostle Peter, though, tells us that even the angels do not bring railing accusations against the Devil (2 Peter 2:11). Nowhere in the New Testament Scriptures do we see the Apostles and early Christians speaking to the Devil in this manner. Carman then says: "I represent a whole new breed of Christian of today. And I'm authorized and deputized to blow you clean away." This is a probable reference to the New Order of the Latter Rain theology which claims that Christ's return will be preceded by a miracle revival whereby Christians will perform miracles and exercise kingdom authority over the powers of this present world. Some of the "prophets" which were popularized by John Wimber and the Vineyard movement, men such as Paul Cain, claim that God is raising up a "new breed" of end time Christian who will take authority over the Devil.

Carman's theology is not only wrong, it is nonsense. He has not blown away the Devil. He has not bound the Devil. He has not arrested the Devil. He has no power to command sickness to depart. He can pray and ask God to remove sickness, and God answers according to His will, but he cannot demand that sickness be healed. No Christian can. When Timothy was sick with frequent infirmities, the Apostle Paul did not command those infirmities to depart. Paul did not curse those infirmities as demonic. He did not say, "I bind you, foul infirmity." No, he said: "Drink no longer water, but use a little wine for thy stomach's sake and thine often infirmities" (1 Tim. 5:23). I will be glad to take any charismatic preacher with me into a hospital and we will demonstrate right there which of us is doctrinally correct in this matter. If a Christian has the power to bind the Devil and to cast out sicknesses, let's see it. In reality, all the charismatic can do is precisely what I do. He can pray for the sickness, and sometimes the prayer is answered and sometimes it is not. Carman is confusing the minds of God's people and leading them away from the truth with his false doctrine.

In typical charismatic fashion Carman rebukes the "demon of alcoholism" and the "spirit of infirmity," demanding that these "demons" depart. He proclaims, "We lay hands on the sick and they recover." In another song, "Our Turn Now," Carman exclaims: "World, you had your turn at bat/ Now stand back and see/ That it's our turn now/ Some things gonna change/ We're gonna bind the/ Devil at every hand by/ the power of Jesus' name." This is unadulterated charismatic kingdom now, dominionism theology. It is dispensational confusion. These things will not come to pass until the Lord Jesus Christ returns and establishes His kingdom.

Steven Curtis Chapman is a member of the Pentecostal Christ Community Church near Nashville, Tennessee. An article in *Newsweek* magazine noted that "Christ Church in Nashville has the hottest choir in town, bar none, and the Pentecostal service on any given Sunday is liable to rock the pews" ("God and the Music Biz," *Newsweek*, May 30, 1994).

Paul Clark, who has been involved in CCM since the Jesus Movement of the '70s, is a Pentecostal who has written songs such as "Latter Rain" and "Believe and Receive."

CCM superstar **Andrae Crouch**, winner of eight Grammy awards, is pastor of Christ Memorial Church in Pacoima, California. Crouch's church is a member of the Church of God in Christ, the largest black American Pentecostal denomination. Word-Faith preacher Kenneth Copeland spoke at his pastoral consecration. Crouch ordained his sister as co-pastor. He says he was called to pastor by being knocked to the floor:

> "It was Sunday morning, and I had my $500 suit on, and I was singing, clapping my hands, and doing a little step, and all of a sudden I hit the floor. The Holy Spirit spoke to me and said, 'Okay Mr. *Through It All*, Mr. *Take Me Back*, Mr. *To God Be the Glory*, you will not get off the floor until you tell Me yes. I don't want uh-huh. I don't want yup. I don't want right on. I want yes. Y-e-s'" (Andrae Crouch, cited by Dave Urbanski, "The Preacher's Life," *CCM Magazine*, February 1997).

Dino Kartsonakis, known popularly simply as **Dino**, was the piano player for the divorced Pentecostal healer-evangelist Kathryn Kuhlman and frequently appears on the Trinity Broadcasting Network program with Paul and Jan Crouch.

CCM trumpeter **Phil Driscoll** attends an independent charismatic church in Cleveland, Tennessee, and continually appears at Charismatic-Pentecostal churches and forums. He has trumpeted, for example, at Kenneth Copeland meetings.

Michael English is a member of the Pentecostal Christ Community Church near Nashville, Tennessee.

The very popular **Don Francisco** moves in the most radical charismatic circles. In November 1986, for example, he had a concert at Vineyard Christian Fellowship Southeast, Denver, Colorado.

Kirk Franklin believes in Pentecostal gifts and phenomena. He believes in Pentecostal tongues and prophecies (Franklin, *Church Boy*, p. 214).

The members of **Ghoti Hook** are Pentecostal and met one another in an Assemblies of God church.

Al Green is a Pentecostal and in 1976 he was ordained as the pastor of the Full Gospel Tabernacle Church in Memphis.

Steve Green's *The Faithful* album (1998) (produced by Phil Naish) has two songs which promote charismatic-ecumenical error: "The River" and "The Great Revival."

> "There's a river ever flowing/ Widening, never slowing/ And all who wade out in it are swept away/ When it ends where its going/ Like the wind, no way of knowing/ Until we answer the call to risk it all/ And enter in. The river calls, we can't deny/ A step of faith is our reply/ We feel the Spirit draw us in/ The water's swift, we're forced to swim/ We're out of control/ And we go where he flows" (Steve Green, "The River").

> "A great movement in every place/ Is going on so fast Eternal light piercing so deep/ I am so convinced/ The prophecies that Jesus spoke/ Will soon all be fulfilled/ Everything will be made clear/ And very soon Jesus will come. Oh, glory hallelujah/ For the Lord is pouring/ A holy fire/ The great revival's started/ Every tongue confessing/ 'Jesus Christ is Lord of all'/ 'Jesus Christ is Lord of all'" (Steve Green, "The Great Revival").

Those familiar with Pentecostal latter-rain doctrine will recognize the river terminology. They believe an end times miracle revival is to precede the return of Christ. The "Laughing Revival" with headquarters in Toronto, Canada, and Pensacola, Florida, uses the "river" terminology to describe their movement. The theme song at the Brownsville Assembly of God in Pensacola is "The River Is Here." The chorus to this song is as follows:

> "The river of God sets our feet a-dancing/ The river of God fills our hearts with cheer/ The river of God fills our mouths with laughter/ And we rejoice for the river is here."

They sing this in the context of such alleged end-times "miracles" as spirit slaying, uncontrollable laughter, and spirit drunkenness.

Steve Green promotes and fellowships with the Promise Keepers organization. It, in turn, has been heavily influenced by John Wimber's Vineyard movement. PK founder Bill McCartney is a member of a Vineyard congregation in Boulder, Colorado, and he was taught to trust his intuitions as "revelation" from God by Vineyard pastor James Ryle. The Vineyard movement also spawned the Laughing Revival. These are different aspects of the same end-times apostasy and they share many of the same unscriptural philosophies.

Note that Steve Green sings that the "river" sweeps people away and makes them "out of control." This is precisely what happens to people who participate in the strange Laughing Revival. People are thrown to the floor and are unable to rise; they become drunken and stagger about, unable to speak plainly. They make animal noises and laugh hysterically. And yet we are told that these things are the works of the Spirit of God in His "latter rain" outpouring. My friends, the "great revival" of which Steven Green sings is not revival; it is apostasy and confusion.

Jack Hayford, author of the song "Majesty" and many other very popular worship songs, is pastor of Church-on-the-Way Foursquare Church, the Pentecostal denominational which was founded by the female pastor Aimee Semple McPherson. Paul and Jan Crouch, of the Trinity Broadcasting Network, and entertainer Pat Boone, are members of Hayford's church. In 1996 Hayford endorsed Robert Schuller's autobiography, *Prayer: My Soul's Adventure with God*, in spite of the fact that Schuller is a dangerous false teacher who has perverted the Gospel by his self-esteem theology. In his book *Self-Esteem: The New Reformation*, Schuller said that sin is merely the lack of self esteem. Writing in the Promise Keepers publication *The Seven Promises of a Promise Keeper*, Hayford stated, "Redeeming worship centers on the Lord's table. Whether your tradition celebrates it as communion, the Eucharist, the Mass or the Lord's Supper, we are all called to this centerpiece of Christian worship" (*Seven Promises*, p. 19). To put the biblical Lord's Supper on the same level as the blasphemous Catholic mass is wickedness. Hayford's very popular song "Majesty" teaches Pentecostal doctrinal error, when it speaks of "kingdom authority." In the Pentecostal-Charismatic context, "kingdom authority" refers to the false doctrine that Christians today have the authority promised for the future kingdom which will be established at Christ's return. Hayford's "kingdom authority" refers to authority to cast out sickness, authority to bind the demonic rulers of this world system, authority to be prosperous.

Dallas Holm, one of the pioneers of Contemporary Christian Music, was trained by the Pentecostal evangelist Dave Wilkerson.

The Imperials are Pentecostal in orientation. Their concerts "always end with the group giving an altar call and praying for those seeking salvation, restoration and healing" (Imperials web site, http://placetobe.org/cmp/artists/index.html).

Phil Keaggy is charismatic and claims to have received the baptism of the Spirit in 1970 at a Kathryn Kuhlman service (Phil Keaggy interview," *Harmony* magazine, 1976, http://www.museweb.com/keaggy/harmony76.html). He was affiliated with the Pentecostal Love Inn Community in Freeville, New York, from 1974 to 1979.

Mylon Lefevre is an elder in the Mt. Param Pentecostal Church (Church of God, Cleveland, Tennessee) near Atlanta.

Petra is charismatic. They performed, for example, at the 15th anniversary celebration of *Charisma* magazine, which promotes the charismatic movement. Guests at the celebration included false prophet Oral Roberts and Charles and Frances Hunter, who teach that every Christian can lay hands on the sick and heal them. Frances Hunter has taken ill and been injured on her healing crusades and has had to seek medical attention when the "healing" failed.

Like Michael English, Curtis Chapman, and several other CCM artists, **Steve Taylor** is a member of the charismatic Christ Community Church near Nashville, pastored by Scott Smith.

Sheila Walsh is a member of a charismatic congregation and has frequently performed in charismatic settings. Together with roughly 20,000 Roman Catholics, she participated in the North American Congress on the Holy Spirit & World Evangelization in New Orleans in 1987. That same year she became the co-host of Pat Robertson's "700 Club."

The **Vineyard** churches, founded by the late **John Wimber**, have had a wide influence with their praise music and are an integral part of the CCM scene. Wimber himself, who was the manager of the secular group The Righteous Brothers before his conversion, wrote many popular songs, and many of the Vineyard churches are noted for their influential music groups. The Vintage Vineyard Music series is advertised as "Vineyard's all-time worship classics THAT CONTINUE TO BE SUNG CROSS-DENOMINATIONALLY IN CHURCHES AROUND THE WORLD." Though Wimber was not Pentecostal, he accepted and popularized many Pentecostal-type practices, including "slaying in the Spirit," prophecy, "words of knowledge," and faith healing.

Greg Volz, who was the singer for Petra from 1979-1985, is a member of Willie Hinn's charismatic church in Vancouver, British Columbia. Willie is the Brother of Benny Hinn.

Wayne Watson is a charismatic-ecumenical CCM musician who moves in a wide range of ecclesiastical circles. In January 1988 he performed at the Assemblies of God-connected Carpenter's Home Church in Lakeland, Florida. In January 1992 he joined hands with many well-known charismatic speakers, including Larry Lea and Jack Deere, and performed for James Robinson's Bible Conference.

THE "LAUGHING REVIVAL" CONNECTION

The dangerously unscriptural "Laughing Revival," with headquarters at the Toronto Airport Christian Fellowship in Toronto, Ontario, and the Brownsville Assembly of God in Pensacola, Florida, has produced music which has been used widely in non-charismatic circles. This music is growing in popularity and influence with each passing month. It is a combination of high-intensity rock music and blues-mood music. The message is simplistic and often unscriptural; the rhythm unbalanced; it is repetitious, hypnotic. It would be impossible to conceive of the Laughing Revival phenomena apart from its rock-mood music. I have attended services at one church which is a headquarters for the Laughing Revival (Holy Trinity Brompton in London, England) and have viewed many video recordings of Laughing Revival services from various parts of the world. The music is always the same type and it is used to prepare the crowds for the "manifestations" (such as spirit slaying and drunkenness).

The Toronto Airport Church was formerly connected with Wimber's Vineyard movement, and though it is no longer a member of the Vineyard association of churches, it continues to have close fellowship with the Vineyard churches and pastors. **David Ruis**, one of the worship leaders at the Toronto Airport church, is a popular song writer in the Vineyard movement. His song "Break Dividing Walls," calling for ecumenical unity, is widely used. **Lindell Cooley**, the music director at the Brownsville Assembly of God in Pensacola, calls his music Vineyard music. The 1997 catalog from Vineyard Music features a "Winds of Worship" series which includes CDs from Toronto and Brownsville, focal points of the "Laughing Revival."

The very popular and influential **Integrity Music** company (Integrity also owns **Hosanna Music**) rose out of the charismatic movement and the music it spreads to 117 countries is of a charismatic nature. Integrity recently recorded an album at the Brownsville Assembly of God. Don Moen is the "creative director" for Integrity. In an interview with the *Pentecostal Evangel*, a magazine published by the Assemblies of God, Moen described the power of the Laughing Revival music in these words: "Because something is imparted when you listen to this tape. I don't want it to sound spooky or mysterious, but there's something powerful about embracing the music of the revival. The fire of the revival can stir in you even as you listen to the songs that took place at the Brownsville revival" ("Don Moen Discusses Music at Brownsville Assembly," *Pentecostal Evangel*, November 10, 1996). The "revival" to which he refers is not a biblical revival; it is a "revival" in which people become drunken and stagger about and fall down and are unable to perform the most basic functions of life. The pastor at Brownsville, John Kilpatrick, has testified that it has taken him a half hour just to put on his socks when he was drunk with the Brownsville revival spirit. He has lain on the church platform for as long as four hours, unable to get up. His wife has been unable to cook their food or clean the house. Whatever this "revival" is, it is not something that is Bible based. Yet Moen testifies that this spirit can be imparted through the music.

Integrity's Hosanna! Music worship tapes include songs by **Robert Gay**, who records music from alleged prophecies given by charismatic "prophets." Gay has written hundreds of choruses, and many of them have been professionally recorded. Integrity has produced twelve of Gay's prophetic songs. Gay claims that the Holy Spirit gives him visions for his songs. Gay is connected with Bill Hamon's Christian International network of supposed prophetic ministries, which promotes the deception that God is continuing to give revelation through prophets and apostles today. Hamon claims that God will soon raise up new apostles who will operate in the miracle-working power of the first-century apostles and who will unite the churches and denominations. He claims that the Laughing Revival and Promise Keepers are part of this restoration process (Hamon, *Apostles, Prophets and the Coming Moves of God: God's End-Time Plans for His Church and Planet Earth*, Santa Rosa Beach, CA: Christian International, 1997).

Integrity's Hosanna! Music worship tapes also include songs of other key churches which have been captured by the Laughing Revival movement. Another one of these is **Hills Christian Life Centre**. Hosanna published an album entitled "Shout to the Lord" which was recorded at this church in AustraliaNew Zealand. It was #2 on the Christian charts in early June 1998. The worship leader at Hills Christian Life Centre is **Darlene Zschech**. Many of the "praise" songs on this album are extremely man centered. The lyrics to the songs often present a theology of "holding out faithful."

> "I love you/ I need you/ Though my world may fall/ I'll never let you go" (Jesus, Lover of My Soul" from "Shout to the Lord").

Instead of the Christian rejoicing in God's promises to keep him, these songs have the Christian promising to hold on to God. It is man-centered theology.

There is also the false Pentecostal latter rain theology in some of the songs.

> "I believe the promise about the visions and the dreams/ That the Holy Spirit will be poured out/ And His power will be seen/ Well the time is now/ The place is here/ And His people have come in faith/ There's a mighty sound/ And a touch of fire/ When we've gathered in one place" ("I Believe the Presence" from "Shout to the Lord").

THE "JESUS ONLY" MUSIC CONNECTION

Many of the most popular "praise songs" today were composed by men and women involved with the Oneness Pentecostal movement, which denies the Trinity and which baptizes only in the name of Jesus. This theology was rejected from the Assemblies of God as false and cultic in the 1920s, yet a recent article in *Charisma* magazine (June 1997) noted that "most popular praise anthems sung in charismatic and evangelical churches today were composed by Oneness believers." The article gave these examples:

Dottie Rambo, who was raised in a Oneness church, wrote "Behold the Lamb," "If That Isn't Love," many and other popular songs.

Joel Hemphill wrote "He's Still Working on Me."

Lanny Wolfe wrote "Greater Is He that Is in Me."

Songwriter **Geron Davis** wrote "Holy Ground" and "In the Presence of Jehovah."

The contemporary Christian recording group **Phillips, Craig And Dean** is composed of three Oneness ministers.

The song "Mercy Seat," which is sung nightly at the Brownsville Assembly of God "revival" in Pensacola, Florida, was written by United Pentecostal Church (a Oneness group) worship leader **Mark Carouthers**.

We do not believe God is the author of the charismatic movement, with its ecumenical goals, its false doctrine, and its strange unscriptural phenomena. The Bible tells us He is not the author of confusion. We believe there are saved people within the movement, but the movement itself is unscriptural. We believe, in fact, that this is part of a movement prophesied in Scripture as the end-times apostasy which will result in a one-world harlot "church." This is described in many New Testament passages (i.e., Matt. 24:3-4,11,24; 1 Timothy 4:1-4; 2 Timothy 3:1-13; 4:4-6; Jude 3-16; 1 John 2:18-19; 1 John 4:1; etc.), culminating in the description given in Revelation 17-18. That there are genuinely saved people in this movement is implied in Revelation 18:4, which says: "And I heard another voice from heaven, saying, Come out of her, my people, that ye be not partakers of her sins, and that ye receive not of her plagues." God calls His people out of the end-time apostasy. We, therefore, reject the charismatic movement AND ITS MUSIC.

CHARACTERISTIC #5 — CONTEMPORARY CHRISTIAN MUSIC CAN BE IDENTIFIED BY ITS WEAK, UNSCRIPTURAL MESSAGE

> "One of the subtlest ways of flattering man is to communicate the gospel in a way he wants rather than the way he needs" (Paul Bassett, cited in *Pop Goes the Gospel*, p. 99).

Defenders of Contemporary Christian Music protest that the music is not important, that only the words to the songs are important. We know this is not true. We know that the music of a song makes a statement just as plainly as the words of that song, and the message preached by CCM music is sensual and unholy. Forgetting the music for a moment, though, what about the words of CCM songs? What about the lyrics? We make three observations: The words to CCM are often not clear because of the rock music; the words are often vague; and the words are often heretical.

FIRST, THE WORDS TO CCM SONGS ARE FREQUENTLY NOT CLEAR.

The first point I would make about the lyrics to CCM is that in a large percentage of Contemporary Christian Music songs the lyrics cannot be understood plainly to the hearers. In light of the rapidly growing popularity of hard rock CCM, I would estimate that this is the case in as many as half of the songs. The music is so loud and riotous that the words simply are not clearly understood.

This is certainly true at many Christian rock concerts. My wife and I attended the Livefest concert near Oklahoma City in June 2001, and it was impossible to understand the words of most of the songs. A man who attended an Audio Adrenaline/dc Talk concert in Rapid City, South Dakota, testified: "All the while the music was so loud if anyone could hear the words it wasn't enough to get a message from; hence, the reaction was to the 'rock' beat not the words" (John Beardsley, "DC Talk Examined," *The Christian Conscience*, June 1996).

Consider the following description of a Sheila Wash concert: "For some of us, however, communication ended when she sang because, more often than not, the band was too loud for us to catch the words" (*Pop Goes the Gospel*, p. 159).

Reviewing a News Boys "Take Me to Your Leader" concert in Rapid City, South Dakota, even the local secular newspaper noted the lack of clarity to the message: "Although most of the choruses are straightforward, THE VERSES ARE HARD TO FOLLOW, A FLAW THAT SERVES TO TRIVIALIZE THE BAND'S CHRISTIAN MESSAGE. ... Built on lyrics that leave too many holes to be filled, the band's message gets lost somewhere in the alternative music" (*Rapid City Journal*, May 13, 1997).

Note the following description of albums by the groups Barnabas and Cruse:

> "A strong rhythm section drives the title cut and 'Auschwitz 87' which opens with solo vocals by, yep, Adolf Hitler. WE CAN'T TELL YOU EXACTLY WHAT THESE SONGS ARE ABOUT BECAUSE THERE'S NO LYRIC SHEET..." (*CCM Magazine*, March 1987, p. 14).

> "It is a good thing that this album [by CRUSE] comes with a lyric sheet, because most of the words do not come through distinctly enough for one to easily follow the message" (*CCM Magazine*, March 1987, p. 19)

It is obvious that the multitudes of professing Christians who listen to hard rock CCM are not very interested in the music's message.

If the words are the only thing that matter and if CCM performers are genuinely concerned about getting across a message that glorifies Jesus Christ, why are the words so unclear in such a large percentage of CCM pieces? It is obvious in such cases that the music takes precedence over the lyrics and it is the rock music which is truly important both to the performers and to the listeners. Of course we realize that these raucous records and concerts are not characteristic of all CCM recordings and performances, but they are characteristic of a large and rapidly growing segment of CCM.

When Christian young people want to defend their love for secular rock music, they argue that they don't listen to the words. When they want to defend their love for Christian rock music, they argue that it is only the words which matter!

It is obvious that the words to the songs are NOT very important in a very large number of cases and that the truly important thing is the sensual experience that CCM listeners have enjoying the music.

SECOND, THE MESSAGE TO CCM SONGS IS WEAK AND VAGUE.

The second observation we make about the lyrics to Contemporary Christian Music is that they are frequently weak, abstract, vague. Noted music authority Dr. Frank Garlock observes that "much of it can be described as trite, shallow, simple, and entertaining."

Ric Llewellyn observes: "Perhaps it is true that music is an art form. But as Christian musicians become more and more 'artistic' the lyrics of Contemporary Christian Music become more and more obscure until they retain virtually no substantial spiritual value. Lyrics become so allegorical that a truly spiritual lesson is imperceptible. This indefiniteness opens the door to many incorrect understandings concerning the point of a particular song, which fosters the acceptance of teachings which are unbiblical and even antibiblical" (Llewellyn, "Christian Rock?," *Foundation*, Vol. VI, Issue 2, 1985, p. 17).

Except for rare exceptions, Contemporary Christian Music (CCM) is either doctrinally weak, or entirely unscriptural. Some years ago I received a letter from a youth leader challenging me that I was wrong in making such statements. He contended that Christian rockers have matured over the past decades and reminded me that even Bob Larson, who once preached against Christian rock, has changed and now promotes the same. He mentioned four groups in particular which he alleged to be doctrinally mature—Petra, White Heart, Steve Camp, and Rez Band—and sent some examples from the music of the groups in an attempt to prove his point.

I took the challenge to go through the several pages of musical lyrics which he sent; and since these were supposed to prove how scripturally mature Christian rock has become, I knew he would send selections representing the very best CCM had to offer. I felt, therefore, that I would probably find some sound music in these examples. How wrong I was!

Let me summarize my findings: There were nine pages of lyrics from the albums of the four groups, and these had words to roughly 50 songs. I had been told that these were examples of the best Christian rock music available. After going through the words to these 50 songs with an open mind, actually thinking that I would find some biblically sound material, I found no more than five which could be termed scripturally sound and edifying. The rest were unbiblical junk. That's the only way to describe it. Consider this one by Petra entitled "Voice in the Wind" —

> "Wind may come wind may go/ Where it blows no one knows/ Chill the bone fan the fire/ Lead the soul to heart's desire/ There's a voice in the wind that calls your name/ If you listen you'll never be the same/ Spirit comes spirit goes/ Whence it comes no one knows/ Giving life making new/ Filling hearts, calling you" (Petra, "Voice in the Wind").

This is supposed to be sound and mature doctrine! And yet lyrics such as these make up the bulk of CCM. The words could mean anything— even a Hindu could be comfortable with such mumbo jumbo.

During the last few months, I have studied hundreds of CCM songs; and I am more convinced than ever that the message of CCM is largely vague and unscriptural.
Stan Moser was one of the most influential producers of Contemporary Christian Music until his retirement in 1995. In an article in *Christianity Today*, he observed, "But to be candid, I look at the majority of the music I hear today and think it's virtually meaningless" (Moser, "We Have Created a Monster," *Christianity Today*, May 20, 1996 p. 27).

Influential CCM writer/performer John Fischer actually calls upon his fellow CCM artists to be vague:

> "Like God, we need to be masters of compelling concealment—hiding the truth, while at the same time, inviting a search. It's a little like when you were a child playing hide and seek, and you actually wanted to be found because you had more fun being 'it' than hiding in the dark. You might want to make a few noises when someone passes by, just to let them know the general area to look in. You might leave clues the way God has done with His universe. Hide the truth. Tuck it into a metaphor or an allegory, but not so far in that it cannot be retrieved. Let it call out from its hiding place to all who care to seek. Just don't be too obvious. Oversimplifying truth profanes God's glory" (John Fischer, "Consider This," *CCM Magazine*, April 1996).

God commands us to "preach the Word." CCM proponents call upon us to conceal the Word! It is true that God conceals wisdom in the natural realm and it is man's task to dig it out, but that is not what we see in the New Testament commands about the Christian life. The message of Christ is to be preached plainly. Christ used parables for the purpose of hiding truth from unbelieving Israel (Matthew 13:10-11), but nowhere do the New Testament epistles indicate that Christians are to imitate this. Christ's parables are plainly interpreted in the Bible. The Apostles did not hide the truth, nor did they instruct the early churches to do so. Paul said: "Seeing then that we have such hope, we use great plainness of speech" (2 Corinthians 3:12). When truth is presented vaguely, truth becomes vague.

Of Charlie Peacock's songs the author of one of his fan websites states: "I'm not even sure I know really what some of the songs really mean, and I've listened quite a bit. If that tells you anything." It tells me a lot! It tells me the lyrics are vague. The message to Peacock's *Everything That's on My Mind* album "doesn't come out and grab you—it's something you have to glean for yourself."

Kerry Livgren's music also illustrates the vagueness of Contemporary Christian Music. The meaning of Livgren's music is rarely plain. He himself describes it as "cryptic" (*Kerry Livgren Getting Electric*, http://placetobe.org/cmp/artists/index.html). He hides Bible truths behind a veil of ambiguity. His 1994 album, *When Things Get*

Electric, contains 13 songs, and not one mentions the name of Christ or contains a clear biblical message. All are vague and strange. Consider, for example, the lyrics to the title song of this album:

> "See the fire streak through the sky/ Children watching and wondering why/ Blameless blood cries from the ground/ Justice sleeping, open your ears to the sound/ Moving waves cover the Earth/ Like a woman who's soon giving birth/ Feel the tension taking it's form/ As dark clouds gather, run for the eye of the storm.
>
> Chorus: "When things get electric, when everything's done/ We'll stand in the open and shine (like the sun)/ This moment's so fleeting, the blink of an eye/ When things get electric, we're all gonna fly/ (it's sweet by and by)" (Kerry Livgren, "When Things Get Electric").

What does this song mean? It could be referring to the coming of Christ, but it could mean many other things, as well, because the meaning is not clear. Without clear meaning there can be no salvation and no Christian growth. The Spirit of God works through the understanding. This is why the Apostle Paul said, "I will sing with the spirit, and I WILL SING WITH THE UNDERSTANDING ALSO" (1 Corinthians 14:15).

This is an hour of incredible spiritual confusion. False christs and false gospels abound. Unless the meaning of a religious or spiritual message is absolutely clear, it leaves room for demonic error and delusion.

Michael W. Smith admits that he does not want the message of his songs to be very plain because that would hurt sales: "I know if I'm too blatant about my Christianity and talk about Jesus I won't succeed in the mainstream. But hey, I'm not an evangelist, I'm a singer" (Monica Langley, "Rock of Ages," *Wall Street Journal*, Sept. 11, 1991, p. 1). A secular paper described the vague nature of a Michael Smith concert in these words: "If you weren't familiar with Michael W. Smith's standing in the world of contemporary Christian music, you might attend one of his concerts and come out none the wiser" (*The Birmingham News*, Birmingham, Alabama, Feb. 12, 1993, p. 5c).

Amy Grant and her husband, Gary Chapman, admit that they purposefully avoid direct messages:

> "Grant and her husband, songwriter Gary Chapman, prefer to 'be a little bit sneaky with the lyrics,' he says. 'We don't want to shove anything down anybody's throat. When you start getting churchy, they start running'" (Jack Kelley, "The Gospel of Grant," *Weekend Post*, Houston, Texas, Nov. 10, 1985).

The Apostles didn't fear getting "a little churchy" in their message! Paul plainly preached the judgment of God and the resurrection of Christ to the idolaters at Athens (Acts 17). Paul's "churchy" message was so foreign to his hearers that some of them thought he was speaking of strange new gods (Acts 17:18). Most mocked and rejected his message, but this did not stop Paul from preaching a plain Gospel to the world because he knew that apart from the plain preaching of the Gospel there is no salvation.

John Gibson describes why he believes Contemporary Christian Music needs to be vague:

> "There are things happening in life all people can relate to. See, to a lot of people, if you sing about Christ, they'll say, 'That's fine, but man, I need a job. Get me a job, and then we'll talk about Christ.' I want to sneak into their hearts with the music. 'Be as wise as serpents and innocent as doves' you know. I think that's the way Jesus did it. He didn't tell them the whole truth. ... I think we kinda gotta do that too. Contemporary Christian music needs to branch out a little more, get a little sneakier. It's warfare, you know" (Jon Gibson, *CCM Magazine*, May 1987, p. 11).

Gibson misuses the Scripture by twisting Matthew 10:16 out of context: "Behold, I send you forth as sheep in the midst of wolves: be ye therefore wise as serpents, and harmless as doves." This verse was part of Christ's instructions to the twelve disciples when He sent them to preach repentance to the nation Israel. He was not instructing them to obscure their message, as Gibson and other CCM performers contend. Christ had already told them that they were to preach a plain message.

> "These twelve Jesus sent forth, and commanded them, saying, Go not into the way of the Gentiles, and into any city of the Samaritans enter ye not: But go rather to the lost sheep of the house of Israel. And as ye go, preach, saying, The kingdom of heaven is at hand" (Matthew 10:5-7).

When the Lord Jesus Christ spoke of being wise as serpents and harmless as doves, He was not speaking of making the Gospel message vague or hiding it in sensual rock music. The Lord's disciples certainly did not understand His meaning in such a fashion. They boldly and plainly preached the Gospel wherever they went. "Therefore they that were scattered abroad went every where preaching the word" (Acts 8:4). This is why they were so continually persecuted by the world. (CCM artists, on the other hand, are often loved and supported by the world.) When the Lord Jesus Christ spoke of being wise as serpents and harmless as doves, He was merely instructing the disciples to be wise and cautious and non-injurious in their dealings with the unsaved and as much as possible to avoid trouble.

Gibson talks of "sneaking" the message of God into people's hearts through obscure music, but the Bible says faith comes by hearing and hearing by the Word of God (Romans 10:17). It is impossible to "sneak" salvation into the hearts of people. Ephesians explains that to be saved people must first hear the word of truth, then they must trust that Word (Ephesians 1:12-13). Romans 6:17 says salvation involves obeying from the heart a specific "form of doctrine." Salvation is a conscious procedure brought about by a plain message.

Finally, for Gibson to say that Jesus Christ "did not tell the whole truth" is blasphemously untrue.

The following two songs from Dakota Motor Company's 1993 *Into the Son* album illustrate the vagueness of this group's music. Both songs are heavy rock:

> "I need a love that will bring me high/ A love that will take my blues away/ I need a love that will light my sky/ A love that will drive my tears away/ I need love, I need You/ Put a rainbow in my view/ After raining down on me/ I need a love that will meet my needs/ So unconditionally/ I need a love that will help me stand/ A love that will show me the way/ I need a love that will take my fear/ When I am feeling afraid" (Dakota Motor Company, "Need a Love," 1993).

This is another ill identified CCM song about love which sounds very much like the "love" secular rock singers praise. Is Dakota Motor Company singing about the love of Jesus Christ? It is not possible to know for sure. God's love to sinners is not known apart from the atonement of Jesus Christ, yet this song does not even mention Christ or the cross. If an unsaved person hears Dakota Motor Company's song, he would easily assume that God's love is entirely unconditional, meaning that God love does not require him to repent or be born again. This is the impression given by the song. The "love" here is entirely man centered. It meets all my "needs." Does the love of God promise to take away all our tears? To the contrary, the Word of God warns that the child of God will suffer much in this world.

> "She's singing in the rain/ And dancing in the sun/ Flowers in her hair on a midnight barefoot run/ Purple pansies with a black velvet face/ No doubt about it, God is in this place/ Sondancer, sondancer girl/ You seem so different, not of this world/ Sea grass grows on the ocean floor/ She swims past way beyond/ The shorebright fishfins cut the water so clear/ No doubt about it, God is here/ Rain comes down on everyone/ Sondancer's eyes are on the Son/ Someone's eyes are set on the pain/ The Son will bring you/ Through the rain/ Set apart running free/ Sondancer girl dance around me" (Dakota Motor Company, "Sondancer," 1993).

This song is more akin to the New Age than to Christianity. From a biblical perspective, its meaning is entirely obscure.

The vague meaninglessness of much of Christian rock music is further illustrated by the lyrics to "Inside" from White Heart's 1995 album by the same name. The song is performed to a heavy, growling, grunge rock style:

> "I wanna feel/ no I wanna dream/ I wanna live on the inside/ Oh I gotta breathe/ gotta pray/ I wanna heal on the inside, I wanna feel/ I wanna feel/ I wanna dream/ I wanna live on the inside/ gotta breathe/ gotta pray/ I wanna heal on the inside/ on the inside/ on the inside/ inside/ inside."

What does the song mean? It can mean anything you please. It therefore means nothing. The Mormon can find his religion here. So can the Hindu, the Catholic mystic, the New Ager, the psychotherapist, the humanist.

Robert Sweet of Stryper made the same admission about one of their albums: "You won't pick up this record (*Against the Law*) and hear anything that says 'God' or 'Christ.' That was intentionally done. We were tired of people coming back with excuses, saying, 'Sorry we can't play this.' MTV's got to play this and the radio's got to play it or it doesn't serve the purpose" (Robert Sweet, Stryper, interview, *CCM Magazine*, August 1990, p. 10).

Christian rocker Mylon LeFevre admits that he often is careful not to be specific in the wording of the lyrics and avoid singing a message which is "religious sounding." "But the album we made for Epic [*Look Up*] is more subtle and still has the Christian message. But it is not so religious sounding. We've been careful to avoid any religious terminology in this record that would turn people off" (LeFevre, cited by Jeff Godwin, *What's Wrong with Christian Rock?*, p. 124).

In their earlier days The Imperials were a traditional Gospel quartet with plain biblical lyrics (generally speaking). Today they use pop music and the lyrics to the songs frequently have been shallow, obscure, and unscriptural:

> "Friend, I know where you're comin' from/ Seems your life's under the gun/ With no real chance of escape/ There is hope right outside your door/ It's what you've been searchin' for/ A love that will never fade/ So don't you run away/ Don't run away/ You can't hide/ Gotta keep reachin'/ You must keep reachin'/ Gotta keep reachin' for higher things" ("Higher Things," The Imperials, 1988, *Free the Fire* album).

What does this song mean? It's hard to tell. If it's for the unsaved, it presents a false gospel. Salvation is not obtained by a continual reaching for God. "But what saith it? The word is nigh thee, even in thy mouth, and in thy heart: that is, the word of faith, which we preach; That if thou shalt confess with thy mouth the Lord Jesus, and shalt believe in thine heart that God hath raised him from the dead, thou shalt be saved" (Romans 10:8,9). If, on the other hand, the song is for the saved, it says our hope is "outside your door." This is false. The Bible says "Christ IN YOU, the hope of glory" (Col. 1:27). The very obscurity of CCM results in false doctrine.

Consider the lyrics to a song from the Imperials 1992 album:

> "If I wanted to change the world/ I would start by loving you/ If loving was all we knew/ Oo baby we could change the world/ We need to change/ We need to change/ We need to change the world/ If I wanted to change the world/ I would start by loving you/ And if loving was all we knew/ Oo baby we could change the world/ I would start by loving you/ That's all I really need to do/ I can't stop loving you/ If I wanted to change the world/ I would start by loving you/ And if loving was all we knew/ Oo baby we would change the world" (Terry Esau, "Change the World," from the Imperials' 1992 album *Stir It Up*).

What does this mean? Who knows. It could mean many things and nothing. Is the singer referring to loving God or loving his girlfriend? The repeated references to "Oo baby" certainly sound like a love song. Further, where does the Bible say that we need to change the world? This song sounds exactly like the message continually presented by secular rock groups.

The song "Lord of the Dance," co-written by Steven Curtis Chapman and Scotty Smith, pastor of Christ Community Church, first appeared on Chapman's 1996 album *Signs of Life*. The song depicts God as the "Lord of the Dance," which is certainly not a scriptural concept. God was the Lord of the type of dancing that King David did, worshipful dancing, but "Lord of the Dance" is sung in the context of the type of dancing which goes on at rock concerts. God is not Lord of sensual, worldly dancing which, due to the fallen nature of man, is at its very heart licentious. It would be more scriptural to say that the Devil is the Lord of the Dance in any rock music context.

> "On the bank of the Tennessee River/ In a small Kentucky town/ I drew my first breath one cold November morning/ And before my feet even touched the ground/ With the doctors and the nurses gathered 'round/ I started to dance/ I started to dance/ A little boy full of wide-eyed wonder/ Footloose and fancy free/ But it would happen, as it does for every dancer/ That I'd stumble on a truth I couldn't see/ And find a longing deep inside of me, it said . . .
>
> Chorus: "I am the heart, I need the heartbeat/ I am the eyes, I need the sight/ I realize that I am just a body/ I need the life/ I move my feet, I go through the motions/ But who'll give purpose to chance/ I am the dancer/ I need the Lord of the dance.
>
> "The world beneath us spins in circles/ And this life makes us twist and turn

and sway/ But we were made for more than rhythm with no reason/ By the one who moves with passion and with grace/ As He dances over all that He has made/ I am the heart, He is the heartbeat/ I am the eyes, He is the sight/ And I see clearly, I am just a body/ He is the life/ I move my feet, I go through the motions/ But He gives purpose to chance/ I am the dancer/ He is the Lord of the dance/ Lord of the dance/ Lord of the dance/ And while the music of His love and mercy plays/ I will fall down on my knees and I will pray."

A Christian message of sorts can be READ INTO this song, that without God life is without meaning, but as the song stands in its own vagueness, there is no clear biblical message. Is God a dancer? The only thing we know about God for certain is the revelation we have in His Word. Where does the Bible portray God as a dancer? It is extremely dangerous to describe God in ways not used in the Bible, because it could be blasphemous. "The Lord of the Dance" could easily be referring to a Hindu god or a New Age christ. Further, the song says every "dancer" will stumble onto truth. This is certainly not true.

The lyrics to the rash of new hard rock "Christian" bands are even more vague than CCM in general. The lyrics to Galactic Cowboy's music, for example, is almost indecipherable. The following are the words to the title song from their 1996 *Feel the Rage* album —

"Take a trip, step outside of this fishbowl life/ Voice recalls, ceramic youth in pots of broken truth/ I feel the rage, comin' off of the stage/ I feel the rage, comin' off of the page/ I feel the rage, comin' off of the page/ Make a wish, clear your mind, let the years rewind/ Poets pain battles fame and becomes its slave/ I feel the rage, comin' off of the stage/ I feel the rage, comin' off of the page/ I feel the [repeated]/ Open mouth, open grave, nothing left to say."

If you don't understand what that means, you are not alone. There is nothing spiritually edifying here, and this is one of the plainest songs on the album!

Most of Ghoti Hook's music is also complete nonsense. Consider the words to the title song on their 1997 debut album, *Banana Man*:

"He might look just a little bit kooky/ But he thinks that's okay/ He needs a job to pay off his mortgage and his Chevrolet/ If tricks you want, then he ain't your person/ All he does is stand/ Except the times when he is running from the policeman/ Banana Man!/ 1 2 3/ I'm Banana Man/ Dance with me!/ It might surprise you he went to college/ And got his degree/ It's hard to find a job with a major in plant psychology/ His identity he tries to keep secret/ But not because he's great/ 'Cause the girls will just keep on laughing, and he'll never get a date."

Every song on Michael W. Smith's top selling *Life the Life* album is vague. Consider

"Love Me Good"—

> "Sometimes I feel like this world/ Is just one big, gigantic merry-go-round/ You gotta hold on tight/ Or you get hurled thru the air/ Yea, life is a 3 ring circus/ With clowns and freaks and camels and such/ And you never know when you might be/ Attacked by the bears/ Give me love, give me love/ Love me good ... Sometimes I wish I was in a movie/ Or some 70s TV thing/ Where every thing gets neatly wrapped up at the end of the show/ Yea, but this ain't Hollywood/ And this sure ain't the Brady Bunch/ And how this plot's gonna all pan out/ I don't really know" (Love Me Good," Michael W. Smith).

My, what a deep, well-expressed Christian message! It reminds me of the Beatles tunes, "Love Me True" and "All You Need Is Love." What love? The love of money? The love of a good time? The love of life? The love of the world? The love of romance? The "love" best understood by the world is lust and sensual passion. Also we need to ask, "Whose love?" It is impossible to know what or who Michael Smith is singing about because his message is incredibly vague. By the way, why does he say that he does not know how it's "all gonna pan out"? Does he not know that the Bible tells us plainly how everything will end? Those who trust Jesus Christ look forward to eternal blessing. Those who reject Jesus Christ will have eternal torment. This present age will end with the Great Tribulation described in Matthew 24 and Revelation 4-18 and elsewhere in Scripture, then the Lord Jesus Christ will return to this earth to establish His kingdom. Why would a Christian sing a song to the world which says he does not know how things will pan out? What Gospel is that? It sounds like the singer's life is as confused as that of the world to whom he is singing.

This reminds me of an article by John Fischer in *Contemporary Christian Music Magazine* in 1995. Fisher is a CCM insider, but he testified to the unscriptural concept of love that is promoted in most CCM songs:

> I noticed it during a coast-to-coast drive across Florida. ... listening all the way to a Christian hit radio station. The focus of almost every song was the love of God, but at the end of this two-hour marathon I can't say I found out anything distinctive about God's love, except that it was real, it drowned me in the sea, it flowed all over me, it put its arms around me and held me close, and it generally made me feel pretty great. But the disturbing fact was that most, if not all of these things, could have just as easily come from someone other than God.
>
> There was no cross in this love. No sin. No guilt. No redemption. No grace. No sacrifice. No obligations. No commitments. No cleansing. No forgiveness. No blood. No death. No heaven. No hell. No savior. No need to be saved. Just love. Lots and lots of it oozing out all over. These were not songs about God's love, they were songs about love in general, with God named or implied as its source.

> I think I might know why this is happening. Now that crossover to commercial success is a real possibility ... the temptation is to write a song on a fence—--general enough for a commercial market but with just enough God in it to insure at least a Christian hit should it fail to get any mainstream attention. This is a dangerous compromise when the love and character of God are at stake (John Fischer, "Watering Down God," *CCM Magazine*, January 1995, p. 76).

Consider the following song by the very popular dc Talk as another prime illustration of this problem of vagueness—

> "You know what I'm going through/ I know (that) it's true/ Cause you've stood in my shoes/ Desire's inside of me/ But, it's hard to believe/ In what you cannot see/ Can you catch the wind? See a breeze? Its presence is revealed by/ The leaves on a tree/ An image of faith in the unseen/ In my mind's eye/ I see your face/ You smile/ As you show me grace/ In my mind's eye/ You take my hand/ We walk through foreign lands/ The foreign lands of life/ In my mind/ I'm where I belong/ As I rest in your arms/ And like a child I hold on to you/ In my moment of truth/ We can ride the storm/ Endure the pain/ You comfort me in my hurricane/ And I'll never be alone again/ ... In my mind I can see your face/ Love pours down in a shower of grace/ Life is a gift that you choose to give/ And I believe that we eternally live/ Faith is the evidence of things unseen/ People tell me that you're just a dream/ But they don't know you the way that I do/ You're the one I live to pursue" ("Mind's Eye," dc Talk).

Nothing is clear about this message. Who are they talking about? Jesus? They don't say. It could just as easily be about Krishna or Buddha or Mary the Queen of Heaven. The listener could easily fit any false god into this song. If the song is about Jesus, what Jesus (2 Corinthians 11:3-4)? The true Jesus of the Bible? Or one of the myriad of false christs in the minds of those who hear dc Talk's music? The song speaks of living eternally, but there is no clear Gospel message so that the hearer can know how to have eternal life. The message of the song is so vague that it is meaningless. A born again Christian can insert Biblical faith into the song. A cultist can insert his heresies into the song. The world can insert its New Age spirituality into the same song.

When I was saved the summer of 1973, one of the first thoughts I had was the realization that I had been deceived by a religious spirit. Before conversion I had pursued an Americanized form of Hinduism through the Self-Realization Fellowship Society (guru Paramahansa Yogananda). I had studied books on Hinduism and the New Age, had practiced meditation, and had made a journey from Florida to California to visit the Self-Realization shrine in Los Angeles. The "god" I had sought during those days was not the God of the Bible. In my rebellion I was led astray by deluding spirits, by doctrines of Devils. During a journey to Los Angeles, I had prayed for a guitar to sing religious tunes. When I won roughly $70 on a slot machine in Las Vegas, I thought God had answered my prayer! In reality, it was the god of this world. After I was saved and began to study the Bible, I knew that I had been deceived.

The entire counter culture hippie movement, of which I was a part, was deceived by New Age spirits, and rock music is filled with a false spirituality, with false gods and false christs. The Beatles helped popularize eastern religions in the West. In late 1970 former Beatle George Harrison recorded "My Sweet Lord," a praise song to the Hindu god Krishna which became a top hit. Young people across North America were singing praises to a pagan idol. The Beach Boys became followers of the Hindu guru Maharishi and recorded an album dedicated to Transcendental Meditation. Jimi Hendrix led his listeners into mystical themes. He believed he was born in outer space and was on earth to fulfill an appointed mission. He conducted a concert in Hawaii in an attempt to build a bridge to "the spiritual centers of the planetary being." The Grateful Dead also tried to lead their listeners into quasi-religious experiences. They performed a 1978 concert at the pyramids in Egypt in an attempt to tap into the religious power alleged to be available at that location (Gans, David, *Playing in the Band: An Oral and Visual Portrait of the Grateful Dead*, pp. 111-120). The Bryds had a 1965 hit based on Ecclesiastes 3 called "Turn! Turn! Turn!" Norman Greenbaum's 1970 hit "Spirit in the Sky" was about "Jesus," but Greenbaum, is a profane man who intersperses his interviews with curse words, admitsted that he was is not even a Christian. That same year there were other religious songs at the top of the charts, including "Jesus Is Just Alright" by the Byrds, "Are You Ready" by Pacific Gas & Electric, "Stoned Love" by the Supremes, "Fire and Rain" by James Taylor, and "Everything Is Beautiful" by Ray Stevens. In 1971, Ocean had the hit "Put Your Hand in the Hand," but again, the singers admit that they did not "feel strongly about the religious angle of the song" (*One Hit Wonders*, p. 298). They simply wanted to cash in on the current popularity of religious pop songs. Pete Townshend of the Who wrote two rock albums (*Tommy* and *Quadrophenia*) about his Hindu god, Meher Baba. Van Morrison sings about spiritual-mystical experiences, but he does not believe that Jesus Christ is God or Savior. The group Earth, Wind and Fire led by Maurice White dealt with "spiritual" themes, but White, who had grown up a Southern Baptist, believed that all religions are one.

The Bible warns that there are many gods and lords and false christs in the world (Matthew 24:4,5,11,24; 1 Corinthians 8:5; 2 Corinthians 11:3-4; 1 John 4:1). After I was saved and came to understand these spiritual truths, I feared that I would be praying to or following a false god or a false christ, and I was very careful to study the Bible diligently that I might not be deceived (John 8:31-32). For many months, when I prayed I did not merely pray "dear Lord" or "dear God" or even "dear Lord Jesus," but I followed the Bible's prayer instructions in Matthew 6:9, Romans 1:8, Hebrews 10:19; 13:15, and elsewhere in detail and carefully prayed something like the following: "Our Father which art in Heaven, I come to you through the blood of your Son Jesus Christ;

hear my prayer and protect me from false spirits. I desire to serve the one true and living God of Heaven and Him alone." I wanted to be absolutely certain that I was not praying to some deluding demon or honoring some false christ, and I am not ashamed of the godly caution I had in those days. My fears were based upon biblical warnings and I did well to be sober and vigilant against the enemy's devices.

The Bible warns about false christs, and we know that the "Christian" world today is filled with them. There is the false wafer Jesus of the Roman Catholic mass (Rome claims the blessed wafer actually becomes Jesus Christ). There is the polygamist Mormon Jesus and the Jehovah's Witness Jesus who is a created being, the Unitarian Jesus who is not God, the Modernist Jesus who was not born of a virgin, the Christian Science Jesus who taught that sin, sickness and death are not real, the Universalist Jesus who will not send anyone to eternal hell, the Prosperity Jesus who was wealthy, the Laughing Revival Jesus who slays people with his spirit and causes them to stagger like drunks, the Self-Esteem Jesus who never called man a sinner, the Revolutionary Jesus who founded Liberation Theology, the Environmental Jesus who wants to save the earth. These are only a few of the false christs in the "Christian" world today.

It is absolutely crucial that Christian music have a plain Biblical message which cuts through the confusion of widespread end times error, but Contemporary Christian Music does not.

Songs such as the previously mentioned "Mind's Eye" by dc Talk which are not clear about who God is and who the Lord Jesus Christ is are dangerous and play right into the hands of the Devil by leaving the hearers open to delusion. The CCM world is filled with songs which present a vague message.

The song "Sinking" by Jars of Clay is another illustration of the dangerous vagueness of CCM:

> "It's not my problem anymore/ You see it never really was/ So you can stop caring as you call it/ And I'll be fine right here/ You see that I can play a pretty convincing role/ So I don't need you, I don't think I need you.
>
> Chorus: "But you see through my forever lies/ And you are not believing/ And I see in your forever eyes/ And you are forever healing/ You can't hear what I'm not saying/ And I can hold out long enough/ Treading water I keep from sinking/ I'm not one for reaching/ You see that I can play a pretty convincing role/ So I don't need you, I don't think I need you."

Of this song, the note at one of the Jars of Clay web sites says: "I think this song shows the attitude of a non-believer hanging on the verge of accepting Christ." The song could just as easily be about any number of other things. It could be a believer describing his backsliding. It is not clear to whom the singer is speaking. Is it God? Is it his girlfriend? Is it his guru? No one can be sure. It can mean anything and nothing.

Jason Martin, singer for Starflyer 59, complains about people pressuring them to make their lyrics clear and biblical: "A lot of bands, the reason they get so turned off, is because you have to put the word 'Jesus' in every line. ... THAT'S WHY SO MANY BANDS GET ALMOST ANTI-JESUS IN THEIR LYRICS, EVEN THOUGH THEY'RE CHRISTIANS" (emphasis added) (Jason Martin of Starflyer 59, *HM*, Mar/Apr 97, p. 21).

That sounds like rebellion to me. Starflyer 59 definitely doesn't put Jesus into every line. In fact, their music is so abstract it is almost meaningless. Consider some examples from *Silver 59*:

> "Lost on words for you/ and I'd better make it soon/ in a world for you/ and the better one you are/ and I'm turning off/ to a place that you don't/ know I'm turning off here - to a place I know" (Starflyer 59, "Monterey," *Silver 59*).

> "And she don't care, well not bad/ and she don't care, well not her/ and her heart it's not there/ and she's just a sled/ and he's just as bad/ and your heart/ it's not there" (Starflyer 59, "Sled," *Silver 59*).

> "Honestly I'd rather sleep but your/ holding me to it all, on the deeper/ side I'm just a ride, your mine, your it/ all, and I'm craving to lift you up, and/ I'm craving to take the fall, on the/ deeper side, I'm just a ride, your/ mine, your it your all" (Starflyer 59, "Hazel Would," *Silver 59*).

> "Happy days are here again and you're not/ cause when she smiles it shakes my sickest phase/ and again, and again, and again/ cause when she smiles it shakes my sickest face" (Starflyer 59, "Happy Days," *Silver 59*).

Contemporary Christian Music fans might argue that I simply don't understand the terminology used by these groups. I would reply that if a message is not plain, it can be understood in any number of ways and it is impossible to know exactly what the right meaning is. The Bible says we are to sing "with the understanding" (1 Corinthians 14:15; Psalm 47:7). The message of God is to be made plain (Proverbs 8:9; Hab. 2:2). If the trumpet makes an uncertain sound who can prepare for war?

AN ASPECT OF THE VAGUENESS OF CCM IS ITS INFREQUENT USE OF THE NAME OF JESUS CHRIST. For example, three of Michael W. Smith's albums—*Change Your World, I'll Lead You Home,* and *Live Your Life*—contain no mention of Jesus Christ. There are over 6,000 words in the lyrics on these records, but not one mention of Jesus.

The name Jesus Christ is not spoken even once in two of the News Boys albums, *Take*

Me to Your Leader and *Going Public*.

The name of Jesus Christ does not appear on Sandi Patty's 1993 album *LeVoyage*.

In fact, the name of Jesus Christ does not appear on hundreds of CCM songs.

By contrast, the names Jesus and Christ appear 1538 times in the New Testament. In each one of the epistles the name of Jesus Christ appears repeatedly—105 times in Romans, 92 times in 1 Corinthians, 56 times in Galatians, 31 times in 1 Peter. The reason is that "there is none other name under heaven given among men, whereby we must be saved" (Acts 4:12) and this is the name "which is above every name" (Philippians 2:9). The Christian's responsibility is to proclaim this wonderful name to a lost and dying world.

Someone might protest that the older traditional hymns do not always contain Jesus' name, either. The very popular song "Never Alone" is an example. Christ is called "My Savior" but his name does not appear.

I have four replies to that. (1) I do not defend songs merely because they are old. There are traditional songs and hymns which contain false doctrine and have vague lyrics. They should be rejected just as surely as those which are contemporary and have the same problems.

(2) It is crucial to note that the theological climate was different in the 19th century and in the early part of this century. The New Age movement had not flourished. Though there were theological differences between denominations, most of them shared certain foundational truths, such as the inerrancy of Scripture and salvation by grace alone through Christ's atonement.

(3) Even though some of the older songs did not name the name of Christ specifically, the words were usually much more precise. Consider the following lyrics from "Never Alone" —

> "He died on Calvary's mountain/ For me they pierced His side/ For me He opened that fountain/ The crimson, cleansing tide/ For me He's waiting in glory/ Upon His heavenly throne."

Although this song does not use the name of Christ, there is nothing vague about its message.

(4) It is also important to remember that the old songs were written for Christians. They were not written to entertain the world and to become top tunes on secular

charts.

ANOTHER ASPECT OF CONTEMPORARY CHRISTIAN MUSIC'S VAGUENESS IS ITS TENDENCY TO ASK QUESTIONS RATHER THAN PROVIDE CLEAR BIBLICAL ANSWERS TO THE GREAT QUESTIONS OF LIFE. Note the following advertisement for an album by the Christian rock group IN-3D: "This band blasts away at conventional Christian music with searing sounds reminiscent of the Police, and thought-provoking lyrics INTENDED TO BE QUESTION-RAISERS. Their artful music is representative of a growing volume of Christian rock, much like U2's, USING AN INDIRECT APPROACH TO EVANGELISM, asking questions about moral issues and the meaning of life, but not necessarily spoon-feeding easy answers. The Chicago-based wave-metal combo explains, 'It's been said that art is not meant to answer questions, but to ask them'" (emphasis added) (Dan and Steve Peters, What about Christian Rock?, p. 121).

It might be true that "art" is not meant to answer questions, but Christian ministry certainly is supposed to answer questions. Ten times in the small epistle of 1 John the Bible states that "we know" the truth. "And we know that the Son of God is come, and hath given us an understanding, that we may know him that is true, and we are in him that is true, even in his Son Jesus Christ. This is the true God, and eternal life" (1 John 5:20). We have a know-so salvation, praise the Lord. We know who God is, what man is, where man came from, how man can be saved, where man is going, what the world is, where the world is headed, what lies beyond death. We know the will of God. We know the work of God. We know the plan of God. We know the love of God. The child of God knows the answer to all of the great mysteries of life, because God has revealed them to us in the Scriptures. It is criminal for professing Christians to merely give the world more questions instead of solid and plain Bible answers to the questions of life.

ANOTHER ASPECT OF THE VAGUENESS OF THE CCM MESSAGE IS ITS FREQUENT REFUSAL TO USE BIBLICAL OR TRADITIONAL CHRISTIAN TERMS. Referring to their 1998 album *Supernatural*, Toby McKeehan of dc Talk says, "When we set out to make this record, we allowed ourselves to roam freely and in doing so, we found that you can venture outside church terms" (*CCM Update*, August 3, 1998).

LeFevre's 1986 album, *Look Up*, designed for the pop rock market, contains lyrics which "avoid religious terminology."

> "But the album we made for Epic [*Look Up*] is more subtle and still has the Christian message. But it is not so religious sounding. We've been careful to avoid any religious terminology in this record that would turn people off" (LeFevre, cited by Jeff Godwin, *What's Wrong with Christian Rock?*, p. 124).

> "It's an anointed record and it's got a good message, but it's very shallow. We really avoided certain words and phrases, you know" (LeFevre, cited by John Styll, *CCM Magazine*, March 1986).

We reject this philosophy of Christian music for the following reasons:

(1) This philosophy denies the power of God's Word. God has promised to bless His Word, not some abstract, ill-defined semblance of Christian thought. It is the Word of God which is "quick, and powerful, and sharper than any twoedged sword, piercing even to the dividing asunder of soul and spirit, and of the joints and marrow, and is a discerner of the thoughts and intents of the heart" (Hebrews 4:12). It is the Word of God which sanctifies. "Sanctify them through thy truth: thy word is truth" (John 17:17). It is the Word of God which we are to preach (2 Timothy 4:2).

(2) Sound doctrine must be stated precisely. False teachers talk about Jesus and God and salvation and grace and mercy and forgiveness. False teachers use the Bible, or we should say they misuse the Bible. They twist verses out of context. 2 Peter 3:16 reminds us that they "wrest" the scriptures. They take sound doctrine and add to it and subtract from it and change it a little. The only protection from theological error is the precise statement of doctrinal truth.

(3) This is the false idea of contextualization. It is the same philosophy which undergirds dynamic equivalency Bible translation. The translator or the singer believes he has the authority to modify God's message to fit the world's terminology and thinking. In reality, when the truth of God is made to conform to the world's cultures, the truth of God is corrupted. The goal of the evangelist, rather, should be to conform the world to the Word of God, not conform the Word of God to the world.

(4) This philosophy believes entertainment is a proper objective of Christian ministry. Toby McKeehan also stated that they didn't feel bound to address strictly biblical themes, that they "felt free to write a song about a loving relationship" (Ibid.). Obviously they believe that entertaining people about the various themes of life is legitimate ministry. We do not believe this. Unless the message of a song is biblically plain nothing of eternal consequence will be accomplished in the listeners lives. Nowhere in the Bible do we have a commission to entertain the world. There is no biblical authority for this type of thinking.

The vagueness which permeates the lyrics of Contemporary Christian Music is apostasy.

CCM musician Dallas Holm, as far back as 1979, noted the hazy nature of Contemporary Christian Music: "Quite honestly, there are a lot of Christian songs I can't figure out. If I, as a Christian, can't figure them out, how in the world is a person out there who isn't even spiritually minded going to figure them out? If I'm failing to communicate the message of Jesus, if anybody sitting out there is wondering what in the world I'm talking about, then I've failed as far as I'm concerned" (Dallas Holm, *CCM Magazine*, July 1998, p. 44).

Holm was right about this problem in 1979, and it has gotten much worse since then. In his 1997 protest against the CCM industry, Steve Camp described the message of CCM songs overall as "a Christ-less, watered-down, pabulum-based, positive alternative, aura-fluff, cream of wheat, mush-kind-of-syrupy, God-as-my-girlfriend kind of thing" (*Dallas Morning News*, Feb. 21, 1998).

He was certainly right about that.

THIRD, THE WORDS TO CCM SONGS ARE SCRIPTURALLY HERETICAL.

The words to Contemporary Christian Music are not only difficult to understand and not only vague, but they frequently present false doctrine.

A POSITIVE-ONLY, NON-JUDGMENTAL DOCTRINE

One of the recurring themes of Contemporary Christian Music is non-judgmentalism. This is no surprise, since the ecumenical world of which CCM is a part focuses on being positive, being tolerant, and not judging. If one accepts this false philosophy of non-judgmentalism, he has no way to protect himself from error, because the God-ordained protection is in judging everything by the Word of God and rejecting that which is contrary to the Scriptures (Psalm 119:128). The protection from error is biblical separation from it (2 Timothy 2:15-18), but there can be no separation unless one first judges the message whether it is true or false.

The following quotes illustrate the non-judgmental philosophy of the CCM world:

> "We've been beating people up with our lyrics, condemning the world harshly. You don't have to tell someone they're locked up in prison——they already know that. They want to know how to get out. Where the key is, and that key is God's love which is more powerful than hatred. This is a pleasant and warm message to the world, one they need and want to hear" (Bebe Winans, *CCM Magazine*, Feb. 1989, p. 17).

> "[Our album *Run to the Light* is] A peace and love type of message. . . . we sorta tamed the message down to peace and love . . . so we wouldn't feel like hypocrites. You know, like Bible-beatin' people and not the whole band was

born again Christians, ya know?" (Brad Holster, member of the CCM group Trouble, *Heaven's Metal Magazine*, Number 18, p. 12).

"We're just gonna present the facts and love one another through thick and thin, and love people and hope that that presents a witness that will attract people to God, rather than turn them off. You turn on the TV and you see these guys screaming and yelling and trying to preach people into the Kingdom of God. I just see more people from our generation turning their backs cold on that. I think that we will draw more people into the Kingdom of God like Stryper, Bloodgood, Barren Cross and these types of ministries have" (Larry Dean, *Heaven's Metal Magazine*, Number 18, p. 10).

"I think the subtle approach reaches a wider audience, when it's right out, it turns 'em off" (Bruce Franklin, member of the CCM group Trouble, *Heaven's Metal Magazine*, Number 18, p. 12).

"He [Mylon LeFevre] doesn't think Christians should condemn others. 'That happened to me as a child, and it's not right. ... We don't holler at people and we don't shake Bibles at them. We just bring the love of Jesus to them'" (*Seattle Post-Intelligencer*, Seattle, Washington, Oct. 11, 1984).

"I'm a singer, not a preacher. I'm not looking to convert anybody. I feel people come to hear my music, not to hear me talk" (Amy Grant, *St. Petersburg Times*, Florida, April 7, 1984, p. 4).

John Fischer is a CCM writer/performer and is also one of the key spokesmen for the CCM movement. He is a regular columnist for *CCM Magazine*. His non-judgmental philosophy is evident from the following statement:

"Some Christian artists will play in clubs and never mention Jesus from stage. They will see this as their calling. Others will feel led to deliver an altar call at every performance. The tendency will be to judge one as being more legitimate than the other, whether by artistic or by ministry standards. Somehow I believe the world is big enough, its need are varied enough and the Holy Spirit is creative enough to legitimize both these approaches. As more and more Christian artists seek acceptance outside the marketing definitions of Christian music, they will face many obstacles. Let's try and make sure at least one of those obstacles doesn't have to be their fellow Christians" (John Fischer, "Between a Rock and a Hard Place," *CCM Magazine*, August 1998, p. 62).

Fischer is saying that it is wrong to judge the difference between a Christian musician who preaches Jesus Christ and one who does not, one who entertains the bar crowd and one who does not. Such thinking certainly does not come from the Bible. The Bible has much to say about music, but nowhere does God's Word give instruction or encouragement for Christians to entertain the world. Where in the New Testament Scriptures do we see anything like crossover Christian music? The Lord Jesus Christ gave us His commission to preach the Gospel to the ends of the earth (Matthew 28; Mark 16; Luke 24; John 20; Acts 1), and that is precisely what the Apostles and first Christians did (Acts 8:4; 17:6). Those who preach the Gospel are certainly to be commended above those who do not! John Fischer might not think it is right to judge musicians by the Word of God, but he is wrong. We are commanded to "prove all things" (1 Thess. 5:21), and that includes musicians. David compared everything to God's Word and rejected everything that was false. "Therefore I esteem all thy precepts concerning all things to be right; and I hate every false way" (Psalm 119:128). Isaiah used the same standard (Isaiah 8:20). One of the Christian's responsibilities is to earnestly contend for the faith once delivered to the saints (Jude 3). That involves comparing everything to the New Testament faith and rejecting everything that is contrary.

Clay Crosse's *Stained Glass* album (1997) (produced by Mark Heimermann and Regie Hamm) contains the song "Love One Another Right." It is written by Regie Hamm, Steve Siler, and Bob Farrell. Note the unscriptural non-judgmental philosophy:

> "We do a pretty good job of throwing sticks and stones/ But everyone's got a closet full of skeleton bones/ No need to tear each other down/ 'Cause we're all standing here on common ground/ If we could love one another/ We could bring Heaven down out of the sky."

The song presents the false ecumenical philosophy that Christians are not to judge sin and error. Since I have my own sins and problems, I have no right to judge any other person, they say. This is not what the Bible says, though. Preaching and teaching is to be judged (1 Cor. 14:29). False teachers are to be judged and rebuked (Titus 3:10-11). Stubborn Christians are to be rebuked sharply (Titus 1:13). Not only am I to avoid the sinful things of this world, but I am commissioned by the Lord to rebuke those who do such things. "And have no fellowship with the unfruitful works of darkness, but rather reprove them" (Eph. 5:11). Paul was not perfect nor sinless but he rebuked Peter publicly for his hypocrisy and compromise (Galatians 2:11-14). We must constantly search our own hearts and avoid being hypocritical, but the man of God does not judge sin because of any perfection in his own life; he judges sin on the authority of the Word of God. We do not exercise our own judgment; the judgment is of God. The modern ecumenist who is fulfilling 2 Timothy 4:3-4 does not understand these weighty matters.

Larry Norman, "the founding father of Christian rock music," does not believe that God will judge sin in the Christian's life:

> "We're taught that God is very judicious, and unrelenting in his ferreting out of your sins, keeping a list and you're going to have to answer for every failing upon your death. That's the God that I was exposed to growing up in America,

but then finding out that God is all-loving toward his own children, his own sheep that know his voice——-that's made the last few years of my life completely different in texture, and I feel that I have a lot of freedom that I never realised was available before" (Interview with Larry Norman, *CrossRhythms*, November 1993).

This is one of those half truths which form a lie. God is all-loving toward his children, but this does not mean He does not ferret out, keep records of, and judge sin. We are motivated by the love of God, but we are also motivated by the fear of God (Heb. 12:28-29). The words "judge" and "judgment" are used more than 200 times in the New Testament. 1 Peter 4:17 says "judgment must begin at the house of God." 1 Peter 4:5 and 2 Timothy 4:1 say God is going to "judge the quick and the dead," meaning He is going to judge the saved and the unsaved. James warned Christians not to sin because if we do we will be condemned by the Lord when He comes (James 5:9). 1 Timothy 5:24 warns that some men's sins follow them to judgment and the context refers to Christians. 2 Corinthians 5:10 warns that the judgment seat of Christ will deal with the good and the bad in the Christian's life. 1 Corinthians 11:31 warns the Christian to judge himself so he will not be judged by the Lord. 1 Corinthians 3:13-14 warns that if a Christian's work does not pass the judgment he will suffer loss because of it. Colossians 3:25 warns that Christ's judgment upon Christians will involve judgment for wrong doing. Further, there is the law of sowing and reaping in this life, and the blood of Christ does not negate that law (Galatians 5:7).

According to the *Huntsville Times* (Huntsville, Alabama), **Steven Curtis Chapman** says he tries to communicate a Biblical world view in a way that will NOT BE "ABRASIVELY PREACHY" (*Huntsville Times*, Oct. 30, 1994). He says his quest for relevance has shown that the best way to communicate his faith is "not to preach fire and brimstone" (Ibid.).

In 1994 **Michael English** confessed to an adulterous affair with another CCM musician, Marabeth Jordon of the group First Call. At the time Mrs. Jordon was the wife of another man. Jordan and English conceived a baby out of wedlock (though it later died). At the fall 1996 National Quartet Convention in Kentucky, English was invited to testify and sing, and he was given multiple standing ovations. When English was introduced, gospel singer J.D. Sumner (of The Stamps) publicly asked him "to forgive people's judging hearts" (Biography of Michael English, http://www.michaelenglish.com/). According to Sumner, the greatest sin is not so much English's vile adultery against his wife or his hypocrisy in performing and recording Christian music even while living in such sin; it is the judgment of that adultery by others. This is yet another illustration of the unscriptural non-judgmental philosophy which permeates the Contemporary Christian Music world.

A web site promoting Michael English contains a statement signed by several hundred CCM lovers which commits them not to judge others. The site is sponsored by Free Indeed Ministries. Note the following statement:

> "From now on, the staff of Free Indeed Ministries will no longer contribute to any conversations that TEAR DOWN, spread rumors, or SERVE ANY FUNCTION OTHER THAN TO UPLIFT. In other words, to quote a popular song, 'IF YOU CAN'T SAY NOTHIN' GOOD, DON'T SAY NOTHIN' AT ALL.' From now on, we are separating ourselves from those that refuse to accept this Biblical command. And we invite you to join us in this. This is a decision that will impact every area of your life, so do not take it lightly! Below you will find the names of all twelve staff members and the hundreds of others that have pledged their support to this pledge" (http://christianmusic.miningco.com/library/blcmweekly.htm).

This statement falsely and dangerously lumps rumor-mongering or gossip together with any judgment of others which is not positive. While the Bible strongly forbids gossiping, it does not forbid exposing sin and error in the lives of public figures. The popular song which Free Indeed Ministries quotes presents false doctrine. The Bible is certainly not all positive. The Lord Jesus Christ did not restrict Himself to positive statements. Neither did the Apostles and preachers in the early churches. A big part of the preacher's job is to "reprove, rebuke, exhort" (2 Timothy 4:2). That is not positive! If the man of God is restricted to being positive and to not judging doctrine, he cannot protect himself and his flock from error and cannot keep the churches pure for the glory of Christ. The Apostle Paul judged the sin at Corinth and rebuked the Christians for their tolerance of sin (1 Cor. 5) and error (2 Cor. 11:1-4).

Mark Lowry's positive-only philosophy is evident in his attitude toward preaching on Hell:

> "I ALSO DON'T BELIEVE IN TELLING PEOPLE TO COME TO CHRIST BECAUSE OF HELL, in scaring people. When we do, we wind up with just another religious person. But if they come to Christ because no one has ever loved them like that before. ... That's the bottom line. Nobody's ever loved you like that before" (Melissa Riddle, "Funny Face," interview with Mark Lowry, *CCM Magazine*, May 1996).

The Lord Jesus Christ did not mind "scaring people." He preached more on Hell than He did on Heaven.

> "And if thy hand offend thee, cut it off: it is better for thee to enter into life maimed, than having two hands to go into hell, into the fire that never shall be quenched: Where their worm dieth not, and the fire is not quenched. And if thy foot offend thee, cut it off: it is better for thee to enter halt into life, than

having two feet to be cast into hell, into the fire that never shall be quenched: Where their worm dieth not, and the fire is not quenched. And if thine eye offend thee, pluck it out: it is better for thee to enter into the kingdom of God with one eye, than having two eyes to be cast into hell fire: Where their worm dieth not, and the fire is not quenched" (Mark 9:43-48).

The Apostles also boldly and plainly preached the judgment of God to produce conviction in sinners and to lead them to Christ. Consider Paul's sermon on Mars Hill: "And the times of this ignorance God winked at; but now commandeth all men every where to repent: Because he hath appointed a day, in the which he will judge the world in righteousness by that man whom he hath ordained; whereof he hath given assurance unto all men, in that he hath raised him from the dead" (Acts 17:30-31). It sounds to me that Paul was not afraid of "scaring people" so they would get saved. Hebrews 6:18 describes salvation as fleeing for refuge in Christ. Fleeing what? Eternal damnation! God's Word repeatedly uses fear to motivate people to do right. At least 24 times the New Testament refers to fearing God (Mt. 10:28; Lk. 1:50; 12:5; 18:2,4; 23:40; Acts 9:31; 10:2,22,35; 13:16,26; Rom. 3:18; 2Cor. 7:1; Eph. 5:21; Col. 3:22; Heb. 10:31; 12:28; 1 Pet. 1:17; 2:17; Rev. 11:18; 14:7; 15:4; 19:5). Judge 23 says some must be saved by fear.

Kathy Troccoli preaches a non-judgmental, anti-fundamentalist philosophy:

> "To me it's very simple: if the world doesn't see God's love in us and our love for each other, they're never going to want what we have. Our dogma and legalism strangle the love of Christ right out of us" (*CCM Magazine*, June 1997).

This sounds good to many ears, but it is impossible to obey the Bible without being deeply concerned about doctrine ("dogma") and obedience to the details of God's Word ("legalism"). Jude 3 explains that God has given one faith to His people and that faith, as recorded in the New Testament Scriptures, is to be preserved and fought for until Jesus returns. It is absolutely impossible to obey Jude 3 and be ecumenical and non-judgmental at the same time. The main thing which divides denominations is doctrine.

Charlie Daniels' 1996 *Steel Witness* album contains the song "New Pharisees," which "speaks about the tendency of modern-day Christians to judge their fellow man, much like the Pharisees of Jesus' day."

The Chinese CCM group **For You** advertises their music as "SPIRITUAL BUT NOT PREACHY" (*The Straits Times*, Singapore, May 18, 2001).

Jason Wade of Lifehouse says, "I think we have a positive message of hope. WE'RE

NOT TRYING TO BLATANTLY PREACH. It all comes down to love" ("The Rock & Roll Gospel according to Lifehouse," *Rolling Stone* magazine, http://www.rollingstone.com/news/newsarticle.asp?nid=13983&cf=13773270).

An ad for "Fuel on the Fire" by **Morgan Cryar** says the song is "a good pop/rock sound for the teenage audience" because the "songs deal with youth issues and situations WITHOUT BEING PREACHY." This is rebellion against the Word of God, because preaching is God's ordained way of proclaiming the truth. The words "preach" and "preaching" are mentioned 141 times in the New Testament. Jesus Christ was a preacher. John the Baptist was a preacher. The Apostles were preachers. A chief characteristic of the apostasy of the end times is to turn away one's ears from the preaching of God's Word (2 Timothy 4:1-4).

Randy Stonehill also has the positive only, judge not philosophy. "I DON'T WANT TO PREACH AT PEOPLE. What I want to do is communicate the truth in the most compelling, fresh, and challenging way I can. I just want to be the best songwriter and performer, unto God, that I can be. That's the main thing" ("Kicking Around with Uncle Rand," *Christian Music Review*, April 1991).

Don Francisco teaches the positive-only philosophy. Consider his testimony: "I knew from my own experience that PAINTING A PICTURE, RATHER THAN POINTING A FINGER, was a much more effective way to get the Gospel into people's heads and hearts." It is strange that the Apostle Paul did not understand this. Consider Paul's sermon to the unsaved pagans on Mars Hill. He preached against their idolatry and warned them of judgment to come (Acts 17). Sounds like "finger pointing" to me, not finger pointing in the sense of a holier-than-thou attitude, but finger pointing in the sense of proclaiming God's righteous judgment and calling men to repentance. Consider, too, Paul's presentation of the Gospel in the book of Romans. It begins with God's holiness and His condemnation of man's sin. Only after this "finger pointing" is completed does he get to the good news toward the end of chapter three that Christ has made the atonement for sin. The love of God is not even mentioned until chapter five of Romans. The preachers in the early churches did not have the philosophy of Contemporary Christian Music. In fact, preachers only 30 years ago did not have this philosophy.

Jon Gibson is another example of this non-judgmental philosophy. He says: "I have matured to the point as a Christian that I stay out of Christ's way. I don't clutter it up with my personal opinion, or religion. I just love people" (Jon Gibson, interview, *Inside Music*, June 1992, p. 20). Gibson thinks Christian love can ignore sin and error, but biblical love is never divorced from knowledge and judgment (Philippians 1:9). Gibson says he wants to stay out of Christ's way and not clutter it up with his opinion or religion, and he uses this statement to excuse himself from exercising judgment and from seeking to correct anyone. To the contrary, Christ has commanded that His people preach His Word (2 Timothy 4:2), contend for the faith (Jude 3), and rebuke sin (Ephesians 5:11).

Amy Grant says: "That's one reason I started writing songs, because I DIDN'T WANT TO IMPOSE MY RELIGION ON ANYONE. This way the audience can sit back and draw its own conclusions. ... My art and the feeling I am trying to communicate through the songs, it would be silly for me to say, this is who God is; I don't have any answers" (Amy Grant, interview, *The Philadelphia Inquirer*, Oct. 21, 1984). This sounds pious to the unsaved world and to an ecumenical generation, but Amy's philosophy is strictly contrary to the Bible. The early Christians did not seek to "impose their religion" on others, but they did preach the Word of God boldly to a lost world. "Therefore they that were scattered abroad went every where preaching the word" (Acts 8:4). We are to hold forth the Word of life to this wicked generation (Philippians 2:15,16). The Christian is supposed to have the answers people need, because we have God's Word (2 Timothy 2:15). Certainly we DO know who God is. "And we know that the Son of God is come, and hath given us an understanding, that we may know him that is true, and we are in him that is true, even in his Son Jesus Christ. This is the true God, and eternal life" (1 John 5:20).

In reviewing **Steve Taylor's** music, the *Seattle Post-Intelligencer* noted that "there is little preaching in his songs. Most of them are metaphoric story-songs written from a Christian perspective" (*Seattle Post-Intelligencer*, Oct. 11, 1984). Taylor admits that people like his concerts because there is no preaching: "Our concerts attract people because THEY KNOW THEY WON'T BE PREACHY or insult their intelligence" (Peters Brothers, *What About Christian Rock*, p. 138). Taylor was quoted as saying: "I don't think people really like to be preached at. One of the reasons Jesus was so effective is because he told parables. I think it's insulting to people's intelligence to preach at them. No one likes to be told what to believe" (*Seattle Post-Intelligencer*, Oct. 11, 1984)Ibid.)..

This unscriptural statement ignores two facts: (1) Jesus Christ was a preacher. At least 30 times the Gospels mention that Christ preached. Christ's ministry began with preaching (Matt. 4:17), and He preached some of the hardest sermons recorded in the Bible (i.e., Mark 9; Matthew 23). (2) Christ's parables were not given for the purpose of not preaching but for the purpose of hiding truth from the willfully blind (Matthew 13:10-11).

One of the songs sung by **Sandi Patty** is "Love in Any Language," which promotes world unity and non-judgmental love.

> "From Leningrad to Lexington, the farmer loves his land/ And daddies all get

> misty-eyed to give their daughter's hand/ Oh maybe when we realize how much there is to share/ We'll find too much in common to pretend it isn't there/ Love in any language/ Straight from the heart/ Pulls us all together/ Never apart/ And once we learn to speak it/ All the world will hear/ Love in any language/ Fluently spoken here..." ("Love in Any Language," by Jon Mohr and John Mays, sung by Sandi Patty).

This is not about biblical love. It is precisely the type of "love" promoted by the Beatles and others within the secular rock world. The only love which can bring men together in true biblical unity is the love of God through the Gospel of Jesus Christ, and the love of God in Jesus Christ divides believers from unbelievers. The Lord Jesus Christ stated: "Think not that I am come to send peace on earth: I came not to send peace, but a sword. For I am come to set a man at variance against his father, and the daughter against her mother, and the daughter in law against her mother in law" (Matt. 10:34,35). The Apostle John testified of this division: "And we know that we are of God, and the whole world lieth in wickedness" (1 John 5:19). The love Sandi Patty sang about , though, is a love which never pulls men apart, never divides. It is the false ecumenical, non-judgmental love which seeks unity apart from truth. There is no true love apart from Jesus Christ, and the love of God in Jesus Christ is to obey God's Word: "For this is the love of God, that we keep his commandments: and his commandments are not grievous" (1 John 5:3). Any message about "love" which does not refer to the one true Gospel of Jesus Christ and obedience to God's Word is a false message.

Bob Carlisle, author of "Butterfly Kisses," has the non-judgmental philosophy of the CCM world.

> "I'm not a finger-pointing kind of song writer or speaker. We're all in this together. In that, the last album was just songs that touch people's everyday experiences. That's what I know" (Interview with Bob Carlisle, *The Lighthouse*, February 1994, http://tlem.netcentral.net/old/carlisle_bob_9402.html).

Leslie Phillips does not hide her belief in non-judgmentalism:

> "I found out that the church really wasn't the place where I had more freedom, it was the opposite: I actually was restricted more. And I always felt like I was swimming upstream in that environment. I guess the main thing is, I want to grow as an artist and I want to be able to write about whatever I want to write about. And I really don't want to be restricted, and I feel like I am in Gospel music. ... The born-again movement is more about obsession and narrow-mindedness and repression and true Christianity is about mercy and freedom and love" (Leslie Phillips, interview, *CCM Magazine*, November 1988, p. 8).

This statement demonstrates a rebellious attitude. True Christianity is about mercy and love, but it is also about repentance and holiness and obedience and fruitfulness and sacrifice and zeal and forbearance and self control and preaching and discipleship.

Terry Taylor, formerly of the Daniel Amos Band, claims that a Christian musician does not have to preach the Gospel plainly, but can provide entertainment and fun:

> "There are some people God has called to evangelism, and they're doing a wonderful job, having results. That's great. God wanted us to do something else, so we got into the area of challenging people, and our ministry basically happens offstage—one-on-one—when we talk with people. IT'S VERY SUBTLE, but God's doing a work! It's entertainment, it's fun, it's a concert—it's all those things—but AT A SUBTLE, DEEPER LEVEL, IT TOUCHES PEOPLE'S HEARTS" (Terry Taylor, cited by Dan and Steve Peters, *What about Christian Rock?*, p. 109).

Taylor is preaching a theme which permeates CCM: the Christian life is about liberty and fun. This is the positive-only, non-judgmental philosophy. How does Taylor know God wanted them to do something else other than plainly preach the Gospel as we see the Christians doing in the Bible (Acts 8:4)? Paul used "great plainness of speech" (2 Corinthians 3:12). The Great Commission is not given merely to preachers or to a few full-time evangelists and missionaries. It is an obligation every born again Christian is to seek to fulfill through the New Testament church (Acts 1:8). Contemporary Christian musicians have no biblical authority to entertain the world. They have no biblical authority to water down the Gospel message so that it is acceptable to the world. They have no authority to make the Christian message vague, to make it man-centered rather than Christ-centered, to make it felt-need centered rather than cross-centered. They have no authority to draw back from preaching plainly that man is sinful and condemned, that God is holy and righteous, that Hell is eternal, that the way of salvation is narrow and requires repentance. It is not the God of the Bible who is leading in this new "contemporary" path. He has already expressed His will in the Scriptures, and we see nothing resembling a Christian rock music program there.

CCM writer/performer **Wayne Watson** says: "I won't write a song that says, 'You better get right with God.' From my own experience I find that way sometimes makes people defensive" (Wayne Watson, *Christian Activities Calendar*, Spring/Summer 1989, p. 11). This is not how the Apostles and early Christians looked at things. They did not appear to mind making people defensive, because they preached boldly against sin and called upon people to repent. Preaching about God's holiness and man's sinfulness has always made people defensive. By the way, this is why the faithful Christians through the centuries have been hated, scorned, persecuted, and martyred. The Word of God has always been offensive and divisive. The only person who can avoid making people defensive and offending people is the person who refuses to obey God's command to preach the truth to a crooked and perverse generation (Luke 24:46-48; Ephesians 5:11; Philippians 2:15,16).

P.O.D. (Payable on Death), a hard rock group from California, also subscribes to the positive-only philosophy: An interviewer with *Pollstar* observed: "While THEY DON'T PREACH or try to ram their spirituality down anyone's throat, they hope that their positive message will have an influence on rock fans" (*Pollstar*, March 20, 2000).

White Heart's unscriptural non-judgmental philosophy is evident in the following statement:

> "So, where do you go when times get tough? You've got to have a powerhouse. You've got to have a place where you can go ... We want to tell people that there are places to go, that we should build communities where they can get strength, NOT TO KNOCK ANYBODY ELSE DOWN, but to find SOMETHING DEEPER WITHIN THEMSELVES" (White Heart, *CCM Magazine*, February, 1991, pp. 20-23).

Of course Christians are to not called to "knock" others down, but they are called to reprove, rebuke, and exhort (2 Timothy 4:2). They are called to reprove the works of darkness (Ephesians 5:11). Also, the message that Christians have for the world is not that we can find something deeper within ourselves, but that the Truth is found in Jesus Christ and in the His Scriptures. Deep within man we find not truth but sin and deception (Jeremiah 17:9; Matthew 15:19-20; Romans 7:18).

MusicLine Magazine describes **Steve Camp's** music in these terms: "Though potent, the message never overwhelms or becomes preachy" (*MusicLine Magazine*, June 1985, p. 20). Camp exhibited his non-judgmental philosophy in the following statement:

> "As an exhorter, I always felt that in order to tell people the correct way to live, my life style had to be perfect, and I'm finding that's not so. I'm finding that they respond more to my weakness" (*CCM Magazine*, November 1986, p. 20).

Camp had the wrong idea about exhortation and preaching (it is possible that he might no longer hold this philosophy). Preaching is not based on the preacher's own moral perfection. The authority for preaching is God's Word, not the preacher's life. The preacher is preaching God, not himself. A preacher should strive to live according to the message he preaches, but no man could ever preach if preaching required any type of moral perfection. "If any man speak, let him speak as the oracles of God..." (1 Peter 4:11). The writers of the Bible were certainly far from perfect. Think of David and Solomon and Jonah and Peter. Steve Camp is not called of God to preach himself, not his strengths nor his weaknesses. He is instructed to preach the Word of God. By the way, I don't want to hear about the weaknesses of Steve Camp or Michael Smith or Amy Grant or anyone else. I want to hear about Jesus Christ and His victory and program.

The very popular CCM musician **Steve Green** also wants the world to know that he supports the non-judgmental philosophy:

> "I do have personal convictions that I conduct my life by, but I'm not going to force my convictions on someone else or try to make them jump through my hoops, through the convictions I have set up for my life" (Steve Green, *MusicLine Magazine*, December 1985, p. 9).

If Steve Green's convictions are not based on the Word of God, of course he is right and he should not urge his convictions upon anyone. If, on the other hand, his convictions are based solidly upon the Word of God, he has every responsibility to urge others to follow them. Timothy was instructed, "Preach the word; be instant in season, out of season; reprove, rebuke, exhort with all longsuffering and doctrine" (2 Timothy 4:2). Green's non-judgmental statement sounds like a clever attempt to escape the responsibility to preach God's standards of holiness and to reprove the works of darkness (Ephesians 5:11).

Note the following words from Steve Green's song "Love One Another" from the 1995 album *The Letter*:

> "Love is there to serve and doesn't seem to mind/ Never has a harsh word to say."

This is the unscriptural definition of love so often promoted by the ecumenical crowd. The love of God does serve and is patient and merciful, but the love of God has many harsh things to say. It has harsh things to say to those who are sinning and unrepentant (Acts 28:25-28). The love of God also has harsh things to say to those who corrupt the Word of God (Acts 13:8-11).

Michael W. Smith, one of the most popular Contemporary Christian Musicians, plainly admits that he is not preachy. "MY SONGS ARE NOT PREACHY — AT ALL . . ." (Michael McCall, *Contemporary Christian*, June 1986, p. 19). Smith presented described his non-judgmental philosophy in an interview in the May 1998 issue of *CCM Magazine*. The unscriptural mindset found among the majority of these musicians is evident throughout the interview. Consider the following excerpt:

> "If Jesus was here today physically, I'm not really sure He'd be in the churches. He'd be hanging out at the bars, with the desperate and the lonely. And I don't think He'd be going in and preaching—I think He'd be going in and

> befriending people. ... For so many years it was like [groaning in mock tones], 'Oh, a Smitty concert. Preaching. Altar call. Fire and brimstone.' A lot of people put me in right-wing, blow-up-abortion-clinic categories. They think all Christians think that way, and it's not true. So when they see my show, they say, 'He's legit. I like that. He's not that right-wing guy. But he's spiritual, and he's got something to say—and he said something that deeply affected me tonight.' That is what you hope for" ("Michael W. Smith Engages Culture," *CCM Magazine*, May 1988, p. 38).

Smith is trying to justify his worldly methods and music and his abstract religious message. His "cross-over" music albums and concerts are designed to appeal to both the "saved" and the unsaved. Smith says he's not sure Jesus Christ would be in churches. That is nonsense, of course, for it was Jesus Christ who founded the church (Matt. 16:18) and who taught the Apostles to make the churches the center of the fulfillment of the Great Commission (see the book of Acts). The church is the pillar and ground of the truth (1 Timothy 3:15). This is not to say that the Lord Jesus Christ is pleased with all churches today. He prophesied that there would be great numbers of false teachers who would lead people astray into error and false churches (Matt. 7:15; 24:3,4,11,24). The Apostles of Jesus Christ made the same warning (1 Tim. 4:1-4; 2 Tim. 3:13; 2 Pet. 2:1; 1 John 2:18-19; 4:1). Christ and the Apostles prophesied a great apostasy, or turning from the one true faith, but they also prophesied that true churches would continue until Christ returns (Matt. 28:18-20). It is true, therefore, that the Lord Jesus Christ would not be in many of the churches which exist today, because they have rejected His Word, but it is not true that the Lord Jesus would reject all churches. He promised to be with the true churches until the end, and we can be sure that He is in the very midst of the true churches today as He was when John saw Him (Revelation 1:12-13).

Smith also says he doesn't think Jesus would be preaching. This statement makes us wonder whether Smith has read the Bible. Christ befriended people, but he also preached, and he preached continually. Many of his sermons are recorded in the Gospels. When Matthew summarized the ministry of Christ, he said, "And Jesus went about all Galilee, TEACHING in their synagogues, and PREACHING the gospel of the kingdom..." (Matt. 4:23). Luke summarized his ministry in these words: "And it came to pass afterward, that he went throughout every city and village, PREACHING and showing the glad tidings of the kingdom of God: and the twelve were with him" (Luke 8:1). Jesus Christ was a Preacher! It was because of His preaching that the crowds turned away from Him (John 6). The Apostles and early Christians followed in Christ's footsteps by preaching wherever they went: "Therefore they that were scattered abroad went every where PREACHING the word" (Acts 8:4). As previously noted, the term "preach" appears 141 times in the New Testament, 37 times in the Gospels alone! The man of God is instructed to "preach the Word" in season and out of season (2 Tim. 4:1-2). We are told that God has chosen to save men by the foolishness of preaching (1

Cor. 1:21).

The passage in 1 Corinthians chapter one reminds us why Contemporary Christian Musicians are so often opposed to biblical preaching. The unsaved hates biblical preaching. The preaching of the cross is foolish to the proud unsaved mind, and it brings the world's reproach upon the preacher. The world did not love the Lord Jesus Christ, and Christ warned:

> "If the world hate you, ye know that it hated me before it hated you. If ye were of the world, the world would love his own: but because ye are not of the world, but I have chosen you out of the world, therefore the world hateth you" (John 15:18,19).

It is possible to "minister" in a compromised, worldly manner so that the unsaved world thinks one is "cool" or "spiritual," but it is not possible to obey the Bible and follow in the footsteps of Christ and the Apostles and the prophets of old and have the unsaved world think one is cool! The Lord Jesus Christ said:

> "Blessed are they which are persecuted for righteousness' sake: for theirs is the kingdom of heaven. Blessed are ye, when men shall revile you, and persecute you, and shall say all manner of evil against you falsely, for my sake. Rejoice, and be exceeding glad: for great is your reward in heaven: for so persecuted they the prophets which were before you" (Matt. 5:10-12)

Jesus also warned: "Woe unto you, when all men shall speak well of you! for so did their fathers to the false prophets" (Luke 6:26).

Smith said the world enjoys his rock music and enjoys the fact that he does not preach hell fire, and so the world counts him "spiritual" and "legit" but not preachy. The term "spiritual" as understood by the world or even by the religious crowd today is meaningless. The world has no idea what true spirituality is. The world does not measure "religion" and "spirituality" by the Bible, but by its own feelings and desires and philosophies. The unregenerate world hates the preaching of the true Gospel of Jesus Christ and the true preaching of the Bible, because it pronounces that all have sinned and come short of the glory of God, and it pronounces God's condemnation upon all men outside of Jesus Christ. It hates the preaching of the true Gospel because it says man's own righteousness, his very best religious, do-good efforts, is as filthy rags before a holy God. The world hates the preaching of the Gospel because it says there is none righteous, no not one, and because it warns that every person who is not born again will not see the kingdom of God but will be tormented forever and ever in the lake of fire, and because it says Jesus Christ alone is the way, the truth, and the life, and there is none other name given under heaven whereby men must be saved, and because it says all other ways are false. The world hates the preaching of the true Gospel because it demands that a man give up his life for Christ's sake and the Gospel's, because it demands that a man come out from among them and be separate, because it demands that we strive to be holy as God is holy. For the world to count someone as spiritual is meaningless from a biblical perspective. The world thinks the pope is spiritual and Native American Indians are spiritual and New Age gurus are spiritual and Hindu mystics are spiritual and Hollywood entertainers are spiritual.

For people to "be deeply affected" by a rock concert does not mean that something spiritual in a biblical fashion is occurring. People are "deeply affected" by all sorts of false religions and cults and experiences and philosophies. People are "deeply affected" by many things which happen in their day to day lives. People are deeply affected by drugs and alcohol and hypnosis and treatment programs, by secular rock songs and by Hollywood movies, by romantic affairs and by other emotionally charged circumstances, by sunsets and mountain scenes. This does not mean they are truly born again or that they are in fellowship with the Lord Jesus Christ of the Bible. The "Christian" world is filled with false christs and false gospels and false spirits. The Apostle Paul warned about these almost 2,000 years ago (2 Cor. 11:1-4), and we are told in Scripture that the religious deception would be much greater just preceding the coming of Christ (Matt. 24:3-4,11,24; 2 Thess. 2:7-11).

In a 1987 interview with *CCM Magazine*, the late **Rich Mullins**, popular CCM writer/performer, said that he was "really sick of all this heavy-handed Christianity," that musicians "should stop preaching unless that's what God has called them to" (*CCM Magazine*, April 1987, p. 12). As we have seen, though, every Christian has a responsibility before God to proclaim the Word of God to this lost world.

Note the lyrics to Mullin's 1995 song "Brother's Keeper":

> "The preacher's thinking thoughts that are wicked/ The lover's got a lonely heart/ My friends ain't the way I wish they were/ They are just the way they are/ I will be my brother's keeper/ Not the one who judges him/ I won't despise him for his weakness/ I won't regard him for his strength/ I won't take away his freedom."

This is another plain statement of the unscriptural non-judgmental philosophy which permeates Contemporary Christian Music. The Lord Jesus Christ warns us against hypocritical judgment (Matthew 7:1-5), but Christians do have a responsibility to judge sin and error (1 Corinthians 2:15; 5:1-13; 6:1-5; 14:29; Philippians 1:9). Mullins also said he would not take away someone's freedom, but Christian freedom is restricted by God's Word (1 Corinthians 8:9; Galatians 5:13; 1 Peter 2:16) and Christians are responsible to judge sin (1 Cor. 5) and to exhort one another daily about sin (Heb. 3:13).

The lyrics to **Donna Summer's** music is described as being "UNPREACHILY AS POSSIBLE, the approach most likely to win the attention of an intelligent non-Christian audience" (*Contemporary Christian Music Magazine*, Oct. 1984, p. 40).

The group **U2** is described by the *Boston Globe* as representing a "NON-DOGMATIC CHRISTIANITY." *CCM Magazine* said U2 has "chosen instead of proclaiming a direct Christian message to act Christianly in the world" (*CCM Magazine*, July 1987, p. 46). This is another way of saying that they are positive and non-judgmental. It is impossible to obey the Bible and have a non-dogmatic Christianity. Jesus Christ is the only Lord and Savior. There is only one Gospel. There is only one Faith. The Apostles and early Christians were most definitely dogmatic in their Christianity. "And we know that we are of God, and the whole world lieth in wickedness. And we know that the Son of God is come, and hath given us an understanding, that we may know him that is true, and we are in him that is true, even in his Son Jesus Christ. This is the true God, and eternal life" (1 John 5:19-20). Further, it is impossible to "act Christianly" without proclaiming a direct Christian message, because Jesus Christ has commanded every Christian to preach the Gospel and to earnestly contend for the faith once delivered to the saints (Mark 16:15; Philippians 2:14-16; Jude 3).

In the summer of 1998 the "Christian" hard rock group **MxPx** were on the "Warped" rock tour as an opening act for the anti-Christian secular rock group Bad Religion. When some Christians protested their alliance with such a wicked group, the members of MxPx complained that their detractors "shouldn't be so negative" (*CCM Magazine*, August 1998, p. 37), demonstrating their unscriptural positive-only philosophy. They even wrote a song to "protest the way some have reacted to their association with artists like Bad Religion." They have confused correction with persecution. They think they are being persecuted because Christians attempt to warn and correct them about things they are doing contrary to the Word of God. The Bible plainly instructs God's people to prove all things (1 Thess. 5:21). The Bereans were commended for doing this (Acts 17:11). The Bible also says Christians are to rebuke sin and error (Ephesians 5:11; Titus 1:13). Those who sought to correct MxPx were not wrong, but the members of the band were so spiritually immature that they could not receive the correction. "The way of a fool is right in his own eyes: but he that hearkeneth unto counsel is wise" (Proverbs 12:15).

We reject Contemporary Christian Music and its unscriptural non-judgmental, positive-only philosophy.

AN ANTI-FUNDAMENTALIST DOCTRINE

Another of the messages which comes across loudly and clearly in Contemporary Christian Music is that of anti-fundamentalism. Consider the following statement by two men who defend CCM:

> "Could it be that the One who 'makes all things new' (Rev. 21:5) is also interested in new music? We think so, and yet, many Christians discriminate against the new and unfamiliar. It's a sort of reverse snobbism which sometimes allows mediocrity under the guise of spirituality, while superficially rejecting even the best contemporary artistic works" (**Dan and Steve Peters**, *What about Christian Rock?*, p. 148).

This statement is very vicious toward Bible-believing people who warn against Christian rock music, and it is a statement filled with error. The authors pretend that those who speak against Christian rock are snobs who merely discriminate against the "unfamiliar." The truth is that large numbers of men and women who warn against Christian rock are godly saints who were heavily involved with rock music prior to their consecration to Christ and who are very familiar with Contemporary Christian Music styles. The authors of the previous statement further pretend that those who reject Contemporary Christian Music practice mediocrity, whereas large numbers of the latter are first-rate musicians and practice the highest standards of musical excellence. The authors of this statement also pretend that those who reject CCM do so "superficially." This is a slander against the many men who have diligently researched CCM in a sincere effort before the Lord to know the truth about this music. In preparation to write this book I have examined the words and music literally to hundreds of CCM songs. Does that type of research produce a "superficial" view of one's subject?

The attitude of the Christian rock crowd has been brashly anti-fundamentalist from the beginning. **Larry Norman** is considered the father of Christian rock music. His 1975 hit "Why Should the Devil Have All the Good Music," one of the theme songs of the CCM scene, promotes the strange philosophy that rock music is something good that Christians need, and that traditional Christian songs, hymns, and spiritual songs are boring "funeral marches." The song oozes with adolescent rebellion, which certainly has no place in the Christian life.

> "I want the people to know/ that he saved my soul/ But I still like to listen to the radio/ THEY SAY ROCK 'N' ROLL IS WRONG/ we'll give you one more chance/ I say I feel so good/ I gotta get up and dance.
>
> "I know what's right/ I know what's wrong/ I don't confuse it/ All I'm really trying to say/ Is why should the Devil have all the good music?/ I feel good every day/ 'Cause Jesus is the rock/ and he rolled my blues away.

> "THEY SAY TO CUT MY HAIR/ THEY'RE DRIVING ME INSANE/ I grew it out long/ to make room for my brain/ But sometimes people don't understand/ What's a good boy doing in a rock 'n' roll band?
>
> "There's nothing wrong with playing blues licks/ But IF YOU GOT A REASON/ TELL ME TO MY FACE / Why should the Devil have all the good music/ There's nothing wrong with what I play/ 'Cause Jesus is the rock/ and he rolled my blues away.
>
> "I ain't knocking the hymns/ JUST GIVE ME A SONG THAT HAS A BEAT/ I ain't knocking the hymns/ Just give me a song that moves my feet/ I DON'T LIKE NONE OF THOSE FUNERAL MARCHES/ I ain't dead yet!
>
> "Jesus told the truth/ Jesus showed the way/ There's one more thing/ I'd like to say/ They nailed him to the cross/ they laid him in the ground/ But they shoulda known/ you can't keep a good man down.
>
> "I feel good every day/ I don't wanna lose it/ All I wanna/ all I wanna know/ Is why should the Devil have all the good music/ I've been filled/ I feel okay/ Jesus is the rock/ and he rolled my blues/Jesus is the rock/ and he rolled my blues/ Jesus is the rock/ and he rolled my blues away" (Larry Norman, "Why Should the Devil Have All the Good Music?").

The philosophy behind this song is the philosophy behind the CCM scene as a whole. It is this: Worldly, sensual music is good and pleasant, and no matter what anyone says and no matter who we offend, we are going to rock and roll. We will dress as we please; we will live as we please. No one is going to judge us. When Larry Norman was in his early teens, his Christian father forbade him to listen to the radio because he was concerned about the influence of rock music on Larry's life. Larry's rebellious attitude toward this fatherly discipline is evident in his music. No one is going to tell him how to wear his hair or what kind of music he can listen to. I remember having precisely the same attitude. When I got out of the Army, I determined that I would never cut my hair again, and I grew it out like a woman's. That was BEFORE I was saved, though!

The attitude of **Amy Grant** and her associates toward biblical fundamentalists is expressed in the following statement:

> "[Amy] doesn't want the conservative fundamentalists coming to the concerts. She wants young people who will get up and move to the beat, people who want to be pinned against the back wall by the volume for two hours. That's what she gives them. ... She has never been the darling of the fundamentalists" (Don Butler, Gospel Music Association executive director, cited by Bob Millard, *Amy Grant*, p. 154).

Not only does the CCM crowd not care about what conservative Bible-believing Christians think about their music, they do even not want conservative Christians at their concerts. They want people who will dance and sway and yield their bodies to the sensual music.

Consider another example of the despicable manner in which those who support CCM look upon men and women of God who warn of the rock music and who attempt to protect God's people from error.

> "These men and others like them, who set themselves up as authorities, as experts in the eyes of many trusting souls, do great violence to the work of countless numbers of their brothers and sisters who are actively trying to do God's will, using rock to speak to a dying world. In the end they do violence to God's work, too. Their views are passed around, augmented and used like whips to herd people into corrals of conformity. Of course, this drives away as many as it herds together" (Steve Lawhead, *Rock Reconsidered*, p. 121).

According to Lawhead, those who warn of CCM are merely trying to manipulate people for their own purposes and to restrict the liberty of people for no good cause. This is slanderous and vicious and exposes the evil motives of those who try to defend this type of music. The truth is that large numbers of godly men and women warn about the dangers of CCM because they love people and are convinced that CCM is dangerous spiritually and morally. This is why they are willing to bear the constant reproach of the ecumenical "liberty" crowd. This is why they are willing to lift a voice against CCM even though it makes them unpopular and even though they lose church members because of their stance. Lawhead claims that to warn people of the dangers of CCM is to "do violence" to people. This is nonsense. No one has ever been injured in any sense by avoiding rock music, secular or "Christian."

Another example of this anti-fundamentalist attitude is in the lyrics to the song "I Want to Be a Clone" by **Steve Taylor**:

> "Be a clone and kiss conviction goodnight/ Cloneliness is next to Godliness, right?/ I'm grateful that they show the way/ 'Cause I could never know the way/ To serve Him on my own, I want to be a clone/ So now I see the whole design/ My church is an assembly line/ The parts are there, I'm feeling fine/ I want to be a clone/ I've learned enough to stay afloat/ But not so much I rock the boat/ I'm glad they shoved it down my throat/ I want to be a clone/ Everybody must get cloned."

These are the words of a rebel, and they are words which encourage rebels. The Bible plainly states that Jesus Christ has established the church and has ordained that pastors and teachers train God's people in faith and practice. Titus was told: "These things speak, and exhort, and rebuke with all authority. Let no man despise thee" (Titus 2:15). Titus, as a pastor and church planter, was given authority to instruct God's people in the right way, and he was to do this with all authority from God. We are to obey them that have the rule over us and submit ourselves (Heb. 13:7,17). It is rebellious nonsense to say that the Christian can "serve Him on my own" and to imply that sound biblical instruction is improper. In a sense, the process of discipleship IS cloning. There was one faith given to the saints almost 2,000 years ago, and we are to keep that exact faith until Jesus comes. Timothy was instructed: "And the things that thou hast heard of me among many witnesses, THE SAME commit thou to faithful men, who shall be able to teach others also" (2 Tim. 2:2). Timothy was also told to "keep that which is committed to thy trust" (1 Timothy 6:20). The preacher's job is to seek to conform the churches and the individual Christians to the New Testament faith in every area. The Lord Jesus Christ commanded that converts are to be taught "to observe all things whatsoever I have commanded you" (Matthew 28:20). In this sense, the church is indeed "an assembly line," Taylor's mocking notwithstanding.

John Michael Talbot is very bold to speak against fundamentalism. Those who create controversy over doctrine and who believe it is wrong to associate with false doctrine are labeled as a "fearful, excluding fundamentalism" by Talbot (Religious News Service, 1996).

Gregory Volz (1950-), former lead singer for the hard rock group Petra, is very plain about his attitude toward Bible-believing fundamentalists: "The church has been bigoted, prejudiced. They'd hear rock and say 'that's the Devil'" (Mark Schwed, "Holy Rollers of Rock," *St. Petersburg Times*, Florida, Jan. 5, 1985). Many rock stars have said rock is of the devil (i.e.., Little Richard, David Bowie). Are THEY bigoted and prejudiced?

Consider the words to "Don't Stop the Music" by **DeGarmo and Key**:

> "I love to hear the music playing slow or fast/ I love the healing message from the distant past/ And if I rearrange it, it remains the same/ I'll change the way I say it but never what I saw/ Don't stop, don't stop the music, you've got to let it play/ Don't stop, don't stop the music, play it in your own way ... I HEAR DISSENTING VOICES QUICK TO DISAGREE/ BUT I'M ON A MUSIC MISSION; THEY DON'T BOTHER ME/ I'll sing those songs that set me free/ Cause kids want to rock" ("Don't Stop the Music," Ed DeGarmo and Dana Key).

The Bible says, "Let us therefore follow after the things which make for peace, and things wherewith one may edify another" (Romans 14:19) and "It is good neither to eat flesh, nor to drink wine, nor any thing whereby thy brother stumbleth, or is offended, or is made weak" (Romans 14:21) and "Let every one of us please his neighbour for his good to edification" (Romans 15:2). DeGarmo and Key are going to rock on "their own way" regardless of who they offend. The CCM rocker knows that he is using music that large numbers of Christian parents do not want their children to listen to and that large numbers of churches reject as worldly. Many of the hard Christian rock songs are described in magazines as numbers "your parents will hate." Such self-willed rebellion, such callousness toward offending godly people, has no place among those who name the name of Christ.

In typical Contemporary Christian Music style, **Mark Lowry** labels standards and ecclesiastical separation "legalism" —

> "Legalism is as sickening today as it was 2000 years ago. It's just wrong. On my new video [*Remotely Controlled*], that's one thing I'm tryin' to take a whack at. Legalism as I know it. And I thank God for the churches I grew up in 'cause that's where I found Christ, but there was a lot of baggage there. It's true of every church. God is probably doing something in most of them. Some people need a charismatic experience. Some need a Calvinist doctrine. And just about the time I think I've got God put in my box, just about the time I've got Him figured out, He's over there loving someone I wouldn't be seen with, working through someone I wouldn't associate with. I tell people at my concerts, 'Isn't that somethin'? We've got Catholics, Presbyterians, Episcopalians, Baptists, and Pentecostals all under one roof! And you know what? Somebody's wrong!' That's why eternity is gonna last so long. God's gotta straighten us out" (Melissa Riddle, "Funny Face," interview with Mark Lowry, *CCM Magazine*, May 1996).

Lowry is correct in observing that there is a right and wrong when it comes to doctrine, but when he claims that God will straighten it all out in Heaven and implies that doctrine should not be divisive in this present world, he is ignoring the Bible's warning about false gospels. The Word of God cautions that those who follow a false gospel are cursed (Galatians 1). It is impossible, therefore, that all of those mentioned by Lowry will be heaven in the first place. Many of those mentioned follow a sacramental faith-works gospel. Many liberals in Protestant denominations are following a universalistic "gospel" of the Fatherhood of God or a social gospel or a golden rule gospel. When Lowry says doctrinal confusion will be straightened out in Heaven, he is also ignoring the fact that it is the Christian's job to defend sound Bible doctrine (Jude 3) and to separate from false doctrine (Romans 16:17). The preacher is not to allow any false doctrine whatsoever (1 Timothy 1:3).

Lowry continues his tirade against legalism:

> "Preachers keep giving people a list of rules instead of 'Love the Lord with all your heart, then do as you please'—because if you love the Lord your God

with all your heart, what you do is gonna please God. It's easier to say 'don't do this, don't do that, do this, and do that,' but you end up a Pharisee. They're taking the easy way out. Man has always loved the law more than grace" (Lowry, Ibid.).

This sounds great, but if preaching the love of God is enough, why are the New Testament epistles filled with specific commandments? Lowry's tirade against "legalism" is a smokescreen for his rebellion against Bible-believing, fundamentalist Christianity. To compare fundamentalists to Pharisees, as is so popular with the ecumenical crowd, is a slander. The Pharisee's problem was his self-righteous pride and rejection of Jesus Christ. The Bible-believing fundamentalist is not self-righteous; he knows and acknowledges readily that he has no righteousness apart from Jesus Christ. The Pharisees rejected the grace of Christ, whereas the fundamentalist exalts the grace of Christ. Legalism is replacing the grace of Christ with works salvation, as we see in the book of Galatians. Many of the denominations have done this, including the Roman Catholic Church, but this is not what the fundamentalist does. He teaches that salvation is by grace alone through faith alone by Christ alone and that works follow as the evidence of salvation. Attempting to take all of the Lord's commandments seriously and apply them to every area of life is not legalism; it is obedience (1 John 5:3).

The lyrics to the following song demonstrate the non-judgmental, anti-fundamentalist philosophy of the **Supertones**:

> "I don't care about your haircut, can't we all just get along?/ Not just get along, but really love and care/ If your eyes are on the Lord you can't see nobody's hair" (Supertones, "Adonai," *Adventures of the O.C. Supertones*, 1996).

It's not true that if your eyes are on the Lord you will not see things such as hair. Those that love the Lord want to obey the Bible in every detail. Jesus Christ said: "If a man love me, he will keep my words" (John 14:23). If hair is entirely unimportant in the Christian life, why does God's Word address it (1 Corinthians 11)? Paul plainly stated that the woman is to have long hair and the man short hair to express their different positions in this world. According to the Bible, hair length even affects angels (1 Cor. 11:10). The rebellious ecumenical crowd, though, pretends that Christian love overlooks such things as clothing and hair length. I can love someone and still be concerned about their hair or dress.

Michael W. Smith also holds the anti-fundamentalist attitude so common among Contemporary Christian Musicians:

> "...you're always going to have those very very conservative people. They say you can't do this; you can't do that ... you can't drink; you can't smoke. ... It's a

pretty bizarre way of thinking" (Michael W. Smith, *The Birmingham News*, Feb. 1993, p. 1B).

A man would have to be biblically ignorant to make such a statement. The Bible, including the New Testament, is filled with restrictions on man's activities! Not only does the Bible contain vast numbers of plain restrictions, but it is also filled with principles which are to be applied to every area of the Christian life.

Deniece Williams reveals her attitude toward biblical fundamentalism:

> "The whole story of 'Footloose' is very close to my life. In the church I grew up in, you couldn't go to dances, you couldn't go to movies, and you couldn't wear pants or sleeveless dresses. There were a lot of 'Thou shalt not's" (Deniece Williams, *CCM Magazine*, January 1987, p. 17).

This is the attitude which is common within Contemporary Christian Music. Those who attempt to apply the Word of God to daily living and to warn against sinful activities are considered legalistic Pharisees. As for the "Thou shalt not's" we are reminded of the commandments of God in the New Testament Scriptures. "For this is the love of God, that we keep his commandments: and his commandments are not grievous" (1 John 5:3). There are denominations which ARE legalistic, in that they teach a works salvation. Some Pentecostal denominations still teach that such things as jewelry or short hair on women will send them to Hell. That is legalism, but it is not legalism to teach that the Christian is obligated to obey the Word of God in order to be fruitful and please the God who saved him.

Teri DeSario makes the following anti-fundamentalist statement:

> "The Christian life is not a bunch of do's and don'ts, but a life of what you can accomplish in Christ" (Dan and Steve Peters, *What about Christian Rock?*, p. 111).

This statement expresses a half-truth. It is true that salvation is by grace alone through faith alone by the shed blood of Jesus Christ alone and that it is not of works. Christians do not get right with God by obedience to commandments. At the same time, the Christian is saved to live a holy life in obedience to God. We are not saved *by* works, but we are saved *to* works (Ephesians 2:8-10; Titus 3:5-8). The New Testament is filled with commandments, with do's and don'ts, which the Christian is to obey. We don't keep them in our own strength, but we are definitely called upon to keep them. It is absolute rebellion to say that the Christian life has nothing to do with keeping commandments. "For this is the love of God, that we keep his commandments: and his commandments are not grievous" (1 John 5:3). The grace of Jesus Christ leads to obedience. "For the grace of God that bringeth salvation hath appeared to all men, Teaching us that, denying ungodliness and worldly lusts, we should live soberly, righteously, and godly, in this present world" (Titus 2:11-12).

Brown Bannister, the producer for Amy Grant, also displays his despite toward fundamentalist Bible-believing Christians in the following statement:

> "That's the problem I'm having with Christian music; it's so formula-oriented. The praise stuff is great, but even the praise stuff is formula. It's like all the same 'Okay, let's name all the names of God in the Bible' and 'Let's say "I will lift my hands"'; … I guess you just kind of run out of things to say when you start talking about that stuff. You're limited to a certain number of phrases that are biblical and scripturally-oriented. … Its very confusing because of the nature of religious education and upbringing and THE SEPARATIST MENTALITY OF MOST CHURCHES AND THEIR CREEDS IN AMERICA AND THEIR OPINIONS ON CULTURE" (Brown Bannister, record producer and promoter, producer for Amy Grant, interview, *CCM Magazine*, October 1988, p. 13).

This influential Contemporary Christian Music producer doesn't like the idea of being restricted by the Bible! He does not like the separatist mentality of churches. He doesn't like churches to apply the Bible to culture. This is the anti-fundamentalist attitude which permeates CCM.

The late **Rich Mullins'** anti-fundamentalism attitude was evident in an interview with *TLeM*, April 1997, five months before his death in an automobile accident:

> "Everything is spiritual. Which is another hang-up I have with Protestantism, and even more specifically with Evangelicalism. It's more like Manicheism than anything else. This dualistic system that says that everything physical is evil, and the only good things are spiritual things. And I go, 'Wow! John wrote a good bit of what he wrote to counter that kind of thinking.' And yet, all these Bible-believing, Bible-thumping born-again-ers are going around professing the very thing that John tried to put out" (Brendt Waters, interview with Rich Mullins, conducted in April 1996, www.tlem.netcentral.net/features/9709/mullins.html).

This is an unscriptural and slanderous statement. Notice how Mullins spoke mockingly of "Bible-thumping born-again-ers." I would be afraid to mock that crowd, seeing that the Apostles and early Christians were definitely "Bible thumpers" and were definitely "born againers"! Mullins built a strawman by describing the "Bible-thumper's" message as saying "that everything physical is evil and the only good things are spiritual things." I don't know any Christian who is saying that everything physical is evil. Though there are doubtless those today who hold such a philosophy, they are primarily in pagan religions and are definitely not within the mainstream of evangelicalism or fundamentalism as Mullins claimed. The things of the world which God made are not evil, but when man takes those things and uses them for evil purposes, they become evil. A guitar or a drum or a piano is not evil in itself, but when it is used licentiously to stir up sensual passions, it is evil. A guitar or a drum or a piano are not evil in themselves, but when they are used licentiously to stir up sensual passions, they are evil. The Bible plainly says that this world is fallen and under the dominion of sinful men and demons, and God's people are to separate from the evil things of this world. The Bible makes a sharp distinction between the holy and the profane (Ezek. 22:26), between the world and God (James 4:4; 1 John 2:15-17). John said, "And we know that we are of God, and the whole world lieth in wickedness" (1 John 5:19).

The rap group **dc Talk** was formed at Jerry Falwell's Liberty University. Their antagonism toward biblical fundamentalists is evident in their music. The song "Time Ta Jam" on their 1989 debut album contained the following insolent lyrics:

> "So hyper fundi, don't be dismayed! Check out the lyrics when the record is played."

The term "hyper fundi" is a sarcastic reference to the fundamentalist who applies the Bible to cultural evils such as rock music. By the way, dc Talk, I have checked out the lyrics to your songs and I reject most of them as vague, man-centered, and heretical.

The anti-fundamentalist attitude of **Caedmon's Call** is evident:

> "It's amazing how we can get caught up in these things. 'Did he say that? I can't believe he said that!' Especially in the Baptist church we're in, our whole idea of Biblical holiness is, 'Don't drink; don't smoke; don't cuss.' True Biblical holiness is a lot more than that. ... the whole Christian subculture in the Bible Belt that says, 'Don't do this. Don't do that. You can't talk about that.' That kind of thing is no different from Jesus' day [the Pharisees]. I've been in their position. I was a Pharisee for many years" (Rob Berman, a conversation with Cliff Young and Todd Bragg, TLeM, *Lighthouse Electronic Magazine*, 1996, http://tlem.netcentral.net/indie/960701/caedmons_call.html).

This statement is a mockery of biblical absolutes. It is impossible to take the Bible seriously without striving to be holy in every area of life, without applying biblical precepts to everything the Christian does. The New Testament is filled with commandments—with do's and don'ts—with things the Christian can and cannot do. It has many commandments against drunkenness and cussing. The attitude expressed by Cliff Young of Caedmon's Call is a smokescreen for rebellion against biblical holiness. He speaks of Baptist churches whose "whole idea of biblical holiness" is don't drink, smoke, or cuss. I have attended, preached in, and studied Baptist churches for 25 years and I don't know of one which limits its doctrine of holiness to a simplistic group of commandments. The rebel only hears that part, though. Young thinks that Phariseeism is requiring commandments. That was not the Pharisee's problem. The Pharisee's root problem was self-righteousness, pride, and the rejection of God's righteousness in Jesus Christ. The Bible-believing fundamentalists that I know (and I know thousands of them) are not self-righteous. They know that they have absolutely no righteousness in themselves, that in their flesh dwelleth no good thing. They are not Christ rejecters; they are Christ lovers. They know that apart from Jesus Christ they are nothing. Zero. They know that holiness is not external; it is the indwelling Spirit of God. To label the Bible-believing fundamentalist a Pharisee is a vicious slander.

Christafari's 1996 album, *Valley of Decision*, includes the song "Modern Day Pharisee," which "swipes at those who judge the band for its appearance or musical style rather than its heart" (Tod Hafer, "Judge Dread: Mark Mohr and Christafari Use Reggae Music to Make a Case for Christianity," *CCM Magazine*, July 1996). This is the anti-fundamentalist attitude which prevails throughout Contemporary Christian Music.

Petra's anti-fundamentalist attitude is evident from their song entitled "Witch Hunt." It was written by Bob Hartman:

> "Another witch hunt looking for evil wherever we can find it/ Off on a tangent, Hope the Lord won't mind it/ Another witch hunt, Takin' a break from all our gospel labor/ On a crusade but we forgot our saber/ ... So send out the dogs and tally ho/ ... No one is safe, No stone is left unturned/ And we won't stop until somebody gets burned..." (Petra, "Witch Hunt")

According to the ecumenical, worldly CCM crowd, it is a witch hunt to judge things by the Word of God and to reprove sin and error. Petra sarcastically pretends that the only thing that is important is preaching the Gospel, and anything else, such as contending for the faith, is a waste of time which displeases the Lord. They slander the biblical fundamentalist as a person with a vain, hurtful agenda. Nothing could be further from the truth. The Apostle Paul spent much of his time defending the Gospel from false teachers and protecting the churches from error. He gave much space to this in his epistles. Paul warned of false teachers and compromisers by name, for example, 10 times in 1 and 2 Timothy alone. Was Paul a witch hunter? At the end of his life he said that he had fought a good fight. What had he fought? He had fought against error. He had fought for the truth. He had fought against the Devil and the Devil's men. The ecumenical CCM crowd is loving and tolerant toward almost anything except conservative Bible preaching.

Another example of the rebellious, anti-fundamentalist attitude that permeates CCM is in the song "Freedom to Move" by **Don Francisco**. Note the words:

> "I believe a believer has the freedom to move!/ Now tell me, mister, what you tryin' to do?/ Those things you're sayin', man, they just ain't true/ You wave the Bible and you scream and you shout/ But you don't have a clue what you're talkin' about/ You been goin' through the churches like a Nazi for Truth/ Sayin' Christian rock music is destroyin' the youth/ Slanderin' your brothers that you don't even know/ Ruinin' reputations every place that you go/ You call it devil music, say it's right from the pit/ Scarin' parents everywhere right out of their wits/ They're goin' to your meetings, buyin' books and buyin' tapes/ But all your're sellin's legalism, guilt and sour grapes. ... Just 'cause you don't like it doesn't mean it's a sin! I know it isn't heavy ministry, the lyrics are light/ But it's got a funky rhythm and the band is really tight/ There's a lot more to life than being down in the groove/ But I believe a believer has the freedom to move/ Won't you get off your soapbox and take off your shoes/ You know it ain't the rhythm, it's the words that you use/ It's not the drums or the electric guitar/ It's all in the motives —- it's in who you really are/ So crank me up some country or some rhythm and blues/ I really don't care what kind of flavour you choose/ Let the lyrics stay clean, let the people all groove/ And say, 'Thank you Jesus, for the freedom to move" (Don Francisco, "Freedom to Move," from the album *Come Away*, 1992).

In a joint interview with Religious Broadcasting, **Phil Keaggy** boldly displayed his anti-fundamentalist attitude:

> "I think also the unity that is so necessary in the body of Christ is important. I admire Charles Colson. He got a lot of flack for writing the book, *The Body*, and being associated with Catholics. I was raised Catholic and my mother's influence was powerful in my life. I came to the Lord when she passed away. She sowed the seeds in my life for me to become a believer. There are divisive voices out there. PEOPLE WHO THRIVE ON DISUNITY ARE THE ONES [TO WHOM] YOU'VE GOT TO SAY, 'I'M NOT GOING TO CONTEND WITH THIS, I'M NOT GOING TO ARGUE, I'M JUST GOING TO GO ABOUT MY BUSINESS'" ("Saran E. Smitha and Christine Pryor, "Integrity Times Two: Michael Card and Phil Keaggy," *Religious Broadcasting*, National Religious Broadcasters, July-August 1995).

The Christian life would be much simpler if one could follow Keaggy's advice and not get involved in contentions about doctrine and Christian living, but faithfulness to the Word of God does not allow it. God requires that His people "earnestly contend for the faith once delivered to the saints" (Jude 3) and reprove the unfruitful works of darkness (Ephesians 5:11). Obedience to such commands does not allow me to follow Keaggy's New Evangelical advice.

Keaggy's unscriptural anti-fundamentalist attitude permeates the world of Contemporary Christian Music, and those who listen to CCM are in great danger of being influenced by this attitude.

A PENTECOSTAL-CHARISMATIC DOCTRINE

We have already seen that the CCM world is permeated with Pentecostal-Charismatic theology. See "Characteristic # 4: CCM Can Be Identified by Its Charismatic Associations."

AN ECUMENICAL DOCTRINE

Another doctrine which permeates Contemporary Christian Music is ecumenism—the call for churches to come together and for Christians to be united regardless of their doctrine and practice. CCM, in fact, is one of the glues of ecumenism. We have already discussed this in Characteristic # 3: CCM Can Be Identified by Its Ecumenism."

A MAN-CENTERED, EXPERIENCE-CENTERED DOCTRINE

Another characteristic of the message of CCM songs is that it is man-centered, felt-need centered, experienced-centered rather than Christ-centered. John Blanchard, who has done research into CCM in Britain, observes: "A great deal of it concentrates on man's felt needs—his loneliness, emptiness, sadness, lack of fulfillment. The songs then invite the hearers to 'come to Jesus' for joy, peace, thrills, happiness, a 'high'" (John Blanchard, *Pop Goes the Gospel*, p. 152).

The man-centeredness of Contemporary Christian Music was recognized in an article in *Good News Broadcaster* almost two decades ago, and things have gotten much worse since then:

> "The lyrics which God honored in the Bible were somewhat different from the average contemporary Christian song. They extolled the greatness of God and His mighty works. His glory was the central theme, and His praise was the aim. If one were to remove all the first and second person pronouns from much of the contemporary Christian music, they would be humming most of the time. God said through Isaiah, 'I will not give my glory unto another' (Is. 48:11) ("Has Conservative Christian Music Had It?" *Good News Broadcaster*, November 1982).

Jon Gibson's music is described in these words: "A Christian perspective is background for Gibson's socially-aware, moral songs ABOUT UNEMPLOYMENT AND GIRLFRIENDS" (*CCM Magazine*, August 1987, p. 34).

Dana Key of the group DeGarmo and Key says: "On *Street Light* we were trying to stick to the street theme and DEAL WITH PROBLEMS PEOPLE WERE DEALING WITH. They weren't biblical themes, and they didn't talk about God a lot" (Dana Key, with the group DeGarmo and Key, interview, *CCM Magazine*, November 1987, p. 20).

A Contemporary Christian Music industry spokesman observes: "You now have songs about pain and death and divorce and sex and relationships and everything that every one of us goes through, whereas at one time contemporary Christian music only talked about the death and resurrection of Christ. We're much more in touch with ourselves and our neighbors, which is the whole idea behind Christ in the first place" (Melissa Helm of Myrrh Records, *MusicLine Magazine*, June 1986, p. 4).

Randy Stonehill does not believe he has to be concerned "with the finer points of theological debate." Instead, his music deals mostly with human experience. "Just look at my song material. It doesn't deal with faith and theology on that level. It is much more of a gut level basic message. ... I try to pick songs that deal with God's grace, God's reality, God's love, our pain, and what kind of confusion we are experiencing in our culture and all of those things" (Devlin Donaldson, "Life Between the Glory and the Fame," *CCM Magazine*, October 1981). This is the experienced-centered approach so common in the lyrics of CCM.

CCM songs invariably present a man-centered message. Jesus is ready to save you from your problems. Joey Belville's song "Redemption" is described as centering "on Belville's failures and frustrations" (*CCM Magazine*, August 1998, p. 20). Jaci Velasquez sings: "If this world is a lonely place for you/ There's a guy that you can trust" (Velasquez, "If This World" from her "Heavenly Places" album). Out of Eden sings: "There's only one who can make you feel secure/ He's waiting just for you" (Out of Eden, "More Than You Know").

Michael W. Smith's 1998 hit "Never Been Unloved" from his "Live the Life" album is a prime example of the man-centeredness of Contemporary Christian Music. As noted earlier, this album was the #3 top album for August 1998, and "Never Been Unloved" was #21 on the CCM chart for August. Note the words:

> "I have been unfaithful/ I have been unworthy/ I have been unrighteous/ I have been unmerciful/ I have been unreachable/ I have been unteachable/ I have been unwilling/ And I have been undesirable/ And sometimes I have been unwise/ I've been undone by what I'm unsure of/ But because of you and all that you went through/ I know that I have never been unloved.

> "I have been unbroken/ I have been unmended/ I have been uneasy/ I have been unapproachable/ I have been unemotional/ I have been unexceptional/ I have been undecided/ I have been unqualified/ I have been unaware — I have been unfair/ I've been unfit for blessings from above/ But even I can see the sacrifice You made for me/ To show that I have never been unloved/ It's

because of you/ And all that You went through/ I know that I have never been unloved" ("Never Been Unloved," Michael W. Smith).

The focus is upon the singer and his moral imperfections. Nineteen of the 26 lines of the song are about the singer. The remaining seven lines speak of a persistent love by an unidentified person. Who is the person who persistently loves Smith? Is it Jesus Christ? We aren't told. It could be a girlfriend or a wife. What about the "sacrifice"? Lovers make sacrifices. Some of the pronouns are capitalized on the song sheet, but most listeners will not have a song sheet before them. The Bible-believing Christian will think of Christ's unfailing love because of Calvary, but the world will think of some other type of love and some other type of sacrifice because of the vagueness of the message.

The Bible is not man-centered like this. Paul did not focus on his failings and imperfections; he exalted Jesus Christ and His victory and purposes. To be very plain, I don't want to hear an endless litany of Michael W. Smith's sins. There is no challenge to holiness in this song. There is no promise of victory. There is no conviction of sin. There is no repentance. Just a steady litany of failure and an abstract notion of being loved.

In contrast to the man-centered message of CCM at large, the Bible instructs us to preach Jesus Christ, to "make known HIS deeds among the people" (Psalm 105:1), to "talk ye of all HIS wondrous works" (Psalm 105:2).

By the way, not only is Smith's popular song vague and man-centered, but it promotes false doctrine. The song implies that no one is ever unloved. If one assumes that the song is about God's love in Jesus Christ (which is not clear), the message is that of universal salvation. There is nothing about repentance and faith in Christ. It is true that God loves the lost world so much that Christ died for it (John 3:16), but it is also true that unless an individual is born again through faith in Jesus Christ he will die and go to eternal hell. There is nothing about these important truths in the song. The unsaved listener is left with the vague impression that he is somehow secure in God's love regardless of how he lives or whether or not he is born again.

A BLASPHEMOUS DOCTRINE

Another characteristic of the message of CCM is its blasphemy. The very popular CCM performer Carman is a key example of this. Carman's *Addicted to Jesus* album contains such blasphemous cuts as the "Holy Ghost Hop." He exclaims:

> "Hey all you brothers and you sisters too/ Don't let tradition tell you what to do/ Release your worries and your fears/ 'cause we've been hoppin' in the church for years/ If King David was here I knew/ that he would do the Holy Ghost Hop with me."

Carman is wrong. David did not dance to rock music. He did not put on a fleshly show. He was not moving his feet to some carnal beat. He danced before the Lord but it was nothing which the world would have appreciated. On the contrary, unsaved people understand and appreciate the type of music and dancing that Carman produces.

On another cut entitled "Come into This House," sung to a heavy rap style, Carman says:

> "I've got news you can choose/ You need to be delivered/ with Christ you win/ without Christ you lose/ BUT IF YOU JAM WITH THE LAMB, YOU'RE SMOOTH/ Cut out the jive, cut into church/ You need a healing' touch/ A big strong hand/ Come rock with the flock/ with the brothers that jam."

The title cut on that album has this flippant message:

> "Addictions you know/ Everybody's got 'em/ From the top to the very/ bottom of the list/ So come get with this/ An addiction you don't wanna miss/ To Christ who paid the price."

These songs present the Lord Jesus Christ as a hip rock musician jamming with the boys.

Carman's *Live...Radically Saved* video depicts Jesus and John the Baptist as hip-hop street kids. Carman says "Jesus is always cool; He's got his thing together." He blasphemously imitates the Lord Jesus walking along in a hip-jive manner, doing "the Messiah walk."

Carman's *Resurrection Rap* video portrays Jesus Christ as a confused street hippie. The crucifixion takes place in a back alley gang fight, and Jesus' body is tossed in a garbage dumpster.

On Carman's *The Standard* album Jesus Christ is blasphemously referred to as "J.C."

> "You take Him high/ You take Him low/ You take J.C. wherever you go/ Now tell me, who...who...who...who...who...who?/ Tell me who's in the house? J.C./ Tell me who's in the house? J.C./ Tell me who's in the house? J.C./ Tell me who's in the house? J.C."

Carman is not the only CCM musician who uses the blasphemous term J.C. to refer to the Lord Jesus Christ. The group called J.C. and Friends explains that their name can stand either for Jesus Christ and his followers or for J.C. Meyers and his pals (*MusicLine Magazine*, October 1985, p. 27).

The following song by Daniel Band further demonstrates the blasphemous and worldly philosophy of many CCM groups:

> "There's a party in Heaven/ The bread is unleaven/ The tree of life is growin' fine/ It's way past eleven/ My number is seven/ The Lamb and I are drinkin' new wine" ("Party in Heaven").

This song is sung to hard rock music. This CCM group seems to think heaven will be a worldly booze party! This is blasphemous.

The manner in which many Christian rockers connect rock music with Jesus Christ is blasphemous:

> "... the only difference [between rock and Christian rock] is the lyrics and then the difference is sometimes subtle ... at the basic root, there's no difference. ... Christianity is about rebellion. JESUS CHRIST IS THE BIGGEST REBEL TO EVER WALK THE FACE OF THE EARTH ... he was crucified for his rebellion. ROCK 'N' ROLL IS ABOUT THE SAME THING—REBELLION ... TO ME ROCK AND THE CHURCH GO HAND IN HAND" (Mark Stuart of Audio Adrenaline, *Pensacola News Journal*, Pensacola, Florida, March 1, 1998, pp. 1,6E).

That is absolute blasphemy. Jesus Christ was not a rebel. A rebel is a law breaker. Christ was the law giver, and He came to earth to fulfill the requirements of His own law (Matt. 5:17-19). Christ was not crucified for rebellion; . He was crucified for testifying that He was God (John 10:33). The wicked rock scene and the true churches of Jesus Christ do not go hand in hand, they stand in direct contradiction to one another.

Petra promotes the blasphemous idea that God is the God of Rock and Roll:

> "God gave rock and roll to you/ Put it in the soul of every one/ If you love the sound/ Then don't forget the source/ You can turn around/ You can change your course/ You can love the Rock/ And let him free your soul" ("God Gave Rock and Roll," Petra).

This song was first sung by secular rock groups Argent and KISS. It is on KISS's *Revenge* album. Petra changed some of the words, but the overall message is the same, that God is the author of rock music. To say that the Holy God of Scripture is the author of filthy rock & roll in any sense whatsoever is blasphemy. The father of rock & roll is a god, but he is not the God of Scripture but the god of this world (2 Corinthians 4:4). I know from experience that the true and living God did not put rock & roll into my soul. It was the Devil who did that to foster my rebellion and licentiousness. The very term "rock & roll," which is commonly shortened to "rock," refers specifically to illicit sexual relations. Most music dictionaries and histories of rock music admit this. The term was popularized in the early 1950s by Alan Freed, one of the first white disk-jockeys to play the new rhythm & blues/country combination. Noting the sexual connotation of the new music, Freed decided to name it after a ghetto term used by blacks for premarital sex in the back seat of a car. (Freed died young of alcoholism.) To try to connect this morally dirty music with a holy God is blasphemous.

Robert Sweet, of the now disbanded Christian rock group Stryper, had the following saying painted on the back of his drummer chair: "JESUS CHRIST ROCKS." This is blasphemy. Jesus Christ is the Rock of Ages, but He does not rock & roll. He does not love to boogie-woogie to sensual music. He does not love to watch girls dance licentiously. He does not enjoy letting the flesh "hang loose." He does not enjoy stirring up rebellious impulses. He does not love anything connected to wicked rock music. He "loved righteousness, and HATED iniquity" (Hebrews 1:9). He is "holy, harmless, undefiled, separate from sinners" (Hebrews 7:26).

Phil Driscoll thinks God is the King of Soul Music:

> "God is the King of Soul; He's the King of all rhythm" (Phil Driscoll, quoted by Tim Fisher, *Battle for Christian Music*, p. 82).

We believe this is a blasphemous portrayal of God. God is not the author of rhythms which stir up illicit passions in men and women, and there are certain rhythms which do exactly that. As we have noted, the very term "rock & roll" itself describes immoral activity; and the musical rhythms associated with rock were designed to encourage this activity. God is also not the author of rhythms which enhance demonic possession, such as the poly-rhythms used by certain African tribes.

Messiah Prophet Band goes even further, calling Jesus Christ the "Master of Metal" —

> "You hear a loud guitar/ You wonder what we are/ You say we're all the same/ You see us dressed in black/ Preparing to attack/ You say it's such a shame/ But do you really know/ The force behind our show/ Our one way ticket home/ WE'RE ROCKIN' FOR THE ROCK/ And we will never stop/ And this you've got to know/ Jesus said upon this Rock my church will stand/ ... HE'S THE MASTER/ THE MASTER OF METAL..." ("Master of Metal," Messiah Prophet Band).

To say that the high and holy Lord Jesus Christ is the Master of rebellious heavy metal rock music is outrageous blasphemy.

The Christian rock group Barren Cross says Jesus Christ is better than marijuana and invites their followers to smoke on His love!

> "Give it a chance, freedom at last/ Yours for free, take and receive/ Better than pot, Jesus rocks/ Come and believe/ You will find out joy will come to

you/ Take it, drink it, no fee, come and believe/ Smoke on His love — believe/ Smoke on His love and you will see the rock — roll/ Believe" (Barren Cross, "Believe").

We are convinced that this is blasphemy.

Note how CCM performer/writer John Fischer describes an imaginary encounter with God:

> "'Wait a minute Kid' [supposedly this is God speaking to Fischer]. Leave it [the radio] on You know, I kind of like this stuff [rock].' I watched in shock as He smiled at me through a casual puff of cigar smoke and swayed His head ever so slightly with the music" (*Contemporary Christian Music Magazine*, July 1984, p. 20).

This is a blasphemous description of God.

The blasphemy of CCM is also illustrated by their use of immoral rock songs. Rez band, for example, sings the song "Bargain" by legendary rock guitarist Pete Townshend of the violent/immoral/occultic rock band, The Who. Townshend wrote "Bargain" as a tribute to his Hindu guru Meher Baba. Townshend has testified: "Baba is Christ, because being a Christian is just like being a Baba lover" (Bob Larson, *Rock*, 1984, p. 140). Consider the words to the song "Bargain" which Rez Band has popularized for Christian young people:

> "I'll pay any price just to get you/ I'll work all my life and I will/ To win you, I'd stand naked, stoned, and stabbed/ I'd call that a bargain/ The best I ever had/ The best I ever had ... I'll pay any price just to win you/ Surrender my good life or bad/ To find you/ I'm gonna drown an unsung man/ I call that a bargain/ The best I ever had..."

Not only is it blasphemous to take a song by an immoral rock star about a Hindu guru and sing it as to Jesus Christ, but the song itself promotes a false gospel. We do not and cannot win the true God by sacrifice and works. Salvation is "not of works, lest any man should boast" (Ephesians 2:8-9). Further, the sinner has no "good life" to surrender. All our righteousness is as filthy rags before God (Isaiah 64:6). There is none that doeth good, no, not one (Romans 3:12).

The Christian rock group Bride has songs like "Scarecrow Messiah" and "Psychedelic Super Jesus. We believe it is blasphemy to refer to Jesus Christ in this manner.

The July 2000 issue of *Charisma*, the very influential Charismatic publication, has an article exhorting the readers to "Get in the Groove." The author, J. Lee Grady, mocks traditional Christian music as "dirge-like" and "lily-white" and something only for "grandmothers." He goes on to make the pretentious claim that worship music in Heaven will feature "a dozen Hammond-B3 organs and a procession of hip-hop [rap] dancers." Not content with this brazen claim, Grady tells us that Jesus Christ "loves all music—even the funkiest" and that Jesus Christ enjoys dancing with the angels and "grooving to the sound of Christian R&B [rhythm and blues] pumped out of a boom box." I believe this is blasphemy.

How does Grady know this? The simple and frightful fact is that he knows no such thing. He is preaching a false christ, but the sad fact is that the entire Contemporary Christian Music movement is preaching the same thing. They tell us that Jesus Christ is not separated from the world, that He loves every sort of music in this wicked world, that He boogies to rock and roll.

I challenge any CCM supporter to show us where the Bible says Jesus Christ dances to rock music. Show us even one instance before or after the Resurrection where Jesus Christ is shaking His body or jiving to the beat of rock-type music. Show us even one little hint that the saints in Heaven are dancing around to anything like rock or rhythm & blues music. The Lord Jesus Christ we see in the book of Revelation following the Resurrection and Ascension is not a grooving Jesus; He is a fearfully holy Jesus. John fell at His feet as dead. The 24 elders are not dancing around with Jesus to some groovy rock beat; they are falling down before Him (Rev. 4:10; 5:8). They are not banging on drums; they are playing harps (Rev. 5:8). There is not the slightest hint of a modern rock dance going on in Heaven.

Grady thinks that Psalm 150 depicts a rock concert, but that is absolute nonsense. The Jews of old observed Psalm 150 in their worship, but they never used anything remotely like rock music. When someone like Grady thinks of drums and loud cymbals, they automatically think of their beloved rock music; but drums and loud cymbals are also components of an orchestra and a marching band. Drums can be used to make all sorts of music other than rock music. Grady says that dancing requires a rock-type drum beat, but that is pure foolishness. I know of no other way to describe it. There are all sorts of dances that do not require a modern dance beat. The Jews and other groups of people have long had traditional dances that were nothing whatsoever like the licentious modern dances associated with rock and rhythm & blues.

At the heart of the battle about music in the churches is the very character of God. Our concept of God will determine what kind of music we use to worship Him and the manner in which we worship Him. If we think that God is a cool dude who hip hops to modern rock music, we will worship him with such music and our lifestyle and very appearance will reflect this concept of God. If, on the other hand, we believe that God is a fearfully holy God before whom the hosts of Heaven fall in awe and reverence, our worship music and our very lifestyle and appearance will reflect holiness and separation from the world.

Those who claim that Jesus Christ grooves to rock music are worshipping a false christ who is different from the christ of the Bible. This is an extremely serious matter.

> "Would to God ye could bear with me a little in my folly: and indeed bear with me. For I am jealous over you with godly jealousy: for I have espoused you to one husband, that I may present you as a chaste virgin to Christ. But I fear, lest by any means, as the serpent beguiled Eve through his subtlety, so your minds should be corrupted from the simplicity that is in Christ. For if he that cometh preacheth another Jesus, whom we have not preached, or if ye receive another spirit, which ye have not received, or another gospel, which ye have not accepted, ye might well bear with him" (2 Corinthians 11:1-4).

AN EASY BELIEVISM, NO REPENTANCE DOCTRINE

Another characteristic of the message of CCM songs is its easy believism and its lack of repentance. Large numbers of CCM musicians do not preach the Gospel plainly so that the world is confronted with its sin and rebellion against Almighty God. At best they present a soft peddle, easy believism, no repentance approach to Christianity. This is the only reason their music can be popular on secular charts. It is for certain that plain Bible preaching would not be Top Ten material! Jesus Christ was not crucified because he encouraged sinners to have strong self esteem; He was crucified because He exposed man's sin. "If I had not come and spoken unto them, they had not had sin: but now they have no cloak for their sin" (John 15:22). The world does not think of itself as wicked and unrighteous. The unsaved will admit that they have problems and shortcomings and faults, but they think of themselves as basically good and deserving of God's favor. This fact of fallen human nature is one reason why the Gospel of Jesus Christ is so offensive to the world. The Bible says man's heart is "deceitful above all things and desperately wicked" (Jeremiah 17:9). It says "all have sinned and come short of the glory of God" (Romans 3:23), "there is none that doeth good" (Romans 3:12), and "there is none righteous" (Romans 3:10). The Bible says the Holy Spirit came to "reprove the world of sin, and of righteousness, and of judgment" (John 16:8), but there is no conviction of sin in the vast majority of CCM songs.

The following statement by the CCM group Age of Faith illustrates the no repentance philosophy which permeates Contemporary Christian Music. The music of this group focuses on human experience and God's grace, but it is a grace which is devoid of repentance.

> "What we are learning is that many of our fans have told us that they have a hard time finding forgiveness for past mistakes. Also that totally believing that God truly forgives. We deal a lot with these issues in this record. We show that God is who he says He is — He never changes — He is enough for us to live this life. Mistakes will be made by us all, but God forgives" (Jimi Ray, Age of Faith, Grey Dot Records web site, http://placetobe.org/cmp/artists/index.html).

Biblical grace is bestowed on the repentant sinner. Repentance has to do with acknowledging that one's actions are sinful before God and are worthy of His judgment; it is being willing to turn from them. Note that Jimi Ray mentioned "mistakes," but he did not mention sin. It is not our mistakes which God forgives; it is sin; and the sin must be acknowledged as such before Him. The Prodigal Son did not say, "I have made a mistake." He said, "Father, I HAVE SINNED AGAINST HEAVEN, AND IN THY SIGHT, and am no more worthy to be called thy son" (Luke 15:21). This is a biblical example of repentance which brings the grace of God. Much of the preaching within the Contemporary Christian Music scene presents an unbiblical grace which does not deal squarely with sin and which does not require repentance. The true grace of God does forgive our sins, but it also teaches "us that, denying ungodliness and worldly lusts, we should live soberly, righteously, and godly, in this present world" (Titus 2:11-12).

We would give dozens of illustrations of the lack of repentance in CCM gospel preaching. John Elefante is an example of this. He preaches a hazy, repentance-less gospel to hard rock music:

> "Hello my good friend/ How have you been doing since I've gone/ Have you shared the love I gave you/ Have you shown the world the truth of who I am/ So let your love be true/ Till I come back to you/ ... You say you don't need Me/ That you'll be alright on your own/ Now you live like a prisoner/ Serving your time all alone/ I can't make you love Me/ I can't make you believe what I say/ So come back to Me, let Me show you the way/ And I'll take you to paradise/ Just listen to My voice inside your heart..." ("Hello My Good Friend (A Letter from the Lord)," John Elefante).

This song is typical of Elefante's music. There is nothing about being born again, nothing about repentance from sin, nothing about the Word of God. It is all experiential and subjective. Do we go to paradise by letting Christ show us the way? That is a work's salvation. In other songs Elefante does mention the cross of Christ, but never does he clarify the Gospel. The exhortation to "listen to My voice inside your heart" is dangerous and unscriptural. Nowhere does the New Testament tell God's people to look into their hearts for truth and guidance. There is an old nature in the heart of man which makes such instruction dangerous (Jer. 17:9; Eph. 4:18; Heb. 3:12).

MISCELLANEOUS OTHER FALSE DOCTRINES

Amy Grant's song "Walking in the Light" teaches the damnable error of baptismal regeneration:

> "The sun woke me up real early/ It's a beautiful morn/ 'Cause I'm goin' down to the river/ To be reborn/ Now me and Jesus did some heavy/ Talkin' last night/ So I'm goin' down to be dipped and/ Come up walkin' in the light" (Amy Grant, "Walking in the Light").

The Audio Adrenaline song "Good People" teaches a universalistic ecumenicalism:

> "I grew up impressed/ by the people I knew in the buckle of the Bible belt/ hopped in a van with a band/ now I've been just about everywhere else/ Met a soldier from Seattle, and a lawyer from the east/ a Texas oil baron and a Roman Catholic priest/ everyday I choose, to walk in their shoes/ cause pretty are the feet of those who bring the good news/ good people, good people everywhere, everywhere/ It's God's people/ Been on the road/ been far from home/ but I found me a friend or two/ time has taught me well/ and I can tell/ you the good things people do/ they really care/ and I've been there/ I've seen it with my eyes/ I can tell/ they're God's people by the goodness in their lives."

We can tell those who are saved by the goodness in their lives? The Bible says those who follow false gospels are cursed of God (Galatians 1), regardless of how spiritual they might appear to be, regardless of their human kindness.

The late Rich Mullins was a very popular CCM writer and performer. He wrote songs popularized by Amy Grant and other well-known singers. His gospel, though, was very murky. In his song "Screen Door" he presents the false gospel of faith plus works:

> "Faith without works baby/ It just ain't happenin'/ One is your left hand/ One is your right/ It'll take two strong arms/ To hold on tight" (Mullins, "Screen Door")

This song presents the false gospel of Roman Catholicism (which Mullins was preparing to join when he was killed) and of every cult. One of the marks of false Christianity is to confuse faith and works, to somehow mix faith and works together for salvation. While it is true that faith without works is dead and that true saving faith produces works, it is not true that faith and works are the two strong arms by which we hold on tight to God and salvation (Ephesians 2:8-10; Romans 11:6), yet that is exactly the heresy what this song teaches.

For more about the message of CCM songs, see Part II, Question # 23.

CHARACTERISTIC #6 — CONTEMPORARY CHRISTIAN MUSIC CAN BE IDENTIFIED BY ITS WORLDLINESS

One of the chief attributes of Contemporary Christian Music is its worldliness or unholiness. Holy means set apart for God, separate, different, distinct. Unholy means not separated from the world, not distinctly different. This is the essence of CCM. It fails to make a plain distinction between the things of the world and the things of God. It is not separated from the world unto God. The Bible, though, is very plain about this subject:

> "**Love not the world**, neither the things that are in the world. If any man love the world, the love of the Father is not in him. For all that is in the world, the lust of the flesh, and the lust of the eyes, and the pride of life, is not of the Father, but is of the world. And the world passeth away, and the lust thereof: but he that doeth the will of God abideth for ever" (1 John 2:15-17).

> "Ye adulterers and adulteresses, know ye not that the **friendship of the world is enmity with God**? whosoever therefore will be a friend of the world is the enemy of God. Do ye think that the scripture saith in vain, The spirit that dwelleth in us lusteth to envy?" (James 4:4,5)

> "And **be not conformed to this world**: but be ye transformed by the renewing of your mind, that ye may prove what is that good, and acceptable, and perfect, will of God" (Romans 12:2).

> "But God forbid that I should glory, save in the cross of our Lord Jesus Christ, by whom **the world is crucified unto me, and I unto the world**" (Galatians 6:14).

> "And have **no fellowship with the unfruitful works of darkness**, but rather reprove them" (Ephesians 5:11).

> "Teaching us that, **denying** ungodliness and **worldly lusts**, we should live soberly, righteously, and godly, in this present world" (Titus 2:12).

> "Pure religion and undefiled before God and the Father is this, To visit the fatherless and widows in their affliction, and **to keep himself unspotted from the world**" (James 1:27).

> "As obedient children, **not fashioning yourselves according to the former lusts** in your ignorance. But as he which hath called you is holy, so **be ye holy in all manner of conversation**; Because it is written, Be ye holy; for I am holy. And if ye call on the Father, who without respect of persons judgeth

according to every man's work, pass the time of your sojourning here in fear" (1 Peter 1:14-17).

"Forasmuch then as Christ hath suffered for us in the flesh, arm yourselves likewise with the same mind: for he that hath suffered in the flesh hath ceased from sin; That he no longer **should live the rest of his time in the flesh to the lusts of men**, but to the will of God" (1 Peter 4:1,2).

"And we know that we are of God, and **the whole world lieth in wickedness**" (1 John 5:19).

"Be ye not unequally yoked together with unbelievers: for **what fellowship hath righteousness with unrighteousness**? and what communion hath light with darkness?" (2 Corinthians 6:14).

"See then that ye walk circumspectly, not as fools, but as wise, Redeeming the time, **because the days are evil**" (Ephesians 5:15,16).

"That ye may be blameless and harmless, the sons of God, without rebuke, **in the midst of a crooked and perverse nation**, among whom ye shine as lights in the world" (Philippians 2:15).

"And that ye may **put difference between holy and unholy, and between unclean and clean**" (Lev. 10:10).

"Her priests have violated my law, and have profaned mine holy things: **they have put no difference between the holy and profane, neither have they showed difference between the unclean and the clean**, and have hid their eyes from my sabbaths, and I am profaned among them" (Ezek. 22:26).

Holiness means separation unto God. The Jews of old were warned to keep the Sabbath holy (Ex. 20:8), meaning they were to set aside the Sabbath for the service of God and not to use it for their own purposes, not to treat the Sabbath as an ordinary day. They were to make a plain distinction between the Sabbath and other days of the week and they were to set it apart by obeying God's law. The Scripture is also called "holy" (Rom. 1:2) because it is distinct from every other writing in the world, it is set apart because it is inspired of God. The Christian, too, is called to be holy in every part of his life (1 Pet. 1:15). He is to be different from the wicked world around him. He is to separate himself from the evil things of this world to live according to God's Word.

CCM often throws up a smoke screen at this point, claiming that separation from the world would require that we move to a remote area and build monasteries. This is not what the Bible means by separation. It does not call for complete isolation, but for distinction. We are to be different. Our lifestyle is to be different. Out philosophy of life is to be different. Our music is to be different.

When the Bible warns of the "world," it is not referring to the natural created things of the world, things such as the trees and animals. It is referring, rather, to the wicked things of the world which come from the heart of fallen men. In 1 John 2:16 the "world" is defined by the Holy Spirit as "the lust of the flesh, and the lust of the eyes, and the pride of life" (1 John. 2:16).

The music of the world is filled with these worldly characteristics. Worldly music is designed largely for the purpose of stirring up and satisfying the fallen nature of man. It appeals directly to the lust of the flesh. On the other hand, godly music does not attempt to satisfy the flesh, but appeals rather to the spiritual side of man. Godly music is the opposite of worldly music.

CCM does not acknowledge this. It claims to be able to use the world's fleshly music to glorify a holy God and to accomplish spiritual purposes. CCM is not holy; it does not make a clear demarcation between worldliness and spirituality. Instead of holiness, CCM practices syncretism, which is combining or synthesizing or uniting differing systems of belief or practice. CCM performer Rick Altizer, in an interview with *CCM Magazine*, stated: "I think Christian music suffers because Christian people by nature are afraid of the world" (*CCM Magazine*, August 1998, p. 18). This strange statement describes the common attitude of the CCM crowd. They think it is wrong to be afraid of the world, but this is utter nonsense. As we have seen, the Bible repeatedly warns God's people to be afraid of the world, because the world is under the dominion of the Devil and man's fallen flesh.

The syncretism practiced by CCM is the exact opposite of holiness and separation from the world.

> "And he hath put a **NEW SONG** in my mouth, even praise unto our God: many shall see it, and fear, and shall trust in the LORD" (Psalm 40:3; see also Ps. 33:3; 96:1; 98:1; 144:9; 149:1; Is. 42:10; Rev. 5:9; 14:3).

Nine times the Bible speaks of a "new song" which God has given His people. The songs we sing in praise to God are not the same as the songs of the world. The "new song" does not mean new in the sense of *time* (such as the 1990s); it means new in the sense of *different* from the song we sang before we were saved. The Christian's music is to be different from that of the world, because we are to be separated from this wicked world and we are not to love the ungodly things of this world. The world is in rebellion against God.

Consider some major areas of CCM's worldliness:

FIRST, CCM HAS A WORLDLY APPEARANCE

Contemporary Christian Music has the same worldly appearance as secular music. There is no holiness of appearance, no separation from the ungodly fashions of the world. Female CCM artists wear the same immodest clothing, the same skimpy outfits, the same low cut blouses, the same tight pants, the same shorts, the same short skirts, as their secular counterparts. Many of the males wear the same long hair and many of the females wear the same short hair as the world. Many of the men wear the same earrings. Many of the CCM groups have the same hard stares as their secular counterparts. A Stryper concert is described as having "all the outward trappings of secular metal—the sass, style, and bombastic bone-jarring sonic barrage of such secular acts as Motley Crue, Ratt, Iron Maiden, or Judas Priest" (*Youth!*, January 1987, p. 8). Stryper has disbanded, but hundreds of new hard rock groups have arisen in its stead.

1 Thessalonians 5:22 commands: "Abstain from all appearance of evil." We see from this verse that evil has an appearance. It is ridiculous to say that one's appearance has no meaning. One's dress almost always makes a statement. The secular rock world knows this very well. Secular rock bands dress in a certain manner expressly because of the evil and rebellion they represent. The women dress immodestly and sensually. Some of the female rockers dress in a masculine fashion. The long hair on males which was commonly associated with rock music's infancy was called a "freak flag," meaning the long hair identified the wearer as a "freak," a term describing a rebellious drug user. The late Jerry Rubin, who helped influence an entire generation of young people, testified that "LONG HAIR is the beginning of our liberation from sexual oppression that underlies the whole military society" (Jerry Rubin, *Do It*). Earrings on men is a fashion which was adopted from the homosexual movement. It is a unisex statement. In Old Testament times earrings were worn by the idolatrous pagans (Judges 8:24). Nowhere in the Scripture do we read of men of God wearing earrings.

God's people are to abstain from all evil appearance and are not to learn the way of the heathen (Jeremiah 10:2).

SECOND, CCM HAS A WORLDLY MANNER OF PRESENTATION.

Contemporary Christian Music also has a worldly manner of presentation. It is entertainment oriented. CCM, like its secular counterpart, has artists, concerts, programs, charts, stars, fans, awards, billings, recording contracts. Even CCM musicians which use folk or Southern gospel styles rather than rock are oriented toward entertainment and closely imitate the world's manners. The Christian rock concerts are worldly. There is dancing, moshing, shrieking:

> "As teenagers' shrieks filled the Dallas Convention Center moments before dc-Talk took the stage Friday night, one of the relatively few grown-ups in the sold-out crowd observed, 'This is just like the BEATLES'" (*Dallas Morning News*, April 27, 1996).
>
> "His [Michael W. Smith] concerts draw hundreds of thousands of fans each year, mostly teenage girls who scream out their AFFECTION FOR HIM non-stop throughout. . . . To his fans, Smith is the absolute greatest there is, BAR NONE..." (*Inside Music*, January/February 1991).
>
> "They're loose again! And this time it's live, unbridled mayhem. ... On stage screaming, stomping, slam dancing, stage diving, pleading and praying. It's the absolute wildest Christian concert ever recorded. . . " (advertisement for One Bad Pig's *Live* album).
>
> "Yes, it looks like a rock concert, it sounds like a rock concert, and in every aspect except for the lyrics, it's just like any standard rock concert by today's teen-oriented bands: plenty of flash and lots of thrash on stage; heads bobbing and bodies moshing in the crowd..." (*Huntsville Times*, Sept. 20, 1998, describing a Christian rock concert).
>
> "CCM fans do in fact deliriously rush the stage and participate in power gestures such as fist thrusts. Both occurred during the 30th Annual Dove Awards, when the Newsboys took the platform, and have been witnessed elsewhere by spectators like Corbitt [author of *Sound of Harvest*]" (John Makujina, *Measuring the Music*, p. 121, f. 73).
>
> "One of the first song routines Carman swings into is a jazzed-up 50's imitation of Elvis Presley called 'Celebrating Jesus.' Carman shakes, stutters and shimmies just like the 'King' himself, as the crowd cheers and be-bops in the aisles" (http://www.av1611.org/question/cqtool.html).

As we see, some "Christian" rock concerts today even feature moshing, head banging, slam dancing, and body surfing. Moshing is a group of rock fans swaying back and forth, slamming into each other. Headbanging is whipping the head back and forth brutally. Body surfing is when someone is lifted up or jumps on top of the crowd and is passed along on the outstretched hands of the people. It is an indecent ritual, as both males and females alike are passed along in this manner, sometimes on their fronts and sometimes on their backs, as the crowd puts their hands on their bodies. The Bible warns that men are not supposed to touch women other than their own wives (1 Corinthians 7:1). The Bible warns "flee also youthful lusts" (2 Timothy 2:22). Moshing and body surfing are a part of concerts performed by dc Talk, Audio Adrenaline, the News

Boys, One Bad Pig, and many other Christian rock groups today. This type of "rioting" is forbidden in the Word of God (Romans 13:13-14).

Another worldly feature of Christian rock is its **repetition**. This is one of the key elements of rock music, of course. The song "The Family Prayer Song" from the *PK Live Worship Album*, repeats the phase "we will serve the Lord" 22 times. Hundreds of examples could be given of the repetition which forms an integral part of CCM songs.

Another worldly aspect of Contemporary Christian Music is its **fan clubs**. Like secular rock stars, each of the popular CCM musicians has Internet fan clubs of enthusiastic followers. They feature gushing praise for their heroes, photographs, details about the artist's life and music, offers of autographed pictures, etc. There are hundreds of these CCM fan club sites on the Internet. There is "A Shrine to Jaci Velasquez" and "The Supertones are Outtasite" and "La la Land" (All Star United) and "Ode to Switchfoot" and "John Elefante Windows." There is "The Commonwealth of Plankeye" by a fan who calls himself "the psychotic one." There are weird sites dedicated to Audio Adrenaline and even weirder sites dedicated to Five Iron Frenzy. A site dedicated to Silage says this "very cool band" is "the cat's pajamas." The "My Tribute to Amy Grant Website" begins with these words of praise: "As you can tell I love Amy Grant. I think she is a great artist as well as a very good looking woman. I am impressed with everything she does..." There is the "Place in This World" site which is "totally devoted to global 'smittyfication,' that is addicting the world to the excellent music of Michael W. Smith." There are at least a dozen web sites dedicated strictly to the CCM rock band Petra. One of these is the "Petra Rocks My World" site. Another describes Petra as "the most incredible, awesome, far-out, hip, cool, radical, enthusiastic, spirit-filled band in the world." There are at least 10 sites devoted to dc Talk, including "a DC Talk Museum," "The Unofficial DC Talk Hangout Place," ("where Jesus freaks hang out") and "The Freakhouse," which features Freak Portraits, Freak Library, Freak Links, even Freak Trivia. Audio Adrenaline has several fan web sites, including such wholesome sounding places as "In Yo Face" and "Realm of the Zombie." (*Zombie* was the name of an Audio Adrenaline album and tour.)

I have examined several dozen of these. In not one case have I found a clear presentation of the Gospel on a CCM fan club site. There might be such a thing, but I haven't found it. From time to time one will find something which indicates an attempt to glorify Jesus Christ, but the overwhelming glory is dedicated to the CCM artist. This is gross worldliness. Can you imagine what the Apostle Paul would have done if some had attempted to establish a Paul fan club and distribute signed Paul photos and Paul "Tough Man for Jesus" T-shirts? He would have denounced such a thing as carnal foolishness (1 Corinthians 1).

THIRD, CCM INCORPORATES WORLDLY TECHNIQUES

Contemporary Christian Music incorporates the world's techniques. Frank Garlock warns:

> "The identical methods employed by the world to make the sound sensual are now being used by many popular contemporary Christian music vocalists. The style itself reflects and projects a philosophy." These techniques include swaying and dancing, scooping (sliding up to a note from an attack below its true pitch), vocal sliding, flipping below and above the actual written melody, whispery, breathy voice, and delayed vibrato.

FOURTH, CCM HAS A WORLDLY LIFESTYLE

The lifestyle common among CCM artists is very worldly. Speaking generally, they love worldly secular rock music, dress in a worldly fashion (short skirts, tight pants, low-cut blouses, bikinis, long hair and earrings on men, etc.), and frequently hang out in worldly places such as bars and nightclubs.

Even cursing and profanity are not uncommon in the CCM world. Charlie Daniels, a country rock CCM performer, used profanity in an interview with the *Huntsville Times* (Huntsville, Alabama) (July 31, 1994). The July-August 1994 issue of *Moody Monthly* admitted that Daniels uses profanity but argued: "For Christians to flatly dismiss musicians because they use four-letter words or sexual references, diminishes the likelihood that people will ever hear our message. ... We have to understand the world's view before we can effectively communicate our view; we have to relate to the people before we can preach to them" (*Moody Monthly*, July-August 1994, p. 57).

This is unscriptural advice. We are not to do evil to reach the world; we are not to relate to the world on the level of sin. The Bible admonishes the Christian to be "wise unto that which is good, and simple concerning evil" (Romans 16:19). The Christian is to have "sound speech, that cannot be condemned; that he that is of the contrary part may be ashamed, having no evil thing to say of you" (Titus 2:8). No corrupt or filthy communication is to proceed out of the Christian's mouth (Ephesians 4:29; Colossians 3:8).

Amy Grant admits that she uses four letter words: "I have a healthy sense of right and wrong, but sometimes, for example, using foul, exclamation-point words among friends can be good for a laugh" (Amy Grant, interview with *Ladies Home Journal*, December 1985, p. 100).

Steve Camp used profanity in a 1986 interview with *CCM Magazine*.

Cliff Young of Caedmon's Call told an interviewer that one of his favorite singers is the immoral, foul-mouthed Alanis Morissette. Young mocked a preacher who warned that Christian musicians should not listen to secular rock, and Young said that he listens to secular rock & rollers because "they are being honest [about] struggles that they go through." He said Christians should not be so concerned that "she [Morissette] says 'damn' and 'hell' in her songs" (Rob Berman, a conversation with Cliff Young and Todd Bragg, http://tlem.netcentral.net/indie/960701/caedmons_call.html). We should note that Morissette says much worse things than "damn" and "hell." *Rolling Stone* magazine describes her music as "uncensored documentation of her psychosexual former Catholic-girl torments" (*Rolling Stone*, No. 720). Morissette admits that she has been sexually active since her childhood and that she is open to sleeping with women. Young said: "I'd rather listen to someone who's being honest and open, cussing in their songs, than someone who's putting up a front and writing a song to get a hit" (Ibid.). Who said we have to make such a silly choice! Why not just listen to wholesome music? Everything is to be done to edification (Ephesians 4:29), and cursing certainly does not edify. Everything is to be done to the glory of Jesus Christ (1 Corinthians 10:31), and He certainly is not glorified by blasphemy and immorality.

Keith Wells of the rock group Roxalt warns that cursing is becoming increasingly common even on "Christian" rock albums: "It seems that some of the new 'Christian' metal bands that are putting out demos now think that they must cuss in order to get their message through. They write lyrics such as 'Satan Sucks' and 'The One who Kicks Satan's ——' and some other choice quotations I won't bring myself to type. ... One more problem I have with the current state of Christian Metal is this: I am hearing of sexual immorality in some of the Christian Bands" (*Heaven's Metal Magazine*, Vol. III, No. 3, p. 16).

It is commonplace for Contemporary Christian Musicians to watch wicked R-rated movies. Some of their interviews mention this. For example, Dove Award winner Ashley Cleveland told an interviewer that two movies she has enjoyed are *Good Will Hunting* and *The Full Monty*. According to Deseret online movie reviews, both are rated R and contain nudity, vulgarity, and profanity, meaning the movies blaspheme the Almighty God. *The Full Monty* is a bawdy British film about a group of unemployed men who decide to become male strippers. Cleveland said that when she was watching this vile film she got a laugh out of wondering how it would be if her husband and his friends would do such a thing. It was a "hilarious thought," she said. *Good Will Hunting* gets its R rating "for almost constant profanity, some very vulgar jokes and references, violence, sex, glimpses of nude paintings and racial epithets." Cleveland says, "I thought that was fantastic. I loved that movie." There is no separation from the world.

We could spend much time on this section. Worldly evils such as immorality and divorce are rampant in CCM circles. Just a few of the divorced or separated or adulterous CCM musicians are Sandi Patty, Deniece Williams, Sheila Walsh, John Talbot, Randy Stonehill, Larry Norman, Tom Howard, Ralph Carmichael, Steve Archer, Amy Grant, Gary Chapman, Stacy Jones of the rap group Grits, Ja'Marc Davis of Raze, and members of the now disbanded Barnabas. Melody Green, widowed wife of Keith Green, recently divorced her second husband, Andrew Sievright.

In April 1994, popular CCM singer Michael English left the Gaither Vocal Band after confessing to an adulterous affair with another CCM musician, Marabeth Jordon of the group First Call. At the time Mrs. Jordon was the wife of another man. Jordan and English conceived a baby out of wedlock (though it later died). English had been named Artist of the Year for 1994. Though English returned his six Dove awards, he was not asked to do so and the Gospel Music Association stated that he can have his awards back anytime he wants them. Later that same year English began recording secular music. In the 1996 album *Freedom Field* he sang: "Old man religion, I've got your name; the best part of my years were wrapped up, tied up in your thang." The single released from this album quickly rose to the top 20 on Billboard's adult contemporary chart.

In 1995, Sandi Patty admitted that she had an adulterous affair with Don Peslis, a divorcee who was working as one of her backup singers. She divorced her husband, John Helvering, and in August 1995, she married her new "love." *Christianity Today* reported that Patty was committing adultery with Peslis as far back as 1991 (*Christianity Today*, September 11, 1995, pp. 72-74). "According to several independent sources who at different times were aware of Patty's activities, she took part in two extramarital relationships, in both cases with married men" (Ibid.). This means that she was living in adultery during most of the years of her "ministry."

Though she admits that she was living in deep sin, and therefore living a gross lie, even while recording popular CCM titles and performing her music in public forums, and even though she blatantly disobeyed the Lord Jesus Christ's command in regard to divorce and remarriage (Matt. 19:9), she remains a favorite CCM musician. Most CCM listeners obviously don't care about biblical truth or morality. Just give them charming voices and gratifying music, and they are content. Her 1997 comeback recording, *Artist of My Soul*, has gained spots on Christian radio play lists nationwide, and she has a growing number of "performance" dates.

In his biography, popular CCM singer Kirk Franklin admits that he lived in deep sin during his teenage years and into his early 20s, even while acting as music director in churches and performing Gospel music in a wide range of forums. He fathered a son out of wedlock in 1990, and as late as 1995 he was still living a promiscuous lifestyle.

He formed his group called The Family in 1992, and by 1995 they had produced two hit Gospel albums and had won Dove, Stellar, and other awards. He was living in fornication all of this time. Of those days he testifies:

> "But there I was, in the odd situation of getting a little bit of exposure and popularity and a little bit of a reputation while my life was still a mess. ... my lifestyle and the casual promiscuity that seems to come along with this crazy business was just killing me. ... my flesh was killing me. ... By January 1995 I knew I couldn't go on with the life I was leading. I didn't want to hurt God, and I knew I'd already been doing that to some degree. ... I know what it's like to be onstage, performing God's music and thinking about who I'll be going home with that night" (Kirk Franklin, *Church Boy*, pp. 136,175,176,195).

Franklin alludes to widespread immorality, even homosexuality, within the Gospel music industry.

> "In the church, especially the African-American church during the seventies and eighties, homosexuality was a big problem. It still is in some places. It's a problem today in gospel music—a major concern—and everybody knows it. ... It seems that more than half the young people involved in dance, music, and the theater are openly gay. ... and the gospel music scene has not been exempt from that" (Ibid., pp. 39,40).

> "That stuff [promiscuity] wasn't happening because that's what I wanted. It was happening because I thought that's just the way it was. A lot of the pastors and preachers and music leaders I had known were doing it. And I honestly thought for a time that that's what you were supposed to do" (Ibid., p. 175).

Mylon LeFevre embarked on his solo career as a "Christian rocker" in 1970, but he admits that he and his fellow band members smoked marijuana together (John W. Styll, "Mylon LeFevre: The Solid Rocker," *CCM Magazine*, March 1986). How many other Christian rockers are living double lives?

Members of the disbanded rock band Stryper admit now that they were drinking and carousing during at least part of their career as "Christian rockers." In 1997 *HM* magazine had an interview with each member of Stryper. Tim Gaines stated that he was intoxicated practically every single day since 1988. The group did not disband until 1992. In a 1998 interview, Michael Sweet admitted that all of the members of Stryper were drinkers:

> "For a while there we all did, we were all drinking. However, I didn't know that it was that bad. ... He [Tim Gaines] never did in public and we never did till the *Against the Law* tour. I don't know if you know a whole lot about that, but ... that was kind of the rebellious tour, a rebellious record and we kind of

vented a lot out of our systems on that record for the bad and we all did some drinking and there are some things that happened that were the exact opposite of what we always stood for" (Interview with Michael Sweet, March 1, 1998, http://www.michaelsweet.com/interview.html).

In another interview Michael Sweet elaborates further:

"We were very sincere and we were serious about our faith and our music and our message but during *Against the Law* we were going onstage and telling people about God and coming offstage and drinking. Going on the bus and having a six pack of beer and a twelve pack of beer and going to the bar at the club we were playing and sitting with people and drinking. That's just not right. It just doesn't mix with telling people not to drink" (Interview with Michael Sweet, May 15, 1998, http://www.getsigned.com/resweet1.html).

In 1989 Stryper toured with secular rock band White Lion. Drummer Greg D'Angelo says, "We threw a party ... About two in the morning ROBERT SWEET WAS WHACKED! DRUNK! He was being dragged around on his tiptoes by two women holding him up!" (*RIP*, June 1989, p. 41).

Examples of the worldliness of the CCM lifestyle could be multiplied exceedingly.

FIFTH, CCM HAS WORLDLY TIES

Contemporary Christian Music is dominated by people with close ties to the world. There is a direct and intimate connection between Contemporary Christian Music and the secular music realm. Phil Driscoll condemns the CCM industry (of which he is a part) when he says a lot of CCM is "so much like the world you can't tell the difference" (*Charisma*, November 1993).

CCM is connected to the world by its financial ties. CCM is big business, a $450 million a year industry. As of 1995, there were 250 radio stations which carried CCM as their primary music format. Revenues from sales of CCM have tripled since the mid-80s, and as of 1992 CCM was a half-billion-dollar-a-year enterprise. One-quarter of the sales in Christian bookstores is from music. This caught the attention of the world, and most of the major CCM producers and distributors are now owned by secular corporations. Word Inc., the largest CCM distributor, is owned by ABC-TV, which is owned by Standard Oil. Word, in turn, owns and/or supports Maranatha, Myrrh, Lexicon, Light, and other CCM producers. Sparrow Records sold out to EMI Music in 1992. Zondervan-owned Benson was purchased in 1993 by Music Entertainment Group in New York. That same year Bertelsmann Music Group (BMG) purchased 50% of Reunion Records and Blanton/Harrell Entertainment. The world owns most of the contemporary

Christian music!

Not only are most CCM record companies owned by the world, but many of the most popular CCM artists are signing recording contracts with secular music companies. For example, the Newsboys 1998 album *Step Up to the Microphone* is being promoted both in Christian (via Star Song) and in secular markets. The latter is being done through Virgin Records, the same company which records the Rolling Stones. Danny Goodwin, Vice President of A&R for Virgin Records, describes their philosophy of music:

> "Our position is, whether these artists are Christians, Jews, Moslems, black, white, Albanian or whatever, they're making great music. And that's what Virgin does—we're in the market to sell what we call quality music to the largest number of people we can" (*CCM Magazine*, August 1998, p. 25).

Many CCM musicians are comfortable working hand in hand with people who produce and distribute the most vile, antichrist rock and roll music.

CCM is connected to the world by its imitation of secular music. This is illustrated by "The Christian Music Comparison Guide" which is designed to help people find "Christian" music which sounds like their favorite secular groups. The fForeword to this *Guide* contains an amazing statement: "It's been interesting to watch just how closely the Christian music industry has begun to mimic its secular counterpart." This *Guide* says that if you like the secular group Crosby, Stills & Nash you might like the Christian artist Michael Card; if you like the secular group Grand Funk Railroad you might like the Christian artist Mark Farner; if you like Judas Priest you might like the Resurrection Band; if you like Kansas you might like Whiteheart; if you like U2 you might like The Julies or Curious Fools; if you like Led Zeppelin you might like Soulfood 76 or Twin sister; if you like Guns 'N' Roses you might like Die Happy; if you like Metallica or Iron Maiden or Kiss or Pearl Jam you might like Tourniquet or Barren Cross or Barebones or Bonedance, etc.

A perfect example of CCM's imitation of secular music is the 1998 album *Surfonic Water Revival*. It is an attempt to Christianize surf-rock music. According to the CCM rockers who designed this album, Heaven could be a "Surfer's Paradise." Note the words to the song "Surfer's Paradise" from this album:

> "It's a dream of mine/ It's always surfin' time/ There's a beach with perfect weather/ And no closing sign/ It's the place to go/ 'Cause your tan never fades there/ And the surf's so fine/ And the junk's all free at the 7-Eleven/ And if you catch the perfect wave/ It'll take you to heaven/ So bring your girl and bring your guy/ And make it on down/ To surfer's Paradise.

"Chorus: Let's get together, yea/ Let's get together (at)/ Surfer's Paradise/ Don't hesitate, don't think twice/ Shorts and bikinis will suffice/ You can wear 'em all day and night/ (At) Surfer's Paradise."

This is worldly. The surfer's scene is one of licentiousness, which the Bible forbids. Many of the surfer songs were about illicit sex, about petting and lusting after half-naked girls, about escaping authority, about avoiding work and responsibility. The music was designed to promote these themes. How foolish to think that Christ can be honored with such music. The Lord Jesus Christ warned that sensual lust, which is a big part of the beach scene, is adultery. When I was saved at age 23 (I grew up in Florida only a short drive from many beaches), God dealt with me about my old ways. He convicted me that it is wrong to lust after bikini-clad girls. I quickly learned that I had to avoid beaches to avoid serious temptation. He convicted me about the evils of rock music. I no longer wanted to bum around and hang out and waste my life as I did before I was saved. Why aren't CCM rockers convicted of these worldly things? Instead of singing about beach nakedness they should be preaching against it. Surfing itself is not wrong, but the surf scene is intimately connected with the licentiousness which the Bible forbids. The same is true for snowboarding. Snowboarding is not wrong, but the snowboard CULTURE is at enmity with God's laws and must be shunned by those who desire to please Christ. The same is true for skateboarding.

dc Talk's 1996 album was titled *Jesus Freak*, copying the world's term for a rebellious counter-culture drug user. dc Talk's Toby McKeehan actually opens some concerts by screaming, "WELCOME TO THE FREAK SHOW!" dc Talk claims that their use of "freak" refers to "an ardent enthusiast" but this is not how the term has been used in the context of American society during the past four decades. Webster's dictionary defines the term not only as an enthusiast, but also as a sexual deviate or a person who uses an illicit drug. I know how the term was used in the '60s and '70s, because I was a rebellious, longhaired, rock-loving, drug-using, hitch-hiking hippie during that era and I gloried in being a "freak." dc Talk has no right to connect the Lord Jesus Christ and Christianity with this term. At best it is confusion.

CCM is also connected to the world by CCM musicians' love for secular music. Contemporary Christian musicians readily acknowledge that they listen to and love secular music. They also perform secular music. There is no separation from the world whatsoever.

Some defenders of Contemporary Christian Music warn about the evil in secular rock and warn that Christians should separate from it, but they turn around and say that it is fine to listen to Christian rock. Steve Peters does this in his 1998 book *Truth about Rock*. This is a strange position because the Christian rock musicians themselves are certainly listening to every form of secular rock.

"FOURTH WATCH cites groups like U2, the Police, Genesis, Pete Townshend, and the Alarm as major influences. MEMBERS LISTEN TO A GREAT DEAL OF MAINSTREAM MUSIC, MAKING NO APOLOGIES FOR IT, and they express a desire to play clubs and other non-church settings" (*CCM Magazine*, April 1987, p. 19).

RANDY STONEHILL "listens to all kinds of music," including hard secular rock (Devlin Donaldson, "Rockin' Randy," *CCM Magazine,* August 1983).

PHIL KEAGGY also has no separation from the world in his music. He performs an unholy combination of secular rock and Christian rock/folk, and those who listen to his music are drawn toward worldly rock & roll. On his 1993 *Crimson and Blue* album, for example, he pays "homage to The Beatles" with several of the songs.

When asked by an interviewer who has influenced her music, CCM singer ASHLEY CLEVELAND replied: "There are at least thirty artists I could name from the late sixties and early seventies that influenced me: Stephen Stills, Joni Mitchell, Neil Young, Elton John, Steely Dan, Led Zeppelin, The Who, Little Feat...and rock-and-roll bands that capitalized on the acoustic guitar's percussive qualities. I really think the acoustic guitar is the ultimate rock-and-roll instrument" (Chris Parks, "Interview with Ashley Cleveland," Feb. 21, 1998, http://www.tollbooth.org/features/cleve.html). When asked what music was currently on her stereo, she replied, "*Living With Ghosts*, Patty Griffin; *What's The Story Morning Glory*, Oasis; *Exile On Main Street*, Rolling Stones" (http://www.ashleycleveland.com/acfacts.htm). In her concerts, Ashley Cleveland performs a very gritty rendition of the Rolling Stones hit "Gimme Shelter."

The GALACTIC COWBOYS singer admits that their biggest influence is the Beatles: "I'd have to say that The Beatles are still the biggest influence on us, all the way around — except for maybe the guitar tones. They were great songwriters and vocalists" (Ben Huggins, cited by Dan Macintosh, *HM* magazine, September-October 1998).

The CCM group 77's says their musical influences are "Led Zeppelin, the Beach Boys, Pearl Jam, and Stone Temple Pilots" ("Biography of the 77's," http://www.cmo.com/cmo/cmo/data/77.htm). 77's performs the Led Zeppelin's song "Nobody's Fault But Mine" on their *Drowning With Land in Sight* album. Led Zeppelin's famous guitarist, Jimmy Page, is a follower of Satanist Aleister Crowley and purchased Crowley's mansion. The Led Zeppelin song "Stairway to Heaven," the most popular rock song of all time, has an ode to Satan in back masking. Led Zeppelin's song "Houses of the Holy" is sung to Satan. (The title song to one of 77's albums is "Pray Naked.")

In an interview with TLeM (*Lighthouse Electronic Magazine*), the members of CAEDMON'S CALL said their greatest love in music is secular rock. They mentioned Indigo Girls, Shawn Colvin, David Wilcox, The Police, Fishbone, 10,000 Maniacs. The group often performs Beatles music. Cliff Young said one of his favorites is the foul-mouthed Alanis Morrisette. He mocked a preacher who warns that Christian musicians should not listen to secular rock, and said that he listens to secular rock & rollers because "they are being honest [about] struggles that they go through."

The members of STRYPER love secular rock music. In a 1995 interview, Michael Sweet, who was the lead singer for Stryper, said: "I'm a fan of all that stuff from the '80s. Groups like Bon Jovi, Van Halen, and Aerosmith. Musically, I like a lot of that stuff, but back when I was a kid what I grew up listening to ranged from Elvis Presley, Jerry Lee Lewis, Fats Domino all the way to groups like Three Dog Night. Credence [Clearwater Revival] was one of my favorite bands and a group called Bad Company. I just loved them and Elvis, of course" (*CCM Magazine*, November 1995).

STEPHEN CURTIS CHAPMAN recorded some of the songs on his *Greatest Hits* album live at Abbey Road Studios in London, the studio where the Beatles recorded their albums. No music group has had a more ungodly and spiritually destructive influence than the Beatles. It is beyond me to understand why CCM musicians by the dozens continue to listen to and glorify this wicked rock group.

The hard rock band COMMON CHILDREN admits that they were influenced by Nirvana. "We listened to Nirvana when they came out and thought they were cool and everything, but our main influences have been Pink Floyd and groups like that" (Chad Benham, interview with Common Children, *RIM magazine*, 1998, http://www.ricochetmusic.com/rim_new/com_children/cc1.htm). Common Children's lead vocalist, Marc Byrd, says: "The thing about Nirvana is they rock, yeah, but Kurt Cobain wrote incredible melodies" (Ibid.). Nirvana, led by Kurt Cobain, was a very dark and occultic band. Cobain, an antichrist blasphemer, killed himself with a shotgun.

AUDIO ADRENALINE'S *Bloom* album includes the song "Free Ride" from the Edgar Winter Group's *They Only Come Out at Night* album. Rock star Edgar Winter was featured on the cover of this wicked album dressed as a homosexual "drag queen." The lyrics to "Free Ride" claim that "all of the answers, are come from within." This is rank heresy, because we know that the answers do not come from within man's fallen heart, but from God's revelation in the Bible.

STEVE CAMP says, "I'll have a Foreigner 4 album going in my car." He also says: "I am dedicated to good music whether it's pop, Christian, gospel, R&B, blues, jazz, classical, rock or whatever. I just love good music" (Steve Camp, *MusicLine* magazine, Feb. 1986, p. 22).

Joey Belville of THE ECHOING GREEN "proudly lists Duran Duran among his biggest influences" (*CCM Magazine*, August 1998, p. 20).

KERRY LIVGREN, formerly the lead guitarist and songwriter for the secular rock group Kansas, left Kansas in 1983 because he wanted to work with those who were likeminded with his new-found Christianity. Since then he has pursued a solo career and recorded Christian albums, but he has also reunited with Kansas (1990-91) on a tour and performed with them on the 1992 *Live at the Whiskey* album.

Some of DC TALK'S musical role models are the Beatles, David Bowie, and The Police, all of which are wicked secular rock groups. dc Talk's album "Free at Last" contains a song titled "Jesus Is Just Alright," which was first sung by the Byrds (the song was later covered by the Doobie Brothers; a "doobie" is a marijuana joint). dc Talk's Kevin Smith admits that he listens to mostly secular rock music (*Flint Michigan Journal*, March 15, 1996, B19). dc Talk opened its "Jesus Freak" concerts with the Beatles' song "Help." They also perform Jimi Hendrix's *Purple Haze*. Hendrix was a drug-crazed New Age occultist. Toward the end of their concerts dc Talk plays the rock song "All Apologies" by the wicked secular rock group Nirvana, formerly led by Kurt Cobain. Terry Watkins notes: "Kurt Cobain is one of the worst Antichrist blasphemers since John Lennon. Kurt Cobain decorated his home with blood-splattered baby dolls hanging by their necks! The inside of Nirvana's album *In Utero*, which is the album dc Talk got 'All Apologies' from, has pictures of chopped up babies! Cobain ran around his neighborhood spraypainting, 'ABORT CHRIST' and 'GOD IS GAY.' Cobain's first band was called 'Fecal Matter.' Cobain killed himself a couple of years ago" (Watkins, *Christian Rock: Blessing or Blasphemy?*)

JARS OF CLAY names Jimmy Hendrix and the Beatles as their inspiration (Dann Denny, "Christian Rock," *Sunday Herald Times*, Bloomington, Ind., Feb. 8, 1998). The lead guitarist for Jars of Clay is said to be a "Beatles fanatic" (*Christian News*, Dec. 8, 1997). When asked by *Christianity Today* to list their musical influences, Jars of Clay members "listed no Christian artists" (*Christianity Today*, Nov. 15, 1999). Jars of Clay performs Ozzy Osbourne's "Crazy Train" during their concerts. Osbourne is the filthymouthed former lead singer for the occultic rock group Black Sabbath. Though members of Black Sabbath today claim it was all done in innocence and "fun," they promoted occultic themes through their music and concerts, including upside down crosses and altar calls for Satan. They blasphemed Jesus Christ and railed against the authority of the God of the Bible. Osbourne has almost died several times because of his outrageous drug abuse and alcoholism. He has dressed in women's clothing and stripped off most of his clothes during concerts. At one point he attempted to kill his wife and had to be jailed. He is deeply scarred by his savage lifestyle and maintains a semblance of normalcy today through the drug Prozac.

JON GIBSON says: "I consider it an honor to tour with Stevie Wonder. I'm thrilled."
AMY GRANT says, "I love to hear Billy Joel, Kenny Loggins and the Doobie Brothers" (*Time*, March 11, 1985). Amy's album *House of Love* includes the environmental-mother-earth song, "Big Yellow Taxi," by new-age-priestess Joni Mitchell (Ibid.). Mitchell is infamous for her open relationship with a spirit she calls "Art." Obviously she is communing with demons, and it is unconscionable for Amy Grant to be promoting Mitchell's music to Christian young people.

DALLAS HOLM claims: "My all-time favorite group was the Byrds."

Dana Key (of DEGARMO AND KEY) notes that he has been influenced most by B.B. King, Jimi Hendrix, and Billy Gibbons (of ZZ Top) (*CCM Magazine*, January 1989, p. 30).

Bob Hartman of PETRA admits that the influences upon their music were the 1970s "guitar heroes" like Hendrix, Clapton, Page and Walsh (*CCM Magazine*, January 1989, p. 31). Petra plays songs by secular rock groups Argent and Kiss.

HOLY SOLDIER plays songs by the Rolling Stones.

The group IN REACH are said to be influenced by secular rock groups like Rush, Deep Purple, and former Beatle Paul McCartney.

The late RICH MULLINS, popular CCM song writer, said, "John Lennon was a big hero of mine."

POINT OF GRACE, on their *Life, Love and Other Mysteries* album, recorded "Sing a Song" by the occultic, antichrist secular group Earth, Wind and Fire.

RACHEL, RACHEL plays songs by Kansas.

REZ BAND sings songs by Jefferson Airplane and the Who, very wicked and openly blasphemous rock groups. Jefferson Airplane's song "The Son of Jesus" says Jesus had a sexual relationship with Mary Magdalene and they produced an illegitimate daughter.

The worldliness of DELIRIOUS is evident in their choice of "musical heroes," which include "U2, Radiohead, Blur and other big British modern rockers" (*CCM* magazine, July 1999, p. 39).

The Christian rock group UNVEILED includes the Rolling Stones occultic song "Sympathy for the Devil" on one of their albums. In an attempt to justify this they said, "We HAD to do this song — we recorded this mostly live about one mile from the Altamont Speedway — and if that doesn't tell you why, you don't know your rock and roll history. [This is where a young man was brutally murdered by the Hells Angels during a Rolling Stones concert in 1969.] And as for the bad word...I think the Devil swears" (http://www.77s.com/music/unveiled/youth_music.lyrics.html#sympathy).

The group DELIVERANCE performs songs by secular rock groups. Their *What a Joke* album has the song "After Forever" by the vile, blasphemous, pagan rock group Black Sabbath.

BOB ROTH, music critic for the magazine *Youth!*, displays his love for secular rock in his articles: "Cloud Nine demonstrates why George Harrison is still having fun. It is a work of love and compassion and hope and silliness. All the stuff the Holy Spirit uses to give us inner power..." (*Youth!*, April 1988). Roth tells his young readers that former Beatle Harrison, a Hindu, is doing the work of love, and he claims that the Holy Spirit produces silliness! Roth even promotes the wicked rock singer Sting of the Police. Roth says, "Sting sings these profound songs in his usual mellow, grainy voice" (Roth, *Youth!*, March 1988). This is what Sting thinks about marriage: "I don't see the point [of being married]. One can procreate without the dreaded ritual ... I am terribly good in bed and I want people to know that..." (Jeff Godwin, *What's Wrong with Christian Rock?*, p. 199). Sting sang "Murder by Numbers," about killing your family or anybody else you "find a bore" (Ibid.). Roth even says it is all right to worship filthy rock stars: "If you are into Bruce [Springsteen] worship, don't feel guilty about buying this disc. (Just admit your addiction!)..." (Roth, *Youth!*, February 1988). If you allow your young people to be influenced by the Contemporary Christian Music world, this is the type of foolish and unscriptural advice they will hear.

MICHAEL W. SMITH admits that his music is influenced by Alan Parsons, one of the most Satanic of rock musicians. One of Parsons songs is titled "Lucifer."

Joel Taylor of UNDERCOVER testifies: "I'm not connected to Christian music at all. I can't stand Christian radio stations."

I went through one issue of *HM* magazine (formerly *Heaven's Metal Magazine*) (May-June 1998) and discovered the following worldly connection: LETHAL MOB noted that they are influenced by gangsta rap. MORTIFICATION testified that they are into Death/

Grind, Black Metal; they play in Melbourne's Hell Club. MAYFAIR LAUNDRY, a group which got its name from a scene in a Beatle's movie, cites influences from the Beatles to Red Hot Chilli Peppers. ZAO says they listen to a lot of Neurosis, Bark Market, Portishead, and Deftones. THE HUNTINGTONS new album pays homage to their favorite band, The Ramones. The producer of this album is Mass Giorgini who also produced albums for The Queers and Screeching Weasel. THE DINGEES told *HM* magazine that their major influences are the Clash, the Specials, and "movies where everything is blowing up." D'GRUVE, which has a "heavy, dark sound," got its name from an early 90s dance hit and cites influences as diverse as the Beatles and Saigon Kick. DALLAS EMBODYMENT, which plays concerts in secular clubs, is described this way: "truly heavy, metal/punk, Kevin peering over his bass ominously and Andrew banging his head full of hair like a true metalhead, shrill close-to-the-mouth hardcore screeching." ULTIMATUM'S new album is described as their most brutal extreme metal onslaught.

CCM is also connected to the world by employing unsaved artists and by performing together with secular groups. It is very common within the CCM industry for unsaved people to be employed as musicians, artists, and producers. Note the following examples of the many which could be given.

Pat Leonard, who played keyboard and synthesizer on Steve Green's first Word album, became Madonna's main producer/songwriter. Leonard was also the producer for Michael W. Smith's *I'll Lead You Home* album. The cover to Steve Green's *It's a Dying World* album was drawn by the same artist who did the Beatles' *Sgt. Pepper* album, which included pictures of satanist Aleister Crowley and LSD proponent Timothy Leary, among others.

dc Talk's video "Jesus Freak" was patterned after one produced by Simon Maxwell for the satanic and blasphemous British rock group Nine Inch Nails (led by Trent Reznor). The members of dc Talk purposefully chose Maxwell as their producer after they viewed a video by Nine Inch Nails. Toby McKeehan said that Maxwell's "style appealed to us" (*Billboard*, November 11, 1995). Nine Inch Nail's blasphemous video, *Closer,* contains a photo of a monkey crucified on a cross.

Carman's 1998 video *Mission 3:16* was filmed partially in Ireland using some of the dancers from the sensual *Riverdance* production (*CCM Magazine*, July 1998, p. 12).

Philip Bailey, who has a gospel album, *The Wonders of His Love*, sang a duet called "Easy Lover" with secular rock star Phil Collins. After some Christian stations refused to play Bailey's gospel songs, he complained that "some of these Christian folks got nothing else to do but sit at home and pick" (*One Hit Wonders*, p. 430).

CCM performer Randy Matthews opened concerts for secular rock groups Lynyrd Skynyrd and ZZ Top.

CCM rock group Tourniquet tours with wicked secular groups such as Atheist. They perform at metal rock festivals with satanist antichrist groups such as Deicide and Morbid Angel. Deicide has a song "Once Upon a Cross" blaspheming Jesus Christ. The inside cover to the album depicts the members of the band cutting Christ open and removing His insides.

One of the largest distributors of background tapes is Soundtraks, based in Oklahoma City. On May 31, 2001, I talked with Don, who works in the production department at Soundtraks, and he plainly told me: "We don't have any spiritual standards for the musicians. Some are out of Nashville. They don't have to go to any church. We just use good musicians. The same musicians are used for Southern Gospel and Contemporary."

The above only uncovers the tip of the iceberg of the CCM connection with the world. Because of this intimate connection, CCM breaks down barriers which should not be broken. CCM creates appetites for the world's music. Note the following testimony of a church music director:

> "Before the Lord saved my soul, I slipped around behind my parent's backs and listened to contemporary Christian music. **This music softened me to the music that I would later come to listen to**. My point is that this type of music softens our young people to actual rock music. I know firsthand."

Christian Rock Is Chum for Secular Rock

One discerning Christian musician describes Christian rock music as "chum" for secular rock. Chumming is a fishing practice. The fisherman uses chum to attract the fish. The chum might be meal and salmon eggs (to attract kokanee) or fish entrails and blood (to attract shark). The fisherman tosses the chum over the side of the boat and if there are fish in the area they will sense the chum and move toward the boat (and the fisherman's waiting lure or net). This is what Christian rock is for secular rock. It creates a desire for worldly music.

Contemporary Christian Music can easily create an appetite for secular music, because there is basically no difference. In a test conducted in a British teen music club, the young people could not tell the difference between secular rock and Christian rock. The May 18, 1998, issue of *Alberta Report* contained an article entitled "Christian and Cool," which described "Christian" musicians playing successfully in secular music clubs in Alberta, Canada. They can make this "cross over" because their music is worldly, and the lyrics to the music are so weak, vague, and inoffensive that the unsaved do not mind that it is somewhat religious in nature. The worldly crowd is there for the music and its effect, not for the words. As long as they can dance and groove to the music, they don't care what the words are. The article mentioned teenagers who wandered into the club "without realizing all the acts were Christian." Why did they not know that the music was Christian? Because it was exactly the same type of music as the world's.

I don't believe that Contemporary Christian Music draws the world to a truly biblical position and lifestyle, but I do believe that Contemporary Christian Music draws professing Christians to the world.

> "The kids that were into Stryper four or five years ago are into thrash right now" (*CCM Magazine*, Feb. 1989, p. 20).

PART II
ANSWERS TO COMMONLY ASKED QUESTIONS

ANSWERS TO COMMONLY ASKED QUESTIONS

The following are questions frequently raised when the topic of Contemporary Christian Music arises.

1. Isn't music neutral?

The idea that music is a neutral force and that any music can be used to glorify God and serve His purposes is one of the key philosophies of the end times apostasy. It is unscriptural and unreasonable to the highest degree. We answer the charge of the neutrality of music in Point One of the Characteristics of Contemporary Christian Music.

2. Isn't the sincerity of the musicians the important thing?

Those who defend Contemporary Christian Music often argue that the only thing that matters is whether or not the musicians are sincere. Note the following statement by Christian rocker Mylon LeFevre:

> "Music is not good or evil because of the formation of the notes or the structure of the beat. Music is good because the heart of the person playing it is innocently and sincerely giving praise to our God" (Christian rock musician Mylon LeFevre, interview by Pastor Rick Anderson, Minneapolis, Minnesota, *Rock Music—What's the Real Message?*, cited by Jeff Godwin, *What's Wrong with Christian Rock?*, p. 122).

We would answer this, first of all, by reminding our readers of the deceptive nature of man's heart.

> "The heart is deceitful above all things, and desperately wicked: who can know it?" (Jeremiah 17:9).

> "He that trusteth in his own heart is a fool: but whoso walketh wisely, he shall be delivered" (Proverbs 28:26).

> "There is a way which seemeth right unto a man, but the end thereof are the ways of death" (Proverbs 14:12).

These verses remind us that man's heart cannot be trusted. One cannot even know his own heart perfectly. It is possible for a man to deceive himself and others. It is therefore impossible to know whether or not someone is sincerely seeking to please God. It is impossible to know for sure whether or not a person has sincere motives for doing what they do. Man's heart is complex, and he often has many motives for what he does.

Secondly, God requires obedience to His Word and does not accept man's sincere disobedience. There are many examples of this in the Bible. Moses was very obedient and sincere before God, but when he disobeyed in the matter of the rock, and struck the rock instead of speaking to it, God judged him and refused to allow him to enter Canaan (Num. 20:7-14). When Aaron's sons offered strange fire, God struck them dead (Leviticus 10:1-7). When Saul disobeyed in the seemingly minor matter of refusing to destroy all of the cattle belonging to the Amalekites, God judged him and removed the kingdom from him (1 Samuel 15). When Uzzah steadied the cart holding the ark, God struck him dead (1 Samuel 6:6-7).

Thirdly, if the only test of the soundness of music is the sincerity of the performers, it would be impossible for the hearer to test it. As already noted, we cannot know for certain the sincerity of the musician. Many Christian rock musicians have admitted that they wrote and performed Contemporary Christian Music even while they were drinking and committing adultery and seeking fortune and fame. The members of the Christian rock band Stryper admit today that they drank and partied in carnal rebellion during part of their touring career. Michael English, Sandi Patty, Kirk Franklin, among others, admit that they were living in fornication and adultery during part of their careers. Mylon LeFevre admits that he wrote and performed music for years before he got right with God, that he was using drugs heavily and drinking and carousing even while producing Christian music. After their success with the *Supernatural* album and tour, Michael Tait of dc Talk admits that he "went through a time where I dabbled in a lot of [wicked] things" (*CCM Magazine*, May 2001, p. 42). He calls this his "dark days." Many CCM spokesmen honestly admit that this type of thing is a big problem in their midst, but a great deal of it is covered up to protect the careers of the worldly musicians and to protect the reputation of the CCM industry. How, then, are we to tell if a musician is sincerely walking with God and performing from a sanctified life? We cannot know this for sure, so it is unreasonable to make this the measure of whether or not the music is sound. The only reasonable test is to examine the character and lyrics of the music itself.

3. Isn't some of CCM acceptable? Why do you have to condemn all of it equally?

First of all, let me say that I have personally examined hundreds of CCM songs in recent months, and I have found that THE VAST MAJORITY of it is unacceptable. We are do not useing extreme examples to paint the entire CCM movement with a broad brush. It is an irrefutable fact that Tthe movement is overwhelmingly ecumenical, charismatic, unscriptural, shallow, and worldly. Exceptions do not overthrow the rule.

Second, I do not condemn sound music, regardless of how new or contemporary it is.

There is some spiritual and sound music being written by contemporary Christian musicians. *Some* of the praise music, for example, is very lovely and Scriptural. If a piece of music is sound, I do not condemn it, though I will warn of its dangerous associations.

Third, I will hasten to add that to find the exceptions one must wade through tons of musical pollution. There are some CCM songs that are not, in themselves, wrong, but they are interconnected with an unscriptural, spiritually-dangerous world. For example, Carman's *I Surrender All* album contains an "Old Rugged Cross Medley" which has some beautiful parts, but the very next cut on the album launches into a sensual heavy boogie-woogie rendition of "Peace Like a River"!

Fourth, CCM creates an appetite for unholy music and leads to secular rock. Contemporary Christian Music uses the world's music, and the world's music appeals to the flesh. The flesh, in turn, is never satisfied. Note the rapid progression of rock music itself, from the very mild character of the '50s to the wildness of the '70s to the insanity of the '90s. We have seen that the CCM musicians themselves love secular rock music. They also perform secular rock music. There is absolutely no separation between CCM and secular rock, and those who listen to CCM are creating and sustaining unholy appetites toward the world.

Fifth, the CCM world is constantly moving, and the movement is toward harder rock and a more obscure, more unscriptural message. The CCM musicians themselves usually move into harder and harder rock. Even those who began with very mild rock have progressed to harder rock. The Gaithers illustrate this. Sandi Patty also illustrates this. She has gone deeper and deeper into hard rock music. Her 1993 album *LeVoyage* does not mention the name of Jesus but it rocks so heavily that *CCM Magazine* made this statement: "...old-line Patty fans are either going to be seeking refunds in droves, or be so flabbergasted at seeing an entirely new side of her..." (*CCM Magazine*, May 1993, p. 40). The dramatic changes which have occurred in CCM in a mere two decades were described by John Fischer in *CCM magazine*: "In 1978, Christian music was unquestionably Christian in content. ... Almost every song had a distinctly gospel message of some sort. Many songs [from the '90s], however, were hardly recognizable as 'Christian' songs, at least not in the traditional sense. Lyrics were sometimes unintelligible; not every song was about Jesus" (John Fischer, "Two Nights Out," *CCM Magazine*, July 1998, p. 145). Consider the following goal dc Talk had for their "Jesus Freak" video: "The intention of the clip was to 'push the envelope' of the Christian music community ... they expect some of the more conservative members of the Christian community to frown on the adventurous clip" (*Billboard*, Nov. 11, 1995). *CCM Magazine* admits that Amy Grant has continually pushed the barriers of Christian music (*CCM*

Magazine, July 1998, p. 42).

As CCM rockers "push the envelope" of acceptability, they are pulling generations of professing Christians with them more deeply into rock music, closer to the world.

The music of Twila Paris is a good example of the danger of CCM. Some of her songs are lovely, with full orchestration, acoustic strings, no rock bass or drums. But there are rock songs on the same albums. For example, her rendition of "When the Roll Is Called Up Yonder" is sung to a funky beat with heavy bass and constant snare drum. The song "We Seek His Face" is sung to a strong disco style rock music. Also many of her songs which begin traditionally end rocky. "Be Thou My Vision," for example, begins with Paris singing to a traditional organ background, then builds into a strong beat with drums and bass guitar. Thus, those who purchase Twila Paris' albums for the non-rock songs will be enticed to enjoy the rock music on the same albums. Lyrically, some of Twila Paris's music contains a plain and scriptural message, but other songs are obscure. Her 1996 song "Love's Been Following You" is an example: "I know sometimes it's hard to believe it/ But love's been following you." What love? How does the listener connect with this love? None of the important questions are answered in the song.

CCM is dangerous. All of its is dangerous. It is moving further and further away from the Word of God. It is moving increasingly deeper into the world. It is taking its listeners not only closer to the world but is yoking them in fellowship with the unscriptural ecumenical-charismatic movement. The only sure protection from its unholy aspects is separation from all of it.

4. What about the miracles which some CCM artists witness?

Mylon LeFevre makes the following claim: "If you come to our concerts, you'll find people getting born again, people getting baptized in the Holy Spirit, people getting healed of physical ailments" (Mylon LeFevre, *Ministries Today*, January-February 1987, p. 30).

We would reply, first, that the Pentecostal "baptism of the Holy Spirit" is not Scriptural. Pentecostals like LeFevre claim the baptism of the Holy Spirit is something which frequently occurs subsequent to salvation as a second blessing, yet nowhere are the believers taught to seek a second blessing or a Spirit baptism. When the Epistles refer to Spirit baptism, they always refer to it in the past tense.

Second, the prophecies about the last days repeatedly warn of end-time deception through lying wonders. The presence of apparent miracles is not evidence that something is true. "For there shall arise false Christs, and false prophets, and shall show great signs and wonders; insomuch that, if it were possible, they shall deceive the very elect" (Matt. 24:24; see also 2 Thessalonians 2:6-12; Rev. 13:13). The unsaved religionists mentioned in Matthew 7:21-23 do "many wonderful works," but Jesus does not know them. The only sure test of a prophet is to compare his teaching and ministry to the Word of God, and when the CCM world is compared with the Word of God, it fails the test. "To the law and to the testimony: if they speak not according to this word, it is because there is no light in them" (Isaiah 8:20).

5. Why does traditional church music seem dull?

First, I don't believe there is anything dull or boring about wonderful traditional hymns such as those written by Fanny Crosby. Those who think these Bible-based hymns are boring or "cheesy" have a worldly appetite and they are yearning for jazzy rhythms rather than focusing on the words of the music. This problem is solved by putting away worldly music and learning to enjoy spiritual music. A spiritual appetite must be created so that one can enjoy spiritual music. This does not necessarily happen overnight.

Second, it is possible to sing spiritual songs and hymns in a boring manner. I have heard it done many times. When the congregational singing is dull and lifeless, the hymns themselves appear dull even if they aren't. The solution to this problem is not the introduction of sensual rock music. The solution rather is to find a church which has a diligent and spiritual song leader and where people love the Lord enough to zealously sing his praises through psalms and hymns and spiritual songs.

Third, I agree that there are boring traditional Christian songs and hymns. When the message is weak or obscure and the melody is uninteresting, the music is boring even to Spirit filled people. There is absolutely no reason why church music should be boring. At times I have found myself wondering why the music leader or the person performing the special music selected certain songs. Are they not thinking about the words? The solution to boring church music, though, is not rock music! It is wise selection of spiritual music and hearty singing of the same.

Fourth, sometimes the song service is boring because of lack of imagination and variety. We have covered this in Part III: Why is the music portion of our church services frequently so lifeless?

Fifth, there are cultural issues which come to bear upon church music. When I visited Ireland and England, I found that many of the church services were dull. Part of the problem was cultural. I simply was not accustomed to the formality of the services or to the music they used. Again, the solution to such problems is NOT rock music.

Fifth, there are denominational differences in church music. Many young people who reject "dull" traditional church music do so because they are familiar with an apostate ritualistic denomination which does not have the power of God. They are familiar with the lifelessness of apostasy. Again, the solution is not rock music or the wildfire of the charismatic movement. It is to find a church which is seriously committed to the Word of God and where the Spirit of God is in control.

6. Can you prove a connection between rock music and voodoo or African paganism?

CCM defenders usually deny that there is a connection between voodoo and African witchcraft and rock music. Steve Lawhead, in his book *Rock Reconsidered*, quotes Tony Palmer: "That rock and its 'evil beat' originated with the slaves of Africa is a racist notion which will not stand up" (*Rock Reconsidered*, pp. 55-60). Dan and Steve Peters present the same nonsense on page 187 of their book *What About Christian Rock?*

Such a denial is absolute spiritual blindness. Dr. William Sargent, head of the Psychological Medicine Department at St. Thomas Hospital in London, says "the Beatles and African witch doctors all practiced a similar type of brainwashing" (*Wichita Beacon*, Feb. 17, 1965, p. 11A). Leonard Seidel, a concert pianist and distinguished lecturer on music, has researched this topic and exposes the lie that there is no connection between voodoo and African paganism and rock music:

> The incessant, poly-rhythms pounded out on cylindrical drums [by African tribals] is the catalyst of rhythm and blues, rock and roll, and today's heavy metal. It is amazing that the reactions we see at a contemporary rock concert are an exact copy of what happened in the Pinkster celebrations [black festivals in New York] or at Place Congo [black slave dancing in New Orleans] during the Antebellum Period. Any analysis that denies this fact renders the church impoverished in its understanding of the African connection to the rock movement of the 20th century.
>
> In *Stairway to Heaven*, Davin Seay quotes Robert Palmer in *Rolling Stone illustrated History of Rock 'N' Roll*, 'In a very real sense rock was implicit in the music of the first Africans brought to North America. And implicit in their music were centuries of accumulated rites, rituals, and religious fervor. The music of those first brutalized and bewildered slaves, ripped from cultures as old as the Pyramids, those ancient chants and tribal stomps, didn't simply evoke the spirits of the forest gods; they animated and immortalized them' (Davin Seay, *Stairway to Heaven*, New York: Ballantine Books, 1986, p. 11).
>
> Implications such as these lead to a deeper investigation and a focus on the slaves who were brought to the Caribbean Isles. One of the most significant books ever published on this subject is the study done by Maya Deren under

the Guggenheim Foundation in 1953 concerning the history of the African tribal origins of demon gods and voodoo meetings in Haiti. The book *Divine Horseman—The Living Gods of Haiti*, deals with the importation of the slaves from the West coast of Africa to the Caribbean Islands. These slaves were taken from the same tribes from which the slaves in the Colonies were taken: Senegalese, Bambaras, Arades, Congos, Kangas, Fons and Fulas. The first slave shipment to Haiti was in 1510.

As with the Colony slaves, THEY BROUGHT WITH THEM ONLY THEIR WORSHIP OF GODS, THEIR DANCES AND THEIR DRUM BEATS. Eileen Southern states: 'There is no question that Haiti was the central place where African religious traditions ... syncretized with Catholic beliefs and practices to produce vaudou, (voodoo) ... the ceremonies centered upon worship of the snake god Damballa through singing, dancing, and spirit possession' (emphasis added) (Eileen Southern, *The Music of Black Americans*, New York: W.W. Horton, 1983, p. 139).

THEIR RELIGIOUS WORSHIP WAS BASED ON DRUMS AND DANCING, and as they worshipped a god or demon, the ultimate experience was to have their bodies possessed by that demon. The rituals were grossly sensualistic and sadistic. Firmly set in the Caribbean Isles, the practice made its way to the shores of the United States primarily through the city of New Orleans. Historically, slaves from Santo Domingo were brought to the States during the Haitian revolution in 1804, but voodoo probably existed before this because the state of Louisiana imported slaves from the West Indies in 1716, and the practice was also reported in Missouri, Georgia and Florida.

The dances of New Orleans were named for the voodoo gods of the worship rituals. The Samba was dedicated to the god 'simbi,' god of seduction and fertility. The Conga was named after the African demon 'congo.' The Mamba was named after the voodoo priestess who offered sacrifices to the demons during the rituals. Sheldon Rodman, author of *Haiti, the Black Republic*, describes these dances and relates them to the dances of today. It is interesting to note that in the 1981 rock album, *My Life in the Bush of Ghosts*, by Brian Eno and David Byrne, they coaxed African spirits from rock's own dim past. [DWC—This album incorporated African tribal drums with electronic rock]

THE MOST POINTED OBSERVATION MADE IN MAYA DEREN'S BOOK CONCERNS THE DRUMMER, THE RHYTHMS AND THE BEAT. 'Of all the individuals related to ritual activity it is the drummer whose role would seem almost analogous to that of an individual virtuoso ... Haitian ritual drumming requires more explicit craft training and practice than any other ritual activity' (Maya Deren, *Divine Horseman—The Living Gods of Haiti*, New Paltz: McPherson & Co., 1953, p. 233).

She observes that the dancers are forced to salute the drummers first before any other part of the ritual is entered into. It is obvious that without the drum, the ritual cannot progress. What a striking parallel to the modern rock band! The drum set is always center stage, usually elevated behind the lead singer. Without the drummer (or in many cases the bass guitarist), the rock band would cease to exist.

Further, Miss Deren writes that it is 'upon the drummer that the burden falls of integrating the participants into a homogeneous collective. It is the drumming which fuses the fifty or more individuals into a single body, making them move as one, as if all of these singular bodies had become linked on the thread of a single pulse—a pulse which beats ... sending the body into a slow serpentine undulation which begins in the shoulders, then the spine, legs and hips' (Deren, *Divine Horseman*, p. 235).

This description is a remarkable parallel to that which takes place at a modern rock concert. One has only to watch a video of the audience to be convinced. The actions would give an observer the impression that some sort of possession has occurred. Miss Deren goes to some length in her book to describe the inanimate object of the drum as being sacred, even to the place of being 'fed food' and guarded by those attending. 'It is the drums and the drum beats per se, which are the sacred sound' (Deren, *Divine Horseman*, pp. 244-246).

Pearl Primus, long noted for her expertise on the voodoo dance, has said, 'The drummers keep up a terrific throb and beat which very easily takes possession of the sensibilities of the worshippers. Observers say that these drums themselves are able to bring a person to a place where it is easy for the deity (loa) to take possession of their bodies—the defenseless person is buffeted by each stroke as the drummer sets out to 'beat the loa (god) into his head: The person cringes with each large (accented) beat as if the drum mallet descended upon his very skull; he ricochets about the place, clutching blindly at the arms extended to support him' (Lecture, Mount Holyoke College, Holyoke, Massachusetts, Mary E. Wooley Hall, 1953).

There can be no denying that there is a strong relationship between what we have uncovered in demonic Haitian voodoo and its counterpart in the city of New Orleans and other southern cities. THERE IS ALSO NO DENYING THAT THE MODERN ROCK AND ROLL MOVEMENT EVOLVED PARTIALLY FROM SOME OF THE DANCES DESCRIBED EARLIER, PROGRESSING THROUGH A NUMBER OF STAGES: RHUMBA DANCING, RHYTHM AND BLUES, ROCK AND ROLL, DISCO, HEAVY METAL AND PUNK ROCK. There are, of course, other elements that make up the evolution of rock music; however, that is not the issue here. Concerning disco, Miss Southern says, 'The insistent pounding rhythms of disco pushed conventional melody and harmonies into subordinate positions ... in a manner that recalled descriptions of juba reciting to accompany dancing on the plantations in the nineteenth century' (Eileen Southern, *The Music of Black Americans*, New York: Norton and Co., 1983, p. 507). ...

Ruth Tooze and Beatrice Krone in their book relate that 'the same instinct for pulsating rhythms that is found in the negro songs is carried over into their use of instruments ... banjos on the plantations and later in the city where they adapted to the trumpet, clarinet and trombone. With their inate talent for improvisation, a new kind of instrumental music was created—we call it jazz' (Ruth Tooze, Beatrice Krone, *Literature and Music*, Englewood Cliffs: Prentice Hall, 1955, p. 105).

It is irrefutable that rock and roll music owes some of its roots to the tribes of Africa. Every analysis written on the subject acknowledges that its roots are deep in 'jazz' and 'rhythm and blues.' Because of the relationship between American Negro music and the African, they have coined a term that is used considerably today, 'Aframerican music' (*Literature and Music*, p. 102). Joseph Machlis says in his voluminous work, *The Enjoyment of Music*, 'Jazz, by a rough definition-of-thumb is an improvisational, Afro-American musical idiom. It makes use of elements of rhythm, melody and harmony from Africa, and of melody and harmony from the European musical tradition. The influence of jazz, and of closely associated Afro-American idioms has been so pervasive, that by now most of our popular music is in an Afro-American idiom, and elements of jazz have permeated a good deal of our concert music as well' (Joseph Machlis, *The Enjoyment of Music*, New York: W. W. Norton, 1963, p. 597).

To declare that these are the only roots of rock music is to mislead and to be less than honest. A careful study of rock music reveals it to be more complex than that; however, TO DENY THAT AN AFRICAN CONNECTION TO THE ROCK RHYTHMS OF OUR DAY DOES NOT EXIST, IS TO BE EQUALLY MISLEADING AND DISHONEST. To declare that a certain rhythm or beat is 'evil' cannot be proved entirely. What is far more important is the historical revelation that demonic activity has been observed in connection with rituals where drums and rhythmic beats have been the catalyst. That this possibility exists should prove a warning to the church that Satan can and will use anything in his power to turn humanity from the worship of a Holy God to himself in order that he might ultimately fulfill his evil purposes and receive the glory (Leonard J. Seidel, *Face the Music: Contemporary Church Music on Trial*, 1988, p. 34-42).

The connection between rock & roll and voodoo has been noted even by unsaved rock musicians. The British rock session drummer, Rocki (Kwasi Dzidzornu), who has recorded with many famous groups such as the Rolling Stones, Spooky Tooth, and Ginger Baker, understood that the music of Jimi Hendrix was akin to voodoo music. Note the following amazing statement from Hendrix's biography:

> "He [Hendrix] had gotten a chance to see Rocki and some other African musicians on the London scene. He found it a pleasure to play rhythms against their polyrhythms. They would totally get outside, into another kind of space that he had seldom been in before. ... Rocki's father was a voodoo priest and

> the chief drummer of a village in Ghana, West Africa. Rocki's real name was Kwasi Dzidzornu. One of the first things Rocki asked Jimi was where he got that voodoo rhythm from. When Jimi demurred, Rocki went on to explain in his halting English that many of the signature rhythms Jimi played on guitar were very often the same rhythms that his father played in voodoo ceremonies. The way Jimi danced to the rhythms of his playing reminded Rocki of the ceremonial dances to the rhythms his father played to Oxun, the god of thunder and lightning. The ceremony is called voodooshi. As a child in the village, Rocki would carve wooden representatives of the gods. They also represented his ancestors. These were the gods they worshiped. They would jam a lot in Jimi's house. One time they were jamming and Jimi stopped and asked Rocki point-blank, 'You communicate with God, do you?' Rocki said, 'Yes, I communicate with God'" (David Henderson, *'Scuse Me While I Kiss the Sky*, pp. 250,251).

As we have noted, there are proponents of "Christian rock" music who label such an idea "racist." In Hendrix's biography, though (which is NOT written by a Christian), we see that the non-Christian son of an actual voodoo priest sees a direct connection between the music of rock star Jimi Hendrix and idolatrous voodoo. Is the black rock drummer Rocki a racist for making such an observation? His remarks cannot be dismissed conveniently as the ranting of a biblical fundamentalist!

Newsweek magazine noted the African and voodoo music connection in disco rock: "From Latin music, it takes the percolating percussion, its sensuous, throbbing rhythms; from Afro and Cuban music, it repeats simple lyric lines like voodoo chants" (*Newsweek*, April 2, 1979, pp. 58,59).

Well-known rock artist Peter Gabriel has no doubt that there is a direct African connection to rock & roll:

> "There are things like the Bo Diddley rhythm that I've heard beat-for-beat in Congolese patterns. Part of what we consider our fundamental rock and roll heritage originated in Africa. Period" (Peter Gabriel, cited by Timothy White, *Rock Lives*, p. 720).

In a 1982 interview with one of the fathers of rock & roll, Jerry Lee Lewis, researcher Steve Turner asked what power falls on Jerry Lee when he performs. Lewis replied: "The power of voodoo" (Turner, *Hungry for Heaven*, p. 26).

Little Richard, another of rock's fathers, has also testified of this connection:

> "My true belief about Rock 'n' Roll—and there have been a lot of phrases attributed to me over the years—is this: I believe this kind of music is demonic.

> ... A lot of the beats in music today are taken from voodoo, from the voodoo drums. If you study music in rhythms, like I have, you'll see that is true ... I believe that kind of music is driving people from Christ. It is contagious" (Little Richard, quoted by Charles White, *The Life and Times of Little Richard*, p. 197).

It would be a simple matter, I suppose, for a proponent of Christian rock music to discount the testimony of Little Richard, perhaps because of his strange personality and his on again, off again relationship with Christianity. But answer me this: Do the defenders of Christian rock really know more about the character of rock and roll than a man like Little Richard, who was one of its creators?

The Rolling Stones and other rock & roll groups have recorded tribal and voodoo occultic drumming ceremonies and incorporated these into their rock music. The Stones' *Goat's Head Soup* album contained such recordings, including the screams of voodoo adherents becoming possessed by *loa* or evil spirits. John Lennon said rock & roll gets through to people because of its voodoo beat: "Because it is primitive enough and has no bull, really, the best stuff, and it gets through to you its beat. Go to the jungle and they have the rhythm and it goes throughout the world and it's as simple as that" (Lennon, *Rolling Stone*, Feb. 12, 1976, p 100). "Tony Sanchez, who traveled with the Stones for many years and who wrote a book about them, described the music at their infamous concert at Altamonte as "pounding voodoo drumming and primitive shrieks" (Sanchez, *Up and Down with the Rolling Stones*, p. 184). In 1981, Brian Eno and David Byrne recorded *My Life in the Bush of Ghosts*, which incorporated satanic African ceremonies with rock and roll. Malcolm McLaren incorporated Zulu tribal music into his 1983 *Duck Rock* album.

7. Didn't Luther use tavern music?

Most books in support of Contemporary Christian Music justify the use of rock music because of Martin Luther's alleged use of secular tavern songs, but this is based on an inaccurate view of Luther's music. In reality, what Luther did is nothing like what Christian rockers are doing today. The following are some of the serious differences between Luther's music and CCM. (A excellent overview of this is found in *Measuring the Music* by John Makujina, chapter 7.)

<u>First, Luther was extremely conscious of the danger of using the world's music and warned that music has the power for good or evil</u>. Note the following quote: "For whether you wish to comfort the sad, to terrify the happy, to encourage the despairing, to humble the proud, to calm the passionate, or to appease those full of hate . . . what more effective means than music could you find?" (Luther, "Preface to Georg Rhau's Symphoniae Iucundae," translated by Ulrich S. Leopold, in *Luther's Works*, vol. 53, 323). He warns that music is "a mistress and governess of those human emotions . . .

which govern men or more often overwhelm them" (Ibid.). Thus it is obvious that Luther did not hold the CCM philosophy that music is neutral and without inherent moral qualities.

Second, though Luther adopted things from secular music, he did so only with extreme caution. Luther carefully changed the music to fit the Christian message. Of his 37 chorales, only one came directly from a secular song, and it was later replaced by a new tune he had written himself. "By avoiding dance tunes and 'de-rhythming' other songs, Luther achieved a chorale with a marked rhythm, but without the devices that would remind the people of the secular world. ... Luther chose only those tunes which would best lend themselves to sacred themes and avoided the vulgar, 'rollicking drinking songs' and dance tunes. ... He carefully tested the melodies he considered, and when necessary molded them into suitability" (Robert Harrell, *Martin Luther: His Music, His Message,* 1980). "He was not content to accept anything uncritically: he was jealous of congruity between the theme of the verse and the spirit of the music. He carefully tested the propriety for their purpose of the melodies he considered, and where necessary molded them into suitability" (Millar Patrick, *The Story of the Church's Song*, p. 74). "Rollicking drinking songs were available in the 16th century too. Luther steered clear of them. He never considered music a mere tool that could be employed regardless of its original association but was careful to match text and tune, so that each text would have its own proper tune and so that both would complement each other" (Ulrich Leupold, an authority on Luther, "Learning from Luther?" *Journal of Church Music*, July-August 1996, p. 5). "It is perhaps in his selectivity of rhythm that we notice the seldom-acknowledged conservatism of Luther. In order for the congregation to sing in unison, a song had to contain some form of rhythm. The plainsong (Gregorian chant), however, lacked the necessary rhythm. On the other hand, dance songs and drinking songs produced a rhythm far too intense and definite for Luther's purposes. Therefore, it is believed that in developing his chorales, Luther managed to discard dance songs altogether and limit the rhythm in other songs" (Makujina, *Measuring the Music*, p. 192).

Third, though Luther wanted to write spiritual songs that were pleasing to young people, he was careful to wean them away from every type of fleshly music. "And these songs were arranged in four parts to give the young—who should at any rate be trained in music and other fine arts—something *to wean them away from love ballads and carnal songs and to teach them something of value in their place*, thus combining the good with the pleasing, as is proper for youth" (emphasis added) (Martin Luther, "Preface to the Wittenberg Hymnal," in *Luther's Works*, vol. 53, p. 316). This is certainly not what we see in CCM! Not only does CCM itself develop worldly appetites in music by uncritically adopting the same, but most of the CCM musicians are hooked directly into secular rock music in their daily lives. We have documented this extensively in the section on the worldliness of rock music.

8. Isn't the issue of music just a matter of different tastes?

There are subjective areas in music, but this is not to say there are no biblical guidelines about music. Everything is to be tested by the Bible. Colossians 3:16 tells us what type of music pleases the Lord. Spiritual songs are not the same as unspiritual, hymns are not the same as rock music, melody is not the same as raucous noise. The Bible also gives instruction about the Christian's affiliation with worldly things, and music which draws the child of God to the world is to be rejected. Further, the Bible gives instruction about the Christian's relationship with doctrinal error, and music which contains the same is to be avoided. Preference refers to personal likes and dislikes. We are not supposed to live like that in our Christian lives. Everything must be brought into subjection to God, and the world, the flesh, and the devil are to be rejected (2 Cor. 10:5; Eph. 4:22-24; Col. 3:3-5).

9. Doesn't the Bible encourage us to use cymbals and stringed instruments and loud sounding instruments?

Yes, but an instrument can be used properly or improperly. Cymbals and stringed instruments are used both in orchestras and in rock bands, but they are used very differently. Stringed instruments can be electrified and used to speak rebellion and to stir up sensual passions, and stringed instruments can also be used to speak peace to troubled souls (1 Samuel 16:23).

10. What is wrong with "soft rock"?

Many Christians who would not listen to "hard rock" nevertheless fill their minds with "soft rock." But is soft rock really innocent and proper for a child of God? Is soft rock a godly influence? Following are six warnings against it.

<u>First, the message of the "soft rock" is often as immoral as that of hard rock</u>. From its earliest days, free sex has been one of the themes that has permeated all of rock music, soft, hard, pop, metal, you name it. It promotes sensual, lustful relationships that are not grounded in marriage. The "love" that is the theme of so much of rock music, is not love at all by God's standards; it is lust. It is very dangerous to allow one's mind to dwell on such things. "But fornication, and all uncleanness, or covetousness, let it not be once named among you, as becometh saints" (Ephesians 5:3).

<u>Second, even soft rock uses sensual "sexy rhythms" that appeal to the flesh</u>. Dr. David Elkind, Chairman, Department of Child Study, Tufts University, warned: "There is a

great deal of powerful sexual stimulation in the rhythm of rock music." Certain kind of rhythms produce certain effects on people. In his history of music in Memphis, Tennessee, author Larry Nager observed that "...the forbidden pleasures of Beale Street had always come wrapped in the PULSING RHYTHMS of the blues" (Larry Nager, *Memphis Beat*). That part of Beale Street near the river was infamous for its bars, gambling dens, and houses of prostitution. Those are the forbidden pleasures referred to by Nager. It is not happenstance that those wicked activities were accompanied by certain types of rhythms. And those old blues and boogie woogie rhythms were not always loud and boisterous. Like rock music, there were soft blues as well as hard. Famous bluesman Robert Johnson knew that his music had a licentious affect on women. He said, "This sound [the blues] affected most women in a way that I could never understand." B.B. King, one of the most famous of the bluesmen, made the same observation in his autobiography: "The women reacted with their bodies flowing to a rhythm coming out of my guitar..." (B.B. King, *Blues All Around Me*). These unsaved blues musicians admit that certain rhythms are sexy. This is a loud warning to those who have ears to hear. "For the flesh lusteth against the Spirit, and the Spirit against the flesh: and these are contrary the one to the other: so that ye cannot do the things that ye would" (Gal. 5:17).

<u>Third by listening to soft rock, one develops an appetite, an addiction, for pop music</u>. Like all appetites, this one is never content. "Hell and destruction are never full; so the eyes of man are never satisfied" (Prov. 27:20).

<u>Fourth, soft rock is a dangerous bridge to the worldly things that permeate the world of rock and roll</u>. "Love not the world, neither the things that are in the world. If any man love the world, the love of the Father is not in him. For all that is in the world, the lust of the flesh, and the lust of the eyes, and the pride of life, is not of the Father, but is of the world. And the world passeth away, and the lust thereof: but he that doeth the will of God abideth for ever" (1 John 2:15-17).

<u>Fifth, the listener has to sort through the huge amount of garbage in pop music to find a few relatively innocent songs</u>. Is this a safe and wise use of this short earthly life? "See then that ye walk circumspectly, not as fools, but as wise, Redeeming the time, because the days are evil. Wherefore be ye not unwise, but understanding what the will of the Lord is" (Ephesians 5:15-17).

Steve Peters, who does not believe all rock & roll is wrong for Christians, nevertheless makes the following important admission: "Just about the time I think I've found a good-clean-acceptable secular musician, they blow it on their next album or tour. And if I have recommended them, suddenly I find myself scrambling to tell thousands of teens who know—I WAS WRONG" (*The Truth about Rock*, p. 90). We would remind

Mr. Peters that he will never undo all the damage he has caused by recommending, even hesitatingly, secular rock. Such recommendations by Christian authority figures are a bright green signal to young people that it is alright to explore the filthy world of rock. VERY few of them will be as cautious about what they listen to as Mr. Peters is.

<u>Sixth, we must be concerned about our influence on others</u>. If I allow myself to listen to "soft rock," it is possible that my influence will encourage others to listen to music that is worse. If a parent, for example, listens to "soft rock," how can he or she consistently and effectively warn young people about the dangers of rock music in general? "All things are lawful for me, but all things are not expedient: all things are lawful for me, but all things edify not. Let no man seek his own, but every man another's wealth. . . . Give none offence, neither to the Jews, nor to the Gentiles, nor to the church of God" (1 Cor. 10:23,24,31). "It is good neither to eat flesh, nor to drink wine, nor any thing whereby thy brother stumbleth, or is offended, or is made weak" (Rom. 14:21).

11. If we assume that Christian rock is demonic, why would the Devil sing about Jesus Christ and the things of God?

Religion has always been one of the Devil's favorite tools. Since the days of the Apostles, the Devil has had thousands of preachers who use the Bible and preach about God and Jesus (Matt. 7:15-23; 2 Corinthians 11:1-10; 2 Peter 2:1; 1 John 2:18-19). The Lord Jesus Christ warned that the end times would be characterized by the multiplicity of false teachers (Matt. 24:11,24). The Devil uses false religion to confuse people and to draw them away from the truth. This is precisely what he is doing with Christian rock music. Through it people are being drawn away from sound Bible doctrine to the ecumenical movement and all of its heresies.

In Acts 16 we have an example of how the Devil will use the name of Jesus and will even preach the truth for his own perverted purposes. A demon-possessed girl followed Paul and his co-workers for many days crying: "These men are the servants of the most high God, which shew unto us the way of salvation" (Acts 16:16-17). Everything the girl said under the power of the demonic influence was absolutely true, but the Bible says Paul was grieved with this and he cast out the demon and stopped her witness. The truth when given in a context of demonic delusion does not glorify God, but produces great confusion. If Paul had not stopped the girl, the people would have thought that her idolatrous, demonic religion was also true and safe for them to follow. The same is true for Christian rock music. Since multitudes of pastors are allowing the use of rock music in the service of Jesus Christ and are not warning about it, an entire generation is growing up with the idea that it is proper and safe to fellowship with the world and to enjoy the things of the world.

12. Didn't God create all music?

God did create music, but the world is no longer in the pristine spiritual condition in which He made it. Man has sinned against God and has created a world in rebellion against Him and against His laws. The Devil is called the god of this world (2 Corinthians 11:4; Ephesians 2:1-2; 1 John 5:19), and there can be no doubt that the god of this world is intimately involved in helping wicked men create music which will satisfy their illicit lusts.

13. Christians are not supposed to judge, are they?

It is absolutely wrong to say that Christians are not supposed to judge as a blanket statement. The Bible forbids certain types of judging and commends other types of judging. The Lord Jesus forbade hypocritical judging in Matthew 7:1-5, but He commended judging false teachers in Matthew 7:15. Romans 14:4-5 warns us not to judge one another in matters of Christian liberty such as in diet and the keeping of holy days, but Romans 14:13 says we are to judge whether or not we are causing our brother to stumble. In 1 Corinthians 14:29 God's people are commanded to judge preaching. Anytime the Word of God is preached or taught, God's people are to test it carefully. This is judging. In Ephesians 5:11 Christians are commanded to reprove the works of darkness. That involves judging. Paul judged Peter and reproved him publicly (Galatians 2:11-14). Paul judged the sin at the church of Corinth (1 Corinthians 5:3). Paul said Christians will judge the world and angels and should therefore judge things in the church (1 Corinthians 6:1-5). Philippians 1:9 says Christian love involves judgment.

14. Aren't Christians only supposed to love? Love is more important than doctrine and standards of living, isn't it?

When Bible-believing Christians take the Word of God and measure leaders, churches, denominations and movements today by it, ecumenical types invariably charge them with a lack of love. A woman recently wrote to me and said:

> "You preach separatism. What about unity? You preach about heresy. WHAT ABOUT LOVE? ... From what I have viewed on your website, you hold your views as high as the Bible itself. What you call 'zeal for the Bible' I call arrogance and pride. If you knew the Bible as well as you claim, then I believe you'd live it. The lost will never be reached through such hatred" (Letter from a reader, May 1997).

This lady was upset about our preaching, but instead of explaining our alleged error carefully from the Bible, she charges us with a lack of love, and this, in spite of her own haughty and incredibly judgmental attitude! To this brainwashed generation, the negative aspects of biblical Christianity are unloving. To carefully test things by the Bible is unloving. To mark and avoid false teachers is hatemongering. To preach high and holy standards of Christian living is legalism. To warn of false gospels and discipline heretics is mean-spirited.

A few years ago, Evangelist Jack Van Impe rejected biblical separatism and went over to the ecumenical philosophy. He said: "Let's forget our labels and come together in love, and the pope has called for that. I had 400 verses on love. Till I die I will proclaim nothing but love for all my brothers and sisters in Christ, my Catholic brothers and sisters, Protestant brothers and sisters, Christian Reformed, Lutherans, I don't care what label you are. By this shall all men know that ye are my disciples if ye have love one to another."

This is the popular view of love, but it is false and dangerous.

ECUMENISTS ARE CONFUSED ABOUT THE DEFINITION OF LOVE. Love is crucial. The Bible says that without love "I am become as sounding brass, or a tinkling cymbal." The Bible tells us that God is love, and those who know God will reflect His love. What is love, though? The ecumenical world is confused about the definition of love. It must be defined biblically. "Love," to human thinking, is a warm feeling or a sensual romantic thought. "Love," to this ecumenical generation, is broadmindedness and non-judgmental tolerance of any one who claims to know the Lord Jesus Christ. This is not what the Bible says about love. Consider the following verses of Holy Scripture:

> "Jesus answered and said unto him, IF A MAN LOVE ME, HE WILL KEEP MY WORDS: and my Father will love him, and we will come unto him, and make our abode with him" (John 14:23).

> "And this I pray, that your LOVE MAY ABOUND YET MORE AND MORE IN KNOWLEDGE AND IN ALL JUDGMENT; That ye may approve things that are excellent; that ye may be sincere and without offence till the day of Christ" (Philippians 1:9-10).

> "For THIS IS THE LOVE OF GOD, THAT WE KEEP HIS COMMANDMENTS: and his commandments are not grievous" (1 John 5:3).

> "And we have confidence in the Lord touching you, that ye both do and will do the things which WE COMMAND YOU. And the Lord direct your hearts into THE LOVE OF GOD, and into the patient waiting for Christ. Now WE COMMAND YOU, brethren, in the name of our Lord Jesus Christ, that ye withdraw yourselves from every brother that walketh disorderly, and not after the tradition which he received of us (2 Th. 3:4-6).

Biblical love is obedience to God and His Word. We see in the last passage cited that the love of God is sandwiched between two verses which emphasize obedience to God's commandments, including separation from disobedient brethren! Love is not a feeling. It is not blissful romanticism. For a woman to love her husband means she submits to and serves him according to the Bible. For a man to love his wife means he treats her in the way the Bible commands. For children to love their parents means they honor and obey their parents as the Bible commands. Love is obedience to God's Word.

Christian love is not an emotion, though emotion is closely associated with it. It is not broadmindedness. It is not non-judgmentalism. It is not non-critical acceptance and tolerance of things that are wrong. Biblical love is careful. It is based on knowledge and judgment from God's Word. It proves all things, and it approves only those things that reflect the will of God.

Was the Lord Jesus Christ unloving when He called Peter a Devil (Matt. 16:23) or when he publicly condemned the Pharisees (Matthew 23)? Was the Apostle Paul unloving when he rebuked Peter publicly for his compromise (Galatians 1)? Was the Apostle Paul unloving when he named the name of false teachers and compromisers such as Hymenaeus and Alexander ten different times in the Pastoral Epistles? Was the Apostle Paul unloving when he forbade women to preach or to usurp authority over men (1 Timothy 2)?

Biblical love does not mean that I ignore things that people do that are wrong and injurious. This is true both in the physical and spiritual realms. For example, to love a murderer, in a biblical sense, does not mean that we ignore his crime. It means that we put him to death for his horrible trespass against the image of God (Genesis 9:5-6). Likewise, to love a false teacher does not mean that I turn a blind eye to his error and strive to have unity with him regardless of his doctrine. It means that I obey the Bible and mark and avoid him (Romans 16:17), that I expose his error publicly to protect those who might be led astray by his teaching.

ECUMENISTS ARE CONFUSED ABOUT THE DIRECTION OF LOVE. Ecumenists are incredibly confused about the definition of love, but they are also confused about the direction of love. *THE FIRST DIRECTION OF LOVE MUST BE TOWARD GOD.* When discussing these matters, ecumenists talk much about love of man, but they talk very little about the love of God. According to the Lord Jesus Christ, though, what is the greatest commandment?

> "Then one of them, which was a lawyer, asked him a question, tempting him, and saying, Master, which is the great commandment in the law? Jesus said unto him, Thou shalt love the Lord thy God with all thy heart, and with all thy soul, and with all thy mind. This is the first and great commandment. And the

second is like unto it, Thou shalt love thy neighbour as thyself" (Matthew 22:35-39).

The first and great commandment is not to love one's neighbor. That is the second commandment. The first and great commandment is to love the Lord God with all the heart, soul, and mind.

Ecumenists point their fingers at the Bible-believing Fundamentalist and charge him with a lack of love toward men because he exercises judgment and discipline and separation. What, though, about love for God and His Word? The Ecumenist tells me that I need to love all the denominations regardless of what doctrine they teach. I reply that I need to love God and His Truth first, and that means that I will obey the Bible, and that means I will measure, mark, and avoid those who are committed to error. A genuine love for God requires that I care more about His Word and His will than about men and their feelings and opinions and programs.

THE DIRECTION OF LOVE NOT ONLY MUST BE TOWARD GOD BUT IT MUST BE TOWARD THOSE WHO ARE IN DANGER. The ecumenical crowd tells me that I need to love the Modernist and the Romanist, etc., but they are practically silent on the subject of love for those who are deceived by the Modernists and the Romanists. We are charged with being unloving, for example, when we expose the fact that John Paul II or Mother Teresa teaches a false sacramental gospel. This is nonsense. The fact is, we love people enough to warn of false gospels so they will not be led astray to eternal Hell. A shepherd who loves wolves more than the sheep is a confused and wicked shepherd.

15. Since God looks on the heart, why are you concerned about appearance?

It is true that God looks on the heart, but the same passage of Scripture also reminds us that man looks on the outward appearance (1 Samuel 16:7). The Christian must be concerned about how his appearance influences others.

Further, God's Word has something to say about man's dress and appearance. When Adam and Eve sinned, one of the first things God did was clothe them properly (Genesis 3:21). Before man sinned his mind was pure and his nakedness was not a problem, but after he sinned his mind became fallen and impure, and in this sinful world steps must be taken to avoid sinful temptations. The Bible forbids a man or woman to look upon the nakedness of someone other than one's own wife or husband (Leviticus 18,20). Therefore it is wrong before God to dress in such a manner that our bodies are displayed to the view of others. The Bible identifies nakedness even as the revealing of the thigh of the leg (Isaiah 47:2,3).

A person can be right in his external appearance and not be right with God in his heart, but when a person is right with God internally he or she will be concerned about dressing modestly.

16. Isn't Christianity all about grace?

Grace is certainly at the heart of Christianity. The true Gospel is called "the grace of Christ" (Galatians 1:6). The grace of God, though, does not produce license; it produces holiness and a zeal for good works.

> "For THE GRACE OF GOD that bringeth salvation hath appeared to all men, TEACHING US THAT, DENYING UNGODLINESS AND WORLDLY LUSTS, WE SHOULD LIVE SOBERLY, RIGHTEOUSLY, AND GODLY, IN THIS PRESENT WORLD; Looking for that blessed hope, and the glorious appearing of the great God and our Saviour Jesus Christ; Who gave himself for us, that he might redeem us from all iniquity, and purify unto himself a peculiar people, zealous of good works" (Titus 2:11-14).

The grace of God teaches men to deny worldly lusts. The "grace" so frequently mentioned by Contemporary Christian Music performers is not biblical grace because it does not produce separation from worldliness. It does not produce peculiar people; it produces worldly people.

17. Kids today aren't listening to traditional Christian music; shouldn't we use rock to reach them?

<u>First, the lost are reached not through music but through the preaching of the Gospel</u>. Nowhere in the Bible do we find that music is for evangelism.

<u>Second, obedience to God does not allow us to use the world's music or methods</u> (Romans 12:1-2; etc.). God is never pleased with disobedience to His Word. As we saw in Question #2, even sincere disobedience is displeasing to God.

<u>Third, the Apostles did not use the entertainment of the world to reach the world</u>. Nowhere do we see Paul attracting people to his preaching through worldly means. The Word of God calls people to holiness, and it is foolish and deceitful to use unholy things to draw people to a holy Christ.

<u>Fourth, what you win people with, you win them to</u>. If people are won through worldly things, how could they ever be expected to separate from the world as the Word of God demands? They can't. Those who are reached through New Evangelicalism, usually become New Evangelical; or, through Pentecostalism, usually become Pentecostal.

Those who are reached through a tainted gospel and unscriptural doctrine usually cleave to those things. What people are won with, they are won to.

18. Making rules and standards about music and clothing, etc., is Pharisaical legalism, isn't it?

"Legalism" is a term frequently used to describe Bible-believing Christians who are zealous for pure doctrine and who desire to maintain holy standards of living in this wicked hour. This "free thinking" attitude was expressed at a "Christian" rock concert called Greenbelt '83: "We don't believe in a fundamentalist approach. We don't set ground rules. Our teaching is non-directive. We want to encourage people to make their own choices." Those who have this type of unscriptural mindset label the old-fashioned Bible Christian as a "legalist" or a "Pharisee."

Note, though, that the Pharisee's error was not his love for the truth and his zeal for Bible righteousness. The Pharisee did not love the truth; he loved tradition (Mt. 15:1-9). If the Pharisee had loved the truth, he would have loved Jesus Christ (Jn. 8:47)! The Pharisee did not love God's righteousness; he loved his own self-righteousness (Lk. 18:9-14). The Pharisee did not have a zeal for God; he had a zeal for his own false religion (Mt. 23:15). To call the fundamental Bible-believing Christian who is saved by the grace of Jesus Christ and who loves the precious Word of God a Pharisee is a wicked slander.

True legalism has a two-fold definition: (1) It is mixing works with grace for salvation (Galatians). (2) It is adding human tradition to the Word of God. The Pharisees committed both of these errors. They taught that the way of salvation was by the keeping of the law, and they made their uninspired tradition authoritative over people's lives without a biblical basis.

For a Bible preacher to proclaim that God's people are to obey the details of God's Word is not legalism; it is faithfulness to God (Matt. 28:20; 2 Tim. 4:1-2; Titus 2:15).

Strict obedience to God's Word is the way of liberty, not bondage (John 8:31-32).

19. Don't 1 Corinthians 6:12 and 10:23 teach that the Christian has liberty in how he lives?

Consider those verses in their context:

> 1 Corinthians 6:12-13 — "All things are lawful unto me, but all things are not expedient: all things are lawful for me, but I will not be brought under the

> power of any. Meats for the belly, and the belly for meats: but God shall destroy both it and them. Now the body is not for fornication, but for the Lord; and the Lord for the body."
>
> 1 Corinthians 10:23-24 — "All things are lawful for me, but all things are not expedient: all things are lawful for me, but all things edify not. Let no man seek his own, but every man another's wealth."

These verses are frequently misused by those who desire liberty to fulfill their carnal desires. These would have us believe that the Apostle Paul is saying the Christian has liberty to wear immodest clothing, watch indecent movies, go to the beach half naked, listen to wicked rock music, and to fellowship with anyone who says he "loves Jesus" regardless of his doctrinal beliefs, etc. Is that what the Holy Spirit through Paul meant by the statement "all things are lawful unto me"? By no means! Obviously there are limitations on the Christian's liberty. The New Testament Scriptures, in fact, put great limits upon our "liberty." We are not free to commit fornication (1 Cor. 6:16-18; 1 Thess. 4:3-6), nor to be involved in any sort of uncleanness (1 Thess. 4:7), nor to fellowship with the unfruitful works of darkness (Eph. 5:11), nor to be drunk with wine (Eph. 5:18), nor to allow any corrupt communication to proceed out of our mouths (Eph. 4:29), nor to allow any filthiness of the flesh or spirit (2 Cor. 7:1), nor to be involved in something which has even the appearance of evil (1 Thess. 5:22), nor to love the things that are in the world (1 John 2:15-17), nor to befriend the world (James 4:4), nor to dress immodestly (1 Tim. 2:9), etc. What, then, did the Apostle mean when he said all things are lawful? He meant that the Christian has been set free by the blood of Christ, free from the wages of sin, free from the condemnation of the law, free from the ceremonies of the Mosaic covenant, but not free to sin or to disobey the Bible, not free to do anything which is not expedient or edifying. He explains himself perfectly in both passages. In 1 Corinthians 6:12-13 he uses the example of eating meat. In 1 Corinthians 8:1-13 and 10:23-28 he uses the example of eating things which have been offered to idols. In all such things, the Christian is free. There are no dietary restrictions for the New Testament Christian as there were under the Mosaic law. We do not have to fear idols; we know they are nothing. This is the type of thing Paul is referring to in 1 Corinthians, if we allow him to explain himself in the very context of the statements, rather than attempt to put some strange meaning upon his words which would fill the Bible with contradiction. He addresses exactly the same thing in Romans chapter 14. The Christian is free from laws about eating and keeping holy days (Rom. 14:2-6). We are not to judge one another in these matters. This does not mean we can't judge anything and that we are free to do whatever we please. Such a philosophy is obviously contrary to the entire tenor of the New Testament and is an appalling perversion of these passages.

FOUR TESTS FOR CHRISTIAN ACTIVITIES

In the two passages we have previously cited in Corinthians Paul gives four tests to determine whether the Christian should allow a certain thing in his life: (1) Does it bring me under its power? (2) Is it expedient? (3) Does it edify? (4) Does it help or hinder my fellow man, does it cause my fellow man to stumble? Again, these are tests which are applied not to sinful things which already are forbidden to the Christian, but to things the Bible does not specifically address. The sincere application of these tests to things commonly allowed in the world of popular Christianity would put a quick stop to many practices. Rock music does bring people under its power; it does not spiritually edify; it is influenced by demons (a simple study of the history of rock music will confirm this) and is not therefore expedient for the Christian who is instructed to be sober and vigilant against the wiles of the Devil. It appeals to the flesh which the Christian is supposed to crucify. Immodest clothing, such as shorts and bathing suits and short skirts, does hinder our fellow man by putting before him a temptation to sin in his thought life; it does not edify those who see us clothed in such a fashion; it does cause others to stumble. Ecumenical relationships between those who believe sound New Testament doctrine and those who do not, hinder my fellow man and cause him to stumble by confusing him about what is true and what is false Christianity, by giving him the impression that doctrine is not important. Such relationships are not edifying because they weaken the believer's spiritual discernment and zeal for the faith once delivered to the saints.

The Bible says we have liberty in Christ, liberty from eternal condemnation, liberty to serve Christ and to enjoy our unspeakably wonderful salvation in Christ, but not liberty to sin, not liberty to do whatever we please with our lives, not liberty to do anything which is not expedient or edifying. The Apostle Paul had such a low view of "personal liberty" that he was willing to forego the eating of meat for the rest of his life if he thought that such eating would offend his brother or cause his brother to stumble (1 Cor. 8:13). He did not have the idea that he was in this world to live as he pleased. Contrast this view of Christian liberty with that which is so popular today. Those who are consumed with their "liberty" will not forego even highly questionable things such as rock music for the sake of glorifying Christ and edifying their fellow man. When confronted with such things, they become puffed up and lash out against a straw man they call "legalism."

20. David danced before the Lord and Psalm 150:4 says we are to praise God with dance. Why are you, therefore, against dancing in churches today?

<u>First, there are two types of dancing mentioned in the Bible: worldly dancing and spiri-</u>

tual dancing. Worldly dancing is practiced by men and women together and is associated with sin and immorality (Ex. 32:19; Job 21:7,11-12; 1 Sam. 30:16; Mt. 14:6). Spiritual dancing is practiced privately or with members of the same sex before the Lord (Ex. 15:20-21; Jud. 11:34; 21:21; 1 Sam. 18:6; 2 Sam. 6:14).

Second, the dancing done by God's people in the Old Testament was completely different from that of the heathen. There are different Hebrew words for these types of dancing. The Hebrew word in Psalm 150:4 is "MACHOWL," which refers to round dancing. The word is translated dance in reference to Israel's dancing in Psalm 30:11; 149:3; Jer. 31:13 and Lam. 5:15. This Hebrew word is never used for heathen dancing. One word used to describe the dancing of the heathen is "CHUWL," which means "to twist or whirl (in a circular or spiral manner), i.e. (specifically) to dance, to writhe in pain (especially of parturition) or fear." This word is found in 58 verses, but it is only translated dance in Judges 21:21 and 23. Elsewhere it is translated "anguish" (Deut. 2:25), "wounded" (1 Chron. 10:3), "grieved" (Esther 4:4), "travaileth" (Job 15:20), "shaketh" (Psalm 29:8), "pained" (Psalm 55:4), etc. Thus it is never used to describe Israel's dancing. Another Hebrew word for dance is "RAQAD." It means "to stamp, i.e. to spring about (wildly or for joy):—dance, jump, leap, skip." It is translated dance three times, in 1 Chron. 15:29 (David's dancing), Job 21:11 (the dancing of the children of the wicked), and Isaiah 13:21 (satyrs dancing). This is the one exception to the rule that different Hebrew words are used to describe the dancing of Israel and that of the heathen. Another Hebrew word for dancing is "CHAGAG." It means "to move in a circle, i.e. (specifically) to march in a sacred procession, to observe a festival; by implication, to be giddy:—celebrate, dance, (keep, hold) a (solemn) feast (holiday), reel to and fro." It is used in 14 verses, but it is usually translated "feast" or "celebrate." It is only translated dance one time, in 1 Sam. 30:16 (dancing of the Amalekites). A final Hebrew word translated dance is "KARAR." This is the Hebrew word translated dance in 2 Sam. 6:14 and 16, describing David's dancing before the Lord, and it is not used in any other passage.

God has strictly commanded Israel that they were not to follow the way of the heathen. They were to be different from the pagan people around them who worshipped idols. "And ye shall not walk in the manners of the nation, which I cast out before you: for they committed all these things, and therefore I abhorred them. But I have said unto you, Ye shall inherit their land, and I will give it unto you to possess it, a land that floweth with milk and honey: I am the Lord your God, which have separated you from other people. . . . And ye shall be holy unto me: for I the Lord am holy, and have severed you from other people, that ye should be mine" (Lev. 20:23-26).

To apply this to our day, it means that Christians must be separate from the world (Romans 12:1-2). We must not conform ourselves to the world's sensual ways, such as their lascivious styles of dancing. Yet if you go to a Christian rock concert, the type of dancing that you see is exactly the same as that of the world. The CCM group Super Chicks is an illustration. The girls dance in a sensual fashion. Kirk Franklin and Mary-Mary are two other examples. They dress inappropriately and dance just like the world. There is no justification for this in the Bible.

<u>Third, Psalm 150 is not a command that every person dance, any more than Psalm 69 is a commandment for Christians to curse their enemies</u>. "Add iniquity unto their iniquity: and let them not come into thy righteousness. Let them be blotted out of the book of the living, and not be written with the righteous" (Psalm 69:27, 28). Most of the things Israel did, we do not do today in the church age. This includes circumcision of baby boys, priests and offerings, temple worship, dietary restrictions, sabbath laws, religious festivals, multiple tithing, and many other things. We determine what part of the Old Testament to keep by comparing it with the New Testament. And there is no instance of dancing in the New Testament.

Jesus didn't dance. The Apostles didn't dance. There was no dancing in the first churches.

The dancing in the Old Testament was associated with God's kingdom (Ps. 149:3; 150:4; Jer. 31:4,13). The reason no dancing is mentioned in the New Testament is probably because this is the period of Christ's rejection and exile. The Bridegroom is away in a far country (Mt. 9:14-15). Contrast this with Rev. 19:7, the marriage of the Lamb. Then will come the time to "be glad and rejoice," and the joyful dancing referred to in Psalm 149 and 150 and Jeremiah 31 will begin! Even so, come Lord Jesus. When the kingdom of God comes again to this earth at the return of Christ, we will dance then, and it will be the right type of dancing.

21. Why do you say that the Pentecostal-Charismatic movement is unscriptural?

An analysis of the Pentecostal-Charismatic movement is beyond the scope of this book, but we have addressed the matter in detail in our 1998 book "The Laughing Revival from Azusa to Pensacola." This is available from Way of Life Literature, http://www.wayoflife.org.

22. By preaching against Christian rock aren't you are hurting people and hindering the ministries of CCM musicians?

Petra's spokesman, Bob Hartman, complains that preaching against Christian rock music is hurtful:

> "It hurts us when some senior pastor says to his youth leader, 'Don't go to this concert.' ... Not only does it deny the kids the opportunity and encouragement to go to the concert, but it hurts terribly our ability to minister. We experience a lot more skepticism" (Hartman, cited by Brian Newcomb, "Petra's Battle," *CCM Magazine*, October 1987).

I can understand why a Christian rocker like Hartman would think like this, but I see it differently.

First, I would reply to him and to other Christian rockers that as a preacher I have a responsibility to deliver the message I believe God has given me. It is not popular to preach against Contemporary Christian Music, even in some fundamental Baptist circles today. I believe a man would have to be certifiably insane to preach against CCM unless he is convinced God gave him this message. I have prayed diligently about the matter of music and whether or not I should resist CCM. I have examined this issue and re-examined it throughout the 25 years I have been saved. As I said at the beginning of this book, I do have a background in music. I played first chair first clarinet during much of my junior and senior high school years. I took private music lessons, won first place ribbons at music competitions both for solos and as a participant in ensembles, was selected to attend a special summer music program at the University of South Florida between my 10th and 11th grades, and had an opportunity to join a symphony orchestra. I also immersed myself in rock music for at least 10 years before I was saved. When I began an intense study into the subject of CCM in recent months, I did so, I believe, with an open mind to obey whatever the Lord showed me. I was willing to re-evaluate my long-standing position against Christian rock, but my concerns were only strengthened and I am more convinced than ever that I must preach against CCM. I understand how difficult it is to be the brunt of preaching, but the man of God is responsible to preach his message regardless of what the hearers think.

Second, if I am right about Christian rock music and it *IS* worldly and unacceptable to God, it is crucial that people hear this message so they can have opportunity to be warned about something which is hurtful to their spiritual well-being and also to the spiritual well-being of the churches.

Third, staying totally away from rock music has never hurt anyone spiritually, but loving it has definitely hurt multitudes. Even if preachers like me are wrong in our assessment of CCM and even if we draw the line against rock music a little too sharply, those who heed our warning will not be hurt by strictly avoiding rock music. It is like alcohol. No one ever became an alcoholic by avoiding alcoholic beverages altogether, but many have been deeply injured by alcohol who thought they could handle it in moderation. Can the Christian rocker promise that young people who are influenced by his music and example will not be drawn into the Devil's snare through entanglement with rock and roll? Can he promise that the young people he draws to rock music will not go on to become addicted to ever more vile forms of rock? Can he promise that they will not be enticed by the licentious lifestyle and rebellious demeanor of secular rock and roll?

23. What about all the young people who are being saved through CCM?

Promoters of Christian rock music claim that the bottom line is that God is blessing it and that many young people are saved through it. Hard rocking Mylon LeFevre claims that tens of thousands have signed decisions cards at his concerts:

> "There are 52,000 people who have signed a little card that says, 'Tonight, for the first time, I understand who Jesus is and how He does things, and I want Him to be my Lord'" (LeFevre, cited by John Styll, "Mylon LeFevre: The Solid Rocker," *CCM Magazine*, March 1986).

This is an amazing statistic by any standard, especially in light of the fact that LeFevre admits that he did not get right with God until 1980 and the aforementioned statement was made in 1986.

Many other CCM performers claim that people are being saved through their ministries. The book *Soul 2 Soul* contains salvation testimonies from CCM groups such as 4 HIM and dc Talk. They claim that people have even been rescued from committing suicide through their music.

I am thankful for every soul who is saved and blessed regardless of whether or not we agree in all matters with those involved. I do believe that some CCM groups are genuinely concerned for the salvation of young people through their music and concerts, and I do believe that some young people are being saved in the context of Contemporary Christian Music.

The fact that people are being saved does not mean a ministry is to be commended in its entirety, though. Many have been saved through Billy Graham's ministry, including my own wife, but this does not mean we should overlook the dangerous and unscriptural methodology of his ecumenical evangelism. Jehoshaphat was a godly king who did many things to glorify God in his life and ministry, but the prophet of God was instructed to rebuke him for his serious disobedience in yoking together with Ahab.

> "And Jehu the son of Hanani the seer went out to meet him, and said to king Jehoshaphat, Shouldest thou help the ungodly, and love them that hate the LORD? therefore is wrath upon thee from before the LORD" (2 Chronicles 19:2).

The disobedience of Jehoshaphat is akin to that of evangelical ecumenists (including those within CCM) today who refuse to practice biblical separation. Just because a church or ministry pleases God in certain areas does not mean that God will not rebuke it for unfaithfulness in others. The Lord's admonitions to the seven churches of Asia in Revelation 2-3 illustrate this. God did not overlook areas of disobedience even in the best of the churches, and it is the preachers whom God uses to rebuke error today (2 Timothy 4:1-2). Paul did not overlook Peter's disobedience in a seeming insignificant matter (Galatians 2:11-13).

I would also remind CCM defenders that God has told us how to do evangelism, and there is absolutely nothing in the Bible about entertainment evangelism or music evangelism. The Bible says that God has chosen to save people through the foolishness of preaching (1 Corinthians 1:21).

I don't believe people are saved *because of* Christian rock music, but *in spite of* it.

Following are the reasons why I question the statistics that are given about great numbers being saved through Christian rock music.

FIRST, THE DECISIONS ARE SUSPECT BECAUSE OF THE MESSAGE. Salvation comes only through repentance and faith in the one true Gospel of Jesus Christ. True salvation comes through true doctrine. Salvation does not come through a false doctrine of the gospel. Note the following Scripture carefully.

> "But God be thanked, that ye were the servants of sin, but YE HAVE OBEYED FROM THE HEART THAT FORM OF DOCTRINE WHICH WAS DELIVERED YOU" (Romans 6:17).

The following verses remind us that salvation comes through hearing and believing the right WORDS of the Gospel:

> "Who shall tell thee WORDS, WHEREBY THOU AND ALL THY HOUSE SHALL BE SAVED" (Acts 11:14).

> "In whom ye also trusted, after that ye heard THE WORD OF TRUTH, THE GOSPEL OF YOUR SALVATION: in whom also after that ye believed, ye were sealed with that holy Spirit of promise" (Ephesians 1:13).

> "For the hope which is laid up for you in heaven, whereof ye heard before in THE WORD OF THE TRUTH OF THE GOSPEL; Which is come unto you, as it is in all the world; and bringeth forth fruit, as it doth also in you, since the day ye heard of it, and knew the grace of God in truth" (Colossians 1:5,6).

A corrupted message of salvation does not produce biblical salvation.

The Bible warns that there are false gospels and false christs.

> "But I fear, lest by any means, as the serpent beguiled Eve through his subtlety, so your minds should be corrupted from the simplicity that is in Christ. For if he that cometh preacheth ANOTHER JESUS, whom we have not preached, or if ye receive ANOTHER SPIRIT, which ye have not received, or ANOTHER GOSPEL, which ye have not accepted, ye might well bear with him" (2 Corinthians 11:3,4).

The Galatians were sharply rebuked because they quickly turned aside to a false gospel:

> "I marvel that ye are so soon removed from him that called you into the grace of Christ unto ANOTHER GOSPEL: Which is not another; but there be some that trouble you, and would pervert the gospel of Christ" (Galatians 1:6,7).

In light of these Bible warnings, we must ask some serious questions about Contemporary Christian Music claims. What gospel, what doctrine of salvation, is being preached? What christ is being presented?

The answer is that the Gospel is rarely clear and sound in the context of an ecumenical-charismatic CCM concert. There are exceptions, of course, but some key men from within the CCM movement have admitted that this is true in general:

> "One of my criticisms of those of us who use music in evangelism is the nature and content of the 'gospel' which is preached. ALL TOO OFTEN, A SUPERFICIAL KIND OF BELIEVISM IS OFFERED, along with promises of large helpings of love, joy and peace" (Graham Kendrick, CCM musician and organizer for British rock festivals, *Pop Goes the Gospel*, p. 142).

> "An analysis of the lyrics of MOST gospel songs indicates A VERY SUPERFICIAL VIEW OF SALVATION and of Christianity" (Garth Hewitt, CCM musician, *Pop Goes the Gospel*, p. 142).

Stan Moser was the former head of Word Records and CEO of Star Song Records. He was one of the pioneers and most important executives in CCM and was the man responsible for signing Amy Grant. In 1995, after 26 years in Contemporary Christian Music, he left it and expressed disgust with what it has become. Note his testimony about the doctrinal content of CCM:

> "But to be candid, I look at THE MAJORITY OF THE MUSIC I HEAR TODAY AND THINK IT'S VIRTUALLY MEANINGLESS. ... I would probably be more inclined to call the industry 'commercial Christian music,' rather than

'contemporary Christian music'" (Stan Moser, "We Have Created a Monster," *Christianity Today*, May 20, 1996, p. 27).

Michael Card, a very popular and influential CCM musician, made the following observation:

"THE LYRICS OF A GOOD NUMBER OF THE SONGS DON'T BETRAY ANYTHING SPECIFICALLY CHRISTIAN — they may have some moral message, but not a lot of the big songs are identifiably Christian. . . 'What happens to the message when we start getting the music to as many people as possible?' There is an essential part of the gospel that's not ever going to sell. The gospel is good news, but it is also bad news: 'You are a sinner, and you are hopeless.' How is a multimillion-dollar record company going to take that? That's a part of the message, too, AND IF THAT'S TAKEN OUT — AND IT FREQUENTLY IS IN CHRISTIAN MUSIC — IT CEASES TO BE THE GOSPEL" (Michael Card, "Can't Buy Me Love," *Christianity Today*, May 20, 1996, p. 25).

There are countless examples we could give of how the Gospel is unclear or is corrupted in Contemporary Christian Music.

Kerry Livgren, former guitarist/songwriter for the secular mega rock group Kansas, claims that many people have been saved through a song he wrote before he became a Christian! "More people have been led to Christ with [the song *Dust in the Wind*] than with everything else I've ever written. Not only did that song not mention Jesus, but I was not a Christian at the time. It just happened to be a truth that the song emphasized" (Kerry Livgren, *CCM Magazine*, Feb. 1989, p. 8).

The late Rich Mullins was a very popular CCM writer and performer. He wrote songs popularized by Amy Grant and other well-known singers. His gospel, though, was very murky. When he was killed in 1997, it was reported that he was in the process of joining the Roman Catholic Church. In his song "Screen Door" he presents the false gospel of faith plus works:

"Faith without works baby/ It just ain't happenin'/ One is your left hand/ One is your right/ It'll take two strong arms/ To hold on tight" (Mullins, "Screen Door")

This song presents the false gospel of Roman Catholicism and of every cult. One of the marks of false Christianity is to confuse faith and works, to somehow mix faith and works together for salvation. While it is true that faith without works is dead and that true saving faith produces works, it is not true that faith and works are the two strong arms by which we hold on tight to God and salvation (Ephesians 2:8-10), yet that is exactly the heresy what this song teaches. "And if by grace, then is it no more of works:

otherwise grace is no more grace. But if it be of works, then is it no more grace: otherwise work is no more work" (Romans 11:6).

The name of Jesus Christ does not appear even once in three of Michael W. Smith's albums—*Change Your World, I'll Lead You Home,* and *Live Your Life.* The lyrics to the albums contain more than 6,000 words, but the name of Jesus is not heard even one time. The Bible says there is none other NAME under heaven given among men whereby we must be saved (Acts 4:12). It is impossible to preach the Gospel clearly without naming the name of Christ Jesus.

Consider the words to the song "Bargain" which Rez Band has popularized for Christian young people:

> "I'll pay any price just to get you/ I'll work all my life and I will/ To win you, I'd stand naked, stoned, and stabbed/ I'd call that a bargain/ The best I ever had/ The best I ever had ... I'll pay any price just to win you/ Surrender my good life or bad/ To find you/ I'm gonna drown an unsung man/ I call that a bargain/ The best I ever had..."

Rez band got this song from legendary rock guitarist Pete Townshend of the violent/ immoral/ occultic rock band, The Who. Townshend wrote "Bargain" as a tribute to his Hindu guru Meher Baba. Townshend has testified: "Baba is Christ, because being a Christian is just like being a Baba lover" (Bob Larson, *Rock*, 1984, p. 140). Not only is it blasphemous to take a song by an immoral rock star about a Hindu guru and sing it as unto Jesus Christ, but the song itself promotes a false gospel. We do not and cannot win the true God by sacrifice and works. Salvation is "not of works, lest any man should boast" (Ephesians 2:8-9). Further, the sinner has no "good life" to surrender. All our righteousness is as filthy rags before God (Isaiah 64:6). There is "none that doeth good, no, not one" (Romans 3:12).

White Heart is a popular CCM group. Note how unclear the gospel message is that they present in "Redemption" from their 1997 album entitled "Jesus" —

> "Stop, do you hear there's something in the distance that is rumbling/ I wonder if it could be the sound of prison walls that are crumbling/ In case you hadn't noticed/ Dead hearts locked up tight as graves are opening/ It's not politics/ Not economical/ Not theological/ Oh it is spiritual, spiritual, spiritual. It is Jesus/ One faith/ One hope/ One love/ One Lord/ Jesus" (White Heart, "Redemption").

Note the following song by the popular CCM group, Delirious. This is "Revival Town" from their *King of Fools* album (which is #13 on the album chart for August 1998):

> "Well I've got a message to bring/ I can't preach but I can sing/ And me and my brothers here/ Gonna play redemption hymns ... Well I've got a story to tell/ About the King above all kings/ He spoke for peace, hope and justice/ Things that we all need today/ You let a broken generation/ Become a dancing generation/ That is revival generation/ You may not hear it on the radio/ But you can feel it in the air."

This doctrinal murkiness is typical of the gospel message preached by most CCM groups today.

The following song is from "Adventures of the O.C. Supertones" (1996) —

> "You probably ask yourself, how'd this Jew boy get so crazy/ Come from kickin' mad knowledge, didn't come from being lazy/ We got the rhythm and the rhythm's got roots/ I'm a crazy little Hebrew onstage wearin' monkey boots/ I love to be onstage and sing and bimskalabimmin/ I love to be out in the crowd a skakin' and a swimmin'/ King David, my great grandfather, was a dancer/ King Solomon, my great grandfather, was a romancer/ Jesus came from Jesse, but Jesse came from Jesus/ Now come to the Lord cuz Lord Jesus frees us."

Is that a plain presentation of the Gospel of Jesus Christ? Could someone be saved through a mixed up message like this? Not according to Romans 6:17.

The following is an eyewitness description of a Deliverance concert:

> "When it came time for the 'preaching,' the members of Deliverance took turns talking about love and victory and not being a 'wimp.' Nothing about repentance. Nothing about salvation or separation from the world. Instead of an altar call, there was a cattle-call yodel where all the Christians were instructed to yell for Jesus" (Jeff Godwin, *What's Wrong with Christian Rock?*, pp. 225,226).

Aaron and Jeoffrey are a father and son music team. As much as we enjoy seeing a close father/son relationship, we cannot support Aaron and Jeoffrey because of their jazzed up worldly music and the unscriptural doctrine they sing. Note the following message from "Moment of Mercy" from *The Climb* album (1997) —

> "We've all been weakened by the choices we have made/ Wrapped in chains it seems we can't undo/ It doesn't matter what we've done or where we've been/ With one honest prayer/ We can be forgiven ... And with a simple act of faith we start to see/ Our failures are forgiven" (Aaron and Jeoffrey, "Moment of Mercy").

This is not the Gospel of Jesus Christ which Paul preached (1 Corinthians 15:1-4). The

Gospel of the Bible says that Jesus Christ died for OUR SINS according to the Scriptures, that He was buried, and that He rose again the third day according to the Scriptures. Aaron and Jeoffrey speak not of forgiveness of sin, but of "failures" and of "choices we have made." A failure or a bad choice is not the same as sin, which is disobedience to God's law. This is a humanistic approach to salvation and it is the common approach found among CCM performers. Further, Aaron and Jeoffrey's gospel is not achieved by faith in the death, burial and resurrection of Christ for sin, but by an "honest prayer" and "a simple act of faith." People can honestly pray many things to God and not be saved, and a simple act of faith in itself does not save. The act of faith must be directed to the death, burial and resurrection of Jesus Christ. Many people have faith in God and faith in God's goodness and faith in God's love who are not saved (James 2:19), because they have not put their trust in the finished cross work of Christ.

The following lyrics by the group Big Tent Revival to the song "Lovely Mausoleum" (from *Open All Nite*, 1996) illustrate the hazy, erroneous CCM gospel -

> "Sunrise open your eyes/ When are you gonna see? New day coming your way/ What is it gonna be? Chorus: Your choice, your voice/ You are in control/ Jesus, Jesus/ He will make you whole" (Big Tent Revival, "Lovely Mausoleum").

There is no Gospel here. What new day is coming my way? What is my choice? I am in control of what? Who is Jesus? What does He have to do with a sunrise for me? How does He make me whole?

Consider Don Francisco. When he does give the gospel in his songs, it is often an unclear message. Consider the words to "Step Across the Line" from his *Forgiven* album: "You gotta take a step across the line/ Let Jesus fill your heart and mind/ I can show you where to look/ but you gotta seek to find." Is that a clear presentation of the gospel? Could someone be born again through that? Contemporary Christian Music evangelism is almost always this hazy. Consider another example. This one is from Francisco's song "I Don't Care Where You've Been Sleeping." "I don't care where you've been sleepin'/ I don't care who's made your bed/ I've already gave my life to set you free/ There's no sin you could imagine/ That's stronger than my love/ And it's yours if you will come back home." It is wonderfully true that Christ died for all of our sins and that His grace is sufficient to forgive any sin, but how do we receive His forgiveness? How can a person be born again? A hazy "come back home" is not the answer. Come back home to what? The unsaved portion of Don Francisco's audience is a mixed multitude of pagans and religious lost. What does "come back home" mean to them? Come back home to the Roman Catholic sacraments? Come back home to baptismal regeneration? Come back home to the "hold on tight because you might lose it" insecurity of an Assemblies of God gospel? Come back home to what? Most CCM musicians do not make the message clear because they do not have a strong understanding of Bible doctrine and because they do not want to cause doctrinal divisions.

Here's another example of Don Francisco's gospel. This one is from his song "Give Your Heart a Home." "If you are tired and weary, weak and heavy laden/ I can understand how it feels to be alone/ I will take your burden/ If you let me love you/ Wrap my arms around you and give your heart a home." Is that the Gospel? It is not the message that the Apostles preached.

CCM performer Dallas Holm was trained by Pentecostal evangelist Dave Wilkerson. Note the following feeling-oriented gospel message from the song "Love Has Come Over Me" (from the album *Chain of Grace*, 1992) —

> "So won't you make a fresh evaluation/ Think about your life, about your soul/ He can touch your heart and make you whole/ Then you will have a wonderful sensation/ When you decide to give Him everything/ Then you'll join the holy celebration/ And lift your voice and begin to sing. Chorus: Because/ Love has come over me/ Captured my spirit/ Set my soul free/ Now I just can't believe/ How different I am since/ Love has come over me."

Is salvation deciding "to give Him everything"? Who is "Him"? There are many false christs and false gods in this world. Which one is Holm singing about? His fans won't know from listening to this song. Is salvation a wonderful sensation? Not necessarily. Salvation is often a sensation of struggle and trial. The hazy message of "love coming over me" is too general to be of help to the young people who listen to CCM. In the context of the ecumenical confusion which surrounds Contemporary Christian Music and the New Age confusion which surrounds young people today, this message could mean almost anything. It could refer to a faithful Catholic attending Mass or a baptismal regenerationist at his baptismal service or a Laughing Revival proponent becoming "drunk in the spirit." The ecumenical movement thrives on hazy doctrine like this.

Note the following "gospel" message by the Imperials:

> "Friend, I know where you're comin' from/ Seems your life's under the gun/ With no real chance of escape/ There is hope right outside your door/ It's what you've been searchin' for/ A love that will never fade/ So don't you run away/ Don't run away/ You can't hide/ Gotta keep reachin'/ You must keep reachin'/ Gotta keep reachin' for higher things" ("Higher Things," The Imperials, 1988, *Free the Fire* album).

What does this song mean? It's hard to tell. If it's for the unsaved, it presents a false gospel, that salvation is obtained by a continual reaching for God. "But what saith it?

The word is nigh thee, even in thy mouth, and in thy heart: that is, the word of faith, which we preach; That if thou shalt confess with thy mouth the Lord Jesus, and shalt believe in thine heart that God hath raised him from the dead, thou shalt be saved" (Romans 10:8,9). If the song, on the other hand, is for the saved, it says our hope is "outside your door." This is false. The Bible says "Christ IN YOU, the hope of glory" (Col. 1:27).

Following is an eyewitness account of the message which was presented by the News Boys on their 1997 "Take Me to Your Leader Tour." This tour was voted #1 by *CCM Magazine*.

> "Then the music stopped and what was to be their gospel message began. The band member who spoke said to the effect, we should have a passion for our faith, that people should see we are different, we should be salty Christians, that we should tell our friends what Jesus did in our lives and how God has changed us. He told how salt preserves, and how we can help stop the spread of decay and corruption and how if we lose our saltiness we are good for nothing. ... In conclusion he said to those who didn't know Jesus to ask those they came with or ask someone around them about what Jesus did in their lives and he said to the effect, before going back into their rock music, 'I know you don't want to hear anymore preaching'" (John Beardsley, "The Invasion Begins: A Review of the News Boys *Take Me to Your Leader* Tour," *The Christian Conscience*, 1997).

That was the only message that was given. The young people were not told about their fallen condition. They were not warned of eternal Hell. They were not told the Gospel. They were not told how to be saved. We must recall, too, that the lyrics to the rock songs performed by the News Boys are vague and almost impossible to understand because of the riotous music. When these elements are combined (no Gospel preaching, vague lyrics, and deafening music), it is impossible to believe that large numbers of young people are being genuinely saved through this medium. Emotional decisions and experiences, vague faith in God, reformation, religious commitments, rebuilding of self esteem—none of these things add up to biblical salvation. Biblical salvation is a supernatural new birth, and it comes through faith in the Gospel.

Reviewing the News Boys *Take Me to Your Leader* concert, even the local secular newspaper noted the lack of clarity to the message: "Although most of the choruses are straightforward, THE VERSES ARE HARD TO FOLLOW, A FLAW THAT SERVES TO TRIVIALIZE THE BAND'S CHRISTIAN MESSAGE. ... Built on lyrics that leave too many holes to be filled, THE BAND'S MESSAGE GETS LOST SOMEWHERE IN THE ALTERNATIVE MUSIC" (*Rapid City Journal*, Rapid City, South Dakota, May 13, 1997).

The WOW 1998 CD contains 30 top CCM songs for the year, thus giving us a clear window into the world of Contemporary Christian Music. The CD jacket says, "This is music that can make an eternal difference," yet there is no clear gospel presentation in the music and it is filled with unclear and false doctrine. How can it then make an eternal difference? Note the following examples, remembering that these are the most popular CCM songs today:

Out of Eden, in their song "More Than You Know," sings: "There's a way out of this world we're livin'/ There's only one who can make you feel secure/ He's waiting just for you." Is the Gospel about making sinners *feel* secure? Who is the person they are singing about? In what sense is "he" waiting for the sinner? No one could get saved through such an unclear gospel.

Caedmon's Call, in "Hope to Carry On," sings: "Love has come and its given me hope to carry on." That is not the gospel. That is unclear. What love? How did it come? What hope has it given?

Rebecca St. James, in "Abba," sings: "You make the road rise up to meet me/ Make the sun shine at my back/ The wind is at my back and the rain falls soft." That is unclear and almost meaningless. Is this the gospel? Is this a description of the Christian life?

Jaci Velasquez, in her song "We Can Make a Difference," sings: "We can make the world a better place/ We can make the sun shine through the rain." What does this mean? Is this the type of message we find in the New Testament epistles?

Petra, in their song "We Need Jesus," sings: "When will the world see that we need Jesus/ If we open our eyes we will all realize that he loves us/ When our hearts are as one and believe that he's the son of our God/ When we share the love of Jesus/ See each other as He sees us/ Then his love will see us through." What does this mean? It is difficult to tell. Are they singing about the world needing Jesus or Christians needing Jesus? Do they mean that when Christians are united the world will believe in Christ? The song is a murky mess, but then, it is good rock music and that is the main thing the Christian rock lover wants.

The message presented by dc Talk is frequently too hazy to be understood. Note the following example from "Mind's Eye" —

> "You know what I'm going through/ I know (that) it's true/ Cause you've stood in my shoes/ Desire's inside of me/ But, it's hard to believe/ In what you cannot see/ Can you catch the wind? See a breeze? Its presence is revealed by/ The leaves on a tree/ An image of faith in the unseen/ In my mind's eye/ I see

your face/ You smile/ As you show me grace/ In my mind's eye/ You take my hand/ We walk through foreign lands/ The foreign lands of life/ In my mind/ I'm where I belong/ As I rest in your arms/ And like a child I hold on to you/ In my moment of truth/ We can ride the storm/ Endure the pain/ You comfort me in my hurricane/ And I'll never be alone again/ ... In my mind I can see your face/ Love pours down in a shower of grace/ Life is a gift that you choose to give/ And I believe that we eternally live/ Faith is the evidence of things unseen/ People tell me that you're just a dream/ But they don't know you the way that I do/ You're the one I live to pursue" ("Mind's Eye," dc Talk).

Nothing is clear about this message. Who are they talking about? Jesus? They don't say. It could just as easily be about Krishna or Buddha. The listener could easily fit any false god into this song. If the song is about Jesus, what Jesus? The true Jesus of the Bible or one of the myriad of false christs in the minds of those who hear dc Talk's music? The song speaks of living eternally, but there is no clear Gospel message so that the hearer can know how to have eternal life.

It is obvious that a large percentage of "decisions" made in the context of Contemporary Christian Music are suspect because the message being presented is either unclear or overtly unscriptural.

SECOND, THE DECISIONS ARE SUSPECT BECAUSE OF THE ATMOSPHERE. Not only are the CCM salvation statistics suspect because of the murky message, they are suspect because of the atmosphere created by the music itself. Powerful music can produce emotional decisions, but biblical salvation is not the product of an emotional decision. It is the product of Holy Spirit-wrought repentance and faith in the Lord Jesus Christ through the preaching of the biblical Gospel. Note the following warnings from men who are very knowledgeable about music:

"The element of relentless beat in rock music increases THE DANGER OF A SHALLOW, EMOTIONAL, UNTHINKING RESPONSE, made at the wrong level and for the wrong reasons" (John Blanchard, *Pop Goes the Gospel*, p. 23)

"In loading our evangelistic programmes with manipulative music, are we not greatly increasing the RISKS OF PRODUCING 'CONVERSIONS' THAT ARE PSYCHOLOGICAL RATHER THAN SPIRITUAL? The set-up could not be more perfect. Impressionable young people can undoubtedly be so conditioned by the music that they are much more likely to accept whatever the preacher says. Add a good communicator and the chances are that he will produce an impressive number of 'decisions.' However, the danger is that these 'decisions' are the result of musical conditioning rather than spiritual conviction" (John Blanchard, *Pop Goes the Gospel*).

"One day I talked with a pastor who had been in charge of follow-up after a large city wide evangelistic campaign. Christian rock had been used prominently throughout the meetings. Several hundred young people had responded to the invitation at the close of the services. This is what he reported: 'A few weeks after the meetings I had difficulty finding any who had signed decision cards. There were none in the churches, none attending Bible studies, NONE GOING ON WITH THE LORD AT ALL.' He concluded that THE YOUNG PEOPLE WERE RESPONDING TO THE MUSIC MORE THAN TO THE MESSAGE" (Lowell Hart, *Satan's Music Exposed*, p. 180).

"Here is the testimony of Phil, a young man who had been saved out of a rock band: 'In 1973 I became a Christian after playing with rock bands and being in the music business for about seven years. ... Some well-meaning Christians encouraged me to 'use my talents for the Lord,' so we formed a group to play what we considered to be the new Christian sound. It was nothing more than secular rock with Christian words. We thought that the type of music we played, the length of our hair and the way we dressed would more effectively reach these young people. We gave our testimonies with soft, slow music in the background. When we gave the invitation sometimes a hundred or more teenagers would come forward. Were these conversions genuine? We decided to begin a follow-up. WE WERE SHOCKED TO FIND THAT ALMOST EVERYONE WHO HAD GIVEN US AN ADDRESS HAD GONE BACK TO THEIR OLD WAYS. I CAN'T THINK OF ONE PERSON I COULD SHOW YOU TODAY AS FRUIT OF OUR MINISTRY. I REALIZE NOW THAT THEY WERE RESPONDING TO THE MUSIC, NOT TO THE HOLY SPIRIT'" (Phil Wilson, June 1978, quoted by Lowell Hart, *Satan's Music Exposed*, pp. 180, 181).

<u>THIRD, THE DECISIONS ARE SUSPECT BECAUSE OF THE MEDIUM.</u> A large percentage of CCM is so loud and raucous that the words are not clear. How can the Gospel be presented in its saving power if the very words are not plain! This exposes the hypocrisy of CCM defenders. They know that the message is frequently unclear, yet they claim that the message is what is important! If they would be honest, I believe they would be forced to admit that what is preeminent to them is their love of sensual music.

A man who attended an Audio Adrenaline/dc Talk concert in Rapid City, South Dakota, testified, "All the while the music was so loud if anyone could hear the words it wasn't enough to get a message from; hence, the reaction was to the 'rock' beat not the words" (John Beardsley, "DC Talk Examined," *The Christian Conscience*, June 1996).

Consider the following description of a Sheila Wash concert: "For some of us, however, communication ended when she sang because, more often than not, the band was too loud for us to catch the words" (*Pop Goes the Gospel*, p. 159).

While visiting in the Nashville, Tennessee, area (one of the headquarters of the commercial music industry in the United States) recently, I listened to WAYFM radio station, which advertises itself as "Christian Hit Radio." They played a skit which made fun of using Bible terms to reach today's generation, alleging that no one can understand terms such as "justification" or "sanctification" or "grace." Instead, "Christian Hit Radio" claims to communicate plainly on a level people today can understand. Having heard that, I listened carefully to song after song to see what message they are presenting. Though I listened off and on for hours, not one song gave a clear Gospel message. There was not even a clear Bible message of any sort. In fact, the words to many of the songs were difficult to impossible to understand. I concluded that while it is true that they are not using difficult Bible terms, they also are not communicating a clear Bible message, so their boast is meaningless. This is true for CCM at large.

FOURTH, THE DECISIONS ARE SUSPECT BECAUSE OF THE FRUIT. If Contemporary Christian Music is of God, the fruit will be genuine salvation, holiness, perseverance, sound doctrine, Christian discipleship. In a nutshell, the fruit will be obedience to the Bible.

> "And hereby we do know that we know him, if we keep his commandments. He that saith, I know him, and keepeth not his commandments, is a liar, and the truth is not in him" (1 John 2:3,4).
>
> "They profess that they know God; but in works they deny him, being abominable, and disobedient, and unto every good work reprobate" (Titus 1:16).
>
> "My sheep hear my voice, and I know them, and they follow me" (John 10:27).
>
> "And every man that hath this hope in him purifieth himself, even as he is pure" (1 John 3:3).
>
> "Therefore if any man be in Christ, he is a new creature: old things are passed away; behold, all things are become new" (2 Corinthians 5:17).
>
> "He that is of God heareth God's words: ye therefore hear them not, because ye are not of God" (John 8:47).

John Blanchard researched 13 missions agencies in Britain to see how many of their missions candidates were converted at Christian rock concerts. Not one was found. The following reply was typical: "I cannot call to mind anybody who has been converted through this type of youth evangelism and has subsequently gone to missionary service" (*Pop Goes the Gospel*, pp. 110-112).

Follow-up on decisions made at Christian rock concerts in Britain found that very few were genuine. For example, of 200 decisions recorded at one youth meeting, only four attended a follow-up session. Of the 100 students who made "decisions" in a school visited by a CCM performance, only one later showed even "a mild interest" in Christian things (*Pop Goes the Gospel*, p. 110).

The Devil has provided many alternatives to the new birth, and multitudes are confused by false professions of salvation. Note the Bible's warnings:

(1) A person can believe in God and not be saved (James 2:19).
(2) A person can pray to Jesus and not be saved (Matt. 7:22-23).
(3) A person can prophesy in Jesus' name and not be saved (Matt. 7:22-23).
(4) A person can do wonderful works in Jesus' name and not be saved (Matt. 7:22-23).
(5) A person can have a zeal for God and not be saved (Rom. 10:2-3).
(6) A person can have a zeal to make proselytes for God and not be saved (Matt. 23:15).
(7) A person can be very interested in Jesus Christ and not be saved (Matt. 19:16-22).
(8) A person can profess to know God and not be saved (Titus 1:16).
(9) A person can follow and serve Christ and not be saved (John 6:70).

<u>FIFTH, THE DECISIONS ARE SUSPECT BECAUSE OF THE SCANT EMPHASIS ON THE GOSPEL</u>. I have been investigating Contemporary Christian Music off and on for 25 years and intently for several months. I have listened to and read the lyrics to hundreds of songs, to many others, visited at least 300 web sites produced by CCM musicians and their fans, listened to CCM radio stations in various parts of the country, etc. There is *some* Gospel preaching done by CCM artists, but this is definitely *not* the main emphasis of the CCM world. In fact, evangelism comes across as a very low priority, generally speaking. *Very* low. Consider the **songs** themselves. Only a VERY tiny percentage of CCM songs present a clear Gospel. Consider the **websites**. The LARGE majority of websites produced by CCM artists or fans do not contain a Gospel message or a challenge to the unsaved. Most **biographies** or interviews of CCM artists do not contain a clear testimony of salvation or any challenge to the unsaved. As we have seen, it is common for CCM **concerts** NOT to give a clear Gospel message. There are exceptions, but we are speaking here of the overall picture.

PART III
THE CHURCH
AND ITS MUSIC

HOW DOES WORLDLY MUSIC ENTER THE CHURCHES?

This question is answered in the Introduction.

WHY IS THE MUSIC PART OF MANY CHURCH SERVICES SO LIFELESS?

I have had the privilege of attending many churches which have truly spiritual and enthusiastic song services. It is a genuine joy to participate in these. The sad truth of the matter, though, is that they are rare. I have loved congregational singing since I was a boy growing up in a Southern Baptist church. I turned my back on the Lord in my teenage years and spent many years away from Him, but after I repented toward God in 1973 and began to attend church of my own accord as an adult, I have continued to love congregational singing. All too often, though, it is not done properly and is dull and lifeless and ritualistic. There are many reasons for this serious problem:

1. The lifelessness is sometimes a reflection of spiritual deadness in the hearts of church members.

> "Public worship is only the manifestation of private worship. The reason our public services are dead is that our private devotional life is dead" (Tim Fisher, *The Battle for Christian Music*, p. 108).

In many instances song services are dull because so many of the members sing only half-heartedly, if at all. It is obvious that most don't have their minds on the service. If someone really desires to lift up his or her voice in praise to God, people look at them like they are strange. Too often we are just going through a religious ritual with our song services. It might as well be a Latin mass, because so few are really thinking about what they are doing. The words are merely being mouthed without consciousness of the glorious message we are singing and without heart-felt enthusiasm toward God. All too often we bring the cares and lusts of the world with us into the church service instead of preparing our hearts by prayer and confession. I speak this to my own shame, as well as to the shame of many others. This is a great sin. It is dangerously close to "having a form of godliness but denying the power thereof," which is a mark of apostasy (2 Timothy 3:5). It is evidence of having left our first love (Revelation 2:4).

2. The lifelessness is caused by treating the music as a ritual to be "gotten through."

The fact that our song services are mere rituals is evident in many ways. It is evident by the aforementioned half-hearted manner with which we sing the songs. It is evident by the fact that many people don't sing at all. It is evident by the way many pastors and special speakers are not attentive to the songs and do not themselves enter heartily into the singing.

The ritualism of our song services is further evidenced by the haphazard manner in which the songs are sung. Though I don't believe the church is under an obligation to sing every stanza of every song, all too often it is evident that the first, second, and third stanza (or the first and last) are sung, not because the lyrics of those particular stanzas have been carefully selected, *but because that is the ritual and no serious thought and preparation has been given to it*! Many times the third stanza is necessary to complete the message of the song. Why skip it? Because that is how we do it, and we don't think about it any more deeply than that. I once thanked Bro. McNeily, one of the song leaders at Fairhaven Baptist Church in Chesterton, Indiana (and a teacher at Fairhaven Baptist College), for singing all of the stanzas of the songs and hymns at a conference I attended there. His reply was informative. He said simply, "We are in no hurry." Amen. Why are we seemingly in such a hurry with our song services? Is it not because it is merely a ritual that we are rushing through with almost no thought?

The ritualism of our song services is also evident by the improper choice of songs. We can't say we are worshipping God when we sing something like "Church in the Wildwood" with its simplistic, nostalgic message which does not turn one's heart in praise to God, or if we sing something which contains actual doctrinal heresy which many of the popular songs and hymns do, or if we sing songs the words of which most people do not understand. If we are going to worship God in song we have to use songs which are worshipful and which are doctrinally sound (He is to be worshipped in truth) and which are understandable. "I will sing with the spirit, and I will sing with the understanding also" (1 Corinthians 14:15).

That is very basic, and the very fact that so many of the songs selected for the song service miss the mark of having a powerful and appropriate message is plain evidence that we are treating the song service as a mere ritual to be gotten through and that the pastor, the song leader, and the congregation are not thinking seriously about what they are doing.

3. The lifelessness is caused by unqualified and unprepared leaders and musicians.

The position of song leader is not insignificant. Just as orchestras need effective conductors and armies need effective officers, churches must have the right song leaders if they are to have effectual song services. An individual can worship God alone effectively if he is so able and inclined, but a congregation must be led. That is why God has ordained leaders and has set forth high qualifications for them. It is true that the New Testament does not spell out the position of song leader or music director, but the Old Testament plainly sets forth this pattern and there is no need to restate it in the New. Common sense dictates its necessity.

> "And Chenaniah, chief of the Levites, was for song: he instructed about the song, because he was skilful" (1 Chronicles 15:22; see also 1 Chronicles 25).

In Israel the music associated with the worship of Almighty God was carefully prepared and skillfully performed with godly oversight. We should have no less in the churches of Jesus Christ. Yet all too often the song service is led by individuals who know almost nothing about what they are doing and/or do not have the enthusiasm and skills and spirituality to do the job. They don't really LEAD the singing. They do little more than announce the song number. Many song leaders don't even look at the congregation. They hide their heads in the song book and mumble along. They give no instructions to the people to lift up their voices diligently or to meditate upon the words of the song, etc. They don't remind the people that we are gathered together to worship the Lord and to edify one another in song. They don't put a lot of prayer and thought into the selection of songs.

No wonder the song service is so dull in these situations, and in my experience this is the situation in a large number of the fundamental Baptist churches. The pastor who selects such an individual and provides him with no training is the responsible party. Apparently that pastor does not think very highly of the song service. No wonder many are tempted to go to a church which has an enthusiastic worship service. No wonder young people think of church as dull. Friends, church does not have to boring! If a church is young and the congregation small, it is understandable that there might not be proper musicians and song leaders. We are referring, rather, to established churches.

4. The lifelessness is caused by ignorance about music.

Oftentimes the chief problem with a church's music program is simple ignorance. In these cases, the pastor does not understand music himself, and he does not provide training for someone who is qualified to direct the music. This is understankable in a new work with a tiny membership, but the pastor should make it one of his priorities to see that a properly trained, spiritually-qualified individual is set over the music. If this is absolutely not possible and absolutely no one is currently available, there is not a lot one can do but pray and be patient. Frequently, though, the problem is a lackadaisical attitude toward church music so that it is not made the priority in prayer and planning that it should be.

For those who speak English there is no excuse for ignorance about spiritual music and effective song leading. There is a wealth of good material available. At the end of this book I have included a list of some of these.

There should be continual education in the church pertaining to music, both positive and negative. Certainly it is that important. We should be continually warning of the danger of worldly music and continually educating on the nature of spiritual music. New members are coming into the church and young people are growing up who need to be trained; and people forget what they learned two or five years ago.

5. The lifelessness is caused by lack of variety and imagination.

All too often there is little or no imagination and serious preparation given to the music service. The same songs are sung every service. "Victory in Jesus" is a wonderful song, but when it is sung every week for fifty years, even a wonderful song can grow tiresome. There are hundreds of songs in the hymnbooks, but many churches sing only a few of them. Variety is the spice of life. The largest book in the Bible is Psalms, and God has provided 150 different psalms in this inspired hymnal. New songs should be introduced regularly and then sung frequently until they become an integral part of the church family's ever-enlarging song repertoire. Singing Scripture is a wonderful way to praise the Lord and edify the saints. During their Sunday evening services, for example, Windsor Hills Baptist Church in Oklahoma City uses Scripture songs produced by North County Baptist Church, 221 W. Ave., Escondido, CA 92027 and Tri-City Baptist Church, 4500 Selsa Rd., Blue Springs, MO 64015. Not only do these introduce variety within the music program, but nothing surpasses the actual words and verses of Scripture for doctrinal purity. Majesty Music recently published a new hymnbook which contains many beautiful songs which were written in the last few decades. (The address for Majesty Music is given at the end of this book under "Helpful Resources on Music.") The music is contemporary in the sense that it is new but it is not contemporary in the sense that it is worldly. (We must warn that some of the new *Patch the Pirate* children's tapes are, in our opinion, moving in the direction of contemporary sounds.) Even the most familiar songs can be made more interesting by imaginative change in the manner of presentation. On some verses the accompanying musicians can drop out while the congregation sings acapello. One verse can be sung by the women, then the next by the men. The choir, singing group, or soloist can be accompanied by the congregation in places. The timing of the song can be altered, etc., etc. There are endless means of singing old songs in new ways.

HOW TO KEEP CONTEMPORARY CHRISTIAN MUSIC OUT OF THE CHURCHES

I hear frequently from people who are broken hearted that the worldly contemporary music has taken over their churches. Let me give an example of what is happening widely among those who only a short time ago would have nothing to do with Contemporary Christian Music. Liberty University was founded by Jerry Falwell, an Independent Baptist preacher. He once had high spiritual standards for music in his church and school and on his Old Time Gospel Hour program, but that is no longer the case, and this exemplifies what is happening on many fronts. For a number of years the school has allowed "Christian" rock concerts on the campus. They are even promoting charismatic music. The October 1997, issue of *Charisma* magazine reported that "Jerry Falwell Is Now Open to Charismatics." The report mentioned that Integrity Music, which is very influential in spreading the contemporary music and which rose out of the charismatic movement, is planning to record a live praise and worship album at Liberty University. The Editor of *Charisma*, Stephen Strang, said that FALWELL ADMITTED THAT "YEARS AGO HE WOULD NOT HAVE ALLOWED THIS TYPE OF MUSIC IN HIS SCHOOL." Strang continued, "Now Liberty is not only co-sponsoring Integrity's live recording, IT IS WORKING WITH INTEGRITY TO ESTABLISH AN INSTITUTE THAT WILL TRAIN A NEW GENERATION OF WORSHIP LEADERS IN LYNCHBURG" (*Charisma*, October 1997, p. 122).

This church and school, which years ago stood for the traditional Christian music that was born out of spiritual revival, has capitulated completely to the siren call of the charismatic-ecumenical Contemporary Christian Music. For several years they have allowed rock concerts to be held on campus for the students. Now it will spread this unscriptural philosophy of music far and wide through its students and the churches under its influence.

WHY IS CCM SWEEPING INTO SO MANY FORMERLY STRONG BIBLE-BELIEVING CHURCHES?

First, CCM is sweeping into so many formerly strong Bible-believing churches because it is pervasive. Unless it is steadfastly resisted, it will be accepted. No church can be neutral in this battle. Even the strongest Bible-believing churches are continually tested in the area of music, and this battle is going to rage ever stronger as the return of Christ draws closer. Church members encounter worldly music on Christian radio and television stations. Further, in most Christian bookstores today one will not find music that is truly spiritual. Instead, the shelves are filled with Christian rock and charismatic "praise" and all sorts of worldly ecumenical beat music.

The companies producing this music are largely owned by secular corporations which have only one motive: profit, money. Nothing truly spiritual and acceptable to the Lord can come out of such a compromised, worldly, unscriptural situation.

Second, the new music is enjoyable. CCM is a great temptation because it is very satisfying to the flesh. This is why one can draw large crowds to attend church if a very rhythmic music is provided, but many of those same people will not come to a prayer meeting or to a preaching service which features traditional Christian music. Worldly music appeals to worldly people. The sad problem is that even the born again child of God has an old nature which enjoys carnal things, and the most spiritually-minded Christian is perpetually tempted by the lusts of his own flesh. It is easy to enjoy Contemporary Christian Music. Just relax and the allow the flesh to have its way.

Third, CCM is the easiest way to draw a crowd. One of the most effective ways for a church to appeal to this present generation is through its music. Pastors are tempted to let down the standard for the sake of increasing the attendance and making the church more popular in the community. If he does not have his eyes directly upon the Lord of His calling, a pastor will think he is in competition with other churches in the area. How can a church compete with Contemporary Christian Music? By providing the same type of music. Pastors all over the land are falling prey to this temptation. It is a sign of spiritual decadence.

Fourth, CCM is entering the homes and churches through children's music. The vast majority of Christian music for children is syncopated and jazzy. Even some of the newer *Patch the Pirate* tapes are troublesome in this regard. (See the article "Be Careful about the Newer Patch the Pirate Tapes" under the Music section of the End Times Apostasy Database at the Way of Life Literature web site — http://www.wayoflife.org.) The following warning is very timely and important: "If you raise your child on seemingly innocent but worldly jingle sounding music they will have a definite thirst for the CCM sound when they become a teenager. You won't be able to say, Oh, now that you're older let me teach you what good music is all about. It will be too late. You need to give them a standard of excellence and spirituality from their earliest years" (David G. Parker, *Music in Our Contemporary Christian Culture*, 1997).

HOW TO KEEP CONTEMPORARY CHRISTIAN MUSIC OUT OF THE CHURCH

How, then, can a church keep the new music out?

1. MAINTAINING SPIRITUAL STANDARDS FOR MUSIC IN THE CHURCH BEGINS WITH THE PASTORS. We believe that everything rises and falls on leadership. It is not enough for a few of the church members to have high standards of music. If the church as a whole is to be protected from the new music, the pastors must understand spiritual music and must have strong convictions and high standards in this area. This must be reflected first of all in their own homes and in the lives of their children. Pastors and deacons do have a greater responsibility to keep their families scripturally sound. God requires this of them (1 Timothy 3:4-5,10-12; Titus 1:6). Those who do not maintain proper scriptural order in their families cease to be qualified to lead the churches. A school principal recently testified to me that he had to tell the teenage children of deacons and pastors in his own church that the music they brought to a church activity was unacceptable. This type of thing will eventually destroy the standards in the church. If the church in general has good standards for music, yet the young people in the homes of the leaders are listening to worldly music, the standard overall will break down quickly. Those young people will set the spiritual tone for the other young people. The parents who try to maintain high standards of music for their children are undermined if the young people in the church leaders' homes flaunt those standards. Further, it is hypocrisy for a pastor to refuse to allow Contemporary Christian Music in the assembly, yet allow it in his own life and family.

2. THE PASTORS MUST TRAIN THE PEOPLE ABOUT SPIRITUAL MUSIC AND MUST WARN THEM OF THE DANGERS OF WORLDLY MUSIC. It does not come "natural" for God's people to reject worldly music. The flesh enjoys it, and the flesh is ever present. Church members must be trained in the area of music just as they must be trained to understand sound doctrine and to win souls to Christ and to have a fruitful Christian home and to practice holiness in every other area. To be effective, the teaching must be very plain and it must be applied so that the people will understand exactly what types of music are helpful spiritually and what types are detrimental. Wise pastors will use every tool available to help the people understand these matters. They will make good literature available. They will bring in speakers who are effective in teaching about Christian music. This is not an insignificant matter. Music is one of the most powerful influences in this world. Note the following statement by the Bible commentator Albert Barnes: "Dr. Johnson once said, that if he were allowed to make the ballads of a nation, he cared not who made the laws. It is true in a more important sense that he who is permitted to make the hymns of a church, need care little who preaches, or who makes the creed. He will more effectually mold the sentiments of a church than they who preach or make creeds and confessions" (*Barnes Notes on the New Testament*, Ephesians-Colossians). The pastor who ignores this issue does so to the spiritual detriment of the church for which God has made him responsible. (Toward the end of this book I have included a list of suggested materials about music and song leading.)

3. THE MUSIC PERSONNEL MUST BE CAREFULLY SELECTED. If a church is to keep Contemporary Christian Music out of its midst, it must be extremely careful about the selection of people who are involved with the music. This includes the music director, church musicians, those who provide special music, and the choir members. The best way to be certain that all involved with the music are committed to maintaining the highest spiritual quality is to have written standards and to go through these with everyone involved. Everyone should be trained in a spiritual philosophy of music and should be fully prepared to recognize and reject worldly music. They must be committed to this philosophy before they are allowed to be involved with the church's music "program." The leaders cannot merely assume that the music personnel understand and agree with these things. The only Christians who understand the issue of Christian music properly are those who have been trained to so understand it. This comes back to the responsibility of the pastors to teach these things. If there is not an ongoing training program pertaining to music, a church will quickly deteriorate in this area, because the pressure to use the new music is constant. Further, the music people must lead by the example of their own lives. If a song director uses spiritual music in the assembly but enjoys worldly music in his car and at home, his example will have a powerful effect upon the church family. I recall one church which used excellent music in the services, but one of the key music personnel loved jazz and other forms of carnal music privately. The young people, particularly, pick up on this kind of double standard.

4. THE HIGHEST STANDARDS MUST BE MAINTAINED FOR WORKERS THROUGHOUT THE CHURCH. One of the most important and effective ways to maintain high spiritual standards of living in a congregation is to have the highest standards for teachers and workers. These are the members who most significantly affect the church body. What they believe and how they live and what their goals are will largely determine that of the entire church. If the church's teachers and workers listen to worldly music, how can it be expected that other members will not follow their example? And how can a church know what its teachers and workers are doing in these areas unless it has written standards and makes certain that the standards are enforced? I have heard pastors say that it is not their business to involve themselves in what the people listen to and what they watch and what they do "in the privacy of their own lives." That philosophy is both unscriptural and unreasonable. It is unscriptural because the Bible says the pastors are placed in the church "to watch for your souls" (Heb. 13:17). The pastors are also in the church for the perfecting and edifying of the body (Eph. 4:11-12). How can a pastor watch for the souls of his church members unless he knows what they are putting into their souls? How can he perfect and edify them unless he knows what is happening in their daily lives? Such a philosophy, therefore, is unscriptural. It is also incredibly unreasonable, because it is saying that the shepherd is not to interfere in the business of the sheep, which is absolute nonsense. A shepherd who does not make it his business to know what the sheep are doing is a lousy shepherd.

5. THE YOUTH GROUP MUST BE LED SPIRITUALLY. The greatest battle over music lies in the region of the young people. In their youthful immaturity they will respond naturally to the "new" things. They will also pressure their parents to weaken the family standards in this area. In fact, those who promote Christian rock music do so in the name of the young people. They claim that the only way to reach the youth is with "their own music." This is nonsense, of course, from a biblical perspective. "For God hath not called us unto uncleanness, but unto holiness" (1 Thess. 4:7). The church is not in the business of entertaining young people, but calling them to discipleship in Christ and separation from the world and holiness of living. It is true that what you win them with you win them to. If a church uses worldly means to win young people, those thus won will be worldly. If a church has an organized youth group, it must be very careful about the selection of those who lead the youth. Young people don't need a "good times Charlie." They don't merely need another buddy who will pal around with them in fun and games. They get plenty of that. What they desperately need, and what the church is required by God to give them, are godly, spiritually mature people who will love them and show them the path of God's perfect will, who will call them to reject the vain, "cool" ways of this present wicked world, who will challenge them to be pure, to pull down the worldly idols from their hearts, to give themselves wholly to the service of Jesus Christ while there is still time, to yield to Christ's command to go into all the world and preach the Gospel to every creature.

6. THE MUSIC SERVICE MUST BE SPIRITUAL AND ENTHUSIASTIC. It is not enough to reject sensual music from the church service. The music must be properly led, spiritual, enthusiastically sung, spiritually performed. There must be a variety so the music service does not become ritualistic and boring. I have attended far too many churches which have a dull music service, with little or no enthusiasm, little or no variety, etc. It is BORING! No wonder young people are bored with churches when this is the case.

I praise the Lord for the many churches which refuse to be infiltrated with worldly music. Those who are standing are not doing so by accident. When the enemy rages against a certain position, the soldier who does not stand firmly will definitely fall.

"The truth of the whole matter is that the mind of today's Christian has become so amalgamated into thinking just like the world, he can no longer differentiate between music that is holy and set apart unto God, from music that is profane and of the flesh. Tolerance sets in when families gravitate to watching the immorality, vulgarity, obscenity, and violence, which at the same time promotes ungodly music into the home by way of television. They soon become so accustomed to it, it no longer offends them. If Christians tolerate the sinful ways of the wicked, they will soon tolerate the music of the wicked, because the two go hand-in-hand. Evidence of this spiritual condition is everywhere today. The path of tolerance leads to the highway of acceptance. Once a person finds CCM acceptable, he will easily embrace it in worship." *Gordon Sears*

PART IV
DIRECTORY OF CONTEMPORARY CHRISTIAN MUSICIANS

DIRECTORY OF CONTEMPORARY CHRISTIAN MUSICIANS

100% PROOF

This British Christian rock group 100% Proof is described as follows in a British magazine:

> "They're the sort of people that my mother told me not to play with. I bet they spit on buses! You won't like this album if you're any kind of weed. ... It's that nasty, noisy, loud heavy metal stuff. Not unlike Quo. Very roots rock 'n' roll. Sounds in places like lunatic music. Exciting, throbbing, subversive rock 'n' roll—just like it should be. Can you describe head-banging as intellectual? ... Good stuff—buy it!" (*Buzz*, December 1981).

2ND CHAPTER OF ACTS

This is one of the early Jesus Movement groups. They put Christian lyrics to soft rock music. The group was composed of three siblings: Annie, Nelly, and Matthew Ward. The group's manager and producer, Buck Herring, is Annie's husband. Herring is the producer for CCM artists Barry McGuire, Phil Keaggy, Terry Talbot, Mike Deasy, Michael and Stormie Omartian, among others. The Wards grew up in a Catholic home, and Annie testifies that the Catholic Church had a great impact on her. "I loved the Church. I didn't know much about God, but I loved the liturgy" (from a booklet accompanying their "20" CD). Before Buck and Annie were married, Buck attended a charismatic church and had a spiritual experience which changed the direction of his life. This is his testimony of what happened:

> "As he stood there, fighting an urge to leave, Buck also experienced a powerful stirring in his heart. The searching question came to him. Are you willing to be foolish in your own eyes—for my sake? He pondered the implications of this query for less than a minute, then by a single act of his will, Buck raised his hands in the air and began to speak words of praise to Jesus" (Ibid.).

Buck shared his religious experience with Annie and gave her a copy of *Good News for Modern Man*. She read Revelation and "felt the same sense of majesty she had felt as a little girl" and "saw Jesus as King of kings and Lord of lords." She sat down at a piano and started to play and sing words, even though she did not know how to play. "Puzzled, Annie stared at the keyboard. Okay, she thought. This song did not come from me. Where did this song come from? In her mind's eye, she pictured Jesus. He was walking toward her, and Annie had the conviction that the song had come from him. What did this mean? Then Jesus spoke to Annie and His words seared into her heart: the only thing I am asking of you is to give your life to Me and let Me live through you" (Ibid.).

This testimony is troubling. Salvation is not giving one's life to the Lord. That is works. Salvation is trusting the death, burial, and resurrection of Christ for forgiveness of one's sin. That and that alone is the Gospel (1 Cor. 15:1-4).

The members of 2nd Chapter of Acts began attending Jack Hayford's Foursquare Pentecostal church in the early 1970s and were discipled by him. Hayford inspired one of the 2nd Chapter's albums, *The Roar of Love*, based on C.S. Lewis's *The Chronicles of Narnia*. Lewis was turning to the Catholic Church before his death. He believed in prayers for the dead and purgatory and confessed his sins regularly to a priest. He received the Catholic sacrament of last rites on July 16, 1963. Lewis also rejected the doctrine of bodily resurrection (*Biblical Discernment Ministries Letter*, Sept.-Oct. 1996) and believed there is salvation in pagan religions. He rejected the doctrine of a literal fiery hell, claiming that hell is not a place but a state of mind. He believed in theistic evolution, but he did not believe the Bible is the infallible Word of God. C.S. Lewis used profanities, told bawdy stories, and frequently got drunk with his students (*World* magazine, May 19, 1990).

The members of the 2nd Chapter of Acts claim that they are guided by prophetic "words" from the Lord. Consider this testimony by Annie: "Some years, He'd tell us, 'You are going to be planted. You will be harvesting in three years, but this year you are going to plant.' Another year He'd say, 'This year you are going to be ushering people into the presence of the Holy Spirit, ' or 'This year is going to be a year of deliverance'" (Ibid.). They recorded their *Hymns* album because of "words" which were delivered to them three times by different individuals who approached them and said: "I believe God has a word for you—that you should do a hymns album." As they were recording this album Buck claims that "the Lord spoke to my heart and said, 'I have chosen you to breathe life back into these songs for your generation.'"

We reject the idea that sound hymns and spiritual songs of the past need to have life breathed back into them through worldly contemporary arrangements.

The members of the 2nd Chapter of Acts hold the false latter rain Pentecostal theology that Christ's return will be preceded by a worldwide miracle evangelistic revival. "The Word of God says that we are to wait for the former and the latter rain, that in the last days God is going to pour out His Spirit. There is coming an outpouring of His Spirit and an ingathering that will make the 'Jesus Movement' of the early '70s pale by comparison. We can see that beginning to happen already. It's gonna rain!" (Buck Herring, Ibid.).

The 2nd Chapter of Acts performed their last concert in August 1988 and disbanded the group to pursue other things.

In spite of their charismatic doctrinal error and their rock music, the members of the 2nd Chapter of Acts were different from the typical Contemporary Christian Music artist today. They rejected the gross commercialism and many of the worldly trappings of CCM. When asked what God wants to say through music today, Buck and Annie testified: "Jesus is Lord! Jesus was never popular. We can't make Him 'more palatable' to our generation. He was despised and rejected. We cannot put him in 20th century trappings and expect that everybody is going to love Him. He is King of kings and He calls you to die to yourself—that will never be popular." We agree with this statement 100%, and it is one of the reasons why we reject the CCM scene, which *does* attempt to present the Gospel in 20th century trappings and *does* attempt to be popular with the world.

4 HIM

4HIM is composed of four male singers: Andy Chrisman, Marty Magehee, Kirk Sullivan, and Mark Harris. The group was formed in 1990 and has recorded seven albums. They have won six Dove Awards, produced a gold album and 19 No. 1 hit songs.

The group is sponsored by the American Bible Society, which produces frightfully corrupt "dynamic equivalency" versions such as the Today's English Version and which works hand-in-hand with the Roman Catholic Church and with theological modernists throughout the world. (See our book *Unholy Hands on God's Holy Book: A Report on the United Bible Societies*, Way of Life Literature, 1701 Harns Rd., Oak Harbor, WA 98277.)

4HIM's song "Great Awakening" from their 1998 *Obvious* album demonstrates their Pentecostal theology:

> "I believe there's a mighty power/ I believe it's a latter rain/ I believe there's a move of God calling us all higher/ Oh I believe these are the days of the great awakening/ More than our hearts can contain/ It is an overflow of God's amazing grace/ Coming to reconcile a world that's lost its way/ Oh, all consuming fire come purify us once again."

Another song on that album is titled "Signs and Wonders."

> "You light the dark/ You are the truth in love/ So we just need to trust the signs and wonders of the heart. ... You sent love to live in us, so we just need to trust the signs and wonders of the heart."

Nowhere in the New Testament are we told to trust "the signs and wonders of the heart." This is an unscriptural experiential approach to Christianity (as opposed to trusting the Bible explicitly rather than looking within oneself for signs) which has produced confusion and shipwreck in its path.

In 1997 4HIM joined Roman Catholic Kathy Troccoli and 40 other CCM artists to record *Love One Another*, a song with an ecumenical theme: "Christians from all denominations demonstrating their common love for Christ and each other." The song talks about tearing down the walls of denominational division. The broad range of participants who joined Kathy Troccoli in recording "Love One Another" demonstrates the ecumenical agenda of Contemporary Christian Music. The song witnessed Catholics, Pentecostals, Baptists, etc., yoked together to call for Christian unity.

AARON AND JEOFFREY

Aaron and Jeoffrey are a father and son music team. As much as we enjoy seeing a close father/son relationship, we cannot support Aaron and Jeoffrey because of their jazzed up music and the unscriptural doctrine they sing. Note the following message from the song "Moment of Mercy" from *The Climb* album (1997) —

> "We've all been weakened by the choices we have made/ Wrapped in chains it seems we can't undo/ It doesn't matter what we've done or where we've been/ With one honest prayer/ We can be forgiven ... And with a simple act of faith we start to see/ Our failures are forgiven."

This is not the Gospel which Paul preached (1 Corinthians 15:1-4). The Gospel of the Bible says that Jesus Christ died for OUR SINS according to the Scriptures, that He was buried, and that He rose again the third day according to the Scriptures. Aaron and Jeoffrey speak not of forgiveness of sin, but of "failures" and of "choices we have made." A failure or a bad choice is not the same as sin, which is disobedience to God's law. This is a humanistic approach to salvation. Further, Aaron and Jeoffrey's gospel is not achieved by faith in the death, burial and resurrection of Christ for sin, but by an "honest prayer" and "a simple act of faith." People can honestly pray many things to God and not be saved, and a simple act of faith in itself does not save. The act of faith must be directed to the death, burial and resurrection of Jesus Christ. Many people have faith in God and faith in God's goodness and even faith in God's love in general who are not saved (James 2:19), because they have not put their trust in the finished cross work of Christ.

Consider another example of the false doctrine that Aaron and Jeoffrey sing:

> "God has a dream/ That your soul should know peace/ Your heart would be free/ God has a dream/ So believe that it's true/ God truly believes in you" ("God Has a Dream," from the album *The Climb*)

My friends, this is false. God loves the sinner and desires that every sinner be saved (John 3:16; 1 Tim. 2:3,4; 2 Peter 3:9), but He does not believe in the sinner. God does even "believe in" His born again children. He knows what is in man. He knows that there is nothing worthy in man. "Now when he was in Jerusalem at the passover, in the feast day, many believed in his name, when they saw the miracles which he did. But Jesus did not commit himself unto them, because he knew all men, And needed not that any should testify of man: for he knew what was in man (John 2:23-25).

In 1997 Aaron and Jeoffrey joined Roman Catholic Kathy Troccoli and 40 other CCM artists to record *Love One Another*, a song with an ecumenical theme: "Christians from all denominations demonstrating their common love for Christ and each other." The song talks about tearing down the walls of denominational division. The broad range of participants who joined Kathy Troccoli in recording "Love One Another" demonstrates the ecumenical agenda of Contemporary Christian Music. The song witnessed Catholics, Pentecostals, Baptists, etc., yoked together to call for Christian unity.

AD. See Terry Livgren.

AGE OF FAITH

The rock band Age of Faith was formed as a duo in 1990 with Jimi Ray as its leader. Ray describes their sound as "a late '80s rock thing" similar to the secular group Bon Jovi (Dave Urbanski, "Age of Faith," *CCM Magazine*, January 1997). After recording two albums and not finding commercial success, the group broke up in 1994 and did not perform or record for two years. During that time Ray's musical tastes changed to harder rock. Instead of receiving his inspiration from Bon Jovi, he "was listening to Counting Crows, Toad the Wet Sprocket, Hootie & the Blowfish—different artists with a rawer sound." In 1996 the group was reformed. Joining Ray in the reconstituted Age of Faith band are Drue Bachmann (bass), Steve Blair (drums), and Daniel Polydores (guitars). In 1997 they recorded a new album, *The Truth*.

The music of this group focuses on human experience and God's grace, but it is a grace which is devoid of repentance.

> "What we are learning is that many of our fans have told us that they have a hard time finding forgiveness for past mistakes. Also totally believing that God truly forgives. We deal a lot with these issues in this record. We show that God is who he says He is — He never changes — He is enough for us to live

this life. Mistakes will be made by us all, but God forgives" (Jimi Ray, Age of Faith, Grey Dot Records web site, http://placetobe.org/cmp/artists/index.html).

Biblical grace is bestowed on the repentant sinner. Repentance has to do with acknowledging that one's actions are sinful before God and are worthy of His judgment; it is being willing to turn from them. Note that Jimi Ray mentioned "mistakes," but he did not mention sin. It is not our mistakes which God forgives; it is our sins; and the sins must be acknowledged as such before Him. The Prodigal Son did not say, "I have made a mistake." He said, "Father, I HAVE SINNED AGAINST HEAVEN, AND IN THY SIGHT, and am no more worthy to be called thy son" (Luke 15:21). This is a biblical example of repentance which brings the grace of God. Much of the preaching within the Contemporary Christian Music scene presents an unbiblical grace which does not deal squarely with sin and which does not require repentance. The true grace of God does forgive our sins, but it also teaches "us that, denying ungodliness and worldly lusts, we should live soberly, righteously, and godly, in this present world" (Titus 2:11-12).

ALTAR BOYS

The rock group Altar Boys (who disbanded around 1990) was composed of Mike Stand (guitar, lead vocals), Ric Alba (bass, vocals), and Jeff Crandall (drums, vocals). They recorded their first album, *Altar Boys*, in 1984 and their last album, *Forever Mercy*, in 1989.

Mike Strand shares his philosophy of evangelism in the following statement:

> "We realized the only way we were going to reach high school and college kids is to play the kind of music they listen to … You have to use the proper form of communication. You can't sing hymns to them and expect them to come running down the aisles. They're just not going to listen" (Mike Strand, cited by Dan and Steve Peters, *What about Christian Rock?*, p. 165).

The Bible nowhere instructs God's people to use music to evangelize the lost. The biblical method of evangelism is preaching the Gospel.

ALTIZER, RICK

CCM performer Rick Altizer, in an interview with *CCM Magazine*, stated: "I think Christian music suffers because Christian people by nature are afraid of the world" (*CCM Magazine*, August 1998, p. 18). This strange statement describes the common attitude of the CCM crowd. They think it is wrong to be afraid of the world, but this is utter nonsense. The Bible repeatedly warns God's people to be afraid of the world, because the world is under the dominion of the Devil, who is called the "god of this world" (2

Cor. 4:4), and also under the dominion of man's fallen nature (1 John 2:15-17). "See then that ye walk circumspectly, not as fools, but as wise, redeeming the time, because the days are evil" (Ephesians 5:15,16).

ARENDS, CAROLYN

In 1997 Carolyn Arends joined Roman Catholic Kathy Troccoli and 40 other CCM artists to record *Love One Another*, a song with an ecumenical theme: "Christians from all denominations demonstrating their common love for Christ and each other." The song talks about tearing down the walls of denominational division. The broad range of participants who joined Kathy Troccoli in recording "Love One Another" demonstrates the ecumenical agenda of Contemporary Christian Music. The song witnessed Catholics, Pentecostals, Baptists, etc., yoked together to call for Christian unity.

ARMAGEDDON

Armageddon is a hard rock group which represents the New Evangelical Campus Crusade for Christ. An Armageddon concert at Ohio State University was described in these words:

> "There lies before me as I write a clipping from the *Ohio State Lantern* (April, 1970), publication of Ohio State University. The clipping contains a picture of Armageddon, a 'nationwide touring group' of young men and mini-skirted young ladies. Their two-hour pop concert, we are informed, 'will include favorite contemporary sounds from such groups as the Beatles, Blood, Sweat and Tears, Brazil '66, and Glen Campbell'" (Charles Woodbridge, *Campus Crusade Examined in the Light of Scripture*, 1970, p. 5).

ASHTON, SUSAN

Susan Ashton (1967-) has become a very popular CCM singer/writer. Her first album, *Wakened by the Wind*, was released in 1991 and became the best-selling album by a new artist under the Sparrow label. In 1992 she was named Favorite New Artist by the readers of *CCM Magazine*. Five singles from her first two albums reached No. 1 on national Christian radio charts.

Ashton is ecumenical and performs in a wide range of denominational situations. She frequently appears in charismatic churches, such as Assemblies of God and Vineyard assemblies, and in various charismatic-ecumenical festivals.

AUDIO ADRENALINE

The popular hard rock group Audio Adrenaline is composed of Mark Stuart (vocals), Will McGinnis (bass), Ben Cissel (drums), Tyler (guitar), and Bob Herdman (keyboards). Former Audio Adrenaline guitarist Barry Blair left the group to become a full-time producer. Two members of the band have shoulder-length hair.

The manner in which Audio Adrenaline connects rock music with Jesus Christ is blasphemous:

> "... the only difference [between rock and Christian rock] is the lyrics and then the difference is sometimes subtle ... at the basic root, there's no difference. ... Christianity is about rebellion. Jesus Christ is the biggest rebel to ever walk the face of the earth ... he was crucified for his rebellion. Rock 'n' roll is about the same thing—rebellion ... to me rock and the church go hand in hand" (Mark Stuart of Audio Adrenaline, *Pensacola News Journal*, Pensacola, Florida, March 1, 1998, pp. 1,6E).

Audio Adrenaline performs secular rock songs on their albums and at their concerts. The *Huntsville* (Alabama) *Times* for March 2, 2000, observed: "If you come to Audio Adrenaline's concert Friday night [$19.50] at Whitesburg Baptist Church, be well-advised. This won't be the Good Time Gospel Hour by a bunch of choirboys. Nope, this is rock 'n' roll-loud, jamming, Christian rock 'n' roll. You might hear some . . . classics, but it's more likely you'll hear 'Free Ride,'—yes, the great rock 'n' roll song by Edgar and Johnny Winter." The song "Free Ride" is also featured on Audio Adrenaline's *Bloom* album. The song is from Edgar Winter Group's *They Only Come Out at Night* album. Rock star Edgar Winter was featured on the cover of this wicked album dressed as a homosexual "drag queen." The lyrics to "Free Ride" claim that "all of the answers, are come from within." This is rank heresy, because we know that the answers do not come from within man's fallen heart, but from God's revelation in the Bible.

The lyrics to Audio Adrenaline's songs are rarely plain. Note the following apparent attempt to give the gospel. It is the hard rock song "Big House" on their 1993 album, *Don't Censor Me*.

> "Come and go with me/ To my Father's house/ ... It's a big, big house/ With lots and lots of room/ A big, big table/ with lots and lots of food/ A big, big yard/ Where we can play football/ A big, big house/ It's my Father's house/ Ibidibidee/ bop bop bow whew! Yeah!/ All I know is a big ole house/ with rooms for everyone/ All I know is lots of land/ Where we can play and run/ All I know is you need love/ And I've got a family/ All I know is you're all alone/ So why not come with me."

What does this song mean? It is not clear. Possibly it means that God has a big house where His children have a good time. If this is what it means, how does one get to God's house? Audio Adrenaline doesn't say. They imply that all a person has to do to go to God's house is to feel all alone and need love and hang around professing Christians ("come along with me"). The line "all I know is you need love" is almost exactly like the line from the Beatle's song—"All you need is love." What love are they talking about? Romantic love? Friendship love? Love of the world? The Lord of God? They don't say. Why not? Why be so vague? If you really care about communicating eternal truths to young people, why not plainly state these truths? Further, why does Audio Adrenaline repeatedly say, "All I know is..."? Don't they know anything else? The Apostle John stated nine times in one short Epistle (1 John) that we know things from God.

The Audio Adrenaline song "Good People" teaches a universalistic ecumenicalism:

> "I grew up impressed/ by the people I knew in the buckle of the Bible belt/ hopped in a van with a band/ now I've been just about everywhere else/ Met a soldier from Seattle, and a lawyer from the east/ a Texas oil baron and a Roman Catholic priest/ everyday I choose, to walk in their shoes/ cause pretty are the feet of those who bring the good news/ good people, good people everywhere, everywhere/ It's God's people/ Been on the road/ been far from home/ but I found me a friend or two/ time has taught me well/ and I can tell/ you the good things people do/ they really care/ and I've been there/ I've seen it with my eyes/ I can tell/ they're God's people by the goodness in their lives."

We can tell those who are saved by the goodness in their lives? The Bible says those who follow false gospels are cursed of God (Galatians 1), regardless of how spiritual they might appear to be, regardless of their human kindness.

In 1997 Audio Adrenaline joined Roman Catholic Kathy Troccoli and 40 other CCM artists to record *Love One Another*, a song with an ecumenical theme: "Christians from all denominations demonstrating their common love for Christ and each other." The song talks about tearing down the walls of denominational division. The broad range of participants who joined Kathy Troccoli in recording "Love One Another" demonstrates the ecumenical agenda of Contemporary Christian Music. The song witnessed Catholics, Pentecostals, Baptists, etc., yoked together to call for Christian unity.
When Pope John Paul II visited the States in January 1999, Audio Adrenaline and other CCM groups joined hands with hundreds of thousands of Catholics to welcome him. Featured at a Catholic youth rally connected with the Pope's visit, were Audio Adrenaline, dc Talk, Rebecca St. James, Jennifer Knapp, The W's, and the Supertones (*CCM Magazine*, April 1999, p. 12). Each attendee received a rosary with instructions about how to pray to Mary.

AVALON

Avalon was formed in 1995 and is composed of Michael Passons, Janna Potter, Nikki Hassman, and Jody McBrayer. At the Avalon web site there are biographical sketches of each member of the group. None of them give a testimony of salvation. They point to secular rock musicians as major influences in their musical development. McBrayer points to Anita Baker, Stevie Wonder and Aretha Franklin. Potter points to Aretha Franklin, Regina Bell, Mahalia Jackson, and Anita Baker.

The hazy nature of much of their music is evident from the lyrics to "This Love" from their 1996 *Avalon* album:

> "I've seen that look a million times/ Disenchanted eyes/ You don't have to say a word/ I know it's love you doubt, but you're lost without it/ You hope for one glimpse of heaven/ You pray for a sign/ But I know where all is forgiven/ Let's go where we know love is alive/ This love can change a life forever/ The only way to start is giving Him our hearts, yea/ His love will piece us back together. This is the way, this is the life/ This love/ It's nothing we could ever earn/ It's unconditional/ It's free, but cost Him everything/ It's this love we need and it's our road to freedom/ So don't underestimate God's love/ It's power to heal/ Come take a drink from the fountain/ Let's go where we know love is alive" ("This Love," written by Chris Rodriguez and Charlie Peacock, sung by Avalon).

This is an attempt to present the Gospel, but the message is too hazy to be effective, unless the hearer already knows the Gospel plainly. Salvation is not by giving Christ my heart. It is by putting my faith in the cross-work of Jesus Christ to redeem me from the punishment due for my sin (1 Corinthians 15:1-4). Why not give a clear Gospel message? Why beat around the bush?

In an interview with *CCM Magazine*, Jody McBrayer says: "I grew up hearing all the don'ts. There's a lot more to God than we think" (Karly Randolph-Pitman, "Graceland," *CCM Magazine*, March 1998). She is right, of course. There is much more to the Christian life than don'ts, but her complaint sounds too much like that we have heard from so many other CCM musicians. They don't like do's and don'ts, but the New Testament is filled with them.

BAILEY, PHILIP

Popular CCM artist Philip Bailey formerly played with the occultic rock group Earth, Wind & Fire. Since becoming a CCM performer, Baily continues to yoke together with the world. He sang a duet called "Easy Lover" with secular rock star Phil Collins.

In his song "The Wonders of His Love," Bailey connects pagan jungle drums with the true and living God.

> "The beating drums in deep forgotten forest floors/ A rhythm dance in tribal doors/ Reach the river shore/ Pounding the wonders of His love..."

Pagan dances do not pound the wonders of God's love; they pound a tribute to the god of this world, Satan, and to the satisfying of the flesh. Pagan drums are used to initiate demon possession and to promote immorality.

BARNABAS

The heavy metal rock group Barnabas was formed in 1978 and disbanded in 1986. It was composed of Kris Klingensmith (drums, lyrics), Nancy Jo Mann (lead vocals), Gary Mann (bass, keyboards), and Brian Belew (guitar). The original guitarist for the band was Monte Cooley. The guitarist for Barnabas' *Find Your Heart a Home* album was Mike Donner. Barnabas appeared in concert in long hair (on the males) and metal rock attire, leather, chains, etc.

Barnabas was so riotous that the lyrics to the songs frequently cannot be understood. The following is a review of one of their albums:

> "A strong rhythm section drives the title cut and 'Auschwitz 87' which opens with solo vocals by, yep, Adolf Hitler. WE CAN'T TELL YOU EXACTLY WHAT THESE SONGS ARE ABOUT BECAUSE THERE'S NO LYRIC SHEET and Nancy Jo Mann's voice can't sustain the clear delivery and energy her three partners deliver" (*CCM Magazine*, May 1987, p. 36).

The members of Barnabas were not concerned that they were offending many pastors. "The group constantly contended with ministers and church organizations who misunderstood the band's image and music and who reviled them as being unchristian and even demonic" ("Barnabas — in Brief," http://www.leconte.com/barnabas/info.htm). Contrast this attitude with that which God requires of His children:

> "But if thy brother be grieved with thy meat, now walkest thou not charitably. Destroy not him with thy meat, for whom Christ died. ... For the kingdom of God is not meat and drink; but righteousness, and peace, and joy in the Holy Ghost" (Romans 14:15,17).

After recording five albums, the group broke up in 1986 with much "pain and disappointment." The end of the band is described as an "emotional crash" which apparently involved the divorce of married band members. Though disbanded, Barnabas "has a loyal and growing fan following throughout the world, thanks to the Internet" (Ibid.).

BARREN CROSS

The following analysis of Barren Cross is from *Focus*, January-February 1987, page 3—

> "Barren Cross, a Christian rock band ... note the sadomasochistic apparel worn in exactly the same fashion as Judas Priest and all other heavy metal rockers. Why does a 'Christian' group wear the trappings of sexual perversion? ... Note the metal studded jacket, belt and metal spiked arm and hand covers. All this is popular gear for sadomasochists. Sadomasochism is the obtaining of sexual pleasure both by inflicting pain upon the partner, and by having pain inflicted upon oneself. The purpose of the metal studs is to draw blood!
>
> "The inner sleeve of this album [*Barren Cross*] contains the following in a letter from the pastor of this group, Bob Beeman. 'I am impressed with their maturity in the Lord and their solid foundation in the scriptures. They not only attend my church, but are involved in teaching and counseling.'
>
> "Not one of their songs presents the way of salvation, or even really tells who our Lord Jesus Christ is. Their sound is indistinguishable from any other heavy metal group. Here are some of their lyrics — judge for yourself, do these present the gospel of Jesus Christ?
>
> "Give it a chance, freedom at last/ Yours for free, take and receive/ Better than pot, Jesus rocks/ Come and believe/ You will find out joy will come to you/ Take it, drink it, no fee, come and believe/ Smoke on His love — believe/ Smoke on His love and you will see the rock — roll/ Believe" (Barren Cross, "Believe").
>
> "We will rock — for the King/ Get yourselves ready to take to the air/ Soon we'll be there — those who live for the King/ We're rockin' steady/ We will rock — to the gates/ We will rock for the King/ We will rock/ Time is running out/ We will rock/ Shout it to the face of the crowd/ We will rock/ Let the people know — make it loud/ We will rock/ The kingdom is at hand/ We will rock/ It's time to make a stand/ Rock for the King" (Barren Cross, "Rock for the King").

BECKER, MARGARET

Margaret Becker claims to have had a spiritual experience which has made her more appreciative of her Roman Catholicism. She does not like the term "born again," though.

> "Asked if she was born again, Becker said, 'I hate to use that term because it's an incorrect term. I like to think of myself as a devout Christian. Born again—that's Christian slang'" (Becker, cited by Dan Maley, "Songs Say It All for Christian Singer," *The Macon Telegraph*, Macon, Georgia, January 1996).

We wonder where Becker got the idea that "born again" is Christian slang? The term is used three times in the Bible, twice by the Lord Jesus Christ. "Jesus answered and said unto him, Verily, verily, I say unto thee, Except a man be born again, he cannot see the kingdom of God" (John 3:3). The Apostle Peter taught that man is born again through God's Word: "Being born again, not of corruptible seed, but of incorruptible, by the word of God, which liveth and abideth for ever" (1 Peter 1:23).

Becker does not use her concerts to preach the Gospel or to call upon people to make commitments to Christ. "I'm not a preacher, I'm not good at that," she said. "I spend a lot of time on my songs, and the speaking or lack of speaking is in the song" (Dan Maley, "Songs say it all for Christian singer," *The Macon Telegraph*, Macon, Georgia, January 1996).

Becker is ecumenical and moves in a wide range of denominational forums. For example, she was scheduled to appear at the First Assembly of God in Warrenton, Virginia, in September 1993. That same month she was featured in a "Margaret Becker Youth Fest" at a large Baptist Bible Fellowship church, Riverdale Baptist Church, Riverdale, Maryland. She was scheduled to appear at a Church of Christ in Converse, Indiana, in March 1994.

The following information is from a report by Don Jasmin in *The Fundamentalist Digest*, May-June 1994: "The *News Journal*, a daily newspaper in Wilmington, Delaware, in a Saturday issue recently featured an article on Becker's musical career. ... Not only is Becker a 'contemporary singer and songwriter,' but following the Amy Grant pattern, according to her own words, she has 'taken very deliberate steps to present ourselves at the next level,' which includes 'hip danceable tunes about relationships, mostly with God.' 'Having performed Christian rock, pop, contemporary and even gospel selections' in her 'gritty alto' voice, 'it seems that Becker has nowhere to go but to secular charts, a la Amy Grant,' according to the article. Reciting a religious history of her life, soon after her supposed new-birth conversion, Becker began 'mixing faith with her music and gained a greater appreciation for her own faith, Catholicism.' 'Now, I'm taking that knowledge with me back to the church of my youth.' Becker declared, 'The familiar prayers and practices are very rich and touch me in a different, more intimate way'" (*The Fundamentalist Digest*, May-June 1994).

Becker has frequently been nominated for Grammy awards. In 1996 *CCM Magazine* named Becker's song "This I Know" the Song of the Year. She co-wrote "Exalt the

Name" which became a No. 1 hit for Sandi Patty.

BELL, STEVE

Steve Bell is a Canadian CCM musician who has produced five albums. In 1999 he debuted his first album on a U.S. label. It is titled *Beyond a Shadow*. After playing secular music in various clubs for 10 years, Bell claims God spoke to him about going into the Christian music field. "God was in the room. I'm not one of those guys who has wondrous kinds of experiences, but I felt God's presence and this heat in my chest" (*CCM magazine*, July 1999, p. 26). Bell's first album was sponsored by a Roman Catholic Jesuit priest.

BEVILL, LISA

In 1997 Lisa Bevill joined Roman Catholic Kathy Troccoli and 40 other CCM artists to record *Love One Another*, a song with an ecumenical theme: "Christians from all denominations demonstrating their common love for Christ and each other." The song talks about tearing down the walls of denominational division. The broad range of participants who joined Kathy Troccoli in recording "Love One Another" demonstrates the ecumenical agenda of Contemporary Christian Music. The song witnessed Catholics, Pentecostals, Baptists, etc., yoked together to call for Christian unity.

BEYOND THE BLUE

In 1997 Beyond the Blue joined Roman Catholic Kathy Troccoli and 40 other CCM artists to record *Love One Another*, a song with an ecumenical theme: "Christians from all denominations demonstrating their common love for Christ and each other." The song talks about tearing down the walls of denominational division. The broad range of participants who joined Kathy Troccoli in recording "Love One Another" demonstrates the ecumenical agenda of Contemporary Christian Music. The song witnessed Catholics, Pentecostals, Baptists, etc., yoked together to call for Christian unity.

BIG TENT REVIVAL
Big Tent Revival is composed of Steve Wiggins (guitar/lead vocals), Randy Williams (guitar), Rick Heil (bass), and Spence Smith (drums).

The following lyrics to the song "Lovely Mausoleum" (from "Open All Nite," 1996) illustrate the hazy, erroneous doctrine of this CCM rock group (some of the members of which have long hair and earrings) —

"Sunrise open your eyes/ When are you gonna see? New day coming your way/ What is it gonna be? Chorus: Your choice, your voice/ You are in control/ Jesus, Jesus/ He will make you whole."

There is no clear gospel here. What new day is coming my way? What is my choice? I am in control of what? Who is Jesus? What does He have to do with a sunrise for me? How does He make me whole? Whole from what?

BLACKWOOD BROTHERS. See J.D. Sumner.

BLAME LUCY

Blame Lucy released its first album, *Going Strong*, in 1998.

> "The main message we are really praying about, sharing about, is that God accepts anyone, as long as they accept Him. ... We want to offer music that they actually want to listen to, and show them that they can have their souls saved at the same time" (Doug Meacham of Blame Lucy, *HM magazine*, May-June, 1998, p. 46).

BLOODGOOD

Bloodgood, who patterned their look after metal rock groups of the 80s (long hair, spandex, leather), released their first album in 1986. It was self titled and was produced by Darrell Mansfield. Their second album, *Detonation*, appeared in 1987. They produced a two-album video collection featuring dancers and visual effects titled *Alive in America* and *Shakin' the World*. The group was composed of Les Carlsen (vocals), Michael Bloodgood (bass/song writer), and David Zaffiro (guitar).

> "We're like Billy Graham with guitars, basically ... rock and roll is neutral. It depends on the spirit" (Michael Bloodgood, *Duluth News Tribune*, October 9, 1987, p. 1C).

One Bloodgood song mocks fallen fundamentalist preachers:

> "He's a sinner though he'd never been found/ He got caught with his own pants down/ Can't imagine how he must have felt/ He should've tightened-up his Bible belt..." (Bloodgood, "Shakin' It").

BOLTZ, RAY

Ray Boltz is known for his mild rock and balladeer style, such as that featured in his hit "I Pledge Allegiance to the Lamb"; but in 2001 he formed a new recording label called

Spindus to produce hard rock groups. The first signing is a band called GS Megaphone, which has a sound similar to the vile secular bands Creed and Pearl Jam.

Ray Boltz praised Mother Teresa in an article in *CCM Magazine:*

> Ray Boltz was one of the privileged that did met the woman born Agnes Gonxha Bojaxhiu [Mother Teresa]. Boltz is a spokesperson for Mission of Mercy, an outreach organization formed in Calcutta, India, the same place that is home to Sister Teresa's Mother House of Missionaries Charity (MC).
>
> Although Boltz describes her as a short, tiny woman, her presence filled the room with that of someone of a much larger stature.
>
> "I was totally in awe," says Boltz of their meeting in 1996. "She was one of the most recognizable women of the century, but you don't want to walk in with the perspective that she is a famous person or that you are a fan. But when she walked in the courtyard at the Mother house, the look on everybody's face was awe! This is Mother Teresa!"
>
> Boltz explains the maxim behind Teresa's work, "Whatever you do, do for Jesus Christ and for the glory of God."
>
> "Mother Teresa was an example to us," says Boltz. "When she started this ministry, she was a teacher. She felt God calling her to minister to the poor. At that time, for a woman to tell her superiors she was called to ministry—that was really out of the ordinary. I am impressed she did not go along with status quo, but followed the call of God. That is refreshing and different and part of why she stands out" (Gregory Rumburg and April Hefner, "The Princess and the Nun, *CCM Magazine*, June 2001).

Mother Teresa was a kind woman, but she preached a false gospel and thereby gave a false hope to those to whom she ministered. We have documented this in our book *Evangelicals and Rome*.

BONO

Bono (1960-) (real name Paul Hewson), lead singer for the megastar secular rock group U2 (formed in 1978), is popular with many Christian youth because he is a professing Christian, as are two other members of the band, Dave Evans ("Edge") and Larry Mullen. The three visited a charismatic house church called Shalom and announced themselves Christians in their teenage years. The U2 drummer, Adam Clayton, does not make any type of Christian profession. In my opinion, he is the most honest of the four band members. At least he does not pretend to have faith in the Bible while living a rock & roll lifestyle.

Bono, Evans, and Mullen admit that they wrestled with quitting rock & roll when they began studying the Bible after their "conversion." They chose to stay with rock & roll and have been moving farther and farther from the Bible ever since. Of that early struggle Bono told a *Rolling Stones* magazine senior editor: "We were getting involved in reading books, the Big Book. Meeting people who were more interested in things spiritual, superspiritual characters that I can see now were possibly far too removed from reality. But we were wrapped up in that."

This business of spiritually-minded Christians being "too far removed from reality" is a common smokescreen used by rebellious types to excuse their worldliness. The Bible says:

> "If ye then be risen with Christ, seek those things which are above, where Christ sitteth on the right hand of God. Set your affection on things above, not on things on the earth. For ye are dead, and your life is hid with Christ in God. When Christ, who is our life, shall appear, then shall ye also appear with him in glory" (Colossians 3:1-4).

Bono mocks as superspiritual those who attempt to turn from the things of this world to set their minds on heavenly things, but the Bible says that is precisely what God wants His people to do.

U2's guitarist, Dave Evans, admits that it is a contradiction for Christians to play in a rock & roll band.

> "It was reconciling two things that seemed for us at that moment to be mutually exclusive. We never did resolve the contradictions. That's the truth. ... Because we were getting a lot of people in our ear saying, 'This is impossible, you guys are Christians, you can't be in a band. It's a contradiction and you have to go one way or the other.' They said a lot worse things than that as well. So I just wanted to find out. I was sick of people not really knowing and me not knowing whether this was right for me. So I took two weeks. Within a day or two I just knew that all this stuff is —— [vulgarity]. We were the band. Okay, it's a contradiction for some, but it's a contradiction that I'm able to live with. I just decided that I was going to live with it. I wasn't going to try to explain it because I can't" (Bill Flanagan, book *U2 at the End of the World*, pp. 47,48).

Note that Evans does not base his decision upon the Word of God. Contrary to Proverbs 3:5,6, he leans on his own desires and understanding.

U2 is frequently mentioned in *CCM Magazine* in a positive light. For example, the December 1998 issue contained a review of U2's "Best of 1980-1990" release. The reviewer said: "...U2 has epitomized the question, 'Is this a Christian band or are its members Christians playing in a band?'" The reviewer praises U2 for its "vivid religious imagery."

In fact, there is very little, if any, evidence in U2's lives, music, or performances that they honor the Word of God. They have been at the heart of the wicked rock & roll scene for almost three decades. They are one of the most popular rock & roll groups alive today and this certainly would not be the case if they were striving to obey the Bible in all things. Their record sales are in excess of 70 million. They have won five awards on the wicked MTV. They have often won *Rolling Stone* magazine's reader's poll titles for most popular rock group. Bono has been named the most popular rock singer. In 1992 "Bono was named premier male sexpot" (*U2: The Rolling Stone Files*, p. xxxvi).

Because of their popularity in the rock music field, the members of U2 have had countless opportunities to testify plainly of their faith in Christ, but Bono says they don't like to discuss their religious beliefs in public. I have read dozens of U2 interviews, but I have never heard them give a clear testimony of the new birth.

The members of U2 don't support any denomination or church. In fact, they rarely attend church, "preferring to meet together in private prayer sessions" (*U2: The Rolling Stone Files*, p. 21). Bono says that he would like to be able to go to a Catholic church or a Protestant one (p. 20). They are "not rabid Bible thumpers" (Ibid., p. 14). In the song "Acrobat," Bono sings, "I'd join the movement/ If there was one I could believe in ... I'd break bread and wine/ If there was a church I could receive in."

One church Bono does attend from time to time is Glide Memorial United Methodist in San Francisco. "When he's in the area Bono is a frequent worshipper at Glide..." (Flanagan, book *U2 at the End of the World,* p. 99). Bono attended Glide Memorial during a special service they had to honor Clinton's 1992 presidential election. Speaking at a meeting connected with the 1972 United Methodist Church Quadrennial Conference, Cecil Williams, pastor of the Glide Memorial Methodist Church in San Francisco, California, said, "I don't want to go to no heaven ... I don't believe in that stuff . I think it's a lot of - - - -." (Here he used a curse word.) Long ago William's church replaced the choir with a rock band, and its "celebrations" have included dancing and even nudity. A Jewish rabbi is on William's staff. After attending a service at Glide Memorial, a newspaper editor wrote, "The service, in my opinion, was an insult to every Christian attending and was the most disgusting display of vulgarity and sensuousness I have ever seen anywhere." In spite of William's apostasy and immorality, his bishop has continued to support him.

The members of U2 do not believe Christianity should have rules and regulations. "I'm really interested in and influenced by the spiritual side of Christianity, rather than the legislative side, the rules and regulations" (Edge, *U2: The Rolling Stone Files*, p. 21).

The lives of the U2 rock stars illustrate their no-rules philosophy. Bill Flanagan, a U2 friend who has traveled extensively with the group, in his book *U2 at the End of the World* describes them as heavy drinkers and constant visitors to bars, brothels, and night clubs. He says, "If I wanted to I could fill up hundreds of pages with this sort of three-sheets-to-the-wind [drunken], navel-gazing dialogue between U2 and me" (p. 145). Bono describes their life on the road as "a fairly decadent kind of selfish-art-oriented lifestyle" (Flanagan, p. 79). Their language is interspersed with the vilest vulgarities and even with profanity. Of Magic Johnson's sexual escapades, Bono says: "Be a sex machine, but for Christ's sake use a condom" (Flanagan, p. 105). When Clinton won the 1992 presidential election, U2 had just traveled from the United States to Canada. Bono said: "Jesus, isn't that just like us! It's a hell of a night to have just left America" (Flanagan, p. 99). Much of Bono's statements cannot be printed in a Christian publication. The cover and lyric sheet to their *Achtung Baby* album contained photos of the band in homosexual drag clothing, a picture of Bono in front of a topless woman, and a frontal photo of Adam Clayton completely nude. Bono has simulated sex with women during his concerts. Their concerts have included video clips portraying nudity and cuss words. One U2 concert series featured a belly dancer. The band members have had serious marital problems and Dave Evans is divorced. Of sex, Bono says: "You know, if you tell people that the best place to have sex is in the safe hands of a loving relationship, you may be telling a lie! There may be other places" (Flanagan, p. 83). For one of their videos U2 dressed up in women's dress like homosexual drag queens. About that, Bono says: "Nobody wanted to take their clothes off for about a week! And I have to say, some people have been doing it ever since!" (Flanagan, p. 58). Bono told the media that he and his bandmates planned to spend New Year's Eve 2000 in Dublin, because "Dublin knows how to drink" (Bono, *USA Today*, Oct. 15, 1999, p. E1).

U2's ambiguous music does not present a clear Christian message, and many of the few songs which do mention Christ do so in a strange, unscriptural manner. "The listener senses something religious is being dealt with but can't be quite sure what" (Steve Turner, *Hungry for Heaven*, p. 172). They never preach the Gospel of Jesus Christ in a plain manner so that their listeners could be born again. They pose moral questions in some of their songs, but they give no Bible answers. "U2 don't pretend to have the answers to the world's troubles. Instead, they devote their energies to letting us know that they are concerned and to creating an awareness about those problems" (*U2: The Rolling Stone Files*, p. 10). What a pitiful testimony for professing Christian musicians who COULD be preaching the light of the Word of God to a dark and hell-bound world.

One of U2's most popular songs even proclaims that they haven't found what they are looking for.

> "You broke the bonds/ You loosed the chains/ You carried the cross/ And my shame/ You know I believe it/ But I still haven't found/ What I'm looking for" ("I Still Haven't Found What I'm Looking For," U2).

This is a strange message for an alleged Christian rock group to broadcast to a needy world! During a Dublin concert, Bono paused in the middle of singing "I Still Haven't Found What I'm Looking For" and shouted, "I hope I never find it!" (*U2: The Rolling Stone Files*, p. xl).

The group is active in political causes, but they are liberal humanistic ones. For example, in 1992 they played a benefit concert for the environmentalist/pacifist group Greenpeace and joined Greenpeace in protesting against a nuclear power plant. One of their hits, "Pride," is a tribute to Martin Luther King; and in 1994 U2 received the Martin Luther King Freedom Award. King was an adulterous, modernistic preacher who taught a false social gospel. U2 supported Bill Clinton in his 1992 run for president. Clinton conversed with them on a national radio talk show during the election campaign and met them in a hotel room in Chicago. At the same time they mocked George Bush during their USA concerts that year. They featured a video clip depicting Bush chanting the words to "We Will Rock You" by the homosexual rock group Queen. Members of U2 performed at Bill Clinton's televised inaugural ball on MTV. Bono thinks Clinton's election was a victory for homosexuals, members of the underclass, women, and artists (Flanagan, p. 100).

Bono's christ appears to be a false one. He says he is "attracted to people like Martin Luther King, Gandhi, Christ, to pacifism" (*U2: The Rolling Stone Files*, p. xxviii). The Lord Jesus Christ of the Bible is not a pacifist. He is not anything like the modernist Martin Luther or the Hindu Gandhi. Christ did instruct His people not to resist evil in the sense of taking up arms for religious causes. When persecuted, we are to endure it (1 Cor. 4:12), but Christ did not teach pacifism. Christ's forerunner, John the Baptist, warned soldiers to be content with their wages, but he did not rebuke them for carrying arms as soldiers (Lk. 3:14). Before his death, Christ instructed his followers to provide swords for themselves (Lk. 22:32-38). Christ said he came not to send peace but a sword (Mt. 10:34). In fact, the Lord Jesus Christ will return on a white horse to make war with his enemies (Rev. 19:11-16). The Christ of the Bible is no pacifist and He did not establish a pacifist movement.

The following quotations demonstrate that U2's "spirituality" is not based on the Bible:

> "... Bono dislikes the label 'born-again Christian'—and he doesn't go to church either. 'I'm a very, very bad advertisement for God...'" (Ibid.).

"Born again Christian Bono has slipped from his saintly ways—with a nine-hour binge which left him 'brainless'... The U2 star ... got struck into beer, wine, cocktails and bubbly celebrating the American release of the band's *Rattle And Hum* film. 'He was slobbering, shouting and showing off,' said a bartender at the Santa Monica niterie that hosted the bash. 'Even the rest of the band told him to calm down. They should have been kicked out but because of who they are we let them stay...'" (*The People*, Oct. 23, 1988, p. 15, cited by Jeff Godwin, *What's Wrong with Christian Rock?*, p. 70).

"A U2 concert aims to raise people's sense of their own worth. 'Its a celebration of me being me and you being you,' as Bono once put it. The music soars and swirls but never bludgeons. ... 'I want people to leave our concerts feeling positive, a bit more free,' says Bono" (Steve Turner, *Hungry for Heaven*, p. 28).

"People expect you, as a believer, to have all the answers, when really all you have is a whole new set of questions" (Bono, cited by Steve Turner, *Hungry for Heaven*, p. 173).

"The link between rock 'n' roll and gospel is not at all tenuous. In my walking into walls spiritually I'm not as alone as I once thought I was. When I look back there's Patti Smith and Bob Dylan and Van Morrison and Elvis Presley—right the way down the line" (Bono, cited by Steve Turner, *Hungry for Heaven*, p. 28).

"Once I thought rock 'n' roll didn't have a place for spiritual concerns. But I've since discovered that a lot of the artists who have inspired me—Bob Dylan, Van Morrison, Patti Smith, Al Green and Marvin Gaye—were in a similar position ... that's why I'm more at ease" (Bono, cited by Steve Turner, *Hungry for Heaven*, back cover).

Bono points to rock stars Bob Dylan, Van Morrison, Elvis Presley, Patti Smith, and Marvin Gaye as an inspiration for spiritual concerns. This is most amazing, as not one of these has a biblical faith in Jesus Christ as God and Redeemer. Not one accepts the Bible as the infallible Word of God. Dylan went through a brief phase of professing faith in Christ in the late 1970s and early 1980s, but he has long since repudiated that. An article in the *San Luis Obispo* (California) *Register* for March 16, 1983, quoted Dylan as saying: "Whoever said I was Christian? Like Gandhi, I'm Christian, I'm Jewish, I'm a Moslem, I'm a Hindu. I am a humanist." Van Morrison believes a New Age sort of hodgepodge theology condensed from his studies in Buddhism, Christianity, Hinduism, and Scientology. He calls himself a "Christian mystic" but does not trust Jesus Christ as God and Savior. Punk rocker Patti Smith curses and blasphemes God on her 1978 *Easter* album. In her song "Gloria" she says: "Jesus died for somebody's sins/ But not mine." She says, "I've been called a blasphemer a thousand times but I said that [in the song 'Gloria'] because I refuse to accept that I came into this world as a sinner" (Patti

Smith, cited by Steve Turner, *Hungry for Heaven*, p. 143). Her heroes in the Bible are Cain, Eve, and Lucifer. Marvin Gaye combined his vile immorality with a profession of faith in Christ. "On his album *Sexual Healing* he recites a list of credits, including one for 'our Lord and Saviour Jesus Christ,' and then glides straight into a song about wanting some woman's body. That's the way he would have liked it to be. He would like to have been able to obey his darkest passions and purify himself at the same time. ... On stage he would strip down to a jock strap" (Ibid.). Elvis Presley did love gospel music and even professed faith in Christ to some people, but he gave no evidence of being a Bible-believing Christian. He constructed "a personalised religion out of what he'd read of Hinduism, Judaism, numerology, theosophy, mind control, positive thinking and Christianity" (Ibid.).

BOONE, DEBBY

"Pat Boone's famous daughter, Debby (1956-), has tried pop, disco and country but is now switching to 'gospel' music (*Birmingham Post-Herald*, March 22, 1985). She was to perform at Samford University as part of her spring tour. Her first solo recording, 'You Light Up My Life,' was a mega hit and she claimed that the four million records it sold was proof of God's blessing. She said she did this song 'for Jesus,' but fundamental Christians objected to the dangerous and scriptural philosophy of the line, 'It can't be wrong when it feels so right.' Debby now plans to be a 'contemporary Christian singer' and sing 'Christian lyrics' set to pop or rock music. She has been concerned for years about her 'goody two-shoes' image, and worried that people considered her shallow and square. She has performed with her dad in Las Vegas, with Dr. Robert Schuller (November 1983); and last year she portrayed a prostitute in a TV movie. Debby, and teens who consider her a role model, needs to read and heed James 4:4" (*Calvary Contender*, April 1985).

BOONE, PAT

Pat Boone (1934-) is a member of Jack Hayford's Foursquare Pentecostal Church. In 1996 Boone released an album of heavy-metal rock songs under the title *Pat Boone in a Metal Mood — No More Mr. Nice Guy*. It contained orchestrated versions of songs by openly demonic rock groups such as Alice Cooper, Guns N' Roses, Ozzy Osbourne, and Judas Priest. On April 15, 1997, Boone's pastor joined him on a Trinity Broadcasting Network broadcast with Paul Crouch and defended his heavy metal album.

Pat Boone's ecumenical philosophy was stated in an interview he gave to the Worldwide Church of God in *The Plain Truth* magazine.

> "We have to allow for each other's doctrinal differences, but agree on the basics. That's where I stand, and why I identify so much with *The Plain Truth*" (Pat Boone,

cited by Sheila Graham, "Up Close and Personal with Pat Boone," *The Plain Truth*, May-June 1997, p. 28).

The Worldwide Church of God no longer denies the Trinity and the Deity of Jesus Christ, as they once did, but they still hold false doctrines such as soul sleep and the annihilation of the unsaved wicked. Timothy was not instructed to allow for doctrinal differences. "As I besought thee to abide still at Ephesus, when I went into Macedonia, that thou mightest charge some that they teach NO OTHER DOCTRINE" (1 Timothy 1:3).

BOOTH, TOM

The *National Catholic Register* for March 8-14, 1998, listed Tom Booth as a Catholic musician.

BOYCE, KIM

Kim Boyce recorded her first album in 1986 and has produced six others since then.

Boyce popularized the old secular rock song "I Just Want to Celebrate" (by Rare Earth) by bringing it out for a Christian audience. The words could have meaning for a New Ager, a cultist, or a follower of a pagan religion: "I just want to celebrate/ Another day of living/ I just want to celebrate/ Another day of life..."

BRIDE

The hard rock group Bride was formed in 1983 in Kentucky by Dale and Troy Thompson. The name of the band originally was Matrix, and it was changed to Bride in 1986. The group recorded three albums with Star Song Communications between 1986 and 1990, achieving four Dove awards and eleven No. 1 radio singles. The group still performs and records.

Bride's worldly attitude is summarized in their song "Rock Those Blues Away" —

> "I don't need nobody to ease my aching mind/ Don't need nobody complaining all the time/ I need to roll those blues, rock those blues away ... Let me tell you honey, what I need/ I need a smooth playing guitar in my hand/ Listen to the rhythm of my hand."

The following is by Terry Watkins from *Christian Rock: Blessing or Blasphemy*:

> Bride has a song in which they speak (truthfully) in the first person for the

Devil. The name of the song is 'I'm the Devil.' Now do you seriously think the Holy Spirit inspired these lyrics?

'I'm the Devil, If you want to loose your freedom/ I'm the Devil, If you have nothing to loose/ I'm the Devil, If you want it all now/ I'm the Devil, COME HERE and take it.'

Believe it or not! At the end of the song they actually give an invitation for the Devil! Here's the unbelievable lyrics!

'Come and take my hand everybody can/ Come and take my hand everybody can/ Listen to it.'

If that wasn't evil enough, at the end of the song they go into a 'voodoo-drum' chanting and you can CLEARLY hear them say, 'in the name of the Devil, in the name of the Lord.'...

Bride is one of the top bands in CCM. They are the winner of several Dove awards. In the song 'Rattlesnake,' they sing, 'Dropping rattlesnakes in the playground/ Are we evil, are we good.' I have a hard time seeing Fanny Crosby singing such ungodly, wicked lyrics! And of course they blaspheme the Lord Jesus Christ. Songs like 'Scarecrow Messiah' (how many scarecrows do you know that DIED on a rugged cross?), 'Psychedelic Super Jesus,' 'Jesus Came Back via Jesus in a Pawn Shop,' to name a few (Terry Watkins, *Christian Rock: Blessing or Blasphemy*).

Here are two other examples of Bride's unscriptural music and their unbridled love for rock music:

"The ones with the power/ They have control/ Their mere words will direct your soul/ My words of steel carry through the night/ Leaving behind the wake of Metal Might..." ("Metal Might," Bride).

"I've got the strings of fire/ Screaming guitars/ Energy that will explode/ Got the golden throat/ To put on the show/ The power I will unload/ Here comes the Bride/ Got feet of brass/ I'm first and last..." ("Here Comes the Bride," Bride).

BROWN, SCOTT WESLEY

Scott Wesley Brown has recorded 18 albums and traveled to 40 countries. He is charismatic and yokes together with ecumenical organizations such as Promise Keepers, Youth With A Mission, Operation Mobilization, and Campus Crusade for Christ. He led the music during the main sessions at the massive New Orleans '87, which I attended with press credentials. There were 20,000 Roman Catholics in attendance (in addition to 20,000 from 40 other denominations), a Catholic mass was held every morning, and a Catholic priest brought the closing message. Scott Wesley Brown was comfortable (apparently) in this type of unscriptural environment.

CAEDMON'S CALL

Caedmon's Call is composed of Cliff Young (vocals, guitar), Derek Webb (guitar, vocals), Danielle Glenn (vocals), Todd Bragg (drums), Randy Holsapple (organ), Garett Buell (percussion), and Aric Nitzberg (bass). Aaron Tate writes the songs for Caedmon's Call. At least two of the men wear earrings. Todd Bragg sports shoulder-length hair.

The name of the group comes from a folk tale about an untalented man who was called by God to sing and who received his songs directly from God.

Their latest album was produced by Don McCollister, who has worked with secular folk/rock groups such as Indigo Girls, R.E.M., and Billy Pilgrim.

They focus their music on the college crowd, performing on large college campuses, but their philosophy is ecumenical and worldly. They perform for the Metro Bible Study, which represents 128 churches in Houston, Texas. The speaker for the Metro Bible Study is David Edwards, a Pentecostal who served on the staff of the Elim Bible Institute for more than 20 years and who was on the steering committee of the North American Renewal Service Committee which sponsored the massive ecumenical-charismatic congresses in 1986, 1987, and 1990. I attended two of these (New Orleans '87 and Indianapolis '90) with press credentials. Half of the tens of thousands in attendance were Roman Catholic and many Roman Catholic priests were featured as speakers. A Catholic mass was conducted every morning of the conferences.

In an interview with TLeM (*Lighthouse Electronic Magazine*), the members of Caedmon's Call said their greatest love in music is secular rock. They mentioned Indigo Girls, Shawn Colvin, David Wilcox, The Police, Fishbone, 10,000 Maniacs. They often perform Beatles music. Cliff Young said one of his favorites is the foul-mouthed Alanis Morrisette. Young mocked a preacher who warns that Christian musicians should not listen to secular rock. Young said that he listens to secular rock & rollers because "they are being honest [about] struggles that they go through." He said Christians should not be so concerned that "she [Morrisette] says 'damn' and 'hell' in her songs" (Rob Berman, a conversation with Cliff Young and Todd Bragg, http://tlem.netcentral.net/indie/960701/caedmons_call.html). We would note that Morissette says much worse things than "damn" and "hell." *Rolling Stone* magazine describes her music as "uncensored documentation of her psychosexual former Catholic-girl torments" (*Rolling*

Stone, No. 720). Young said: "I'd rather listen to someone who's being honest and open, cussing in their songs, than someone who's putting up a front and writing a song to get a hit" (Ibid.). Who said we have to make such a silly choice! Why not just listen to wholesome music? Everything is to be done to edification (Ephesians 4:29), and cursing certainly does not edify. Everything is to be done to the glory of Jesus Christ (1 Corinthians 10:31), and He certainly is not glorified by cursing and immorality.

Young also defended listening to the vulgar rock singer David Wilcox: "I don't see any immorality in songs like 'Boob Job.' If anything, he's looking down on stuff like that. If you look at the Bible, it's not a cute little book with sweet little stories. It's one of the most graphic, dirtiest, gross, powerful, dark, yet enlightening books" (Ibid.). This is amazing. We wonder what kind of Bible Cliff Young has. I've been studying the Bible for 25 years and have never found it to be graphic or gross or dirty or dark. Whenever the Bible deals with anything touching on immorality, it does so in a sensitive and holy manner so that the reader's thoughts are not perverted. This is certainly not the way that the rock world deals with immorality.

The anti-fundamentalist attitude of Caedmon's Call is evident:

> "It's amazing how we can get caught up in these things. 'Did he say that? I can't believe he said that!' Especially in the Baptist church we're in, our whole idea of Biblical holiness is, 'Don't drink; don't smoke; don't cuss.' True Biblical holiness is a lot more than that. ... the whole Christian subculture in the Bible Belt that says, 'Don't do this. Don't do that. You can't talk about that.' That kind of thing is no different from Jesus' day [the Pharisees]. I've been in their position. I was a Pharisee for many years" (Cliff Young, Ibid.).

This statement is a mockery of biblical absolutes. It is impossible to take the Bible seriously without striving to be holy in every area of life, without applying biblical precepts to everything the Christian does, without guarding the tongue. The New Testament is filled with commandments—with do's and don'ts—with things the Christian can and cannot do. It has many commandments against drunkenness and cussing. The very appearance of evil is to be avoided (1 Thess. 5:21). The attitude expressed by Cliff Young of Caedmon's Call is a smokescreen for rebellion against biblical holiness. He speaks of Baptist churches whose "whole idea of biblical holiness" is don't drink, smoke, or cuss. I have attended, preached in, and studied Baptist churches for 25 years and I don't know of one which limits its doctrine of holiness to a simplistic group of commandments like that. The rebel only hears that part, though. Young thinks that Phariseeism is requiring commandments. That was not the Pharisee's problem. The Pharisee's root problem was self-righteousness, pride, and the rejection of God's righteousness in Jesus Christ. The Bible-believing fundamentalists that I know (and I know thousands of them) are not self-righteous. They know that they have absolutely no righteousness in themselves, that in their flesh dwelleth no good thing. They are not Christ rejecters; they are Christ lovers. They know that apart from Jesus Christ they are nothing. Zero. They know that holiness is not external; it is the indwelling Spirit of God. To label the Bible-believing fundamentalist a Pharisee is a vicious slander.

Cliff Young also said in the interview that being forced to listen only to Christian music as he was growing up "hurt my walk and my effectiveness as a Christian" (Ibid.). To listen only to wholesome music is injurious! To be separated from vile secular rock music is injurious! What unscriptural nonsense.

In a 2001 interview with Echo magazine, Young condemned "Christian-cultural-Bible-Belt-legalism" which says, "Stay away from this and stay away from that."

Caedman's Call does not believe there should be a split between Christian and secular music:

> "We don't really believe in a split between Christian and mainstream music. I think there are Christians and non-Christians and the music they write reflects the kind of people they are" (Biography, Caedman's Call web site, http://www.wbr.com/alliance/caedmonscall/cmp/bio.html).

This amazing statement reminds me of the warning in the Word of God about the apostate priests of old. They "put no difference between the holy and profane" (Ezekiel 22:26).

CAMP, STEVE

Steve Camp (1956-) made a profession of faith at age five but became serious about serving Jesus Christ as a junior in high school in the early 1970s and was "taught the art and craft of songwriting" by Larry Norman. Camp produced his first album in 1978 and has recorded 15 more since then.

Steve Camp married his wife Kim in 1988 and has four children.

Camp has changed much during his career in Christian music. In the 1980s he was the typical non-judgmental, easy-prayerism CCM musician. In 1986 *MusicLine* magazine described Camp's music in these terms: "Though potent, the message never overwhelms or becomes preachy" (*MusicLine* magazine, June 1985, p. 20). Camp further described his non-judgmental philosophy in the following statement:

> "As an exhorter, I always felt that in order to tell people the correct way to live, my life style had to be perfect, and I'm finding that's not so. I'm finding that

they respond more to my weakness" (*CCM Magazine*, November 1986, p. 20).

This is the wrong idea about exhortation and preaching (and it is possible that he no longer holds it). Preaching is not based on the preacher's own moral perfection. The authority for preaching is God's Word, not the preacher's life. The preacher is preaching God, not himself. A preacher should strive to live according to the message he preaches, but no man could ever preach if preaching required any type of moral perfection. "If any man speak, let him speak as the oracles of God..." (1 Peter 4:11). The writers of the Bible were certainly far from perfect. Think of David and Solomon and Jonah and Peter. The man of God is not called of God to preach himself, not his strengths nor his weaknesses. He is instructed to preach the Word of God.

Camp admits that he has changed much in the last decade. In a 1993 interview with TLeM (*Lighthouse Electronic Magazine*), he described the message he preaches at his concerts, and it is the clearest presentation of the Gospel I have heard from a CCM musician:

> "But at the end of each concert, I do about a half hour of teaching time in the Word before giving the invitation. Because, I really want people to be confronted with the reality of a few things. Number one, of their own depravity. Number two, the reality of sin. Number three, the reality of the Lordship of Jesus Christ and why He came and who He is as God in human flesh and what it cost Him at Calvary for the penalty of our sins. And, number four, the wonderful victory and glory that He has in the cross if we come professing our faith in Jesus Christ, placing no confidence in ourselves but solely abandoning ourselves in Him and His saving grace.
>
> "Music has such a powerful emotional element, that I don't want people to simply make a response on that night due to their emotions were kindled, due to the fact that they've given an emotional response. I did that for a long time until I really woke up to the fact that that's not really the Gospel. But when you simply present the hard truth and the wonderful truth of the Gospel according to Jesus, then the fruit is of the Lord" (Steve Camp, interview, TLeM, April 1993, http://tlem.netcentral.net/old/camp_steve_9304.html).

We don't agree with Camp's music, described as "up-tempo, driving beat usually coupled with some incredible piano licks," or his concerts. We don't see the Apostles and early churches using anything like a rock concert to draw a crowd, but Camp gives an excellent description of the biblical manner of presenting the Gospel and of the dangers of shallow, emotional decisions. Many fundamental Baptists could learn much from his statement.

In 1997 Camp published a protest titled "A Call for Reformation in the Contemporary Christian Music Industry." He criticized the message of most CCM songs as "a Christless, watered-down, pabulum-based, positive alternative, aura-fluff, cream of wheat, mush-kind-of-syrupy, God-as-my-girlfriend kind of thing." He observed that "the serpentine foe of compromise has invaded the camp through years of specious living, skewed doctrine and, most recently, the secular ownership of Christian music ministries. ... Departure from the Word of God is now clearly evidenced in our music, lyrics, business practices and alliances."

Camp's Call for Reformation contained many insights into the unscriptural character of CCM, but he did not call for the Bible's solution to such rebellion, which is separation from it. He called for separation from the secular music companies, but he did not call for separation from the compromised Christian music industry itself and from those who are living and teaching in disobedience to the Word of God.

Steve Camp organized The CAUSE in April 1985, which brought together more than 90 popular musicians to record the song "Do Something Now." CAUSE stood for Christian Artists United to Save the Earth. Proceeds went to Compassion International for hunger relief.

Camp holds the false philosophy that music is neutral.

> "I am dedicated to good music whether it's pop, Christian, gospel, R&B, blues, jazz, classical, rock or whatever. I just love good music" (Steve Camp, *MusicLine* magazine, Feb. 1986, p. 22).

CARD, MICHAEL

Michael Card (1956-) is a very popular CCM musician. As of 1997 he had produced 18 albums and won seven Gospel Music Association Dove Awards.

Card was discipled by Dr. William Lane of Western Kentucky University. Under Lane's tutelage Card completed his Master's thesis and was accepted as a candidate for a Ph.D. program in 1980 (James Long, "Michael Card: Where Are the Average Looking Artists?," *CCM Magazine*, December 1995). Instead of pursuing the Ph.D., though, Card launched his career in the Christian music industry. Lane was listed in 1994 as a member of the Jesus Seminar, which denies that Jesus Christ is God and questions the authenticity of most parts of the Gospels.

At Michael Card's official web site there is a list of the books which have most influenced his thoughts about God. The list includes several modernistic and Roman Catholic authors without any warning to the viewers about their theological heresies and false gospels. These include Dietrich Bonhoeffer, Malcolm Muggeridge, F.F. Bruce, and Henri Nouwen. Bonhoeffer rejected such doctrines as the virgin birth, bodily resurrection, and substitutionary atonement of Jesus Christ. According to Bonhoeffer, it is a "cardinal error" to regard Christianity as a religion of salvation. Card specifically mentions Muggeridge's blasphemous book *Jesus Rediscovered*, in which he denied the virgin birth, deity, and bodily resurrection of Jesus Christ. F.F. Bruce denied the eternal fire of Hell and promoted the damnable annihilation theory of judgment. Henri Nouwen is a liberal Catholic priest who has supported homosexuality and liberation theology.

Card is radically ecumenical. In 1996 he produced an album (*Brother to Brother*) jointly with fellow CCM performer John Michael Talbot, who is a Roman Catholic and prays to Mary. Of this venture, Card testified: "Doing this project has enabled us to become real friends. And along the way, the denominational lines have become really meaningless to me, and to John, too" (*CCM Magazine*, July 1996).

To say that denominational division is meaningless is to say that doctrine is not important, because doctrine is one of the key things which divides denominations and churches! Some churches teach sound doctrine about Jesus Christ and some teach false doctrine. Some teach sound doctrine about salvation; some, false. Some teach sound doctrine about baptism; some, false. Some teach sound doctrine about the Holy Spirit; some, false. Some teach sound doctrine about the New Testament church; some, false. Timothy's job in Ephesus was to "charge some that they TEACH NO OTHER DOCTRINE" (1 Timothy 1:3). When a church stands upon the whole counsel of New Testament doctrine, it automatically becomes divided from churches which are committed to different doctrine. This cannot be avoided, and it is not wrong. In fact, God forbids sound churches from associating with those who hold different doctrine (Romans 16:17). To say that the denominational lines pertaining to Romanism are meaningless is to say that false doctrines such as the mass, the papacy, the priesthood, sacramental salvation, prayers to the dead, Mary the Queen of Heaven, Purgatory, etc., are unimportant.

Card and Talbot embarked on a concert tour which included concerts in eight cities, "with the audience mix estimated at 50 percent Catholic and 50 percent Protestant" (*Charisma*, December 1996, p. 29). In March 1996 they performed together for the largest gathering of Catholics in America at the Los Angeles Religious Education Congress. Roughly 20,000 "clergy and laity" attended this congress. Both men also spoke at the formation retreat for the Catholic Musicians Association. Talbot is the president of this new association.

On their album Talbot and Card sing: "There is one faith/ One hope and one baptism/

One God and Father of all/ There is one church, one body, one life in the spirit/ Now given so freely for all."

What one faith, baptism, and church? The Roman Catholic faith is not the Bible faith. It's infant baptism certainly is not biblical baptism. The Roman church is not the New Testament church found in Scripture. Consider what the Vatican II Council said about purgatory: "The doctrine of purgatory clearly demonstrates that even when the guilt of sin has been taken away, punishment for it or the consequences of it may remain to be expiated or cleansed. They often are. In fact, in purgatory the souls of those who died in the charity of God and truly repentant, but who had not made satisfaction with adequate penance for their sins and omissions are cleansed after death with punishments designed to purge away their debt" (Vatican II documents, Apostolic Constitution on the Revision of Indulgences, 3).

Purgatory means to cleanse or purify. This Catholic doctrine is a plain and open denial of the perfect sufficiency of the atonement of the Lord Jesus Christ to take away all sin. The Bible says, "For by one offering he hath perfected for ever them that are sanctified" (Heb. 10:14). Rome has a faith, a baptism, and a church, but it is not the one we read about in the Holy Scriptures. Why, then, would Michael Card pretend that he and John Talbot are singing about the same thing? If Card believes Talbot's faith is the one true faith, why does he not become a Roman Catholic?

It is painfully obvious that doctrinal truth means nothing to these CCM performers. If Talbot really took his Catholic doctrine seriously, he would not yoke together with those who deny that doctrine, and if Card really took his evangelical doctrine seriously he would not yoke together with a man who denies that doctrine. If the Pope is truly the Vicar of Christ and the head of all Christians, it would be wicked to deny it; but if the Catholic papacy is nothing but a man-made tradition, it is wicked to believe it. If Mary is truly the immaculate, ever-virgin Queen of Heaven, it would be wicked to deny it; but if the Catholic Mary is a demonic idol, it is wicked to believe it. If the Catholic priesthood really is ordained by God, it would be wicked to deny it; but if it has no authority from God and is merely a tradition of man, it is wicked to accept it. There is no middle ground here. There can be no fellowship between those who hold doctrines this diverse. The Bible says those who teach doctrine contrary to that which the Apostles delivered are to be marked and avoided (Romans 16:17). The Bible wisely asks: "Can two walk together, except they be agreed?" (Amos 3:3).

In 1996 Michael Card performed at the Temple Baptist Church of Detroit, Michigan, long a key church in the Baptist Bible Fellowship headquartered in Springfield, Missouri. The church has been pastored by such famous BBF leaders as G.B. Vick and Truman Dollar. The pastor today is Bradley Powell. In recent years Jack Van Impe has been a member (*Calvary Contender*, October 1, 1996).

Card is highly critical of the Christian music industry, charging that it is driven by "competition, commercialism and individualism" and that it is "getting worse faster than any of us can imagine" (*CCM Magazine*, December 1995). He charges that Christian music is quickly becoming not Christ-centered or even song-centered, but "is becoming so much an artist/personality/celebrity-centered thing" (Ibid.). We could not agree more, but an even greater problem is the false doctrine and unscriptural unity which permeates CCM.

CARLISLE, BOB

In his late teens Bob Carlisle (c.1954-) was involved in the Jesus movement in California in the 1970s and played in two long-haired Christian pop bands, Good News and Psalm 150. By the time the latter had broken up, Carlisle said he had become "disillusioned with the Christian music business" because "there weren't enough places to tour that could financially support a big band and their families" ("Biography of Bob Carlisle," http://www.bobcarlisle.com/biography.htm). He complained about small love offerings in churches.

He moved into secular music, singing for hire, writing pop music, playing in night clubs. During one of his night club performances he repented and rededicated his life to God. Soon thereafter he joined Randy Thomas and Sam Scott to form a new Christian rock band named Allies. The band split up in 1992, after recording six albums. Since then Carlisle has had a solo career. The single title song from his latest album, *Butterfly Kisses*, has become a huge commercial success and has been high on secular charts. It is a amiable little pop song about a father's love for his young daughter, but it also contains false doctrine:

> "Butterfly kisses after bedtime prayer/ Stickin little white flowers all up in her hair/ 'Walk beside the pony/ daddy, it's my first ride'/ 'I know the cake looks funny/ daddy, but I sure tried'/ Oh, with all that I've done wrong/ I MUST HAVE DONE SOMETHING RIGHT/ TO DESERVE A HUG EVERY MORNING/ And butterfly kisses at night."

CCM musicians who crossover to the secular music arena invariably argue that they are reaching the world with the Gospel, that Christian music should not be shut up in the churches but should go out into the world, where the message of Christ is desperately needed. The Gospel DOES need to be preached to the world, but one of the problems with this argument by CCM crossover musicians is that their music almost never contains a clear Gospel message. At best it presents a vague religiosity or spirituality. Like

Carlisle's "Butterfly Kisses," the crossover songs also frequently contain outright false doctrine. Do we "deserve" the blessings of life? The world thinks so. The world does not think of itself as wicked and unrighteous. The unsaved will admit that they have problems and shortcomings and faults, but they commonly think of themselves as basically good and largely deserving of God's favor. This fact of fallen human nature is one reason why the Gospel of Jesus Christ is so offensive to the world. The Bible says man's heart is "deceitful above all things and desperately wicked" (Jeremiah 17:9). It says "all have sinned and come short of the glory of God" (Romans 3:23), "there is none that doeth good" (Romans 3:12), and "there is none righteous" (Romans 3:10). Crossover CCM musicians do not preach the Gospel plainly so that the world is confronted with its sin and rebellion against Almighty God. At best they soft peddle an easy believism, no repentance approach to Christianity. This is the only reason their music can be popular on secular charts. It is for certain that plain Bible preaching would not be Top Ten material! Jesus Christ was not crucified because he encouraged sinners to have strong self esteem; He was crucified because He exposed man's sin. "If I had not come and spoken unto them, they had not had sin: but now they have no cloak for their sin" (John 15:22).

Carlisle admits that as a teen he loved worldly music and that he still does today. He "fell head over heels in love" with soul music represented by Otis Redding, Wilson Pickett, and James Brown, and he admits in recent interviews that his "heart is still there." This love for the world is evident in his music.

Carlisle has the non-judgmental philosophy of the CCM world.

> "I'm not a finger-pointing kind of song writer or speaker. We're all in this together. In that, the last album was just songs that touch people's everyday experiences. That's what I know" (Interview with Bob Carlisle, *The Lighthouse*, February 1994, http://tlem.netcentral.net/old/carlisle_bob_9402.html).

How can the Spirit of God be pleased with such a message when the Bible says He came to "reprove the world of sin, and of righteousness, and of judgment" (John 16:8)? That sounds like "finger pointing" to me. There is no conviction of sin in the vast majority of CCM lyrics. The Dove Award is named after the Holy Spirit, but we are convinced that He is not pleased with many of the things which are done in His name within Contemporary Christian Music.

CARMAN (CARMAN DOMINIC LICCIARDELLO)

Carman (1956-) sang in bars during his teen years and formed a group called The Broken Hearts. In 1976 he accepted Christ as his Savior after attending an Andrae Crouch concert at Disneyland in California. He published his first album in 1980. In 1981 Bill Gaither invited him to tour with the Gaither Trio. Carman is a member of the charismatic Higher Dimensions Evangelistic Center in Tulsa, Oklahoma, pastored by Carlton Pearson. He is one of the highest paid CCM musicians. On October 22, 1994, he set the record for the highest attendance at a Christian concert with more than 71,000 people filling the Dallas Texas Stadium. In 1995 he signed with secular record company Liberty Records for a roughly five million dollar bonus (*Shout*, Dec. 1995, p. 35). His 1994 *Raising The Standard* tour drew a total attendance of 1.1 million people. Of the top 75 all-time best-selling Christian albums, seven belong to Carman (*CCM Magazine*, July 1998, pp. 107-108). He has had nine gold and two platinum albums and videos. He has won six Dove Awards and has twice been voted *Billboard Magazine's* Contemporary Christian Artist of the Year.

Carman has made great efforts to reach young people evangelistically. Much of his music is geared to evangelism. His official website is one of the very few CCM sites which has a presentation of the Gospel. He claims that thousands have been saved through his concerts, and we hope this is the case. We don't question the man's sincerity in seeing unsaved people come to Jesus Christ, nor do we fault his zeal in this most important endeavor. The Bible instructs us to "prove all things," though, and what we do seriously question is his music, his method, and his message.

Carman's *Addicted to Jesus* album contains such blasphemous cuts as the "HOLY GHOST HOP." He exclaims:

> "Everybody used to do the twist/ The mashed potato and it goes like this/ The funky chicken, monkey too/ There wasn't nothing' they would not do/ But there's a new dance no one can stop/ A leap for joy we call the Holy Ghost Hop.
>
> "Now get ready, hold steady/ Don't deny it, just try it/ Be bold now, let it go now/ Give the Holy Ghost control now.
>
> "Hey all you brothers and you sisters too/ Don't let tradition tell you what to do/ Release your worries and your fears/ 'Cause we've been hopping in the church for years/ If King David was here I know that he/ Would do the Holy Ghost Hop with me" ("The Holy Ghost Hop" by Carman).

Carman is wrong. David did not dance to rock music. He did not put on a fleshly show. He was not moving his feet to some carnal beat. He was not entertaining anyone. He danced before the Lord but it was nothing which the world would have appreciated or paid money to see. To the contrary, even unsaved people understand and appreciate the type of music and dancing that Carman produces.

On another cut entitled "Come into This House," sung to a heavy rap style, Carman says:

> "I've got news you can choose/ You need to be delivered/ with Christ you win/ without Christ you lose/ BUT IF YOU JAM WITH THE LAMB, YOU'RE SMOOTH/ Cut out the jive, cut into church/ You need a healing' touch/ A big strong hand/ Come rock with the flock/ with the brothers that jam."

The title cut on that album has this flippant message:

> "Addictions you know/ Everybody's got 'em/ From the top to the very/ bottom of the list/ So come get with this/ An addiction you don't wanna miss/ To Christ who paid the price."

Carman's unscriptural and dangerous charismatic theology comes across loud and clear in his music. In his song "Satan, Bite the Dust," Carman claims that he has "been sent with a warrant from the body of Christ" to arrest the Devil and to run every unclean spirit out of town. He claims to have the authority to cast out "depression, strife, disease and fear." In this strange song Carman asserts, "Satan, you coward, you molester of souls, I command you to appear." The Apostle Peter, though, tells us that even the angels do not bring railing accusations against the Devil (2 Peter 2:11). Nowhere in the New Testament Scriptures do we see the Apostles and early Christians speaking to the Devil in this manner. Carman then says: "I represent a whole new breed of Christian of today. And I'm authorized and deputized to blow you [Satan] clean away." This is a probable reference to the New Order of the Latter Rain theology which claims that Christ's return will be preceded by a miracle revival whereby Christians will perform miracles and exercise kingdom authority over the powers of this present world. Some of the "prophets" which were popularized by John Wimber and the Vineyard movement, men such as Paul Cain, claim that God is raising up a "new breed" of end-time Christian who will take complete authority over the Devil.

Carman's theology is not only wrong, it is nonsense. He has not blown away the Devil. He has not bound the Devil. He has not arrested the Devil. He has no power to command sickness to depart. He can pray and ask God to remove sickness, and God answers according to His will, but he cannot demand that sickness be healed. No Christian can. When Timothy was sick with frequent infirmities, the Apostle Paul did not command those infirmities to depart. Paul did not curse those infirmities as demonic. He did not say, "I bind you, foul infirmity." No, he said: "Drink no longer water, but use a little wine for thy stomach's sake and thine often infirmities" (1 Tim. 5:23). I will be glad to take any charismatic preacher with me into a hospital and we will demonstrate right there which of us is doctrinally correct in this matter. If a Christian has the power to bind the Devil and to cast out sicknesses, let's see it. In reality, all the charismatic can do is precisely what I do. He can pray for the sickness, and sometimes God heals and sometimes He doesn't, according to His will. Carman is confusing the minds of God's people and leading them away from the truth with his false doctrine.

In typical charismatic fashion Carman rebukes the "demon of alcoholism" and the "spirit of infirmity," demanding that these "demons" depart. He proclaims, "We lay hands on the sick and they recover." Carman and his Pentecostal preacher friends who claim that healing is in the atonement are false teachers. They claim to have the authority to lay hands on the sick and they will recover, but in reality they do not have this authority and tens of thousands of sick and afflicted have attended Pentecostal healing meetings to no avail.

In another song, "Our Turn Now," Carman exclaims:

> "World, you had your turn at bat/ Now stand back and see/ That it's our turn now/ Some things gonna change/ We're gonna bind the/ Devil at every hand by/ the power of Jesus' name."

This is unadulterated charismatic Kingdom Now, dominionism theology. These things will not come to pass until the Lord Jesus Christ returns and establishes His kingdom.

The following description of three of Carman's videos/albums is by former rock guitarist Terry Watkins:

> Blasphemy saturates Christian rock, such as the blasphemous 'humor' of Carman Dominic Licciardello, better known as Carman. His blasphemous, street-jive, dialogue between John the Baptist and Jesus Christ as teenagers on his video *Live...Radically Saved* is disgusting! Here's a sample of Carman's blasphemy:
>
> JOHN: 'Hey man, Hey cuz, Whatchoo doin man? I ain't seen you in a long time. HEY, BABY.' (John calling Jesus baby!)
>
> Jesus turns and says, 'Hey, what's up, John?' See, Jesus is always cool; he's always together. He's got his thing together, y' know.
>
> Then Carman blasphemously imitates the Lord Jesus Christ walking hip-jive doing what Carman calls 'THE MESSIAH WALK.' UNGODLY! BLASPHEMY!
>
> JOHN: 'This is wild, brother, now I don't know. Man, I never had anybody in my family MAKE IT BIG... Listen to it.'
>
> Jesus 'MADE IT BIG'? Jesus Christ died a curse for sinful man! See Gal. 3:13; 2 Cor. 5:17! Jesus Christ was 'despised and rejected of men' (Isa. 53:3).

Is 'MAKING IT BIG' being beaten, smitten, spit upon, mocked and crucified?

Carman's *Resurrection Rap* video is some of the lowest BLASPHEMY I've ever seen! In the video, Carman portrays the Lord Jesus Christ as a confused street hippie, while the Pharisees and apostles are black street gang members! The crucifixion takes place, not on Calvary—but in a back alley gang fight! The Lord Jesus Christ is buried in a GARBAGE DUMPSTER. ...

On Carman's *The Standard* album is the sacrilegious (at least!) 'Who's in the House,' in which Carman crudely refers to the Lord Jesus Christ as 'J.C.':

'You take Him high/ You take Him low/ You take J.C. wherever you go/ Now tell me, who...who...who...who...who...who?/ Tell me who's in the house? J.C./ Tell me who's in the house? J.C./ Tell me who's in the house? J.C./ Tell me who's in the house? J.C./ Jesus Christ is in the house today.'

Now, in your wildest dreams, could you possibly imagine the Apostle Paul referring to the Lord Jesus Christ as J.C.? Here's what the Apostle Paul says about the name of Jesus Christ in Philippians 2: 'Wherefore God also hath highly exalted him, and given him a NAME [not the initials J.C.!] which is above every NAME: That at the NAME of Jesus every knee should bow, of things in heaven, and things in earth, and things under the earth' (Philippians 2:9-10) (*Christian Rock: Blessing or Blasphemy?* by Terry Watkins, former rock guitarist, Dial the Truth Ministries, http://www.av1611.org/crock.html#Carman Res Rap).

Carman's *Live...Radically Saved* video includes "a jazzed-up 50s imitation of Elvis Presley called 'Celebrating Jesus.' Carman shakes, stutters and shimmies just like the 'King' himself, as the crowd cheers and be-bops in the aisles. ... Elvis admirers would surely say, 'What's the big deal?' That's exactly the point. It should be a very big deal when Christians glamorize a sex pervert, drug addict and pathetic tool of Satan like Elvis" (Jeff Godwin, *What's Wrong with Christian Rock?*, pp. 184,185).

Carman's 1998 video *Mission 3:16* was filmed partially in Ireland using some of the dancers from the sensual and indecent *Riverdance* program (*CCM Magazine*, July 1998, p. 12).

In 1997 Carman joined Roman Catholic Kathy Troccoli and 40 other CCM artists to record *Love One Another*, a song with an ecumenical theme: "Christians from all denominations demonstrating their common love for Christ and each other." The song talks about tearing down the walls of denominational division. The broad range of participants who joined Kathy Troccoli in recording "Love One Another" demonstrates the ecumenical agenda of Contemporary Christian Music. The song witnessed Catholics, Pentecostals, Baptists, etc., yoked together to call for Christian unity.

CARMICHAEL, RALPH

Ralph Carmichael is one of the fathers of Contemporary Christian Music. The following biography describes his role:

> Carmichael's crusade to contemporize Christian music had begun as early as 1947. 'Way back then,' Carmichael explains, 'there was a rhythmic sound that people were listening to on their radios. Just a gentle bass and then a backbeat on the guitar was all there was to it. We had music that could be played on keyboards that fit into those tempo slots, but the minute you put the bass and guitar and drums with it, and got it to where it was the sound the populace was listening to, then the church folk took exception to it. They would listen to it so long as it wasn't church music, but then they would come to church on Sunday and it had to be just the keyboards again. I couldn't figure that out, because I knew that I liked the sound. I love the strings. I loved the pulse, the rhythms. I didn't understand why we were always having to sing in half notes and quarter notes and whole notes. You could never use the strings, the brass, the woodwinds.' [Note from Bro. Cloud: There is nothing wrong with strings or brass in themselves. The problem is the misuse of these instruments in producing sensual rhythms which do not fit the holy message of Christ.]
>
> Carmichael began to search for ways to make those sounds and use them in the Christian field. ... When Carmichael was about eighteen, his ideas started to develop and his experimentation with sounds began. When he was twenty-one, he organized a band and traveled on holidays. 'We would get thrown out of churches,' he recalls. 'We had it all there—four trumpets, four trombones, five saxes, rhythm, and sixteen male singers. Things really started to happen when we went on television. We began to be accepted using strings and a moderate beat, too. There were several years when everything was comfortable because we had fought that battle and they were listening to the strings. I had made an album entitled *102 Strings*, and we were doing big things with big choirs.'
>
> Just when Carmichael had 'won the battle,' secular music began changing, making a turn toward rock. 'Some musicians made that transition,' Carmichael adds. 'By that time I had started to do some secular things. I was experimenting and learning my lessons, ALWAYS HOPING THAT WHAT I LEARNED IN THE SECULAR FIELD I COULD BRING OVER AND USE IN THE CHRISTIAN FIELD. I didn't like rock. My daughter used to buy rock records and I would break them. I remember the day I went out to my car and I found her station on! We developed this 'her' station/'my' station syndrome. She would play the rock and I wouldn't play it. I would play only my station. I wouldn't even let her buy rock records with her allowance.
>
> 'Then one day Roger Williams called and asked, "Can you write rock?" Well,

of course that was getting into my pocketbook, so I said yes, and hung up the phone asking myself, "Why did I say that?"' Roger Williams isn't a rock musician, but things were happening in the commercial field with the influence of rock, so we recorded with a moderate rock beat. It was even eighth notes, if that made it rock. The song was "Born Free," and it was a hit! So my daughter came home from school one day and she had bought *Born Free*, as did about two or three million other people. She flipped the album down and said, "Is that the same Ralph Carmichael that doesn't like rock?" She had caught me!' (Paul Baker, *Contemporary Christian Music*, 1985, pp. 12-14).

Note that Carmichael was opposed to rock music at first and that he changed his opinion NOT because of the Bible but because of money.

Carmichael went on to write the music for Billy Graham's 1965 film, *The Restless Ones*. He used bass guitar and drums to produce a rock sound. Baker observes: "Although by today's standard the music would seem tame, it caused waves among the conservative church goers because of its contemporary nature" (Ibid.). Churches which had previously resisted the use of rock music began to accept it because of Billy Graham's immense popularity and the fact that his name was behind the film.

Carmichael has been married and divorced several times.

CAROUTHERS, MARK

Mark Carouthers is a member of a United Pentecostal Church, which denies the Trinity. The song "Mercy Seat," which is sung nightly at the Brownsville Assembly of God "revival" in Pensacola, Florida, was written by Carouthers.

CASH, JOHNNY

Johnny Cash (1932-), who has been called "a living folk hero," has spent four decades in the music business. He first played "Cry, Cry, Cry" at Sun Records in 1955. "Since then, he's written more than a thousand songs, performed for audiences all over the world, scored tons of hits, written two books, hosted his own television program, acted in films and TV shows" (Biography of Johnny Cash, imusic, http://imusic.com/showcase/country/jcash.html).
Cash professes faith in Jesus Christ. Among his earliest musical influences was Southern gospel, and he has frequently returned to those roots. He has been married to his wife, June Carter, since 1962. Before their marriage, June Carter was a member of the famous Gospel singers, the Carter Family. In 1995 he wrote a song for her, "Meet Me in Heaven." Of it he says: "I always wanted to write a song called 'Meet Me in Heaven' because those words are on my brother's [who died from an accident at age 14] and

my father's tombstones. That song is one of those songs of peace that comes with my faith."

We are glad that Johnny Cash believes in the Lord Jesus Christ and has confidence in God's grace, but beyond his basic faith in Christ, there are serious problems biblically with his theological views and practices and his close, uncritical relationship with the world. His theology is a strange mixture of Pentecostalism, Ecumenism, and New Age.

The following is by Terry Watkins from *Christian Rock: Blessing or Blasphemy*:

> Johnny's latest album is on the American (formerly Def American) record label owned by Rick Rubin. Rubin also is the producer for Cash's album. Rubin is also the producer and American is the home for Slayer, Danzig, Black Crowes, Red Hot Chili Peppers, et al. The group Danzig's logo is a picture of a demon strangling the Lord Jesus Christ while blood is coming out of Jesus's bulging eyes! The inside of Danzig's album *Lucifuge* depicts Glenn Danzig wearing the cross of Jesus Christ — upside down — with a demon's head in the middle of the cross. Boldly written at the top is part of John 8:44, 'Ye are of your father the Devil, and the lusts of your father ye will do.' Glenn Danzig is a hard-core satanist. To show his utter hatred for Jesus Christ, one of his songs is titled 'Snakes of Christ.' Now you want to hear the unbelievable? Not only did Johnny Cash record a song on American label produced by Rick Rubin — but on the album he sings a song written by satanist Glenn Danzig! The name of the song? You guessed it — Thirteen! ...
>
> Here's what Johnny says about this album: 'This is what I've always wanted to do, and I was able to do it with Rick. I think I'm more proud of it than anything I've ever done in my life. I don't think I ever worked so well with a producer in my entire career.'
>
> The *Birmingham News*, Feb. 11, 1996, p. 5F, had an ad for Silverstar gambling casino in Mississippi. Featured in the ad was none other than Mr. Johnny Cash, who was scheduled to perform at the gambling casino (Feb. 29, 1996). But of course, compared with recording a song by satanist Glenn Danzig (who obviously would get royalties from Cash recording his song), performing in a gambling casino is next to going to church (Terry Watkins, *Christian Rock: Blessing or Blasphemy*).

THE CATHEDRALS

This popular Southern gospel group was formed in 1964 at charismatic evangelist Rex Humbard's Cathedral of Tomorrow church, where it was founded. The original members were Glen Payne, George Younce, Bobby Clark, and Danny Koker. After performing on Humbard's television broadcast for four years, the Cathedrals left in 1968 to become an independent quartet. In the mid-1970s, Bill Gaither invited the Cathedrals to perform at his Praise Gathering in Indianapolis, Indiana. George Younce calls

Gaither "the contemporary Christian music scene's guiding force" and Gaither's Praise Gathering "an annual three-day celebration of contemporary Christian music" (*The Cathedrals*, pp. 180,181). The Cathedrals have performed at Billy Graham crusades.

The Cathedrals were the first Southern gospel group to perform at the Praise Gathering. In 1977 the Cathedrals won four Dove Awards.

The Cathedrals were ecumenical from their conception within Rex Humbard's ministry. After Humbard visited the Catholic pope in Rome in 1980, he gave this testimony: "As we talked together, I sensed more and more that our mission is the same: to build the body of Christ; to uplift the brethren in the Lord; to win the world for the kingdom; to share that shining message that Jesus gave us to share. ... 'You are loved'" (Rex Humbard, *Answer*, March 1980). Humbard attended the 1975 Full Gospel World Convention in Anaheim, California. The theme was tearing down all barriers between the denominations, and Catholics were prominently featured. Roman Catholic priest John Bertolucci was a main evening speaker. He told about "gorgeous experiences" with charismatic masses and said, "...you know the Lord is doing a whole new thing—He's pouring out His Spirit on all flesh ... on all denominations ... on everybody and this is ... the Lord's ecumenism." At the same meeting, female charismatic preacher Kathryn Kuhlman told of her meeting with the pope and stated, "I want you to know that Pope Paul would have fit in very well with this great world-wide convention of the FGBMFI." In spite of this, Humbard gave the following endorsement of Kuhlman: "God has laid His hand upon Kathryn Kuhlman for this moment and this hour to reveal His supernatural power to the church and I thank God for her faithfulness and power" (*FEA News & Views*, Jul.-Aug. 1975).

CHAGALL GUEVARA. See Steve Taylor.

CHAPMAN, GARY. See Amy Grant.

CHAPMAN, STEVEN CURTIS

Steven Curtis Chapman (1963-) is "the most honored Christian artist of the 1990s" (*CCM* magazine, July 1999, p. 28). He has won 38 Dove Awards and three Grammys for Best Pop/ Contemporary Gospel. He has four gold albums (sold 500,000 units) and one platinum (sold one million units). Thirty of his singles have been No. 1. His concert tours are attended by hundreds of thousands.

Chapman is a member of the Pentecostal Christ Community Church near Nashville, Tennessee. An article in *Newsweek* magazine noted that "Christ Church in Nashville has the hottest choir in town, bar none, and the Pentecostal service on any given Sunday is liable to rock the pews" ("God and the Music Biz," *Newsweek*, May 30, 1994). The Christ Church choir performed "Put a Little Love in Your Heart" with Dolly Parton during the 1993 Country Music Association Awards. Lindell Cooley, the worship leader at Brownsville Assembly of God in Pensacola, Florida, was in charge of music at Christ Church before he moved to Pensacola.

In recent years, Steven Chapman has "embraced high energy rock" and some elements of rap (*Moody Monthly*, Nov. 1994). An article in the *Tennessean*, September 21, 1996, observed that Chapman had "taken a radical left turn with his music."

Some of the songs on his 1997 *Greatest Hits* album were recorded live at Abbey Road Studios in London, the studio where the Beatles recorded their albums. Why would a Christian desire to produce an album at the studio made famous by an antichrist rock group which has influenced multitudes of young people to reject the Word of God?

According to the *Huntsville Times* (Huntsville, Alabama), Chapman says he tries to communicate a biblical world view in a way that will not be "abrasively preachy" (*Huntsville Times*, Oct. 30, 1994). He says his quest for relevance has shown that the best way to communicate his faith is "not to preach fire and brimstone" (Ibid.). Contrariwise, the Lord Jesus Christ *was* a "fire and brimstone" preacher (Mk. 9:44-48).

The song "Lord of the Dance," co-written by Chapman and Scotty Smith, pastor of Christ Community Church, first appeared on Chapman's 1996 album, *Signs of Life*. The song depicts God as the "Lord of the Dance," which is certainly not a scriptural concept. God was the Lord of the type of dancing that King David did, but "Lord of the Dance" is sung in the context of the type of dancing which goes on at rock concerts. God is not Lord of sensual, worldly dancing which, due to the fallen nature of man is, at its very heart, licentious. It would be more scriptural to say that the Devil is the Lord of the Dance in any rock music context. Consider the words to "Lord of the Dance"—

> "On the bank of the Tennessee River/ In a small Kentucky town/ I drew my first breath one cold November morning/ And before my feet even touched the ground/ With the doctors and the nurses gathered 'round/ I started to dance/ I started to dance/ A little boy full of wide-eyed wonder/ Footloose and fancy free/ But it would happen, as it does for every dancer/ That I'd stumble on a truth I couldn't see/ And find a longing deep inside of me, it said . . .
>
> Chorus: "I am the heart, I need the heartbeat/ I am the eyes, I need the sight/ I realize that I am just a body/ I need the life/ I move my feet, I go through the motions/ But who'll give purpose to chance/ I am the dancer/ I need the Lord of the dance.

"The world beneath us spins in circles/ And this life makes us twist and turn and sway/ But we were made for more than rhythm with no reason/ By the one who moves with passion and with grace/ As He dances over all that He has made/ I am the heart, He is the heartbeat/ I am the eyes, He is the sight/ And I see clearly, I am just a body/ He is the life/ I move my feet, I go through the motions/ But He gives purpose to chance/ I am the dancer/ He is the Lord of the dance/ Lord of the dance/ Lord of the dance/ And while the music of His love and mercy plays/ I will fall down on my knees and I will pray."

A Christian message of sorts can be READ INTO this song, that apart from God life is without meaning; but as the song stands in its own vagueness, there is no clear biblical message. Is God a dancer? The only thing we know about God for certain is the revelation we have in His Word. Where does the Bible portray God as a dancer? It is extremely dangerous to describe God in ways not used in the Bible, because it could be blasphemous. "The Lord of the Dance" could easily be referring to a Hindu god or a New Age christ. Further, the song says every "dancer" will stumble onto truth. This is certainly not true.

Chapman's song "I Will Not Go Quietly" was part of the soundtrack for the wicked PG-13-rated 1998 Hollywood movie, *The Apostle*, which depicts a drunken, womanizing Pentecostal preacher who kills the lover of his unfaithful wife in a murderous rampage, then flees to another part of the country, changes his name to "The Apostle E.F.," and starts a new church. There he has an affair with another woman. Though the star of *The Apostle*, Robert Duvall, is an extremely talented actor, he has played roles in many vile and immoral movies. Even so, he is featured in Chapman's video for "I Will Not Go Quietly."

CHRISTAFARI

Christafari is a reggae band which was formed in 1989 by Mark Mohr (1972-). He was raised in a Christian home but turned his back on the Lord and got involved in drugs, immorality, and a Jamaican cult, Rastafarianism. In 1989 Mohr attended a Christian camp and, in his own words, "It was at this time that I re-surrendered my life to Christ." This, of course, is not biblical salvation. I read several Mohr interviews, but in none of them does he give a clear testimony of when he was born again. He believes the Lord spoke to him through 1 Corinthians 7:24 to stay involved in the reggae music scene. "I really felt the Lord impressing on my heart to start the first Christian reggae band." Such an interpretation of 1 Corinthians 7:24 ignores the context and is a perversion of the passage. 1 Corinthians 7 is speaking of marriage, circumcision, and slavery. The Christian who is married when he gets saved is to be content to remain married. The Christian who is a Gentile when he gets saved is to remain a Gentile. The Christian who is a servant is to be content to remain a servant. The passage is *not* talking about remaining in a wicked industry like rock music, pornography, the liquor or drug business, etc. 2 Corinthians 6:17 describes God's will for the latter: "Wherefore come out from among them, and be ye separate, saith the Lord, and touch not the unclean thing; and I will receive you."

Mohr attended the New Evangelical BIOLA University in Oregon. He pursued a degree in Christian Education and Pastoral Studies and wrote the songs for Christafari's first two albums. In addition to performing and producing with Christafari, Mohr has started churches in Jamaica and is an associate pastor at the Sanctuary in Mount Juliet, Tennessee. Mohr's wife, Vanessa, was a vocalist and dancer with his band before they were married in 1995.

Christafari's mission statement is the clearest we have seen among CCM groups: "Christafari commits to preach the gospel of Jesus Christ clearly through music, the spoken word and their lives, as illustrated in the Holy Bible, in order to win souls for Christ's kingdom in accordance with His great commission." The lyrics to many of their songs are biblical and plain. It is sad that they try to use the world's sensual music to attempt to accomplish the work of a holy Christ. Some of their music sounds like African tribal music.

Christafari's music is pure reggae. It has heavy "jungle" drums and the vocals are similar in many cases to rap. A large percentage of the lyrics are difficult or impossible to understand.

The photo of Christafari on their 1996 *Valley of Decision* album portray them with hard stares. Three of the musicians have long womanish hair.

Christafari's *Valley of Decision* album includes the song "Modern Day Pharisee," which "swipes at those who judge the band for its appearance or musical style rather than its heart" (Tod Hafer, "Judge Dread: Mark Mohr and Christafari Use Reggae Music to Make a Case for Christianity," *CCM Magazine*, July 1996).

The following Christafari song expresses in a very harsh manner the anti-fundamentalist attitude which prevails throughout Contemporary Christian Music.

> "Judgment! Enough of them run up their mouths with their bad lip service/ Blah blah boom boom/ They say that they are bonafide but them bones fe fry/ They try to give you respect but they give you disrespect/ Contangarous/ Friendenemy/ They are a big disturbance/ Modern Day Pharisee you didn't have to judge me/ Modern Day Pharisee you can do no wrong, no wrong/ I said you can do no wrong, no wrong.

> "Look the way you live your righteousness worn on your sleeve/ Your working so hard to be good to convince that you've done your duty/ You are a pillar of society/ A righteous man you claim to be/ So well respected in your church, you know it's by grace you've been saved and that not of your works/ Modern Day Pharisee.
>
> "You tie your heavy load and throw it upon my back/ And if I stumbled and fell to the floor you'd pursue with a vicious attack/ You love to sit and accuse and go so far to inflict abuse?/ Are you really out for blood?/ Don't forget that we all fall short of the glory of God Modern Day Pharisee/ Modern Day Pharisee you love to shine brightly/ Modern Day Pharisee you didn't have to judge me.
>
> "Boy you go on like you are the article/ But you're artificial back stabber/ Go have His mercy. ...
>
> "Modern Day Pharisee, Concrete hearts!/ You give a tenth faithfully and even fast maybe twice a week/ Yet you judge me from the start?/ Don't you know that the Lord only sees what is there in you heart Modern Day Pharisee/ Modern Day Pharisee you love to shine brightly/ Modern Day Pharisee you didn't have to judge me.
>
> "They're a brood of vipers/ They would pluck you off one by one just like a sniper/ They lash out their tongue like a lethal weapon/ They don't deal with a relationship (with God) just religion."

The ecumenical crowd exercises love and tolerance for everyone except the "Bible thumper"! Christafari obviously has been reproved by fundamental Bible believers. They did not like it, and they lash back with this song. They slander fundamentalists by labeling them Pharisees, by claiming they are unloving and insincere hypocrites, vipers who simply want to put people into legalistic bondage. No doubt there are religious Pharisees in the world today, but to label someone a Pharisee because they take a fundamentalist stand against rock music and such things is ridiculous. Was the Apostle John a legalistic Pharisee when he demanded that Christians not love the world nor the things which are in the world? Was James a legalistic Pharisee when he said that friendship with the world is enmity with God? Was Paul a legalistic Pharisee when he instructed Christians about the significance of hair length?

As for hurting people, to follow the fundamentalist lifestyle and to reject all rock music has never injured anyone; but to accept rock music and to fellowship with the wicked rock crowd has destroyed countless people spiritually and morally. Christafari charges fundamentalists with only caring about religion and not about a relationship with God. This is a vicious slander. The Bible-believing fundamentalists that I know (and I know thousands of them) understand that a relationship with God through Jesus Christ is everything. They have no time for man-made religion and extra-biblical tradition. That is why they reject Roman Catholicism and any other form of Christianity which is contrary to the Word of God.

In 1997 Christafari joined Roman Catholic Kathy Troccoli and 40 other CCM artists to record *Love One Another*, a song with an ecumenical theme: "Christians from all denominations demonstrating their common love for Christ and each other." The song talks about tearing down the walls of denominational division. The broad range of participants who joined Kathy Troccoli in recording "Love One Another" demonstrates the ecumenical agenda of Contemporary Christian Music. The song witnessed Catholics, Pentecostals, Baptists, etc., yoked together to call for Christian unity.

In 1997, the members of Christafari, minus founder Mark Mohr, formed a new reggae band called Temple Yard. Their debut album was self titled. Band members said "a difference in long-term visions prompted the split" (*Charisma*, March 1999, p. 110).

CHRISTIAN, CHRIS

Chris Christian changed his name from Lon Christian Smith when he began his career in pop music. He runs the LCS Music Group, which has had 20 gold and platinum records. He is also president of Home Sweet Home Productions. "He's written songs for Sheena Easton, B.J. Thomas, and Olivia Newton-John, with one of his earliest songs recorded by Elvis Presley" (Kit Frieden, "Christian Music Guru Says There's 'No Such Thing,'" *The Patriot*, Harrisburg, Penn., Nov. 29, 1986). He is known in the recording industry as the discoverer of Amy Grant.

After obtaining a degree from the Church of Christ Abilene Christian College, Christian went to Nashville to seek his fame and fortune in music. He performed in the Grand Ole Opry, provided backup guitar for various groups, played in the group Cotton, Lloyd & Christian, then formed Home Sweet Home Productions.

The lyrics to his songs often "have a double meaning that don't always give the song away as religious in nature." The song "Safe," which was produced by Christian's Home Sweet Home Productions, was not even written by a Christian, yet many Christian hearers probably think it is about the Lord Jesus Christ. The lyrics state: "I'm safe, safe inside your love. And there ain't anything I can't face, safe inside your hiding place."

Chris Christian has the CCM philosophy that music is neutral:

> "There's no such thing as Christian music. Music is generic" (Chris Christian, Kit Frieden, "Christian Music Guru Says There's 'No Such Thing,'" *The Patriot*, Harrisburg, Penn., Nov. 29, 1986).

CHURCH, CHARLOTTE

"Charlotte Church was originally marketed by the recording labels as a super sweet, innocent teenaged Welsh girl who sings hymns. Lots of church going older folks (at least over here [Singapore] and in the UK) bought her first album and she was considered a great singing sensation. The latest newspaper picture of her has her belting it out in skin-tight black leather pants, bustier. The newspaper used the word 'raunchy' to describe her new image. Of course all this is just marketing and packaging and it's another attempt by the recording companies to christianize what is essentially a secular style, approach and attitude to music" (Letter from Jesse Sng, Oct. 31, 2001).

CLARK, PAUL

Paul Clark (c.1952-) formed his first band in junior high school after seeing the Beatles on the Ed Sullivan show. He got involved in the hippie drug scene, but during his first year in college in 1970 he determined to be a disciple of Christ. "I was an 18-year-old hippie, trying to find God. One day, I received a box of books from my grandmother. I chose one and read it from cover to cover in one day. At the end of the book was a prayer to follow Jesus as his disciple. The next morning brought more than another pristine Rocky Mountain day. I sat on my porch and felt so new, so clean and so thankful" (Paul Clark Web Site, http://placetobe.org/cmp/artists/index.html).

Clark then became involved in the Jesus Movement of the '70s and has continued writing and performing Contemporary Christian Music. He has recorded 15 albums and written more than 300 songs, as well as produced projects for other artists.

Clark is a Pentecostal who has written songs such as "Latter Rain" and "Believe and Receive."

CLEVELAND, ASHLY

Ashly Cleveland's (1957-) music includes "reflective folk songs to straight-ahead rock and roll." She told an interviewer that she is convinced that the authors of the old hymns she has recorded are "rolling perpetually in their graves," since her blues–based rock & roll interpretations are, to say the least, unorthodox (Shirley Simmons and Nita Andrews, "Interview with Ashley Cleveland," *Mars Hill Review*, Summer 1997, pp. 116-124).

Cleveland was born in Tennessee but grew up in northern California. Though she was reared in a Presbyterian church, she says, "I always knew that I was a closet Pentecostal" (Ibid.). In the half dozen or so interviews I read, she never gives a clear testimony of when and how she was born again. Cleveland's first child was eight years old when Cleveland married her husband, Kenneth Greenburg. She has two children by this marriage.

Cleveland's producers are her husband, Kenny, and Brown Bannister, who also produces Amy Grant. In 1985 she moved to Nashville and performed on some 200 albums as a background studio singer. Most of the albums were not Christian. She sang, for example, on Joan Baez's 1992 album, *Play Me Backwards*. Her first album, *Big Town*, appeared in 1991. For her 1993 album, *Bus Named Desire*, she was nominated for a Dove Award for "New Artist of the Year." In 1994 she won a Dove Award for her work on the album *Songs from the Loft*. In 1996 she won a Grammy for Best Rock Gospel Album for *Lesson of Love*.

When asked by an interviewer who has influenced her music, she replied: "There are at least thirty artists I could name from the late sixties and early seventies that influenced me: Stephen Stills, Joni Mitchell, Neil Young, Elton John, Steely Dan, Led Zeppelin, The Who, Little Feat...and rock-and-roll bands that capitalized on the acoustic guitar's percussive qualities. I really think the acoustic guitar is the ultimate rock-and-roll instrument" (Chris Parks, "Interview with Ashley Cleveland," Feb. 21, 1998, http://www.tollbooth.org/features/cleve.html). When asked what music was currently on her stereo, she replied, "*Living With Ghosts*, Patty Griffin; *What's The Story Morning Glory*, Oasis; *Exile On Main Street*, Rolling Stones" (http://www.ashleycleveland.com/acfacts.htm). In her concerts, Ashley Cleveland performs a very gritty rendition of the Rolling Stones' hit "Gimme Shelter."

Cleveland does not like fundamentalist Christianity. She changed the words to the lyrics of "Power in the Blood" from "would you be free of your passion and pride" to "would you be free of your pettiness and pride." She told an interviewer that the pettiness refers to "conservative bastions" such as taboos against certain kinds of indecent clothing, tattoos, etc. She has at least two tattoos, because "I really enjoy poking at conservative bastions" (Shirley Simmons and Nita Andrews, "Interview with Ashley Cleveland," *Mars Hill Review*, Summer 1997). She says:

> "I still have those seeds of rebellion that refuse to leave me [laughs] that show up here and there. I can't say that I work diligently to get rid of them, I guess as I get older they're my last vestiges of youth and I cling to them. ... I disdain the trend that conservative Republicans represent Christianity. So, I hardly ever resist an opportunity to take a little shot at that. ... That is pretty much the form that my rebellion takes. It's difficult for me to sit quietly under somebody

else's authority and so that's the other form" (Ibid.).

She told an interviewer that two movies she has enjoyed are *Good Will Hunting* and *The Full Monty*. According to Deseret online movie reviews, both are rated R and contain nudity, vulgarity, and profanity, meaning the movies blaspheme the Almighty God. *The Full Monty* is a bawdy British film about a group of unemployed men who decide to become male strippers. Cleveland said that when she was watching this vile film she got a laugh out of wondering how it would be if her husband and his friends would do such a thing. It was a "hilarious thought," she said. *Good Will Hunting* gets its R rating "for almost constant profanity, some very vulgar jokes and references, violence, sex, glimpses of nude paintings and racial epithets." Cleveland says, "I thought that was fantastic. I loved that movie."

In her song "Skintight," from the 1993 album, *Bus Named Desire*, Ashley Cleveland sings about fornication:

> "Glad you could make it over/ Step in the room/ Shake off the night/ Can't take it any longer/ Promise you do, even you might ... Maybe that's why love like mine is skin tight/ Love like mine is skin tight/ Move a little closer/ Take in the view, lower the light/ I wanna be your lover/ To find truth and bring it to light..." (Ashley Cleveland, "Skintight").

Cleveland's 1998 album contains a cover of the Rolling Stones hit "Gimme Shelter."

COMMON BOND

Common Bond is a music and drama team from the Kalamazoo, Michigan, Youth for Christ.

Ken Samuels of Common Bond says they "have to completely disassociate from anything people commonly associate with religion" (*CCM Magazine*, April 1987, p. 13). This is a strange goal for professing Christian musicians. What are things commonly associated with Christian religion? The Bible, Jesus Christ, the cross, the Gospel, preaching, heaven, hell. Common Bond wants to disassociate from such things so they will not be rejected by the worldly crowd.

COMMON CHILDREN

The hard rock band Common Children was formed in 1993 by Marc Byrd (vocals), Drew Powell (bass), and Hampton Eugene (drums). Their 1996 debut album, *Skywire*, was compared to various secular grunge bands, particularly Nirvana. Byrd says: "The thing about Nirvana is they rock, yeah, but Kurt Cobain wrote incredible melodies" (Chad Benham, interview with Common Children, *RIM*, Ricochet Internet Magazine, 1998, http://www.ricochetmusic.com/rim_new/com_children/cc1.htm).

Byrd also says. "I'll admit, yes, we were influenced by Nirvana. We listened to Nirvana when they came out and thought they were cool and everything, but our main influences have been Pink Floyd and groups like that" (Ibid.). Nirvana, lead by Kurt Cobain, was a very dark and occultic band. The antichrist Cobain killed himself with a shotgun.

COOLEY, LINDELL

Lindell Cooley (1963-) is the music director at the Brownsville Assembly of God in Pensacola, Florida, the headquarters for the "Pensacola Outpouring," an offshoot of the Toronto Laughing Revival. He grew up in a Pentecostal home and claims to have begun speaking in tongues at age 10. Pentecostal preachers prophesied that he would have a worldwide ministry through music. The music of his childhood was jazzy Pentecostal styles, Black spirituals, and soul music.

> "Well, I have a strong soulful side in me because I grew up with all those A.A. Allen records, and other albums by Andrae Crouch, Aretha Franklin, and Billy Preston, who had a big hit tune with the line, 'Will it go 'round in circles?' I loved that kind of syncopated, high-energy soul style. I loved all the Motown stuff, so I had a good handle on secular music too..." (Cooley, *A Touch of Glory*, p. 39).

Prior to becoming the music minister at Brownsville Assembly of God in 1995, Cooley was in charge of music at Christ Church near Nashville, Tennessee. This is the home for many well-known country and CCM musicians. In 1993 he led the Christ Church choir in performing "Put a Little Love in Your Heart" with Dolly Parton at the Country Music Association awards. After leaving there in at the end of 1993, Cooley attended an Episcopal church for awhile as he reconsidered his relationship with Pentecostalism.

Just before he became the music leader at the Brownsville Assembly of God, Cooley attended the Toronto Laughing Revival meetings. Of his experience in Toronto, Cooley testifies:

> "... I felt the fire of God come on me too! ... My experience with God in Toronto did something so powerful in me that it even changed my music tastes—in a radical way. All of a sudden I couldn't get enough 'California beach music' from Vineyard" (Cooley, *A Touch of Glory*, p. 114).

Cooley calls the music he is playing at Brownsville Assembly of God "Vineyard music."

The 1997 catalog from Vineyard Music features a "Winds of Worship" series which includes CDs from Toronto and Brownsville.

In a perceptive article on the music at Brownsville, Pastor Joseph Chambers makes the following comments:

> "The music minister at Brownsville Assembly of God in Pensacola, Florida, Lindell Cooley, defined the music of the 'revival' as 'honky music.' That word is an excellent description of Beatle's music, as well as Pensacola's music. The dictionary defines 'honky' as an adjective, which means 'cheap entertainment or jangly piano music' (*Chambers English Dictionary*, W&R Chambers, Ltd., 1990, p. 683). Jangly music is dissonant, described as 'not agreeing or harmonizing in sound, a combination of musical sounds that call for resolution or produces beats' (Ibid., p. 412). This is clearly Beatles' music and it is an excellent description of the music that has invaded the church. **Instead of quieting the human spirit, as music was created to accomplish, it arouses the human spirit and guides the person into unfamiliar realms of the emotions. It is perfect for creating altered states or a hypnotic condition.** It is clearly music designed to do the opposite of what our creator ordained.
>
> "There are two main songs that appear to help drive the Pensacola impartations. The first is what appears to be the theme, *The River Is Here*. ... This song is New Age to the core. It is void of truth, treats God in a generic fashion, and suggests that God's grace and glory flows from a river. Notice the term, 'And all who touch it can be revived.' Standing in the Brownsville church, I watched almost everyone dance, jump, jerk, shake, or swoon to this song. It captured the crowd, but it absolutely was not the Holy Spirit. After forty-five years of [experiencing and practicing] Biblical worship, it clearly showed no kin [to true worship].
>
> "The other song is on the opposite side of the pendulum. The above song is hypnotic in a mood-altering fashion. The second song gets you read to be zapped. It is named *Fire in His Eyes*, and is usually sung right before Evangelist Hill takes the services. ... I have no way of knowing the mind of the composer, but it certainly does not fit historic theology.
>
> "Jesus is not riding a white horse, but is seated at the right hand of the Father. He will ride this horse after the Rapture and the Great Tribulation when He returns to fight the Battle of Armageddon. Revelation, chapter six, suggests a White Horse rider with a crown and a bow, but this is judgment against the wicked and is certainly not when the saints ride. Most Bible teachers call this rider the Antichrist or the going forth of righteousness and judgment.
>
> "This appears to be in perfect accord with the theology of the Vineyard Church and their Joel's Army of conquerors. It is called Dominion Theology

and denies the traditional Rapture of the church. The words of these two songs are certainly confusing, but the spirit ... is even more dangerous. Why would we even consider this kind of music to sing to the Lord Jesus Christ? The truth is that we would not, because this music is not sung to Jesus Christ; it is sung to a new Jesus and by a totally different spirit.

"The transition from honoring the Lord Jesus with singing and praise to honoring a false Jesus takes place first in the soul. The worshipper is not conscious of this transition and may be absolutely sincere and honest. The best way to notice that this transition has begun is the new arrogance and unapproachableness of those passing through this paradigm. The word paradigm describes the New Age idea of transition between two world views. ... **It's easy to make the transition. Leave your theology at home. Don't question the big name who is dispensing this power. Open up and drink. Do not ask questions, for questions and biblical reasoning is a solid block against this change.** Even a young Christian with little experience is a stalwart against this deception if they cling to the Word of God and refuse to be swooned by the crowd controllers. ...

"Dr. David A. Noebel said of the Beatles' Music, 'The hard fact is that in this present revolutionary era, heavy beat music has become the catalyst for the young radicals in their announced plans not only to destroy Western culture, but to dethrone God. And few can really deny that the Beatles have and are playing a strategic and crucial role in the spiritual and cultural demise of the West and in the proposed destruction of Christianity throughout the world' (David A. Noebel, *The Beatles, A Study in Drugs, Sex and Revolution*, p. 8).

"The Beatles' music has finished duping the world and is now in the sanctuary" (Joseph Chambers, "Beatles' Music at Pensacola," *The End Times*, March-April 1997, p. 3).

Pastor Chambers is an old-line Pentecostal and we differ with him theologically on some issues, but we are thankful for his stand against the charismatic rock-mood music and we agree with his assessment of the music at Brownsville.

The following is a description of the music service at Brownsville Assembly of God:

"Thump ... Thump ... Thump ... Thump ... It begins with a drummer laying down a slow beat that goes on for several minutes, a steady, inescapable, portentous heartbeat. The guitarist and the organist join in, along with a choir of several dozen singers clad in purple robes with gold sashes. From the first note, the people are up out of the pews and on their feet, clapping in time or dancing with eyes closed and hands raised. In front of the first row, teenagers pogo up and down, a sort of Pentecostal mosh pit. IF IT WEREN'T FOR THE CROSS AND THE STAINED GLASS BEHIND THE ALTAR, YOU MIGHT

THINK YOU WERE AT A ROCK-AND-ROLL SHOW. The first song ends to wild cheers. A second begins, then a third and a fourth. ... It's a half-hour into the service and not a word has yet been preached" (*Washington Post*, April 27, 1997).

The music which is coming out of the Laughing Revival is not coincidental. A certain type of music produces a certain type of response and creates a certain type of atmosphere. There is a type of music which accompanies the sensual atmosphere of a nightclub. There is another type of music which lifts the spirit to commune with the holy God of Creation and which creates an atmosphere of conviction and worship in Spirit and truth. These two types of music are not compatible. The atmosphere and response created by Fanny Crosby's "He Hideth My Soul" is not the same as that created by the Beatles' "I Wanna Hold Your Hand."

Likewise, there is a type of music which fits the context of spiritual abandon, doctrinal carelessness, and fleshly sensuousness associated with the charismatic movement. It is a very different type of music than that which has traditionally been used by God's people. Charismatic musicians see little or no distinction between worldly music and godly music. They lack spiritual discernment. They think music is neutral, that only the words have meaning. They refuse to acknowledge that the music itself carries a message even without the words, and that the message of the music must match the message of the words. To use sensual music in an attempt to glorify the holy God is great confusion.

CRAWFORD, BEVERLY

In 1997 Beverly Crawford joined Roman Catholic Kathy Troccoli and 40 other CCM artists to record *Love One Another*, a song with an ecumenical theme: "Christians from all denominations demonstrating their common love for Christ and each other." The song talks about tearing down the walls of denominational division. The broad range of participants who joined Kathy Troccoli in recording "Love One Another" demonstrates the ecumenical agenda of Contemporary Christian Music. The song witnessed Catholics, Pentecostals, Baptists, etc., yoked together to call for Christian unity.

CROSSE, CLAY

Clay Crosse (1967-) is a relative new comer to the CCM scene. In 1995 he received the Dove Award for New Artist of the Year. By 1998 Ssix of his singles hadve reached No. 1 and his first two albums havde sold more than 400,000 copies. He is was one of the top 30 CCM artists of 1998. He has been married to his wife, Renna, since 1991 and has two childrenone child and another due in October 1998. An article in *CCM Magazine* reported that in 1998 Cross admitted to his wife that he had long been addicted to pornography, and he began then to seek help. He testified, "Because I valued being an open-minded Christian, I allowed things into my life that someone who's trying to be Christ-like should not. It filtered in through TV shows, comedians. I'd go see movies that really pushed the envelope, arguing that they had artistic value, even if I knew they weren't the kind of things I should be seeing as a Christian" (Melissa Riddle, "Brave New World," *CCM Magazine*, May 2000, p. 51). This is a loud warning about the easy-going, do-your-own-thing philosophy which has permeated Contemporary Christian Music today. Those who warn against unwholesome movies, sensual music, immodest dress, etc., are called legalists and Pharisees, but godly boundaries protect people from moral and spiritual destruction. Clay Crosse learned this the hard way.

Crosse is affiliated with the ecumenical World Vision and reveals his ecumenical philosophy in the song "Saving the World" —

> "So many preachers/ So many churches and denominations/ Got their opinions and their documents/ And statements and beliefs/ And sometimes there's a miscommunication/ And we complicate the truth/ And convolute the story/ But as far as I recall/ I do believe it all comes down to a man dying on a cross/ Saving the world/ Rising from the dead/ Doing what he said he would do/ Loving everyone."

While it is true that the denominational divisions have complicated the truth and that there is miscommunication between professing Christians, Crosse leaves his listeners with the false and dangerous impression that doctrine and statements of faith are unimportant and unnecessary, that all that is important is the central fact of Christ's death and resurrection and some sort of ill-defined universal love. The words to this song reflect the ecumenical philosophy of organizations such as Promise Keepers and March for Jesus. We must put aside doctrinal disputes and have unity among all who "love Jesus." This ecumenical philosophy lightly passes over the Bible's warnings about false teachers. It ignores the Bible's prophecies of worldwide apostasy. It fails to address Paul's warning that there are false christs and false gospels.

In 1997 Clay Crosse joined Roman Catholic Kathy Troccoli and 40 other CCM artists to record *Love One Another*, a song with an ecumenical theme: "Christians from all denominations demonstrating their common love for Christ and each other." The song talks about tearing down the walls of denominational division. The broad range of participants who joined Kathy Troccoli in recording "Love One Another" demonstrates the ecumenical agenda of Contemporary Christian Music. The song witnessed Catholics, Pentecostals, Baptists, etc., yoked together to call for Christian unity.

On Crosse's *Stained Glass* album (1997) (produced by Mark Heimermann and Regie Hamm) is the song "Love One Another Right." It is written by Regie Hamm, Steve Siler, and Bob Farrell. Note the following unscriptural philosophy:

> "We do a pretty good job of throwing sticks and stones/ But everyone's got a closet full of skeleton bones/ No need to tear each other down/ 'Cause we're all standing here on common ground/ If we could love one another/ We could bring Heaven down out of the sky."

The song presents the false ecumenical philosophy that Christians are not to judge sin and error. Since I have my own sins and problems, I have no right to judge any other person, they say. This is not what the Bible says, though. Preaching and teaching is to be judged (1 Cor. 14:29). False teachers are to be judged and rebuked (Titus 3:10-11). Stubborn Christians are to be rebuked sharply (Titus 1:13). Not only am I to avoid the sinful things of this world, but I am commissioned by the Lord to rebuke those who do such things. "And have no fellowship with the unfruitful works of darkness, but rather reprove them" (Eph. 5:11). Paul was not perfect or sinless but he rebuked Peter publicly for his hypocrisy and compromise (Galatians 2:11-14). The man of God does not judge sin because of perfection in his own life but on the authority of the Word of God.

CROUCH, ANDRAE

Andrae Crouch (c.1942-) is a CCM superstar. He is the winner of eight Grammy awards. His group Andrae Crouch and the Disciples was the first CCM group to sell one million records.

Crouch is also pastor of Christ Memorial Church in Pacoima, California. Crouch's church is a member of the Church of God in Christ, the largest black American Pentecostal denomination. He became the pastor of the church when his brother, who was the previous pastor, died of cancer in 1995. Crouch began his musical career playing the piano at age 11 in his father's church. In the 1970s he formed a group called The Disciples, and since then he has exercised vast influence within Contemporary Christian Music.

From 1981 to 1996 Crouch's music producer was Bill Maxwell, who also produced albums for Keith Green.

Crouch has written many songs which have become modern Christian classics, including "Jesus Is the Answer," "The Blood Will Never Lose Its Power," and the lovely "Through It All."

Crouch says he was called to pastor by being knocked to the floor:

> "It was Sunday morning, and I had my $500 suit on, and I was singing, clap-

ping my hands, and doing a little step, and all of a sudden I hit the floor. The Holy Spirit spoke to me and said, 'Okay Mr. *Through It All*, Mr. *Take Me Back*, Mr. *To God Be the Glory*, you will not get off the floor until you tell Me yes. I don't want uh-huh. I don't want yup. I don't want right on. I want yes. Y-e-s'" (Dave Urbanski, "The Preacher's Life," *CCM Magazine*, February 1997).

After he was called to preach, Crouch left his luxurious home with a swimming pool in a wealthy neighborhood and moved into the small house which had belonged to his father, the former pastor of Christ Memorial. Of his ministry in a Latino-Black neighborhood, Crouch says: "I don't know how many teenage kids from the neighborhood I've buried who never even went to church, never even heard 'Amazing Grace.' And there I am, talking to this dead kid's friends, and I see the young body in the casket, never to walk this earth again. I cry all the time. And I cannot rest. I cannot rest" (Dave Urbanski, "The Preacher's Life," *CCM Magazine*, February 1997).

Crouch holds the CCM philosophy that music is neutral. Producer Bill Maxwell, a longtime Crouch compatriot, agrees. "Andrae has no boundaries. He always liked good music, whether it was the Beatles or black gospel" (*CCM Magazine*, February 1997). The music for Crouch's 1994 album is described as mixing "reggae, calypso, and African rhythms respectively" (*World*, August 13, 1994).

Though his denomination forbids women pastors, Crouch defiantly ordained his twin sister, Sandra Crouch, as assistant pastor of the church on August 1, 1998 (*Los Angeles Times*, July 26, 1998). Sandra is also a professional singer and Grammy winner. She has worked with Michael Jackson, Diana Ross, Neil Diamond, and Julio Iglesias. Crouch said, "I don't see anywhere in the Word that women can't be ordained" (*Charisma*, October 1998, p. 50). 1 Timothy 2:12 plainly forbids a woman to teach or usurp authority over men. The woman's role in the church is in teaching children and other women (Titus 2:3-5), not men. There were no female apostles and no female pastors in the apostolic churches. One of the requirements for the pastor is that he be the "husband of one wife" (1 Timothy 3:2; Titus 1:5-6). No woman fulfills this qualification. Crouch uses human reason as his authority: "I figure if they're [women] good enough to cook you food, they're good enough to feed you spiritual food" (Ibid.). This sounds plausible but it doesn't have any biblical authority behind it. Whether or not to ordain a woman has nothing to do with whether she is "good enough" to do the job. No one, man or woman, is really "good enough" to be a pastor. It is an high and holy office which a sinner can hold only by the grace of Jesus Christ. God has give us the instructions for the operation of the church, and He has plainly restricted the office of the pastor to men. Women and men have different roles in society and in the church. Doctrine and practice cannot be established upon human reason. Crouch has no biblical authority to ordain a woman as a pastor.

Crouch has a close, non-critical relationship with the unholy secular music industry, recording with many well-known secular musicians. Crouch and his choir sang the soundtrack of Disney's New Age children's movie *The Lion King* and performed on Madonna's 1989 blasphemous album *Like a Prayer*. He worked on Steven Spielberg's film *The Color Purple*. He has collaborated in music with Diana Ross, Stevie Wonder, Elton John, B.B. King, Michael Jackson, and many others. On the wall of his office is a platinum CD of Michael Jackson's 1995 double album with an inscription thanking him for arranging the music for this album which sold 11 million copies (*Charisma*, October 1998, p. 50). Crouch argues that he is being salt and light in the darkness of the secular music industry, but does his non-critical relationship with these secular musicians not encourage Christian young people that it's O.K. to be involved in that type of music and thereby bring injury to their spiritual and moral lives? Elton John, for example, is an admitted bi-sexual and his music is very immoral, rebellious, New Age, even antichrist. The same is true for Michael Jackson. Fletcher Brothers, who operates a home dedicated to rescuing young people from moral destruction, says: "America will probably never know how extent the damages are that Michael Jackson has brought upon her young people—not until eternity. Many of his popular songs contain illicit sex..." (*The Rock Report*, p. 47). Nothing good can come from young people being encouraged that it is fine to listen to music produced by such people.

CROW, ROBIN

"There are artists who do nothing but play praise music for believers. Great. My music is not praise or evangelism. I don't even call it a ministry, because that puts a hundred expectations on you before you ever play a note" (Robin Crow, interview, *Contemporary Christian Music Magazine*, August 1983, p. 28).

CROW, SHERYL

The *National Catholic Register* for March 8-14, 1998, listed Sheryl Crow as a Catholic musician.

CRUSE

Cruse plays such loud, riotous rock music that their lyrics cannot be understood. Following is a description by a reviewer: "It's a good thing that this album comes with a lyric sheet, because most of the words do not come through distinctly enough for one to easily follow the message" (*Contemporary Christian Music Magazine*, January 1985, p. 28).

CRYAR, MORGAN

Morgan Cryar (1959-) has been involved professionally with CCM since 1981. His debut album, *Keep No Secrets*, was released in 1985. Since then he has produced four others. He entered college with the goal of becoming a pastor, but went into the music field instead. He toured with Petra in the 1980s in a band called King's X. He was married to his wife, Melanie, in 1982, and as of 1996 they had five children.

> "A good pop/rock sound for the teenage audience. The songs deal with youth issues and situations WITHOUT BEING PREACHY" (an ad for "Fuel on the Fire" by Morgan Cryar).

DAKOTA MOTOR COMPANY

The Dakota Motor Company was formed in 1994 and features Peter King (guitar), Melissa Brewer (lead singer), Derik Toy (bass), Elliot Chenault (lead guitar), and Chuck Cummings (drums).

Peter King, who is a professional surfer, has a contract with wicked MTV to host "Sandblast" and to do "sports-oriented stuff, some of the special events, like 'Beach House' and the vacation deals, as well as some celebrity interviews" (Peter King, interview, *CCM Magazine*, February 1996). By his example, King is telling young people that it is alright to watch the vile MTV.

The group's philosophy is evident from the following statements:

> "We are just trying our hardest to be a really good rock band; that's our goal ... to have a lot of [musical] integrity. ... But really, we want to play for fans of music, not fans of Christianity ... We're getting paid to play every night, pretty much, and we believe that we're getting paid to perform a concert, not a ministry. ... Rock 'n' roll, as far as I'm concerned, is just rock 'n' roll, and I love it for what it is. I don't think there's anything wrong with that. ... I don't care if you're Jewish, Buddhist, black, white, green, Mormon, Christian or not, I want to play Dakota's music for you, and I want that music to impact your life. Not because I'm selfish, but because I want you to dig my music. I mean, that's why we do this" (Peter King, *CCM Magazine*, July 1996).
> "We're definitely not cheerleaders ... We feel that people are paying to see a show; they're paying for music, not a Bible study. I know a lot of people will come expecting the same Christian show that happened the week before, or the week before that. But don't come to see Dakota just because we're Christians. We love playing music for the sake of playing music" (Peter King, *CCM Magazine*, February 1996).

At least The Dakota Motor Company is honest and forthright about what they are doing. Their first priority with music is to rock & roll!

The following two songs from Dakota Motor Company's 1993 *Into the Son* album illustrate the vagueness of this group's music. Both songs are heavy rock:

> "I need a love that will bring me high/ A love that will take my blues away/ I need a love that will light my sky/ A love that will drive my tears away/ I need love, I need You/ Put a rainbow in my view/ After raining down on me/ I need a love that will meet my needs/ So unconditionally/ I need a love that will help me stand/ A love that will show me the way/ I need a love that will take my fear/ When I am feeling afraid" (Dakota Motor Company, "Need a Love," 1993).

This is another ill identified CCM song about love which sounds very much like the "love" secular rock singers praise. Is Dakota Motor Company singing about the love of Jesus Christ? It is not possible to know for sure. God's love to sinners is not known apart from the atonement of Jesus Christ, yet this song does not even mention Christ or the cross. An unsaved person hearing Dakota Motor Company's song, would easily assume that God's love is entirely unconditional, meaning that God accepts him as he is and that he does not need to repent or be born again. This is the impression given by the song. The love here is entirely man centered. It meets all my "needs." Does the love of God promise to take away all our tears?

> "She's singing in the rain/ And dancing in the sun/ Flowers in her hair on a midnight barefoot run/ Purple pansies with a black velvet face/ No doubt about it, God is in this place/ Sondancer, sondancer girl/ You seem so different, not of this world/ Sea grass grows on the ocean floor/ She swims past way beyond/ The shorebright fishfins cut the water so clear/ No doubt about it, God is here/ Rain comes down on everyone/ Sondancer's eyes are on the Son/ Someone's eyes are set on the pain/ The Son will bring you/ Through the rain/ Set apart running free/ Sondancer girl dance around me" (Dakota Motor Company, "Sondancer," 1993).

This song is more akin to the New Age than to Christianity. It would have fit perfectly on the Beatle's *Sgt. Pepper* album. From a biblical perspective, its meaning is entirely obscure.

DANA

Dana (pronounced Donna) was a popular mainstream musician in Northern Ireland before relocating to America. She is a Roman Catholic and records for the Catholic-owned Heartbeat Records, based in Donnelson, Iowa. Her album *The Rosary*, about

Mary the Queen of Heaven, has sold more than 200,000 copies. She performed for Pope John Paul II at the World Youth Day in Denver, Colorado, in 1993. In fact, she wrote the theme song for that event.

Dana's album "No Greater Love" was the first release of Krystal Records in 1988. Krystal was founded by the Roman Catholic Daughter's of St. Paul. One of the songs on this album was "Totus Tuus," which means "Totally Yours" and which is Pope John Paul II's motto. The words, which are embroidered on his papal robes, refer to his dedication to Mary. Some have falsely claimed that the motto refers to the pope's dedication to Jesus Christ, but in his own book, *Crossing the Threshold of Hope* (Alfred A. Knopf, 1994), John Paul II testifies that *Totus Tuus* describes his devotion to Mary.

Dana is one of the most popular Catholic CCM musicians and, like Michael Talbot, is pushing for ecumenical unity. She has an album titled "We Are One Body" and has performed at the Christian Booksellers Association.

DANIEL AMOS BAND

The Daniel Amos band, from California, released its first album in 1976. The group was one of the first Christian hard rock groups. The original members were Terry Taylor, Jerry Chamberlain, Steve Baxter, and Marty Dieckmeyer. Other members have included Ed McTaggart, Mark Cook, Alex MacDougal, Rob Watson, Tim Chandler, and Greg Flesch.

The following song by Daniel Amos Band demonstrates the worldly philosophy of this group:

> "There's a party in Heaven/ The bread is unleaven/ The tree of life is growin' fine/ It's way past eleven/ My number is seven/ The Lamb and I are drinkin' new wine" ("Party in Heaven").

This song is sung to hard rock music. This CCM group apparently thinks Heaven will be something like a worldly booze party!

Terry Taylor claims that a Christian musician does not have to preach the Gospel plainly, but can provide entertainment and fun:

> "There are some people God has called to evangelism, and they're doing a wonderful job, having results. That's great. God wanted us to do something else, so we got into the area of challenging people, and our ministry basically happens offstage—one-on-one—when we talk with people. It's very subtle, but God's doing a work! It's entertainment, it's fun, it's a concert—it's all those

things—but at a subtle, deeper level, it touches people's hearts" (Terry Taylor, cited by Dan and Steve Peters, *What about Christian Rock?*, p. 109).

How does Taylor know God wanted them to do something else other than plainly preach the Gospel as we see the Christians doing in the Bible (Acts 8:4)? The Great Commission is not given merely to preachers or to a few full-time evangelists and missionaries. It is for every born again Christian to fulfill through the New Testament church (Acts 1:8). Contemporary Christian musicians have no biblical authority to entertain the world. Christian music is to teach and admonish (Col. 3:16). They have no biblical authority to water down the Gospel message so that it is acceptable to the world. They have no authority to make the Christian message vague, to make it man-centered rather than Christ-centered, to make it felt-need centered rather than cross-centered. They have no authority to draw back from preaching plainly that man is sinful and condemned, that God is holy and righteous, that Hell is eternal, that the way of salvation is narrow and requires repentance. It is not the God of the Bible who is leading in this new "contemporary" path. He has already expressed His will in the Scriptures, and we see nothing resembling a Contemporary Christian Music program there.

The Daniel Amos band still works together irregularly. Terry Taylor continues to influence CCM. He is the A&R director at KMG Records and continues to produce and perform. He produced *Surfonic Water Revival: New Surf Music for the Redeemed Masses*, which focuses on "the whole era of surf music, from the primitive, garagey stuff to the real orchestrated, *Pet Sounds* kind of thing." The album is described as follows by Kent Songer, KMG vice-president: "*Surfonic* contains all the elements that make for successful musical genres—honesty, fun, memorable hooks, fun, the ability to do rockin' cuts or ballads and, of course, fun" (*7Ball*, July-August 1998, p. 26).

The Apostles describe the Christian life in terms of fearing God, self-denial, separation from the world. Christian rockers describe the Christian life in terms of fun, fun, fun.

DANIELS, CHARLIE

Country/bluegrass musician Charlie Daniels has produced 29 albums, two of them Christian. Unlike the average popular country-rock performer, Daniels has remained married to the same woman for 35 years and has traveled with his wife for the last 15 or so. This is commendable.

"The July-August *Moody Monthly* favorably reviewed a country rock 'gospel' album by Charlie Daniels, and said he 'could certainly use our prayers as he embarks on an adventure of attracting his secular listeners to these new lyrics' (p. 36). An interview with Daniels in the July 31 *Huntsville Times* quoted him using profanity. But *Moody* says:

'For Christians to flatly dismiss musicians because they use four-letter words or sexual references, diminishes the likelihood that people will ever hear our message. ... We have to understand the world's view before we can effectively communicate our view; we have to relate to the people before we can preach to them' (p. 57)" (*Calvary Contender*, Sept. 1, 1994).

This is unscriptural advice. We are not to do evil to reach the world. The Bible admonishes us to be "wise unto that which is good, and simple concerning evil" (Romans 16:19). The Bible also warns: "Let no corrupt communication proceed out of your mouth, but that which is good to the use of edifying, that it may minister grace unto the hearers" (Eph. 4:29).

Daniels' 1996 *Steel Witness* album contains the song "New Pharisees," which "speaks about the tendency of modern-day Christians to judge their fellow man, much like the Pharisees of Jesus' day."

Daniels hammered this same theme in a 1994 interview: "I'm not a religious person. I'm a person that's been bought and paid for by the blood of Jesus Christ. I'm not religious, per se. I'm not a Pharisee. I don't believe in certain rules and that things have to be that way. I don't like to judge people. I get judged a lot by critics and that sort of thing" (*The Lighthouse*, June 1994). While we are glad that Charlie Daniels is trusting the blood of Christ for his salvation, he is wrong to claim that the Christian life has nothing to do with rules. There are 88 specific laws or rules for the Christian in the book of Ephesians alone. The child of God is not saved BY good works, but he is saved UNTO good works (Ephesians 2:8-10). It is not Phariseeism to strive to be faithful to the Word of God and to judge everything by the Word of God. Phariseeism was adding human commandments to the Word of God and rejecting the grace of Christ for a works salvation. Those who label Fundamentalist Bible believers Pharisees are slanderers. We have discussed the issue of Phariseeism in the "Questions and Answers" section of this book.

In the same interview, Daniels said: "One of the things that I wish did not exist in the Church, in the Body of Christ, is people going against each other, saying, 'I don't believe the way you do, so you're wrong and I can't have anything to do with you...' and so on—existing as if their own little corner of the world is the only part of it they should live in. I don't believe in that. I think that's wrong" (Charlie Daniels, *The Lighthouse*, June 1994). This is the unscriptural philosophy that is at the heart of the ecumenical movement. Timothy was told not to allow any other doctrine (1 Timothy 1:3). Every Christian is to earnestly contend for the faith once delivered to the saints (Jude 3). That means that it is every Christian's task to know sound New Testament doctrine and to defend it against all error. Romans 16:17 goes on to require that we separate from those who teach false doctrine. That is a very narrow view of doctrine, but it is what the Word of God teaches. The Apostle Paul "went against" many professing Christians because of their false doctrine. Ten times in the epistles to Timothy alone he warned of false teachers and compromisers by name (1 Tim. 1:20; 2 Tim. 1:15; 2:17; 3:8; 4:10,14).

DAVIS, GERON

Songwriter Geron Davis is committed to "Jesus Only" doctrine, which denies the Trinity and baptizes only in Jesus' name. He wrote "Holy Ground" and "In the Presence of Jehovah."

DC TALK

The rock group dc Talk was formed in 1989 by students from Jerry Falwell's Liberty University, Toby Mckeehan, Michael Tait, and Kevin Smith. Toby wears two ear rings and has long hair. Their interviews contain offensive and vulgar words such as "crappy" and "freaking." The Bible says we should use only "sound speech, that cannot be condemned; that he that is of the contrary part may be ashamed, having no evil thing to say of you" (Titus 2:8).

The three met at the charismatic Heritage USA when Falwell was attempting to rescue the PTL Club after Jim Bakker was arrested. The origin of this rock group, therefore, is related to the compromise of Jerry Falwell in associating with the worldly/unscriptural PTL Club. After dc Talk was formed, they were allowed to sing at a Liberty University chapel service (*Calvary Contender*, July 15, 1991).

In 1991 Falwell stated: "During Toby, Michael, and Kevin's tenure at Liberty University, it was obvious to me that God had great plans for these three young men and their powerful program..." (*Calendar* magazine, Spring/Summer 1991, p. 8). Terry Watkins observes: "That's quite a statement by Brother Falwell, considering that Kevin was kicked out of Liberty for a 'drinking' problem!"

The group was praised in Falwell's June 1996 *National Liberty Journal*: "This year's top artists are Liberty University's own dc Talk, whose *Jesus Freak* CD experienced never-before-seen sales figures for gospel music." In April 1996 hard rocking dc Talk drew the largest concert crowd in the history of Falwell's university.
In an interview with *CCM Magazine* about their 1998 album, *Supernatural*, the members of dc Talk described their objective in these words:

> "'We are not ministers,' says McKeehan. 'DC TALK IS A BUSINESS, but in

the midst of our business, we pray that God ministers to people through our lives. Max adds, 'DC TALK IS AN ENTERTAINMENT GROUP. But when you dig deep into what we do or you dig into what we say, therein lies where the Holy Spirit interacts with the people" (emphasis added) (April Hefner, "Supermen," *CCM Magazine*, October 1998, p. 38).

The name dc Talk refers to Washington D.C., where the band members are from.

Michael Tait admits that he loves the "look at me" aspect of rock. "I've always wanted to be the front guy of a band of guitar-toting, drum-slinging rock 'n' rollers because my personality is one of such flamboyancy and energy. Rock 'n' roll embodies and exudes all of that" (*CCM Magazine*, May 2001, p. 43). Kevin Max also admits that they are self-possessed with their music, just like secular rockers: "As a performer, you're constantly neurotic about what you look like, how you're performing on stage, what you come off like to the public" (Ibid., p. 44).

Some of dc Talk's musical role models are the Beatles, David Bowie, and The Police, all of which are wicked secular rock groups. Kevin Smith admits that he listens to mostly secular rock music (*Flint Michigan Journal*, March 15, 1996, p. B19). dc Talk opened its "Jesus Freak" concerts with the Beatles' song "Help." They also perform other secular rock songs at their concerts, including drug inspired "Purple Haze" by Jimi Hendrix. Toward the end of their concerts they played the rock song "All Apologies" by the secular rock group Nirvana, formerly led by Kurt Cobain. Terry Watkins notes: "Kurt Cobain is one of the worst ANTICHRIST blasphemers since John Lennon. Kurt Cobain decorated his home with blood-splattered baby dolls hanging by their necks! The inside of Nirvana's album *In Utero*, which is the album dc Talk got 'All Apololgies' from, has pictures of chopped up babies! Cobain ran around his neighborhood spray-painting, 'ABORT CHRIST' and 'GOD IS GAY.' Cobain's first band was called 'Fecal Matter.' Cobain killed himself a couple of years ago" (Watkins, *Christian Rock: Blessing or Blasphemy?*). During their 1999 "Supernatural Experience" tour, dc Talk performed "Hello Good-bye" by the Beatles, "Jesus Is Just Alright" by the Doobie Brothers, "Give Peace a Chance" by the late New Ager John Lennon, "That's the Way I Like It" by the Sunshine Band, and "Le Freak" by Chic (*CCM Magazine*, April 1999, p. 55).

dc Talk hired Simon Maxwell to produce their "Jesus Freak" video. Maxwell was hired because dc Talk had seen his work with the antichrist rock group Nine Inch Nails. Toby McKeehan said that Maxwell's "style appealed to us" (*Billboard*, Nov. 11, 1995). The Maxwell-produced Nine Inch Nails video *Closer* features a monkey crucified on a cross! Nine Inch Nails lead singer Trent Reznor backs the satanist group Marilyn Manson, which has a blasphemous album titled "Antichrist Superstar."

dc talk admits that they want to push the envelope with their music and videos. Following is their stated goal with the video *Jesus Freak*: "the intention of the clip was to 'push the envelope' of the Christian music community ... they expect some of the more conservative members of the Christian community to frown on the adventurous clip" (*Billboard*, Nov. 11, 1995).

The members of dc Talk do not belong to any organized Christian denomination or church affiliation.

dc Talk's antagonism toward biblical fundamentalists is evident in their music. The song "Time Ta Jam" on their 1989 debut album contained the following insolent lyrics:

> "So hyper fundi, don't be dismayed! Check out the lyrics when the record is played."

In other words, dc Talk is mocking biblical fundamentalists ("hyper fundi")who are opposed to the use of rock music. They are saying that only the message matters. The hypocrisy of this view is evident by the fact that the message presented by dc Talk often is obscured by their heavy rock music. Further, the message is frequently abstract. Note the following example from "Mind's Eye"—

> "You know what I'm going through/ I know (that) it's true/ Cause you've stood in my shoes/ Desire's inside of me/ But, it's hard to believe/ In what you cannot see/ Can you catch the wind? See a breeze? Its presence is revealed by/ The leaves on a tree/ An image of faith in the unseen/ In my mind's eye/ I see your face/ You smile/ As you show me grace/ In my mind's eye/ You take my hand/ We walk through foreign lands/ The foreign lands of life/ In my mind/ I'm where I belong/ As I rest in your arms/ And like a child I hold on to you/ In my moment of truth/ We can ride the storm/ Endure the pain/ You comfort me in my hurricane/ And I'll never be alone again/ ... In my mind I can see your face/ Love pours down in a shower of grace/ Life is a gift that you choose to give/ And I believe that we eternally live/ Faith is the evidence of things unseen/ People tell me that you're just a dream/ But they don't know you the way that I do/ You're the one I live to pursue" ("Mind's Eye," dc Talk).

Nothing is clear about this message. Who are they talking about? Jesus? They don't say. It could just as easily be about Krishna or Buddha. The listener could easily fit any false god into this song. If the song is about Jesus, what Jesus? The true Jesus of the Bible or one of the myriad of false christs in the minds of those who hear dc Talk's music? The song speaks of living eternally, but there is no clear Gospel message so that the hearer can know how to have eternal life. In fact, this dc Talk song could be about a girl, a lover. There are secular rock songs which have a similar message.

Notice how dc Talk describes John the Baptist:

> "There was a man from the desert with naps in his head/ The sand that he walked was also his bed/ The words that he spoke made the people assume/ There wasn't too much left in the upper room/ With skins on his back and hair on his face/ They thought he was strange by the locusts he ate/ The Pharisee's tripped when they heard him speak/ Until the king took the head of this Jesus freak" ("Jesus Freak," dc Talk).

To dc Talk, John the Baptist was a strange Jesus freak! A freak is a term popularized during the hippie era of the 1960s and '70s. It referred to a drug using counter culture rebel. dc Talk claims that they use the term merely to refer to an "enthusiast," but that is not how the term has been used in American society during the past four decades. I know the term well, because I was a "freak" before I was saved. To apply this term to a John the Baptist is foolish. The term freak implies rebellion, but the Christian is called to submission not only to God but also to parents and employers and church and government. Freak implies dissatisfaction, but the Christian has found complete satisfaction in Jesus Christ. Freak implies resentment toward life, but the Christian has faith that God is in complete control of his life. Christians are not freaks, and the venerable John the Baptist, who was exalted by Jesus Christ as the greatest man who ever lived, was not a freak.

In dc Talk's Kevin Smith joined Roman Catholic Kathy Troccoli and 40 other CCM artists to record *Love One Another,* a song with an ecumenical theme: "Christians from all denominations demonstrating their common love for Christ and each other." The song talks about tearing down the walls of denominational division. The broad range of participants who joined Kathy Troccoli in recording "Love One Another" demonstrates the ecumenical agenda of Contemporary Christian Music. The song witnessed Catholics, Pentecostals, Baptists, etc., yoked together to call for Christian unity.

When Pope John Paul II visited the States in January 1999, dc Talk and other CCM groups joined hands with hundreds of thousands of Catholics to welcome him. Featured at a Catholic youth rally connected with the Pope's visit, were dc Talk, Audio Adrenaline, Rebecca St. James, Jennifer Knapp, The W's, and the Supertones (*CCM Magazine*, April 1999, p. 12). dc Talk's Kevin Max praised the Catholic youth for coming out to hear the Pope, describing John Paul II as "someone with something of substance to say" (Ibid.). Each attendee received a rosary with instructions about how to pray to Mary.

After their success with the *Supernatural* album and tour, Michael Tait admits that he "went through a time where I dabbled in a lot of [wicked] things" (*CCM Magazine*, May

2001, p. 42). He calls this his "dark days."

DEGARMO & KEY

DeGarmo & Key, composed of Memphis friends Eddie DeGarmo and Dana Key, appeared in the late 1970s. Their "This Time Thru" album appeared in 1978, and they have produced 14 others since then. *CCM Magazine* notes that they immediately "pushed the sonic envelope." In January 1985 DeGarmo & Key's video *666* was rejected by the secular MTV for "senseless violence." An edited version appeared on MTV three months later, and DeGarmo & Key became the first Christian musicians to have a video on wicked MTV. They were also the first Christian rock group to receive a Grammy nomination.

One of the DeGarmo & Key's focuses in recent years has been to encourage kids to read their Bibles. They started the Biblical Literacy Foundation with the aim of getting a million kids to read the Bible at the same time on one day in 1995. Key says: "One of the real famines we see in American Christianity is the fact that there's a lot of Christians that have mastered all the Christian clichés, but don't have any content. They have all the right T-shirts, but they don't know what the slogan on the T-shirt means in terms of what God says in His Word. We're trying to get people to read the Bible on a daily basis" (*The Lighthouse*, June 1994). This is certainly an accurate assessment, and they have a good goal. The problem is that they promote the corrupted NIV version of the Bible, they are ecumenical in their approach to churches, and they mix their youth ministry in with rock music. "We still feel it's our calling to tell kids about that and there's no better way than through rock music. We have definitely made a rock record" (DeGarmo, Ibid.). DeGarmo & Key's 13-week Sunday School curriculum is based on songs from one of their rock albums.

DeGarmo and Key's music is man-problem-centered rather than Christ-centered.

> "On *Street Light* we were trying to stick to the street theme and deal with problems people were dealing with. They weren't biblical themes, and they didn't talk about God a lot" (Dana Key, with the group DeGarmo and Key, interview, *CCM Magazine*, November 1987, p. 20).

Note the following unscriptural statement comparing New Age with Christianity:

> "What's strange about the New Age is that it has several things in common with Christianity. It wants to deal with the world's problems and increase people's self-esteem, which I think Christianity has an interest in as well" (Dana Key, *Media Update*, September-October 1989, p. 3).

Bible-believing Christianity does *not* focus on dealing with the world's problems. It focuses on preaching the Gospel to the ends of the earth and rescuing souls from eternal Hell before the door of salvation is closed and Christ returns to judge the world. Bible Christianity also does not focus on increasing people's self-esteem; it focuses on dying to self, not building up self, on Christ-esteem rather than self-esteem. The Bible's call to die to self is exactly the opposite to the New Age call to celebrate oneself.

Consider the words to "Don't Stop the Music" by DeGarmo and Key:

> "I love to hear the music playing slow or fast/ I love the healing message from the distant past/ And if I rearrange it, it remains the same/ I'll change the way I say it but never what I saw/ Don't stop, don't stop the music, you've got to let it play/ Don't stop, don't stop the music, play it in your own way ... I HEAR DISSENTING VOICES QUICK TO DISAGREE/ BUT I'M ON A MUSIC MISSION; THEY DON'T BOTHER ME/ I'll sing those songs that set me free/ Cause kids want to rock" ("Don't Stop the Music," Ed DeGarmo and Dana Key).

This is a rebellious song. The Bible says, "Let us therefore follow after the things which make for peace, and things wherewith one may edify another" (Romans 14:19) and "It is good neither to eat flesh, nor to drink wine, nor any thing whereby thy brother stumbleth, or is offended, or is made weak" (Romans 14:21) and "Let every one of us please his neighbour for his good to edification" (Romans 15:2). The philosophy of Contemporary Christian Music is commonly the opposite to these Scriptural injunctions. DeGarmo and Key are going to rock "their own way" regardless of who they offend. They are going to use rock "cause the kids want it." Well, kids want a lot of wrong things. Does the Bible tell us to give them whatever they want? The CCM rocker knows that he is using music that large numbers of Christian parents do not want their children to listen to and that large numbers of churches reject as worldly. Many of the hard Christian rock songs are described in magazines as numbers "your parents will hate." Such self-willed rebellion, such callousness toward offending godly people, such dishonor toward parental concerns, has no place among those who name the name of Christ. Note that Degarmo and Key claim that music remains the same no matter how it is arranged. That is the false view that music is neutral.

DeGarmo & Key's *Street Light* album is described by former rock musician Jeff Godwin:

> "The *Street Light* album is a perfect example of the pasteurized pap masquerading as Christian soul winning. ... Jesus is a mystery man, a kind of galactic Santa Claus. He's never presented as the personal Lord, Master and Savior all true disciples know. Compromising 'Christian' rock like the *Street Light* LP has turned true Christianity into a fairyland of mass market religion. Blinded by the bright lights and deafened by the roar, the fans never know the differ-

ence" (Jeff Godwin, *Dancing with Demons*, p. 318).

DELIRIOUS

The rock group Delirious is composed of Martin Smith (vocals, guitar), Stewart Smith (drums), Jon Thatcher (bass), Tim Jupp (keyboard), and Stuart Garrard (guitar). The group, first named Cutting Edge, started in 1992 as a youth worship band at Arun Community Church, a charismatic congregation in England that is associated with the "Toronto Blessing," otherwise known as the "Laughing Revival." [See the author's book *The Laughing Revival: From Azusa to Pensacola*, available from Way of Life Literature.] Their music is used widely in the Laughing Revival churches such as the Toronto Airport Christian Fellowship in Ontario and the Brownsville Assembly of God in Pensacola, Florida (Clive Price, "A Delirious New Sound," *Charisma*, December 1999, p. 65). Their song "I've Found Jesus" is a theme song at the charismatic Teen Mania conferences. Delirious is at the forefront of the current Contemporary Praise music phenomenon, having authored several popular praise songs, including "I Could Sing of Your Love Forever," "The Happy Song," and "Did You Feel the Mountains Tremble?"

By 2001, the group had sold more than one million records and was "considered by many to be the forerunners of the modern worship music movement" (Christianbook.com). Delirious' summer 2001 tour of the United Kingdom in support of secular rock bands Bon Jovi and Matchbox 20 were attended by over 300,000 people.

The worldliness of Delirious is evident in their choice of "musical heroes," which include "U2, Radiohead, Blur and other big British modern rockers" (*CCM* magazine, July 1999, p. 39). When the group played at Walt Disney World in Orlando, Florida, an observer noted that "crowds of believers and unbelievers alike dance with wild abandon" to their rock songs. "As one non-Christian told them once: 'I'm not into your religion, but I love your music'" (*Charisma*, December 1999, p. 64).

Delirious' 1999 *Mezzamorphis* album includes the song "It's OK," which contains crude swearing in one line.

Though they claim that they are playing rock music to reach the world for Christ, they also claim that they can do this without a clear Bible message in their songs.

> "What we're about is the challenge to communicate that in a way that does truly communicate to folk outside of the church. TO GET IT ACROSS IN A WAY THAT ISN'T JUST LIMITED TO LANGUAGE. I think we're getting there" (emphasis added) (Martin Smith, cited in "A Delirious New Sound," *Charisma*, December 1999, p. 68).

The Lord Jesus Christ has not instructed His people to reach the world without language! We have a definite Gospel message that is to be preached in a precise biblical manner. This is how the Apostles and early Christians reached the world in their day, and it is how Christians are to reach the world today. The world is not reached for Christ with a rock song that contains a vague religious message.

Their 1998 album, *King of Fools,* is filled with strange, hazy messages and unscriptural doctrine. Their charismatic-ecumenical philosophy is evident in the song "Revival Town" —

> "Well I've got a message to bring/ I can't preach but I can sing/ And me and my brothers here/ Gonna play redemption hymns/ We're not on our own you know/ It's all around the world/ Cos this is the freedom generation/ Living for revival in this time/
>
> Chorus: "Hallelujah, you've turned my mourning into dancing/ Revival town/ That's what they're calling this place now/ Revival town/ It'll put a smile on your face now/ Revival town.
>
> "Well I've got a story to tell/ About the King above all kings/ He spoke for peace, hope and justice/ Things that we all need today/ You let a broken generation/ Become a dancing generation/ That is revival generation/ You may not hear it on the radio/ But you can feel it in the air" (Delirious5, "Revival Town," *King of Fools*).

This song, like a large percentage of the songs played by the new CCM groups, is almost meaningless because its message is so unclear. Delirious claims they are "gonna play redemption hymns," but there is no clear Gospel presented in these songs. The name of Jesus Christ is not even mentioned in the song. When "dancing generation" is mentioned in the context of the type of hard rock music which Delirious plays, it refers not to something spontaneous like David did before the Lord but to something carnal and worldly. The world would not have appreciated what David did, but the world loves the type of dancing associated with rock music.

The song "All the Way" is even stranger. Consider the carnal terminology these rock musicians use to describe their relationship with the Lord Jesus Christ:

> "Come close to me, too close for words/ And still my beating heart/ I find your thoughts without one glance/ We're going all the way ... With you I'm washed as white as snow/ And all crimson stain becomes just a shadow/ You know I would be blind without you/ So light up my way to find my way home again/ Today, today, today, we're going all the way."

Secular rockers sing songs like this about their lovers. I believe it is blasphemous to speak like this of the Christian's relationship with Christ.

Consider the words to the title song, "King of Fools" —

> "Walking with you/ Blindly follow out upon the/ Water runs down/ You've become the very best of friends/ I'll live for you and try to be the king of fools/ I'll long for you and walk before the king of all. Joy has found me/ Living life without you would be/ Hell or heaven/ Soon we'll find the greatest king of fools."

Contemporary Christian Music fans might argue that I simply don't understand the terminology used by these groups. I would reply that if a message is not plain it can be understood in any number of ways, and there is no doubt that the message preached in these CCM songs is unclear. The Bible says we are to sing "with the understanding" (1 Corinthians 14:15; Psalm 47:7). The message of God is to be made plain (Proverbs 8:9; Hab. 2:2). If the trumpet makes an uncertain sound who can prepare for war?

With their 1999 album, *Mezzamorphis*, Delirious announced that they are pursuing a more mainstream (secular) audience. They want to continue to "present a message of faith," but one that is "less explicitly stated" than their earlier albums (*CCM* magazine, July 1999, p. 39). As we have seen, their faith was never explicitly stated, and if it is even less so now they will be stating absolutely nothing! As to their goal in music: "We are artists, first and foremost, and want to create great art first and foremost. ... At the end of the day, we just want to be writing and playing great music." At least they are honest about their musical objective. One of their new songs, "It's OK," uses cursing. "She's as pretty as hell and her eyes have no home." Sparrow records wanted to leave that song off the album, but the band members insisted that it stay. Martin Smith says: "It's back on the album now, which we feel great about."

Delirious claims that they worship God by performing in immoral rock music venues. They have toured with the secular rock band Bon Jovi, for instance; and in a recent interview with *CDNow* editor Brian Mansfield, Delirious's lead man Martin Smith claims that their secular concerts are "not much different" from their "more worship-oriented" concerts. Smith said, "...when we're playing in a mainstream situation [secular rock and roll concerts], I want to get everyone there worshipping God, but I can't speak that language. I have to encourage them in a different way. You have to get in the back door and let God move on the music in a sovereign way, and stir people's hearts, open them up. Music is the language of the spirit. Music, even without words, can cut a man in two, and God can get in there." Where does the Bible say that music can "cut a man in two" so that God can minister to him? The Bible is SOLE basis for faith and practice, yet there is no scriptural basis for using Christian rock music to minister to the unsaved. At the typical Christian rock concert, one cannot even understand the words of the songs. Young people don't attend Bon Jovi concerts to hear the gospel, and Delirious doesn't clearly preach the gospel at such concerts. Yet it is the gospel of Jesus Christ, and that only, which is the power of God unto salvation, not vaguely worded Christian rock songs performed by people who are committed to looking and sounding as much like the world as possible.

DELIVERANCE

The "speed metal" band Deliverance was formed in 1985 in Los Angeles. The group is composed of Jimmy Brown (vocalist/guitar), Jeff Mason (drums), Manny Morales (bass), and Matt Winslow (guitar). Their first album, in 1987, was titled *California Metal*. They describe their music as "alternative because of the Bowiesque [referring to bisexual rock star David Bowie] or Pink Floydish elements" (Interview with Deliverance, *TLeM*, June 1996). In 1991 they did a video, *Weapons of Our Warfare*, which ran for 12 weeks on wicked MTV "on the top three on Headbangers Ball." It contained no clear Gospel message, so it didn't help the unsaved; but it did encourage professing Christians that it is alright to watch the vile programming spewing forth from MTV.

The following is an eyewitness description of a Deliverance concert which occurred on April 7, 1989. The report is given by a former rock musician:

> "There were no seats; everyone stood or sat on the floor. Once Deliverance hit the stage, their 'music' threw the fans into instant fits of demonic Devildance. When the drummer poured on the gas, a young man next to us leaped off the ground, his arms flinging right and left while his head jerked back like he'd been hit with a tire jack. Lost in the jet-engine roar, his body convulsed and twitched in spastic seizures. His eyes were tightly shut. We dove into a corner to keep from being slugged by his swinging fists. Others were doing the same thing all over the room. When it came time for the 'preaching,' the members of Deliverance took turns talking about love and victory and not being a 'wimp.' Nothing about repentance. Nothing about salvation or separation from the world. Instead of an altar call, there was a cattle-call yodel where all the Christians were instructed to yell for Jesus" (Jeff Godwin, *What's Wrong with Christian Rock?*, pp. 225,226).

Deliverance not only patterns themselves after worldly secular rock groups, they perform songs by these groups. Their *What a Joke* album has the song "After Forever" by the immoral/occultic group Black Sabbath, who blasphemed the cross of Jesus Christ during their concerts.

DENE, TERRY

British-born Terry Dene (born Terry Williams) (1938-) had hits in the 1950s, including "A White Sport Coat" and "Stairway of Love." He divorced his wife at the end of that decade and became an alcoholic. He then turned to Christianity and recorded three gospel albums, but in the 1980s he returned to rock & roll and formed a group called the Dene-Aces. He continues to perform rock music in the 1990s.

DENVER, JOHN

The late rock singer John Denver (1943-1997), real name Henry John Deutschendorf Jr., was one of the top five recording artists in the sales history of the music industry. He died in a plane crash when the experimental private jet he was piloting crashed into the sea off the coast of California. He was considered to be born again by some, but in reality he was a New Age pantheist. In 1976 he established the Windstar Foundation for environmental education and other efforts "toward a sustainable future for the world." He said:

> "I'm a global citizen. I've created that for myself, and I don't want to step away from it. I want to work in whatever I do—my music, my writing, my performing, my commitments, my home and personal life—in a way that is directed towards a world in balance, a world that creates a better quality of life for all people" (John Denver biography, imusic, http://imusic.com/showcase/country/johndenver.html).

John Denver followed est (Erhard Seminar Training). On the inside cover to his *Back Home Again* album he stated: "Participating in est has created an amazing amount of space for joy and aliveness in my life. It pleases me to share est with you." He dedicated his Wingsong album "to Werner Erhard and everyone in est." "Erhard basically has a pantheist view of life. We are all just little 'gods.' There is neither wrong nor right. This movement is subtly based on Zen Buddhism and teaches the disciple never to use the rational mind, but to open up to the so-called 'ever present now'" (Mundy, *The Role of Rock*, p. 177).

The following is Denver's testimony:

> "It was during the summer of 1971 that Denver and his wife Annie moved to Aspen. There he had his 'born again' experience. From it he emerged an eco-aware pantheist. Pantheism is the belief that God and the law and the forces of nature are one. It happened this way — while camping out at an 11,000 foot high lake in the Rockies, he and some friends witnessed a spectacular meteor shower. He claims he watched it for 2 hours and saw it 'rainin' in the

sky.' Afterwards he wrote his famous 'Rocky Mountain High' hit. The artist believes the flowers are his sisters and brothers. He also believes the Rocky Mountains are living and will never die. He talks of having an on-going relationship with God, of being God, and told a news reporter he'd rather get stoned than drunk. Perhaps his *Rocky Mountain High* comes from Rocky Mountain hash. During an interview in Australia, he stated, 'Sure, I enjoy hash. I have a lot of fun with the stuff.' He doesn't believe it should get out of hand, though and has stated, 'I do not think marijuana is harmful, if handled responsibly'" (*Focus*, October 1986, page 8).

DE'VINE, MIKE

"Mike De'Vine left the obscene 'savaging women' 2 Live Crew rap group in 1989, sick of the life-style. He's now a hip hop artist who thinks he is on the verge of breaking into the big time gospel market. The January 26 *Rocky Mountain News* [Denver, Colorado] said he is looking to Promise Keepers as a pulpit and has met with PK founder Bill McCartney. He says McCartney is interested in him coming aboard to rap before stadiums full of men, and a PK official said: 'We would certainly be interested in him since he can reach out to youth'" (*Calvary Contender*, March 1, 1996).

DINO

Piano player extraordinaire Dino Kartsonakis, known popularly simply as Dino, was the piano player for the divorced Pentecostal healing evangelist Kathryn Kuhlman. He is at home on the ecumenical-charismatic Trinity Broadcasting Network program headed by Paul and Jan Crouch.

DORSEY, THOMAS

Thomas Dorsey (1899-1993) was a popular blues singer, pianist, guitarist, and songwriter, who became a pioneer in the field of gospel music. In the 1920s, he played with the Hokum Boys, which also featured Tampa Red (Hudson Whittaker) on guitar. They were famous for their openly sexual lyrics. "The two became so notorious for their cunningly erotic blues they coined a word for the style (*hokum*) and the new duo proceeded to scandalize the churches with their 1928 recording of the highly erotic 'Tight Like That'" (*Black Gospel: An Illustrated History of the Gospel Sound*, p. 40). By the end of the 1920s, Dorsey stopped recording secular blues and devoted himself to "sacred blues." He recorded many well-known gospel songs, such as "There Shall Be Peace in the Valley." He pioneered the intermingling of sensual dance music with Christian lyrics. He did not renounce his early career in sleazy blues, and looked back with "evident fondness" to those days. He was "thoroughly unrepentant of his early career" (*Black Gospel*, p. 39). "He was appointed choir director at the Pilgrim Baptist Church in Chicago, a life-long job, but stayed loyal to his former blues acolytes, since unlike many religious people, he never rejected the secular music" (*MusicHound Blue: The Essential Album Guide*).

DRISCOLL, PHIL

CCM trumpeter Phil Driscoll (1947-) has won four Dove Awards and a Grammy, as well as numerous other recognitions. He often has been voted one of the most popular CCM musicians in *CCM Magazine* polls. As a freshman at the Southern Baptist Baylor University in Texas, Driscoll formed Baylor's first jazz band ("Phil Driscoll's Biography," http://www.gospelcom.net/ phildriscoll/biography/index.html). By the time he graduated he was appearing on Ed Sullivan and other television shows. For several years he collaborated with and performed with secular rock groups, including Blood, Sweat & Tears and Joe Cocker. He wrote three of Cocker's hits (*Southern Lady*, *Wasted Years*, and *Boogie Baby*). In 1978 Driscoll left secular music "to pursue a calling within contemporary Christian music circles."

Driscoll attends an independent charismatic church in Cleveland, Tennessee, and continually appears at Charismatic-Pentecostal churches and forums. He has trumpeted, for example, at Kenneth Copeland meetings and at the radically ecumenical Washington for Jesus rallies. He has also been featured at Jerry Falwell's Liberty University.

Driscoll has also performed at the Tom Skinner Memorial Leadership Conference (Biography, Ibid.). The respected Fundamental Evangelistic Association of Los Osos, California, had the following warning about Skinner:

> "Black Evangelist Tom Skinner writes, 'make no bones about it. I'm a revolutionary.' His latest book, *Words of Revolution*, is a clever mixture of new evangelical thought phrased in revolutionary language. He claims that 'Jesus Christ came to break the system,' and 'to put in a new system called the Kingdom of God.' He claims that 'it is the responsibility of the church to go into the world to change the world.' He plays down Heaven and Hell and emphasizes the here and now. He calls our Lord Jesus Christ 'a gutsy radical, contemporary revolutionary with hair on His chest and dirt under his fingernails.' In spite of this, Skinner is much in demand as a speaker in New Evangelical circles. What a shame" (*F.E.A. News & Views*, March-April 1971).

Driscoll is openly critical of many aspects of Contemporary Christian Music. He has stated that the gospel music industry, for the most part, is "market-driven, not Spirit-led" and "a lot of contemporary Christian music is so much like the world you can't tell the difference" (Driscoll, cited by Marsha Gallardo, "Money or Ministry?," *Charisma*, November 1993). He is critical of watering down the message of the music to appeal to a secular audience. "I believe in crossover music as long as you take the cross over."

In these matters we would certainly agree with Driscoll, but he himself is caught up in the worldly-ecumenical aspects of CCM.

Phil Driscoll holds the ecumenical philosophy: "In the Nov. 23, 1987, *Today's Banner*, Driscoll said: 'I have felt in my heart for a long time that music was the power that God would use to transcend every denomination, every barrier that has kept God's people apart.' His *Make Us One* was the theme song for the April 1988 Washington For Jesus charismatic rally" (*Calvary Contender*, January 1, 1989).

Phil Driscoll thinks God is the King of Soul Music:

> "We've had the mistaken impression for too long that somehow the Creator doesn't have rhythm. God is the King of Soul; He's the King of all rhythm" (Phi Driscoll, cited by Dan and Steve Peters, *What about Christian Rock?*, p. 187).

DUNCAN, BRYAN

Bryan Duncan (1953-) grew up in a pastor's home and testifies that rock & roll music became his means of escape:

> "I think music became a kind of salvation for me. It was a way of expressing my frustrations about feeling trapped. IF I WAS ANGRY I COULD PLAY ROCK 'N ROLL. THAT CERTAINLY EXPRESSED ANGER BETTER THAN ANYTHING ELSE. So it was, in some ways, my saving grace."

Duncan is right in saying that rock & roll expresses anger. It appears that the rebellious youth loved rebellious music. Why was he feeling trapped? Why did he need "saving grace" in rebellious music instead of in a relationship with Jesus Christ? Instead of expressing anger and feelings of entrapment, the young Bryan Duncan could have been expressing praise, submission, and obedience. In none of his interviews or biographies on the Internet does he give a testimony of salvation.

Duncan helped organize the Sweet Comfort Band when he was in college and played in it from 1972 to 1984. He has since launched a solo music career. His "trademark" is "infectious, groove-oriented, blue-eyed soul" and "falsetto howls/squeals." His concerts feature Duncan "dancing like James Brown."

> "Bryan Duncan lets his energy get to him sometimes, even during his concerts. Recently, while playing a gig at Nyack College (a Christian college in New York), Bryan decided to jump out into the audience and begin dancing

with a certain promotion director from a certain Christian radio station. And he did all this while still playing his guitar and singing. What a talented guy!" (*CCM Magazine*, December 1986, p. 14).

He often hints at a dark time of the soul, a time of deep sin, that he went through in recent years because of constant touring, being away from his family, having no practical connection to a church.

Duncan joined the group Anointed and Crystal Lewis in the 1997 Big Voice Tour, which promoted ecumenical unity: "In God's eyes, we are all one big family, and should be of one mind, of one voice. The tour is one of unity."

His concerts do not feature "a lot of Christian terminology" —

> "Because I don't use a lot of Christian terminology in my concerts, I want to make sure people know what I really think about my faith, where my heart is. I'm not sure you'd get the impression I'm as committed to my faith as I am, simply from seeing my concerts. For me, presenting my faith from the stage feels weird, like prostitution or something. I guess it's because you are doing something that is designed to make money or at least entertain people that have paid to see you....
>
> "There's a problem here, because you're doing something that you make money from, and when it becomes the way you make a living, it's almost like a conflict of interest to present your faith as something genuine. Maybe that's why I'm less likely to make big statements on stage about how God's gonna change your life, and what He's gonna do in your life, things like that. Although I've got to say, after going through the things I have in the last few years, I can really look back and say, 'God has been faithful to me, even when I was really, really angry with Him.' So I guess I could get up on stage and say, 'God is faithful,' but it just sounds so glib" (Tom Granger, "Bryan Duncan Mows His Lawn," http://place2b.org/cmp/duncan/bsr6.html).

Testifying that God is faithful sounds glib? What unscriptural nonsense. Duncan is correct, though, in admitting that what he and most other commercial CCM musicians are doing is commercial entertainment.

DYLAN, BOB

From my "hippie" days prior to conversion in 1973, I remember rock legend Bob Dylan (1941-) (real name Robert Zimmerman) very well. It was in 1962 that Dylan legally changed his name and produced his debut album. His famous song "The Times They Are A-Changin" appeared in 1964. I had started listening to rock music intently in the early 1960s, and I was consumed with that type of music until I was saved in 1973. That era was the heyday of Dylan's career, and I still recall the haunting, sensual nature of his music. He helped to popularize the merging of folk and rock music and sang some very immoral songs as well as songs with pacifistic, civil rights, socialistic, humanistic, and new age themes. He was one of the chief poets of the rock generation. His songs posed many interesting questions, but he had no answers. In "Blowing in the Wind," he asked such things as, "How many roads must a man walk down before he is called a man?" What is the answer? "The answer, my friends, is blowing in the wind..." What does that mean? It means he doesn't know the answer and he is not sure anyone knows the answer. Sadly, that is the philosophy of most of Dylan's fans because they have rejected the blessed Word of God. His vast influence has been anything but wholesome and godly. There was violence at some Dylan concerts. For example, in Slane, Ireland, in July 1984, the police had to barricade themselves inside their station as mobs of Dylan fans besieged them, rioting, breaking windows, and overturning cars.

In 1978 Dylan attended a home Bible study with his girlfriend at the time, Mary Alice. She had recently re-dedicated her life to Christ. Dylan's testimony was as follows: "One thing led to another ... until I had this feeling, this vision and feeling. I truly had a born-again experience, if you want to call it that. It's an over-used term, but it's something that people can relate to" (Steve Turner, *Hungry for Heaven*, p. 160). The Bible study eventually formed into the Hollywood (California) Vineyard Fellowship associated with the late John Wimber. Dylan spent three and a half months at the church's School of Discipleship, and his next two albums, *Slow Train Coming* and *Saved*, were gospel albums of sorts.

Dylan soon repudiated any claim to Christian faith and went back to his standard rock music. The July 21, 1983, issue of the *Washington Post* noted that Dylan believes in reincarnation and that "everyone is born knowing the truth." An article in the *San Luis Obispo* (California) *Register* for March 16, 1983, quoted Dylan as saying: "Whoever said I was Christian? Like Gandhi, I'm Christian, I'm Jewish, I'm a Moslem, I'm a Hindu. I am a humanist." In recent years Dylan has practiced Lubavitch Hasidism, an ultra-orthodox form of Judaism, suggesting he has returned to his Jewish roots.

In September 1997, Dylan performed before Pope John Paul II at a Roman Catholic youth festival in Bologna, Italy. A crowd of 300,000 young people attended the festival. The 56-year-old Dylan sang two songs directly to the pope. Dylan then took off his cowboy hat and bowed before him. The Catholic organizer of the festival, Cardinal Ernesto Vecchi, said that he had invited Dylan because he is the "representative of the best type of rock" and "he has a spiritual nature."

ELEFANTE, JOHN

John Elefante (1960-) became a Christian in 1980, and in 1981 he became the lead singer for the popular secular rock group Kansas. The founder of Kansas, Kerry Livgren, had also become a Christian not long before and was beginning to incorporate some Christianized lyrics into Kansas' music. Kansas' lead singer, Steve Walsh, due to philosophical and other differences, had left the band in 1981 to begin an unsuccessful solo career. Elefante took Walsh's place and performed with Kansas for three years until it disbanded in 1983. (The group was reconstituted in 1986 by Walsh, with new members, and continues to produce albums and tour on the oldies circuits.)

Elefante has pursued a career in music in the Christian field since leaving Kansas. (Two other Kansas band members, Kerry Livgren and bassist Dave Hope, went on to form the Christian rock group AD.) Elefante still wears long hair and an earring, and his music is largely abstract. He preaches a hazy, repentance-less gospel to hard rock music:

> "Hello my good friend/ How have you been doing since I've gone/ Have you shared the love I gave you/ Have you shown the world the truth of who I am/ So let your love be true/ Till I come back to you/ ... You say you don't need Me/ That you'll be alright on your own/ Now you live like a prisoner/ Serving your time all alone/ I can't make you love Me/ I can't make you believe what I say/ So come back to Me, let Me show you the way/ And I'll take you to paradise/ Just listen to My voice inside your heart..." ("Hello My Good Friend (A Letter from the Lord)," John Elefante).

This song is typical of Elefante's music. The message is vague. There is nothing clear about being born again, nothing about repentance from sin, nothing about the Word of God. It is all experiential and subjective. Do we go to paradise by letting Christ show us the way? That is a works salvation. In other songs Elefante does mention the cross of Christ, but never, to my knowledge, does he clarify the Gospel. The exhortation to "listen to My voice inside your heart" is dangerous and unscriptural. Nowhere does the New Testament tell God's people to look into their hearts for truth and guidance. There is an old nature in the heart of man which makes such instruction dangerous (Jer. 17:9; Eph. 4:18; Heb. 3:12). There are also demonic voices which seek to deceive (2 Cor. 11:13-15).

ENGLISH, MICHAEL

Popular CCM singer Michael English (1962-) began his music profession singing in Southern gospel groups. According to his biography, he became a Christian at age seven "in a small but vibrant Pentecostal Church in Wallace, North Carolina" (Biography of Michael English, www.michaelenglish.com/). After high school he toured with The Singing Americans and the Goodmans. He later joined the Gaither band, then launched a successful solo career. His first album appeared in 1992 and his second, a year later. In 1992 he was voted Best New Artist by the Gospel Music Association. For three years in a row he won the Male Vocalist of the Year title. In 1994 English was named Artist of the Year and received six Dove Awards.

Within 24 hours of receiving the awards, English confessed to an adulterous affair with another CCM musician, Marabeth Jordon of the group First Call. At the time Mrs. Jordon was the wife of another man. Jordan and English conceived a baby out of wedlock (though it later died). English returned his six Dove awards, though he was not asked to do so and the Gospel Music Association stated that he can have his awards back anytime he wants them. Warner Alliance canceled English's contract.

In English's press release about this affair there was no mention of sin. "I feel it is necessary to announce my withdrawal from Christian music because of mistakes that I have recently made."

English is a member of Christ Community Church in Franklin, Tennessee (near Nashville), which is attended by many other well-known CCM and country musicians, including Steven Curtis Chapman and country star Wynonna Judd.

> "Christ Church in Nashville has the hottest choir in town, bar none, and the Pentecostal service on any given Sunday is liable to rock the pews. But earlier this month when word came of two out-of-wedlock pregnancies in the congregation, the reverberation could be heard in all 50 states. Wynonna Judd held a press conference and said she had conceived and had no immediate plans to wed. The week before, the Gospel Music Association had announced that married Christian pop singer Michael English had impregnated Marabeth Jordan, who is a singer with the trio First Call—and somebody else's wife. ... 'It's kind of a wake-up call,' says Rev. Scotty Smith, who counseled English, Jordan and executives at Warner Alliance.
>
> "Yet the call went unheeded among Christian contemporary-music fans, who made a distinction between the ironies of English's sin—he and Jordan had just done a benefit tour for unwed mothers—and his songs. They snatched up any of his albums still on the racks. CHRISTIAN RADIO STATIONS THAT BANNED HIS MICHAEL BOLTONISH HITS WERE BARRAGED WITH NASTY CALLS. 'THEY WERE MORE ANGRY WITH US THAN WITH MICHAEL ENGLISH,' says Mark De Young at WNAZ in Nashville. 'They weren't condemning of him at all'" (emphasis added) ("God and the Music Biz," *Newsweek*, May 30, 1994).

Later in 1994 English began recording secular music. He recorded the song "Healing" with Wynonna. The song was featured in the R-rated movie *Silent Fall*. Professional movie reviewer Chris Hicks says *Silent Fall* received it's R rating for "violence, gore, profanity, and vulgarity."

A photo of English adorns the cover of his 1996 album, *Freedom*. He has long hair, scruffy beard, an earring, and a hard, rebellious stare. In the song *Freedom Field* from this album, English sings:

> "Old man religion, I've got your name/ The best part of my years were wrapped up, tied up in your thang/ Should you wake one early morning, to the sound of breaking chains/ I'll be dancin', I'll be dancin'."

It sounds like English is blaming religion for his problems, that he is looking upon religion as a bondage. If this is not his meaning, it certainly is how many country-rock music fans look at religion. In this song English makes no distinction between true religion and false. The Bible uses the term "religion" five times. Three times it refers to the "Jews religion" (Acts 26:5; Galatians 1:13,14) and two times it refers to "pure religion" (James 1:26,27). One of the marks of pure religion is to keep oneself "unspotted from the world." Many within Contemporary Christian Music would label James a Pharisaical legalist for demanding separation from worldliness.

The single released from English's *Freedom* album quickly rose to the top 20 on Billboard's adult contemporary chart.

The songs are basically trashy rock music. The beat is very heavy. Lots of pounding drums and bass guitar. Actually there is not a significant difference between Michael English's secular albums and his "Christian" albums. The music is the same and the lyrics are even similar. In *Freedom*, he sings about love in a worldly fashion after the manner of unsaved rockers. Consider the following:

> "I see you standing there/ Those simple things you wear/ Oh it makes me crazy/ You take it so casually/ You've got that look in your eyes/ As you pass me by/ And I just can't keep from wonderin' why/ And you say. ... I wanna know what your love is like/ What you feel inside/ Every time I look into your eyes/ I gotta know if you want it too/ Girl and if you do/ Then let me ask you this question/ Baby what have we got to lose..." ("I Wanna Know," from Michael English's *Freedom* album).

This is about "love" on a purely physical, lustful level. At least that is the way most unsaved rock lovers will understand it. There is nothing about marriage in the song. It could easily be applied by the hearer to any pre-marital or extra-marital situation. Why would a Christian sing songs like this? English is not edifying society with these songs.

As a "cross over" artist, he has the ear of a secular audience. His albums are sold in secular rock music stores and are given air play on secular rock stations, but he is preaching nothing biblically convicting to this audience.

> "I've seen the seven wonders of the world/ I've seen the beauty of diamonds and pearls/ But they ain't nothin' baby/ Your love amazes me. ... I've prayed for miracles that never came/ Got down on my knees out in the pourin' rain/ But only you could save me/ Your love amazes me/ Don't you ever doubt this heart of mine/ You're the only one for me/ You give me hope you give me reason" ("Your Love Amazes Me," from Michael English's "Freedom" album).

This is blasphemy. He sings that he has prayed for miracles but the only thing that could save him is some romantic sweetheart! Why would a professing Christian sing something this unscriptural?

English is perfectly at home in the wicked world of rock and roll. He toured as the "opener" for the secular rock group Foreigner, a group which glorifies immoral sexual relations.

After letting his hair grow long, hanging out at bars, dating a stripper, and landing in jail (*CCM Magazine*, July 2000, p. 29), English began making a return to Christian music in 1997. In fact he never really stopped producing Christian albums or performing background for them. In 1995 and 1996 he produced albums for The Gaither Vocal Band, The Stamps, and The Martins, and performed as background singer on several Christian albums. At the fall 1996 National Quartet Convention in Kentucky, English was invited to testify and sing, and he was given multiple standing ovations. When English was introduced, gospel singer J.D. Sumner (of The Stamps) publicly asked him "to forgive people's judging hearts" (Biography of Michael English, http://www.michaelenglish.com/). According to Sumner, the great sin is not so much English's vile adultery against his wife or his hypocrisy in performing and recording Christian music even while living in such sin; it is the judgment of that adultery by others. This is yet another illustration of the unscriptural non-judgmental philosophy which permeates the Contemporary Christian Music world. In May 1997 English accepted an invitation to sing on Paul Crouch's Trinity Broadcasting Network ("Faith sustains English during transitional times in career," *Grand Rapids Press*, Nov. 6, 1997).

In a 1998 concert at the Monroe Church of God, Monroe, Georgia, English gave an apology about his failure, though he still did not call it sin: "I messed up really bad about three and a half years ago. I let a lot of people down. I let my family down. I let my friends down. And most of all, I let God down. And I'm really regretful for doing that. I'm really, really sorry from the bottom of my heart" (Michael English, Fan Web site, http://members.aol.com/ MEWebpage/testimony.html).

In February 2000, Michael English entered a drug rehab program to kick an addiction to hydrocodone after police began an investigation into possible illegal activities in this connection. They found more than 80 prescriptions which had been filled in less than three years. In June the police charged English with 12 counts of fraudulently obtaining the prescription sedative.

FARNER, MARK

Mark Farner (1948-) is the former singer for the popular '70s rock group Grand Funk Railroad. After a Christian conversion experience of some sort he moved from secular rock to Christian rock.

He took the Grand Funk Railroad song "Some Kind of Wonderful," which was about sensual lust, and made it into a song (allegedly) about Jesus Christ:

> "When He holds me in His arms/ You know it sets my soul on fire/ Yea when my savior's lovin' me/ My old heart becomes filled with desire/ When He wraps His lovin' arms around me/ It 'bout drives me out of my mind/ ... Well my Jesus, He's alright/ My savior is clean out of sight/ Don't ya know that He is some kind of wonderful" (Mark Farner, "Some Kind of Wonderful").

This song illustrates much that is wrong with Contemporary Christian Music. Instead of seeking to bring the world up to the level of the Word of God and the Holy God of the Bible, it brings the things of Christ down to the level of the world. This is an impossible task which results in a debased form of Christianity. Originally Farner's song was about holding a girl in his arms. I believe it is blasphemous to take a lustful rock song and sing it to Jesus Christ. Not only so, but the song, even with the word changes ("he" instead of "her" and "Jesus" instead of "baby") contains false teaching. The Lord Jesus Christ does not stir up the "old heart's desires," because the old heart is fallen in sin and is at enmity with God (Jeremiah 17:9; Ephesians 4:22-24). Further, Jesus Christ is not just "alright." He is Almighty God and has a name above all names. He is "the King eternal, immortal, invisible, the only wise God" (1 Timothy 1:17). The Jesus worshipped by much of the CCM world is a false christ, a worldly humanistic christ who does not convict of sin, does not call to repentance and separation from the world, and does not rebuke false doctrine and compromise of the truth.

FENHOLT, JEFF

At age 21, Jeff Fenholt (1949-) played the part of Jesus in the original Broadway play

Jesus Christ Superstar. This blasphemous 1970 musical was authored by Tim Rice and Andrew Lloyd Webber, agnostics who desired to debunk what they felt was the myth of Jesus Christ's deity. In *Jesus Christ Superstar* they portrayed Christ as a confused philosopher who had a secret love affair with Mary Magdalene, who died for nothing, and did not rise from the dead. The play actually glorifies and justifies Judas Iscariot. Instead of Christ being resurrected, Judas comes back from the dead and rebukes Christ. The album that accompanied *Jesus Christ Superstar* has sold 15 million copies and spun off hit singles. Fenhold makes a bold profession of faith in Christ and has various charismatic Christian ministries, but he continues to wear his wearhair long like a woman's and at his web site (as of December 23, 1999) he features information about how to attend *Jesus Christ Superstar* and features the actual lyrics to the blasphemous songs. There is no word of warning about any of this readily made for those who visit the site, unless one happens to read far into . The only mention that something is wrong with the play is deep within one of the articles. at the site.

Fenholt admits that he was deeply involved with the occult and was probably demon possessed. One day a charismatic Catholic and others laid hands on him and prayed for him in "tongues."

> "They dropped their hammers, jumped down and laid hands on me, speaking in tongues. I hit the deck. I felt a weight come off my back like the weight of the world. It was as if my back opened up and an anvil was lifted out of it. I said, 'If this is Jesus, I want to accept Jesus as my Lord and Saviour.' I knelt right there and accepted Jesus as my Saviour. They took me right down to the beach and baptized me" ("Out of Darkness," from Fenholt's official web site).

Fenfolt claims that he spoke in "tongues" during this experience:

> "I got back down on my knees; I prayed the prayer to receive Jesus; I got filled with the Holy Ghost. I didn't have time to hear any of the stuff, why you shouldn't pray in tongues. I was prayin' in tongues within ten seconds" (Fenholt, "I God Saved," from his official web site).

Jeff Fenholt is a charismatic who for many years has had a program on the Trinity Broadcasting Network and also has hosted various Praise the Lord functions for Paul and Jan Crouch. He is affiliated with Word-Faith preachers such as Kenneth Copeland. His wife was a Roman Catholic who allegedly was led to the Lord by a charismatic Catholic priest. At his website, Fenholt promotes the false idea that there are saved Catholics who are still committed to the Catholic church.

> "I praise God that I married this young Catholic woman, Maureen Hope Marie McFadden. Then she became Fenholt. I call her Reeni. She went to a priest

> who was a member of the Charismatic Movement. How many know there are Catholics who are saved, and love Jesus Christ? Praise the Lord Jesus Christ. This priest lead my wife to the Lord, introduced her to Jesus. And she began to pray to Jesus. She no longer lit candles. Or maybe she did, I don't know. All I know is her prayers changed. She began to say things like this, 'I bind you, satan, in the name of Jesus'" (Fenholt, "Jesus Understands," from his official web site).

Jeff Fenholt has adopted the heresy that music is neutral and that the only thing that matters is the condition of the performer's heart. Thus he believes it is proper to use rock music as long as the words are not ungodly. He made this statement in a media interview in Russia that is cited in Jeff Godwin's video *What Is Wrong with Christian Rock*.

> "If the heart of the musician belongs to the devil, then the music belongs to the devil. My heart belongs to Jesus, so my music belongs to the Lord."

At his concerts, Fenholt sings secular rock songs and blasphemously turns them into something allegedly about Jesus Christ. A video clip of a Fenholt concert in Russia shows him playing Elvis Presley's "Jailhouse Rock" in English with some words added about Jesus ("come on everybody, let's rock; Jesus is the rock") while Russian young people are rocking away to the sensual, rebellious beat.

FISCHER, JOHN

John Fischer (c.1947-) is a CCM performer/writer and has had wide influence through his pen. He is a regular columnist for *CCM Magazine*. Fischer was involved in the pioneer days of Christian rock music, and he believes that God told him that it is not wrong to listen to groups like the Beatles:

> "[In 1963] I was in high school hearing a Beatles' song and loving the music and feeling guilty about it. I was raised as a Christian not to like that kind of music, that that music was bad, [but I was] having a sense that God didn't think it was bad. I [had a sense of] God saying 'Do you like this music? Well, how does it make you feel? How do I make you feel? The same way? I make you feel happy? I make you feel upset? Well then, why don't you write the music about Me?' You know, it was just plain as day. And so I just started doing it. I had my first contract to record in late '69. And I would say 1970 is when everything exploded, as far as I remember ... Groups just suddenly came out of the woodwork everywhere. Many of them were musicians already who were becoming Christians, and they were just being saved—almost as if Christ had just plucked them out and saved them and sent them out singing new music" (John Fischer, cited by April Hefner, "Don't Know Much about History," *CCM Magazine*, April 1996).

Few men have had a more morally and spiritually destructive influence in this world than the Beatles. There can be no doubt that there are occultic powers behind the Beatles' music, yet it is loved widely by the CCM crowd. Many examples of this can be found in the pages of this book. Many CCM groups even perform Beatles songs during their concerts. I have read hundred of pages of interviews and testimonies of CCM musicians and not once have I read a warning about the Beatles.

Note how Fischer describes an imaginary encounter with God:

> "'Wait a minute Kid' [supposedly this is God speaking to Fischer]. Leave it [the radio] on. You know, I kind of like this stuff [rock].' I watched in shock as He smiled at me through a casual puff of cigar smoke and swayed His head ever so slightly with the music" (*Contemporary Christian Music Magazine*, July 1984, p. 20).

This is a blasphemous description of God.

Fischer's unscriptural philosophy is evident from the following statement:

> "I'd love to see the labels fall off. I'd love to not have to call things Christian or secular anymore. ... I'd rather we weren't so trapped in dogma, so busy confirming what we already know, so eager to hear what we already agree with, that we miss another point of view that might just happen to come from God. I'd love to see Christians less concerned about getting the words right and more concerned about the heart" (John Fischer, *CCM Magazine*, March 1990, p. 52).

This is completely contrary to the teaching of the Word of God. Fischer wants to stop putting a difference between Christian and secular, but God rebuked the prophets and priests of old precisely because "they put no difference between the holy and profane" (Ezekiel 22:26). John the Apostle put a huge difference between Christian and secular when he stated: "And we know that we are of God, and the whole world lieth in wickedness" (1 John 5:19). Fischer wants Christians to stop being trapped in dogma, but what is dogma? It is doctrine or teaching, which is precisely why God gave His Word. The Bible is given for doctrine (2 Timothy 3:16-17). Timothy was instructed to stand fast in the doctrine he had been taught by the Apostle and to impart the exact same doctrine to others. "'And the things that thou hast heard of me among many witnesses, THE SAME commit thou to faithful men, who shall be able to teach others also" (2 Timothy 2:2). Timothy was to allow NO OTHER DOCTRINE to be taught (1 Timothy 1:3). The faith once delivered to the saints is to be defended by every generation of Christians (Jude 3). This means God's people are to know the sound doctrine of the Word of God and they are to fight for it against anything that is contrary to it. Doctrine is a basis of separation (Romans 16:17). It is impossible to stand for sound doctrine without being deeply concerned about "getting the words right." Doctrine is given to us in words, and it is promoted and defended by words, and if those words are not right the doctrine is not right. Fischer wants less concern for doctrinal truth and more concern for the heart. The attitude and motives of the heart are very important before God, but the heart is not the standard for truth; it is too undependable. The heart of man is deceitful above all things and desperately wicked (Jeremiah 17:9). We can judge a person's doctrine, but it is not possible to judge the sincerity of his heart.

In an article in *CCM Magazine*, August 1998, John Fischer made the following amazing statement which illustrates the non-judgmental philosophy which permeates Contemporary Christian Music:

> "Some Christian artists will play in clubs and never mention Jesus from stage. They will see this as their calling. Others will feel led to deliver an altar call at every performance. The tendency will be to judge one as being more legitimate than the other, whether by artistic or by ministry standards. Somehow I believe the world is big enough, its needs are varied enough and the Holy Spirit is creative enough to legitimize both these approaches. As more and more Christian artists seek acceptance outside the marketing definitions of Christian music, they will face many obstacles. Let's try and make sure at least one of those obstacles doesn't have to be their fellow Christians" (John Fischer, "Between a Rock and a Hard Place," *CCM Magazine*, August 1998, p. 62).

Fischer is saying that it is wrong to judge the difference between a musician who preaches Jesus Christ and one who does not. Such thinking certainly does not come from the Bible. The Bible has much to say about music, but nowhere does God's Word give instruction or encouragement for Christians to entertain the world. Where in the New Testament Scriptures do we see anything like crossover Christian music? The Lord Jesus Christ gave us His commission to preach the Gospel to the ends of the earth (Matthew 28; Mark 16; Luke 24; John 20; Acts 1), and that is precisely what the Apostles and first Christians did. Those who preach the Gospel are certainly to be commended above those who do not! John Fischer might not think it is right to judge musicians by the Word of God, but he is wrong. We are commanded to "prove all things" (1 Thess. 5:21), and that includes musicians. David compared everything to God's Word and rejected everything that was false (Psalm 119:128). Isaiah used the same standard (Isaiah 8:20). One of the Christian's responsibilities is to earnestly contend for the faith once delivered to the saints (Jude 3). That involves comparing everything to the New Testament faith and rejecting everything that is contrary.

FIVE IRON FRENZY

The eight-member band Five Iron Frenzy dressed in Star Trek outfits for their SkaMania tour in 1999, and their between-song banter consisted mostly of Star Trek-related dialogue ("Where No Ministry Has Gone Before," *Christianity Today*, May 24, 1999, p. 75). Lead vocalist Reese Roper said, "Our band is about being obedient to God. And God doesn't want us to preach all the time. ... It's wrong to put God in a box, to say that he only works through bands that preach at shows. He's so much bigger than that. ... some kids would have left [the concert] if they heard us preaching. They would have just walked out."

FRANCISCO, DON

Don Francisco moves in the most radical charismatic circles. In November 1986, for example, he had a concert at Vineyard Christian Fellowship Southeast, Denver, Colorado. The Vineyard movement, founded by the late John Wimber, has promoted such unscriptural notions as extra-biblical prophecy, slaying in the spirit, miracle evangelism, and the laughing revival. Francisco's music is a mixture of "folk, rock and blues" (from the cover to his *Early Works* album). He teaches the positive-only philosophy which is typical of the charismatic-ecumenical-New Evangelical movements that are permeating Christianity in these apostate last hours. Consider his testimony:

> "I knew from my own experience that painting a picture, RATHER THAN POINTING A FINGER, was a much more effective way to get the Gospel into people's heads and hearts."

It is strange that the Apostle Paul did not understand this. Consider Paul's sermon to the unsaved pagans on Mars Hill. He preached against their idolatry and warned them of judgment to come (Acts 17). Sounds like "finger pointing" to me, not finger pointing in the sense of a holier-than-thou attitude, but finger pointing in the sense of proclaiming God's righteous judgment and calling men to repentance. Consider Paul's presentation of the Gospel in the book of Romans. It begins with God's holiness and His condemnation of man's sin. Only after this "finger pointing" is completed, does he get to the good news that Christ has made the atonement for sin. The love of God is not even mentioned until chapter five of Romans. The preachers in the early churches did not have the philosophy of modern Contemporary Christian Music. In fact, preachers only 50 years ago did not have this philosophy.

When Don Francisco does give the gospel in his songs it is an unclear message. Consider the words to "Step Across the Line" from his *Forgiven* album: "You gotta take a step across the line/ Let Jesus fill your heart and mind/ I can show you where to look/ but you gotta seek to find."

Is that a clear presentation of the gospel? Could someone be born again through that?

Contemporary Christian Music evangelism is almost always this hazy.

Consider another example. This one is from Francisco's song "I Don't Care Where You've Been Sleeping." "I don't care where you've been sleepin'/ I don't care who's made your bed/ I've already gave my life to set you free/ There's no sin you could imagine/ That's stronger than my love/ And it's yours if you will come back home."

It is wonderfully true that Christ died for all of our sins and that His grace is sufficient to forgive any sin, but how do we receive His forgiveness? How can a person be born again? A hazy "come back home" is not the answer. Come back home to what? Come back home how? The unsaved portion of Don Francisco's audience is a mixed multitude of pagans and religious lost. What does "come back home" mean to them? Come back home to the Roman Catholic sacraments? Come back home to baptismal regeneration? Come back home to the "hold on tight because you might lose it" insecurity of an Assemblies of God gospel? Most CCM musicians do not make the message clear because they do not have a strong understanding of Bible doctrine and because they do not want to cause doctrinal divisions.

Here's another example of Don Francisco's gospel. This one is from his song "Give Your Heart a Home." "If you are tired and weary, weak and heavy laden/ I can understand how it feels to be alone/ I will take your burden/ If you let me love you/ Wrap my arms around you and give your heart a home." Is that the Gospel? It is not the message that the Apostles preached.

FRANKLIN, KIRK

Kirk Franklin (1972-) has taken the CCM world by a storm. His first two albums sold a combined 3 million copies. At eleven, Franklin was appointed music minister at Mt. Rose Baptist Church in Ft. Worth, Texas. It was then that he began to write, arrange, and rearrange Christian music. "My first triumph," recalls Franklin, "was turning Elton John's 'Benny & The Jetts' into a gospel tune" ("Kirk Franklin and the Family," http://www.gofishnet.com). We would not call that a triumph; we would call it a disgrace. Why do we need to take music created by a bisexual rock star and attempt to turn it into something associated with the holy Savior?

In his biography, Franklin admits that he lived in deep sin during his teenage years and into his early 20s, even while acting as music director in churches and performing Gospel music in a wide range of forums. He fathered a son out of wedlock in 1990, and as late as 1995 he was still living a promiscuous lifestyle. He formed his group called The Family in 1992, and by 1995 they had produced two hit Gospel albums and had won

Dove, Stellar, and other awards. He was living in fornication all of this time. Of those days he testifies:

> "But there I was, in the odd situation of getting a little bit of exposure and popularity and a little bit of a reputation while my life was still a mess. ...my lifestyle and THE CASUAL PROMISCUITY THAT SEEMS TO COME ALONG WITH THIS CRAZY BUSINESS was just killing me. ... my flesh was killing me. ... By January 1995 I knew I couldn't go on with the life I was leading. I didn't want to hurt God, and I knew I'd already been doing that to some degree. ... I know what it's like to be onstage, performing God's music and thinking about who I'll be going home with that night" (Kirk Franklin, *Church Boy*, pp. 136,175,176,195).

Franklin alludes to widespread immorality, even homosexuality, within the Gospel music industry.

> "In the church, especially the African-American church during the seventies and eighties, HOMOSEXUALITY was a big problem. It still is in some places. IT'S A PROBLEM TODAY IN GOSPEL MUSIC—A MAJOR CONCERN—AND EVERYBODY KNOWS IT. ... It seems that more than half the young people involved in dance, music, and the theater are openly gay. ... and the gospel music scene has not been exempt from that" (Ibid., pp. 39,40).

> "That stuff [promiscuity] wasn't happening because that's what I wanted. It was happening because I thought that's just the way it was. A lot of the pastors and preachers and music leaders I had known were doing it. And I honestly thought for a time that that's what you were supposed to do" (Ibid., p. 175).

We cannot fathom how Franklin could grow up in churches and think that immorality is justified. This sounds like a convenient excuse. Be that as it may, note that Franklin plainly testifies that fornication, adultery, and homosexuality are rampant in Gospel music circles.

In 1997, Franklin and Nu Nation had a hit titled "Stomp." It was very popular on secular charts. To a strong "hip-hop" beat they sang that Jesus' love made them want to dance and rock and roll: "It gets me high, up to the sky/ And when I think about Your goodness/ It makes me wanna stomp."

One of the performers for "Stomp" was rapper Cheryl "Salt" James of Salt 'N' Pepa. She has blasphemously stated in interviews that she believes in "Jesus and recreational sex."

Franklin claims that music is neutral and that any music can glorify God. "This album [1998] represents every style of music in our culture—jazz, gospel, blues, hip-hop, rock, ballads, blues, classical, you name it. They say music is universal, but the message is specific. If this music is universal, it's all ours; it's the message within it that makes the difference. ... The gospel is the message, and as long as the music is dedicated to Jesus, He makes it pure" (Franklin, *Church Boy*, pp. 225,226).

We have exposed this error in earlier sections of the book. We would ask Franklin one question, though. Where does the Bible say that the Lord Jesus purifies anything that is dedicated to Him, regardless of the character of the thing being dedicated? Paul warned the Corinthians that to take things from idolatry and to intermingle them into their Christian lives is an abomination to God (1 Cor. 10:18-23). Christ does not sanctify evil things. Franklin and other CCM musicians refuse to believe that rock music is evil, but tens of thousands of men and women of God are convinced that they are wrong and that they are doing great damage to the cause of Christ by attempting to use the world's music in the service of Christ. If rock music is evil as many believe, it is unacceptable to God and is not sanctified simply because it is dedicated to Christ. Where does the Bible say that only the sincerity and devotion of the minister is important? Was Moses not sincere when he struck the rock instead of speaking to it? Yet God judged him severely and refused to allow him to go into the Promised Land (Num. 20:7-14). Was Uzzah not sincere when he steadied the cart holding the ark? Yet God struck him dead (1 Sam. 6:6-7).

Franklin is ecumenical and easy-going about Bible doctrine. He believes in Pentecostal tongues and prophecies (Franklin, *Church Boy*, p. 214), and at one point he was music minister at a Seventh-day Adventist church. In his biography he says nothing to warn his readers about the doctrinal heresies of Seventh-day Adventism (*Church Boy*, p. 122). The *Way of Life Encyclopedia of the Bible & Christianity* exposes the danger of SDA doctrine.

Franklin's unscriptural philosophy of Christian ministry can be discerned from the following statement:

> "We're just trying to create an atmosphere, because we know that society has been turned off by organized religion. We know that the people aren't trying to hear about Christianity. Nobody's really trying to hear about that. We present it in a way that it's not corny, it's not boring, it's not for your grandma" (Kirk Franklin, Sept. 11, 1997, http://www.mtv.com/mtv/news/gallery/g/gods970911.html).

Franklin, like many Contemporary Christian Musicians, considers traditional Bible Christianity as it has been practiced in years past as boring and corny. He believes the Gospel of Jesus Christ has to be made cool and palatable to the world. This is contrary to what the Lord's Apostles practiced and taught. We don't wrap the Gospel in a worldly package to make it more acceptable to the unsaved. We don't use worldly methods to attract men to a holy Gospel. That is confusion. When God grants men conviction of their sin and repentance, they are ready to turn from the world and its vain pleasures. They yearn for something holy. When the Lord gave me repentance at age 23, frankly, I was *ready* to sing the traditional songs and hymns. I stilled loved rock music for a short time, but I also knew that it was deeply associated with evil and I yearned for something different, something holy and separate from this wicked world. I did not find the old hymns boring or corny. In fact, I did enjoy the very songs and hymns my grandmother loved. Though I was a rock-loving hippie I didn't need any type of rock music to draw me to the Gospel, and I didn't need rock music to help me enjoy Christian worship.

Franklin defends his close relationship with the licentious world of secular rock by claiming to be a light in the darkness. His philosophy of witnessing, though, is not scriptural. He holds the standard non-judgmental philosophy of the ecumenical movement.

> "Sometimes I'm an ear. They [secular musicians] know they're talking to somebody who's not going to judge them. ... You know, to reach the secular world, you don't beat them over the head with the Bible. You do it the way Jesus did it. You feed them first, then you preach to them" (Kirk Franklin, *CCM Magazine*, December 1998, p. 38).

This is a false statement. In His earthly ministry, Christ preached to people long before He ever fed them. The first thing the Lord Jesus Christ did in His ministry was proclaim: "Repent: for the kingdom of heaven is at hand" (Matt. 4:17). Christ's "negative" preaching caused the crowds to stop following Him (John 6:61-66). Christ preached righteousness and holiness (Matt. 5-7). The unsaved world has always found such preaching to be "judgmental." The fact that it is God's judgment and not man's makes no difference to those who are rebellious. Ephesians 5:11 says: "And have no fellowship with the unfruitful works of darkness, but rather reprove them." If Franklin would obey this he would not be so popular in the secular music field.

Franklin mocks Bible-believing Christians who do not like his rock music. His 1998 album, *The Nu Nation Project,* contains a skit titled "The Car," which depicts someone searching for more traditional gospel music on the radio. When the person comes across Franklin's rock music, instead, he snorts: "Oh, Lord Jesus! That's that old Kirk Franklin mess ... I'd know that old filth anywhere." Franklin and his fellow CCM artists intend to rock on regardless of who they offend and regardless of whether or not they cause young people to go astray into the filthy world of rock music.

Like many other CCM musicians, Franklin slanders "old fashioned" Bible-believing

Christians as "hard-nosed traditionalists" and "legalists."

> "The only thing those hard-nosed traditionalists can see is that these musicians are really wild and seem pretty far out for gospel singers. Ever since that first meeting back in 1992 when we laid out the basic outlines of the Family, we've been concerned about the legalism in the church. We've been hurt by it, but I can honestly say it's a lot better today than it was five years ago. Those who live by rigid legalism may not be able to see the obvious. And too often they can't even see how their attitudes are driving young people out of the church and into the streets and the gangs and the clubs" (Kirk Franklin, *Church Boy*, p. 173).

This statement is laughable in light of Franklin's immorality and the immorality practiced by other members of his group. (Franklin's keyboard player, Bobby Sparks, has been with Franklin's group since its inception, but he did not "give his life to the Lord" until August 1997. Prior to that Sparks was living in deep sin, yet he was playing Gospel music.) Those who take their stand on the Bible and preach against loving the world and who preach holy living are slanderously called legalists. We would remind Franklin that it is not legalism to strive to obey God's commands and to preach obedience and holiness. Note what the Lord Jesus said about the commandments:

> "For verily I say unto you, Till heaven and earth pass, one jot or one tittle shall in no wise pass from the law, till all be fulfilled. Whosoever therefore shall break one of these least commandments, and shall teach men so, he shall be called the least in the kingdom of heaven: but whosoever shall do and teach them, the same shall be called great in the kingdom of heaven" (Matthew 5:18,19).

Further, Franklin confuses persecution with correction. He says he has been hurt by those who criticize his lifestyle and music. It is never pleasant to be corrected for sin, but such correction is not persecution nor is it hurtful (except to the old sinful, proud self). A father rebukes his children because he loves them. The Lord Jesus rebukes those He loves (Revelation 3:19), and we are warned that His correction is not pleasant and we must beware of fainting under it (Heb. 12:5). One of the preacher's chief tasks is to reprove and rebuke (2 Timothy 4:1-2). The Scriptures are given by God "for reproof, for correction, for instruction in righteousness" (2 Timothy 3:16-17). Those who repent when they are rebuked learn to appreciate the correction, but those who harden their hearts and refuse to repent hate those who rebuke them. The book of Proverbs frequently warns that a person's attitude toward correction reveals the condition of his heart and determines whether he is wise or foolish.

> "Reprove not a scorner, lest he hate thee: rebuke a wise man, and he will love thee" (Prov. 9:8).

"He is in the way of life that keepeth instruction: but he that refuseth reproof erreth" (Prov. 10:17).

"A fool despiseth his father's instruction: but he that regardeth reproof is prudent" (Prov. 15:5).

"Correction is grievous unto him that forsaketh the way: and he that hateth reproof shall die" (Prov. 15:10).

"A scorner loveth not one that reproveth him: neither will he go unto the wise" (Prov. 15:12).
"A reproof entereth more into a wise man than a hundred stripes into a fool" (Prov. 17:10).

The world recognizes Franklin's defiant attitude. A review of his 1998 album in the *Dallas Morning News* (Oct. 2, 1998) is titled "Rebellious Franklin Pledges Nu Nation under God." The article observes: "The Fort Worth rapper-songwriter-producer spends two tracks on his new CD, 'The Nu Nation Project,' reminding listeners what a rebel and outcast he is. ... He's a provocateur and proud of it."

GAITHERS

The very popular Bill and Gloria Gaither are graduates of Anderson College, a Church of God school, and attend a Nazarene church. Though not Pentecostal, they have a close, non-critical relationship with the ecumenical-charismatic movement. They provided the music one evening at Indianapolis '90, a large ecumenical charismatic gathering I attended with press credentials. One-half of the 25,000 participants were Roman Catholics. A Catholic mass was held each morning during this conference, and Catholic priest Tom Forrest from Rome brought the closing message. Roughly 40 other denominations were present. The Gaithers were at home in this unscriptural gathering and entertained the mixed multitude with their lively music.

During a concert tour in New England in 1986, Bill Gaither admitted that he had changed his musical style due to the influence of the "world's culture." He said he believed there was a place for Christian rock, and he expressed his philosophy of music in these words: "God speaks through all different kinds of art forms and musical styles and musical forms" and the "format itself is not necessarily spiritual or non-spiritual" (*FBF News Bulletin*, March-April 1986, p. 3). Gaither is promoting the Devil's lie that music is neutral and that any type of music can be used to glorify God.

The following is an eyewitness description of the Gaither's appearance at the Southern Baptist Convention in St. Louis in 1980: "The Bill Gaither Trio entertained 15,000

Southern Baptists on Sunday evening with a musical program worldly enough to make any true believer weep. The music was so loud that some people left and others put their hands to their ears to block the intense amplification of the music" (Robert S. Reynolds, "Southern Baptists on the Downgrade," Report on the 1980 SBC Convention in St. Louis, *Foundation*, Volume VI, Issue 1, 1985, p. 9).

The Gaithers have increasingly used rock styles. During the disco craze in the late 1980s, the Gaither Trio recorded a disco album (*Calvary Contender*, August 15, 1989). The Gaithers have a song titled "Singin' with the Saints" which is a boogie-woogie version of "He Keeps Me Singing." This is confusion.

Bill Gaither has mentored many of the popular CCM artists, including Sandi Patty, Russ Taff, Michael English, Carman, and the members of Whiteheart (*CCM Magazine*, July 1998, p. 20).

In 1999, Bill Gaither joined forces with dc Talk founder Toby McKeehan to "create a new modern worship music label, 40 Records" (*CCM magazine*, July 1999, p. 11). The goal is "to stretch the boundary of worship music" and to "give a youthful spirit to worship music for ANY DENOMINATION…" Speaking of the new music company, Gaither said: "I view building bridges of understanding of different cultures and PHILOSOPHICAL POINTS OF VIEW as part of my calling. UNITY DOES NOT DEPEND ON OUR CONSENSUS OF OPINION, but on our unity in Christ." This is a false and dangerous statement. Biblical unity *does* depend on a consensus of opinion about doctrine. Ephesians 4:1-6, which speaks of Christian unity, says there is only "one faith" (verse 5). This refers to the body of truth delivered by the Holy Spirit to the Apostles and recorded in the New Testament Scriptures. Philippians 1:27 also speaks of Christian unity, and it demands "one mind striving together for the faith of the gospel." That is not a description of modern ecumenism. Timothy was instructed to allow "no other doctrine" in the churches he was overseeing (1 Timothy 3:16). Paul taught the church at Rome that false doctrine is the basis for separation (Romans 16:17). Like Gaither, McKeehan and dc Talk are unscripturally ecumenical and even accept Roman Catholics as brothers and sisters in Christ in spite of Rome's false gospel. When Pope John Paul II visited the States in January 1999, dc Talk and other CCM groups joined hands with hundreds of thousands of Catholics to welcome him. Featured at a Catholic youth rally connected with the Pope's visit, were dc Talk, Audio Adrenaline, Rebecca St. James, Jennifer Knapp, The W's, and the Supertones (*CCM Magazine*, April 1999, p. 12). dc Talk's Kevin Max praised the Catholic youth for coming out to hear the Pope, describing John Paul II as "someone with something of substance to say" (Ibid.). Each attendee received a rosary with instructions about how to pray to Mary.

The Gaithers promote false doctrine through their music. The Gaither Vocal Band *Wings* album (1988) contains a cut "What Once Was a River," which teaches the error of latter rain theology.

> "It's time. The prophecies are here/ The Spirit's moving swifter. The last days are near/ Young men will see visions. Old men will dream dreams/ I will pour out my Spirit in those days like will never before seen/ What once was a river now is a flood/ What once was a taste of His glory now is a feast of His love/ The windows of heaven have opened above."

The Gaithers frequently perform and record songs which present an ecumenical philosophy. "Songs that Answer Questions" from their *Back Home in Indiana* album has the following lyrics:

> "Don't want to spend my life a preachin' sermons/ that give answers to the questions no one's asking anywhere/ When there's so much pain and hurting/ there's no time to be searching/ for the needles in the haystacks that aren't there/ I wanna spend my time a wearin' myself out for Jesus/ with the news a cure's been found to heal our land/ Stead of making lists, inventing creeds/ that aren't concerned with people's needs/ I'll show 'em how to touch the nail scarred hand/ Don't wanna spend my time prayin' prayers/ Bombarding heaven with requests to rain down fire on saints who care [unclear]/ In our methods we may differ, but if Christ the Lord we live for/ May we not forget the enemy is OUT THERE."

This song contains half-truths and subtle errors, which are more dangerous than plain and obvious errors. While it is true that God's people are to be concerned about suffering and are to be showing people how to "touch the nail scarred hand," it is not true that preaching is to be limited merely to answering questions people have. The preacher is instructed to preach the whole counsel of God and the whole Word of God (Acts 20:27; 2 Tim. 3:16-17; 4:1-2). The Bible warns that it is apostate people who will desire teachers who teach merely what they want to hear, what they feel a need for (2 Timothy 4:3-4). This sounds very much like what the Gaithers are singing about. It is also not true that "a cure's been found to heal our land." The cure provided by the Gospel is the cure for personal salvation, not national salvation. The Apostles did not try to "heal the land," they preached the Gospel and discipled believers. It is also not true that it is wrong to "make lists" or "invent creeds" that aren't concerned with people's needs. The lists and creeds mentioned in this song refer to doctrinal studies and statements of faith. Doctrinal studies must, first of all, faithfully represent Bible truth, regardless of whether or not it meets "people's needs." Sound Bible doctrine does meet man's deepest needs, of course, but that does not mean that Bible doctrine meets the *felt needs* of unsaved or carnal people. The unsaved or carnal man does not feel he has a need to be told he is a sinner or that he is has no righteousness before God or that he is to repent or that he is to die to self or that he is to separate from the world or that there is an eternal hell, etc., but sound Bible doctrine tells him all of these things. The unsaved crowd does not believe it needs any of the Bible, really! This song encourages the hearers to despise doctrinal studies and research and teaching and statements of faith, which is the attitude typically found in the ecumenical movement. It is also not true that the divisions among Christians are merely about differing methods or that differing methods are not important. Take baptism, for example. Some denominations "baptize" infants. That is their "method." Some baptize only those who have trusted Jesus Christ as their Savior. Some sprinkle; others immerse. These are differing methods, but they are not insignificant and cannot be ignored. It is also not true that the "enemy" is limited to things outside of the churches. The Bible warns of false teachers, false christs, false spirits, false gospels, deluding spirits, doctrines of devils—all of which will be found within churches and among professing Christians. It is also not true that fundamentalists are praying for fire to fall on those with whom they disagree doctrinally. That is a nonsensical, actually a vicious, slander. The unscriptural and very dangerous message of this song is put across by the effective means of pleasant country-rock music and by the use of repetition.

Another ecumenical Gaither song is "Jesus Built This Church on Love" from their *Back Home in Indiana* album. The lead on the song is performed by Candy "Hemphill" Christmas, who travels with the Gaithers. The song is sung at many of the Gaither concerts. It is done in the style of a mid-tempo jazzy black spiritual with heavy drums and bass guitar.

> "Do you ever just get to wonderin'/ 'bout the way things are today?/ So many on board this gospel ship/ Trying to row in a different way/ If we'd all pull together/ Like a family me and you/ We'd come a lot closer to doin'/ what the Lord called us to do.
>
> Chorus: "Jesus built this church on love/ and that's what it's all about/ Trying to get everybody saved/ not to keep anybody out..."

This song implies that the divisions within Christianity are largely if not entirely man-made and unnecessary, that if professing Christians would merely "pull together" and exercise love the divisions would be healed. It is a feel-good sentiment, a nice fairy tale which has wide appeal, but it is unreasonable and unscriptural. The Lord Jesus Christ and the Apostles warned repeatedly that false teachers would lead many astray, that there would be false christs, false spirits, false gospels, false churches, doctrines of devils (Matt. 7:15-23; 24:3-5,11,24; Acts 20:28-30; 2 Cor. 1:1-4; Galatians 1; 1 Tim. 4:1; 2 Tim. 3:13; 4:3-4; 2 Pet. 2; 1 John 4:1; Jude; etc.). The book of Revelation predicts a one-world end-time harlot Christian religion (Rev. 17). Those who preach an ecumenical unity rarely even mention these Bible warnings and never focus on them. They do not tell us where these false christs, false gospels, false spirits, false teachers, and false churches are in Christianity today. They imply, rather, that the denominational divisions are largely unnecessary and petty which could be overcome by a little ecumenical love. There are many problems among Christians which can be healed through love, but it simply is not true that love will heal the major divisions within Christianity. The differences between denominations involve serious doctrinal issues which cannot be ignored and which cannot be solved through sentimental songs. This Gaither song also says the churches are "not to keep anybody out." That is openly contrary to the Bible's command to separate from error and to exercise church discipline (Rom. 16:17; 1 Corinthians 5; 2 Cor. 6:14-18; 1 Tim. 6:3-5; 2 Tim. 2:16-21; 3:5; 2 John 8-11; Rev. 18:4). Another ecumenical Gaither song is "Loving God, Living Each Other" from the album by that name.

> "They pushed back from the table/ To listen to his words/ His secret plan before he had to go/ It's not complicated/ Don't need a lot of rules/ This is all you need to know/ We tend to make it harder/ Build steeples out of stone/ Fill books with explanations of the way/ But if we'd stop and listen/ And break a little bread/ We would hear the Master say/ It's Loving God, loving each other/ Making music with my friends/ Loving God, loving each other/ And the story never ends."

The song contains more half truths and subtle errors. Love is a very important part of the Christian life, but true Christian love is obeying God's Word (John 14:23; 1 John 5:3). To say that we "don't need a lot of rules" ignores the fact that the New Testament is literally filled with commandments! To say that we don't need to "fill books with explanations of the way" ignores the fact that the Bible instructs us to "Study to show thyself approved unto God, a workman that needeth not to be ashamed, rightly dividing the word of truth" (2 Tim. 2:15). It ignores the fact that the Bible is given for "doctrine" (teaching) (2 Tim. 3:16) and that preachers are instructed to teach other men (2 Tim. 2:2), that older women are instructed to teach younger women (Titus 2:3-5), etc. Bible teaching certainly involves "filling books with explanations of the way." That is precisely what the Apostles did in the Epistles. The Bible itself contains 66 books with explanations of the way! This Gaither song presents a sentimental, ecumenical approach to the Christian life and ministry which is simplistic and appealing to a modern crowd but which is patently contrary to the Scriptures. The unscriptural message of this song is put across by the very effective means of pleasant country-rock music and by the use of repetition.

The Gaithers represent the very heart and soul of Southern gospel music today. In recent years they have held "homecoming" specials which have brought together most of the well known Southern gospel groups. These include members of the Statesmen, the

Blackwood Brothers, the Cathedrals, the Goodman's, the Speer Family, the Florida Boys, the Gatlin Brothers, and many others. Those who have attended these gatherings have put their stamp of approval upon the ecumenical-charismatic-rock music side of Southern gospel by not separating from those who are guilty of these things and by not lifting their voices to reprove them. The Bible instructs us to "have no fellowship with the unfruitful works of darkness, but rather reprove them" (Eph. 5:11). Revelation 18:4 warns God's people to come out from among the apostasy of the last hours "that ye be not partakers of her sins." COMPLICITY WITH DOCTRINAL AND SPIRITUAL ERROR MAKES ME A PARTAKER WITH THAT ERROR. 2 John warns that even to bid God speed to a false teacher makes me "partaker of his evil deeds" (2 John 11). I realize this is a very hard line and one that is completely foreign to the thinking of this ecumenical-crazed age, but this is what the Word of God says. I also realize that the Gaithers have produced some lovely Christian music, but this is no excuse for disobedience to God's Word. When the Gaithers greet 12,000 Roman Catholics, including many priests and nuns, as brethren in Christ, as they did at Indianapolis '90, they are partakers of the evil deeds of Rome and God's people should protest.

It is very dangerous to bring the jazzed up music and the ecumenical philosophy of these groups into our churches and homes.

GAINES, BILLY AND SARAH

In 1997 Billy and Sarah Gaines joined Roman Catholic Kathy Troccoli and 40 other CCM artists to record *Love One Another*, a song with an ecumenical theme: "Christians from all denominations demonstrating their common love for Christ and each other." The song talks about tearing down the walls of denominational division. The broad range of participants who joined Kathy Troccoli in recording "Love One Another" demonstrates the ecumenical agenda of Contemporary Christian Music. The song witnessed Catholics, Pentecostals, Baptists, etc., yoked together to call for Christian unity.

GALACTIC COWBOYS

The Galactic Cowboys, from Houston, Texas, was originally called The Awful Truth. The name was changed in 1990. The band is composed of Ben Huggins (vocals), Monty Colvin (bass), Wally Farkas (guitar), and Alan Doss (drums). The band has "a real dirty grunge-like sound." They play in night clubs. For example, they are billed to play at Tramps in Manhattan on October 7, 1998.

They have produced five albums, two on Geffen Records (who publish vile secular rock groups such as Guns 'n' Roses and Nirvana) and three on Metal Blade Records.

The group's singer admits that their biggest influence is the Beatles:

> "I'd have to say that The Beatles are still the biggest influence on us all the way around — except for maybe the guitar tones. They were great songwriters and vocalists" (Ben Huggins, cited by Dan Macintosh, *HM* magazine, September-October 1998).

The lyrics to Galactic Cowboy's music is almost indecipherable. The following are the words to the title song from their 1996 *Feel the Rage* album —

> "Take a trip, step outside of this fishbowl life/ Voice recalls, ceramic youth in pots of broken truth/ I feel the rage, comin' off of the stage/ I feel the rage, comin' off of the page/ I feel the rage, comin' off of the page/ Make a wish, clear your mind, let the years rewind/ Poets pain battles fame and becomes its slave/ I feel the rage, comin' off of the stage/ I feel the rage, comin' off of the page/ I feel the.../ Open mouth, open grave, nothing left to say."

If you don't understand what that means, you are not alone. There is nothing spiritually edifying here, and this is one of the plainest songs on the album!

GAY, ROBERT. See Laughing Revival.

GHOTI HOOK

The members of Ghoti Hook are Adam Neubauer (drums), Joel Bell (vocals/guitar), Christian Ergueta (bass), and Jamie Tolosa (guitar). Ghoti Hook means Fish Hook. The band members are Pentecostal and met one another in an Assemblies of God church.

Their fall 1998 album features covers of songs by secular rock and country groups such as Willie Nelson, The Cars, Violent Femmes, and The Pixies.

Most of Ghoti Hook's music is complete nonsense. Consider the words to the title song on their 1997 debut album, *Banana Man*:

> "He might look just a little bit kooky/ But he thinks that's okay/ He needs a job to pay off his mortgage and his Chevrolet/ If tricks you want, then he ain't your person/ All he does is stand/ Except the times when he is running from the policeman/ Banana Man!/ 1 2 3/ I'm Banana Man/ Dance with me!/ It might surprise you he went to college/ And got his degree/ It's hard to find a job with a major in plant psychology/ His identity he tries to keep secret/ But not because he's great/ 'Cause the girls will just keep on laughing, and he'll never get a date."

Not only does Ghoti Hook not preach a plain biblical message in their music, they do not preach during their concerts, either.

> "Sometime people give us a hard time because we don't mention God onstage. ... I know that a lot of other bands and people are called to talk about God onstage a lot more than we do, and that's great, but we just feel that our calling is to get people interested in our MUSIC, interested in US..." (Ghoti Hook, *HM* magazine, formerly *Heaven's Metal Magazine*, Issue #67, pp. 34-35).

GIBSON, JON

Jon Gibson's music is described as "soulful pop sound." He has also been one of those instrumental in introducing rap music into Christian circles. In the mid-1980s he worked with Michael Jackson on "So Shy." In 1987 Gibson recorded a song entitled "the Wall" with Kirk Burrell for Gibson's 1988 album, *Change of Heart*. This was the first contemporary Christian song to feature rap music. Burrell went on to become a rap superstar known as M.C. Hammer. In 1989 Gibson teamed with Stevie Wonder for a remake of "Have a Talk with God." The duet was released on Gibson's 1989 release *Body & Soul* (Jon Gibson, Biography for *Love Education* (1995), BMP Management, TLeM Christian Music Resources, http://tlem.netcentral.net/cmr/database/g/gibson_jon.html).

"The two main influences in Jon Gibson's music are Stevie Wonder and Jesus Christ—in that order. Wonder's touch is obvious in every syllable of Gibson's vocal performance. A Christian perspective is background for Gibson's socially-aware, moral songs about unemployment and girlfriends" (*CCM Magazine*, August 1987, p. 34).

Gibson's non-judgmental philosophy is evident from the following statement:

> "I have matured to the point as a Christian that I stay out of Christ's way. I don't clutter it up with my personal opinion, or religion. I just love people" (Jon Gibson, interview, *Inside Music*, June 1992, p. 20).

Gibson thinks Christian love can ignore sin and error, but biblical love is never divorced from knowledge and judgment (Philippians 1:9). Gibson says he wants to stay out of Christ's way and not clutter it up with his opinion or religion, and he uses this statement to excuse himself from exercising judgment and from seeking to correct anyone about anything. To the contrary, Christ has commanded that His people preach His Word (2 Timothy 4:2), contend for the faith (Jude 3), and rebuke sin (Ephesians 5:11).

Gibson's unscriptural philosophy is further evident in the following statement:

> "There are things happening in life all people can relate to. See, to a lot of people, if you sing about Christ, they'll say, 'That's fine, but man, I need a job. Get me a job, and then we'll talk about Christ.' I want to sneak into their hearts with the music. 'Be as wise as serpents and innocent as doves' you know. I think that's the way Jesus did it. He didn't tell them the whole truth. ... I think we kinda gotta do that too. Contemporary Christian music needs to branch out a little more, get a little sneakier. It's warfare, you know" (Jon Gibson, *CCM Magazine*, May 1987, p. 11).

Gibson misuses the Scripture by twisting Matthew 10:16 out of context: "Behold, I send you forth as sheep in the midst of wolves: be ye therefore wise as serpents, and harmless as doves." This verse was part of Christ's instructions to the twelve disciples when He sent them to preach repentance to the nation Israel. He was not instructing them to obscure their message, as Gibson and other CCM performers contend. Christ had already told them that they were to preach a plain message.

> "These twelve Jesus sent forth, and commanded them, saying, Go not into the way of the Gentiles, and into any city of the Samaritans enter ye not: But go rather to the lost sheep of the house of Israel. And as ye go, preach, saying, The kingdom of heaven is at hand" (Matthew 10:5-7).

When the Lord Jesus Christ spoke of being wise as serpents and harmless as doves, He was certainly not speaking of making the Gospel message vague or hiding it in sensual rock music. The Lord's disciples did not understand His meaning in such a fashion. They boldly and plainly preached the Gospel wherever they went. "Therefore they that were scattered abroad went every where preaching the word" (Acts 8:4). This is why they were so continually persecuted by the world. (CCM artists, on the other hand, are often loved and supported by the world.) When the Lord Jesus Christ spoke of being wise as serpents and harmless as doves, He was merely instructing the disciples to be wise and cautious and non-injurious in their dealings with the unsaved and as much as possible to avoid trouble.

Gibson talks of "sneaking" the message of God into people's hearts through obscure music, but the Bible says faith comes by hearing and hearing by the Word of God (Romans 10:17). It is impossible to "sneak" salvation into the hearts of people. Ephesians explains that to be saved people must first hear the word of truth, then they must trust that Word (Ephesians 1:12-13). It is a very conscious procedure brought about by a plain message.

GOODMAN, VESTAL

In 1997 Southern gospel legend Vestal Goodman joined Roman Catholic Kathy Troccoli and 40 other CCM artists to record *Love One Another*, a song with an ecumenical theme: "Christians from all denominations demonstrating their common love for Christ and each other." The song talks about tearing down the walls of denominational division. The broad range of participants who joined Kathy Troccoli in recording "Love One Another" demonstrates the ecumenical agenda of Contemporary Christian Music. The song witnessed Catholics, Pentecostals, Baptists, etc., yoked together to call for Christian unity.

GRANT, AMY

Amy Grant (1960-) is one of the most popular figures in Contemporary Christian Music. She has sold nearly 18 million records worldwide, won five Grammys, 17 Dove awards, been voted "Artist of the Year" four times. "She has performed from the White House to The Grand Ole Opry to Monday Night Football." She has appeared on *The Today Show*, *Good Morning America*, *The Grammy Awards*, *Arsenio Hall*, *The Tonight Show*, and many other such forums.

Grant grew up in a wealthy Church of Christ family near Nashville and began writing and singing folk/pop music as a young teenager. She signed her first recording contract at age 15. Amy was baptized in the baptismal regenerationist Church of Christ in the seventh grade. When she left home, she joined the charismatic Belmont Assembly in Nashville. She attended the Southern Baptist-affiliated Furman University in Greenville, South Carolina.

In January 1999, Grant and her husband of 16 years, Gary Chapman, announced their separation. She filed for divorce in March 1999, citing "irreconcilable differences." They have three children. Although she claims that she did not commit adultery, Grant began dating her friend, country singer Vince Gill, even before her divorce was finalized; and she admits that she had a close emotional relationship with him for a long time. In an interview with *CCM Magazine*, Grant's ex-husband Gary Chapman testified that Amy came to him in late 1994 and said: "I don't love you anymore You're the biggest mistake I've ever made. ... I've given my heart to another man" (*CCM Magazine*, January 2000, p. 36). It was not until three years later, in 1997, that Gill divorced his wife. Chapman said that he believes Amy's relationship with Gill was the primary cause of the divorce (Ibid.).

In March 2000, Amy married Vance Gill.

In an interview with *CCM Magazine*, Grant notes that she and her husband went through numerous counseling sessions beginning in 1986. Not only did this counseling not save her marriage, some of it apparently contributed to it. She quotes one counselor who gave her the following unscriptural advice:

> "Amy, God made marriage for people. He didn't make people for marriage. He didn't create this institution so He could just plug people into it. He provided this so that people could enjoy each other to the fullest" ("Judging Amy," *CCM Magazine*, November 1999, p. 36).

Grant concluded from this that "if two people are not thriving healthily in a situation, I say remove the marriage [and] let them heal" (Ibid., p. 36).

In August 1998, Grant told her husband: "I believe and trust that I've been released from this [marriage]" (Ibid., p. 35). She came to this foolish conclusion although she had no biblical grounds for separation or divorce and her husband was committed to the marriage. Only the Lord knows the woman's heart, but it is appears that she had committed herself to marrying another man to whom she had already given her heart. She admits that she saw in Vince Gill "a true complement" to herself.

In contrast to Grant's delusion about being released from her marriage, the Bible is very clear about God's will:

> "And unto the married I command, yet not I, but the Lord, LET NOT THE WIFE DEPART FROM HER HUSBAND: But and if she depart, let her remain unmarried, or be reconciled to her husband: and let not the husband put away his wife" (1 Corinthians 7:10,11).

> "The Pharisees also came unto him, tempting him, and saying unto him, Is it lawful for a man to put away his wife for every cause? And he answered and said unto them, Have ye not read, that he which made them at the beginning made them male and female, And said, For this cause shall a man leave father and mother, and shall cleave to his wife: and they twain shall be one flesh? Wherefore they are no more twain, but one flesh. What therefore God hath joined together, let not man put asunder. They say unto him, Why did Moses then command to give a writing of divorcement, and to put her away? He saith unto them, Moses because of the hardness of your hearts suffered you to put away your wives: but from the beginning it was not so. And I say unto you, WHOSOEVER SHALL PUT AWAY HIS WIFE, EXCEPT IT BE FOR FORNICATION, AND SHALL MARRY ANOTHER, COMMITTETH ADULTERY: AND WHOSO MARRIETH HER WHICH IS PUT AWAY DOTH COMMIT ADULTERY" (Matthew 19:3-9).

Amy Grant's husband did not want the marriage to end and he sought to save it. He told *CCM Magazine*: "For five years after I was told that I was no longer loved and that she wanted out of the marriage, I refused that because of the kids." He testified of getting down on his knees and begging her not to leave. Contrary to Amy's self-esteem psychobabble about God releasing her from the marriage, Chapman does not believe the divorce is God's will. He says: "It was not God's will that we divorced. It wasn't. That was not His plan. ... Did we allow God to do all He could do? Unquestionably no. No, we did not. 'Irreconcilable differences' [the basis upon which the divorce was sought] is such a lame and hollow phrase. That's what you say when you're afraid to say anything. It's the legalese that allows you to walk away. From my vantage point, we had one irreconcilable difference: I wanted her to stay, and she wanted to leave. Everything else, God could have reconciled" (*CCM Magazine*, January 2000, pp. 36,37).

In typical CCM fashion, Amy Grant lashes out at those who would judge her. Note the following statements from her interview:

> "Let's get real. Humanity is humanity. You want to know what my real black ugly stuff is? Go look in a mirror and everything that's black and ugly about you, it's the same about me. ... No one is ever changed because of judgment. ... It doesn't make one person more holy to point out the sin of another person" (Amy Grant, *CCM Magazine*, November 1999, p. 38).

While it is true that all are sinners, it is not true that Christians have no right to judge sin. When a member of the church at Corinth committed fornication and brought reproach upon the name of Christ, the congregation followed the Amy Grant philosophy and refused to exercise judgment. Paul rebuked them for their tolerance and lack of judgment in the matter.

> "For I verily, as absent in body, but present in spirit, HAVE JUDGED ALREADY, as though I were present, concerning him that hath so done this deed, In the name of our Lord Jesus Christ, when ye are gathered together, and my spirit, with the power of our Lord Jesus Christ, To deliver such an one unto Satan for the destruction of the flesh, that the spirit may be saved in the day of the Lord Jesus" (1 Corinthians 5:3-5).

Christians ARE responsible to reprove sin in the lives of others with the goal of bringing the sinner to repentance.

> "And have no fellowship with the unfruitful works of darkness, but rather reprove them" (Ephesians 5:11).

> "Them that sin rebuke before all, that others also may fear" (1 Timothy 5:20).

> "This witness is true. Wherefore rebuke them sharply, that they may be sound in the faith" (Titus 1:13).

> "But exhort one another daily, while it is called To day; lest any of you be hardened through the deceitfulness of sin" (Hebrews 3:13).

> "Brethren, if any of you do err from the truth, and one convert him; Let him know, that he which converteth the sinner from the error of his way shall save a soul from death, and shall hide a multitude of sins" (James 5:19,20).

The love of Christ does not overlook sin. The Lord Jesus Christ said, "As many as I love, I rebuke and chasten: be zealous therefore, and repent" (Revelation 3:19).

Grant has made 15 albums. Her self-titled debut album sold over 50,000 copies in 1977. Amy was only 17 years old. Her music has moved increasingly toward heavy rock. Her 1982 album, *Age to Age*, was the first album on a Christian label to go platinum, meaning it sold more than one million copies. $200,000 was spent in its production. Of this album, Amy testified: "I wanted to make a record that musically would fit right between Madonna and Huey Lewis" (*Rolling Stone*, June 6, 1985, p. 10). In 1983, she won her first Grammy. The next year she won her second. Since then she has won three more. She made history by being the first to be named Top Female Gospel Vocalist three years in a row. By 1995, she had sold 18 million records. Of the top 20 all-time best-selling Christian albums, eight belong to Amy Grant: *Heart in Motion* (5,846,000), *Home for Christmas* (3,624,000), *House of Love* (2,605,000), *Lead Me On* (1,671,000), *The Collection* (1,634,000), *A Christmas Album* (1,275,000), *Unguarded* (1,267,000), *Age to Age* (1,243,000), and *Straight Ahead* (1,133,000) (*CCM Magazine*, July 1998, pp. 107-108). Her 1984 album, *Straight Ahead*, was number one on the Gospel chart for 53 consecutive weeks.

By 1984 her tours were reaching half a million fans and grossing $1.5 million. The 1985 amount reached $2.5 million. That year Amy Grant was ranked with female vocalist secular superstars Diana Ross, Tina Turner, Cyndi Lauper, and Madonna, in terms of concert attendance.

She has also been the most successful "cross over" CCM artist. Her 1985 album, *Unguarded*, was the first to be distributed jointly by CCM label Myrrh in the "Christian" market and by A&M Records in the secular market.

Amy Grant and her husband admit that they purposefully avoid direct messages so the secular fans won't reject their music:

> "Grant and her husband, songwriter Gary Chapman, prefer to 'be a little bit sneaky with the lyrics,' he says. 'We don't want to shove anything down anybody's throat. When you start getting churchy, they start running'" (Jack Kelley, "The Gospel of Grant," *Weekend Post*, Houston, Texas, Nov. 10, 1985).

When challenged about yoking together with secular companies and distributing music to a secular audience, CCM artists invariably reply that they do this to gain a wider audience for the Christian message. The gross duplicity of that argument is evident in the vagueness of the lyrics to the "cross over" albums. They are reaching a secular audience, but they are not reaching that audience with a clear Gospel message. *At best,* the message is vaguely religious. There is no clear Gospel in Amy Grant's cross over albums. As we have seen, Amy and her husband admit that they are "sneaky" with the message. Notice how she describes the songs on her 1997 album, *Behind the Eyes* —

> "These songs are not about life being perfect. THEY ARE NOT ABOUT CONVINCING ANYBODY OF ANYTHING, but I'm willing to stand behind every one of these songs and say, 'Either you like them or not but they are all meaningful for me'" ("Amy Grant," imusic, http://imusic.com/showcase/contemporary/amygrant.html).

Behind the Eyes is the first of Amy's albums to make NO mention of God or Jesus Christ and to have no explicitly Christian lyrics. In an interview with *Christianity Today*, Grant testified: "I don't know if 'Behind the Eyes' is a Christian record. Being able to label it Christian or non-Christian is not the point for me" (*Christianity Today*, Dec. 8, 1997). Although it is not a Christian record in any sense, Grant's *Behind the Eyes* album won the 1998 Gospel Music Association Dove Award for Pop/Contemporary album of the year!

One of the songs on *Behind the Eyes* is "Like I Love You." Amy told imusic, a secular entertainment distributor, that this song is about loving oneself!

> "Amy suddenly realized she was singing to herself on many of the songs on the new album. 'It's strange, if you ask me what that song is about, ["Like I Love You"] I would say, "This is how I believe we all want to be loved." But if you're going to love anybody else, you have to be able to love yourself — and that's not the blatant selfishness of "I want things to go my way." It has to do with issues of respect and not abandoning yourself'" (Ibid.).

As if North American culture needs another dose of self esteem!

The song "Somewhere Down the Road" presents a universalistic false gospel. Though a large part of Amy Grant's intended audience is the unsaved, she gives them no Gospel so they can be saved. Instead, she comforts them with vague promises about God's love toward them that they are in no position to enjoy. The message therefore becomes false and wicked. What do Amy's unsaved listeners think when they hear the following lyrics?

> "Somewhere down the road/ There'll be answers to the questions/ ... Though we cannot see it now/ ... You will find mighty arms reaching for you/ And they will hold the answers at the end of the road" (Amy Grant, "Somewhere Down the Road").

If her listeners think about God at all through the lyrics to this song (it is never absolutely clear that she is singing about God) they will think merely that some sort of God (Grant never defines him) will work everything out for them somehow in the end. This is not true, though. The only way God is going to work things out for individual sinners and they only way He reaches out to them is through the new birth in Jesus Christ. In Christ and in Christ alone are the answers. Any "hope" outside of this is a false hope. Anyone can find comfort in Amy Grant's music. The New Ager, the Hindu, the Mormon, the baptismal regenerationist, anyone. Her music is that vague.

Note the following unscriptural message in the song "Turn the World Around" from the *Behind the Eyes* album:

> "We're all the same it seems/ Behind the eyes/ Broken promises and dreams/ In good disguise/ All we're really looking for is somewhere/ Safe and warm/ The shelter of each other in the storm. Chorus: Maybe one day/ We can turn and face our fears/ Maybe one day/ We can reach out through our tears/ After all it's really not that far/ To where hope can be found."

It is unconscionable for a Christian to sing to the unsaved about "hope," about searching for a shelter from the storms of life, without giving them a clear presentation of the Gospel. The unsaved have absolutely no hope apart from salvation in the Lord Jesus Christ. The destiny of every person apart from Jesus Christ is eternal Hell. Instead of presenting the Gospel, Amy Grant gives a hazy message about reaching out for some mystical hope in a place that is not far away. What place? What hope? How does a person reach it? Not only is Amy's gospel hazy; it is false. Is hope gained by turning and facing our fears? She leaves her listeners with this unscriptural impression.

By communicating a vague gospel Amy Grant is actually communicating a false gospel.

Some of the songs *on Behind the Eyes* focus on humanitarian themes, but not from a biblical perspective. The song "Turn This World Around" is about the plight of the homeless in America, but it does not explain to the hearers that this plight is largely one of their own making. Instead, the song uses the issue of homelessness to call for some vague humanitarian unity: "The hunger and longing every one of us knows inside/Can be the bridge between us if we tried." Secular music distributor imusic notes that this universalistic statement "may well sum up the album's humanitarian themes." Amy Grant is singing about some of the same themes that the unsaved world is singing about.

Articles about Amy Grant in the secular media invariably reveal that she is loved not for her Christian message but for her sensuality. She is not popular for her lyrics; she is popular for her sensual music (with or without lyrics), her voice, and her sexuality, which she admittedly flaunts. Even her voice is described in sensual terms, as "alluring and seductive."

People magazine noticed Amy's lack of holiness in the performance of the video for the song "Baby, Baby." "There's saintly Amy cuddling some hunky guy, crooning 'Baby, Baby' into his ear and looking pretty SLEEK AND SINFUL..." (*People*, July 15, 1991 p. 71). Amy Grant admits that "I'm trying to look SEXY to sell a record..." (*Rolling Stone*, June 6, 1985, p. 10). When asked about the controversy surrounding this video, Amy replied: "The whole thing just seemed very boring to me. Besides, shooting the video was a blast. *It's fun to flirt* if you're a happily married woman" (*Woman's Day*, Dec. 22 , 1992 , p. 35).

The song "Baby, Baby" from Grant's 1991 album, *Heart in Motion,* became the first song by a "Christian artist" to take the No. 1 spot on *Billboard* magazine (a secular chart). That album became the number one best-selling "Christian" album of all time, though it has no clear Gospel message. Nine of the eleven songs, mostly sung to heavy rock music, do not mention Jesus Christ or God and have no clear Christian message of any sort. They are primarily about romance. The two songs which do mention God present a hazy, unclear message. Consider the words to one of these, "Ask Me" —

> "She's coming to life again/ He's in the middle of her pain/ In the middle of her shame/ Mercy brings life/ He's in the middle/ Mercy in the middle."

Amy Grant's unscriptural philosophy is evident in statements she and her associates have made to the press:

> "I have a healthy sense of right and wrong, but sometimes, for example, using foul, exclamation-point words among friends can be good for a laugh" (Amy Grant, interview with *Ladies Home Journal*, December 1985, p. 100).

> "[Amy] doesn't want the conservative fundamentalists coming to the concerts. She wants young people who will get up and move to the beat, people who want to be pinned against the back wall by the volume for two hours. That's want she gives them. Besides, Amy never had the traditional Gospel music fans, so how could she turn them off? She has never been the darling of the fundamentalists" (Don Butler, Gospel Music Association executive director, cited by Bob Millard, *Amy Grant*, p. 154).

> "It seems to me that people who are most adamantly against premarital sex have experienced some kind of pain in their own lives. Like the people who say absolutely NO to rock 'n' roll. Chances are it has something to do with a past sadness..." (Amy Grant, interview, *Ladies Home Journal*, December

1985, p. 210).

"I'm a singer, not a preacher. I'm not looking to convert anybody. I feel people come to hear my music, not to hear me talk" (Amy Grant, *St. Petersburg Times*, Florida, April 7, 1984, p. 4).

"I'm not a preacher. I'm not a reaper, either. And I don't even know if I'm really a sower. Sometimes I think I'm simply the package stuck up on a stick at the end of the row that says, 'This is what's available here ... this is what you'll find in this row if you're interested'" (Amy Grant, *Religious Broadcasting*, April 1986).

"I don't feel like it's my mission in life to preach to people. I feel like it's just my gift to communicate life as I see it" (Amy Grant, *Family Weekly*, August 11, 1985).

"Why isolate yourself? Your life isolates you enough. I'm isolated when I walk into a room and somebody says, She's a Christian and NOBODY OFFERS ME A JOINT and all the coke [cocaine] disappears..." (emphasis added) (Amy Grant, quoted by Bob Millard in his book *Amy Grant*, New York, 1986, p. 169).

"I've become disillusioned, and that's why my lyrics are less idealistic. I'm realizing that the world isn't a perfect place, and God can't solve everyone's problems" (Amy Grant, interview, *Family Circle*, September 9, 1986, p. 24).

"If an audience feels I've walked away from God because I no longer talk about Him onstage, then that's their loss" (Amy Grant, Ibid.).

"I get tired of Christians trying to tell me what being a Christian is. I get tired of that kind of Christianity. ... People asking, 'Have you had your quiet time today?' We have such a regimented idea of what Christianity is" (Amy Grant, 1980, cited by Bob Millard, *Amy Grant*, p. 107).

"That's one reason I started writing songs, because I didn't want to impose my religion on anyone. This way the audience can sit back and draw its own conclusions. ... My art and the feeling I am trying to communicate through the songs, it would be silly for me to say, this is who God is; I don't have any answers" (Amy Grant, interview, *The Philadelphia Inquirer*, Oct. 21, 1984).

"I want to play hardball in this [music] business. ... I want to be on the same level professionally with performers in all areas of music. I love to hear Billy Joel, Kenny Loggins and the Doobie Brothers. Why not? I aim to bridge the gap between Christian and pop" (Amy Grant, interview, *Time*, March 11, 1985).

"Christians can be sexy. What I'm doing is a good thing" (Amy Grant, interview, *People*, July 15, 1991).

[The following is Amy's own description of her actions before a crowd of

30,000 young people in Kissimmee, Florida, in 1978.] "We're sitting there, I do my sound check. All these girls are in halter tops, great figures, everybody's wearing nothing, we're in Floriday [her way of pronouncing Florida]. I'm eighteen and I know what they're thinking. I said, 'I really want to know Jesus and I really want to love him except ... my hormones are on ten and I see you all ... sitting out there getting chummy and praying together—and we're horny. My feeling is why fake it? I'm not trying to be gross, I'm saying let's be honest about what's coming down'" (Bob Millard, *Amy Grant*, 1986, p. 103).

Amy's *House of Love* album includes the environmental-mother-earth song, "Big Yellow Taxi," by Joni Mitchell. Mitchell is infamous for her open relationship with a spirit she calls "Art." Obviously, she is communing with demons, and it is unconscionable for Amy Grant to be promoting Mitchell's music to Christian young people.

Grant's song "Walking in the Light" teaches the damnable error of baptismal regeneration:

"The sun woke me up real early/ It's a beautiful morn/ 'CAUSE I'M GOIN' DOWN TO THE RIVER/ TO BE REBORN/ Now me and Jesus did some heavy/ Talkin' last night/ So I'm goin' down to be dipped and/ Come up walkin' in the light" (Amy Grant, "Walking in the Light").

Grant's song "Faithless Heart" is about a woman who has adulterous desires:

"Faithless heart/ At times the woman deep inside me wanders far from home/ And in my mind I live a life that chills me to the bone/ A heart, running for arms out of reach/ But who is the stranger my longing seeks?" (Amy Grant, "Faithless Heart").

Amy Grant's producer, Brown Bannister, reveals his unscriptural philosophy and his despite toward Bible-believing fundamentalist churches in the following interview:

"That's the problem I'm having with Christian music; it's so formula-oriented. The praise stuff is great, but even the praise stuff is formula. It's like all the same 'Okay, let's name all the names of God in the Bible' and 'Let's say "I will lift my hands"'; ... I guess you just kind of run out of things to say when you start talking about that stuff. You're limited to a certain number of phrases that are biblical and scripturally-oriented. ... Its very confusing because of the nature of religious education and upbringing and the separatist mentality of most churches and their creeds in America and their opinions on culture" (Brown Bannister, record producer and promoter, producer for Amy Grant, interview, *CCM Magazine*, October 1988, p. 13).

In October 1996 Amy Grant's former husband, Gary Chapman, was named host of the licentious television show "Prime Time Country" on TNN, The Nashville Network.

The confusion caused by yoking together with the world to provide entertainment was evident during Amy Grant's 1995 *House of Love* tour. The tour was financed by the retailing corporation Target. Target's parent company, Dayton Hudson Corporation, in turn donates money to Planned Parenthood. Though Amy Grant does not defend abortion herself and is a supporter of Nashville's Crisis Pregnancy Support Center, she has in this manner helped fund Planned Parenthood, which supports abortion on demand. For this reason her tour was picketed by members of Operation Rescue who distributed a handout requesting that people write Grant and "ask her to stop supporting child killing."

Amy Grant has given an interview to the Roman Catholic youth magazine *YOU* (*The Fundamentalist Digest*, May-June 1992). She did not warn the young people that Rome's sacramental gospel leads to eternal destruction.

Roman Catholic Kathy Troccoli was the backup singer for Amy Grant before Troccoli began her own recording career in 1982 (*St. Petersburg Times*, Religious section, Nov. 9, 1985, p. 3).

In 1997 Amy Grant and Gary Chapman joined Troccoli and 40 other CCM artists to record *Love One Another*, a song with an ecumenical theme: "Christians from all denominations demonstrating their common love for Christ and each other." The song talks about tearing down the walls of denominational division. The broad range of participants who joined Kathy Troccoli in recording "Love One Another" demonstrates the ecumenical agenda of Contemporary Christian Music. The song witnessed Catholics, Pentecostals, Baptists, etc., yoked together to call for Christian unity.

In 1994, the Catholic St. John's University gave its highest award, the Pax Christi, to Amy Grant (*Houston Chronicle*, May 7, 1994). Pax Christi is the radical International Catholic Peace Movement (*Calvary Contender*, June 1, 1994).

GREEN, AL

Gospel/Rhythm & Blues singer Al Green (c.1946-), who began his career in the mid 1960s, is an inductee into the Rock and Roll Hall of Fame. The *Rolling Stone Encyclopedia of Rock* observes that he "embodies both the sacred and the profane in soul music." As he was growing up, he sang with his father as part of the family gospel group, The Green Brothers. In the mid-1960s he formed his own group, Al Green and the Creations, before becoming lead singer with The Soul Mates. Their song "Back Up Train" became a Top 5 Rhythm & Blues hit. In 1969, Green began his solo career. In the 1970s he was the "most popular purveyor of soul music," selling more than 20 million records.

In 1974, Green was attacked in a motel room by a spurned lover. She poured scalding hot food on him, then shot herself to death. This shocking event caused him to return to church. His 1976 album, *Full of Fire,* contained three rather obscure "spiritual tunes." In his 1977 recording, *The Belle Album,* "Green effectively brings God into the love song, but without introducing Him by name" (Steve Turner, *Hungry for Heaven,* p. 61). Green said the album worked well because "it channeled both religion and rock 'n' roll and it channeled them so well." This is an attempt to merge Christ and the world, and it is an impossible task.

In 1983, he recorded his first all-gospel album, *The Lord Will Make A Way,* and during the next few years, he recorded 10 gospel records. Beginning in 1987, he had more secular music hits, including "Everything Is Gonna Be Alright" and "Put a Little Love in Your Heart."

Green is a Pentecostal and in 1976 he was ordained as pastor of the Full Gospel Tabernacle Church in Memphis. He did not give up his pop career, and he preaches at his church only when he is not on tour (*Rolling Stone Encyclopedia of Rock & Roll*, p. 396). He claims that God told him to continue singing his old secular hits. "I prayed about it and was told, 'you sing all your songs. I gave you all your songs, all those good songs. They're about love and about people and they're about happy endings and life. Sing your songs.' So I started singing 'em" (Al Green, cited by Larry Nager, *Memphis Beat*, p. 210). I don't know who Al Green was talking with, but the holy God of the Bible would not have said that. The "love" Al Green and other rhythm & blues performers sing about is not godly love, but is forbidden lust and non-judgmental emotionalism. God is a God of love and great compassion. He offers salvation to any sinner who repents of his sin and trusts Jesus Christ as his Savior, but God is not all-accepting and non-judgmental. He accepts sinners solely based on the shed blood of Jesus Christ. He requires repentance from sin and holiness of life and does not allow sinners to live like they please. He does not allow men to make up their own religious philosophy. Those who refuse to walk the Bible way are rejected and judged. Green's song "Put a Little Love in Your Heart" is an example of a song that promotes an unbiblical philosophy of love, and we can be certain that God does not inspire such songs.

Al Green performed at the opening of the Rock & Roll Hall of Fame in Cleveland, Ohio.

Jeff Godwin notes that in 1989 Al Green sang a duet, "Put a Little Love in Your Heart," with secular rock singer Annie Lennox who appears in concert with a butch hair cut, clad in leather pants and a lacy bra. Lennox is with the secular rock group Eurythmics, which took its name from an occultic style of music developed by Dr. Rudolph Steiner (1861-1925). Like Satanist Aleister Crowley, Steiner was a member of the Order of the

Golden Dawn. Eurythmics uses combinations of rhythm and light and movement to create occultic objectives and to draw "astral light" into the individual "who becomes the bearer of the spirit self." From a Biblical perspective, we know that this refers to demons entering people. Demonic powers are very much at work within rock music, and it is blatant disobedience to the Scriptures for a professing Christian to join forces with immoral and occultic rock musicians.

> "Be ye not unequally yoked together with unbelievers: for what fellowship hath righteousness with unrighteousness? and what communion hath light with darkness? And what concord hath Christ with Belial? or what part hath he that believeth with an infidel? And what agreement hath the temple of God with idols? for ye are the temple of the living God; as God hath said, I will dwell in them, and walk in them; and I will be their God, and they shall be my people. Wherefore come out from among them, and be ye separate, saith the Lord, and touch not the unclean thing; and I will receive you" (2 Cor. 6:14-17).

The song which Green and Lennox sang, "Put a Little Love in Your Heart," is a 1960s "anthem to New Age unity." The words are as follows:

> "Think of your fellow man/ Lend him a helping hand/ Put a little love in your heart/ You see it's getting late/ Oh please don't hesitate/ Put a little love in your heart ... If you want the world to know/ We won't let hatred grow/ Put a little love in your heart/ And the world will be a better place/ And the world will be a better place/ For you and me/ You just wait and see, people now..."

Jeff Godwin observes: "The Green/Lennox collaboration is the ultimate in New Age 'paradigm shift' (new frame of reference). If you really want the world to be a better place, throw a 'Christian' singer and an antichrist transvestite together. Their very presence on the same stage proves 'love' is the answer to all our problems, and the occult eurythmy of the light and sound drives that point into the minds of millions. ... The words to this song sound good until you peer beyond the light and smoke. This kind of deception is so slick and subtle, multitudes have been taken in by it. Many an angry CCM fan will argue, 'It talked about love and God loves the world, so what's the problem?' The problem is the love they are promoting is Satan's phony New Age love, not the true love of Jesus Christ" (*What's Wrong with Christian Rock?*, p. 82).

GREEN, KEITH

Keith Green (1953-1982) was one of the most influential names in Contemporary Christian Music in the late 1970s and early 1980s. His first album appeared in 1977 and sold a then unheard of 300,000 copies. With his wife, Melody, he founded Last Days Ministries. The Greens were discipled by Kenn Gulliksen, founder of a Vineyard Christian Fellowship.

His Pentecostal theology aside, he took some stands which were not popular or common to the CCM world. He preached boldly against the errors of Roman Catholicism. He preached repentance and warned against "easy believism." He preached against careless, fruitless, discipleless Christianity. He refused to charge for attendance at his concerts, and he dedicated the profits of his music to missions and to fight world hunger.

He brazenly defended the use of rock music in the service of the Lord, though. In July 1982, he was killed in a plane crash. Earlier that year he had published a book titled *Can God Use Rock Music?* in which he strongly argued for the use of rock music by Christians and he denounced those who warn against it. Note the following excerpt from this book:

> "...I believe that music, in itself, is a neutral force. Let me give you a better example. Take a knife for instance. With it, you can cut bread, carve a roast, loose someone who's been bound by ropes, or you can do harm and even kill somebody" (Keith Green, *Can God Use Rock Music?*).

To compare music to a knife is nonsense. A knife is indeed a neutral force until it is used in a certain manner. A musical composition, though, is not neutral because it presents a specific message by the particular arrangement of rhythm, melody, harmony, etc. The knife would better be compared to musical notes and components. These are neutral as long as they are not arranged into a musical composition.

Melody Green kept Last Days Ministries going until 1996, when it closed its doors. Keith Green's music is still available in Christian book stores and he is still voted one the most popular CCM musicians. After Keith's death, Melody Green remarried, to Andrew Sievright, and subsequently divorced him.

GREEN, STEVE

The very popular Steve Green (1957-) has recorded 21 albums, produced 17 No. 1 hits, and has received six Dove Awards and four Grammy nominations. He was born and raised in Argentina as a missionary kid. At 16 he began writing songs and playing the guitar for hours at a time. When he returned to the States at age 18 he entered an eight year period of rebellion.

> "I was tired of being alone, and I was tired of being different. I felt that Christianity was restrictive. I'd heard some people felt you didn't have to live as stringent a lifestyle as I had been taught. I wanted to find out who those people were...and join them! I didn't want to completely abandon ship, but I did want to do some skiing in the water. I wanted to get to heaven, but I wanted to do it my way. That attitude led to eight years of spiritual decline. The upbringing I

had was great. The convictions my parents had, they had for the right reasons. It's just that sometimes kids pick up on the rules and miss the heart. That's what I did. If my parents did something or didn't do something because of their love for the Lord, I didn't do it because Dad said not to do it, but I missed the 'love the Lord' part. So when I came back to the States, I was already kicking against what I perceived as rules. When I got out from under the rules, I soon tossed off all restraint" (James Long, interview with Steve Green, *CCM Magazine*, March 1996).

Steve Green was still in a condition he describes as "spiritual coldness" when he began playing music in Christian bands. He released his first single in 1975. He tutored with Larry Norman for a year and a half, then signed to Word Records in 1977. Green's first album with Word, *Sayin' It with Love*, was released in June 1978. According to his own testimony, though, it was not until 1984 that Green truly got right with the Lord. He admits that "I had been a hypocrite, spouting off about God, without really knowing what I was talking about" (Ibid.).

Green is married and has two children.

Pat Leonard, who played keyboard and synthesizer on Green's first Word album, became Madonna's main producer/songwriter. The cover to Green's *It's a Dying World* album was drawn by the same artist who did the Beatles' occultic, drug-inspired, New Age *Sgt. Pepper* album.

Steve Green has sung at ecumenical forums such as the Religious Broadcasters Association annual convention, Moody Bible Institute's Founders Week, Billy Graham crusades, and Promise Keepers rallies. Green has performed at a half dozen Promise Keepers meetings since 1993. At the Promise Keepers Atlanta Clergy Conference in 1996, Green sang, "Let the Walls Come Down," referring to PK's goal of breaking down walls between denominations. Several Catholic priests were present at that conference, and Dr. Ralph Colas, who attended the event, described it in these words: "The big beat, contemporary music brought the ministers to their feet. ... Steve Green belted out repeatedly 'Let the Walls Come Down.' The 40,000 clergy shouted, whistled, clapped, and cheered as they worked to a higher and higher pitch of emotion." Dr. Colas noted further: "While there may be some good things said at a PK conference, this meeting included compromise, ecumenism, apostasy, Jesuit casuistry (end justifies the means), and hyper-emotionalism, along with a theology based on relationships rather than Biblical truth" (*Calvary Contender*, April 15, 1996).

Steve Green's *The Faithful* album (1998) (produced by Phil Naish) has two songs which promote charismatic-ecumenical error:

> "There's a river ever flowing/ Widening, never slowing/ And all who wade out in it are swept away/ When it ends where its going/ Like the wind, no way of knowing/ Until we answer the call to risk it all/ And enter in/ The river calls, we can't deny/ A step of faith is our reply/ We feel the Spirit draw us in/ The water's swift, we're forced to swim/ We're out of control/ And we go where he flows" (Steve Green, "The River").

> "A great movement in every place/ Is going on so fast Eternal light piercing so deep/ I am so convinced/ The prophecies that Jesus spoke/ Will soon all be fulfilled/ Everything will be made clear/ And very soon Jesus will come/ Oh, glory hallelujah/ For the Lord is pouring/ A holy fire/ The great revival's started/ Every tongue confessing/ 'Jesus Christ is Lord of all'/ 'Jesus Christ is Lord of all'" (Steve Green, "The Great Revival").

Those familiar with Pentecostal latter-rain doctrine will recognize the river terminology. They believe an end-time miracle revival is to precede the return of Christ. The "Laughing Revival," with headquarters in Toronto and Pensacola, uses the "river" terminology to describe their movement. The theme song at the Brownsville Assembly of God in Pensacola is "The River Is Here." The chorus to this song is as follows:

> "The river of God sets our feet a-dancing/ The river of God fills our hearts with cheer/ The river of God fills our mouths with laughter/ And we rejoice for the river is here."

As we have seen, Steve Green promotes and fellowships with the Promise Keepers organization. It, in turn, has been heavily influenced by John Wimber's Vineyard movement. PK founder Bill McCartney is a member of a Vineyard congregation in Boulder, Colorado, and he was taught to trust his intuitions as "revelation" from God by Vineyard pastor James Ryle. The Vineyard movement also spawned the Laughing Revival. These are different aspects of the same end-time apostasy and they share many of the same unscriptural philosophies.

Note that Steve Green sings that the "river" sweeps people away and makes them "out of control." This is precisely what happens to people who participate in the strange Laughing Revival. People are thrown to the floor and are unable to rise; they become drunken and stagger about and are unable to speak plainly. They make animal noises and laugh hysterically. And yet we are told that these things are the works of the Spirit of God in His "latter rain" outpouring. My friends, the "great revival" of which Steven Green sings is not revival; it is apostasy and confusion.

Steve Green also wants the world to know that he supports the non-judgmental philosophy:

> "I do have personal convictions that I conduct my life by, but I'm not going to force my convictions on someone else or try to make them jump through my hoops, through the convictions I have set up for my life" (Steve Green, *MusicLine Magazine*, December 1985, p. 9).

If Steve Green's "convictions" are not based on the Word of God, if they are merely his own "preferences," of course he is right and he should not urge his "convictions" upon anyone. If, on the other hand, his convictions are based solidly upon the Word of God, he has every responsibility to urge others to follow them. Timothy was instructed, "Preach the word; be instant in season, out of season; reprove, rebuke, exhort with all longsuffering and doctrine" (2 Timothy 4:2). Green's non-judgmental statement sounds like a clever attempt to escape the responsibility to preach God's standards of holiness and to reprove the works of darkness (Ephesians 5:11).

In January 1988, Green performed at the Assemblies of God-connected Carpenter's Home Church in Lakeland, Florida. It was at this church that the Laughing Revival began under the ministry of Rodney Howard-Browne, who blasphemously calls himself "the Holy Spirit bartender."

GRITS

This rap/rock group was formed out of the Silicon Valley Vineyard Church in California. This is the group of churches founded by the late John Wimber. The name Grits stands for Grammatical Revolution in the Spirit. The two rappers call themselves Bonafide (Teron Carter) and Coffee (Stacy Jones). In an article in the July 1999 issue of *CCM* magazine, Carter and Jones complain about "the negative stereotypes" or rap music. The two are preparing to enter the secular rap field. "We getting ready to make a major push into the mainstream." Their unscriptural philosophy is evident from the following statement: "What kids are listening to, we need to counter that. We can't come out there with 'Jesus loves you,' when kids are out there with real issues and real problems" ("Smoke Signals," *CCM* magazine, July 1999, p. 35). This is worldly nonsense. The Apostles and evangelists of the first century were not afraid of preaching "Jesus loves you" to a pagan world. Jones is divorced.

HAMMOND, FRED

Fred Hammond grew up in Detroit, Michigan, and began singing in a Pentecostal church. Even then he was attracted to the jazzy tunes, and there were songs "his strict Apostolic church wouldn't let him sing because they were too 'bluesy'" ("I'll Just Keep Praising Him," *Charisma*, July 2000, p. 52). Hammond has never gotten over his love for music with a hard beat, but times have changed and most churches today have adopted his worldly taste in music. Hammond and his group, Radical for Christ, are extremely influential in the Contemporary Praise field. His 1999 *Pages of Life* album sold more than a million copies, and his *Purpose by Design* album, released in March 2000, is even more popular. It was No. 1 on *Billboard's* gospel charts for six weeks. in the mid-1990s Hammond entered a partnership with Integrity Music to "develop a praise and worship line for the urban church." *Praise in the House* was released in 1995 and became the first of a series of popular "In the House" recordings.

Hammond claims that his music comes through revelations from God. He claims that while on tour in 1993 he had a vision of God sitting on His throne and beside Him was a special vault of songs. God supposedly said to Hammond, "These are songs I really love." Hammond also saw a vase, which God used to pour out songs. A few months later, Hammond allegedly had another vision, and God told him that 1993 began a new season in music. Hammond believes that these visions indicate God's pleasure with contemporary praise music. Hammond also tells of a prophecy which was given to him by a minister of a Charismatic church in 1993. The prophecy commanded Hammond to do praise and worship music "with the things inside of you—every beat, every note and chord that you ever grew up with" (*Charisma*, July 2000, p. 56). Thus he believes that God Himself has confirmed His pleasure with using any worldly music for the service of Jesus Christ.

In an interview with *Charisma* magazine, Hammond said: "I need something that catapults me into the stratosphere financially. I don't need to be just pretty well off. I need to be wealthy, extremely wealthy, and I don't even mind saying it." He goes on to say: "I want to set up big outdoor concerts where we actually feed the people—feed them naturally and spiritually; sing and don't do it shabby—do it like the world would do it" (*Charisma*, July 2000, p. 6). It is not wise nor scriptural to desire to be wealthy or to want to do things "like the world would do it."

HART, SARAH

The *National Catholic Register* for March 8-14, 1998, listed Sarah Hart as a Catholic musician. In 1997 Hart joined Roman Catholic Kathy Troccoli and 40 other CCM artists to record *Love One Another*, a song with an ecumenical theme: "Christians from all denominations demonstrating their common love for Christ and each other." The song talks about tearing down the walls of denominational division. The broad range of participants who joined Kathy Troccoli in recording "Love One Another" demonstrates the ecumenical agenda of Contemporary Christian Music. The song witnessed Catholics, Pentecostals, Baptists, etc., yoked together to call for Christian unity.

HARTMAN, BOB. See Petra.

HAYFORD, JACK

Jack Hayford (1934-), author of the song "Majesty" and many other very popular worship songs (more than 400 total), is pastor of Church-on-the-Way Foursquare Church, Van Nuys, California. Foursquare is the Pentecostal denominational which was founded by the female pastor Aimee Semple McPherson. Paul and Jan Crouch, of the Trinity Broadcasting Network, and entertainer Pat Boone, are members of Hayford's church. The Foursquare denomination believes that physical healing is promised in the atonement of Jesus Christ, that the baptism of the Holy Spirit is evidenced by speaking in tongues, and that a believer can lose his salvation. McPherson was very influential in the promotion of the unscriptural latter rain theology. She claimed that physical healing is part of the gospel. The "foursquare" gospel she promoted was Jesus Christ as Savior, Baptizer in the Holy Spirit, Healer, and Coming King. She claimed that she had obtained this gospel through a vision in 1922, in which God showed her that the Gospel was for body and soul and spirit. McPherson's ministry at times featured the unscriptural and dangerous spirit slaying phenomenon.

In 1996 Hayford endorsed Robert Schuller's autobiography, *Prayer: My Soul's Adventure with God*, in spite of the fact that Schuller is a dangerous false teacher who has perverted the Gospel by his self-esteem theology.

Writing in the Promise Keepers publication *The Seven Promises of a Promise Keeper*, Hayford stated, "Redeeming worship centers on the Lord's table. Whether your tradition celebrates it as communion, the Eucharist, the Mass or the Lord's Supper, we are all called to this centerpiece of Christian worship" (*Seven Promises*, p. 19). To put the biblical Lord's Supper on the same level as the blasphemous Catholic mass is extreme error.

Hayford's very popular and lovely song "Majesty" teaches Pentecostal doctrinal error, when it speaks of "kingdom authority." In the Pentecostal-Charismatic context, "kingdom authority" refers to the false doctrine that Christians today have the authority promised for the future kingdom which will be established at Christ's return. Hayford's "kingdom authority" refers to authority to cast out sickness, authority to bind the demonic rulers of this world system, authority to be prosperous.

HEAR THE LIGHT

This Christian rock group's *Barnabus* album was described as follows in the British CCM

Magazine *Buzz*: "This is music to hit yourself on the head to. Who cares if the lyrics are a bit simple, even banal in places? The album runs from solid rock through to electric blues and ends up at heavy metal. There are times when the female vocalist sounds like Janis Joplin and at others her voice is like wailing banshees in the night" (*Buzz*, September 1981). How edifying!

HEARTBEAT RECORDS

This is a Catholic-owned record label based in Donnelson, Iowa. It was founded in 1989. It's most popular musician is Dana, who has recorded more than a dozen albums, including "The Rosary" and "We Are One Body," which calls for ecumenical unity. Susan Stein, an executive with Heartbeat, makes no pretense of her yearning for unity between Catholics and evangelicals:

> "I would like Protestants and Catholics to set aside what are basically petty differences. We [Catholics] are different, but we are Christ-centered. And we would like to see the evangelical market be more open to listening to their fellow Christians, to be a bit less judgmental and a bit more open to understanding" (Stein, quoted in Steve Rabey, "Association Formed to Support Catholic Music," *CCM Update*, May 27, 1996).

HEMPHILL, JOEL

Joel Hemphill is committed to "Jesus Only" doctrine, which denies the Trinity and baptizes only in Jesus' name. He wrote "He's Still Working on Me."

HERRING, BUCK. See 2nd Chapter of Acts.

HEWSON, BONO. See Bono.

HOLM, DALLAS

Dallas Holm (c.1947-), who was trained by the Pentecostal evangelist Dave Wilkerson, was one of the pioneers of Contemporary Christian Music. He started singing in 1970 and has recorded 30 albums. He was one of the first Christian musicians to have a gold album (500,000 copies). He was the first to win Dove Awards for "Song of the Year," "Songwriter of the Year" and "Male Vocalist Of the Year." He is married and has three children.

For many years Holm's music was folk or very soft rock style, but the release of his 1990 album marked a move toward heavier rock.

Note the following feeling-oriented gospel message from the song "Love Has Come Over Me" (from Holm's album *Chain of Grace*, 1992) —

> "So won't you make a fresh evaluation/ Think about your life, about your soul/ He can touch your heart and make you whole/ Then you will have a wonderful sensation/ When you decide to give Him everything/ Then you'll join the holy celebration/ And lift your voice and begin to sing. Chorus: Because/ Love has come over me/ Captured my spirit/ Set my soul free/ Now I just can't believe/ How different I am/ Since love has come over me."

Is salvation deciding "to give Him everything"? Who is "Him"? There are many false christs and false gods in this world. Which one is Holm singing about? His listeners won't know from hearing this song. Is salvation a wonderful sensation? Not necessarily. Salvation is often a sensation of struggle and trial. The hazy message of love coming over me is too general to be of help to the young people who listen to CCM. In the context of the ecumenical confusion which surrounds Contemporary Christian Music, this message could mean almost anything. It could refer to a faithful Catholic attending Mass or to a baptismal regenerationist at his baptismal service or a Laughing Revival proponent becoming "drunk in the spirit." The unholy ecumenical movement thrives on hazy doctrine like this.

HOSANNA MUSIC. See Integrity Music.

IMPERIALS

The Imperials was formed in 1964 by Jake Hess and Armond Morales (1933-). Hess had performed with Hovie Lister and the Statesmen for many years. Bill Gaither calls the Imperials "one of the first contemporary gospel music groups" (Gaither, *Homecoming*, p. 153). The original members were Hess, Morales, Gary McSpadden, and Shirl Nielson, and there have been more than 20 different members through the years. The group has recorded 40 albums. The Imperials has won four Grammy's, 13 Dove Awards, and has had 17 No. 1 songs.

Morales is the lone remaining member of the original group, having been with the Imperials for 30 years. During that time the group has undergone a metamorphous in style, from Southern gospel to contemporary to rock. *Lighthouse Magazine*, which is rock oriented, has taken note that the music of the Imperials has changed radically. Their 1987 album, *This Year's Model*, "took a sharp turn to a youthful techno pop/rock sound that caused many long time Imperial fans to fall by the wayside" (Stephen Trickey, "The Imperials: Reaching the Church in the 90s with Music and Ministry," *The Lighthouse Electronic Magazine*, December 1996). In reality, the Imperials had become extremely jazzy long before 1987. Many of the songs on 1970s and early 1980s albums had a heavy boogie-woogie/disco dance rhythm.

As a matter of fact, the Imperials, like many Southern gospel groups, were jazzy and entertainment-oriented from their inception. There is an undated photo of Elvis Presley with the Imperials in the July 1998 issue of *CCM Magazine*. In the mid to late 1990s a determination was made to take the group back somewhat in the direction of its roots. Of their 1996 album, *Til He Comes*, Morales said: "If you enjoyed the Imperials music 10 years ago, you will enjoy 'Til He Comes.'" The problem is that the Imperials even 10 years ago were too jazzy and their music too entertainment-oriented. By 1965 all five members of the Imperials had near shoulder-length hair.

The group is Pentecostal in orientation. Their concerts "always end with the group giving an altar call and praying for those seeking salvation, restoration and healing" (Imperials web site, http://placetobe.org/cmp/artists/index.html).

The Imperials are also very ecumenical. In 1992, for example, they conducted concerts at the First Assembly of God in Virginia Beach, Virginia, and at the Lancaster Bible College the same month. They frequently appear on the radically ecumenical Trinity Broadcasting Network. On August 21, 1998, they appeared at Focus on the Family in Colorado Springs, Colorado.

As noted, in their earlier days The Imperials were closer to a traditional gospel quartet with plain biblical lyrics (generally speaking). Today they use pop music and the lyrics to the songs frequently have been shallow, obscure, and unscriptural:

> "Friend, I know where you're comin' from/ Seems your life's under the gun/ With no real chance of escape/ There is hope right outside your door/ It's what you've been searchin' for/ A love that will never fade/ So don't you run away/ Don't run away/ You can't hide/ Gotta keep reachin'/ You must keep reachin'/ Gotta keep reachin' for higher things" ("Higher Things," The Imperials, 1988, "Free the Fire" album).

What does this song mean? It's hard to tell. If it's for the unsaved, it presents a false gospel. Salvation is not obtained by a continual reaching for God. "But what saith it? The word is nigh thee, even in thy mouth, and in thy heart: that is, the word of faith, which we preach; That if thou shalt confess with thy mouth the Lord Jesus, and shalt believe in thine heart that God hath raised him from the dead, thou shalt be saved" (Romans 10:8,9). If, on the other hand, the song is for the saved, it says our hope is "outside your door." This is false. The Bible says "Christ IN YOU, the hope of glory" (Col. 1:27).

Consider the lyrics to a song from the Imperials' 1992 album:

> "If I wanted to change the world/ I would start by loving you/ If loving was all we knew/ Oo baby we could change the world/ We need to change/ We need to change/ We need to change the world/ If I wanted to change the world/ I would start by loving you/ And if loving was all we knew/ Oo baby we could change the world/ I would start by loving you/ That's all I really need to do/ I can't stop loving you/ If I wanted to change the world/ I would start by loving you/ And if loving was all we knew/ Oo baby we would change the world" (Terry Esau, "Change the World," from the Imperials' 1992 album, *Stir It Up*).

What does this mean? Who knows. It could mean many things and nothing. Is the singer referring to loving God or loving his girlfriend? Where does the Bible say that we need to change the world? This song could easily be sung by secular pop groups.

IN-3D

The rock group IN-3D began in 1994. "The name IN-3D is a metaphor for the Trinity and how as a band we want to display all parts of GOD and not leave the smallest thing out" (IN-3D web site).

One feature of Contemporary Christian Music at large is its tendency to ask questions rather than provide clear biblical answers. Note the following advertisement for an album by this group:

> "This band BLASTS AWAY AT CONVENTIONAL CHRISTIAN MUSIC with searing sounds reminiscent of the Police, and thought-provoking lyrics intended to be question-raisers. Their artful music is representative of a growing volume of Christian rock, much like U2's, USING AN INDIRECT APPROACH TO EVANGELISM, asking questions about moral issues and the meaning of life, but not necessarily spoon-feeding easy answers. The Chicago-based wave-metal combo explains, 'It's been said that art is not meant to answer questions, but to ask them'" (Dan and Steve Peters, *What about Christian Rock?*, p. 121).

It might be true that "art" is not meant to answer questions, but Christian ministry certainly is supposed to answer questions. Ten times in the small epistle of 1 John the Bible states that "we know" the truth. "And WE KNOW that the Son of God is come, and hath given us an understanding, that we may know him that is true, and we are in him that is true, even in his Son Jesus Christ. This is the true God, and eternal life" (1 John 5:20). We have a know-so salvation, praise the Lord. We know who God is, what man is, where man came from, how man can be saved, where man is going, what the world is, where the world is headed, what lies beyond death. We know the will of God. We know the work of God. We know the plan of God. We know the love of God. The child of God knows the answer to all of the great mysteries of life, because God has revealed them to us in the Scriptures. It is criminal for professing Christians to merely give the world more questions instead of solid and plain biblical answers to the mysteries of life.

IN REACH

A review of In Reach by *CCM Magazine* noted that they play in secular rock venues and are influenced by secular rock groups such as Rush, Genesis, Deep Purple, Paul McCartney, and Journey (*CCM Magazine*, August 1992, p. 11).

INTEGRITY MUSIC

The very popular and influential Integrity Music company (also owns Hosanna Music) arose out of the charismatic movement, and the music it spreads to 117 countries is of a charismatic nature. Integrity recently recorded an album at the Brownsville Assembly of God (home of the "Pensacola Outpouring"). Don Moen is the "creative director" for Integrity. In an interview with the *Pentecostal Evangel*, a magazine published by the Assemblies of God, Moen described the power of the Laughing Revival music in these words: "Because something is imparted when you listen to this tape. I don't want it to sound spooky or mysterious, but there's something powerful about embracing the music of the revival. The fire of the revival can stir in you even as you listen to the songs that took place at the Brownsville revival" ("Don Moen Discusses Music at Brownsville Assembly," *Pentecostal Evangel*, November 10, 1996). The "revival" to which he refers is not a biblical revival; it is a "revival" in which people become drunken and stagger about and fall down and are unable to perform the most basic functions of life. The pastor at Brownsville, John Kilpatrick, has testified that it has taken him a half hour just to put on his socks when he was drunk with the Brownsville revival spirit. He has lain on the church platform for as long as four hours, unable to get up. His wife has been unable to cook their food or clean the house. Whatever this "revival" is, it is not something that is Bible based. Yet Moen testifies that this spirit can be imparted through the music.

Integrity's Hosanna! Music worship tapes include songs by **ROBERT GAY**, who records music from alleged prophecies given by charismatic "prophets." Gay has written hundreds of choruses, and many of them have been professionally recorded. Integrity has produced twelve of Gay's prophetic songs. Gay claims that the Holy Spirit gives him visions for his songs. Gay is connected with Bill Hamon's Christian International network of supposed prophetic ministries, which promotes the deception that God is continuing to give revelation through prophets and apostles today. Hamon claims that God will soon raise up new apostles who will operate in the miracle-working power of the first-century apostles and who will unite the churches and denominations. He claims that the Laughing Revival and Promise Keepers are part of this restoration process (Hamon, *Apostles, Prophets and the Coming Moves of God: God's End-Time Plans for His Church and Planet Earth*, 1997).

Integrity's Hosanna! Music worship tapes also include songs of other key churches which have been captured by the Laughing Revival movement. Another one of these is **HILLS CHRISTIAN LIFE CENTRE**. Hosanna published an album entitled "Shout to the Lord" which was recorded at this church in New Zealand. It was #2 on the Christian charts in early June 1998. The worship leader at Hills Christian Life Centre is **DARLENE ZSCHECH**. Many of the "praise" songs on this album are extremely man centered. The lyrics to the songs often present a theology of "holding out faithful."

> "I will never be the same again/ I've closed the door/ I will walk the path/ I'll run the race" ("I Will Never Be" from *Shout to the Lord*).

> "I love you/ I need you/ Though my world may fall/ I'll never let you go" (Jesus, Lover of My Soul" from *Shout to the Lord*).

Instead of the Christian rejoicing in God's promises to keep him, these songs have the Christian promising to hold on to God. It is man-centered theology.

There is also the false Pentecostal latter rain theology in some of the songs.

> "I believe the promise about the visions and the dreams/ That the Holy Spirit will be poured out/ And His power will be seen/ Well the time is now/ The place is here/ And His people have come in faith/ There's a mighty sound/ And a touch of fire/ When we've gathered in one place" ("I Believe the Presence" from *Shout to the Lord*).

J.C. AND FRIENDS

The group called J.C. and Friends explains that their name can stand either for Jesus Christ and his followers or for J.C. Meyers and his pals (*MusicLine Magazine*, October 1985, p. 27). We believe it is blasphemous to call Jesus Christ "J.C."

JAHN, SARA

In 1997 Sara Jahn joined Roman Catholic Kathy Troccoli and 40 other CCM artists to record *Love One Another*, a song with an ecumenical theme: "Christians from all denominations demonstrating their common love for Christ and each other." The song talks about tearing down the walls of denominational division. The broad range of participants who joined Kathy Troccoli in recording "Love One Another" demonstrates the ecumenical agenda of Contemporary Christian Music. The song witnessed Catholics, Pentecostals, Baptists, etc., yoked together to call for Christian unity.

JARS OF CLAY

Jars of Clay sprang upon the CCM scene like gangbusters. Their 1995 debut album sold over two million copies to become the best-selling debut in Christian music history. The video associated with the album was broadcast on MTV and VH1. Their 1997 album, *Much Afraid*, debuted at No. 8 on the Billboard 200 chart (*CCM Magazine*, July 1998, p. 42). Secular rock magazines *Rolling Stone* and *Spin* have interviewed the members of the band. Jars of Clay performs as the opening act for the rock group Sting. The band members are from a wide variety of theological backgrounds, "ranging from Presbyterian and Episcopalian to the General Association of Regular Baptists" (*Christianity Today*, Nov. 15, 1999, p. 38). Their music is so worldly that it is popular in homosexual clubs in New York City (Ibid.).

Jars of Clay names Jimmy Hendrix and the Beatles as their inspiration (Dann Denny, "Christian Rock," *Sunday Herald Times*, Bloomington, Ind., Feb. 8, 1998). The lead guitarist for Jars of Clay is said to be a "Beatles fanatic" (*Christian News*, Dec. 8, 1997). When asked by *Christianity Today* to list their musical influences, Jars of Clay members "listed no Christian artists" (*Christianity Today*, Nov. 15, 1999). Jars of Clay performs Ozzy Osbourne's "Crazy Train" during their concerts. Osbourne is the filthy-mouthed former lead singer for the occultic rock group Black Sabbath. Though members of Black Sabbath today claim it was all done in innocence and "fun," they promoted occultic themes through their music and concerts, including upside down crosses and altar calls for Satan. They blasphemed Jesus Christ and railed against the authority of the God of the Bible. Osbourne has almost died several times because of his outrageous drug abuse and alcoholism. He has dressed in women's clothing and stripped off most of his clothes during concerts. At one point he attempted to kill his wife and had to be jailed. He is deeply scarred by his savage lifestyle and maintains a semblance of normalcy today through the drug Prozac.

Dan Haseltine of Jars of Clay says, "We don't want to be called a 'Christian band' because it is a turn-off" (*Alabama Baptist*, August 20, 1998).

Why does the world love Jars of Clay? The answer is simple. They play the world's music and they have the world's philosophy. Some would argue that Jars of Clay performs in wicked settings because they desire to be a light in the darkness. What light does their music carry, though? What is their goal with the music? Is it to win sinners to Jesus Christ? Is it to proclaim the Bible faithfully to a lost and Hell-bound world? Consider the following excerpt from an interview with Dan Haseltine by the Religious News Service:

> "The topics we deal with are universal in many ways. And we're not only singing to Christians, so why would I want to write a song that uses all this language that only Christians would understand? That would be shooting ourselves in the foot. An artist spends most of life in a prison tainted by his experience. Ours is tainted by our experience of being in church and being Christian. Hopefully, people who hear us are going to go 'Wow! That was a good song!' And we hope some people get some hope out of our music. Anything else is great" (Steve Rabey, Religious News Service, reprinted from *The Christian News*, Dec. 8, 1997, p. 17).

Haseltine complained that "a lot of agendas get thrown at a band when you call it Christian," and he told Religious News Service that Jars of Clay has no agenda. That means they have no specific goal with their music. They do not want to be bound by any specific "agenda." In fact, Haseltine believes that to be defined as Christian in a traditional church sense is "a prison" for "an artist." Does God give a Christian "artist" a different plan or "agenda" than He gives to other Christians? What do they think the Bible is? It is God's agenda for the believer! Every believer has been given the same agenda! God's perfect will is spelled out in the New Testament Scriptures and is given in the context of sound apostolic churches. Christian liberty is not liberty to do what we please, liberty to feed the flesh. That is not liberty; it is license. Christian liberty is liberty to obey God in all matters and to walk in His perfect will as expressed in His Word.

> "As free, and not using your liberty for a cloak of maliciousness, but as the servants of God" (1 Peter 2:16).

> "For, brethren, ye have been called unto liberty; only use not liberty for an occasion to the flesh, but by love serve one another" (Galatians 5:13).

> "For this is the love of God, that we keep his commandments: and his commandments are not grievous" (1 John 5:3).

> "While they promise them liberty, they themselves are the servants of corruption: for of whom a man is overcome, of the same is he brought in bondage" (2 Peter 2:19).

By their own testimony, Jars of Clay's agenda is not to obey the Word of God in every detail. They merely want to make people feel good and have "some hope" in a general, ill-defined sense. They speak of "Jesus," but what Jesus? Is it the Jesus Christ of the Bible, the holy, sinless, Son of God, the only Savior of the world, who is coming again to judge the world in righteousness; or it is some humanistic, man-made, feel-good Jesus?

Their song "Liquid" from the 1997 *Much Afraid* album has the following lyrics:

> "Arms nailed down/ are you tellin' me something?/ Eyes turned out/ are you looking for something?/ This is the one thing/ The one thing that I know/ Blood-stained brow/ are you dying for nothing?/ Flesh and blood/ is it so elemental?/ This is the one thing/ The one thing that I know/ Blood-stained brow/ He wasn't broken for nothing/ Arms nailed down/ He didn't die for nothing/ This is the one thing/ The one thing that I know."

The song says Christ didn't die for nothing, but it doesn't say why He died! Why not? Why be so vague?

Their song "Sinking" is another illustration of the vagueness of Jars of Clay's music:

> "It's not my problem anymore/ You see it never really was/ So you can stop caring as you call it/ And I'll be fine right here/ You see that I can play a pretty convincing role/ So I don't need you, I don't think I need you.
>
> Chorus: "But you see through my forever lies/ And you are not believing/ And I see in your forever eyes/ And you are forever healing/ You can't hear what I'm not saying/ And I can hold out long enough/ Treading water I keep from sinking/ I'm not one for reaching/ You see that I can play a pretty convincing role/ So I don't need you, I don't think I need you."

Of this song, the note at one of the Jars of Clay web sites says: "I think this song shows the attitude of a non-believer hanging on the verge of accepting Christ." The song could just as easily be about any number of other things, though, because it is vague. It could be a believer describing his backsliding. It is not clear to whom the singer is speaking. Is it God? Is it his girlfriend? Is it his guru? The hearer cannot be sure. It can mean anything and nothing. No wonder Jars of Clay is popular with the world. The world doesn't mind religious sentiment in music as long as it is non-dogmatic and non-convicting.

When Pope John Paul II visited the States in January 1999, Jars of Clay and other CCM groups joined hands with hundreds of thousands of Catholics to welcome him. Featured at a Catholic youth rally connected with the Pope's visit, were dc Talk, Audio Adrenaline, Rebecca St. James, and Jars of Clay (Music and Entertainment News, http://www.theenews.com/news/slug-12599_ dctalk-pope.html).

KARTSONAKIS, DINO. See Dino.

KEAGGY, PHIL

Phil Keaggy (1951-) is considered one of the foremost Christian guitarist/songwriters. In 1998 he won a Dove Award for Instrumental Album of the Year. He played in several rock bands in his teen years, and in 1968 he joined John Sferra to form a rock group called the Glass Harp. Bass player Dan Pecchio joined them about a year later, and they produced their first album in the fall of 1970. Earlier that same year Keaggy made a commitment to Christ in an Assemblies of God church, following the death of his mother in an automobile accident. Like most CCM musicians, Keaggy does not describe his salvation in clear biblical terms in his interviews or at his web site. He continued to play with Glass Harp for a couple more years, opening for secular rock groups such as Chicago, Janis Joplin, Alice Cooper, the James Gang, and Iron Butterfly. In 1972 he left Glass Harp due to philosophical differences to do solo work and to began playing in Christian circles. During the last half of the 1970s he worked with Buck Herring and the 2nd Chapter of Acts. Later he formed the Phil Keaggy Band. He won his first Dove Award in 1988.
Keaggy married in 1973, and he and his wife Bernadette have three children.

Though the Catholic-raised Keaggy made a commitment to Christ of some sort in an Assemblies of God church in 1970, he has not rejected Roman Catholicism and he is very ecumenical. Keaggy joined Catholic John Michael Talbot on his newest album, *Cave of the Heart*. Note the following statement from a 1995 interview:

> "... the Gospel is preached in many Catholic churches, and the truth is known there. ... Over the years, I've been a part of many nondenominational churches and denominational churches, but I have even a higher regard and respect for my Catholic upbringing, because I believe it planted the seeds of faith in me. And I read books that give me a greater understanding of the Catholic faith today. I'm not a practicing Catholic, but I believe that I'm a true believer who responds to the truth that is there. Because it's ancient tradition; it goes way back. I think Martin Luther had some great ideas, and showed us that we're saved by grace through faith, but he was a Catholic when he posted all that up! ... I have great fellowship with my Catholic brethren today. I have some dear friends across the country that I've made. That's a whole other subject; but I think when the Lord looks at his Bride, he doesn't see the walls that we use to divide ourselves from each other. He sees one body, and that body is comprised of his children, those who he bought and paid for with his blood ... I love the liturgy; I think liturgy with the Spirit is one of the most powerful ways of communicating the life of God to us" (Phil Keaggy, cited by Tom Loredo, "Phil Keaggy in His Own Words," *Way Back Home*, December 1995).

It is true that Catholicism can plant general seeds of faith in God which can sometimes be watered by the Gospel, but to imply that Catholic churches preach the Gospel is completely untrue. It is true that Martin Luther was a Catholic when he first made his protest against Rome, *but he did not learn salvation by grace alone from Roman Catholicism.* He learned it from the Bible IN SPITE OF Rome, and Rome quickly condemned him. Rome's Council of Trent, which was responding to Luther, boldly cursed anyone who says that salvation is by grace alone through faith alone by the blood of Christ alone without works or sacraments, and Trent has never been rescinded. Any Catholic church which preaches the true Gospel that salvation has nothing whatsoever to do with works or sacraments (and I don't know of any) is preaching contrary to what Roman Catholicism teaches in its official proclamations. The Catholic Church plainly states that salvation is by grace PLUS works and sacraments. Not only does the Catholic Church deny the Gospel of the grace of Christ by its formal declarations, but in many other ways, as well. The all-sufficiency of Christ's once-for-all atonement is denied by the Catholic Mass, which alleges to be a continual re-offering of Christ's sacrifice. The all-sufficiency of Jesus Christ is also denied by the Catholic priesthood, which alleges to stand between the believer and Christ. The all-sufficiency of Christ is further denied by the Catholic sainthood, which alleges to mediate between men and God. Keaggy says he loves the Catholic liturgy, but it is contrary to the Bible. There is no mass in the Bible. In fact, there are no sacraments in the New Testament Scriptures. Sacraments are supposed to be channels of grace, but the ordinances of true New Testament churches (believer's baptism and the Lord's Supper) are not channels of grace but are symbols and simple reminders only.

Keaggy discounts the importance of sound doctrine when he says that God does not see differences between churches and denominations. The Lord Jesus Christ warned that there would be many false teachers who would lead many astray from the truth (Matt. 7:15). He warned that as His return draws nearer, false teachers would increase (Matt. 24:11,24). The Apostles likewise warned of a great apostasy or turning away from the true New Testament faith, of the rise of many false teachers, of the creation of false churches (1 Timothy 4; 2 Timothy 3-4; 2 Peter 2; 1 John 2,4; Jude; Revelation 17). If God sees all denominations as a part of His one body, where are the false teachers? Where are the false churches? Where is the spirit of antichrist?

The following is from a more recent interview:

> "I'm just pro-Jesus. I'll go into any church where His name is honored. I don't know where it will take me. I just know that Christians need to love each other" (Phil Keaggy, cited by Dave Ubanski, "Fret Not," *CCM Magazine*, Nov. 1998, p. 36).

This sounds good to many, but Keaggy ignores the Bible's warning that there are false christs (2 Cor. 11:3-4). The "Jesus" honored by many churches is an unscriptural Jesus, and the Bible warns that God's people are not to fellowship with these (2 John 10-11). Christian love is important, but the Bible says that true love is obeying God's commandments (1 John 5:3).

In an interview with Religious Broadcasting, Keaggy further emphasized his ecumenical philosophy:

> "I think also the unity that is so necessary in the body of Christ is important. I admire Charles Colson. He got a lot of flack for writing the book, *The Body*, and being associated with Catholics. I was raised Catholic and my mother's influence was powerful in my life. I came to the Lord when she passed away. She sowed the seeds in my life for me to become a believer. There are divisive voices out there. People who thrive on disunity are the ones [to whom] you've got to say, 'I'm not going to contend with this, I'm not going to argue, I'm just going to go about my business'" ("Saran E. Smitha and Christine Pryor, "Integrity Times Two: Michael Card and Phil Keaggy," *Religious Broadcasting*, National Religious Broadcasters, July-August 1995).

The Christian life would be much simpler if one could follow Keaggy's advice and not get involved in contentions about doctrine and Christian living, but faithfulness to the Word of God does not allow it. Keaggy says he is not going to "contend," but God requires that His people "earnestly contend for the faith once delivered to the saints" (Jude 3) and reprove the unfruitful works of darkness (Ephesians 5:11). Obedience to such commands does not allow me to follow Keaggy's New Evangelical advice.

Keaggy's unscriptural ecumenical philosophy and anti-fundamentalist attitude is perfectly at home in the world of Contemporary Christian Music.

Some of Keaggy's music is simple folk strings style, and some of the lyrics to his songs are lovely and scriptural. The song "Disappointment" is an example. Consider the first stanza:

> "Disappointment—HIS appointment, change one letter/ Then I see, that the thwarting of my purpose is God's better choice for me/ His appointment must be blessing, though it may come in disguise/ For the end from the beginning, open to His wisdom lies/ Disappointment—HIS appointment, whose?/ The Lord's who loves me best/ Understands and knows me fully, who my faith and love would test/ For like loving, earthly parent, He rejoices when He knows/ That His child accepts unquestioned all that from His wisdom flows."

Keaggy is charismatic and claims to have received the "baptism of the Spirit" in 1970 at a Kathryn Kuhlman service (Phil Keaggy interview," *Harmony* magazine, 1976, http://www.museweb.com/keaggy/harmony76.html). He was affiliated with the Pentecostal Love Inn Community in Freeville, New York, from 1974 to 1979.

As with most CCM artists Keaggy has no separation from the world in his music. He performs an unholy combination of secular rock and Christian rock/folk, and those who listen to his music are drawn toward worldly rock & roll. On his 1993 *Crimson and Blue* album, for example, he pays "homage to The Beatles" with several of the songs. The Beatles have done more to further the Devil's program in this generation than any other music group. It is unconscionable for a Christian to pay homage to these wicked people and to their demonically-inspired music, thereby encouraging Christian young people to think that rock & roll is harmless.

Keaggy had a large role in producing the 1998 album *Surfonic Water Revival*. It is an attempt to Christianize surf-rock music. According to the CCM rockers who designed this album, Heaven might be a "Surfer's Paradise." Note the words to the song "Surfer's Paradise" from this album. It is written by Terry Scott Taylor and performed by All Star United with Phil Keaggy:

> "It's a dream of mine/ It's always surfin' time/ There's a beach with perfect weather/ And no closing sign/ It's the place to go/ 'Cause your tan never fades there/ And the surf's so fine/ And the junk's all free at the 7-Eleven/ And if you catch the perfect wave/ It'll take you to heaven/ So bring your girl and bring your guy/ And make it on down/ To surfer's Paradise.
>
> Chorus: "Let's get together, yea/ Let's get together (at)/ Surfer's Paradise/ Don't hesitate, don't think twice/ Shorts and bikinis will suffice/ You can wear 'em all day and night/ (At) Surfer's Paradise."

This is worldly foolishness. God's Word forbids half-nakedness. The Lord Jesus Christ warned that sensual lust, which is a big part of the beach scene, is adultery. When I was saved at age 23 from a hippie lifestyle (I grew up in Florida only a short drive from many beaches), God dealt with me about my old ways. He convicted me that it is wrong to lust after bikini-clad girls. I understood that I had to avoid beaches to avoid temptation. He convicted me about the evils of rock music. I no longer wanted to bum around and hang out and waste my life as I did before I was saved. Why aren't CCM rockers convicted of these worldly things? Instead of singing about beach nakedness they should be preaching against it. Surfing itself is not wrong, but the surf scene is intimately connected with the licentiousness which the Bible forbids. The same is true for snowboarding. Snowboarding is not wrong, but the snowboard culture is at enmity with God's laws and must be shunned by those who desire to please a holy Christ. The same is true for skateboarding.

KENDRICK, GRAHAM

The following is excerpted from an excellent article by Alan Morrison (pastor of the International Baptist Church in Eindhoven, the Netherlands) entitled "The New Style of Worship and the Great Apostasy." [Used by permission, Diakrisis International, Bordeauxlaan 41, Achtse Barrier, 5627 GR Eindhoven, The Netherlands, AM@diakrisis.org (e-mail).] The entire article is available on the Diakrisis web site at http://www.diakrisis.org/articles.htm.

> As a graphic illustration of the kind of "Christianity" which lies behind the new hymnody, consider the following interview with that veteran of the New Style of Worship, Graham Kendrick, conducted by the supremo of the cult-like Jesus Army Fellowship, Noel Stanton:
>
> NS: "What are the landmarks in your life?"
>
> GK: "I remember when I was about five years old my mother reading us a bedtime story which included a simple explanation of the gospel and asking us if we wanted to invite Jesus to forgive our sins. I remember kneeling down by myself and praying. I felt an excitement deep inside me that surprised me. During teenage years I began to examine if it was first hand or second hand".
>
> NS: "You were a rebel?"
>
> GK: "It was the 60s and I tended towards the cynicism of the time. Certainly I was determined to discover more".
>
> NS: "Did that lead to Baptism in the Spirit?"
>
> GK: "I've never been a crisis person but I came out of one particularly drab Christian Union meeting at college thinking 'There must be more than this'. So I set out to seek for more of God. I had met one or two people who seemed to have been profoundly affected by the Holy Spirit. I tracked down a housegroup and knocked on the door, not knowing anybody there, and asked people to pray for me afterwards. It was later that night when I was cleaning my teeth ready to go to bed that I was filled with the Holy Spirit! That was a real watershed in my Christian experience".
>
> NS: "When was this?"
>
> GK: "It was about 1971, when the charismatic renewal movement was in its early days and was quite controversial. Lots of people would warn you off and say it was of the devil! Tongues were as controversial then as the current manifestations of shaking and falling are now" (*Jesus Life Magazine*, from the Jesus Army Fellowship website at http://www.jesus.org.uk/kendrick.html. This interview was also reproduced on "The Graham Kendrick Website" under the

link "Graham's Christianity").

This brief testimony displays all the inadequacies and dead-ends of the modern understanding of what it means to become a Christian. While we are aware that such interviews do not necessarily contain every facet of a person's conversion, the fact remains that — having been asked to identify the landmarks in his Christian life, Mr. Kendrick places the emphasis not on the holiness of God, the demands of the Gospel or the atonement of Christ but on his own feelings and experiences. This is symptomatic of a grave crisis in the modern evangelical scene, and one which has worked its way into churches through the New Style of Worship songs which they sing today. We have no desire to enter into ad hominem contentions, but it is surely valid for us to highlight what we believe to be unhealthy and even dangerous ideas in the testimony of a keynote composer in the New Style of Worship scene, who plainly wields considerable influence over gullible and vulnerable young people.

Firstly, while there is a verbal mention of sin and forgiveness in this interview with Kendrick, there is not the slightest indication of true repentance and an understanding of what sin is all about. Surely this is the most important aspect of a conversion experience, as shown in those examples in the Early Church, when folk were "cut to the heart" (e.g. Acts 2:37). While we do not at all deny that small children can be regenerated and converted — recognising that their understanding of the Gospel will not be identical to that of a university professor — there must surely be a real awareness first of the need for forgiveness and a subsequent desire for repentance, otherwise conversion becomes a mere mental assent.

(It should be pointed out here that there are two equal and opposite errors into which we can fall on the experience of conversion. One is what is known as 'Sandemanianism' — named after Robert Sandeman, 1718-1771, the Scottish minister who first publicly propounded this doctrine — which involves the idea that a person merely needs to give verbal assent to the propositions contained in the Gospel in order to be saved, without any evidence of a heart change or regeneration. The other is what we can call 'Preparationism' — whereby a person is persuaded of the need to enter into a massively overprolonged (or even indefinite) period of intense preparation for conversion, during which he must go through the most oppressive heart-searching rigours, without which he cannot be saved. We must always be sure that our evangelism does not encourage either "easy-believism" or its opposite: bondage-making preparationism. They lie at contrary ends of the spectrum, but both are deadly, conversion-stifling errors.)

Secondly, a child who is genuinely regenerated will surely not subsequently become an adolescent rebel, with a tendency to partake in "the cynicism of the time", as Kendrick puts it. It seems to be taken for granted in so many evangelical churches today that even youngsters who profess Christianity will still go on to be teenage rebels who need to express themselves in rock music, foppish clothes, and the raucous multi-media experiences of the world. But such out-and-out rebellion belongs to the fallen nature and should not be a feature in a believer's life of any age.

Thirdly, in this testimony, there is that typical feature of neo-evangelicalism: the desire for increasingly exciting experiences. Regardless of what Mr. Kendrick says here, he was indeed a "crisis person" who was seeking a "crisis experience". Is there not a link here back to that early prayer of his which engendered "an excitement deep inside me" but which apparently failed to kindle godly sorrow and contrition? The Christian Union meeting, he believed, was not good enough for him. But instead of seeking out some orthodox Christians who promote sound doctrine to point him in the right direction, like so many immature, misguided seekers he goes in search of sensational "pyrotechnics". From the present writer's experience of this kind of complaint, that "particularly drab Christian Union meeting at college" could easily have been made up of godly youngsters singing hymns in the old-style and bowing quietly in prayer before the Lord (without the almost mandatory trance-induced arm-waving and gibberish kind of "tongues-speaking" one finds among most university and college Christian Unions today). This is considered dull and boring in the kind of circles where CCM is extolled, and especially among carnal youngsters who have been processed on the easy-believist conveyor belt of evangelism.

The housegroup scene has always been a pastoral minefield, and if you go down that pathway you are far more likely to wind up in a cult rather than a sound assembly!

Fourthly, the account of being "filled with the Holy Spirit" is decidedly suspect. Christians are certainly instructed to "go on being filled with the Spirit" (Eph. 5:18) throughout their Christian lives; but it is so typical of the sensation-seeking, crisis-loving evangelicals of today to highlight one incident as their supposed "baptism in the Spirit". And is it not strange that what Kendrick describes as "a real watershed" in his Christian experience should occur entirely as an incidental experience while he happened to be "brushing his teeth"? Frankly, we find it hard to credit the fact that in a serious interview, designed to display the testimony of the work of God in his life and his faith in the Son of God, we should read such a flippant narrative. This is entirely in keeping with the superficial nature of the New Style of Worship as a whole; and the question must be asked here: Is it right for churches to worship God from a hymnbook of which almost 10% of the songs were written by a man whose testimony would not even obtain membership for him in our churches? (*Mission Praise* contains 8.5% of Graham Kendrick songs. *Songs of Fellowship* contains 10%.)

Surely there is a clear connection between the truncated "Christianity" of this "conversion" experience, and that which the New Style of Worship is promoting in churches today. This is a plain example of "easy believism", with a subsequent psycho-religious catharsis masquerading as an "infilling of the Spirit". Such phenomena form the undergirding theology which governs the style and content of the New Style of Worship songs, which are deliberately manipulative of a bogus spiritual experience. A person who has had a superficial "conversion" experience will always spend his or her time seeking a more profound "second blessing". Consequently, in place of the simple desire for reverential praise of the Triune God, we find that the search for an ever-greater "high" also becomes the goal of worship. Hence, these songs are often used to bring a person into what is known as an "altered state of consciousness" (Alan Morrison, "The New Style of Worship and the Great Apostasy," Diakrisis International, The Netherlands; the entire article is available on the Diakrisis web site at http://www.diakrisis.org/articles.htm).

KING'S X

The King's X is composed of Doug Pinnick (bass, lead singer), Ty Tabor (guitar, vocals), and Jerry Gaskill (drums, vocals). It was formed in the late 1980s, and though it has not claimed to be a Christian band, some CCM fans have considered it as such.

> "When King's X broke into the music scene a decade ago, its penchant for avoiding cigarettes and alcohol and not cursing during interviews gained the group a Christian following. The trio, however, never considered itself a Christian band" (Brian Aberback, "Onward, Says an Ex-Christian Soldier," *Bergen County Record*, New Jersey, October 2, 1998).

In recent interviews, band spokesman Doug Pinnick leaves no doubt about his spiritual condition and lifestyle.

> "Doug Pinnick has a message for fans who look to him as a paragon of Christian virtue: 'I *WILL* let you down.' The bassist and lead singer of King's X is tired of people expecting him to uphold the beliefs he once espoused. 'People complain that I've changed or let them down because they've seen me drinking or cursing,' Pinnick said recently by phone. ... Following the lead of his grandmother's hellfire-and-brimstone approach to religion, Pinnick embarked on a path of self-torture. 'I was convinced that God made me to destroy me and send me to hell,' said Pinnick. A turning point came four years ago. 'At that time I felt like, "What am I doing? I feel like I live in hell [already]."' Pinnick had had enough. 'I said to myself, 'Stop the madness.' Pinnick still believes in the basic tenets of Christianity such as the Ten Commandments, but no longer considers himself a devout follower" (Ibid.).

It sounds like Pinnick has never understood the Gospel of the grace of Jesus Christ, that he looked upon Christianity as some sort of works religion whereby he was forced to earn God's favor by his own efforts. It appears that he was attempting by his own self will to be religious, and he finally gave up the effort and gave himself over to licentiousness. We pray he will come to understand that true Christianity is not merely a list of dos and don'ts but a personal and living relationship with God through faith in Jesus Christ. The basic tenet of Christianity is not the Ten Commandments but the Cross of Jesus Christ and His lovely grace!

KNAPP, JENNIFER

Jennifer Knapp's first album, *Kansas*, appeared in 1998 and was very popular. At her web site, she describes the album as "just a reflection of all the music I've grown up listening to. It's what has really spoken to my heart, musically." In 1999 she is scheduled for a 60-city tour with dc Talk. Though she plays acoustic guitar and some folk stylings, on tour she uses an "aggressive three-piece band" that gives her songs "a much more hard-edged tenor" and "at times drowned out her passionate vocals" (*CCM Magazine*, April 1999, p. 55).

Jennifer's music, like much of CCM, is oriented toward self and feeling. It presents a vague religiosity instead of a clear biblical gospel. For example, in the song "Whole Again" from *Kansas* she sings:

> "Daddy, daddy do you miss me. The way I crawled upon your knee. Those childish games of hide and seek seem a million miles away. Am I lost in some illusion. or am I what you thought I'd be. Now it seems I've found myself in need to be forgiven. Is there still room upon that knee? If I give my Life if I lay it down can you turn this Life around, can I be made clean by this offering of my soul. Can I be made whole again? Have I labored all for nothing. Trying to make it on my own. Fear to reach out to the hand of one who understands me say I'd rather be here all alone. It's all my fault I sit and wallow in seclusion. As if I had no hope at all, I guess truth becomes you I have seen it all in motion that Pride comes before the fall. Can I offer up this simple prayer. Pray it finds a simple ear. A scratch in your infinite time. Not withstanding my failings not withstanding my crime!" (Jennifer Knapp, "Whole Again," *Kansas*).

What does this song mean? It is impossible to know. Is it about her earthly father or is it about God or both? It is unclear. What does she mean by being made clean by the offering of her soul? She asks questions ("Can I be made whole again") but does not answer them in a biblical fashion. She prays to be accepted to God "not withstanding my failings and my crime" but she does not explain that this can only happen through the blood of Jesus Christ.

Most of her songs are like this. Consider the words to "His Grace Is Sufficient"—

> "I've exhausted every possible solution, I've tried every last game there is to play. In this search for the Christ like perfection I'm convinced I've only left my God ashamed. I cry I wonder can he hear my despair. Afraid to lift my hands afraid he doesn't care. And if he answers and I fall again can I still be his daughter can I still depend on him. When I'm down search every mistake, looking for new regrets. Sometimes I forget, I forget that his grace is sufficient for me. That it's deeper and wider than I can conceive. His Grace is sufficient for me. My convictions seem to fade with desperation, my hope declines with each and every tear. My sin an anchor and this grace just an illusion. The gavels heavy and justice is near. Up comes the light and finds the stains on my hands. Up comes my pride, I hide, I know he won't understand. Cause it's deeper than deep and it's wider then wide. Why did I ever doubt now I'm dying inside. (chorus). His Grace is sufficient!" (Jennifer Knapp, "His Grace Is Sufficient," *Kansas*).

This song is allegedly about God's grace but there is absolutely nothing clear about what God's grace is and how it is obtained. The listener is left with no biblical gospel. A Hindu or a New Ager or a Muslim could sing this song to their false gods because it does not have enough biblical content to define the truth.

One of the songs on Knapp's *Kansas* album does give a plainer message. The final words to the song "Trinity" are as follows—

> "Raise your hands sing praises to the Lord. He's the King and he'll reign forevermore. He died on the cross of Calvary. He died to save a wretch like me!"

The tiny gospel message in this song cannot make up for all of the vagueness and unscriptural thinking that permeates most of her songs, though.

In light of the lack of biblical clarity in her music, it is no surprise that Jennifer Knapp joined other CCM groups and hundreds of thousands of Catholics to welcome Pope John Paul II to the States in January 1999. Featured at a Catholic youth rally connected with the Pope's visit, were Knapp, dc Talk, Audio Adrenaline, Rebecca St. James, The W's, and the Supertones (*CCM Magazine*, April 1999, p. 12). Each attendee received a rosary with instructions about how to pray to Mary. The music and philosophy of most influential CCM groups does not refute Catholic doctrine.

KRIPPAYNE, SCOTT

In 1997 Scott Krippayne joined Roman Catholic Kathy Troccoli and 40 other CCM artists to record *Love One Another*, a song with an ecumenical theme: "Christians from all denominations demonstrating their common love for Christ and each other." The song talks about tearing down the walls of denominational division. The broad range of participants who joined Kathy Troccoli in recording "Love One Another" demonstrates the ecumenical agenda of Contemporary Christian Music. The song witnessed Catholics, Pentecostals, Baptists, etc., yoked together to call for Christian unity.

LANGDON, DANNY

The *National Catholic Register* for March 8-14, 1998, listed Danny Langdon as a Catholic musician.

LEFEVRE, MYLON

Mylon LeFevre (c.1948-) grew up in a family which performed Southern gospel. He left the family group in the 1960s over "group tensions and a dispute about his sideburns" (*CCM Magazine*, July 1998, p. 76). His music has had a rebellious character ever since. He embarked on a rock & roll career and released his first solo album in 1970. It was supposed to be a "Christian" rock album, but LeFevre admits that he and his fellow band members smoked marijuana together and he soon fell away from church (John W. Styll, "Mylon LeFevre: The Solid Rocker," *CCM Magazine*, March 1986). After performing with some of the most famous rock groups, such as The Who, the Rolling Stones, and Little Richard, and becoming a slave to drugs, LeFevre made a recommitment to Jesus Christ in 1980. (He had been recording and performing Christian music with Phil Keaggy and others since 1976.) In the 1980s he formed the "Christian rock" group Broken Heart, and they released their first album, *Brand New Start*, in 1982. His 1985 album was the absurd and unscriptural *Sheep in Wolves Clothing*. In 1992 he had a heart attack and his health problems forced the retirement of Broken Heart.

LeFevre is an elder in the Mt. Param Pentecostal Church (Church of God, Cleveland, Tennessee) near Atlanta.

LeFevre has a zeal to preach Christ to those who attend his concerts, and thousands have made professions of faith of some sort. He claims that he writes songs with fasting and prayer (*Broken Heart News*, cited in *The Contemporary Christian Music Debate*, p. 189). By 1989 LeFevre claimed that 160,000 young people had signed decision cards at his concerts (Jerry Wilson, "Rock Evangelist for the 90s," *CCM Magazine*, July 1990, p. 30).

LeFevre very aggressively promotes a non-judgmental philosophy: "He doesn't think Christians should condemn others. 'That happened to me as a child, and it's not right. ... We don't holler at people and we don't shake Bibles at them. We just bring the love

of Jesus to them'" (*Seattle Post-Intelligencer*, Seattle, Washington, Oct. 11, 1984).
LeFevre's Pentecostal doctrine is evident by the following statement: "If you come to our concerts, you'll find people getting born again, people getting baptized in the Holy Spirit, people getting healed of physical ailments" (Mylon LeFevre, *Ministries Today*, January-February 1987, p. 30).

As noted previously, one of LeFevre's videos was called "Sheep in Wolves' Clothing." The Lord Jesus Christ warned that false teachers are wolves in sheep's clothing, but Christian rockers claim to be sheep in wolves' clothing! What incredible confusion.

LeFevre's 1986 album, *Look Up*, was designed for the pop rock market and contains lyrics which are supposed to present a Christian message, but in typically abstract CCM style:

> "But the album we made for Epic [*Look Up*] is more subtle and still has the Christian message. But it is not so religious sounding. We've been careful to avoid any religious terminology in this record that would turn people off" (LeFevre, cited by Jeff Godwin, *What's Wrong with Christian Rock?*, p. 124).
>
> "It's an anointed record and it's got a good message, but it's very shallow. We really avoided certain words and phrases, you know" (LeFevre, cited by John Styll, *CCM Magazine*, March 1986).

LeFevre promotes the false idea that music is neutral and that any music can be used to glorify God as long as the performer is sincere:

> "Music is not good or evil because of the formation of the notes or the structure of the beat. Music is good because the heart of the person playing it is innocently and sincerely giving praise to our God" (Mylon LeFevre, cited by Jeff Godwin, *What's Wrong with Christian Rock?*, p. 122).
>
> "Rock 'n' roll is not evil. Rock 'n' roll is rock 'n' roll. It's a form of music" (LeFevre, cited by John Styll, *CCM Magazine*, March 1986).

Any bar owner knows that music is not neutral. Why does the owner of a tavern or a night club choose a certain kind of music? Because that type of music creates the right atmosphere to promote the fleshly activities of that establishment. If a tavern owner attempted to play traditional hymns, he would create an entirely different atmosphere which would not be conducive for the type of recreation his patrons are engaged in.

In 1997 well-known Pentecostal leader David Wilkerson (of *Cross & Switchblade* fame) identified LeFevre's music as demonic. Wilkerson's newsletter in August of that year described Wilkerson's impressions while attending a concert:

"At first, I couldn't believe what I was seeing on stage. Suddenly I was on the ground, on my back, weeping and sobbing and groaning in the Spirit. I sat up and took another look at the stage. I WAS HORRIFIED BY WHAT I SAW IN THE SPIRIT! I SAW DEMONIC IMAGES RISING FROM THAT STAGE! I HEARD SATAN LAUGHING! (Wilkerson's emphasis) It was an overt manifestation of Satan — worse than anything I've ever seen on the streets of New York."

LEVITICUS

The following is a description of Leviticus performing at a bar in Omaha, Nebraska: "Leviticus came out and rocked the place. What was amazing is that people flooded the dance floor, after the second song. This was hard-driving Christian heavy metal from Sweden!" (*Heaven's Metal Magazine*, Number 18, p. 24).

LIBERATED WAILING WALL

The Liberated Wailing Wall is a group of Christian Jews associated with the Jews for Jesus organization. They are very charismatic and ecumenical and appear in a wide variety of denominational forums. The Liberated Wailing Wall appeared at Morris Cerullo's Deeper Life Conference in 1975. One of the featured speakers was Catholic priest Michael Manning. In 1987 the Liberated Wailing Wall joined hands with 20,000 Roman Catholics and with members of 40 other denominations to participate in New Orleans '87. There was a Catholic mass every morning during the conference, and the final message was delivered by Catholic priest Tom Forrest. In February and March 1994, the Liberated Wailing Wall were scheduled to perform at First Coast Baptist Church in Jacksonville, Florida; at Peace Lutheran Church, Palm Bay, Florida; at Christ United Methodist Church, Venice, Florida; and at the First Broad Street Methodist Church in Kingsport, Tennessee.

LIFEHOUSE

Lifehouse is currently composed of Jason Wade, Sergio Andrade, and Rick Woolstenhulme. They got their start at the Malibu Vineyard Church in Malibu, California. Wade grew up in a missionary home, but his parents were divorced when he was 12, and he later fell in love with grunge music. He says Kurt Cobain was "a major influence." Wade and Andrade formed a "trashy, just-no-good garage band" in high school. At the same time they were part of a charismatic youth group at the Malibu Vineyard Church. They started getting a name playing Friday night rock concerts at the church, featuring a light show and smoke machines.

Lifehouse doesn't like to be called a Christian band. Wade says, "I don't even like the word religion. My music is spiritually based, but we don't want to be labeled as a 'Christian band,' because all of a sudden people's walls come up and they won't listen to your music and what you have to say" (David Wild, "The Rock & Roll Gospel according to Lifehouse," *Rolling Stone* magazine, June 7, 2001, http://www.rollingstone.com/news/newsarticle.asp?nid=13983&cf=13773270).

Lifehouse toured as a second stage opener with the immoral Pearl Jam rock band in 2000.

The members of Lifehouse hold the non-judgmental philosophy that is typical of CCM in general. Jason Wade of Lifehouse says, "I think we have a positive message of hope. WE'RE NOT TRYING TO BLATANTLY PREACH. It all comes down to love" (David Wild, Rolling Stone magazine, Ibid.).

LISTER, HOVIE

Hovie Lister (1926-) is one of the most renowned Southern gospel musicians. He was raised in a Holiness Baptist Church, which has a doctrine of sanctification more akin to Nazarene and Wesleyan Methodist than to traditional Baptist. As a teen he attended a music school operated by the Stamps-Baxter Music Company and determined to be in a prosperous gospel quartet. By 1948 he formed the Statesmen (there were actually five in the group, a vocal quartet and Lister at the piano), which quickly became one of the most famous of all Southern gospel groups. For 12 years, during the 1950s and '60s, Lister pastored a Southern Baptist church in Marietta, Georgia, while continuing with his music career.

Hovie Lister was one of Elvis Presley's favorite gospel singers.

Lister, at least at one point in his career, did not believe it was right for gospel singers to offer their services to the world to sing secular music. In 1954, following their successful appearance on the popular Authur Godfrey Talent Scouts program, the Statesmen turned down lucrative offers by secular corporations (Taylor, *Happy Rhythms*, p. 46). Lister did much, though, in his own way to bring worldly methods and sounds into church music. (This does mean, of course, that the Statesmen sang ONLY jazzy music. Some of their numbers were nice renditions of good Christian music. An example was the beautiful "What a Savior," featuring lyric tenor Rosie Rozell.) The flamboyant Lister popularized an entertainment-oriented, jazzy gospel music presentation. Lister and the Statesmen went so far beyond that which was traditionally acceptable in Christian music in the middle of this century that some Christian radio stations would not play their music. In fact, some stations broke their records in protest! This occurred in 1955 when they recorded some gospel songs with a "New Orleans jazz flavor." The instrumental group which backed the Statesmen on the album included country guitarist Chet Atkins, Ernie Newton on the stand-up bass guitar, and Farris Coursey on drums. This was essentially a country-rock band. (The Statesmen thus pioneered the CCM practice of using unsaved musicians on their recordings.) Hovie Lister played the boogie-woogie piano. One preacher who protested called it "stripping music" (Taylor, p. 55).

Though the Statesmen did not accept contracts to move entirely into the secular music field, they did sell their services to the Nabisco Company in the 1950s. Hovie became their spokesman. He also emceed for Nabisco commercials and the group performed on the Nabisco television show. "In their personal appearances, the Statesmen participated in a complete merchandising campaign on behalf of their sponsor..." (Taylor, p. 53). One photo in David Taylor's history of the Statesmen shows the group performing in front of a large wall mural of a woman dressed in a short skirt as "the Sweetheart of the South" for Nabisco Vanilla Wafers. This was part of Nabisco's advertising campaign surrounding the Statesmen. For their work with Nabisco the group recorded music with Wade Creager's dance orchestra at the Biltmore Hotel in Atlanta.

Many preachers condemned the Statesmen's showmanship and bluesy rhythms and their yokes with the world through their Nabisco television programs, movie soundtracks, and pop market recordings for RCA (which were recorded with the accompaniment of unsaved musicians). *Moody Monthly* ran an article which called the Statesmen "a sideshow," comparing them to a carnival attraction. A Birmingham church warned that "they've simply jazzed up religious songs to be-bop rhythms for a fast buck." A *Saturday Evening Post* article, June 23, 1956, about the Statesmen noted that "most churchmen regard gospel singing in this commercial dress with disfavor."

The group was called the "Sensational Statesmen" because of their energetic showmanship. They danced and pranced, even jumped on top of the piano. Jake Hester said, "When I was on top of the piano bench, Hovie was on top of the piano." A writer for *Billboard* magazine described their performance as "electrifying." Recalling the first time he saw the Statesmen in Nashville, Bill Gaither says, "The crowd just went crazy when they came on!" In his history of Southern gospel, Gaither admits that Hovie Lister's "approach was loud, fast, swingy, and pop" and that "he would do whatever it took to get the loudest applause, the biggest laugh" (Bill Gaither, *Homecoming*, p. 133). A *Time* magazine article about the Southern gospel quartets of the 1950s described their concerts as "swinging from rowdy boogie to fervent waltzes, all in praise of the Lord."

The Statesmen's bass singer, Jim "Big Chief" Wetherington, moved his legs in ways strangely reminiscent of how Elvis moved to rock & roll. Jake Hess, another member of the original Statesmen, noted: "He went about as far as you could go in gospel music.

The women would jump up, just like they do for pop shows" (Peter Guralnick, *Last Train for Memphis*, p. 48). Rock historian Peter Guralnick observes that "preachers frequently objected to the lewd movements." Some conservative Christian radio stations broke Statesmen records on the air to protest their jazzy music.

Note the following description of the Statesmen by rock & roll researcher Steve Turner:

> "White quartet singing had developed in the 1920s ... they began to develop showmanship and gimmicks during the 1940s. ... Hovie Lister, a dashing young man with long, dark wavy hair and an Errol Flynn mustache, LOVED TO SHAKE IT ALL UP FOR THE LORD. He joined with Crumpler and Jake Hess to form the Statesmen Quartet, which was to become one of the first supergroups of white gospel, catapulting the music to commercial acceptability and SETTING THE STYLE FOR EMERGENT ROCK 'N' ROLLERS BRED ON HOLY MUSIC.
>
> "Although much was made of the evils of dancing, show business, jukeboxes and television, THE SUCCESS OF THE GOSPEL QUARTETS WAS LARGELY DUE TO THEIR PRESENTING MUCH OF THE SAME GLOSS AND EXCITEMENT in an acceptable context. The songs were about loving your neighbor, being holy and not giving in to 'modern religion,' but THE PERFORMANCES DREW FROM POP, BLUES, COUNTRY, RAGTIME AND JAZZ. ...
>
> "Don Butler, now director of archives for the Nashville-based Gospel Music Association, was the Statesmen Quartet's manager during the 1950s. 'They were sensational,' he remembers. 'Hovie Lister had no peer in showmanship. He created a tremendous rapport with the audience. HE COULD TURN THEIR EMOTIONS ON AND OFF JUST LIKE THAT. They also had highly polished harmonies and arrangements. HOVIE WOULD JUMP ONTO A PIANO AND SHAKE HIS LONG BLACK HAIR INTO HIS FACE WHILE THE REST OF THE GROUP DANCED ON STAGE. They were the first quartet to use four individual microphones. Before that everyone had gathered around one mike'" (emphasis added) (Steve Turner, *Hungry for Heaven*, pp. 29-31).

Of the group's objective Lister said: "We went out to have fun. We went out there fully aware that we had a goal to reach and that was to entertain those people. And we were going to do it whatever it took. If it meant Jake getting up on the piano bench, we did it" (Taylor, p. 35). Speaking with the *Saturday Evening Post* in the mid-1950s, Lister said:

> "If it takes shaking my hair down, beating a piano like Liberace or Piano Red to keep those young people out of beer joints and the rear seats of automobiles, I'll do it. The devil's got his kind of entertainment. We've got ours. They criticize me, say I'm too lively for religion, but I get results. That's what counts" (Furman Bisher, "They Put Rhythm in Religion," *Saturday Evening*

Post, June 23, 1956).

Lister's philosophy was pragmatism; whatever works is right. This is exactly the same New Evangelical philosophy which permeates the Contemporary Christian Music field today. Hovie Lister and the Statesmen were forerunners to CCM. God has not instructed us to do whatever "gets results," but to obey His Word regardless of the results. The sole authority for faith and practice is the Bible. If it is Scriptural it is right; if it is not Scriptural, it is wrong, regardless of how well it appears to work. God's Word plainly forbids His people to love the world. It is therefore impossible to please God by adapting the things of the world to the service of Christ. Liberace was a homosexual entertainer who helped corrupt the morals of America. I believe it is a serious error to adopt his sensual, worldly ways to Gospel music. Where does God's Word encourage us to copy the world? To be holy, means to be set apart from and different from the world. Nowhere do we see the Lord Jesus Christ or the Apostles entertaining people in the name of the ministry. We do not see them putting on some sort of worldly show to draw a crowd. We do not see them adapting themselves to the spirit of the age. We do not see them attempting to manipulate people by worldly means. The Apostle Paul plainly stated that he depended solely upon the power of the Holy Spirit. "For I determined not to know any thing among you, save Jesus Christ, and him crucified. And I was with you in weakness, and in fear, and in much trembling. And my speech and my preaching was not with enticing words of man's wisdom, but in demonstration of the Spirit and of power: That your faith should not stand in the wisdom of men, but in the power of God" (1 Corinthians 2:2-5).

Some of the Statesmen Quartet's music was brought over from the swinging black gospel. "So many of their early hits began to stray away some from the southern, singing convention style—the music that was coming out of Stamps-Baxter—and basically were coming out of the black tradition" (Taylor, *Happy Rhythms*, p. 32).

In one of their early hits, *Happy Rhythm* (1950), the Statesmen Quartet actually used the phrase rock and roll to describe what they were doing! "There's a happy rhythm keeps a-rockin' and a-rollin'." This was set to a "rollicking, boogie setting" (Taylor, p. 34). Their 1961 album contained the song "God Is God," "featuring a rockabilly Chet Atkins guitar solo which was similar to early Elvis Presley releases" (Taylor, p. 86).

In the 1950s, the Statesmen represented the Nabisco company nationally through a television program and with their concert appearances. Lister was Nabiso's pitch man, and "in their personal appearances, the Statesmen participated in a complete merchandising campaign on behalf of their sponsor." They sang some secular songs on the program and were backed up by secular musicians, such as country guitarist Chet Atkins. They also recorded soundtracks with Wade Creager's nine-piece dance orchestra from

Atlanta's Biltmore Hotel. In 1953 the Statesmen sang at the funeral of country music legend Hank Williams, who died at age 29 from a life of drug and alcohol abuse.

In the 1970s, the Statesmen, with many personnel changes but with Hovie Lister still at the helm, added more contemporary numbers to their already somewhat jazzed up traditional fare. For example, they recorded songs by Christian rockers Larry Norman ("Sweet Song of Salvation") and Mylon LeFevre ("You're on His Mind"). They even recorded Simon and Garfunkel's "Bridge over Troubled Water," which is not a Christian song. By 1973 two members of the group, Sherrill Nielsen and Tim Baty, sported shoulder length hair. The group had grown to six members with the addition of bass guitarist Baty.

Three of the Statesmen died young. The Statesmen's first tenor, Bobby Strickland, was killed in a car accident at age 33. Denver Crumpler died in 1958 at age 44 of a heart attack. Jim "Big Chief" Wetherington died in 1973 at age 51 of a heart attack. Cat Freeman left the group in 1958 because of a divorce and other reasons.

In the 1980s Hovie Lister joined Rosie Rozell, Jake Hess, J.D. Sumner, and James Blackwood to form Masters V. They performed from 1981 to 1988. By then Sumner was the sole remaining original member, and he renamed the group J.D. Sumner and the Stamps.

In the 1990s Hovie Lister has worked closely with Bill Gaither. Gaither produced a "Bill Gaither Remembers The Statesmen" video in 1990. Three of the old Statesmen were present: Hovie Lister, Jake Hess, and Jim Hill. The show was telecast nationally on Pat Robertson's ecumenical-charismatic *700 Club*. Following this, Gaither organized a reunited Statesmen Quartet called the New Statesmen. They debuted in January 1992 and toured for a year and a half. Jake Hess retired from the road in June 1993. In September 1993 Lister had surgery for throat cancer, but he began singing again the following year.

Hovie Lister has moved farther and farther into the field of secular music. He is on the board of directors for the Georgia Music Hall of Fame, which honors all sorts of worldly musicians, including rock & rollers. He is a Governor on the Board of Directors of the Atlanta Chapter of the NARAS, which bestows the worldly Grammy Awards to recording artists.

See the chapter on "Southern Gospel Music" for more information about the Statesmen.

LITTLE RICHARD

Richard Wayne Penniman (1935-), known by his rock & roll name Little Richard, is one of the founders of modern rock music. He was among the first ten inductees into the Rock and Roll Hall of Fame in 1986. He grew up in a Seventh-day Adventist family and learned to play the piano and sing at church. When he was 13, his father (who ran bootleg whiskey) kicked him out of the house because of his bi-sexuality and rebellion. He tried to play and sing in some Baptist churches but was kicked out for screaming the hymns. By 1950 Little Richard was a homosexual "drag queen," wearing dresses and make-up. He was arrested at least twice for lewd conduct. In 1955 he had his first big hit, "Tutti Frutti."

Little Richard continues to dress somewhat in a feminine fashion and use women's makeup, though he is married and is the father of children. In his 1984 authorized biography, *The Life and Times of Little Richard* by Charles White, Little Richard was quoted as saying: "Homosexuality is contagious. It's not something you're born with."

Little Richard is a classic case of double mindedness (James 1:5-8; 4:7-9). He has been in and out of rock as well as in and out of religion. In 1957 he quit his successful rock career, claiming he had been warned of his own damnation in a vision. He attended Oakwood College in Huntsville, Alabama, and was ordained a minister in the Church of God of the Ten Commandments. In 1964 he returned to recording and performing rock music. In the mid-1970s he was addicted to a wide variety of illegal drugs. In the late 1970s he again renounced rock, drugs, and homosexuality and once more began preaching and singing gospel music, this time for the Universal Remnant Church of God. In 1985 he launched another comeback in the rock world.

Little Richard has testified that rock music is demonic:

> "My true belief about Rock 'n' Roll—and there have been a lot of phrases attributed to me over the years—is this: I believe this kind of music is demonic. ... A lot of the beats in music today are taken from voodoo, from the voodoo drums. If you study music in rhythms, like I have, you'll see that is true ... I believe that kind of music is driving people from Christ. It is contagious" (Little Richard, quoted by Charles White, *The Life and Times of Little Richard*, p. 197).

Little Richard's theology is a homogenous mixture of Bible and New Age. In 1985 he summarized his views: "I can't go to a Bible study. Most of my inspiration comes directly from God's Spirit. ... There are good people in all churches. Some Buddhists really love God. Some Jehovah's Witnesses, too. It doesn't matter what church you belong to! Only God can read a man's heart" (*Contemporary Christian Music Magazine*,

February 1985, p. 2).

LIVGREN, KERRY

Kerry Livgren (c.1951-) was the lead guitarist/songwriter for the superstar secular rock band Kansas, which was formed in 1970. He was converted to Christianity in July 1979 and began incorporating some rather nebulous Christian lyrics into Kansas' music. Kansas' lead singer, Steve Walsh, left the band in 1981 to begin a solo career. John Elefante, who had become a Christian one year earlier, took Walsh's place and performed with Kansas for three years until it disbanded in 1983. (The group was reconstituted in 1986 by Walsh, with three original and some new members, and continues to tour on the oldies circuits and record albums.)

In 1980 Kerry Livgren released his first solo album, *Seeds of Change*, which featured the occultic Ronnie James Dio, David Pack of Ambrosia, drummer Barriemore Barlowe of the antichrist rock group Jethro Tull, among others.

After leaving Kansas, Livgren and Kansas bassist Dave Hope, who had also received Christ during his years with Kansas, went on to form the Christian rock group AD. Livgren and Hope were joined by vocalists Michael Gleason and Warren Ham and by drummer Dennis Holt. The group toured from 1983 to 1985, released four albums, and disbanded in 1986. Hope moved to Destin, Florida, after the disbanding of AD and became a youth leader in the charismatic St. Andrews by the Sea Episcopal Church.

Livgren pursued a solo career in producing and writing. In 1989 Livgren won a Dove Award for Instrumental Album of the Year for his album, *One of Several Possible Musiks*. In the mid-1990s Livgren formed his own independent label, Numavox (which means voice of the spirit), as well as a new recording group, Corps de Pneuma (Army of Spirits).

In 1990-1991 Livgren re-united with Kansas for a European and then a domestic tour, and he has maintained a relationship with the group since then. "It has grown into a working relationship in which I participate in some Kansas-related activities, writing for the band, etc." Livgren performed on Kansas' 1992 album, *Live at the Whiskey*. Livgren also rejoined Kansas for a reunion album in 2000, "Somewhere to Elsewhere." Livgren wrote the songs and appeared in at least one of the concerts to advertise the album.

Livgren describes his conversion to Christianity in intellectual terms:

> "I became a believing Christian in the summer of 1979 during the Monolith tour. It was, in many ways, a process of elimination for me, as I had gone

through most of the world's belief systems, from philosophy to Eastern thought. Jeff Pollard, of Louisiana's LeRoux, was on the tour with us. We engaged in a series of friendly theological debates during which I became convinced of the historical and spiritual truths about Jesus Christ. I remain convinced 17 years later" (Don Palmer, Kerry Livgren Interview, *AOR Classics*, a British magazine, April 1996).

During his years in the Atlanta area, Livgren started the Grace Fellowship Church in his living room and it has grown into a large congregation. He moved back to his home state of Kansas in 1993.

At the Kerry Livgren/Numavox web site is a detailed Bible study defending the Deity of Jesus Christ.

The meaning of Livgren's music is rarely plain. He himself describes it as "cryptic" (*Terry Livgren Getting Electric*, http://placetobe.org/cmp/artists/index.html). He hides Bible truths behind a veil of ambiguity. His 1994 album, *When Things Get Electric*, contains 13 songs, not one of which mentions the name of Christ or contains a clear biblical message. All are vague and strange. Consider, for example, the lyrics to the title song of this album:

> "See the fire streak through the sky/ Children watching and wondering why/ Blameless blood cries from the ground/ Justice sleeping, open your ears to the sound/ Moving waves cover the Earth/ Like a woman who's soon giving birth/ Feel the tension taking it's form/ As dark clouds gather, run for the eye of the storm.
>
> Chorus: "When things get electric, when everything's done/ We'll stand in the open and shine (like the sun)/ This moment's so fleeting, the blink of an eye/ When things get electric, we're all gonna fly/ (it's sweet by and by)" (Kerry Livgren, "When Things Get Electric").

What does this song mean? It could be referring to the coming of Christ, but it could mean many other things, as well, because the meaning is not clear. Without clear meaning there can be no salvation and no Christian growth. The Spirit of God works through the understanding. The Apostle Paul said, "I will sing with the spirit, and I will sing with the understanding also" (1 Corinthians 14:15).

This is an hour of incredible spiritual confusion. False christs and false gospels abound. Unless the meaning of a religious or spiritual message is absolutely clear, it leaves room for demonic error and delusion.

Livgren claims that many people have been saved through a song he wrote *prior to his conversion*:

> "More people have been led to Christ with [the Kansas megahit *Dust in the Wind*] than with everything else I've ever written. Not only did that song not mention Jesus, but I was not a Christian at the time. It just happened to be a truth that the song emphasized" (Kerry Livgren, *CCM Magazine*, Feb. 1989, p. 8).

Note the lyrics to *Dust in the Wind*.

> "I close my eyes only for a moment and the moment's gone/ All my dreams pass before my eyes a curiosity/ Dust in the wind/ All we are is dust in the wind/ Same old song, just a drop of water in an endless sea/ All we do crumbles to the ground though we refuse to see/ Dust in the wind/ All we are is dust in the wind/ Don't hang on; nothing lasts forever but the earth and sky/ It slips away and all your money won't another minute buy/ Dust in the wind/ All we are is dust in the wind" ("Dust in the Wind," Kansas, 1977).

This song is performed to an acoustic guitar and orchestral strings background, with some non-obtrusive bongo drums toward the end. The message speaks of the vanity and brevity of life, but there is no Gospel in it. How is it possible that many people have been saved through this song?

LOVE SONG

The band Love Song was formed by members of Chuck Smith's Calvary Chapel in California in the early 1970s. It was composed of Chuck Girard, Tom Coomes, Fred Field, and Jay Truax. Prior to this Girard had sung in the secular rock groups The Castells and the Hondells. Love Song recorded their namesake album in 1972 and *Final Touch* in 1974. The title song to their 1972 album became a No. 1 single in the Philippines.

Their song "Little Country Church" described the changes which occur when churches move from traditional to contemporary worship styles.

> "Preacher isn't talkin' 'bout religion no more/ He just wants to praise the Lord/ People aren't as stuffy as they were before/ They just want to praise the Lord."

In other words, pastors no longer worry about such "stuffy" things as how people live. This song promotes the non-judgmentalism philosophy of Contemporary Christian Music. The Apostles were very concerned about religious things! Their epistles are filled with instruction about sound Christian religion. They said true religion is "To visit the fatherless and widows in their affliction, and to keep himself unspotted from the world" (James 1:27). Any preacher that is faithful to God will be "talking about" true Bible religion.

Following the lead of Calvary Chapel philosophy, Love Song was very ecumenical. For example, in 1972 they performed at a "Jesus Joy Solid Rock Gathering," a Labor Day concert in Madison Square Garden. Among the speakers was Catholic priest Jack Sutton and radical leftist Tom Skinner.

Love Song broke up in the mid-1970s, but the members continue to be influential in Contemporary Christian Music. Tom Coomes, for example, has been an integral part of Maranatha! Music. He also leads worship teams for Billy and Franklin Graham ministries and for Promise Keepers.

LOWRY, MARK

Singer/comedian Mark Lowry (1958-) has been performing music professionally since age 10, when he appeared at the International Song Festival in Memphis (now called the National Quartet Convention) and was given a recording contract soon thereafter. He recorded two albums, including one with the London Symphony Orchestra. In addition to his solo work, he sings with the Gaither Quartet. He grew up in a Baptist home and played in theaters around Houston.

> "My dad would let me be in the plays, but he wouldn't let me dance 'cause we were Baptist. [The cast] would dance around me, but I couldn't do it" (Melissa Riddle, "Funny Face," interview with Mark Lowry, *CCM Magazine*, May 1996).

Lowry attended Jerry Falwell's Liberty University and describes the early part of his career:

> "I started honing my craft in independent, fundamental, legalistic, wonderful and-I-thank-God-for-them Baptists churches—not all legalistic, I take that back—but I wore my suits and ties and my Jerry Falwell haircut..." (Ibid.).

That was before Falwell became ecumenical and began to support Christian rock music, etc. In typical Contemporary Christian Music style, Mark Lowry labels standards and ecclesiastical separation "legalism" —

> "Legalism is as sickening today as it was 2000 years ago. It's just wrong. On my new video [*Remotely Controlled*], that's one thing I'm tryin' to take a whack at. Legalism as I know it. And I thank God for the churches I grew up in 'cause that's where I found Christ, but there was a lot of baggage there. It's true of every church. God is probably doing something in most of them. Some people need a charismatic experience. Some need a Calvinist doctrine. And just about the time I think I've got God put in my box, just about the time I've

> got Him figured out, He's over there loving someone I wouldn't be seen with, working through someone I wouldn't associate with. I tell people at my concerts, 'Isn't that somethin'? We've got Catholics, Presbyterians, Episcopalians, Baptists, and Pentecostals all under one roof! And you know what? Somebody's wrong!' That's why eternity is gonna last so long. God's gotta straighten us out" (Ibid.).

Lowry is correct in observing that there is a right and wrong when it comes to doctrine, but when he claims that God will straighten it all out in Heaven and implies that doctrine should not be divisive in this present world, he is ignoring the Bible's warning about false gospels. Paul warned of false christs, false spirits, and false gospels (2 Cor. 11:1-4). The Word of God cautions that those who follow a false gospel are cursed (Galatians 1). It is impossible, therefore, that all of those mentioned by Lowry will be heaven in the first place. Many of those mentioned follow a sacramental faith-works gospel. Many liberals in Protestant denominations are following a universalistic "gospel" of the Fatherhood of God or a social gospel or a golden rule gospel. When Lowry says doctrinal confusion will be straightened out in Heaven, he is also ignoring the fact that it is the Christian's job to defend sound Bible doctrine (Jude 3) and to separate from false doctrine (Romans 16:17). The preacher is not to allow any false doctrine whatsoever (1 Timothy 1:3).

Lowry continues his tirade against legalism:

> "Preachers keep giving people a list of rules instead of 'Love the Lord with all your heart, then do as you please'—because if you love the Lord your God with all your heart, what you do is gonna please God. It's easier to say 'don't do this, don't do that, do this, and do that,' but you end up a Pharisee. They're taking the easy way out. Man has always loved the law more than grace" (Lowry, Ibid.).

This sounds great, but if preaching the love of God is enough why are the New Testament epistles filled with specific commandments? Lowry's tirade against "legalism" is a smokescreen for his rebellion against Bible-believing, fundamentalist Christianity. To compare fundamentalists to Pharisees, as is so popular with the ecumenical crowd, is a slander. The Pharisee's problem was his self-righteous pride and rejection of God's salvation in Jesus Christ. The Bible-believing fundamentalists that I know are not self-righteous; they know and acknowledge readily that they have no righteousness apart from Jesus Christ. The Pharisees rejected the grace of Christ, whereas the fundamentalist exalts the grace of Christ. Legalism is replacing the grace of Christ with works salvation, as we see in the book of Galatians. Many of the denominations have done this, including the Roman Catholic Church, but this is not what the fundamentalist does. He teaches that salvation is by grace alone through faith alone by Christ alone and that works follow as the evidence of salvation. Attempting to take all of the Lord's commandments seriously and apply them to every area of life is not legalism; it is obedience.

Lowry's ecumenical, positive-only philosophy is evident in his attitude toward preaching on Hell: "I also don't believe in telling people to come to Christ because of hell, in scaring people. When we do, we wind up with just another religious person. But if they come to Christ because no one has ever loved them like that before.... That's the bottom line. Nobody's ever loved you like that before" (Ibid.).

The Lord Jesus Christ preached more on Hell than He did on Heaven. Consider His sermon in Mark 9:

> "And if thy hand offend thee, cut it off: it is better for thee to enter into life maimed, than having two hands to go into hell, into the fire that never shall be quenched: Where their worm dieth not, and the fire is not quenched. And if thy foot offend thee, cut it off: it is better for thee to enter halt into life, than having two feet to be cast into hell, into the fire that never shall be quenched: Where their worm dieth not, and the fire is not quenched. And if thine eye offend thee, pluck it out: it is better for thee to enter into the kingdom of God with one eye, than having two eyes to be cast into hell fire: Where their worm dieth not, and the fire is not quenched" (Mark 9:43-48).

The Apostles also boldly and plainly preached the judgment of God to produce conviction in sinners and to lead them to Christ. Consider Paul's sermon on Mars Hill: "And the times of this ignorance God winked at; but now commandeth all men every where to repent: Because he hath appointed a day, in the which he will judge the world in righteousness by that man whom he hath ordained; whereof he hath given assurance unto all men, in that he hath raised him from the dead" (Acts 17:30-31). Paul didn't mind "scaring people" about Hell. Jude plainly says some are to be saved by fear (Jude 23).

In 1997 Lowry joined Roman Catholic Kathy Troccoli and 40 other CCM artists to record *Love One Another*, a song with an ecumenical theme: "Christians from all denominations demonstrating their common love for Christ and each other." The song talks about tearing down the walls of denominational division. The broad range of participants who joined Kathy Troccoli in recording "Love One Another" demonstrates the ecumenical agenda of Contemporary Christian Music. The song witnessed Catholics, Pentecostals, Baptists, etc., yoked together to call for Christian unity.

In an article in *CCM Magazine*, Lowry praised Mother Teresa and Princess Diana. "Diana and Mother Teresa were using their influence for good. One from a palace and the other from poverty. That's what we all should do" (Gregory Rumburg and April

Hefner, "The Princess and the Nun," *CCM Magazine*, June 2001). Lowry had no word of warning about Mother Teresa's false gospel that has caused multitudes to die with a false hope. We have described Mother Teresa's doctrinal beliefs in our book *Evangelicals and Rome*.

MCGUIRE, BARRY

Barry McGuire (1935-) was a folk/rock singer with The New Christy Minstrels and later branched out into a solo career. He wrote the mega-hits "Green, Green" and "Eve of Destruction" (1965). In the early '70s, McGuire became a Christian. He went on to record Christian albums, including a live album with the 2nd Chapter of Acts.

In the mid-1990s McGuire began performing and touring with John Michael Talbot's brother, Terry. They did roughly 40 concerts in 1995 and more than 70 in 1996. McGuire describes these as follows: "What we are doing isn't so much ministry—we just want to bring some joy and laughter. There are lots of other good ministers out there. We want to bring wholesome entertainment. Not everything we sing is necessarily Christian. We will sing songs like 'Help,' 'Blowin' in the Wind,' and 'When the Ship Comes In.' These songs can move people. We still do 'Eve of Destruction'" (McGuire, interviewed by Devlin Donaldson, http://placetobe.org/cmp/artists/index.html).

The McGuire-Talbot music is folk and soft rock and some of the folk music they play might indeed be "wholesome entertainment," as they say. Note, though, that McGuire and Talbot play songs by the Beatles. I believe it is absolutely unconscionable for Christian musicians to encourage an appetite for Beatles' rock music in young people. No rock group has had a more spiritually destructive influence than the Beatles. There were certainly controlled by demons as they captured the hearts of an entire generation with their "magical mystery" music and carried millions of young people along on their journey to eastern religion and drug abuse. The Beatles continue to exercise a vast influence, and young people need to be warned to stay away from them and the world of licentious rock and roll which the Beatles helped to create.

Of his faith in God McGuire says: "I don't know where God is taking me. But I know I am right where God wants me. I know that God is in control of my life. One time a guy said to me, 'You're a fatalist.' I said, 'Absolutely. My faith is in the hands of my God, and I know I can trust Him. Is trusting God fatalism? If it is, then I am.' It's really simple. It takes all the pressure out of life" (*CCM Magazine*, April 1996).

This is a wonderful expression of faith in God, and I am glad that Barry McGuire trusts the Lord. We would remind McGuire and his listeners, though, that "faith cometh by hearing, and hearing by the Word of God" (Romans 10:17). I cannot know I am "right where God wants me" unless I am living in accordance with the Bible.

For many years McGuire was involved with the ecumenical World Vision.

Barry McGuire's song about his conversion and his new life in Christ, "Cosmic Cowboy," does not present the way of salvation and demeans the Person and Work of Christ which He undertook on our behalf.

"Christian youth are afflicted with the 'Cosmic Cowboy Syndrome' when it comes to a real understanding of who Jesus Christ is and what He has accomplished. The character and philosophy of a Christian musician is easily adopted by his listeners, and will draw them away from the firm foundation of the Word" (Ric Llewellyn, "Christian? Rock," *Foundation*, Vol. VI, Issue 2, 1985, p. 18).

MASEN, SARAH

In 1997 Sarah Masen joined Roman Catholic Kathy Troccoli and 40 other CCM artists to record *Love One Another*, a song with an ecumenical theme: "Christians from all denominations demonstrating their common love for Christ and each other." The song talks about tearing down the walls of denominational division. The broad range of participants who joined Kathy Troccoli in recording "Love One Another" demonstrates the ecumenical agenda of Contemporary Christian Music. The song witnessed Catholics, Pentecostals, Baptists, etc., yoked together to call for Christian unity.

MASON, BABBIE

In 1997 Babbie Mason joined Roman Catholic Kathy Troccoli and 40 other CCM artists to record *Love One Another*, a song with an ecumenical theme: "Christians from all denominations demonstrating their common love for Christ and each other." The song talks about tearing down the walls of denominational division. The broad range of participants who joined Kathy Troccoli in recording "Love One Another" demonstrates the ecumenical agenda of Contemporary Christian Music. The song witnessed Catholics, Pentecostals, Baptists, etc., yoked together to call for Christian unity.

MATTHEWS, RANDY

Randy Matthews founded the Jesus House in Cincinnati, Ohio, in 1971. He recorded the first contemporary album for Word publishing. His philosophy is as follows: "For the masses today, the greatest medium for expressing the gospel is rock 'n' roll. It's not even a musical form anymore; it's a culture, and it's a lifestyle. The pulpit of this generation and the next is the guitar" (Randy Matthews, *CCM Magazine*, July 1998, p. 20).

His music was so hard that at the Jesus '74 concert in Mercer, Pennsylvania, he was unplugged and shooed from the stage. Only a few years later, though, the hard rock style had become acceptable in CCM circles.

MELENDEZ, TONY

Tony Melendez is an armless musician who plays the guitar with his feet. He is a Roman Catholic and was a founding member in 1996 of the Catholic Musicians Association which was organized by John Michael Talbot. In 1990 Melendez recorded an album for Star Song entitled *Ways of the Wise*, but the album didn't sell well and Melendez was dropped from the label's roster. In 1997 he recorded *Hands in Heaven* on the Angelus label.

MESSIAH PROPHET

Messiah Prophet produced two albums, *Rock the Flock* (1984) and *Master of the Metal* (1986). Their hard rock style is described as follows: "[They] have a style that always remains close to Iron Maiden ... comparisons can be made with a mixture of secular artists like Nazareth, AC/DC, Def Leppard and Led Zepplin" (*The Revealer Magazine*, Summer 1987, p. 8).

The blasphemous, unscriptural message of this group is evident in the following lyrics:
> "You hear a loud guitar/ You wonder what we are/ You say we're all the same/ You see us dressed in black/ Preparing to attack/ You say it's such a shame/ But do you really know/ The force behind our show/ Our one way ticket home/ WE'RE ROCKIN' FOR THE ROCK/ And we will never stop/ And this you've got to know/ Jesus said upon this Rock my church will stand/ ... HE'S THE MASTER/ THE MASTER OF METAL..." ("Master of Metal," Messiah Prophet Band).

To say that the high and holy Lord Jesus Christ is the Master of rebellious heavy metal rock music is outrageous.

MG THE VISIONARY

This rap group is riding the new wave of popularity for "Christian" hip-hop music. *CCM Magazine* notes: "After nearly 20 years lobbying for position in the Christian scene, rap and hip-hop may be digging their way out of the underground. With the evolving success of the genre in the general market, a handful of Christian labels have turned attention to the music hoping to ride the wave of popularity" (*CCM Magazine*, May 2000, p. 11). MG The Visionary explains why young people like hip-hop: "Now-a-days people want to shake their booties. You can't deny it. Yes, it sounds funny, but it's the truth.

You can mosh, you can slam and rock out. But what music just lets you, and actually calls you, to groove and feel the soul, feel the natural rhythm God has given us?"

Rap music emphasizes the beat to an extreme degree. It is overwhelmingly sensual. It's goal is to move the body.

MG the Visionary explains why young people like hip-hop: "Now-a-days people want to shake their booties. You can't deny it. Yes, it sounds funny, but it's the truth. You can mosh, you can slam and rock out. But what music just lets you, and actually calls you, to groove and feel the soul, feel the natural rhythm God has given us?"

Without knowing it, MG the Visionary, in his trashy language, has explained exactly what is wrong with hip-hop from a biblical perspective. It is true that there are "natural rhythms" within men, but those rhythms and impulses have been corrupted through the fall. The Bible says there is within man a carnal nature that loves evil and that is at enmity against God. Just because something is "natural" does not make it right. It is natural to be naked, but God clothed the man and the woman after they sinned, because their hearts had become darkened with evil thoughts. That is why the Bible forbids nakedness and immodesty. The Lord Jesus warned that for a man even to look upon a woman lustfully is adultery. The Bible says there is a conflict between the Spirit and the flesh. They are not friends, and they are not to be syncretized. The lust of the flesh is part of the world, and God's Word commands Christian to love *not* the world. When young people are shaking their bodies to the beat of hip-hop, they are not consumed with the glory of Jesus Christ and the holiness of God. They are consumed with carnal things, with the lusts of the flesh and the lusts of the eyes. Girls who love to dance to hip-hop do not dress modestly, and the fellows who dance to hip-hop to not want them to dress modestly.

Unsaved people look at the lust of the flesh as a wonderful thing, a natural thing which should be enjoyed to the fullest. "If it feels good, do it," is the world's philosophy. "Hey, what could be wrong with looking at a woman shaking herself to the beat?" the worldly man says. "Didn't God make me like that? What's wrong with dancing? What's wrong with showing a little flesh? It's natural, isn't it?" God looks at the lust of the flesh, though, as a wicked thing which has corrupted His world. The Lord Jesus Christ died to save people from "the corruption that is in the world through lust" (1 Peter 1:4).

Christianity that is syncretized with the world is apostate Christianity, and that is precisely what we find on every hand today. That is how the Roman Catholic Church was formed in the fourth century. It was a yoking together of churches with the world. Contemporary Christian Music attempts to do the same thing. Peter described false Christians as those who "walk after the flesh in the lust of uncleanness" (2 Peter 2:10). Further, we are told that false Christians "allure through the lusts of the flesh, through much wantonness" (2 Peter 2:18). That sounds exactly like CCM to me.

MULLINS, RICH

Rich Mullins (1956-1997), who died in an automobile accident, was a very popular CCM song writer and performer. He wrote songs recorded by such megastars as Amy Grant. He opened most of his concerts with "Hallelujah" sung in Beach Boys style. He grew up around Quakers and the Church of Christ. His brother David is pastor at Oak Grove Christian Church in Beckley, West Virginia. A few years ago Rich was a member of Wichita's Central Christian Church (baptismal regeneration) and attended a Quaker university. At the time of his death it was reported that Rich Mullins was taking the final steps to enter the Roman Catholic Church. He was attending mass at least weekly, and the night before he died, Mullins talked on the phone with priest Matt McGinness, communicating his readiness to say his first confession and to be confirmed. McGinness describes the conversation as follows:

> "There was a sense of urgency. He told me, 'This may sound strange, but I HAVE to receive the body and blood of Christ.' I told him, 'That doesn't sound strange at all. That sounds wonderful.' Rich finally sounded like he was at peace with his decision" (Terry Mattingly, "Rich Mullins—Enigmatic, Restless, Catholic," www.gospel.com.net/tmattingly/col.05.06.98.html).

Priest Mattingly's testimony that Rich Mullins was taking the last step to become a Catholic when he died is disputed by some. Brian William, who runs a website featuring Rich Mullins information, makes the following comment: "I really don't have the answer to that [as to whether or not Mullins' became a Catholic], and I don't think anybody really does. There was a priest in Wichita who claimed that Rich had gone through the entire training program to learn what it is the RCC believes and was only days away from taking his first Mass and entering into full communion with the Roman Catholic church. Meanwhile, his family and friends said that although he was very interested in learning more about Catholicism and always had had a strong respect and admiration for a lot of things the RCC did, he also had a number of issues with them and wasn't able to reconcile his differences with them so he wasn't interested in actuutally becoming Catholic himself" (E-mail from Brian William to Jose Mandez, Feb. 9, 2000).

I believe priest Mattingly's testimony because Rich Mullins' music reflected both his ecumenism and his growing Catholicism. The last project he completed was called *Canticle of the Plains* and was based on the life and legend of the Catholic St. Francis of Assisi. There was nothing scriptural about the ministry of St. Francis of Assisi.

The following is what Mullins' told Brendt Waters of TLeM during Gospel Music Association Week in April 1996:

> "Beaker [who co-wrote music with Mullins] and I both first got really interested in religious orders. I had read a book called *Exploring Spiritual Direction* by Alan Jones. THAT WHOLE EVANGELICAL DISCIPLESHIP THING REALLY TURNED ME OFF, AS MOST EVANGELICAL THINGS DO. I was just so depressed from meeting all these kids that were turning into caricatures of great old men or great old women, these great saints. People were thinking [that] the way to become spiritual is to imitate the lives of really spiritual people. Well, in Catholicism, spiritual direction is something like discipleship, only their idea is that you don't become like me, you become like you. In Catholicism—and this is one of the places in which Catholicism is much more appealing to me than Protestantism, and certainly more than Evangelicalism—our identity as being a creature, as being someone uniquely created, is much more 'in your face' than in Protestantism. PROTESTANTISM IS KIND OF LIKE 'CHRISTIANITY LITE' TO ME. It's kind of like we want to be Christians, but we really take science more seriously than we take Christianity. We take what we think we know more seriously than what we believe. AND I THINK THERE IS NOTHING MORE USELESS TO ME THAN WHAT WE NOW KNOW, because tomorrow we're going to 'now' know something completely different and contradictory" (emphasis added).

Mullins obviously loved Catholic "spirituality" even though the same is not based on the Bible. Note, too, that more than a year before his death Mullins had largely rejected "evangelicalism" and "Protestantism" and did not believe in a settled doctrinal faith.

The song "Creed" on Mullins' *Songs* album contains the words: "I believe in the Holy Spirit/ One Holy Church, the communion of Saints." On the booklet accompanying the CD the lyrics to this song are superimposed on a photo of a Catholic Madonna (which blasphemously depicts Mary as the sinless Queen of Heaven). Consider some of the lyrics to another Mullins' songs:

> "To say that time is short/ Just means the time is now/ Every tongue will confess/ And every knee is going to bow/ Don't have to be no hunger/ Don't have to be no war" (Rich Mullins, "Alrightokuhhuhamen").

On the literature accompanying the "Songs" CD, the lyrics to theis song ("Alright ok uhhuh amen") are superimposed on a picture of a Catholic Madonna holding a Rosary. The Rosary, of course, is largely a prayer to Mary as the Queen of Heaven. Some have claimed that Mullins did not believe in praying to Mary, but if he did not, it is very puzzling why he would feature a Rosary on his album. Surely he understood that his listeners would identify the Rosary with Catholic prayers to Mary and would assume that he believed in the same.

The following Mullins' song presents the false gospel taught by Catholicism and every other cult.

> "Faith without works baby/ It just ain't happenin'/ One is your left hand/ One is your right/ It'll take two strong arms/ To hold on tight" (Rich Mullins, "Screen Door").

One of the marks of false Christianity is to confuse faith and works, to mix faith and works together for salvation. While it is true that faith without works is dead and that true saving faith produces works, it is not true that faith and works are the two strong arms by which we hold on tight to God and salvation (Ephesians 2:8-10; Romans 11:6), yet that is exactly the heresy what this song teaches.

The following Mullins' song teaches heresy about the Lord Jesus Christ.

> "You was a boy like I was once/ But was you a boy like me?/ I grew up around Indiana/ You grew up around Galilee/ And if I ever really do grow up/ Lord I want to grow up and be just like you/ ... And I really may just grow up/ And be like You some day" (Rich Mullins, "Boy Like Me/ Man Like You").

Christ was a boy, but He was NOT a boy like you or me. And though the child of God will one day be like the Lord Jesus in some ways, in that we will have glorified resurrection bodies, we will never be "just like" Jesus, because He "only hath immortality, dwelling in the light which no man can approach unto; whom no man hath seen, nor can see: to whom be honour and power everlasting" (1 Timothy 6:16). It is a common practice within CCM to bring Christ down to a level below that which is revealed in Scripture.

In a 1987 interview with *CCM Magazine,* Mullins made the following statement:

> "I'm really sick of all this heavy-handed Christianity. Musicians take themselves too seriously. They should have more fun, and they should stop preaching unless that's what God has called them to. If I want to hear a sermon, I'll go to my church, thank you" (Rich Mullins, *CCM Magazine*, April 1987, p. 12).

That is an unscriptural attitude toward Christian music. Colossians 3:16 says Christian music is to be a channel for "teaching and admonishing." That sounds like preaching to me! It is also an unscriptural attitude toward preaching. Preaching is to be done "in season and out of season." It is not something restricted to church. Preaching is also not restricted to preachers. It is every Christian's job to exhort others in holiness and faith. "But exhort one another daily, while it is called To day; lest any of you be hardened through the deceitfulness of sin" (Hebrews 3:13; see also Heb. 10:25).

In a 1996 interview, Mullins said that he did not believe in doctrinal statements:

> "I don't like the terms liberal and conservative. I think I'm more conservative than most conservatives and more liberal than most liberals. ... I think that all these doctrinal statements that all the congregations come up with over the years are basically just not very worthwhile. ... But I think our real doctrine is that doctrine that is born out in our character" (Rich Mullins, cited by Christopher Coppernoll, *Soul 2 Soul*, pp. 48-49).

This is an unscriptural attitude toward doctrine. Doctrine and character are two different things and it is a very serious error to confuse them. The Bible never puts doctrine and Christian living in contrast to one another as Mullins did. Sound doctrine is important, and sound Christian living is important. They are not at odds. The two Greek words translated "doctrine," *didaskalia* and *didache*, are also translated "teacheth" (Rom. 12:7) and "learning" (Rom. 15:4). These words are used more than 140 times in the N.T., which shows how important doctrine is before God. Other terms which refer to doctrine are "truth" (1 Tim. 2:4), "the faith" (1 Tim. 3:9; 2 Tim. 3:8; Tit. 1:13; Jude 3), "wholesome words" (1 Tim. 6:3), and "sound words" (2 Tim. 1:13). Doctrine (and its companion terms) are referred to 59 times in the Pastoral Epistles alone. "The truth" is referred to 10 times in 2 and 3 John alone. Defining sound doctrine and avoiding false doctrine is one of the chief responsibilities of the churches.

Mullins' anti-fundamentalism attitude was evident in an interview with *TLeM*, April 1997: "Everything is spiritual. Which is another hang-up I have with Protestantism, and even more specifically with Evangelicalism. It's more like Manicheism than anything else. This dualistic system that says that everything physical is evil, and the only good things are spiritual things. And I go, 'Wow! John wrote a good bit of what he wrote to counter that kind of thinking.' And yet, ALL THESE BIBLE-BELIEVING, BIBLE-THUMPING BORN-AGAIN-ERS are going around professing the very thing that John tried to put out" (Brendt Waters, interview with Rich Mullins, conducted in April 1996, www.tlem.netcentral.net/features/9709/mullins.html).

This is an unscriptural and slanderous statement. Notice how Mullins spoke mockingly of "Bible-thumping born-again-ers." I would be afraid to mock that crowd, seeing that the Apostles and early Christians were definitely "Bible thumpers" (quoting the Scriptures continually) and were definitely "born againers"! The Lord Jesus Christ founded the "born againer" movement when He said, "Verily, verily, I say unto thee, Except a man be born again, he cannot see the kingdom of God" (John 3:3). Mullins built a strawman by describing the "Bible-thumper's" message as saying "that everything physical is evil and the only good things are spiritual things." I don't know anyone who is saying that everything physical is evil. Though there are perhaps those today who hold such a philosophy, they are primarily in pagan religions and are definitely not within the mainstream of evangelicalism or fundamentalism as Mullins claimed. The things of the world which God made are not evil, but when man takes those things and uses them for evil purposes, they become evil. A guitar or a drum or a piano are not evil in themselves, but when they are used licentiously to stir up sensual passions, they are evil. The Bible plainly says that this world is fallen and under the domination of sinful men and demons, and God's people are to separate from the evil things of this world. The Bible makes a sharp distinction between the holy and the profane (Ezek. 22:26), between the world and God (James 4:4; 1 John 2:15-17). John said, "And we know that we are of God, and the whole world lieth in wickedness" (1 John 5:19).

Like all Contemporary Christian Music "artists," Mullins believed in the mythical "neutrality of music." In a 1997 interview with Artie Terry, Professor of Communications, Wheaton College, Mullins made the following statement: "...you know, everyone's worried about what kids listen to. Tipper Gore is all on a roar about it, and I wish she'd go someplace else and roar. There's a... I think the reason why people like bad music is because they're not exposed, in a positive way, to good music. And I don't think that Bach is necessarily good and 'Ice T' [an immoral rapper] is necessarily bad. I'm not sure that those labels apply in music" (Rich Mullins, interview on radio station WETN, Wheaton College, April 17, 1997).

Earlier in this book we have exposed the error of this thinking.
At the time of his death, Mullins was deeply influenced by Native American culture. He claimed to have watched the New Age Hollywood movie *Dances with Wolves* 70 times, and *CCM Magazine* notes that "his fascination with Native American culture was legendary" (*CCM Magazine,* July 1998, p. 85). He had moved to a Navajo reservation in 1996.

Though we must reject Rich Mullins' doctrinal stance, we credit him for attempting to live up to his convictions. He disliked the gross commercialism which characterizes Contemporary Christian Music, and he reportedly gave much of the proceeds from his music to charities. "He had all his earnings sent to elders at his church, who paid him an average American worker's salary and donated the rest to charity. By the end of his life, Mullins was getting $1,000 a month and living in a trailer on a Native American reservation, teaching children music. He never even knew how much money he was making. When Arvin, who produced several of his records, asked Mullins why, Mullins answered, 'Because if I knew, it would be so much harder to give away'" ("Is Profit a Problem in Christian Music?" *Pittsburgh Post-Gazette,* Sunday, Feb. 13, 2000).

A tribute album, *Awesome God: A Tribute to Rich Mullins*, was released in November 1998. On this album Mullins' songs are covered by Amy Grant, Michael W. Smith, Jars of Clay, dc Talk's Kevin Max, Caedmon's Call, Gary Chapman, Third Day, Chris Rice, Billy Crockett, Billy Sprague, Ashley Cleveland, and Carolyn Arends.

MXPX

MxPx was formed in 1994 and became the best-selling band on the label Tooth & Nail, which produces albums for Alternative Christian groups. In 1998 MxPx signed with the secular company A&M Records, which also publishes Amy Grant. The band's name originally was Magnified Plaid, which they shortened to M.P. One member of the band writes periods as small x's, thus resulting in the name MxPx.

The band is comprised of three members: Tom Wisniewski (guitar), Mike Herrara (bass/lead singer), and Yuri Ruley (drums).

In the summer of 1998 they were on the "Warped" rock tour as an opening act for the anti-Christian secular rock group Bad Religion. When some Christians protested their alliance with such a wicked group, the members of MxPx complained that they "shouldn't be so negative" (*CCM Magazine*, August 1998, p. 37), demonstrating their unscriptural positive-only philosophy. They claim they are being light in darkness by performing in wicked rock concerts with vile secular rock bands, but in reality they are encouraging young people to attended these demonic, immoral events and that it is harmless to listen to wicked rock music. They even wrote a song to "protest the way Christians have reacted to their association with artists like Bad Religion." They have confused correction with persecution. They think they are being persecuted because some attempt to warn and correct them about things they are doing contrary to the Word of God. The Bible plainly instructs God's people to prove all things (1 Thess. 5:21). The Bereans were commended for doing this (Acts 17:11). The Bible also says Christians are to rebuke sin and error (Ephesians 5:11; Titus 1:13). Those who sought to correct MxPx are not wrong, but the members of the band wouldn't receive the correction. "Hear counsel, and receive instruction, that thou mayest be wise in thy latter end" (Prov. 19:20).

Speaking of their 1998 album, *Slowly Going the Way of the Buffalo*, Herrera admits that the message is not openly biblical: "But don't expect a lot of biblical paraphrase from it. With this new album, you won't find many Christian buzzwords" (Herrera, *HM* magazine, September-October 1998).

The unscriptural philosophy of this group is evident from an interview with *CCM Magazine*: "We'd like Christians to be the standard, not the minority [in the world]. More accepted and less weird. ... From the very beginning, we didn't really play 'Christian' or 'secular' shows. We didn't realize there was a difference..." (Mike Herrara, *CCM Magazine*, August 1998, p. 37).

Consider Herrara's statement in light of the following two verses:

> "And we know that we are of God, and the whole world lieth in wickedness" (1 John 5:19).

> "If the world hate you, ye know that it hated me before it hated you. If ye were of the world, the world would love his own: but because ye are not of the world, but I have chosen you out of the world, therefore the world hateth you" (John 15:18,19).

These verses remind us that Christians who are obeying the Word of God will never be completely accepted by the world. We are not of this world. We are strangers and pilgrims in the world. Note that this CCM group does not even realize that there is a difference between Christian and secular! It reminds us of the apostate condition of Israel of old: "Her priests have violated my law, and have profaned mine holy things: THEY HAVE PUT NO DIFFERENCE BETWEEN THE HOLY AND PROFANE, NEITHER HAVE THEY SHOWED DIFFERENCE BETWEEN THE UNCLEAN AND THE CLEAN, and have hid their eyes from my sabbaths, and I am profaned among them" (Ezek. 22:26).

The band's philosophy is also evident in the following statement by Herrara: "We're Christians, but we're not missionaries. We're not trying to save everybody. It just happens to be what we believe" (Mike Herrara, *The Rocket Magazine*, The Northwest Music Magazine, 1996).

Contrast this with Christ's command in the Great Commission: "And he said unto them, Go ye into all the world, and preach the gospel to every creature" (Mark 16:15). Every Christian has been commissioned by Christ to be a missionary in the sense of presenting the Gospel to the unsaved. The early Christians preached the Gospel wherever they went. "Therefore they that were scattered abroad went every where preaching the word" (Acts 8:4).

The spiritual shallowness of MxPx lyrics is illustrated by the song "Southbound" from their 1996 *Life in General* album —

> "It's all the same/ same old town with a different name/ That's fine with me/ There's only one place I wanna be/ Southbound on I-5/ Windows down and music on the stereo/ I'm drivin' and I'm dreamin'/ There's no place I'd rather go/ Staring at the white lines on the side of the road/ (Playing every night, with

the occasional fight)/ Been on the road awhile/ I gotta get back to a place with style/ Hang out, havin' fun/ I gotta get back to the beach in the sun" ("Southbound," MxPx).

In 1997 MxPx signed with secular recording company A&M Records (which produces wicked rock groups such as Sting).

NAILED

Nailed is a popular hard rock band based in Knoxville, Tennessee. The band members look just like the world and their music sounds just like the world. Lead guitarist Scottie Hoaglan has very long hair, a nose pin, and tattoos all over his arms. Songs such as "Hell to Pay" and "Bleed Me" from their 1999 *Entity* album are described as "top-notch productions with energizing choruses and a dark feel that will instantly win over fans of Tool, Stavesacre and Alice in Chains" (*7Ball*, July-August 1999, p. 27). The three secular groups to whom Nailed is compared are extremely wicked.

NEWSBOYS

The Newsboys are a hard rock group. Their music "has run the gamut from punkish rock to a turn at rap and Euro-flavored techno pop." The band members are from Australia, New Zealand, and America. They are Phil Joel (bass), Jody Davis (guitar), Jeff Frankenstein (keyboard), Peter Furler (lead singer), and Duncan Phillips (drums). Co-founder/lead singer John James left the group in late 1997. They are managed by Wes Campbell. One member sports long womanish hair; another has an earring.
Their albums are as follows: *Read All About It* (1988), *Hell Is for Wimps* (1990), *Boyz Will Be Boyz* (1991), *Not Ashamed* (1992), *Going Public* (1994), *Take Me to Your Leader* (1996), and *Step Up to the Microphone* (1998). In 1990 they signed with the Christian label Star Song, and in 1996 they signed with the secular label Virgin Records, which also produces for the Rolling Stones. From 1991 to 1996 their albums were produced by Steve Taylor.

Their first two albums sold 30,000 each. Their fourth album, *Not Ashamed (1992)*, sold 400,000 and received a Grammy nomination. They have received two Dove awards for rock music.

In a 1996 interview Peter Furler said: "Our first three or four records weren't very deep, but neither was our experience in the faith" (*CCM Magazine*, February 1996).

The Newsboys 1998 album, *Step Up to the Microphone,* is being promoted both in Christian (via Star Song) and in secular markets. The latter is being done through Virgin

Records. Danny Goodwin, Vice President of A&R for Virgin, describes their philosophy of music: "Our position is, whether these artists are Christians, Jews, Moslems, black, white, Albanian or whatever, they're making great music. And that's what Virgin does—we're in the market to sell what we call quality music to the largest number of people we can" (*CCM Magazine,* August 1998, p. 25).

Many CCM musicians are comfortable working hand in hand with people who produce and distribute the most vile rock and roll music, whereas the Bible says, "Wherefore come out from among them, and be ye separate, saith the Lord, and touch not the unclean thing; and I will receive you" (2 Cor. 6:17).

Newsboys concerts feature many of the same things found at secular rock concerts: dancing, moshing, stage diving, crowd surfing. There have been numerous accidents relating directly or indirectly to moshing at Newsboys concerts ("To Mosh or Not to Mosh," *CCM Magazine,* February 1996).

In 1997 Newsboys' Phil Joel joined Roman Catholic Kathy Troccoli and 40 other CCM artists to record *Love One Another*, a song with an ecumenical theme: "Christians from all denominations demonstrating their common love for Christ and each other." The song talks about tearing down the walls of denominational division. The broad range of participants who joined Kathy Troccoli in recording "Love One Another" demonstrates the ecumenical agenda of Contemporary Christian Music. The song witnessed Catholics, Pentecostals, Baptists, etc., yoked together to call for Christian unity.

NORMAN, LARRY

Larry Norman was one of the pioneers of "Jesus Rock" in the late 1960s. *Time* magazine once called him "the poet laureate of Jesus Music," and the British CCM magazine *CrossRhythms* labeled him "the founding father of contemporary Christian music." It has been said that he was the first to combine rock and roll with Christian lyrics. He formed his first rock band, the People, in 1967. His debut album, *Upon This Rock,* was released by Capitol Records. It was banned by most Christian bookstores at the time.

Norman married in 1973 but experienced serious marital problems caused at least partly by his wife, Pamela's, jet set lifestyle as a model. They were separated in 1978, and she divorced him in 1980 ("Only Visiting This Planet," interview with Larry Norman, *CrossRhythms*, November 1993; Steve Goddard and Roger Green, "Interview with Larry Norman, *Buzz magazine,* May 1981). Norman has one son from the marriage.

He formed Solid Rock Records after leaving MGM Records in 1974 and produced albums for himself and other CCM musicians, including such well-known names as Randy Stonehill, Daniel Amos, and the late Mark Heard. At least three of the musicians associated with Solid Rock (Larry Norman, Randy Stonehill, and Tom Howard) went through divorce. Solid Rock was dissolved in the late 1970s, and Norman has spent much of his time touring in Europe and Australia since then. He had two heart attacks in 1992, and was again hospitalized with heart problems in 1993.

Norman's 1975 hit, "Why Should the Devil Have All the Good Music," is one of the theme songs of the CCM scene. It promotes the strange, rebellious philosophy that rock music is something good that Christians need, and that traditional Christian songs, hymns, and spiritual songs are boring "funeral marches." The song oozes with adolescent rebellion, which certainly has no place in the Christian life.

> "I want the people to know/ that he saved my soul/ But I still like to listen to the radio/ They say rock 'n' roll is wrong/ we'll give you one more chance/ I say I feel so good/ I gotta get up and dance.
>
> "I know what's right/ I know what's wrong/ I don't confuse it/ All I'm really trying to say/ Is why should the Devil have all the good music?/ I feel good every day/ 'Cause Jesus is the rock/ and he rolled my blues away.
>
> "THEY SAY TO CUT MY HAIR/ THEY'RE DRIVING ME INSANE/ I GREW IT OUT LONG/ TO MAKE ROOM FOR MY BRAIN/ But sometimes people don't understand/ What's a good boy doing in a rock 'n' roll band?
>
> "There's nothing wrong with playing blues licks/ But if you got a reason/ tell me to my face / Why should the Devil have all the good music/ There's nothing wrong with what I play/ 'Cause Jesus is the rock/ and he rolled my blues away.
>
> "I ain't knocking the hymns/ JUST GIVE ME A SONG THAT HAS A BEAT/ I ain't knocking the hymns/ Just give me a song that moves my feet/ I DON'T LIKE NONE OF THOSE FUNERAL MARCHES/ I ain't dead yet!
>
> "Jesus told the truth/ Jesus showed the way/ There's one more thing/ I'd like to say/ They nailed him to the cross/ They laid him in the ground/ But they shoulda known/ you can't keep a good man down.
>
> "I feel good every day/ I don't wanna lose it/ All I wanna/ all I wanna know/ Is why should the Devil have all the good music/ I've been filled/ I feel okay/ Jesus is the rock/ and he rolled my blues/ Jesus is the rock/ and he rolled my blues/ Jesus is the rock/ and he rolled my blues away" (Larry Norman, "Why Should the Devil Have All the Good Music?").

The philosophy behind this song is the philosophy behind the CCM scene as a whole. It is this: Worldly, sensual music is good and pleasant, and no matter what anyone says and no matter who we offend, we are going to rock. When Larry Norman was in his early teens, his Christian father forbade him to listen to the radio because he was concerned about the influence of rock music on Larry's life. Larry's rebellious attitude toward this type of fatherly discipline is evident in his music. No one is going to tell him how to wear his hair or what kind of music he can listen to. I remember having precisely the same attitude. When I got out of the Army, I determined that I would never cut my hair again, and I grew it out like a woman's. That was BEFORE I was saved, though!

Norman is non-denominational, in fact, almost anti-denominational. When asked the simple question by *Buzz* magazine about what church he attended, he became very defensive and absolutely refused to answer, except to say that "I think it's unimportant" and "I just don't like the question." He also said, "I'm non-denominational in my thinking." He implied that he believes it is an "obsessive compulsion" to meet at regular weekly times for church. The Bible warns about Norman's lackadaisical attitude toward church attendance. "Not forsaking the assembling of ourselves together, as the manner of some is; but exhorting one another: and so much the more, as ye see the day approaching" (Heb. 10:25).

Larry Norman does not believe that God will judge sin in the Christian's life: "We're taught that God is very judicious, and unrelenting in his ferreting out of your sins, keeping a list and you're going to have to answer for every failing upon your death. That's the God that I was exposed to growing up in America, but then finding out that God is all-loving toward his own children, his own sheep that know his voice—that's made the last few years of my life completely different in texture, and I feel that I have a lot of freedom that I never realised was available before" (*CrossRhythms*, November 1993).

This is one of those half truths which form a lie. God is all-loving toward his children, but this does not mean He does not ferret out, keep records of, and judge sin. We are motivated by the love of God, but we are also motivated by the fear of God (Heb. 12:28-29). The word "judgment" is used more than 200 times in the New Testament. 1 Peter 4:17 says "judgment must begin at the house of God." 1 Peter 4:5 and 2 Timothy 4:1 say God is going to "judge the quick and the dead," meaning He is going to judge the saved *and* the unsaved. James warned Christians not to sin because if we do we will be condemned by the Lord when He comes (James 5:9). 1 Timothy 5:24 warns that some men's sins follow them to judgment, and the context is speaking of Christians. 2 Corinthians 5:10 warns that the judgment seat of Christ will deal with the good and the bad in the Christian's life. 1 Corinthians 11:31 warns the Christian to judge himself so he will not be judged by the Lord. 1 Corinthians 3:13-14 warns that if a

Christian's work does not pass the Lord's judgment he will suffer loss because of it. Colossians 3:25 warns that Christ's judgment upon Christians will involve punishment for wrong doing. Further, there is the law of sowing and reaping in this life, and the blood of Christ does not negate that law (Galatians 5:7).

ONE BAD PIG

The advertisement for One Bad Pig's live album, *Blow the House Down,* describes this "Christian" performance as follows: "They're loose again! And this time it's live, UNBRIDLED MAYHEM ... On stage screaming, stomping, slam dancing, stage diving, pleading and praying. It's the absolute wildest Christian concert ever recorded..."

OUT OF THE GREY

In 1997 Out of the Grey joined Roman Catholic Kathy Troccoli and 40 other CCM artists to record *Love One Another,* a song with an ecumenical theme: "Christians from all denominations demonstrating their common love for Christ and each other." The song talks about tearing down the walls of denominational division. The broad range of participants who joined Kathy Troccoli in recording "Love One Another" demonstrates the ecumenical agenda of Contemporary Christian Music. The song witnessed Catholics, Pentecostals, Baptists, etc., yoked together to call for Christian unity.

PARIS, TWILA

Twila Paris grew up in a Christian home and, according to her testimony, placed her faith in Christ at age four. She has produced 13 albums since 1979. She has won Dove Award for Female Vocalist of the Year two times. Fourteen of her singles have been No. 1 on Christian radio charts. She has written popular contemporary worship hymns. Some of her songs contain a plain and scriptural message. Consider, for example, "The Lamb of God" —

> "Your only son, no sin to hide/ But You have sent Him from Your side/ To walk upon this guilty sod/ And to become the Lamb of God/ Your gift of Love they crucified/ They laughed and scorned Him as He died/ The humble King they named a fraud/ And sacrificed the Lamb of God.
>
> Chorus: Oh Lamb of God, Sweet Lamb of God/ I love the Holy Lamb of God/ Oh wash me in His precious blood/ My Jesus Christ, the Lamb of God.
>
> "I was so lost, I should have died/ But You have brought me to Your side/ To be led by Your staff and rod/ And to be called the Lamb of God."

The lyrics to many of her songs, though, are vague.

Some of her songs are lovely, with full orchestration, acoustic strings, no rock bass or drums, no syncopation. But there are rock songs on the same albums. For example, her rendition of "When the Roll Is Called Up Yonder" is sung to a funky beat with heavy bass and constant snare drum. The song "We Seek His Face" is sung to strong disco style rock. Also many of her songs which begin with nice strings or organ music end rocky. "Be Thou My Vision," for example, begins with Paris singing to a traditional organ background, then builds into a strong beat with rock drums and bass guitar.

Of her 1993 album, *Beyond a Dream*, Twila Paris said: "This album is very current. It talks about how to face what's going on in the world, NOT FROM THE POINT OF ME BEING SOME SORT OF AN AUTHORITY, BUT FROM THE STRUGGLES THAT I'M GOING THROUGH and writing as I go through them. It was also the biggest stretch for me so far, artistically. Brown and Paul had me singing like I've never sung before" (http://placetobe.org/cmp/artists/index.html).

This is the standard CCM approach: non-judgmental, non-authoritative, non-dogmatic. No wonder the world finds such music popular. Can you imagine the Apostle Paul recording an album which would be applauded by the world?

Twila Paris's, uncle, Loren Cunningham, founded the charismatic-oriented, radically ecumenical Youth With A Mission (YWAM). Her father, Oren Paris, runs the Youth With A Mission near his Arkansas home. Twila has been associated with YWAM since 1976. In an interview with a YWAM leader in New Orleans in 1987, I was told that a large number of the short-term workers with YWAM are Roman Catholics. Youth With A Mission was perfectly at home at New Orleans '87, with its Catholic masses and Catholic priests as speakers, with its slaying in the spirit and phony "tongues." In 1984, YWAM adopted a policy allowing staff to work with Catholics when it was possible and desirable. Since then, YWAM has installed a Catholic, Rob Clarke, as director of its discipleship training school in Dublin. Al Akimoff, YWAM's director for Slavic Ministries, says YWAM's missionaries are not aiming to lure Catholics out of their churches. Rob Clarke, YWAM's Roman Catholic national director in Ireland, says, "We are trying to get away from the idea of simply 'converting' Catholics—that is turning them into Protestants—and towards a framework of ministry within the Catholic Church" (*Fundamentalist Digest*, May-June 1993). In January 1997 Youth With a Mission leader Bruce Clewett (national director of YWAM in Austria) participated in a historic ecumenical worship service at the Catholic City Cathedral of St. Stephen's in Vienna (*Charisma*, May 1997).

Twila Paris collaborated with Wheaton College professor Robert Webber to write *In This Sanctuary,* a book on public worship. Webber was trained at fundamentalist Bob Jones University, but he rejected fundamentalism and moved through Presbyterianism to Episcopalianism. He has promoted formal Catholic-style church liturgy among evangelicals. He has long been associated with the radical *Sojourners* magazine and with liberal political causes. In his book *Evangelicals on the Canterbury Trail: Why Evangelicals Are Attracted to the Liturgical Church,* Webber "predicts a new openness in which both evangelicals and Catholics will find increased value in each other's heritage in a work of the Holy Spirit toward greater Christian wholeness—in which the liturgical church will play an important part." On page 30 he spoke of the "mystery of God's saving presence in Christ communicated through worship and the sacraments." This is the chief error of the false sacramental doctrine of Rome and other sacramental denominations. The New Testament nowhere says God's saving presence in Christ is communicated through sacraments. God's salvation comes directly to the believer through faith in Christ by the power of the indwelling Holy Spirit. The New Testament church has no sacraments (meaning ordinances which are channels of grace); it has simple ordinances which are memorials, symbolic reminders of Christ. On pages 62 and 63 of his book, Webber says that Pope John XXIII and the Roman Catholic Vatican II Council assisted in his "pilgrimage into an identity with the universal church." Webber states that his model is Billy Graham who "has worked with every Protestant denomination; he has made friends in the Orthodox church as well as in the Catholic church" (p. 73).

In 1980 Webber stated: "The authoritative basis for Christian truth does not rest on a doctrine of verbal inerrancy, but Apostolic tradition" (*Blu-Print*, Sept. 30, 1980). This, of course, is the false Catholic view that exalts tradition to a place of authority alongside of the Bible.

Webber was on the convening committee for *The Chicago Call: An Appeal to Evangelicals* in 1977, which urged evangelicals to be more concerned about sacraments and tradition, to be involved in social change and environmental protection, among other things. *The Chicago Call* also desired ecumenical unity. Among the 46 church leaders who took part in drafting the *Call* were two Roman Catholic priests, Benedict Viviano and Jon Alexander. Note three statements from this *Call*:

> "We deplore the tendency of evangelicals to understand salvation solely as an individual, spiritual and otherworldly matter to the neglect of the corporate, physical and this-worldly implication of God's saving activity....
>
> "We affirm that the Bible is to be interpreted in accordance with the best insights of historical and literary studies, under the guidance of the Holy Spirit, with respect for the historic understanding of the church....

> "We deplore the scandalous isolation and separation of Christians from one another. We believe such division is contrary to Christ's explicit desire for unity among his people and impedes the witness of the church in the world. Evangelicalism is too frequently characterized by an ahistorical, sectarian mentality. We fail to appropriate the catholicity of historic Christianity, as well as the breadth of the biblical revelation" (The Chicago Call, 1977, cited in Richard Quebedeaux, *The Worldly Evangelicals*, 1978, Harper & Row: San Francisco, pp. 159-160).

These statements play right into the hands of the Roman Catholic Church, which claims that the Bible can only be properly interpreted in light of church tradition and which believes that the "church" is a universal (catholic) body and that the division of Christians from mother Rome is a sin. Also note the call for a "holistic view of salvation" which downplays the biblical truth that salvation is an individual being saved from the consequences of sin and focuses rather on the salvation of society, something the New Testament never does. We never see the Apostles trying to change society or build a more just world. They spent their energies preaching the Gospel and discipling the saints through the establishment of sound churches. Contrary to *The Chicago Call*, the New Testament approach to life is very much "otherworldly" minded.

> "If ye then be risen with Christ, SEEK THOSE THINGS WHICH ARE ABOVE, where Christ sitteth on the right hand of God. SET YOUR AFFECTION ON THINGS ABOVE, NOT ON THINGS ON THE EARTH. For ye are dead, and your life is hid with Christ in God. When Christ, who is our life, shall appear, then shall ye also appear with him in glory" (Colossians 3:1-4).

False teachers like Robert Webber remind us of those mentioned in Philippians:

> "(For many walk, of whom I have told you often, and now tell you even weeping, that they are the enemies of the cross of Christ: Whose end is destruction, whose God is their belly, and whose glory is in their shame, WHO MIND EARTHLY THINGS.) For our conversation is in heaven; from whence also we look for the Saviour, the Lord Jesus Christ. Who shall change our vile body, that it may be fashioned like unto his glorious body, according to the working whereby he is able even to subdue all things unto himself" (Philippians 3:18-21).

In 1990 Webber admitted that he is a "new-model evangelical" who does not believe that God sends people to eternal hell. Webber said that "God accepts those who trust him, regardless of the interpretation they give to that trust" (*Calvary Contender*, Oct. 1, 1990).

In 1997 Webber was one of 16 writers who responded to Pope John Paul II's book *Crossing the Threshold of Hope*. The responses were published in *A Reader's Companion* to *Crossing the Threshold of Hope*. In his comments Webber said that salvation is a process which begins at baptism. "Today, when people say to me, 'When were you saved?' I always answer, 'At my baptism.' I see the whole of my Christian life as a calling to live out my baptism. ... Salvation as a process moving from evil to ultimate good is a constant calling." The man is becoming more spiritually blind with each passing year.

We have taken the time to look at Robert Webber, because in so doing we learn much about the Contemporary Christian Music scene. Twila Paris moves freely and comfortably in this scene. She has worked closely with many of the well-known CCM musicians, including Sandi Patty, Kathy Troccoli, Amy Grant, Steve Curtis Chapman, Brown Bannister, and Cindy Morgan. Sadly, her close association with Robert Webber speaks volumes about the theological confusion that permeates CCM.

PARSONS, SQUIRE

Squire Parsons illustrates the unscriptural ecumenism of Southern Gospel today. His 1999 schedule includes performances at United Methodist, Nazarene, Church of God, Free Methodist, Quaker, Wesleyan, and Pentecostal Holiness churches.

PASCHAL, JANET

In 1997 Janet Paschal joined Roman Catholic Kathy Troccoli and 40 other CCM artists to record *Love One Another*, a song with an ecumenical theme: "Christians from all denominations demonstrating their common love for Christ and each other." The song talks about tearing down the walls of denominational division. The broad range of participants who joined Kathy Troccoli in recording "Love One Another" demonstrates the ecumenical agenda of Contemporary Christian Music. The song witnessed Catholics, Pentecostals, Baptists, etc., yoked together to call for Christian unity.

PATILLO, LEON

Leon Patillo's album "The Sky's the Limit" presents the false idea that individuals can do anything we put our minds to. "The inspirational title cut expresses the universal theme that we as individuals can do anything, when we put our minds to it, because 'the sky is the limit'" (*Contemporary Christian Music Magazine*, May 1984, p. 39).

In his video "Love Calling," Patillo sings the following hazy message:

> "Earth people/ Please come in/ I am not alien/ This is love calling/ Please come in/ I want to be your friend/ I don't want to harm you/ It's the last thing on my mind/ I just want to share my love with all of mankind..."

As these words are sung people on the video are doing the funky chicken dance.

PATTY, SANDI

Sandi Patty is one of the most popular CCM singers. Since her first album was released in 1979 she has sold more than 11 million records, has received 35 Dove Awards and five Grammys. She has often been named one of the favorite vocalists in readers polls conducted by Christian magazines. Year after year she has been honored by the Gospel Music Association. In 1995 she was named Female Vocalist of the Year for the 11th straight year. Of the top 50 all-time best-selling Christian albums, six belong to Patty (*CCM Magazine*, July 1998, pp. 107-108). She is one of the highest paid Gospel entertainers in the world. In 1988 she averaged $75,000 for a two-hour performance (Don Cusic, *Sandi Patti*, New York, 1988, pp. 211-212).

Sandi Patty is a member of the Church of God, Anderson, Indiana. Though not Pentecostal herself, Patty moves freely in charismatic circles. She has entertained audiences as diverse as Billy Graham crusades, Jerry Falwell meetings, Southern Baptist Convention annual conferences, and Pope John Paul II masses (she performed at a papal mass in Los Angeles in September 1987).

Not only has Sandi Patty put her stamp of approval upon Roman Catholicism by her performance for the pope, she has consistently promoted the unscriptural ecumenical-charismatic cause. In 1985 she was one of the 60 "well known Christian artists" who gathered in Nashville under the name "CAUSE—Christians Artists United to Save the Earth." The group included Amy Grant, Bill Gaither, and Doug Oldham. The session opened with a communion service followed by prayers, a prophecy, and hymns. Oldham, who used to be associated with Jerry Falwell, has performed with Billy Graham and Pat Boone, and sings each year at a Southern Baptist church in Huntsville, Alabama. "A few years ago he said music will bring all churches together into the ecumenical movement" (*Calvary Contender*, January 1, 1986).

In 1997 Sandi joined Roman Catholic Kathy Troccoli and 40 other CCM artists to record *Love One Another*, a song with an ecumenical theme: "Christians from all denominations demonstrating their common love for Christ and each other." The song talks about tearing down the walls of denominational division. The broad range of participants who joined Kathy Troccoli in recording "Love One Another" demonstrates the ecumenical agenda of Contemporary Christian Music. The song witnessed Catholics, Pentecostals, Baptists, etc., yoked together to call for Christian unity.

In 1997 Sandi Patty returned to the top of the "Christian music charts" with a new recording only two years after admitting that she had an adulterous affair with Don Peslis, a divorcee who was working as one of her backup singers. Patty divorced her husband, John Helvering, and in August 1995, she married her forbidden, adulterous "lover." *Christianity Today* reported that Patty was committing adultery with Peslis as far back as 1991 (*Christianity Today*, September 11, 1995, pp. 72-74). "According to several independent sources who at different times were aware of Patty's activities, she took part in two extramarital relationships, in both cases with married men" (Ibid.). This means that she was living in adultery during most of the years of her Christian music career.

A 1995 *World* magazine article stated that Sandi Patty has been in psychological counseling since 1989 and she "attributes her pattern of 'keeping secrets' to her childhood molestation, the memory of which she recovered in therapy" (*World*, September 16, 1995). This is psychobabble nonsense. The Bible nowhere says that our sin can be blamed on things which happen to us in our childhood. Nowhere in the Word of God are Christians taught to dig through their childhood memories to find the key to their adult actions.

Rick Miesel wisely observes: "Patty's rising popularity [after her acknowledged adultery and the divorce of her husband] is indicative of the trashed condition of Christians who claim the name of Christ but will not follow the doctrines of the Bible. Marrying a partner in adultery does not make the relationship right. It constitutes a continual condition of disobedience to God. How does one repent of adultery while one continues in an ongoing relationship with a former accomplice in adultery? Sin is further compounded while it festers under the unholy sanctions of a compromised institution. ... by God's standards Sandi Patty simply moved from adultery into a sinful divorce and then into marriage with her adultery partner, who divorced his wife" (*PsychoHeresy Awareness Letter*, March-April 1998, pp. 1,8).

It is not surprising that Sandi Patty has gone deeper and deeper into hard rock music. Her 1993 album, *LeVoyage,* does not mention the name of Jesus but it rocks so heavily that *CCM Magazine* made this statement: "...old-line Patty fans are either going to be seeking refunds in droves, or be so flabbergasted at seeing an entirely new side of her..." (*CCM Magazine*, May 1993, p. 40).

One of the songs sung by Sandi Patty is "Love in Any Language," which promotes world unity and non-judgmental love.

> "From Leningrad to Lexington, the farmer loves his land/ And daddies all get misty-eyed to give their daughter's hand/ Oh maybe when we realize how much there is to share/ We'll find too much in common to pretend it isn't there/

Love in any language/ Straight from the heart/ Pulls us all together/ Never apart/ And once we learn to speak it/ All the world will hear/ Love in any language/ Fluently spoken here..." ("Love in Any Language," by Jon Mohr and John Mays, sung by Sandi Patty).

This is not about biblical love. The only love which can bring men together in true biblical unity is the love of God through the Gospel of Jesus Christ. The love of God in Jesus Christ divides believers from unbelievers. The Lord Jesus Christ stated: "Think not that I am come to send peace on earth: I came not to send peace, but a sword. For I am come to set a man at variance against his father, and the daughter against her mother, and the daughter in law against her mother in law" (Matt. 10:34,35). The Apostle John testified of this division: "And we know that we are of God, and the whole world lieth in wickedness" (1 John 5:19). The love Sandi Patty sings about in this song, though, is a love which never pulls men apart, never divides. It is the false ecumenical, New Age, non-judgmental love which seeks unity apart from truth. There is no true love apart from Jesus Christ, and the love of God in Jesus Christ is to obey God's Word: "For this is the love of God, that we keep his commandments: and his commandments are not grievous" (1 John 5:3). Any message about "love" which does not refer to the one true Gospel of Jesus Christ and obedience to God's Word is a false message.

PEACE, MICHAEL

Christian rap singer/drummer Michael Peace displays his unscriptural philosophy as follows:

> "I know we're something now, y'all, if we have Jesus/ I didn't come to tell you, you're a sinner/ You can be a bunch of winners for Jesus..." (*Charisma*, February 1990, p. 42).

PENNIMAN, RICHARD. See Little Richard.

PENROSE, PETER

In 1997 Peter Penrose joined Roman Catholic Kathy Troccoli and 40 other CCM artists to record *Love One Another*, a song with an ecumenical theme: "Christians from all denominations demonstrating their common love for Christ and each other." The song talks about tearing down the walls of denominational division. The broad range of participants who joined Kathy Troccoli in recording "Love One Another" demonstrates the ecumenical agenda of Contemporary Christian Music. The song witnessed Catholics, Pentecostals, Baptists, etc., yoked together to call for Christian unity.

PETRA

Petra was formed in 1972 by guitarist Bob Hartman (1949-) and was the unofficial house band at The Adam's Apple, a "Jesus Freak" hangout in Ft. Wayne, Indiana (*CCM Magazine*, July 1998, p. 36).

Petra's first album appeared in 1974 but was not popular because their hard rock style was not yet widely accepted among professing Christians. By 1980 this begin to change rapidly and by 1984 the band had sold over a million records. Their 1984 album, *Beat the System*, hit the big time. It was distributed on A&M Records to secular record stores. The album contained songs which illustrate the unscriptural philosophy of the group. The song "Witch Hunt" slanders biblical fundamentalism, and the song "God Gave Rock and Roll to You" blasphemously states that God is the author of rock music and that it is God who puts rock music into the hearts of people. Petra got the latter song from secular rock group Argent. It was also performed by the wicked band KISS. Petra's 1987 album, *This Means War*, was even more popular, and the rapid sale of albums and the vast array of *This Means War* paraphernalia, including stickers, balloons, book covers, buttons, posters, etc., proved to be a gold mine to the band. Their 1990 album, *Beyond Belief*, won a Grammy and "brought them superstar status." Their 1991 album, *Unseen Power*, sold well over 300,000 copies and won a Grammy. Attendance at their concerts grew from an average of roughly 750 in 1981 to more than 8,000 in 1988.

Petra has produced a total of 18 albums and has sold more than six million of themalbums. They have won three Grammys and nine Dove Awards. Petra has been the winner of *CCM Magazine* Readers' Polls at least 24 times.

The band currently is composed of Bob Hartman (songwriting, management), Louie Weaver (drums), John Schlitt (lead vocals), Ronny Cates (bass), Jim Cooper (keyboard), David Lichens (guitar). Lichens has replaced Hartman as lead guitarist. Hartman is still affiliated with Petra but no longer be tours.

Of the group's name, Hartman says: "For me the name Petra has a duel meaning. It means rock music, but it also means that we stand upon the rock of our belief in Christ" (*CCM Magazine*, July 1998, p. 38).

Petra has a plain goal of ministering spiritually to those who attend their concerts. They have toured with popular campus speaker Josh McDowell of Campus Crusade for Christ. His conclusion was that "I've never worked with people more godly than the guys in Petra" (*The Contemporary Christian Music Debate*, pp. 175,176).

While we are glad that they have a good testimony, we cannot support Petra because of their rock music and charismatic-ecumenical doctrine. Note the following testimony about the effect of a Petra concert:

> "Have you ever seen a bunch of young people (be they Lutheran, Presbyterian, or Baptist, charismatic or evangelical) setting aside their religious idiosyncrasies to jump and shout when Petra walks on stage?... THE SHARED EXPERIENCE WILL SEND THEM BACK TO THEIR OWN CHURCHES LESS THEOLOGICALLY EXCLUSIVE. From that moment on, they are 'not of this world' with all of its petty ecclesiastical divisions" (emphasis added) (Bob Larson, *Contemporary Christian Music Magazine*, December 1985).

Petra performed at the 15th anniversary celebration of *Charisma* magazine, which promotes the charismatic movement. Guests at the celebration included false prophet Oral Roberts and Charles and Frances Hunter, who teach that every Christian can lay hands on the sick and heal them. (Frances Hunter has taken ill and been injured on her healing crusades and has had to seek medical attention when the "healing" failed.)

As already mentioned, Petra popularized among Christian young people the song "God Gave Rock and Roll to You"

> "God gave rock and roll to you/ Put it in the soul of every one/ If you love the sound/ Then don't forget the source/ You can turn around/ You can change your course/ You can love the Rock/ And let him free your soul" ("God Gave Rock and Roll," Petra).

This song was first sung by secular rock groups Argent and KISS. It is on KISS's *Revenge* album. Petra changed some of the words, but the overall message is the same, that God is the author of rock music. This is absolute nonsense, of course. To say that the Holy God of Scripture is the author of filthy rock & roll is blasphemy. The father of rock & roll is a god, but he is not the God of Scripture but the god of this world (2 Corinthians 4:4). I know from experience that the true and living God did not put rock & roll into my soul. It was the Devil who did that to foster my rebellion and licentiousness.

Petra's anti-fundamentalist attitude is evident from their aforementioned song entitled "Witch Hunt." It was written by Bob Hartman:

> "Another witch hunt looking for evil wherever we can find it/ Off on a tangent, Hope the Lord won't mind it/ Another witch hunt, Takin' a break from all our gospel labor/ On a crusade but we forgot our saber/ ... So send out the dogs and tally ho/ ... No one is safe, No stone is left unturned/ And we won't stop until somebody gets burned..." (Petra, "Witch Hunt")

According to the ecumenical, worldly CCM crowd, it is a witch hunt to judge things by the Word of God and to reprove sin and error. Petra sarcastically pretends that the only thing that is important is preaching the Gospel, and anything else, such as contending for the faith, is a waste of time which displeases the Lord. They slander the biblical fundamentalist as a person with a vain, hurtful agenda. Nothing could be further from the truth. The Apostle Paul spent much of his time defending the Gospel from false teachers and protecting the churches from error. He gave much space to this in his epistles. Was Paul a witch hunter? At the end of his life he said that he had fought a good fight. What had he fought? He had fought against error. He had fought for the truth. He had fought against the Devil and the Devil's men. The ecumenical CCM crowd is loving and tolerant toward almost anything except conservative Bible preaching.

Greg Volz, who was the lead singer for Petra from 1979-1985, is also very plain about his attitude toward Bible-believing fundamentalists: "The church has been bigoted, prejudiced. They'd hear rock and say 'that's the Devil'" (Mark Schwed, "Holy Rollers of Rock," *St. Petersburg Times*, Florida, Jan. 5, 1985). When Volz joined Petra, he had turned down an offer to sing for the popular secular rock band R.E.O. Speedwagon; but after leaving Petra Volz formed a secular rock band, Pieces of Eight, with former Paul McCartney drummer Joe English. Volz is a member of Willie Hinn's charismatic church in Vancouver, British Columbia. Willie is the brother of Benny Hinn.

Some of the Petra songs are very scriptural and outspoken about Bible truth, but even these are hidden behind a mask of hard rock music. An example is the song "Creed" on their *Beyond Belief* album:

> "I believe in God the Father — maker of heaven and earth/ And in Jesus Christ His only son/ I believe in the virgin birth/ I believe in the Man of Sorrows bruised for iniquities/ I believe in the Lamb who was crucified and hung between two thieves/ I believe in the resurrection on the third and glorious day/ And I believe in the empty tomb and the stone that the angel rolled away/ He descended and set the captives free/ And now He sits at God's right hand and prepares a place for me/ This is my creed — the witness I have heard/ The faith that has endured/ This truth is assured/ Through the darkest ages past/ Though persecuted, it will last/ And I will hold steadfast to this creed."

These words are scriptural, but they are hidden beneath loud, growling, angry rock and roll. The result is confusion. The words preach one thing; the music preaches something entirely different.

Hartman, complains that preaching against Christian rock music is hurtful:

> "It hurts us when some senior pastor says to his youth leader, 'Don't go to this

concert.' ... Not only does it deny the kids the opportunity and encouragement to go to the concert, but it hurts terribly our ability to minister. We experience a lot more skepticism" (Hartman, cited by Brian Newcomb, "Petra's Battle," *CCM Magazine*, October 1987).

I can understand why a Christian rocker like Hartman would think like this, but I see it differently.

First, the pastor has the authority and responsibility before God to set the standards for the young people in his church. Hebrews 13:17 says: "Obey them that have the rule over you, and submit yourselves: for they watch for your souls, as they that must give account, that they may do it with joy, and not with grief: for that is unprofitable for you." Hartman is actually stirring up rebellion against pastoral authority with his statement.

Second, I would reply to him and to other Christian rockers that as a preacher I have a responsibility to deliver the message I believe God has given me. It is not popular to preach against Contemporary Christian Music, even in some fundamental Baptist circles today. I believe a man would have to be certifiably insane to preach against CCM unless he is convinced God gave him this message. I have prayed diligently about the matter of music and whether or not I should resist CCM. I have examined this issue and re-examined it throughout the 25 years I have been saved. I do have a background in music. I played first chair first clarinet during much of my junior and senior high school years. I took private music lessons, won first place ribbons at music competitions both for solos and as a participant in ensembles, was selected to attend a special summer music program at the University of South Florida between my 10th and 11th grades, and was invited to join a symphony orchestra. I also immersed myself in rock music for 10 years before I was saved. When I began an intense study into the subject of CCM in recent months, I did so, I believe, with an open mind to obey whatever the Lord showed me. I was willing to re-evaluate my long-standing position against Christian rock, but my concerns were actually strengthened and I am more convinced than ever that I must preach against CCM. I understand how difficult it is to be the brunt of preaching, but the man of God is responsible to preach his message regardless of what the hearers think.

Third, if I am right about Christian rock music and it *IS* worldly and unacceptable to God, it is crucial that people hear this message so they can have opportunity to be warned about something which is hurtful to their spiritual well-being and also to the spiritual well-being of the churches.

Fourth, staying totally away from rock music has never hurt anyone spiritually, but loving it has definitely hurt multitudes. Even if preachers like me are wrong in our assessment of CCM and even if we draw the line against rock music a little too sharply, those who heed our warning will not be hurt by strictly avoiding rock music. It is like alcohol. No one ever became an alcoholic by avoiding alcoholic beverages altogether, but many have been deeply injured by alcohol who thought they could handle it in moderation. Can the Christian rocker promise that young people who are influenced by his music and example will not be drawn into the Devil's snare through entanglement with rock and roll? Can he promise that the young people he draws to rock music will not go on to become addicted to ever more vile forms of rock? Can he promise that they will not be enticed by the licentious lifestyle and rebellious demeanor of secular rock and roll?

PHILLIPS, LESLIE

For five years Leslie Phillips (1962-) performed and wrote as a contemporary Christian artist. She made her first album, *Beyond Saturday Night*, in 1983, and her last, *The Turning*, in 1987. A 1984 article in *Harpers* called her "The Queen of Christian Rock." "Leslie Phillips is on the cutting edge of the New Music. And she's no square. If ever there was a Queen of Christian Rock, she's it."

In 1987 Phillips left the Christian music industry for the secular:

> "Many fans of contemporary Christian music were shocked when singer Leslie Phillips announced she was leaving the gospel music world to sign a recording contract with a secular record label. At a California concert in May, Phillips' new material, black miniskirt, and nonchurchy stage talk were more than many fans could handle. An estimated 1,500 people walked out during the performance. 'I've never seen an audience react that way in my eight years of promoting,' says Robberson, who promoted the concert and formerly managed Phillips. 'Fans were disappointed and surprised, and I was in shock myself...' (*Christianity Today*, Oct. 2, 1987, p. 59).

She did not try to hide her unscriptural philosophy:

> "I found out that the church really wasn't the place where I had more freedom, it was the opposite: I actually was restricted more. And I always felt like I was swimming upstream in that environment. I guess the main thing is, I want to grow as an artist and I want to be able to write about whatever I want to write about. And I really don't want to be restricted, and I feel like I am in Gospel music. ... The born-again movement is more about obsession and narrow-mindedness and repression and true Christianity is about mercy and freedom and love" (Leslie Phillips, interview, *CCM Magazine*, November 1988, p. 8).

> "People are tired of Christian songs that are only praise and worship. The

church forced the 'old' taste in music on kids. We're breaking the stereotype" (Leslie Phillips, cited by Carol Leggett, *Amy Grant*, 1987, p. 112)

"Escaping from the Sunday-morning world of white pompadours, fixed smiles, and emotional lip-synching, Phillips discovered that there were ways to express her Christianity that required less control. 'Black gospel is very sensual, and it celebrates that. I believe that Jesus was a very secular, life-embracing person, when you get right down to it. He didn't hang out with the church hierarchy of the day; he hung out with the street people and the rebels. A lot of Christians have lost that part of him. That's kind of sad, but now I'm a lot more comfortable saying what I want to say. Bob Marley, Sam Cooke, and even Elvis Presley were able to colour their pop music with spiritual concerns, and I think that's a heckuva lot more healthy'" (Sam Phillips, cited by Ken Eisner, *The Georgia Straight*, Feb. 10-17, 1989).

Bob Marley, Sam Cooke, and Elvis weren't born again Christians.

In a May 1987 interview with *CCM Magazine*, Phillips spoke of her love for the Beatles: "[In the 1987 album *The Turning*] I just sort of returned to what I loved originally. You know, returning to your roots and all that. The Beatles were the first rock group I remember hearing, and I dearly love them. They were spectacular, even in their mistakes. There was a spirit in that kind of music that we don't have today."

She is now known as Sam Phillips and has produced four albums since her departure from the Christian music industry in 1987. One of these was *Martinis & Bikinis*. She also acted in the 1995 R-rated movie *Die Hard with A Vengeance*. It was rated R for "violence, gore, profanity, vulgarity, and sex."

PHILLIPS, CRAIG AND DEAN

The contemporary Christian recording group Phillips, Craig and Dean is composed of three Oneness ministers. The oneness Pentecostal doctrine denies the Trinity.
In 1997 Phillips, Craig and Dean joined Roman Catholic Kathy Troccoli and 40 other CCM artists to record *Love One Another*, a song with an ecumenical theme: "Christians from all denominations demonstrating their common love for Christ and each other." The song talks about tearing down the walls of denominational division. The broad range of participants who joined Kathy Troccoli in recording "Love One Another" demonstrates the ecumenical agenda of Contemporary Christian Music. The song witnessed Catholics, Pentecostals, Baptists, etc., yoked together to call for Christian unity.

PIERCE, JONATHAN

In 1997 Jonathan Pierce joined Roman Catholic Kathy Troccoli and 40 other CCM artists to record *Love One Another*, a song with an ecumenical theme: "Christians from all denominations demonstrating their common love for Christ and each other." The song talks about tearing down the walls of denominational division. The broad range of participants who joined Kathy Troccoli in recording "Love One Another" demonstrates the ecumenical agenda of Contemporary Christian Music. The song witnessed Catholics, Pentecostals, Baptists, etc., yoked together to call for Christian unity.

PINNICK, DOUG. See King's X.

P.O.D.

P.O.D. is a rap/hardcore band from San Diego, California. The name stands for Payable On Death. The members of P.O.D. wear tattoos and earrings and otherwise look like the world, and P.O.D. even tours with vile rock bands such as Korn. The band claims they play concerts with secular groups and record on a secular label "to be heard by the lost people." Note the following statement by Sonny Samilpa of P.O.D. "A secular label will help us be heard by the lost people. ... if they hear the music first, people will not be as quick to judge the Gospel being preached through the lyrics. That way, they can hear that not all Christian music is cheesy" (Sonny Samilpa, POD, *HM magazine*, May-June 1998, p. 48).

In the minds of these musicians, traditional Christian music is "cheesy." Thus they flippantly dismiss God's command to use "psalms, hymns, and spiritual songs." They think that the world can be drawn to Christ by a strange, clandestine message disguised by sensual music. In fact, P.O.D. doesn't have to worry about people judging the gospel preached through their songs, because it isn't there. Note the following two examples of their lyrics:

> "I see you people babble on and on and on graven/ Images, golden idols and false icons I'm seeking/ Wisdom like Solomon but my antennae keeps on/ Picking up evil transmissions at headquarters I/ Receive my mission blow up the ruler of the air (Eph 2:2)/ Like nuclear fission so I analyze my weapons laser/ Guided rifles that shoot spiritual wisdom I think I see/ Enemy warriors fragile heathens tryin' to run stuff/ Like mayors so with brotha's that snuff punks I set up/ Time bombs to destroy the strongholds of babylon" (P.O.D., "Breathe Babylon").
>
> "What's the problem son? You said you wanted some/ But when I started rocking POD got the job done/ My Lord said hard, hard is how you hit 'em/

> One blow with the mic and the quickness is how I get 'em/ Alternative thrash can you deal with it?/ Funk and groove with a hip hop feel to it/ Giving you a style with a different kind of sound/ So keep on rockin even when we bring it down/ Bring it down, bring it down, bring it down ya'll/ Bring it down, bring it down, bring it down/ Bring it down, bring it down, bring it down ya'll/ But don't change the funky funky sound" (P.O.D., "Can You Feel It?").

I challenge anyone to find the biblical gospel in those lyrics, and they are representative of all of their songs. The main message in "Can You Feel It" is that you can keep on rocking no matter what and that God Himself loves rock music. The message to "Breathe Babylon" is so obscure that it is meaningless. It is obvious that it is the hard rock music itself that really matters to P.O.D. and their followers.

In a 2001 interview with Theresa McKeon of Shoutweb titled "P.O.D. The Fundamental Elements of God Rock," the members of P.O.D. (Sonny, Traa, and Marcos) cussed and otherwise demonstrated their worldliness even while claiming to love the Lord. (Many young people who write to me to defend Christian rock music curse at me.) Sonny said "Jesus was the first rebel. He was the first punk rocker going against all the rest of it." When Shoutweb observed that P.O.D. is "making it cool for kids to be who they are" and "it's not like every kid has to choose to be good or evil," Sonny made the following amazing statement: "It's not even that they're evil. I mean, I like Slayer. I like Manson. I like this music and this dark imagery. They are people that are saying, 'Yeah dude, I'm Catholic. I believe in God.' But it's cooler to be into the dark stuff. ... We're not trying to be the 'white stuff' and they're the dark stuff." P.O.D. is not trying to make a difference between good and evil, light and darkness, but the Bible does. "And we know that we are of God, and the whole world lieth in wickedness" (1 John 5:19). "For ye were sometimes darkness, but now are ye light in the Lord: walk as children of light" (Ephesians 5:8).

Sonny went on to admit that he not only listens to vile secular rock music, but he watches R-rated movies. He justified that sort of thing, claiming that he has liberty in Christ make such choices, and that Christianity is not "putting on shackles." He is confusing liberty with license. "For, brethren, ye have been called unto liberty; only use not liberty for an occasion to the flesh, but by love serve one another" (Galatians 5:13).

Sonny criticized kids "who want to segregate themselves from the rest of the world," but the Bible warns, "Ye adulterers and adulteresses, know ye not that the friendship of the world is enmity with God? whosoever therefore will be a friend of the world is the enemy of God" (James 4:4).

PRESLEY, ELVIS

Elvis Presley (1935-1977) is aptly called the "King of Rock & Roll." He produced 94 gold singles, 43 gold albums; and his movies grossed over $180 million. Further millions were made through the sale or merchandise. He is the object of one of "the biggest personality cults in modern history." Twenty years after his death, hundreds of thousands each year stream through his Graceland mansion in Memphis, Tennessee; and the annual vigil held to commemorate his death is attended by thousands of dedicated fans, many of whom weep openly during the occasion.

Elvis grew up in a superficially "religious family," attending off and on First Assembly of God Church in East Tupelo, Mississippi, then First Assembly of God in Memphis. His father and mother were not committed church members, though, and Elvis himself never made a profession of faith or joined the church. The pastor in Memphis, James E. Hamill, says Elvis did not sing in church or participate in a church group (Steve Turner, *Hungry for Heaven*, p. 20). His father, Vernon, was "a weakling, a malingerer, always averse to work and responsibility" (Goldman, *Elvis: The Last 24 Hours*, p. 16). Vernon went to prison for check forgery when Elvis was a child. Later Vernon was kicked out of his hometown in Mississippi for moonshining. After the death of Elvis's mom, Vernon remarried, but his second wife left him because of his adultery with another woman. Elvis's mother was "a surreptitious drinker and alcoholic." When she was angry, "she cussed like a sailor" (Priscilla Presley, *Elvis and Me*, p. 172). She was "a woman susceptible to the full spectrum of backwoods superstitions, prone to prophetic dreams and mystical intuitions" (*Stairway to Heaven*, p. 46).

There is a saying, "The blues had a baby and named it rock & roll." Elvis Presley was a key figure in the birth of that baby. Elvis "spent much of his spare time hanging around the black section of town, especially on Beale Street, where bluesmen like Furry Lewis and B.B. King performed" (*Rolling Stone Encyclopedia of Rock*, p. 783). B.B. King said: "I knew Elvis before he was popular. He used to come around and be around us a lot. There was a place we used to go and hang out on Beale Street" (*A Time to Rock*, p. 35). Elvis also listened to radio WDIA, "a flagship blues station of the South that featured such flamboyant black disk jockeys as Rufus Thomas and B.B. King" (*Rock Lives*, p. 38). Elvis's first guitarist, Scotty Moore, learned many of his guitar licks from an old black blues player who worked with him before he teamed up with Elvis (Scotty Moore, *That's Alright, Elvis*, p. 57). Sam Phillips, owner of Sun Records, was looking for "a white man with a Negro sound and the Negro feel," because he believed the black blues and boogie-woogie music could become tremendously popular among white people if presented in the right way. Phillips had said, "If I could find a white man who had the Negro sound and the Negro feel, I could make a billion dollars." He found his man in

Elvis, and in 1954 he roared to popularity with "That's All Right, Mama," a song written by black bluesman Arthur "Big Boy" Crudup. The flipside of that hit single was "Blue Moon of Kentucky," which was a country song that Elvis hopped up and gave "a bluesy spin." Their first No. 1 hit single, "Mystery Train," was also an old blues number. Six of the 15 songs Elvis recorded for Sun Records (before going over to RCA-Victor a year later) were from black bluesmen.

There was also a strong Southern gospel music element in Elvis's music, which has been described as "blues laced with country and country tinged with gospel" (*Rolling Stone Encyclopedia*, p. 782). Elvis loved gospel quartets and black spirituals and attended Southern gospel singings as well as black church singings, but he did not surrender to Christ and pursued, instead, the world, the flesh, and the Devil.

It is important to understand that the Southern gospel groups that Evis loved were as much jazzy entertainers as soul winners. The Delmore Brothers, for example, "mixed sacred lyrics, blues and boogie with spectacular commercial results" (*Stairway to Heaven*, p. 49). Another group, the Melody Masters, presented "a rambunctious type of program" (Taylor, *Happy Rhythms*, p. 22). Of of the singers in the Melody Masters, Wally Varner, admits that "in those days gospel music wasn't as spiritual, it was more entertaining."

The pioneer of the ragtime gospel piano style was Dwight Brock, who played in one of the Stamps quartets.

> "Brock played a rhythm piano style; some thought it sounded a little like Dixieland [jazz] or razzamatazz. ... Thousands of pianists would copy his style in the years to come. ... IT WAS REVOLUTIONARY BECAUSE IT JAZZED UP GOSPEL MUSIC JUST ENOUGH FOR THE SECULAR PUBLIC TO CATCH ON. Dwight's nephew, Brock Speer, who sings bass for the Speer Family today, said when his uncle was a boy in the early teens—he was born in 1905—he heard a circus drummer playing SYNCOPATED RHYTHMS on snare drums, and said to himself, 'I wonder if I could do that on the piano?'" (*The Music Men*, pp. 38,39).

The following is a description of the type of gospel quartets that most strongly influenced Elvis:

> The white gospel quartets of the 1950s, when [Elvis] Presley started to study them, were every bit as exciting as their black counterparts, USING SHOWBIZ HYPE, WHIPPING UP CROWDS AND CREATING STARS. Reporting on an all-night sing in Atlanta, Georgia, for *The Saturday Evening Post* (June 1956), Furman Bisher compared the audience response to the Oak Ridge Quartet to bobby soxers' swooning for Frank Sinatra. 'Women out there

shrieked, and a couple of young girls rushed to the stage edge to snap pictures of the tenor who was holding that high note the way a trumpet player prolongs a "ride,"' wrote Bisher. ...

Presley idolized such gospel stars for the rest of his life. His particular favorites were J.D. Sumner, the tall, stringy bass vocalist with the Blackwood Brothers, who also went to the First Assembly of God Church in Memphis, and Jake Hess and Hovie Lister of the Statesmen Quartet (which actually had five members). An ordained minister, LISTER IS OFTEN CREDITED WITH BRINGING SHOW BUSINESS TO QUARTET SINGING. At the time he said, 'If it takes shaking my hair down, beating a piano like Liberace or Piano Red to keep these young people out of beer joints and the rear seats of cars, I'll do it. The Devil's got his kind of entertainment. We've got ours. They criticize me, say I'm too lively for religion, but I get results. That's what counts.'

White quartet singing had developed in the 1920s ... they began to develop showmanship and gimmicks during the 1940s. ... Hovie Lister, a dashing young man with long, dark wavy hair and an Errol Flynn mustache, LOVED TO SHAKE IT ALL UP FOR THE LORD. He joined with Crumpler and Jake Hess to form the Statesmen Quartet, which was to become one of the first supergroups of white gospel, catapulting the music to commercial acceptability and SETTING THE STYLE FOR EMERGENT ROCK 'N' ROLLERS BRED ON HOLY MUSIC.

Although much was made of the evils of dancing, show business, jukeboxes and television, THE SUCCESS OF THE GOSPEL QUARTETS WAS LARGELY DUE TO THEIR PRESENTING MUCH OF THE SAME GLOSS AND EXCITEMENT in an acceptable context. The songs were about loving your neighbor, being holy and not giving in to 'modern religion,' but THE PERFORMANCES DREW FROM POP, BLUES, COUNTRY, RAGTIME AND JAZZ. ...

Don Butler, now director of archives for the Nashville-based Gospel Music Association, was the Statesmen Quartet's manager during the 1950s. 'They were sensational,' he remembers. 'Hovie Lister had no peer in showmanship. He created a tremendous rapport with the audience. HE COULD TURN THEIR EMOTIONS ON AND OFF JUST LIKE THAT. They also had highly polished harmonies and arrangements. HOVIE WOULD JUMP ONTO A PIANO AND SHAKE HIS LONG BLACK HAIR INTO HIS FACE WHILE THE REST OF THE GROUP DANCED ON STAGE. They were the first quartet to use four individual microphones. Before that everyone had gathered around one mike' (emphasis added) (Steve Turner, *Hungry for Heaven*, pp. 29-31).

Bill Gaither, in his history of Southern gospel, admits that Hovie Lister's "approach was loud, fast, swingy, and pop" and that "he would do whatever it took to get the loudest applause, the biggest laugh" (Bill Gaither, *Homecoming*, p. 133). In fact, some conservative Christian radio stations broke Statesmen records on the air to protest their jazzy music.

It was to this type of Southern gospel—the showmanship, entertainment, jazzed-up type—that Elvis Presley was drawn. James Wetherington of the Statesmen, who was called "The Chief," would even shake his leg in a fashion similar to the way Presley did (though not nearly as lasciviously!).

By 1956, Presley was a national rock star and teenage idol, and his music and image had a tremendously unwholesome effect upon young people. Parents, pastors, and teachers condemned his sensual music and suggestive dancing and warned of the evil influence he was exercising among young people. They were right, but the onslaught of rock & roll was unstoppable. When asked about his sensual stage gyrations, he replied: "It's the beat that gets you. If you like it and you feel it, you can't help but move to it. That's what happens to me. I can't help it" (*Hungry for Heaven*, p. 21). Elvis correctly observed the power of the rock & roll beat.

Between March 1958 and March 1960 Elvis served in the army, then resumed his music and movie career where he had left off. He had many top ten hits in the first half of the 1960s. In 1961, Priscilla Beaulieu moved in with Elvis and his father and stepmother in his Graceland mansion. They finally married May 1, 1967, and exactly nine months later, on February 1, 1968, Elvis's only child, Lisa Marie, was born.

Elvis did not drink, but he abused drugs most of his life. He began using amphetamines and Benzedrine to give him a lift when he began his rock & roll career in the first half of the 1950s. It is possible that they were first given to him by Memphis disk jockey Dewey Phillips, who helped popularize Elvis's music by playing his songs repeatedly (Goldman, p. 9). The drugs "transformed the shy, mute, passive 'Baby Elvis' of those years into the Hillbilly Cat.'" He also used marijuana some and took LSD at least once. In her autobiography, Priscilla Presley says that Elvis was using drugs heavily by 1960 and that his personality changed dramatically because of the drugs. After the breakup of his marriage in 1973, Elvis "was hopelessly drug-dependent." He abused barbiturates and narcotics so heavily that he destroyed himself. He died on August 16, 1977, at age 42 in his bathroom at Graceland, of a shutdown of his central nervous system caused by polypharmacy, or the combined effect of a number of drugs. There is some evidence, in fact, that Elvis committed suicide (Goldman, *Elvis: The Last 24 Hours*, pp. 161-175). He had attempted suicide in 1967 just before his marriage. Fourteen drugs were found in his body during the autopsy, including toxic or near toxic levels of four. Dr. Norman Weissman, director of operations at Bio-Sciences Laboratories, where the toxicity tests were performed, testified that he had never seen so many drugs in one specimen. Elvis's doctor, George Nichopolous, had prescribed 19,000 pills and vials for Elvis in the last 31.5 months of his life. Elvis required 5,110 pills per year just for his sleeping routine. Elvis also obtained drugs from many other sources, both legal and illegal! It was estimated that he spent at least $1 million per year on drugs and drug prescribing doctors (Goldman, p. 56). Dr. Nichopolous's head nurse, Tish Henley, actually lived on the grounds of Graceland and monitored Elvis's drug consumption. In 1980 Nichopolous was found in violation of the prescribing rules of the Tennessee Board of Medical Examiners, and he lost his license for three months and was put on probation for three years. In 1992 his medical license was revoked permanently.

After a protracted legal battle, Elvis's daughter, Lisa Marie, inherited his entire estate, now valued at over $100 million. Graceland was made into a museum, and it is visited by more than 650,000 per year.

Elvis was self-centered to the extreme. Though he gave away many expensive gifts, including fancy automobiles and jewelry, it was obvious that he used these to obtain his own way. "But when his extravagant presents fail to inspire a properly beholden attitude, the legendary Presley generosity peels off, revealing its true motive as the desire for absolute control" (Goldman, p. 104). He could not take even kind criticism and was quick to cut off friends who crossed him in any way. "A little Caesar, he made himself all-powerful in his kingdom, reducing everyone around him to a sycophant or hustler" (Goldman, *Elvis: The Last 24 Hours*, p. 15). He was hyper critical, sarcastic, and mean-spirited to people around him. When Elvis first began touring with Scotty Moore and Bill Black, they traveled in the automobile owned and maintained by Moore's wife, Bobbie. She worked at Sears and was the only one who had a steady paying job at the time. When Elvis became an overnight star and began to make big money, he purchased a Lincoln, but he never made any attempt to replace Bobbie's car or to pay back what she had put into it for them. Elvis promised Scotty Moore and Bill Black, the members of his first band, that he would not forget them if they prospered financially, but he did just that. While Elvis was making tens of thousands of dollars by 1956 and 1957, Moore and Black were paid lowly wages and were finally let go to fend for themselves as best they could. Elvis never gave his old friends automobiles or anything of significant value. Reminiscing on those days, Scotty Moore says, "He promised us that the more he made the more we would make, but it hasn't worked out that way. The thing that got me, the thing that wasn't right about it, was the fact that Elvis didn't keep his word. ... We were supposed to be the King's men. In reality, we were the court jesters" (Moore, *That's Alright, Elvis*, pp. 146,155). Elvis turned them "out to pasture like broken-down mules, without a penny." Elvis kept up this pattern all his life. Bobby West served his cousin Elvis faithfully for 20 years, and was rewarded in 1976 by being fired with three day's notice and one week's pay. Delbert West (another cousin) and

Dave Hebler were similarly treated.

Elvis often exhibited a violent, even murderous, rage. He was "notorious for making terrible threats." He cooked up murder plots against a number of people, including the man his ex-wife ran off with and three former bodyguards who wrote a tell-all book about him. He threw things at people and even dragged one woman through several rooms by her hair. He drew and fired his guns many times when he could not get his way, firing into ceilings, shooting out television sets. When his last girlfriend, Ginger Alden, attempted to leave Graceland against his wishes, he fired over her head to force her to stay. Elvis hit Priscilla, his wife, at least once, giving her a black eye. He also threw chairs and other things at her.

Elvis cursed and profaned the Lord's name continually in his ordinary conversation.

Elvis was a fornicator and adulterer. He had "a roving eye." "His list of one-night stands would fill volumes" (Jim Curtin, *Elvis*, p. 119). He slept with countless girls before his marriage to Priscilla Beaulieu, and had multiple affairs after his marriage. Priscilla was only a 14-year-old ninth grader when Elvis began dating her in 1959 during his army tour in Germany. At the time he met Priscilla, he had an even younger girl living in his house (Moore, *That's Alright, Elvis*, p. 162). Elvis corrupted the shy, teenaged Priscilla. He gave her liquor and got her drunk. He got her hooked on pills. He taught her to dress in a licentious manner. He encouraged her to lie to her parents. He led her into immorality and pornography. He taught her to gamble. He used hallucinogenic drugs with her. (These are facts published in Priscilla's autobiography.) In 1962 Priscilla moved in with Elvis at his Graceland mansion in Memphis and they lived together for five years before they married in May 1967. (The marriage was probably due to pressure put on Elvis by his manager, who was worried about the star's public image.) Elvis and Priscilla had constant problems in their marriage and were divorced in 1973. Elvis had many adulterous affairs during his marriage, and Priscilla admits two affairs of her own. Scotty Moore's second wife, Emily, said she felt sorry for Priscilla because of all of the women Elvis was seeing. Elvis seduced his stepbrother Billy's wife, Angie, and destroyed their marriage. He then banished Billy from Graceland.

Elvis lived for pleasure but was utterly bored with life before he was 40 years old. Elvis sought to be rich, but it came with a curse attached to it and most of his riches disappeared into thin air. Though Elvis's music, movies, and trademarked items grossed an estimated two or more BILLIONS of dollars during his lifetime, he saw relatively little of it and most of what he did receive was squandered on play things. By 1969, he was so broke that he was forced to revive his stage career. He had no investments, no property except that surrounding Graceland, and no savings. His manager, Colonel Parker, had swindled or mismanaged him out of a vast fortune. (On Parker's advice, for example, Elvis sold the rights to his record royalties in 1974 for a lump sum which netted him only $750,000 after taxes.)

Elvis's music was reflective of his lifestyle: sensual and licentious. Many of his performances were characterized by hysteria and near rioting. Females attempted to rip off Elvis's clothes. There were riots at his early concerts. "He'd start out, 'You ain't nothin' but a Hound Dog,' and they'd just go to pieces. They'd always react the same way. There'd be a riot every time" (Scotty Moore, p. 175). In DeLeon, Texas, in July 1955, fans "shredded Presley's pink shirt—a trademark by now—and tore the shoes from his feet." At a 1956 concert in Jacksonville, Florida, Juvenile Court Judge Marion Gooding warned Elvis that if he did his "hip-gyrating movements" and created a riot, he would be arrested and sent to jail. Elvis performed flatfooted and stayed out of trouble.

Elvis's first band was composed of three members, Elvis, lead guitarist Scotty Moore, and bass guitarist Bill Black. The lives of all three men were marked by confusion and tragedy. Elvis died young and miserable. When asked about his severe narcotic usage in the years before his death, Elvis replied, "It's better to be unconscious than miserable" (Goldman, p. 3). Bill Black, who formed the Bill Black Combo after his years with Elvis, died in 1965 at age 29 of a brain tumor. Scotty Moore was divorced multiple times. He also had multiple extra-marital affairs. When he had been married only three months to his first wife, he fathered a child by another woman, a nightclub singer he met on the road. The little girl was born the night Elvis, Moore, and Black recorded their first hit at Sun Records. During his second marriage, Moore fathered another out-of-wedlock child. In 1992, at age 61, Moore filed for bankruptcy.

Elvis performed and recorded many gospel songs. As we have seen, in the early 1950s he attended all-night gospel quartet concerts at the First Assembly of God and Ellis Auditorium in Memphis and befriended such famous groups as the Blackwood Brothers and the Statesmen. When he was 18, Elvis auditioned for a place in the Songfellows Quartet, but the position was given to James Blackwood's nephew Cecil. Later, as his rock & roll career was prospering, Elvis was offered a place with the Blackwood Brothers, but he turned it down. Even after he became famous, Elvis continued attending Southern gospel sings and the National Quartet Convention. In the early years of his rock & roll career, he sang some with the Blackwood Brothers and the Statesmen at all-night sings at Ellis Auditorium in Memphis (Taylor, *Happy Rhythms*, p. 117). Elvis told pop singer Johnny Rivers that he patterned his singing style after Jake Hess of the Statesmen Quartet (*Happy Rhythm*, p. 49). The Jordanaires performed as background singers on Elvis Presley records and as session singers for many other raunchy rock and country recordings. Members of the Speer Family (Ben and Brock) also sang on Elvis recordings, including "I've Got a Woman" and "Heartbreak Hotel." The Jordanaires provided vocals for Elvis's 1956 megahit "Hound Dog." The Jordanaires toured with Eddy

Arnold as well as with Elvis. They also performed on some of Elvis's indecent movies. J.D. Sumner and the Stamps toured with Elvis from 1969 until his death in 1977, performing backup for the King of Rock & Roll in sin-holes such as Las Vegas nightclubs. Ed Hill, one of the singers with the Stamps, was Elvis's announcer for two years. It was Hill who concluded the Elvis concerts with: "Ladies and gentlemen, Elvis has left the building. Goodbye, and God bless you." (During the years in which Sumner and the Stamps were backing Elvis Presley at Las Vegas and elsewhere, Sumner's nephew, Donnie, who sang in the group, became a drug addict and was lured into the licentious pop music field.) Sumner helped arrange Elvis's funeral, and the Stamps, the Statesmen, and James Blackwood provided the music.

Elvis's love for gospel music is not evidence that he was born again. His on-again, off-again profession of faith in Christ also was not evidence that he was saved. Three independent Baptist preachers have testified that Elvis told them that he had trusted Jesus as his Savior in his younger years but was backslidden. There was no biblical evidence for that, though. We must remember that Elvis grew up around churches and understood all of the terminology. There was never a time, though, when Elvis's life changed. Empty professions of faith do not constitute biblical salvation. "Therefore if any man be in Christ, he is a new creature: old things are passed away; behold, all things are become new" (2 Cor. 5:17). Elvis liked some gospel music but he did not like Bible preaching. He refused to allow anyone, including God, tell him how to live his life. That is evidence of an unregenerate heart.

We agree with the following sad, but honest, assessment of Elvis's life: "Elvis Presley never stood for anything. He made no sacrifices, fought no battles, suffered no martyrdom, never raised a finger to struggle on behalf of what he believed or claimed to believe. Even gospel, the music he cherished above all, he travestied and commercialized and soft-soaped to the point where it became nauseating. ... Essentially, Elvis was a phony. ... He feigned piety, but his spirituals sound insincere or histrionic" (Goldman, *Elvis: The Last 24 Hours*, pp. 187,188).

The Bible warns that friendship with the world is enmity with God (James 4:4); and while we hope Elvis did trust Jesus Christ as God and Savior before he died, there is no evidence that he truly repented of his sin or separated from the world or believed in the Christ of the Bible. The book he took to the bathroom just before he died was either *The Force of Jesus* by Frank Adams or *The Scientific Search for the Face of Jesus*, depending on various accounts. Both books present an unscriptural, pagan christ. Elvis never made a public profession of faith in Christ, was never baptized, and never joined a church. Pastor Hamill, former pastor of First Assembly of God in Memphis, says that Presley visited him in the late 1950s, when he was at the height of his rock & roll powers, and testified: "Pastor, I'm the most miserable young man you've ever seen. I've got all the money I'll ever need to spend. I've got millions of fans. I've got friends. But I'm doing what you taught me not to do, and I'm not doing the things you taught me to do" (Steve Turner, *Hungry for Heaven*, p. 20).

Elvis did not believe the Bible in any traditional sense. His christ was a false one. Elvis constructed "a personalised religion out of what he'd read of Hinduism, Judaism, numerology, theosophy, mind control, positive thinking and Christianity" (*Hungry for Heaven*, p. 143). The night he died, he was reading a book about psychic energy (Goldman, *Elvis: The Last 24 Hours*, p. 140). Elvis loved material by guru Paramahansa Yogananda, the Hindu founder of the Self-Realization Fellowship. (I studied Yogananda's writings and belonged to his Fellowship before I was saved in 1973.) In considering a marriage to Ginger Alden (which never came to pass) prior to his death, Elvis wanted the ceremony to be held in a pyramid-shaped arena "in order to focus the spiritual energies upon him and Ginger" (Goldman, *Elvis: The Last 24 Hours*, p. 125). Elvis traveled with a portable bookcase containing over 200 volumes of his favorite books. The books most commonly associated with him were books promoting pagan religion, such as *The Prophet* by Kahilil Gibran; *Autobiography of a Yogi* by Yogananda; *The Mystical Christ* by Manley Palmer; *The Life and Teachings of the Master of the Far East* by Baird Spalding; *The Inner Life* by Leadbetter; *The First and Last Freedom* by Krishnamurti; *The Urantia Book*; *The Rosicrucian Cosmo-Conception*; the *Book of Numbers* by Cheiro; and *Esoteric Healing* by Alice Bailey. Elvis was a great fan of occultist Madame Blavatsky. He was so taken with Blavatsky's book *The Voice of Silence*, which contains the supposed translation of ancient occult Tibetan incantations, that he "sometimes read from it onstage and was inspired by it to name his own gospel group, Voice" (Goldman, *Elvis*, p. 436). Another of Elvis's favorite books was *The Impersonal Life*, which supposedly contains words recorded directly from God by Joseph Benner. Biographer Albert Goldman says Elvis gave away hundreds of copies of this book over the last 13 years of his life.

Elvis was sometimes called the evangelist by those who hung around him, and he called them his disciples; but the message he preached contained "strange permutations of Christian dogma" (*Stairway to Heaven*, p. 56). Elvis believed, for example, that Jesus slept with his female followers. Elvis even had messianic concepts of himself as the savior of mankind in the early 1970s. He read the Bible aloud at times and even conducted some strange "Bible studies," but he had no spiritual discernment and made up his own wild-eyed interpretations of biblical passages. His ex-wife, Priscilla, joined the Church of Scientology, as did his daughter, Lisa Marie, and her two children.

Elvis prayed a lot in his last days, asking God for forgiveness, but the evidence points to a Judas type of remorse instead of godly repentance. "For godly sorrow worketh repentance to salvation not to be repented of: but the sorrow of the world worketh death" (2

Cor. 7:10). One can have sorrow or remorse for the consequences of one's sin without repenting toward God and trusting God's provision for sin, which is the shed blood of Jesus Christ. Judas "repented himself" in the sense that he was sorry for betraying Jesus, and he committed suicide because of his despair, but he did not repent *toward God* and trust Jesus Christ as his Savior (Matt. 27:3-5). True biblical salvation is "repentance toward God, and faith toward our Lord Jesus Christ" (Acts 20:21). Had Elvis done this he would have been a new man (2 Cor. 5:17) and would have seen things through the eyes of hope instead of through the eyes of despair. He would have had supernatural power, and there would have been a change in his life. The spiritual blindness would have fallen from his eyes and he would have cast off his eastern mysticism and cleaved to the truth. Elvis's guilt and sorrow produced no perceptible change in his life.

RAMBO, DOTTIE

Dottie Rambo was raised in a Oneness Pentecostal church which denies the Trinity. She wrote "Behold the Lamb" and other popular contemporary songs.

RELIENT K

The Christian rock band Relient K was featured in a November 2001 advertising campaign for Abercrombie & Fitch (A&F). This company is infamous for its use of scantily clad and seductively posed young people in its commercials and catalogs. Bill Johnson, president of the American Decency Association, rightly criticized Relient K for its association with such an immoral company, saying: "I am very disappointed and very troubled that a Christian band . . . that is naming Jesus Christ in its music and ministry, would in any regard feel comfortable aligning themselves with a corporation so blatant in targeting our youth through sexually erotic images" (*Religion Today*, Nov. 5, 2001). Wendy Wright, a director with Concerned Women of America, added that the association between Relient K and A&F sends a mixed message: "A young person could easily come to think that you can be a Christian and still promote and be involved in pornography."

REPP, RAY

Ray Repp is a Catholic musician who composed a series of folk masses in the 1970s.

REZ (RESURRECTION) BAND

The Resurrection Band was formed in 1972 as an outreach of Jesus People USA, an ecumenical charismatic community in Chicago. They produced the "first real heavy metal rock album totally produced by Christians" (*CCM Magazine*, July 1998, p. 22). The Jesus People USA have done much good through such efforts as reaching street people, feeding the hungry, visiting prisons, and helping the handicapped. The founder of the Resurrection Band, Glenn Kaiser, and another band member, John Herrin, are elders in the JPUSA church. Two other band members are deacons.

Kaiser describes the group's ecumenical philosophy:

> "Jesus prayed that all of His followers 'may be one' (John 17:20-23). ... Ninety-nine percent of all true Christians believe in the same basic Bible doctrines. But when hairs are split ... so are we—one from another. ... Over the years, I have had the pleasure of meeting true Christians in nearly every kind of denominational (large and small) and inter- or nondenominational church" (Kaiser, *The Responsibility of the Christian Musician*, pp. 53-55).

Kaiser misrepresents Christ's prayer in John 17. The Lord Jesus was not asking Christians to build ecumenical unity. He was praying to God the Father to create supernatural unity among those who are born again. That prayer was answered. Those who are born again are members of the same family. Christ certainly did not pray that His people will ignore false doctrine and sin for the purpose of creating a man-made unity. That would be contrary to the teaching of many other passages. Timothy, for example, was instructed not to allow ANY OTHER DOCTRINE (1 Timothy 1:3). That is an extremely narrow view of doctrinal soundness. Such an attitude toward doctrine will not allow a Christian to be ecumenical, because he cannot ignore false doctrine.

Kaiser's idea that 99% of "true" Christians believe the same basic doctrines is simply not accurate. The largest group of professing Christians are Roman Catholics—roughly one billion strong. Roman Catholicism teaches all sorts of unscriptural doctrines, such as the mass as a re-sacrifice of Christ, baptism as regeneration, the pope as the holy father, Mary as the Queen the Heaven, the priests as representatives of Christ, the sacraments as means of salvation, and purgatory as the means of purification. Perhaps Kaiser and the Resurrection Band do not consider Roman Catholics true Christians. If so, why did he not warn about Catholic doctrine in his book and why does he not why does he not warn of CCM musicians who are themselves Catholic or of those who treat Romanists as if they are true Christians? Another large group of professing Christians are members of various Protestant denominations, such as Lutheran and Episcopalian. Both of these teach a form of infant baptism and baptismal regeneration. This one heresy alone would require that we mark and avoid them in obedience to Romans 16:17. Another large group are Pentecostals, many of whom have perverted the doctrine of the Holy Spirit and denied the doctrine of eternal security. These are doctrinal errors which cannot be ignored for the sake of ecumenism.

The Resurrection Band loves to play secular rock songs and thereby they create a taste in Christian young people for that unholy music. For example they sing the song "Bargain" by legendary rock guitarist Pete Townshend of the violent/immoral/occultic rock band, The Who. Townshend wrote "Bargain" as a tribute to his Hindu guru Meher Baba. Townshend has testified: "Baba is Christ, because being a Christian is just like being a Baba lover" (Townshend, cited by Bob Larson, *Rock*, 1984, p. 140). Consider the words to the song "Bargain" which Rez Band has popularized for Christian young people:

> "I'll pay any price just to get you/ I'll work all my life and I will/ To win you, I'd stand naked, stoned, and stabbed/ I'd call that a bargain/ The best I ever had/ The best I ever had ... I'll pay any price just to win you/ Surrender my good life or bad/ To find you/ I'm gonna drown an unsung man/ I call that a bargain/ The best I ever had..."

Not only is it blasphemous to take a song by an immoral rock star about a Hindu guru and sing it as to Jesus Christ, but the song itself promotes a false gospel. We do not and cannot win the true God by sacrifice and works. Salvation is "not of works, lest any man should boast" (Ephesians 2:8-9). Further, the sinner has no "good life" to surrender. All our righteousness is as filthy rags before God (Isaiah 64:6). There is none that doeth good, no, not one (Romans 3:12).

Another song by Rez is "Silence Screams." Notice the strange lyrics:

> "The folly in our passions/ The prisons of desire/ The foolishness of bigots/ Tinder for the fire/ In bitterness and exile/ As foolish as it seems/ In the coldest, darkest spirit/ Silence screams/ Silence screams/ The echoes roar/ Silence screams forevermore..."

RICHARD, CLIFF

Cliff Richard (1940-) is one of the most popular rock singers in Britain. He began his career in pop music in 1958. During his first five years he sold 5.5 million singles. He appeared in his first film in the late 1950s and began appearing in a television series in 1961. His 1961 movie, *The Young Ones,* was the second biggest box office hit of the year. He has retained his popularity through the years, and even in the 1990s his singles continue to reach the top ten on the charts. His 1987 album, *Always Guaranteed,* became his highest selling studio album of all time. In 1989 he celebrated thirty years in "show business" with two sellout Wembley Stadium shows performing to 144,000 people. Ticket sales for his 1995 tour through South East Asia, Australia, New Zealand, and South Africa exceeded half a million. A string of shows celebrating his 40th show biz anniversary are sellouts. In a 1998 poll conducted by the British Market Research Bureau for British music magazine *Mojo,* Richard was voted the seventh greatest pop artist of all time. The Beatles are No. 1, and Elvis Presley is No. 2. Richard is ranked the tenth highest selling artist of all time, having sold over 280 million albums and singles worldwide. In 1995 Cliff Richard became the first pop star to be knighted by the Queen of England.

At a Billy Graham crusade in London in 1966 Cliff Richard professed faith in Christ and has since appeared in many Christian forums, including Billy Graham evangelistic crusades, to share his faith.

At the same time, though, he has retained his close fellowship with the world, touring with secular rock artists such as Olivia Newton John. He has also continued to sing sensual songs, such as "Devil Woman," "Born to Rock 'n' Roll," "Move It," "Do You Wanna Dance," "What Would I Do for the Love of a Girl," and "One Time Lover Man."

> "Come on pretty baby lets a move it and a groove it/ Well shake oh baby shake oh honey please don't lose it/ It's rhythm that gets into your heart and soul/ Well let me tell you baby it's called rock 'n roll" (Cliff Richard, "Move It").

In 1976 his song "Devil Woman" became a huge hit in the United States, reaching No. 6 on the charts and selling over one million copies.

> "I've had nothing but bad luck/ Since the day I saw the cat at my door/ So I came here to you sweet lady/ Answering your mystical call/ Crystal ball on the table/ Showing the future the past/ Same cat with them evil eyes/ And I know it was a spell she'd cast" (Cliff Richard, "Devil Woman").

In 1985, Richard recorded "Slow Rivers" with bi-sexual rock star Elton John. Richard's 1988 single, "Mistletoe and Wine," rose to number one and became the highest selling single of the year. His 1995 single, "Misunderstood Man," was banned by BBC's Radio 2 for being "too raunchy." In 1996, Richard's musical, *Heathcliff*, opened in London. Joining Richard in the creation of this musical were Olivia Newton John, John Farrar, and Tim Rice. The latter was the co-author of the blasphemous 1970 musical *Jesus Christ Superstar*. Rice and co-collaborator Andrew Lloyd Webber were agnostics who desired to debunk what they felt was the myth of Jesus Christ's deity. In *Jesus Christ Superstar* they portrayed Christ as a confused philosopher who had a secret love affair with Mary Magdalene, who died for nothing, and did not rise from the dead.

In 1997, Cliff Richard contributed a song to the Princess Diana tribute album which was released following her death. In June 1998 he performed "Do You Wanna Dance," "Move It," and other songs before 15,000 at the Princess Diana Memorial Concert. Richard's 1998 album, *Real As I Wanna Be*, is largely produced by Peter Wolf who has produced for The Rolling Stones and Aretha Franklin.

There is no Gospel presentation at any of the Cliff Richard web sites. Everything is in praise of Cliff Richard with nothing said in praise of Jesus Christ.

RICHARD, LITTLE. See Little Richard.

ROSE, ROGER

"[Roger Rose's] attempts to avoid church talk and cliché result in some fresh, invigorating images. In 'Living Dead,' the line 'I need life blood' is, Rose suggests, 'another way of getting at Jesus' words that we need to be born again without using those now too familiar words" (*CCM Magazine*, March 1987, p. 14).

RUIS, DAVID

David Ruis, one of the worship leaders at the Toronto Airport church, is a popular song writer in the Vineyard movement. The Toronto Airport Church was formerly connected with Wimber's Vineyard movement, and though it is no longer a member of the Vineyard association of churches, it continues to have close fellowship with the Vineyard churches and pastors. Ruis's song "Break Dividing Walls," calling for ecumenical unity, is widely used.

> "There is a place of commanded blessing/ Where brethren in unity dwell/ A place where anointing oil is flowing/ And we live as one/ You have called us to be a body/ You have called us friends/ Joined together in the bond of the Spirit/ Unto the end/ Father we join with the prayer of Jesus/ As you are so let us be one/ Joined together in unity and purpose/ All for the love of Your Son/ We will break dividing walls/ We will break dividing walls/ We will break dividing walls/ In the name of your Son/ We will break dividing walls/ We will break dividing walls/ And we will be one."

ST. JAMES, REBECCA

The Australian-born Rebecca St. James' (1977-) real name is Rebecca Smallbone. Like many CCM musicians, there are many commendable things about her life and ministry. She is from a large, close-knit Christian family (seven children). Her father is her manager, and family members travel with her on music tours. They seek to be ministry focused rather than entertainment or business focused. She refuses to be caught up in the "cross-over" frenzy, wisely noting that "We're not trying to water down our lyrics so that other people can maybe suddenly be interested in our message. At the end of the day, I don't think that formula works" (*Charisma*, April 1999, p. 54).

Sadly, though, her charismatic doctrine and rock music make it impossible for us to recommend her. In Australia, the Smallbones attended the Hills Christian Life Centre, which is a headquarters for the "Laughing Revival" type phenomenon similar to that being experienced in Toronto and Pensacola.

When Pope John Paul II visited the States in January 1999, Rebecca St. James and other CCM groups joined hands with hundreds of thousands of Catholics to welcome him. Featured at a Catholic youth rally connected with the Pope's visit, were St. James, dc Talk, Audio Adrenaline, Jennifer Knapp, The W's, and the Supertones (*CCM Magazine*, April 1999, p. 12). Each attendee received a rosary with instructions about how to pray to Mary.

In an interview with *Charisma* magazine, Rebecca made the following statement that indicates the confusion of her doctrinal position:

> St. James, who attended Hills Christian Life Centre in Australia—a bustling charismatic congregation in Sydney—is quick to point out that her ability to speak boldly to her generation isn't self-derived. In fact, she says, many times the Holy Spirit has guided her words, especially in sensitive situations.
>
> 'One time I was asked in a concert, "Do Mormons go to heaven?" ' she recalls. 'It really caught me off guard, but I sensed the Holy Spirit leading me to say, 'Only God can judge a person's heart.' I know that answer didn't come from me (St. James, cited by Lindy Warren, "A Saint at Age 21," *Charisma*, April 1999, p. 46).

Of course, Rebecca is only 21 and it is understandable if she is unable to give a proper biblical reply to some questions. Her answer, though, does not merely reflect biblical ignorance; it plainly reflects her unscriptural, "judge-not" charismatic philosophy. No one who believes Mormon doctrine will go to Heaven, because the Mormon organization teaches a false gospel. We do not have to wait to see how God will judge such cases. The Bible already tells us. Galatians 1 says anyone who believes or preaches a false gospel is cursed of God. Rebecca should have used that occasion to warn her fans that there are many false gospels (2 Cor. 11:1-4) and to exhort them to be certain that that they are born again through faith in the gospel of the Bible. Instead, she gave them a false answer that implied that might be possible for a Mormon to go to Heaven. For Rebecca St. James to claim that God gave her that unscriptural answer illustrates the serious problem with charismatic ministries and their false doctrine of revelation knowledge.

SERVANT

Servant is described as follows: "This Christian rock band features 'edgy, rhythmic, treble rock and an aggressive stage performance...' Not only is their show 'filled with the salvation message,' but it is augmented with smoke-bombs and flash-pots. Their 1983 tour was billed as 'The Largest Christian Rock-Gospel Show in America.' Such a contradictory testimony immediately suggests an irony. The salvation message is punctuated by smoke-bombs and presented a la P.T. Barnum. The frivolity of a 'show' detracts immensely from the gravity of the Gospel" (Ric Llewellyn, "Christian? Rock," *Foundation*, Vol. VI, Issue 2, 1985, p. 18).

SEVEN DAY JESUS

Seven Day Jesus is a hard rock group composed of Brian McSweeney (lead singer/writer), Wes Simpkins (bass), Chris Beaty (guitar), and Matt Sumpter (drums). The name of the group refers to serving Jesus Christ seven days a week. The group's performances are intended to minister to young people, but they also admit that they simply love rock music:

> "When asked if they view Seven Day Jesus as a ministry, an art form, or entertainment, they collectively agreed that '...even if we weren't Christians, we would still be playing rock music because this is what we love'" (*CCM Magazine*, June 1996).

SIXPENCE NONE THE RICHER

Sixpence None the Richer published their first album in 1993. At that time the group was a duo composed of vocalist Leigh Bingham (1977-) and guitarist Matt Slocum (1974-). By the time their second album, titled "This Beautiful Mess," came out in 1995, the group had grown by two members. As of 1999, the core of Sixpence None the Richer is a quintet. Matt and Leigh (whose last name was changed to Nash after her marriage) were joined by Dale Baker, Sean Kelly, and Justin Cary. Their second album won the Dove Award for Modern Rock Album of the Year in 1996.

The group's name came from a passage in the book *Mere Christianity* by C.S. Lewis. Slocum and Nash told *The Lighthouse* magazine (January 1994) that they are both C.S. Lewis fans. Lewis was turning to the Catholic Church before his death. He believed in prayers for the dead and purgatory and confessed his sins regularly to a priest. He received the Catholic sacrament of last rites on July 16, 1963. Lewis also rejected the doctrine of bodily resurrection and believed there is salvation in pagan religions. He questioned the doctrine of a literal fiery hell, claiming that hell is not a place but a state of mind. He believed in theistic evolution, but he did not believe the Bible is the infallible Word of God. C.S. Lewis used profanities, told bawdy stories, and frequently got drunk with his students (*World* magazine, May 19, 1990).

Like most CCM musicians, the members of Sixpence None the Richer love secular rock music. When asked what music she listens to by The Lighthouse magazine, Nash replied that she loves people like Whitney Houston and Natalie Merchant of 10,000 Maniacs (*The Lighthouse*, January 1994).

The lyrics to the Sixpence None the Richer rock songs are typically vague, as lyrics to the following two songs illustrate:

> "Dreams, inconsistent angel things/ Horses bred with star laced wings/ But it's so hard to make them fly/ Fly, fly" (Sixpence None the Richer, "We Have Forgotten," *This Beautiful Mess*).

> "This is my 45th depressing tune/They're looking for money as they clean my artistic womb/And when I give birth to the child I must take flight/'Cause the black in our pocket won't let us fight a proper fight" (Sixpence None the Richer, "Anything," *This Beautiful Mess*).

Sixpence None the Richer performed for a youth event in Boston sponsored by Roman Catholic Cardinal Bernard Law (letter from Gay Guptill, April 30, 2000).

In 1999, Sixpence None the Richer broke into pop music stardom with the song "Kiss Me." Sixpence None the Richer is a popular Contemporary Christian Music group that broke into pop music stardom in 1999 with a song titled "Kiss Me." In an Associated Press interview, the publicist for the group responded to their critics (who say the group should not be producing worldly music) with these words: "We're not preachers. But there are some very narrow-minded believers who think the message, not the music, is the only thing that's important" (Jay Swartzendruber, ("Between rock and a hard place," *Chicago Tribune*, Nov. 24, 2000, p. 3). He also said, "We don't consider ourselves a Christian band." Referring to a church singing tour, band members "complained of pressure to give religious speeches after they played." Worldly-minded musicians who think "music" is more important than truth, who don't have a testimony for Jesus Christ on their lips, have no business in churches.

SMITH, MICHAEL W.

Michael W. (Whitaker) Smith (1957-) is one of the most popular CCM musicians. Of the top 100 all-time best-selling Christian albums, eight belong to Smith (*CCM Magazine*, July 1998, pp. 107-108). In 1982 Smith became Amy Grant's keyboardist, but he was quickly vaulted to musical fame in his own right. As of April 2000, he had 26 No. 1 songs, a platinum and six gold records, two Grammys and career sales of more than 7 million records. He says: "I became a Christian when I was 10, and I was extremely fired up. I wore a big wooden cross around my neck and carried a Scofield Bible" (April

Hefner, "Mike and the Mechanics," *CCM Magazine,* September 1995). As he grew older he turned rebellious and went out into the world, playing in a secular rock band and using drugs. In 1979 he had a crisis experience which caused him to change directions and he joined a Christian band called Higher Ground. He also joined Belmont Church near Nashville, a Church of Christ congregation which had moved into the charismatic movement. His pastor was Don Finto, who has since retired. I heard Finto speak in 1987 at the North American Congress on the Holy Spirit & World Evangelization in New Orleans. Of the roughly 40,000 in attendance, 50% were Roman Catholic. A Catholic mass was conducted each morning of the convention, and priest Tom Forrest from Rome brought the final message. In a message I heard Forrest preach in 1990 in Indianapolis, he said that he was thankful for purgatory, because he could only go to Heaven through purgatory. This is the type of ecumenical confusion that Michael W. Smith learned to support during the almost 20 years he was a member at Belmont Church.

In 1981 he was married to his wife, Debbie, and they have five children.

Smith testifies that he has had many charismatic experiences, though he doesn't like the label "charismatic" because of "negative baggage associated with the term." At a Full Gospel Business Men's meeting he was "slain in the spirit" for 15 minutes and "laughed all the way home" (*Charisma,* April 2000, p. 55). Another time he felt "a bolt of electricity go through my body from the top of my head to my toes—wham!" He also started laughing uncontrollably—"rolling on the floor," "hyperventilating"—on that occasion. This fit of "holy laughter" happened during a prayer meeting for his son who had been diagnosed with "a rare behavior disorder for which there was no reliable cure."

Inside Magazine interviewed Michael W. Smith in 1991 and noted that his music is influenced by Alan Parsons. The interviewer said: "There's also the influence of such groups as Alan Parsons in your music. It's especially noticeable on the first record, the *Michael W. Smith Project*" (*Inside Music,* January/February 1991, p. 23). This is a reference to Alan Parson's album, *The Alan Parsons Project.* Smith's quick reply was "DEFINITELY!" Alan Parsons is one of the most occultic rock musicians. One of his songs is openly titled "Lucifer," and much of his music is openly blasphemous against the one true and living God.

The following statements illustrate Smith's unscriptural philosophy of life and ministry:

> ""...you're always going to have those very very conservative people. They say you can't do this; you can't do that ... you can't drink; you can't smoke. ... It's a pretty bizarre way of thinking" (Michael W. Smith, *The Birmingham News*, Feb. 1993, p. 1B).

> "I know if I'm too blatant about my Christianity and talk about Jesus I won't succeed in the mainstream. But hey, I'm not an evangelist, I'm a singer" (Michael W. Smith, cited by Monica Langley, "Rock of Ages," *Wall Street Journal*, Sept. 11, 1991, p. 1).

Three of Michael W. Smith's albums—*Change Your World*, *I'll Lead You Home*, and *Live Your Life*—contain no mention of Jesus Christ. There are over 6,000 words in the lyrics on these records, but there is not one mention of Jesus.

The following description exposes the worldly character of a Michael W. Smith concert:

> "Smith, with synthesizers blaring, drums blazing, and guitars screeching, sent a young crowd into a frenzy from beginning to end" (Richard Linihan, *Tulsa Tribune*, cited by Jeff Godwin, *What's Wrong with Christian Rock?*, p. 61).

In 1993 Smith performed for the World Youth Day in Denver, Colorado, an event sponsored by the Roman Catholic Church. Pope John Paul II was in attendance.

Smith and guitarist-songwriter Billy Sprague performed with Roman Catholic Kathy Troccoli at a concert in November 1985 in Tampa, Florida. The concert was sponsored by Youth for Christ and the First Assembly of God of Clearwater, Florida (*St. Petersburg Times*, Florida, Nov. 9, 1985, Religious Section, p. 3).

In 1997 Smith joined Troccoli and 40 other CCM artists to record *Love One Another*, a song with an ecumenical theme: "Christians from all denominations demonstrating their common love for Christ and each other." The song talks about tearing down the walls of denominational division. The broad range of participants who joined Kathy Troccoli in recording "Love One Another" demonstrates the ecumenical agenda of Contemporary Christian Music. The song witnessed Catholics, Pentecostals, Baptists, etc., yoked together to call for Christian unity.

Smith's 1998 single "Live the Life" was "inspired by the life of the Catholic St. Francis of Assisi" ("New Releases October 28, 1997," Christian Music Online, http://christianmusic.miningco.com/library/blcmweekly.htm).

See also the chapter titled "Michael W. Smith's Worship Album Performed in a Laughing Revival Church."

SOUTHERN GOSPEL

See Part V: Southern Gospel.

In the Directory of Contemporary Christian Musicians see also Cathedrals, Gaithers, Imperials, Hovie Lister, and J.D. Sumner.

SPURR, THURLOW. See The Spurrlows.

SPURRLOWS

The Spurrlows were formed in the late 1950s by Thurlow Spurr. At the time, he was with the ecumenical Youth for Christ (YFC) in Winston-Salem, North Carolina. In 1960 Spurr left YFC to be full-time with the singing group. "As the years progressed, the style of the music they performed paralleled more and more of the current popular styles in secular music; the group developed an increasingly contemporary sound. By the late sixties, they were mixing in rock numbers at a regular pace" (Paul Baker, *Contemporary Christian Music*, 1985, p. 11). The group, sponsored by the Chrysler Corporation, toured high schools across America. "They did their Chrysler work in school assemblies by day, and performed both secular and Christian contemporary music in local churches and auditoriums by night. More than a million people heard the Spurrlows each year" (Ibid.). The Spurrlows and another group which came out of Youth for Christ, the Continentals, were very influential in breaking down church barriers against using secular sounds. The contemporary music of these groups gained even wider influence when it was recorded by Ralph Carmichael. Thurlow Spurr headed up music for Oral Roberts television programs and became the music director for Jim Bakker's PTL network. Many Christian radio stations banned his music in the 1960s, but by the '70s his worldly styles were widely accepted.

SQUAD FIVE-O

Squad Five-O is a punk-ska rock band. They are "big metal fans" and love wicked rock groups such as Motley Crue, Nikki Sixx, and Seven Seconds. Lead singer Jeff Fortson says, "We love that stuff" (Interview with *HM Magazine*, March 26, 1998, http://place2b.org/cmp/hmmag/). Fortson wears black under his eyes when performing because "one of my favorite punk bands, Seven Seconds, Kevin Seconds, their lead singer, he used to put the black marks under his eyes." Squad Five-O recorded a Motley Crue song called "Raise Your Hand to Rock." Fortson argues that Motley Crue is not necessarily evil, that "music is music" (Ibid.). That is nonsense. Even the *Rolling Stone Encyclopedia of Rock* describes Motley Crue as "fast-living, hard-driving postadolescent REPROBATES" and their concerts as "a leering embrace of all things hedonistic." The *All Music Guide to Rock* observes that Motley Crue savored "the joys of trashy, unapologetically decadent fun." Their music glorified such evil things as strippers ("Girls, Girls, Girls") and service to the Devil ("Shout at the Devil"). Motley Crue's bassist, Nikki Sixx, was addicted to heroin; and the band's lead vocalist, Vince Neil, was convicted of vehicular manslaughter after he killed one person and seriously injured two others in a drunken accident. From a biblical standpoint, Motley Crue was definitely an evil band, and their music both reflected and communicated that evil. Christians have no business fellowshipping with the wicked world of rock & roll. By their worldly example groups like Squad Five-O are telling young people it is fine to listen to wicked, blasphemous rock & roll.

STAMPS QUARTET. See J.D. Sumner.

STARFLYER 59

The hard rock band Starflyer 59 was formed in 1993 by Jason Martin (1975-) and went through a complete personnel change during its first two years. It is currently composed of Martin (vocals/song writing), Eric Campuzano, and Wayne Everett.

The group's 1995 album, *Gold*, is described as "thoroughly modern 'modern rock,' mixing mostly DARK AND MOODY sounds with BROODING vocal arrangements." Starflyer's label, Tooth and Nail Records, calls it "noise pop art rock" (Ibid.).

Asked to describe his music, Martin says: "I think Starflyer 59 is just rock 'n' roll" (*CCM Magazine*, December 1995).

When asked how they came up with their heavy, droning sound, Martin replies: "Partially, probably on accident. Just bands I was listening to at the time were bands like the Boo Radleys, Red House Painters. With the combination of like three or four bands that I was really into just kinda, I don't know, it just came out sounding like that. It wasn't like I tried to have any particular sound. We went into the *Silver* album, and we'd only been a band a few months, and it just kinda turned out sounding like it did. It was kinda weird—no real plan in mind" (Starflyer 59 interview, *HM* magazine, March-April 1997).

These are the kind of spiritually immature, mixed up people who are creating much of Christian rock music.

Martin complains about people pressuring them to make their lyrics clear and biblical: "A lot of bands, the reason they get so turned off, is because you have to put the word 'Jesus' in every line. ... THAT'S WHY SO MANY BANDS GET ALMOST ANTI-JESUS IN THEIR LYRICS, EVEN THOUGH THEY'RE CHRISTIANS" (emphasis added) (Jason Martin of Starflyer 59, *HM*, Mar/Apr 97, p. 21).

The rebellion of Christian rock is evident in this statement. Starflyer 59 definitely doesn't put Jesus into every line. In fact, their music is so abstract it is almost meaningless. Consider some examples from *Silver 59*:

> "Lost on words for you/ and I'd better make it soon/ in a world for you/ and the better one you are/ and I'm turning off/ to a place that you don't/ know I'm turning off here - to a place I know" (Starflyer 59, "Monterey," *Silver 59*).
>
> "And she don't care, well not bad/ and she don't care, well not her/ and her heart it's not there/ and she's just a sled/ and he's just as bad/ and your heart/ it's not there" (Starflyer 59, "Sled," *Silver 59*).
>
> "Honestly I'd rather sleep but your/ holding me to it all, on the deeper/ side I'm just a ride, your mine, your it/ all, and I'm craving to lift you up, and/ I'm craving to take the fall, on the/ deeper side, I'm just a ride, your/ mine, your it your all" (Starflyer 59, "Hazel Would," *Silver 59*).
>
> "Happy days are here again and you're not/ cause when she smiles it shakes my sickest phase/ and again, and again, and again/ cause when she smiles it shakes my sickest face" (Starflyer 59, "Happy Days," *Silver 59*).

The lyrics to Starflyer's second album, *Gold*, does not have any songs which speak about God. "Instead, there are songs about girls—many songs about girls—girls and the lack thereof" (TLeM review of Starflyer 59's *Gold* album).

A description of Starflyer 59's *Silver* album: "the songs ran together into one wall of sonic mud, and the words were unintelligible" (*7 Ball*, Sept.-Oct. 1997).

When Martin was asked what 10 songs he would choose if he were stranded on an island and could only have 10, he listed: "Finest Kiss" by Boo Radleys, "Ceremony" by New Order, "Last Night I Dreamed Somebody Loved Me" by The Smiths, "Solid Gold" by Luxury, "Ana" by Pixies, "Andmoreagain" by Love, "Bye Bye Color" by L.S.U., "Ocean Rain" by Echo & The Bunnymen, "Girlfriend in a Coma" by The Smiths, "Grace Cathedral Park" by Red House Painters" (Interview with Jason Martin, *Blue Star Journal*).

All of these are secular rock songs. The Pixies, for example, are described by *Rolling Stone Encyclopedia of Rock* as "the Beach Boys on acid." The Smiths lyrics "disclosed a sexually ambiguous point of view" (meaning they promote both heterosexuality and homosexuality), while their music was "trancelike guitar-based."

STATESMEN QUARTET. See Hovie Lister.

STEVENS, MARSHA

Marsha Stevens (c. 1954-) is the author of the popular song "For Those Tears I Died (Come to the Water)." She has toured with the Children of the Day as well as solo and has provided vocals on several of the Maranatha and Praise albums.

In 1979, she divorced her husband of seven years (she has two children by that marriage) because she had "fallen in love with a woman." She said: "When I came out as a born again lesbian, I didn't anticipate that people would come unglued the way they did. Once the church found out, people came over and told me to take the 'Jesus Is Lord' sign off my door. People would rip the pages out of their hymnals containing my songs and send them to me with hate mail."

She quit her music career for about five years, but claims that God showed her that He accepts her as she is and, "I found that the Word still burned in my heart and I could not contain it. I began to sing again." She performs in a variety of liberal denominational churches as well as the Universal Fellowship of Metropolitan Community Churches. She started her own label called BALM (Born Again Lesbian Music) and performs between 150 and 200 concerts a year. Two of her songs are "The Body of Christ Has AIDS" and "Love Is the Only Law."

She lives with her "partner," Suzanne McKeag, and they travel together to concerts. In her December 1998 newsletter, she noted that she had to leave Suzanne for three days in an RV park "with a 'Christian' group parked next door who made it a point to tell her that gay people are going to hell."

Her ministry is recommended by Dr. Mark Allen Powell, Professor of New Testament, Trinity Lutheran Seminary. He is the author of "An Encyclopedia of Contemporary Christian Music." He states: "The Mother of Contemporary Christian Music continues to capture hearts for Jesus. Argue interpretations of Scripture and debate the ethics and origins of homosexuality all you want - no one with sensitivity to things of the Spirit can deny God is using Marsha Stevens to bring the love and mercy of Christ to people whom God apparently has not forgotten."

Stevens claims to have been saved in 1969 when she was a teenager. This is how her salvation is described at her web site: "In 1969, Marsha Stevens was a troubled adolescent when she had her first conscious encounter with Christ while participating in a Bible study group. In the vision this encounter evoked, she saw herself walking with Jesus near a deep blue river and this experience both changed and saved her life. Following it, she composed the folk hymn, 'For Those Tears I Died (or Come To the Water).' The song has now become a standard of Christian hymnals and it launched her career as a Christian singer/songwriter."

This is not a biblical salvation testimony, and it is no wonder that she has become apostate. To see oneself walking with Jesus near a deep blue river is not the same as confessing and repenting of one's sin and trusting the blood of Christ for forgiveness.

STONEHILL, RANDY

Randy Stonehill (1952-) is one of the pioneers of Contemporary Christian Music, dating back to the "Jesus Movement" of the 1970s. He grew up in a non-Christian family and began writing and performing music in his early teens, playing in minor rock bands in high school. He notes that it was the Beatles who gave him the inspiration to play rock and roll: "Really it was after I saw the Beatles. I saw them on television when I was twelve and I knew that that was what I wanted to do" (Stonehill, cited by Devlin Donaldson, "Life Between the Glory and the Fame," *CCM Magazine*, October 1981). In 1970 Stonehill left home to seek fame and fortune in Los Angeles. There he met some Christian musicians, including Larry Norman, and had a conversion experience in August 1970. He immediately became involved with the Christian folk/rock scene. For many years he worked with Larry Norman and his Solid Rock Records. By the end of the 70s Stonehill's relationship with Norman had deteriorated seriously and he launched out on his own.

Stonehill's first marriage lasted five years and ended in divorce. He has been married to his second wife, Sandi, since 1980 or 81. He has a daughter, Heather, who was born in 1982.

Stonehill's first album, *Born Twice*, was released in 1971. By 1995 he had recorded 16 albums.

Stonehill frequently admits that he has had a lot of resistance from conservative Christians who think his music is worldly:

> "The years 1974-78 were a real low point in my career. I was getting a lot of flack from the church, and Christian rock was generally looked on with disdain and distrust" (Stonehill, cited by Davin Seay, "Randy Stonehill: Waking up from the Longest Dream," *CCM Magazine,* November 1985).
> "And the other side of the coin was that the more traditional elements of the church ... were raising an eyebrow and saying, 'How dare you? How dare you cheapen the Gospel by trying to share it this way?'" (Stonehill, cited by Chris Willman, "Randy Stonehill: Turning Twenty," *CCM Magazine*, August 1990).
>
> "A lot of the old-school thinkers of the Church were just up in arms, saying

> 'you can't do this. Rock and roll is of the Devil. How dare you cheapen the gospel in this way.' ... We said 'music belongs to God, and it can be used or misused" (Randy Stonehill, cited in "Kicking Around with Uncle Rand," *Christian Music Review*, April 1991).
>
> "Frankly, I would suspect that it would be easier to be truer to your spirituality and artistry in mainstream music than within the confines of the church. I think the church, as I said, has a hidden agenda. There are guidelines and if you rock the boat, you don't smell right to them anymore and, all of a sudden, you're on the periphery, you're ostracized" (Randy Stonehill, *Christian Music Review*, April 1991).

Stonehill doesn't seem to like biblical guidelines, but God certainly requires that His people work within a Bible framework. Our liberty is restricted by the Word of God. This is not a "hidden agenda" in a Bible-believing church; it is an open agenda!

Stonehill admits that he is rarely in church: "When other people are going to Bible studies and Sunday services, I try to have the Church of the Airplane, the Church of the Taxi, or the Church of the Hotel Room" (*CCM Magazine*, November 1985).

Stonehill does not believe he has to be concerned "with the finer points of theological debate." Instead, his music deals mostly with human experience. "Just look at my song material. It doesn't deal with faith and theology on that level. It is much more of a gut level basic message. ... I try to pick songs that deal with God's grace, God's reality, God's love, our pain, and what kind of confusion we are experiencing in our culture and all of those things" (Devlin Donaldson, "Life Between the Glory and the Fame," *CCM Magazine*, October 1981). This is the experienced-centered approach so common in the lyrics of CCM.

Stonehill also does not want to preach via his music: "I don't want to preach at people. What I want to do is communicate the truth in the most compelling, fresh, and challenging way I can. I just want to be the best songwriter and performer, unto God, that I can be. That's the main thing" ("Kicking Around with Uncle Rand," *Christian Music Review*, April 1991).

Of his 1975 album, *Welcome to Paradise*, Stonehill says, "It helped them [the hearers] understand that God really is involved in their humanity and that this relationship can be celebrated through rock 'n' roll" (*CCM Magazine,* November 1985).

Like most Contemporary Christian Music performers, Stonehill "listens to all kinds of music," including hard secular rock (Devlin Donaldson, "Rockin' Randy," *CCM Magazine,* August 1983). Though he says he wishes the secular rock group U2 would be forthright in presenting the Christian message, he also says that "their music is great and they're really making a statement artistically" (*CCM Magazine,* November 1985). Under the entry on U2 in this "Directory of CCM Musicians" we have shown that there is nothing biblical about this secular rock group.

Stonehill's philosophy is expressed in the following statement:

> "Rock music is the only type of music some kids will listen to. If we don't put Jesus into modern music, some of them might never really hear the message!" (Stonehill, cited by Paul Davis, "Wanting to Do Something Monumental in Music,' *New Music*, No. 16, 1979).

There are many problems with this philosophy, not the least of which is that the "Jesus message" commonly inserted into Christian rock is abstract and insufficient and often patently unscriptural. It is *exceedingly* rare that Christian rock contains a clear Gospel message. In reality, what Christian rockers are doing is entertaining young people with rock music and pampering them with a vague religiosity.

Stonehill plays in a wide variety of ecumenical settings. For example in April 1990 he performed at Kingsley United Methodist Church in Erie, Pennsylvania. The United Methodist denomination is one of the most liberal groups in America. It is a member of the World Council of Churches. Its pulpits are filled with men who deny that the Bible is the infallible Word of God and who question and deny the deity, virgin birth, vicarious atonement, and resurrection of Christ.

STRYKEN

The song "Rock On" by Stryken has the following silly, unscriptural lyrics:

> "Come on everybody/ Put your hands above your head/ Today we're screamin'/ 'Cause tomorrow you might be dead/ The earth is shakin/, and the clouds are rolled away/ Come on everybody/ Get ready for the Judgment Day/ Rock on, Got my feet on the ground/ Got my eyes on Heaven/ Rock on..."

STRYPER

Brothers Michael (1963-) and Robert Sweet (c.1965-) were the guitarist and drummer for Stryper. They had a "secular" rock group called Roxx Regime in the early 1980s. The Sweet family had converted to Christianity in 1975 via a Jimmy Swaggart television broadcast, but the Sweet brothers did not get serious about Christ until 1983. At that time, joined by Tim Gaines on bass and Oz Fox (real name Richard Martinez), they refashioned Roxx Regime into the "Christian" heavy rock group Stryper. Roxx Regime dressed in tight black leotards with yellow, and so did Stryper. They continued to dress the same and to put on hard rock concerts. The only thing that changed was some of the words to the songs. It is admitted by former members of Stryper that they even continued to be involved in licentious partying during at least part of their concert career.

Band member Oz Fox explained where the name Stryper came from:

> "Enigma [their record label] wanted us to come up with a new name because the old name didn't have what it needed. One day Robert came up with 'Stryper' because it rhymed with 'hyper' and because we were already using stripes in our outfits and on the equipment. So we spelled it with a 'Y'" (*Youth!*, January 1987, p. 10).

Stryper's first album, *The Yellow and Black Attack*, sold 150,000 copies. Their second album, *Soldiers Under Command*, came a year later, in 1985, and sold more than 280,000 copies. It was obvious that the Christian world at large, which had rejected hard "Christian" rock music in the 1970s, was ready for it by the mid-1980s.

Their 1986 album was *To Hell with the Devil*, and it was even more popular than the first two. An associated video clip "was the number one most requested video on MTV in May 1987" (Godwin, *Dancing with Demons*, p. 274).

> "Speak of the Devil/ He's no friend of mine/ to turn from him/ is what we've got in mind/ To hell with the Devil/ To hell with the Devil.

> "Just a liar and a thief/ the word tells us so/ we'd like to let him know/ where he can go/ To hell with the Devil/ To hell with the Devil.

> "When things are going wrong/ you know who to blame/ He will always live/ up to his name/ To hell with the Devil/ To hell with the Devil.

> "He's never been the answer/ there's a better way/ We are here to rock you/ and to say/ To hell with the Devil/ To hell with the Devil" (Stryper, "To Hell with the Devil").

Stryper's "To Hell with the Devil" promotes the unscriptural and dangerous idea that Christians have the power to ridicule and bind the Devil or even to send the Devil to Hell. Satan is not in Hell today and he will not be in Hell until Christ returns (Revelation 20). Actually, he will never be in Hell itself, but in the Lake of Fire. The Bible instructs us that even the archangel Michael dared not bring a railing accusation against the Devil (Jude 9). As for binding the Devil, we don't have that authority. We can resist him, but we cannot bind him. Even the Apostle Paul was hindered by the Devil at times. "Wherefore we would have come unto you, even I Paul, once and again;

but Satan hindered us" (1 Thessalonians 2:18).

In 1997 *HM* magazine had an interview with each member of Stryper. Tim Gaines stated that he was intoxicated practically every single day since 1988. In a 1998 interview, Michael Sweet admitted that all of the members of Stryper were drinkers:

> "For a while there we all did, we were all drinking. However, I didn't know that it was that bad. ... He [Tim Gaines] never did in public and we never did till the *Against the Law* tour. I don't know if you know a whole lot about that, but ... that was kind of the rebellious tour, a rebellious record and we kind of vented a lot out of our systems on that record for the bad and we all did some drinking and there are some things that happened that were the exact opposite of what we always stood for" (Interview with Michael Sweet, March 1, 1998, http://www.michaelsweet.com/interview.html).

In another interview Michael elaborates a bit more:

> "We were very sincere and we were serious about our faith and our music and our message but during *Against the Law* we were going onstage and telling people about God and coming offstage and drinking. Going on the bus and having a six pack of beer and a twelve pack of beer and going to the bar at the club we were playing and sitting with people and drinking. That's just not right. It just doesn't mix with telling people not to drink" (Interview with Michael Sweet, May 15, 1998, http://www.getsigned.com/resweet1.html).

Stryper disbanded in 1992 when Michael Sweet left "over artistic differences" to pursue a solo career. He has recorded three albums since his departure from Stryper. In a 1995 interview he said that he remains proud of Stryper:

> "The Stryper thing ... I never want to shed that. It's something that I'm very proud of. I'm not ashamed of that at all. I feel that was a rare, once in a lifetime thing. It was such an incredibly powerful ministry, a lot more powerful than most people realize" (Michael Sweet, cited by Tod Chatman, "Will the Real Michael Sweet Please Stand Up," *CCM Magazine*, November 1995).

Oz Fox and Tim Gaines have a band called SinDizzy. Robert Sweet is playing with a new band called Blank.

The positive-only, non-judgmental philosophy of Robert Sweet is evident from the following statement at his web site:

> "To explain myself further, I would like to emphasize a few things. I am not a Republican who hates Democrats, nor a conservative who hates liberals. I PREACH NO RELIGION! I AM NOT A FINGER POINTER NOR A BIBLE

> BASHER. I'm not a pro-lifer who would hate and kill one who holds the view of pro choice. I am not a homophobic. I'm simply a musician who hopes to show the reality of JESUS in some way to all those whose path I cross" ("A Letter from Robert," Robert Sweet web site, http://members.aol.com/RobrtSweet/index.html).

Robert Sweet also says:

> "I don't believe that believing in hope is a joke. I truly feel if everyone on this planet would take to heart the brilliant words of JESUS, war would simply be no more. Racism would disappear. The needs of the homeless and starving would be met. Senseless drive-bys and other shootings would cease to exist. Dissension would end. One could always leave their doors unlocked, and peace could truly be given a chance, as John Lennon once pleaded" ("A Letter from Robert," Robert Sweet web site).

This statement demonstrates a gross lack of biblical understanding. There are many problems with this statement. (1) The Bible plainly says that people in this present fallen world are not going to take the words of Jesus seriously. The Holy Spirit prophesied that evil men will increase (2 Timothy 4:13). (2) Even if men would somehow attempt to live by the words of Jesus, they would still be sinners and there would still be sin, because "all have sinned and come short of the glory of God" (Romans 3:23). (3) What people need is not merely to follow Christ's teaching but to be born again through faith in His blood atonement. "For in Christ Jesus neither circumcision availeth any thing, nor uncircumcision, but a new creature" (Galatians 6:15). Instead of mouthing unscriptural statements like this, Robert Sweet should be preaching the glorious Gospel of Jesus Christ; yet his web site contains no presentation of the Gospel.

The members of Stryper love secular rock music. Michael Sweet says:

> "I'm a fan of all that stuff from the '80s. Groups like Bon Jovi, Van Halen, and Aerosmith. Musically, I like a lot of that stuff, but back when I was a kid what I grew up listening to ranged from Elvis Presley, Jerry Lee Lewis, Fats Domino all the way to groups like Three Dog Night. Credence [Clearwater Revival] was one of my favorite bands and a group called Bad Company. I just loved them and Elvis, of course" (*CCM Magazine*, November 1995).

The following is by Terry Watkins from *Christian Rock: Blessing or Blasphemy*:

> With long womanish hair, earrings, mascara, lip-gloss, eye shadow and effeminate clothes, Stryper demolished any convictions left in Christian music! How Christians tolerate such ungodly behavior is frightening! And despite the Bible's clear warnings! 1 Corinthians 6:9 says '... Be not deceived: neither fornicators ... NOR EFFEMINATE ... shall inherit the kingdom of God.' The

demonic creatures from the bottomless pit in Revelation 9:8 are described as 'their faces were as the faces of men. And they had hair as THE HAIR OF WOMEN...'!

Stryper is not exactly 'good little Christian boys.' In 1989 Stryper toured with secular rockers White Lion. Drummer Greg D'Angelo says, 'We threw a party ... About two in the morning ROBERT SWEET WAS WHACKED! DRUNK! He was being dragged around on his tiptoes by two women holding him up!' (*RIP*, June, 1989, p. 41). Stryper also toured with the perverted secular group WASP (whose name stands for We Are Sex Perverts). WASP singer Blackie Lawless drinks blood on stage from a human skull. WASP spreads their satanic message, as they tell young people the vicious lie that Lucifer loves them. They're drunk on his love and magic, in 'Sleeping in the Fire': 'Taste the LOVE, THE LUCIFER'S MAGIC That makes you numb; You feel what it does and you're drunk on LOVE; YOU'RE SLEEPING IN THE FIRE!'

The back of WASP's album reads, 'The gods you worship are steel, AT THE ALTAR OF ROCK AND ROLL YOU KNEEL.' The concert tour was called 'HEAVEN AND HELL'!

'...what fellowship hath righteousness with unrighteousness? and what communion hath LIGHT with DARKNESS? And what concord hath CHRIST with BELIAL...' (2 Corinthians 6:14-15).

Stryper Bass player Steve Gaines says, '... we NEVER wanted to get caught up in the whole Christian music scene in the first place...' (*Inside Music*, Oct/Nov 90, p. 16). Robert Sweet confesses, '... we're about the MOST UNRELIGIOUS Christian band you could imagine...' (*Hit Parader*, Nov. 1986, p. 21). And according to lead singer, Michael Sweet, 'We don't consider ourselves to be overly religious ... In fact, religion has NOTHING to do with what Stryper's all about' (*Hit Parader*, Feb. 1987, p. 41).

Stryper guitarist Oz Fox's real name is Richard Martinez. Why does Richard use the name Oz Fox? Because of an obsession with satanic rocker OZZY OSBOURNE! In fact, on their *Reason for the Season* album, Stryper's guitarist is listed as 'OZZIE' Fox!

The name Stryper supposedly comes from Isaiah 53:5 ('with his STRIPES we are healed'), but in *Youth* magazine, Stryper guitarist Oz Fox tells the real reason: 'One day Robert came up with Stryper because it rhymed with hyper...' (*Youth*, Jan. 1987, p. 10). It has nothing to do with Isaiah 53! They admittedly didn't make the connection to Isaiah 53 till somebody showed them!

Stryper wears the number '777,' supposedly depicting the Biblical number of perfection. But '777' is highly esteemed in witchcraft and satanism! Satanist Aleister Crowley wrote a book titled *Liber 777*. The satanic group Danzig has a song titled '777.' *The Treasury of Witchcraft* says of the number seven: 'this number, in occult rites, possessed mystic implications ... POWERFUL: TRIPLE REPETITION is characteristic of magic ritual' (*Treasury of Witchcraft*, p. 23).

Stryper wears the colors yellow and black. But did you know yellow and black is the color of the Devil's livery or clothing! 'According to mediaeval legend, the livery of the Devil is Black and Yellow; Black indicating Death, Yellow implying Quarantine' (*Treasury of Witchcraft*, Wedeck, p. 111).

A poster dated August 13, 1982, for the band Roxx Regime with Michael and Robert Sweet, has 777's displayed in the corners! And they're called the 'yellow and black attack'—the same as Stryper.

Their conversion to Christ took place in 1983—a year later!—but they're displaying the 777's and 'yellow and black' the year before they're saved!

Stryper's unique triangle logo (with a curved bottom, outline around the edge and rays emitting) on the cover of *In God We Trust* is nearly an exact copy of satanist Aleister Crowley's infamous triangle! Could the Holy Spirit of the Bible possibly be the one inspiring these Christian rock stars to copy satanic symbols! Not once ... but over and over and over!

On Stryper's video *In The Beginning*, you see scores of young people flashing the 'satanic salute'! (Godwin, *Dancing with Demons*, p. 274). And what about the cover on *To Hell With the Devil*? Why are the winged-members of Stryper wearing a satanic Pentagram and throwing someone into hell? It is NO coincident that the creatures coming out from hell in Revelation 9:7-8 are described as, 'their faces were as the faces of men. And they had HAIR as the hair of women.'

Robert Sweet makes a startling admission to the truth about rock music in *RIP* magazine: 'As a matter of fact, the band was one thing that was making us turn and walk the OPPOSITE DIRECTION from Christianity, because, let's face it, when you're out there playing rock 'n' roll, and you're having a real good time doing your own thing it's not that you hate God or anything—you just don't want to think about Christ, because what he does is he exposes a lifestyle. If you're doing something you like doing, AND GOD SAYS NOT TO DO IT then you're not going to pay attention' (*RIP*, April 1987, p. 49) (Terry Watkins, *Christian Rock: Blessing or Blasphemy*).

The following quotes from members of the Stryper band illustrate their unscriptural philosophy:

> "We're not religious fanatics who are trying to convert everybody we meet. We're not trying to shut down rock radio stations or make magazines go out of

business. We honestly believe that Jesus Christ is the Savior, but we're about the most unreligious Christian band you could imagine. Religion is real for us, but so is rock and roll..." (Robert Sweet, *Hit Parader*, November 1986, p. 21).

"We always had this attitude that we didn't want to be characterized as this little religious band sold in religious bookstores and happy and content to play in a church for love offerings. I mean, all that's wonderful, but our whole goal and vision was to be a real rock 'n' roll band to reach a real world..." (Robert Sweet, *Milwaukee Journal*, Milwaukee, Wisconsin, August 25, 1987, p. 11).

"[We don't go to church a lot.] A lot of people think that's actually a part of Christianity. It can be, if it helps you grow in the Lord ... But, if you look through the Bible, so many men, take John the Baptist for example, he never darkened the doors of a church in his life. Let's put it this way — religion is man reaching up to God with sincerity, and most of the time failing. Christianity is God reaching down to man" (Robert Sweet, *Hard Rock Video*, pp. 55, cited by Wilson Ewin, *The Pied Piper of the Pentecostal Movement*, 1986, p. 58).

"You won't pick up this record (*Against the Law*) and hear anything that says 'God' or 'Christ.' That was intentionally done. We were tired of people coming back with excuses, saying, 'Sorry we can't play this.' MTV's got to play this and the radio's got to play it or it doesn't serve the purpose" (Robert Sweet, Stryper, interview, *CCM Magazine*, August 1990, p. 10).

"I was basically the same guy as far as the way I look now. But, I hadn't really given my life to God ... [Being a Christian] doesn't necessarily mean that you become this type of religious person and you change the way you look, etc. You can do that if you want, but it is not a priority" (Robert Sweet, *Robert Sweet's Story*, Stryper fan club promotional material).

"If a kid turns on the television and sees Jimmy Swaggart, he's going to change the channel—if he happens to go to church, chances are he'll start to get bored and want to leave—a lot of Christians are stuck in traditional ways" (Oz Fox, Stryper, cited by Lenny Seidel, *Face the Music*, p. 70).

"We listen to just about everybody. From Whitney Houston to Judas Priest. We like music in general. If we closed our minds to one particular way or one particular thing in music we wouldn't be artists. We wouldn't be able to write the kind of music we write. Of course, we're rooted and grounded so it doesn't hurt us. Somebody who can't handle themselves, listening to that kind of music might make them want to go out and booze and party and whatever" (Oz Fox, Stryper, *Youth!*, January 1987, p. 11). [Brother Cloud: That is precisely what Stryper ended up doing!]

"My influences were the same as most everybody else's. I didn't listen to religious music. I was into Zeppelin and Kiss. All the hard rock bands were playing the music I loved. Religious music always disappointed me" (Robert

Sweet, Stryper, interview, *Hit Parade*, November 1986, p. 21).

Two Stryper fans were injured in Australia when they were pushed through a plate glass window as 1,500 young people shoved forward in an attempt to see the rock band at a record store. Speaking with the press about this, Robert Sweet said: "What happened on Saturday was purely rock and roll. It shows we're not wimpy religious Christian guys, but a real rock and roll venture" (*The Sun*, April 4, 1989, p. 7). Though he said he was sorry people got hurt, Sweet also stated that he and the other members of Stryper "don't mind people being wild..." The Bible, though, repeatedly warns against rioting (Prov. 28:7; Romans 13:13; Titus 1:6; 1 Peter 4:4). It was "riotous living" that was the downfall of the rebellious Prodigal Son (Luke 15:13).

The following is an eye-witness description of a 1987 Stryper concert in Indianapolis, Indiana:

> They boogied, they leaped and they danced until the roar from the audience even drowned out their music (not an easy thing to do). Oz spun in circles like a hairy zebra-striped top as he played. After a couple of songs, the band stopped to catch their breath. That's when Michael Sweet said, 'Let's hear it for Hurricane (the licentious rock group who opened the concert for Stryper)! We're brothers and we love these guys a lot, and we love you. You'll be seein' more bands Rockin' for the man upstairs, I'm sure. You sure are a Rockin' crowd! How many Rock & Rollers have we got out there? Come on! LOUDER!'
>
> The deafening screams of Stryper's congregation, the blinding banks of strobing floodlights and the stomach-flapping volume created a scene of complete chaos. Michael looked up at his drum-pounding brother and yelled, 'Robert! Robert! Come on down!' Bob descended from his platform and stood on the lip of the stage. As Mike handed him an armful of books, he shouted, 'Here's something we always throw out to the crowd.' Bob pitched Bibles like baseballs, but no one bothered to mention it was the holy Word of God or that it had the power to change lives forever....
>
> After Robert returned to his drummer's perch, Michael screamed into the microphone, 'YEAH! He's the one and only way!' Then the band launched into 'The Way' and 'Calling on You.' Long, drawn out bass, drum and guitar solos followed, just like at any other rock concert. Oz Fox fell to his knees, mouth open, head bobbing and hair flying as he cranked out a sizzling and scorching mega-decibel lead that quickly degenerated into white noise. It sounded like a sawmill that had just been hit by a Cruise missile. All this was your basic brand of rock star ego-tripping. I asked myself: 'How does this junk glorify Jesus Christ?'
>
> When the band lit into 'You Won't Be Lonely,' girls screamed until their voices gave out, spurred on by Michael's hip bouncing wiggle. 'Battle Hymn of the

Republic' finally closed the concert. As the boys from Stryper walked into the wings, Clowes Hall erupted into a deafening bellow — 'STRY-PER! STRY-PER! STRY-PER! STRY-PER!' The Lord Jesus was the last thing on anyone's mind.

Band member Oz Fox says: 'We don't like to tell people we're a Christian band, because the metalheads would be turned off. I'm not saying Christian bands are bad, but a lot of times it's not what the kids want to hear. The kids'll say, "I don't want to go see THAT, I don't want to have somebody preaching at me...: So we tell people we are "God rock"' (*Youth!*, January 1987, p. 8).

After five minutes of roaring pandemonium, Stryper returned. A thunderous ovation shook the roof. A sweat-soaked Michael Sweet declared, 'We don't sing about sex and booze, and we don't sing about drugs.' Stryper may not sing about sex, booze or drugs, but they sure didn't say much about Jesus Christ, either! It seems impossible, but the volume of their final encore increased to the point that the inside of my ears began to hum (even through the ear protectors).

Finally, after the last atom bomb crash of head-ripping, lightning blast of thunder, Michael Sweet, his back to the crowd, lifted his guitar high above his head in the classic pose of Rock & Roll defiance. Grabbing the microphone, he shouted, 'Anyone who's not a Christian, try our God, Jesus Christ.'

And then they were gone.

There was no altar call and no plea to accept Jesus Christ as Lord, Master and Savior. All Stryper could manage was a half-hearted yodel to 'try Christ' like some kind of new improved anti-perspirant. ... That is exactly what happened at Clowes Hall on March 25, 1987. No Christian witnessing was done. No instruction was given about the importance of the Bible, repentance, salvation, forgiveness or holiness (Jeff Godwin, *Dancing with Demons*, pp. 289-292).

SUMMER, DONNA

"[Donna Summer's lyrics] Stand as directly and unpreachily as possible, the approach most likely to win the attention of an intelligent non-Christian audience" (*Contemporary Christian Music Magazine*, Oct. 1984, p. 40).

SUMNER, J.D.

J.D. (John Daniel) Sumner (1924-1998) was one of the most influential Southern gospel performers, music writers, and publishers. Born in Lakeland, Florida, and reared in Assemblies of God churches, Sumner began his gospel quartet career in 1943 with the Sunshine Boys, a 'cowboy quartet' that made more than a dozen movies with western stars Eddie Dean and 'The Durango Kid'" (southerngospel.org). Sumner and the Sunshine Boys were infamous for their worldly lifestyles. They smoked, drank, cavorted with women, etc. "The Blackwoods, three months before their air tragedy, were not the only ones who referred to him and his cohorts in the Sunshine Boys as infidels" (Gaither, Homecoming, p. 160). In 1954 Sumner joined the famous Blackwood Brothers, following the death of R. W. Blackwood and Bill Lyles in an airplane crash. For eleven years Sumner sang with the Blackwood Brothers. In 1964 the Blackwood Brothers purchased the Stamps Quartet, and Sumner took over the quartet. He stayed with them until his death.

Sumner twice recorded a double-low C and at one time he was listed in the Guinness Book of World Records as the world's lowest bass singer. He wrote some 500 songs during his career.

Sumner was not merely a gospel singer; he was an entertainer. When Sumner took over the Stamps Quartet in 1965 he brought in "a live stage band, colorful 'loud' stage wear, and A NEW SOUND for Gospel Music with a lot of young people involved" (Harold Timmons, "Memories of J.D. Sumner," http://southerngospel.org/jd2.html). Sumner and other top-line gospel quartets jazzed up their presentations and were considered worldly by many sincere Christians. Sumner's friends, Hovie Lister and the Statesmen, went so far beyond that which was traditionally acceptable in Christian music in the first half of this century that some Christian radio stations would not play their music.

Sumner was also a businessman. The well-known Southern gospel quartets, in fact, were born in the early part of this century as business enterprises. The "inventer" of the gospel quartet was James Vaughan, who hired a professional male quartet in 1910 to represent his publishing company. The Vaughan Quartet performances at churches, revivals, and conventions, were a means whereby Vaughan sold music. "In this way the groups promoted their sponsor and created a market for the songbooks" (David L. Taylor, Happy Rhythm, p. 7). By the late 1920s Vaughan had 16 full-time quartets on the road. In 1924 the V.O. Stamps Music Company was founded by Virgil Stamps, and they, too, put quartets to work. In 1929 this company became the famous Stamps-Baxter Music Company. J.D. Sumner also helped found a publishing enterprise called Gospel Quartet Music Company, as well as a record company, Skylite Recordings, in 1959.

The Stamps Quartet performed regularly in concert with rock & roll king Elvis Presley from 1969 to 1977. Sumner even sang on Presley records such as "Burning Love," "American Trilogy," and "Way Down" (southerngospel.org). In a 1990 Associated Press interview, Sumner said Presley "was a good man and as deeply religious a person as I've ever known. I've talked more about Jesus Christ and prayed more with Elvis

Presley than anyone I've ever known" (Ibid.). This statement reveals an extreme lack of spiritual and doctrinal discernment on the part of Sumner. Presley did love Southern gospel and Negro spiritual music and he talked about Jesus Christ, but Presley's christ was a false one of his own creation, and he gave no evidence of being a Bible-believing Christian. He never made a public profession of faith in Christ, did not believe the Bible is the infallible Word of God, was never baptized and never joined a church. Elvis constructed "a personalised religion out of what he'd read of Hinduism, Judaism, numerology, theosophy, mind control, positive thinking and Christianity" (Steve Turner, *Hungry for Heaven*, p. 143).

J.D. Sumner conceived of the National Quartet Convention, which was founded as a joint venture by the Blackwood Brothers and the Statesmen. The first was held in 1956 and drew 10,000 Southern gospel music fans.

Sumner died of a heart attack at age 73 in November 1998, and his funeral was held at the Pentecostal Christ Church in Nashville, Tennessee.

SUPERTONES

The Supertones are a very popular Christian rock group. The members are Tony Terusa (bass), Jason Carson (drums), Brian Johnson (guitar), Matt Morginsky (vocals), Dan Spencer (trombone), Dave Chevalier (saxophone), and Darrin Mettler (trumpet).

When someone criticizes The Supertones' rock music, their defenders rejoin that it is the words to their music that matters. The problem with this is that the lyrics to The Supertones' music are vague and strange and rarely present a clear biblical message: Consider, for example, the following words from *Adventures of the O.C. Supertones* (1996):

> "You probably ask yourself, how'd this Jew boy get so crazy/ Come from kickin' mad knowledge, didn't come from being lazy/ We got the rhythm and the rhythm's got roots/ I'm a crazy little Hebrew onstage wearin' monkey boots/ I love to be onstage and sing and bimskalabimmin/ I love to be out in the crowd a skakin' and a swimmin'/ King David, my great grandfather, was a dancer/ King Solomon, my great grandfather, was a romancer/ Jesus came from Jesse, but Jesse came from Jesus/ Now come to the Lord cuz Lord Jesus frees us."

The lyrics to the following song demonstrates the non-judgmental, anti-fundamentalist philosophy of the Supertones:

> "I don't care about your haircut, can't we all just get along?/ Not just get along,

but really love and care/ If your eyes are on the Lord you can't see nobody's hair" (Supertones, "Adonai," *Adventures of the O.C. Supertones*, 1996).

It's not true that if your eyes are on the Lord you will not see things such as hair. Those that love the Lord want to obey the Bible in every detail. Jesus Christ said: "If a man love me, he will keep my words" (John 14:23). If hair is entirely unimportant in the Christian life, why does God's Word address it (1 Corinthians 11)? Paul plainly stated that the woman is to have long hair and the man short hair to express their different positions in this world. According to the Bible, hair length even affects angels (1 Cor. 11:10). The rebellious ecumenical crowd, though, pretends that Christian love overlooks such things as clothing and hair length. I can love someone and still be concerned about biblical standards for hair or dress.

The Supertones' non-judgmental philosophy permeates Contemporary Christian Music. This is one reason why it is so dangerous for Christian young people to listen to it. Not only does CCM use the world's music, it preaches unscriptural philosophies.

The following are some of the lyrics from "The Supertones Strike Back" (1997)—

> "So come on put a glide in you stride, and a dip in yo hip/ Best back the heck up, cuz' hip-hop rolls from my lips/ I spit when I rap, saliva flies when I sing/ God gives me gifts, just look at my ring/ Look less at me and look more to Christ/ Grace has saved me and His grace will suffice/ So I jump for Jesus, it's Jesus who frees us/ Let's get dumb like Beavis, I don't care who sees us" ("Supertones Strike Back").

> "I will keep fighting to the knockout, even if I'm knocked out/ Hitting hard, I'm hittin' for the belt/ My soul will keep going 'till my body buckles/ I will drop my bloody knuckles/ Carry us to Heaven by the truckfulls/ I will be as stubborn as a pitbull/ Neutral as a Nazi, resolute like Ghandi/ I will keep preaching 'till I'm took out/ Till I'm in Heaven en route/ No sell out!" (Supertones, "Perseverance of the Saints").

By their frequent and uncritical reference to worldly and pagan things such as Beavis and Ghandi, the Supertones are encouraging young people that such things are harmless.

When Pope John Paul II visited the States in January 1999, The Supertones were among the CCM groups that joined hands with hundreds of thousands of Catholics to welcome him. Featured at a Catholic youth rally connected with the Pope's visit, were the Supertones, dc Talk, Audio Adrenaline, Rebecca St. James, Jennifer Knapp, and The W's (*CCM Magazine*, April 1999, p. 12). A large group of nuns and Dominican priests "danced with abandon" at the Supertones rock music. Each attendee received a rosary with instructions about how to pray to Mary.

SWEET, MICHAEL. See Stryper.

SWEET, ROBERT. See Stryper.

SWITCHFOOT

This California-based Christian rock band is composed of two brothers Jon and Tim Foreman, and Chad Butler. Their first album, *The Legend of Chin*, was produced by Charlie Peacock. The song "Sooner or Later" deals with doubt and was inspired by the liberal theologian Soren Kierkegaard. Jon Foreman says: "Kierkegaard inspired that song with his book *Fear and Trembling*. With his theological writings, he ushered in a whole new era of philosophy, and he deealt with the issue of holy doubt quite a bit" (*Fuelmagazine*, Spring-Summer 1999, p. 23). Foreman gives no hint of warning about Kierkegaard's false gospel and heretical theology.

TABER, TIM

In 1997 Tim Taber joined Roman Catholic Kathy Troccoli and 40 other CCM artists to record *Love One Another*, a song with an ecumenical theme: "Christians from all denominations demonstrating their common love for Christ and each other." The song talks about tearing down the walls of denominational division. The broad range of participants who joined Kathy Troccoli in recording "Love One Another" demonstrates the ecumenical agenda of Contemporary Christian Music. The song witnessed Catholics, Pentecostals, Baptists, etc., yoked together to call for Christian unity.

TAFF, RUSS

Together with roughly 20,000 Roman Catholics and 20,000 others representing 40 denominations, Russ Taff participated in the North American Congress on the Holy Spirit & World Evangelization in New Orleans in 1987. There was a Catholic mass every morning, and the final message was delivered by Catholic priest Tom Forrest from Rome.

TAKE 6

Take 6 is a Seventh-day Adventist group. They participated in the Billy Graham rally in New York's Central Park, September 22, 1991 (*Calvary Contender*, October 1, 1991).

TALBOT, JOHN MICHAEL

John Michael Talbot (1955-) is an extremely popular Contemporary Christian Music recording artist, with (with roughly 35 albumssales of 4 million. Billboard magazine named him the number one male Christian recording artist. Talbot) who regularly appears in concert with CCM musicians representing a wide variety of denominational backgrounds. Though Talbot He is a charismatic Roman Catholic who prays to Mary and believes in dreams and other forms of extra-biblical revelation, regularly appears in concert with CCM musicians representing a wide variety of denominational backgrounds. . He became a lay "brother" in the order of Secular Franciscans in 1979 and lives in Little Portion Hermitage in Eureka Springs, Arkansas. This is the home of the Brothers and Sisters of Charity, "an integrated monastic community of families, celibates and singles" founded by Talbot. It is formally recognized by the Catholic Church as a "Public Association of the Faithful." In 1989 Talbot broke the vow of celibacy he had taken in 1979 and married Viola Pratka. His first marriage ended in divorce in 1977 before he became a Catholic. He has a daughter, Amy, from that marriage.

In his early teens, Talbot joined his brother, Terry, in the rock band Mason Proffit. They opened for Janis Joplin and other well-known groups. Sometime around 1971 he converted to Christianity and in 1973 he left the band. By 1976 he recorded his first Christian album, *Reborn, John Michael Talbot*. The following overview of Talbot's religious experiences is from *Rock—Making Musical Choices* by Richard Peck:

> John Michael Talbot notes that after his divorce he thought of giving up his music. Searching for counsel, he visited Alverna—a Franciscan retreat near his parents' home in Indianapolis, Indiana. Eventually, Talbot decided to make his home in this Roman Catholic retreat.
>
> At an appropriate time, John talked with his religious superiors about his music. Talbot entered the CCM movement after leaving the successful secular group Mason Profit. His early albums presented a conservative, Protestant theology. He performed often in Bible-preaching (though neo-evangelical) churches. Clearly, John could be useful to the Roman Church.
>
> "Think twice," the priest advised. Aside from the matter of talent, the Franciscan continued, "there is another consideration perhaps just as important, if not more so. You may want to keep in touch with Protestant evangelical Christianity, instead of withdrawing from it. I think God has chosen you as a bridge builder."
>
> The remainder of Talbot's account shows him progressively falling under the spell of Romanist error. He soon concluded that the Protestant Reformation had no basis, and that to deny the authority of the Roman Catholic Church

was to deny the church that "gave us the Scriptures." Wholly caught up in the philosophy of his new religion, Talbot was soon received into the Roman Catholic Church.

The charismatic emphasis, though without tongues, is also seen in Talbot's experience. Dreams and other direct "revelations" from God account for his increasing conviction that the Roman Church holds the key to the future (Richard Peck, *Rock—Making Musical Choices*).

Talbot says: "Music is an extension of my life. When I became a Christian, my music became Christian music. When I became Catholic, my music became Catholic music" (B. Cole Bennett, "John Michael Talbot: An Encounter with the Counter-Culture," *Shout!* magazine, February 1996).

Talbot's albums were the first by a Catholic artist to be accepted by both Protestant and Catholic listeners. "In 1988, *Billboard Magazine* reported that Talbot out-ranked all other male Christian artists in total career albums sold. After more than three million sales with Sparrow Records, making him Sparrow's all-time best-selling recording artist, John Michael Talbot started a new record label in 1992 called Troubadour for the Lord" ("John Michael Talbot," Talbot's web site).

His music is mostly acoustic folk and ballad style, but he also incorporates chanting and a wide variety of other music forms into his albums. Talbot promotes the false philosophy of the neutrality of music:

> "We need to know rock 'n' roll. We need to know the gentleness of a folk tune. We need to know the majesty of Handel's Messiah. We need to know the awesome reverence of the Gregorian chant" (John Talbot, *CCM Magazine*, July 1998, p. 28).

In his book *Simplicity*, Talbot stated: "Personally, I have found praying the Rosary to be one of the most powerful tools I possess in obtaining simple, childlike meditation on the life of Jesus Christ." The Rosary is largely a prayer to Mary as the Queen of Heaven. In 1984 Talbot said: "I am also feeling the presence of Mary becoming important in my life. ... I feel that she really does love me and intercedes to God on my behalf" (*Contemporary Christian Music Magazine*, November 1984, p. 47).

In an article entitled "Our Fathers, and Our Divided Family," in the Catholic charismatic magazine *New Covenant*, Talbot called for Christian unity on the basis of the Roman Catholic papacy:

> "A Roman Catholic, I respect other Christians. We are especially close to those who value apostolic tradition as well as Scripture. But even in this we

face further debates that are obstacles to complete Christian unity. THIS IS WHY THE CATECHISM OF THE CATHOLIC CHURCH INSISTS THAT SCRIPTURE, TRADITION AND MAGISTERIUM ARE NECESSARY FOR A FULLY UNIFIED PEOPLE. WE ROMAN CATHOLICS FIND THIS IN THE POPE AS BISHOP OF ROME, TOGETHER WITH THE BISHOPS OF THE CHURCHES IN FULL COMMUNION WITH ROME. This has theologically freed us to develop the greatest mystical and functional unity in Christendom. It has also given us an authority that enables us to enter into interfaith and ecumenical dialogue without defensiveness. ... May we all hear these ancient truths and experience real conversion of heart" (John Talbot, "Our Fathers, and Our Divided Family," *New Covenant*, September 1997, p. 21).

Talbot says Catholic tradition and the papacy are equal in authority with the Scripture. He says true Christian unity can be found only in fellowship with the pope of Rome. He prays that his readers will hear this message and experience conversion to Rome. What could be more unscriptural? The Apostle Paul said anyone, even an angel from heaven, who preaches a false gospel is cursed of God (Galatians 1). The Roman Catholic popes, with their sacramental gospel and blasphemous claims and titles, have been under this curse from their unscriptural origin. Nowhere does the New Testament say the Apostles passed on their authority at death. The true Apostles were given miracle-working signs to authenticate their calling (2 Cor. 12:12). Nowhere does the New Testament establish a pope over all of the churches, and nowhere do we see Peter acting or living as a pope. We don't need the so-called "church fathers" to explain to us the rule of faith and practice; God has given us an infallible and sufficient rule in the Scriptures (1 Tim. 3:16,17) which were completed during the days of the Apostles and which were sealed with a solemn seal in Revelation 22:18,19.

There is room, though, for Talbot's apostate theology in the doctrinally confused world of Contemporary Christian Music. He is considered a brother in Christ and is welcomed with open arms, in the face of God's commands that we mark and avoid those who promote doctrine contrary to that taught by the Apostles (Romans 16:17-18). This is one of the many reasons why we refuse to have anything to do with CCM and its rebellious musicians and worldly musical styles. The Devil is using the ecumenical thrust of CCM to break down the walls between truth and error toward the completion of the one-world apostate "church." Referring to the mixed crowds who attended the Talbot/Card concerts in Catholic churches, Talbot said that he delights to see Protestants who never would have darkened the doorstep of a Catholic church come to one of his concerts. "All of a sudden they say, 'Hey, I feel very much at home here. That doesn't mean necessarily I want to be a Roman Catholic, but I feel very much at home worshipping God with other people who are not that different from me'" (John Talbot, quoted in "Interfaith Album Strikes Sour Note," Peter Smith, Religious News Service, Dec. 8, 1996). Surveys show that 60 percent of Talbot's listeners are non-Catholic.

In 1996 Talbot produced an ecumenical album (*Brother to Brother*) jointly with fellow CCM performer Michael Card. Of this venture, Card testified: "Doing this project has enabled us to become real friends. And along the way, the denominational lines have become really meaningless to me, and to John, too" (*CCM Magazine*, July 1996).

To say that denominational division is meaningless is to say that doctrine is not important, because doctrine is one of the key things which divides denominations and churches. Some churches teach sound doctrine about Jesus Christ and some teach false doctrine. Some teach sound doctrine about salvation; some, false doctrine. Some teach sound doctrine about baptism; some, false doctrine. Some teach sound doctrine about the Holy Spirit; some, false doctrine. Some teach sound doctrine about the New Testament church; some, false doctrine. Timothy's job in Ephesus was "that thou mightest charge some that they TEACH NO OTHER DOCTRINE" (1 Timothy 1:3). When a church stands upon the whole counsel of New Testament doctrine, it automatically becomes divided from churches which stand for different doctrine. This cannot be avoided, and it is not wrong. In fact, God forbids sound churches from associating with those who hold different doctrine (Romans 16:17).

In 1996 Talbot was instrumental in forming the Catholic Musicians Association to encourage Catholic musicians and to help them find a place in the more mainstream Contemporary Christian Music world. Joining Talbot at the founding meeting in April 1996 were Tony Melendez, Dana, Susan Stein (executive of Heartbeat Records), Paulette McCoy (Oregon Catholic Press), and Catholic church officials and professionals involved in marketing and publicity (Steve Rabey, "Association Formed to Support Catholic Music," *CCM Update*, May 27, 1996). At the meeting Stein said she "would like Protestants and Catholics to set aside what are basically petty differences" and she urged evangelicals "to be a bit less judgmental and a bit more open to understanding" (Ibid.).

TAYLOR, STEVE

Like Michael English, Curtis Chapman, and several other CCM artists, Steve Taylor (c.1960-) is a member of Christ Community Church near Nashville. Taylor has been married to his wife, Debbie, since 1986.

Taylor performed and produced Christian music from 1983 to 1990 (recording six albums), then formed a secular rock band called Chagall Guevara and was committed to it for a couple of years. He said he got fed up with criticism about his hard music style and other aspects of his CCM career (Interview with Steve Taylor, *The Lighthouse*, November 1993). Other members of Chagall Guevara were Wade James, Mike Mead, L. Arthur Nichols, and Dave Perkins. Chagall Guevara released an album on MCA Records in 1991. Of this venture Taylor says:

> "All of us are Christians. None of us are ashamed of our faith, but it's like everyone had their guard up, and I think some of us in the band were almost paranoid about being associated with gospel music" (Interview with Steve Taylor, *The Lighthouse*, November 1993).

In 1992 Taylor returned to Christian music (or that which he and his friends call Christian music). For the production of his 1998 album, *Squint*, Taylor was joined by three of the members of his rock band: Mike Mead, Wade James, and Phil Madeira.

Taylor says his goal for young people is "develop a world view, and to question authority..." (Peters Brothers, *What about Christian Rock?*, p. 138). His philosophy is further described as follows:

> "There's a whole segment of youth culture that the church isn't reaching. I believe that type of music [Christian rock] can break through the walls and say 'Maybe you've been lied to about Christianity'" (Steve Taylor, *Contemporary Christian Music Magazine*, June 1984, p. 44).

Taylor seems to be saying that young people need a new type of Christianity, a Christianity which allows them to keep their sensual lifestyles, their rock music, their counter culture attitudes, a Christianity which has few rules, a Christianity which focuses on liberty and fun.

Taylor produced albums for the hard rock group Newsboys from 1991 to 1996. This included *Boyz Will Be Boyz* (1991), *Not Ashamed* (1992), *Going Public* (1994), and *Take Me to Your Leader* (1996). (The Newsboys 1998 album, *Step Up to the Microphone*, was not produced by Taylor.)

In reviewing Taylor's music, the *Seattle Post-Intelligencer* noted that "there is little preaching in his songs. Most of them are metaphoric story-songs written from a Christian perspective" (*Seattle Post-Intelligencer*, Oct. 11, 1984). Taylor was quoted as saying: "I DON'T THINK PEOPLE REALLY LIKE TO BE PREACHED AT. One of the reasons Jesus was so effective is because he told parables. I think it's insulting to people's intelligence to preach at them. No one likes to be told what to believe" (Ibid.).

Taylor is certainly correct in saying that people in general don't like to be preached at. It happens to be because we are sinners and by nature we don't like to be corrected. Taylor's statement ignores two facts: (1) Jesus Christ was a preacher. At least 30 times the Gospels mention that Christ preached. Christ's ministry began with preaching (Matt. 4:17), and He preached some of the hardest sermons recorded in the Bible (i.e., Matthew 23; Mark 9). (2) Christ's parables were not given for the purpose of not preaching but for the purpose of hiding truth from the willfully blind (Matthew 13:10-11).

Taylor's song "I Want to Be a Clone" mocks biblical fundamentalism:

> "Be a clone and kiss conviction goodnight/ Cloneliness is next to Godliness, right?/ I'm grateful that they show the way/ 'Cause I could never know the way/ To serve Him on my own, I want to be a clone/ So now I see the whole design/ My church is an assembly line/ The parts are there, I'm feeling fine/ I want to be a clone/ I've learned enough to stay afloat/ But not so much I rock the boat/ I'm glad they shoved it down my throat/ I want to be a clone/ Everybody must get cloned" (Steve Taylor, "I Want to Be a Clone").

These sound to me like the words of a rebel, and these are words which encourage rebels. The Bible plainly states that Jesus Christ has established the church and has ordained that pastors and teachers train God's people in faith and practice. Titus was told: "These things speak, and exhort, and rebuke with all authority. Let no man despise thee" (Titus 2:15). Titus, as a pastor and church planter, was given authority to instruct God's people in the right way, and he was to do this with all authority from God. We are to obey them that have the rule over us and submit ourselves (Heb. 13:7,17). It is rebellious nonsense to say that the Christian can "serve Him on my own" and to imply that sound biblical instruction is improper. In a sense, the process of discipleship IS cloning. There was one faith given to the saints almost 2,000 years ago, and we are to keep that exact faith until Jesus comes. Timothy was instructed, "And the things that thou hast heard of me among many witnesses, THE SAME commit thou to faithful men, who shall be able to teach others also" (2 Tim. 2:2). Timothy was also told to "keep that which is committed to thy trust" (1 Timothy 6:20). The preacher's job is to seek to conform the churches and the individual Christians to the New Testament faith in every area. The Lord Jesus Christ commanded that converts are to be taught "to observe all things whatsoever I have commanded you" (Matthew 28:20). In this sense, the church is indeed "an assembly line," Taylor's song notwithstanding.

TAYLOR, TERRY. See Daniel Amos Band.

THIRD DAY

In 1997 Third Day's Tai Anderson joined Roman Catholic Kathy Troccoli and 40 other CCM artists to record *Love One Another*, a song with an ecumenical theme: "Christians from all denominations demonstrating their common love for Christ and each other." The song talks about tearing down the walls of denominational division. The broad range of participants who joined Kathy Troccoli in recording "Love One Another" demonstrates the ecumenical agenda of Contemporary Christian Music. The song witnessed

Catholics, Pentecostals, Baptists, etc., yoked together to call for Christian unity.

TOURNIQUET

Tourniquet is a very popular hard rock group, which began as a "powermetal/thrash" band and has branched out into other forms of rock. The band was formed in 1990 and has had many personnel changes. As of 1998 the group was composed of Ted Kirkpatrick (drums), Luke Easter (vocals), Vince Dennis (bass), and Aaron Guerra (guitar/vocals). Guy Ritter was the original vocalist. Between 1990 and 1998 Tourniquet produced eight albums and five videos. Their first album, *Stop the Bleeding*, had vocals described as "alternating between high-pitched screams and more main stream metal vocals."

Their song "You Get What You Pray For," from *Stop the Bleeding*, was No. 1 for 24 consecutive weeks. Tourniquet tours with some of the most wicked secular rock groups, such as the antichrist group Atheist. Terry Watkins notes that at the Milwaukee Metal Festival Tourniquet shared "the stage with such ungodly groups as Deicide and Morbid Angel. Deicide (whose name means the death of God) are hard-core Satanists. Deicide has an album titled *Once Upon the Cross*; the cover shows a cloth covering the crucified Lord Jesus Christ with blood from each wound. On the inside of the album they have taken the Lord Jesus Christ and cut Him open and are in the process of removing His insides" (Terry Watkins, *Christian Rock: Blessing or Blasphemy?*).

Tourniquet's song "White Knucklin' the Rosary" is about the problem of praying only when one is in trouble. That is a good theme, but it is heresy to sing as if the Rosary were a biblical prayer. The Rosary is largely a prayer to Mary, the alleged Queen of Heaven. It is blasphemous to think that we can pray to Mary or to any other sinner. Jesus Christ alone is the Mediator between God and men (1 Timothy 2:1-6).

TROCCOLI, KATHY

CCM singer Kathy Troccoli (1958-) is very popular. She has produced five albums since 1982, and she took five years off from her music career during that time. Her 1995 album, *Sounds of Heaven*, spawned five No. 1 singles. Troccoli has been nominated five times as the Gospel Music Association female vocalist of the year.

Troccoli is a Roman Catholic. She was mentioned in an article in the *National Catholic Register* in March 8-14, 1998, which stated that she and other Catholic musicians are using their music to "evangelize" evangelical young people into the Catholic faith. In an interview with *CCM Magazine* in 1997 she said: "But I'd been very judgmental toward the Catholic church for years, and I've recently been able to go back to it without having a chip on my shoulder. I now have a much greater capacity for—as the album says—*Love and Mercy*."

Troccoli preaches an ecumenical, non-judgmental, anti-fundamentalist philosophy:

> "To me it's very simple: if the world doesn't see God's love in us and our love for each other, they're never going to want what we have. Our dogma and legalism strangle the love of Christ right out of us" (*CCM Magazine*, June 1997).

This sounds good to many ears, and there is no doubt about the importance of Christian love; but it is impossible to obey the Bible without being deeply concerned about doctrine ("dogma") and obedience to the details of God's Word ("legalism"). Jude 3 explains that God has given one faith to His people; and that faith, as recorded in the New Testament Scriptures, is to be preserved and fought for until Jesus returns. It is absolutely impossible to obey Jude 3 and be ecumenical and non-judgmental at the same time. The main thing which divides denominations is doctrine.

Troccoli's 1997 album, *Love One Another*, has an ecumenical theme: "Christians from all denominations demonstrating their common love for Christ and each other" (Dave Urbanski, "Chatty Kathy," *CCM Magazine*, June 1997). The recording of the title song involved 40 CCM artists: Amy Grant, Gary Chapman, Clay Crosse, Sandi Patty, Michael W. Smith, Carman, Tony Vincent, Jonathan Pierce, Mark Lowry, Phillips, Craig and Dean, Aaron and Jeoffrey, Jaci Velasquez, Lisa Bevill, Scott Krippayne, Sarah Masen, Babbie Mason, Sara Jahn, Carolyn Arends, Vestal Goodman, Paul Vann, Billy and Sarah Gaines, Tim Taber, Sarah Hart, Peter Penrose, Janet Paschal, Beverly Crawford, Phil Joel of the Newsboys, Kevin Smith of dc Talk, Tai Anderson of Third Day, plus the members of Out of the Grey, Beyond the Blue, 4 HIM, Christafari, and Audio Adrenaline. Like most CCM songs, this one is owned by a secular corporation. It is copyrighted 1996 by Sony/ATV Songs, Tree Publishing, Pants Down Music, and Radioquest Music Publishing. The song talks about tearing down the walls of denominational division.

> "Look around the world today/ There is anger there is hate/ And I know that it grieves His heart/ When His people stand apart/ Cause we're the only Jesus they will see/ Love one another, and live as one in His name/ Love one another we can tear down walls by His grace" ("Love One Another").

The broad range of participants who joined Kathy Troccoli in recording "Love One Another" demonstrates the ecumenical agenda of Contemporary Christian Music. The song witnessed Catholics, Pentecostals, Baptists, etc., yoked together to call for Christian unity. The New Testament repeatedly warns of widespread apostasy among those who claim to be Christians, yet the ecumenical movement ignores apostasy and calls for almost unqualified unity among professing Christians. While there is little doubt that God is grieved by some of the divisions among Bible-believing Christians, it is not true that the heart of God is grieved by all divisions within Christianity, because there are divisions He Himself has commanded. He has commanded that His people separate from those who follow doctrinal error.

Kathy Troccoli is a national spokesperson for Chuck Colson's Prison Fellowship ministry.

The worldly, sensual nature of her music is described in a review of one of her albums: "On a first listen, 'Images' hits like a great party record. Sequencers stutter and shake; explosive, violent drums syncopate dangerously off the beat; and untamed guitar solos writhe and snake through dense jungles of reverberation" (*CCM Magazine*, December 1986, p. 32).

TROUBLE

The following quotes by members of the group Trouble illustrate their non-judgmental philosophy:

> "[Our album *Run to the Light* is a] peace and love type of message. . . . we sorta tamed the message down to peace and love ... so we wouldn't feel like hypocrites. You know, like Bible-beatin' people and not the whole band was born again Christians, ya know?" (Brad Holster, member of the CCM group Trouble, *Heaven's Metal Magazine*, Number 18, p. 12).

> "I think the subtle approach reaches a wider audience, when it's right out, it turns 'em off" (Bruce Franklin, member of the CCM group Trouble, *Heaven's Metal Magazine*, Number 18, p. 12).

U2. See Bono.

UNDERCOVER

Undercover is "a Christian alternative rock band from Southern California, styles ranging from punk/new wave to dark, heavy rock. Since 1982, they've released albums dealing with what it is to be a Christian and the struggles of day-to-day life, the albums becoming more introspective and thoughtful as the band has matured" (Undercover web site). The band has recorded eight albums.

> "I'm not connected to Christian music at all. I can't stand Christian radio stations, and Christian TV makes me barf" (Joel Taylor of Undercover, interview, *CCM Magazine*, June 1986, p. 15).

VANN, PAUL

In 1997 Paul Vann joined Roman Catholic Kathy Troccoli and 40 other CCM artists to record *Love One Another*, a song with an ecumenical theme: "Christians from all denominations demonstrating their common love for Christ and each other." The song talks about tearing down the walls of denominational division. The broad range of participants who joined Kathy Troccoli in recording "Love One Another" demonstrates the ecumenical agenda of Contemporary Christian Music. The song witnessed Catholics, Pentecostals, Baptists, etc., yoked together to call for Christian unity.

VELASQUEZ, JACI

Jaci (pronounced Jackie) Velasquez (1979-) released her first album, *Heavenly Place*, in 1996 when she was only 16 years old. It quickly became the fastest-selling debut for a solo musician, produced five No. 1 hits, and won her the Dove Award for New Artist of the Year. The album has sold more than 500,000 copies. Her second album, self-titled, appeared in 1998. Her singing style is very sensual after the fashion of popular female rock singers such as the Spice Girls. Her songs are filled with breathiness, moaning, sighing, and high pitched vocal gymnastics.

Jaci cites Amy Grant among her greatest influences ("Personal Information on Jaci Velasquez," http://www.ajy.net/jaciv/jacibio.html). "She counts her greatest moment as an artist as her performances at a Billy Graham Crusade" (Ibid.). At such a forum she was yoked together with the most radical type of ecumenism, which includes practically every Protestant denomination, regardless of how liberal and unscriptural, plus Seventh-day Adventism and Roman Catholicism.

In 1997 Jaci joined Roman Catholic Kathy Troccoli and 40 other CCM artists to record *Love One Another*, a song with an ecumenical theme: "Christians from all denominations demonstrating their common love for Christ and each other." The song talks about tearing down the walls of denominational division. The broad range of participants who joined Kathy Troccoli in recording "Love One Another" demonstrates the ecumenical agenda of Contemporary Christian Music. The song witnessed Catholics, Pentecostals, Baptists, etc., yoked together to call for Christian unity.

VENGEANCE

The thrash/metal group Vengeance was put together by Bob Beamon. They are described as "the most extreme thrash/speed metal ever put out in a Christian setting. The vocals sound like demons. They sound angry and rebellious" (Al Menconi, supporter of Christian rock, *Media Update*, January-February 1989, cited by Jeff Godwin,

What's Wrong with Christian Rock?, p. 230).

> "I want (my) head chopped off/ You'll see (my) body rot/ But then (I'll) reign with Christ/ And then you will fry …" (song ends with tortured human screams) (Vengeance, "Beheaded").

Vengeance sings songs by wicked secular rock groups, thus creating in Christian youth a taste for this filthy music. For example, they perform "Space Truckin'" by the occultic/immoral rock group Deep Purple. The lyrics to "Space Truckin'" were written by Ian Gillan, who sang with the occultic band Black Sabbath. Following are the words to this foolish song:

> "The fireball that we rode was moving/ But now we've got a new machine/ Yeah, Yeah, Yeah, Yeah, the freaks said/ Man those cats can really swing/ They got music in their solar system/ They've rocked around the Milky Way/ They dance around with Borealice/ They're space truckin' every day…" ("Space Truckin'," by Vengeance).

VIGILANTES OF LOVE

Vigilantes of Love is led by Bill Mallonee. The 1997 Vigilantes of Love album *Slow Dark Train* contained a song titled "Love Cocoon." Note the following lyrics:

> "Honey, I wanna attack your flesh with glad abandon/ I wanna look for your fruits/ I wanna put my hands on 'em."

VINCENT, TONY

In 1997 Tony Vincent joined Roman Catholic Kathy Troccoli and 40 other CCM artists to record *Love One Another*, a song with an ecumenical theme: "Christians from all denominations demonstrating their common love for Christ and each other." The song talks about tearing down the walls of denominational division. The broad range of participants who joined Kathy Troccoli in recording "Love One Another" demonstrates the ecumenical agenda of Contemporary Christian Music. The song witnessed Catholics, Pentecostals, Baptists, etc., yoked together to call for Christian unity.

VINEYARD CHURCHES. See Wimber, John.

VOLZ, GREGORY. See Petra.

VOX, BONO. See Bono.

WALSH, SHEILA

The Scottish Sheila Walsh released her first album, *Future Eyes,* in early 1982. It contained experimentation with "British new wave" rock music. Walsh is a member of a charismatic congregation and has frequently performed in charismatic settings. Together with roughly 20,000 Roman Catholics (and 20,000 representing roughly 40 other denominations), she participated in the charismatic-ecumenical North American Congress on the Holy Spirit & World Evangelization in New Orleans in 1987. That same year she became the co-host of Pat Robertson's *700 Club.* Five years later she entered a psychiatric hospital for a month then began an extended series of psychiatric treatments. She left the *700 Club* and divorced her husband. By 1996 she had remarried, was working on a degree in theology, and had begun a writing career (*CCM Magazine*, July 1996).

WATSON, WAYNE

Wayne Watson (1955-) recorded his first album in 1980 and it immediately yielded a No. 1 hit single, "Touch of the Master's Hand." He has had 34 Top 10 singles. Watson is a charismatic-ecumenical CCM musician who moves in a wide range of ecclesiastical circles. In January 1988, for example, he performed at the Assemblies of God-connected Carpenter's Home Church in Lakeland, Florida. In January 1992 he joined hands with many well-known charismatic speakers, including Larry Lea and Jack Deere, and performed for James Robinson's Bible Conference.

Watson's positive-only, non-judgmental philosophy comes across loud and clear: "I won't write a song that says, 'You better get right with God.' From my own experience I find that way sometimes makes people defensive" (Wayne Watson, *Christian Activities Calendar*, Spring/Summer 1989, p. 11).

WHITE HEART

The long-haired members of White Heart are Rick Florian (lead), Bill Smiley (guitar), Mark Gersmehl (keyboard), Brian Wooten (guitar), Anthony Sallee (bass), and Jon Knox (drums). The group began in 1982. They recorded three albums with Word Records. In 1985 White Heart moved to Sparrow, and in 1990, to Star Song.

White Heart's unscriptural philosophy is evident in the following statement:

> "So, where do you go when times get tough? You've got to have a powerhouse. You've got to have a place where you can go ... We want to tell people that there are places to go, that we should build communities where they can

get strength, NOT TO KNOCK ANYBODY ELSE DOWN, but to find SOMETHING DEEPER WITHIN THEMSELVES" (White Heart, *CCM*, February, 1991, pp. 20-23).

Note the unscriptural non-judgmental philosophy. Of course Christians are to not called to "knock" others down, but they are called to reprove, rebuke, and exhort (2 Timothy 4:2). They are called to reprove the works of darkness (Ephesians 5:11). Also, the message that Christians have for the world is not that we can find something deeper within ourselves, but that the Truth is found in Jesus Christ and in the His Scriptures. Deep within man we find not truth but sin and deception (Jeremiah 17:9).

The vague meaningless of much of White Heart's music is illustrated by the lyrics to "Inside" from their 1995 album by the same name. The song is performed to a heavy, growling, grunge rock:

> "I wanna feel/ no I wanna dream/ I wanna live on the inside/ Oh I gotta breathe/ gotta pray/ I wanna heal on the inside, I wanna feel/ I wanna feel/ I wanna dream/ I wanna live on the inside/ gotta breath/ gotta pray/ I wanna heal on the inside/ on the inside/ on the inside/ inside/ inside."

What does the song mean? It can mean anything you please. It therefore means nothing. The Mormon can find his religion here. So can the Hindu, the Catholic mystic, the New Ager, the psychotherapist, the humanist.

WILLIAMS, DENIECE

Deniece Williams (1950-) began her career in 1971 singing with Stevie Wonder's group Wonderlove on tour with the Rolling Stones. She began a solo career in 1976 with Kalimba, a production company owned by Maurice White of the rock band Earth, Wind and Fire. In 1986 she recorded her first Christian album. That same year she was married, but by 1991 she and her husband were divorced. "Time away from home created a troubled marriage" (Deniece Williams, *CCM Magazine*, September 1998, p. 43).

Williams performed at a Catholic mass conducted by Pope John Paul II during his visit to Los Angeles, California, in September 1987 (*San Francisco Chronicle*, July 18, 1987).

Williams reveals her attitude toward biblical fundamentalism:

> "The whole story of *Footloose* is very close to my life. In the church I grew up in, you couldn't go to dances, you couldn't go to movies, and you couldn't wear pants or sleeveless dresses. There were a lot of 'Thou shalt not's" (Deniece Williams, *CCM Magazine*, January 1987, p. 17).

This is the attitude which is common within Contemporary Christian Music. Those who attempt to apply the Word of God to daily living and to warn against sinful activities are considered legalistic Pharisees. As for the "Thou shalt not's" we are reminded of the commandments of God in the New Testament Scriptures. "For this is the love of God, that we keep his commandments: and his commandments are not grievous" (1 John 5:3).

WIMBER, JOHN, & AND THE VINEYARD

The Vineyard Churches, founded by the late John Wimber (1934-1997), have had a wide influence with their praise music. Wimber himself, who was the manager of the secular group The Righteous Brothers before his conversion, wrote many popular songs, and many of the Vineyard churches are noted for their influential music groups. The *Vintage Vineyard Music* series is advertised as "Vineyard's all-time worship classics THAT CONTINUE TO BE SUNG CROSS-DENOMINATIONALLY IN CHURCHES AROUND THE WORLD." (As of 1990, 52 of the 53 songs in the *Vineyard Songbook* did not mention the cross of Jesus Christ.) Wimber conducted many "signs and wonders" conferences in various parts of the world, teaching the error that effective evangelism requires the working of miracles. Wimber spread great confusion through his allowance for extra-biblical revelation. Music groups from the Vineyard movement have performed at the influential Urbana youth conferences, sponsored by the InterVarsity Christian Fellowship, since 1990. A *Charisma* magazine report on Urbana '90, noted that "delegates swayed and clapped to the beat" of the 11-piece Vineyard group. The music group had the young people raise their hands for "prayer for inner healing." (A Roman Catholic priest led one seminar at Urbana '90.) The Promise Keepers movement was founded by men involved in the Vineyard. PK founder Bill McCartney is a member of a Vineyard church in Boulder, Colorado. The pastor of that church, James Ryle, and Randy Phillips, another member of his church, also are leaders in Promise Keepers. Ryle teaches that God is still raising up prophets in the churches and claims to receive many revelations from God through dreams and visions. In 1990 he claimed that he saw in a vision that the Beatles got their magically popular music sound from an anointing by God, and that God eventually removed His anointing because they abused it. God allegedly implied to Ryle in the vision that He would place that same anointing upon musicians "in the church" in these last days.

Though Wimber was not Pentecostal, he accepted and popularized many Pentecostal-type practices, including "slaying in the Spirit," prophecy, "words of knowledge," and Pentecostal-style faith healing.

Wimber frequently spoke on the same platform with Roman Catholic priests and apparently saw no serious problem with their doctrine. In 1986 Wimber joined Catholic priest Tom Forrest and Anglican Michael Harper at the European Festival of Faith, an ecumenical meeting in Birmingham, England. The Festival leaders and the 8,000 participants sent the Pope of Rome a message: "We are ready to join you in the united evangelism of Europe" (*Australian Beacon*, March 1988).

Wimber was a featured speaker at the North American Congress on the Holy Spirit & World Evangelization in Indianapolis, August 1990. In that forum he joined hands with roughly 12,000 Roman Catholics, including countless priests and nuns. A Catholic mass was held every morning of the convention. I was present at this conference with press credentials and heard Wimber speak.

In October 1991, the John Wimber conference in Sydney, Australia, featured Catholic priests Tom Forrest and Raniero Cantalamessa, as well as Catholic layman Kevin Ranaghan. Forrest is the priest who at Indianapolis '90 said he praises God for purgatory. Cantalamessa is the papal preacher at the Vatican. Ranaghan claims that the Roman Catholic Church alone contains the fullness of God and truth and that the Pope is the infallible head of all churches. In spite of their blasphemous heresies, these men were featured by Wimber as Spirit-filled men of God.

In his church planting seminar Wimber said there is nothing scripturally wrong with the Catholic practice of seeking healing through relics: "In the Catholic church for over a 1,200 year period people were healed as a result of touching the relics of the saints. We Protestants have difficulty with that ... but we healers shouldn't, because there's nothing theologically out of line with that" (John Wimber, *Church Planting Seminar*).

Wimber actively encouraged the reunification of Protestants with the church of Rome. "During the Vineyard pastors' conference, he went so far as to 'apologize' to the Catholic church on behalf of all Protestants ... He stated that 'the pope, who by the way is very responsive to the charismatic movement, and is himself a born-again evangelical, is preaching the Gospel as clear as anyone in the world today'" (John Wimber, *Church Planting Seminar*, audio tapes, 5 volumes, unedited, 1981, cited by Pastor John Goodwin).

WINANS, BEBE AND CECE

Bebe (1962-) and CeCe (1964-) Winans form the popular brother/sister pop-R&B duo. In 1982 they began performing on the Pentecostal *PTL Club*. They have since won many Grammys, Dove, and other music awards. They have had secular hits such as "Addictive Love," "It's OK," and "I'll Take You There." Many of their other songs are written so vaguely that they could be about God or about one's earthly lover.

The non-judgmental philosophy of BeBe Winans is evident from the following statement:

> "We've been beating people up with our lyrics, condemning the world harshly. You don't have to tell someone they're locked up in prison—they already know that. They want to know how to get out. Where the key is, and that key is God's love which is more powerful than hatred. This is a pleasant and warm message to the world, one they need and want to hear" (BeBe Winans, *CCM Magazine*, Feb. 1989, p. 17).

Winans also holds the false philosophy that music is neutral:

> "We believe all music comes from God, and that liberates us to express ourselves in a wider range of artistic expression than some others" (BeBe Winans, *CCM Magazine*, Feb. 1989, p. 21).

THE W'S

The music of the W's is described in a CMRH review as follows:

> "The W's have taken the craze of the 40's, swing music, and have modernized it with a healthy dose of 90's alternative and ska. Their music is catchy, even addictive, with lots of unconventional musical instruments (well, conventional for contemporary Christian artists at least). Like the OC Supertones, they spice up their music with saxophones, clarinets, trombones, trumpets, and the like. But while the Supertones present the image of seriousness — with the coats and ties, and matching black sunglasses — the W's go quite the other direction. 'Wacky' comes to mind, as do 'rowdy' and 'disheveled.' The end result is a band with a sound you'll not soon forget, and an image that's offbeat enough for them to stand out" (David Longenecker, *Christian Music Review Headquarters*, Dec. 20, 1998).

The last thing Christian teenagers need is to be encouraged to be rowdy and disheveled! I would like to know what Scriptures encourage this activity.

The W's are performing with dc Talk on their 1999 "Supernatural Experience" tour.

When Pope John Paul II visited the States in January 1999, The W's and other CCM groups joined hands with hundreds of thousands of Catholics to welcome him. Featured at a Catholic youth rally connected with the Pope's visit, were The W's, Jennifer Knapp, dc Talk, Audio Adrenaline, Rebecca St. James, and the Supertones (*CCM Magazine*, April 1999, p. 12). Each attendee received a rosary with instructions about how to pray to Mary.

WOLFE, LANNY

Lanny Wolfe is committed to "Jesus Only" doctrine, which denies the Trinity and baptizes only in Jesus' name. He wrote "Greater Is He that Is in Me."

ZAO

Zao, a rock band described as "hardcore music at an extreme level," went through almost a complete personnel change recently. The band currently is composed of Jesse Smith (drums), Russ Cogdell (guitar), Brett Detar (guitar), and Daniel Weyandt (vocals).

I would describe Zao's "music" as raunchy, growling, screeching, depressing noise layered with the screams of the damned! Some of their songs are not quite so hard, but this is exactly how I would describe the pieces I have listened to.

The following is a description of Zao in concert by a Zao fan:

> "Like Black Flag or Unbroken in their seminal heydahs, Zao are frightening to behold—knocking over cymbal stands, hurling guitars into the air and screaming aloud during moments that are otherwise silent. Smith has been known to shout into a drum mic once in a while during a song. On one occasion, Weyandt's raw emotion bubbled over so distinctly that he vomited all over the stage" (Zao web site, http://placetobe.org/cmp/artists/index.html).

"Question: What do you want to accomplish spiritually or in a ministry sense with the new record? Answer: We are trying to stay away from any Christian formulas for ministry. ... Just because we are Christian in this band, that does not entitle kids to expect a spiritual circus at every show" (Jesse and Dan of ZAO, *HM magazine*, May-June 1998, p. 25). Jesse also said, "I don't want to be held back by an 'a.k.a. Christian' tag. I want to play for as many people as we can. Hopefully by next year we'll be headlining for bands like Slayer" (*Fuelmagazine*, Spring-Summer 1999, p. 21).

Zao drummer Jesse Smith said the band listens to all sorts of filthy secular rock music. "I like so much stuff, the new PJ Harvey; Jimmy Eat World is awesome! I'm pretty much the guy in the band that likes everything. I like Matchbox 20, Girls Against Boys, Third Eye Blind, and then I like scary stuff like Neurosis. Most of the guys in the band are into other stuff. Scott's into a lot of death metal and Dan and Russ are into indie bands. We try to get our hands on anything that is just pushing the evenlope" (*Fuelmagazine*, Spring-Summer 1999, p. 21).

ZSCHECH, DARLENE

See Laughing Revival.

PART V
SOUTHERN GOSPEL

SOUTHERN GOSPEL MUSIC

Southern gospel is not a single style of music but is a classification for a broad range of harmonizing, country-tinged Christian music which originated in the southeast part of the United States. Some Southern gospel is lovely and spiritual and seeks not to entertain the flesh but to edify the spirit. (There are also quartets which are not Southern gospel in style. An example is the Old Fashioned Revival Hour Quartet which was featured on Charles Fuller's radio program.) We praise the Lord for all Christian music, Southern or otherwise, which rejects worldly rhythms, which has scriptural lyrics, which seeks solely to glorify Jesus Christ and edify the saints, and which is produced by faithful Christians. Sadly, though, much of the Southern gospel incorporates worldly pop, country, ragtime, jazz, boogie-woogie, and rock rhythms, and is oriented toward entertainment. It is the latter that is closely akin to Contemporary Christian Music. As a matter of fact, commercial Southern gospel is one of the branches of the larger CCM world.

I grew up with Southern gospel. The Southern Baptist churches my mom and dad attended in Florida would have all-day sings on some Sundays. Following the morning service, we would have a glorious "dinner on the ground," featuring tables piled high with the tastiest dishes the church ladies could concoct. The kids would romp around as the tables were prepared, then the pastor would pray and everyone would gorge themselves on whichever foods suited their fancy. The variety was incredible. When the meal was finished and the tables cleared, everyone gathered back in the church auditorium for the sing. There would be some congregational singing, then the quartets would start up. Usually these were local groups, but sometimes a professional group would be available. I always liked the congregational singing best.

History of Southern Gospel

As we will see, Southern gospel brought four significant changes to Christian music in North America in the 1920s, '30s, '40s and '50s. (1) They commercialized it. (2) They took it out of the churches and put it into hands of publishers and promoters. (3) They jazzed it up with worldly styles. (4) They turned it into entertainment. Gospel music publisher Harper and Associates advertised their Southern gospel music as "Family entertainment with a message, entertainment that a Fair or civic organization can sponsor and not feel like they're getting too churchy." This sounds exactly like the Contemporary Christian Music approach. The Stamps Quartet of the 1930s "not only sang the most popular gospel songs of the day, but gave an all-around entertainment program" (Bob Terrell, *The Music Men*, p. 39).

Professional Southern gospel quartets were born in the early part of this century as business enterprises. Prior to that quartets were mixed (men and women) and "sang in their churches simply for the spiritual edification of the congregation" (*The Music Men*, p. 54). The inventor of the professional male gospel quartet was a Nazarene, James Vaughan, who hired a quartet in 1910 to represent his music publishing company (which he had founded in 1902). The Vaughan Quartet performances at churches, revivals, and conventions were a means whereby Vaughan sold music. "In this way the groups promoted their sponsor and created a market for the songbooks" (David L. Taylor, *Happy Rhythm*, p. 7). By the late 1920s Vaughan had 16 full-time quartets on the road. In 1921 the pioneering Vaughan cut the first record for his new recording company, and in 1922 he built the first radio station in Tennessee, all with the goal of promoting his music. In 1924 the V.O. Stamps Music Company was founded by a Baptist, Virgil Stamps; and he, too, put quartets to work. In 1929 this company became the famous Stamps-Baxter Music Company. These companies established influential music training schools and created the hugely popular all-day and all-night gospel music sings.

The new "Southern gospel" style featured "tag lines in accompanying voices, chromatic lower-neighbor note and passing notes, and in the refrain a walking bass lead with several interjections. The harmony was simple and very rhythmic. A ragtime style was added later to the piano accompaniment (commonly called the 'stomp beat'), which made the sacred and the secular indistinguishable" (H.T. Spence, *Confronting Contemporary Christian Music*, p. 120).

The pioneer of the ragtime gospel piano style was Dwight Brock, who played in one of the Stamps quartets.

> "Brock played a rhythm piano style; some thought it sounded a little like Dixieland [jazz] or razzamatazz. ... Thousands of pianists would copy his style in the years to come. ... IT WAS REVOLUTIONARY BECAUSE IT JAZZED UP GOSPEL MUSIC JUST ENOUGH FOR THE SECULAR PUBLIC TO CATCH ON. Dwight's nephew, Brock Speer, who sings bass for the Speer Family today, said when his uncle was a boy in the early teens—he was born in 1905—he heard a circus drummer playing syncopated rhythms on snare drums, and said to himself, 'I wonder if I could do that on the piano?'" (*The Music Men*, pp. 38,39).

Though the seeds for these things were present in the 1920s and '30s, it was not until the 1940s that Southern gospel began to promote an entertainment-oriented, jazzed up approach to Christian music on a large scale. Prior to that the quartets were not very flashy. For example, W.B. Walbert, the manager of the Vaughan Quartet during the 1920s, "was a spiritual man who did not believe that a quartet should do anything showy to detract from the gospel messages in the songs" (*The Music Men*, p. 33). This attitude did not prevail, though, and even Walbert's own son, James, began playing the piano backwards, playing with his elbows, and otherwise putting on a show to entertain the crowds.

Two of the most influential groups in this direction were the Blackwood Brothers and the Statesmen. Prior to this, professional gospel quartets commonly sang without musical accompaniment or with traditional strings. The Ranger Quartet, for example, often sang with a guitar. The Statesmen were one of the first professional quartets to feature the piano; and it was not just ANY piano, it was Hovie Lister's ragtime, honky-tonk piano. Sadly, this style has dominated popular Southern gospel ever since. (This does not mean, of course, that the Statesmen sang ONLY jazzy music. Some of their numbers were nice renditions of good Christian music. An example was the beautiful "What a Savior," featuring lyric tenor Rosie Rozell.)

The following brief history of Southern gospel is by a man who researches rock music. He has correctly observed the close connection between jived up Southern gospel of the 1940s and '50s and early rock & roll.

> "The white gospel quartets of the 1950s, when [Elvis] Presley started to study them, were every bit as exciting as their black counterparts, USING SHOW-BIZ HYPE, WHIPPING UP CROWDS AND CREATING STARS. Reporting on an all-night sing in Atlanta, Georgia, for *The Saturday Evening Post* (June 1956), Furman Bisher compared the audience response to the Oak Ridge Quartet to bobby soxers' swooning for Frank Sinatra. 'Women out there shrieked, and a couple of young girls rushed to the stage edge to snap pictures of the tenor who was holding that high note the way a trumpet player prolongs a "ride,"' wrote Bisher. ...
>
> "Presley idolized such gospel stars for the rest of his life. His particular favorites were J.D. Sumner, the tall, stringy bass vocalist with the Blackwood Brothers, who also went to the First Assembly of God Church in Memphis, and Jake Hess and Hovie Lister of the Statesmen Quartet (which actually had five members). An ordained minister, LISTER IS OFTEN CREDITED WITH BRINGING SHOW BUSINESS TO QUARTET SINGING. At the time he said, 'If it takes shaking my hair down, beating a piano like Liberace or Piano Red to keep these young people out of beer joints and the rear seats of cars, I'll do it. The Devil's got his kind of entertainment. We've got ours. They criticize me, say I'm too lively for religion, but I get results. That's what counts'" (emphasis added) (Steve Turner, *Hungry for Heaven*, pp. 29-31).

Lister's philosophy was pragmatism; whatever works is right. This is exactly the same New Evangelical philosophy which permeates the Contemporary Christian Music field today. Hovie Lister and the Statesmen were forerunners to CCM. God has not instructed us to do whatever "gets results," but to obey His Word regardless of the results. The sole authority for faith and practice is the Bible. If it is Scriptural it is right; if it is not Scriptural, it is wrong, regardless of how well it appears to work. God's Word plainly forbids His people to love the world. It is therefore impossible to please God by adapting the things of the world to the service of Christ. Liberace was a homosexual entertainer who helped corrupt the morals of America. I believe it is a serious error to adopt his sensual, worldly ways to Gospel music. Where does God's Word encourage us to copy the world? To be holy, means to be set apart from and different from the world. Nowhere do we see the Lord Jesus Christ or the Apostles entertaining people in the name of the ministry. We do not see them putting on some sort of worldly show to draw a crowd. We do not see them adapting themselves to the spirit of the age. We do not see them attempting to manipulate people by worldly means. The Apostle Paul plainly stated that he depended solely upon the power of the Holy Spirit. "For I determined not to know any thing among you, save Jesus Christ, and him crucified. And I was with you in weakness, and in fear, and in much trembling. And my speech and my preaching was not with enticing words of man's wisdom, but in demonstration of the Spirit and of power: That your faith should not stand in the wisdom of men, but in the power of God" (1 Corinthians 2:2-5).

Now we continue with Steve Turner's overview of the history of Southern gospel:

> "White quartet singing had developed in the 1920s ... they began to develop showmanship and gimmicks during the 1940s. ... Hovie Lister, a dashing young man with long, dark wavy hair and an Errol Flynn mustache, LOVED TO SHAKE IT ALL UP FOR THE LORD. He joined with Crumpler and Jake Hess to form the Statesmen Quartet, which was to become one of the first supergroups of white gospel, catapulting the music to commercial acceptability and SETTING THE STYLE FOR EMERGENT ROCK 'N' ROLLERS BRED ON HOLY MUSIC.

> "Although much was made of the evils of dancing, show business, jukeboxes and television, THE SUCCESS OF THE GOSPEL QUARTETS WAS LARGELY DUE TO THEIR PRESENTING MUCH OF THE SAME GLOSS AND EXCITEMENT in an acceptable context. The songs were about loving your neighbor, being holy and not giving in to 'modern religion,' but THE PERFORMANCES DREW FROM POP, BLUES, COUNTRY, RAGTIME AND JAZZ. ...

> "Don Butler, now director of archives for the Nashville-based Gospel Music Association, was the Statesmen Quartet's manager during the 1950s. 'They were sensational,' he remembers. 'Hovie Lister had no peer in showmanship. He created a tremendous rapport with the audience. HE COULD TURN THEIR EMOTIONS ON AND OFF JUST LIKE THAT. They also had highly

polished harmonies and arrangements. HOVIE WOULD JUMP ONTO A PIANO AND SHAKE HIS LONG BLACK HAIR INTO HIS FACE WHILE THE REST OF THE GROUP DANCED ON STAGE. They were the first quartet to use four individual microphones. Before that everyone had gathered around one mike'" (emphasis added) (Steve Turner, *Hungry for Heaven*, pp. 29-31).

Bill Gaither, in his history of Southern gospel, admits that Hovie Lister's "approach was loud, fast, swingy, and pop" and that "he would do whatever it took to get the loudest applause, the biggest laugh" (Bill Gaither, *Homecoming*, p. 133).

The Statesmen's bass singer, Jim "Big Chief" Wetherington, moved his legs in ways strangely reminiscent of how Elvis moved to rock & roll. Jake Hess, another member of the original Statesmen, noted: "He went about as far as you could go in gospel music. The women would jump up, just like they do for pop shows" (Peter Guralnick, *Last Train for Memphis*, p. 48). Rock historian Peter Guralnick observes that "preachers frequently objected to the lewd movements." Some conservative Christian radio stations broke Statesmen records on the air to protest their jazzy music.

Describing the popular Southern gospel quartets of the 1940s and 1950s, Wally Varner of the Melody Masters testifies: "I guess the Melody Masters were one of the wildest organizations, for the lack of a better word, that I've ever worked with. I used to turn flips and things like that. ... In those days GOSPEL MUSIC WASN'T AS SPIRITUAL, IT WAS MORE ENTERTAINING. We had a rambunctious type of program, but we also had some beautiful singing that we would settle down to" (Taylor, *Happy Rhythms*, p. 22). Another popular group, The Delmore Brothers, "mixed sacred lyrics, blues and boogie with spectacular commercial results" (David Seay, *Stairway to Heaven*, p. 49).

Southern gospel in the 1970s was still entertainment oriented and highly competitive. "All-night sings occasionally resembled singing contests, as groups often appeared more interested in 'putting it to' one another onstage than entertaining and ministering to the audience" (Ibid., p. 111).

Worldliness

There have been two distinct sides or camps to Southern gospel. We would label them conservative and contemporary. The conservative Southern gospel people have used music solely to glorify Jesus Christ and edify the saints. They have refused to jazz up the music with worldly rhythms and sounds. The singers and musicians who represent this category have tended to live godly, Christ-honoring lives. The contemporary side has used music for entertainment. They have sought to jazz up Christian music with the world's rhythms. The singers and musicians in this category have tended to live spiritually careless, worldly lives.

This distinction has been evident from the inception of Southern gospel. Even in the 1920s, '30s, and '40s, there were many churches which refused to participate in the "jazzy" side of Southern gospel and which refused to allow worldly Southern gospel musicians to ply their wares. One of the reasons why so many of the popular Southern gospel groups of that era sang in school auditoriums and other secular venues was because "some churches would not permit these 'jazzy' singers to perform in church houses" (*The Music Men*, pp. 64,65).

The two different camps within Southern gospel was already evident in the 1920s. James Vaughan did have a commercial goal with his music, but his goal was the spiritual edification of his hearers and he did not introduce worldliness into the music. He "emphasized holiness and living a sanctified life, separated from the world" and his groups "avoided any style that would draw attention to oneself" (*Homecoming*, p. 76). Vaughn lived an exemplary Christian life and "never used tobacco in any form, never swore an oath, and never drank intoxicating beverages" (*The Music Men*, p. 28). He "knew the Bible as few men did." V.O. Stamps, on the other hand, exemplified the worldly camp. Stamps was a heavy smoker and a glutton who died young of diabetes. He would order two-pound steaks and follow that up with three pieces of pie. At one of his All-Night Broadcasts he drank 46 sodas, most of them Coca-Colas (*The Music Men*, p. 122). This camp within Southern gospel was far less careful about spiritual matters and had no conviction about putting on a show with their music. The Stamps Quartet even in the early years was described as "an entertaining fivesome" (*The Music Men*, p. 39). Their theme song was "Give the World a Smile," which featured strong rhythm with the bass singing melody and the upper voices singing an afterbeat. "Then, on the repeat chorus, they sang a boom, boo, pang, pang effect like a rhythm guitar" (Ibid.). Their ragtime pianist was the aforementioned Dwight Brock, who "jazzed up gospel music just enough for the secular public to catch on."

Many of the popular Southern gospel groups of the 1950s and '60s were characterized by worldliness. Drinking, smoking, womanizing, and divorce has been a common feature of Southern gospel. The Statesmen's first tenor, Bobby Strickland observed that Southern gospel quartets often reach a certain level and "then something happens." He believed the reason for this was that "they don't live right" (*The Music Men*, p. 97). J.D. Sumner and the Sunshine Boys were infamous for their worldly lifestyles. They smoked, drank, cavorted with women, etc. "The Blackwoods, three months before their air tragedy, were not the only ones who referred to him [Sumner] and his cohorts in the Sunshine Boys as infidels" (Gaither, *Homecoming*, p. 160). The Sunshine Boys were formed by Ace Richman, a swing band entertainer who saw that gospel quartets were financially profitable. When he added "Western swing" to gospel songs, he saw that "people liked them even better" (*The Music Men*, p. 190). Richman was "the man who put swing into gospel." The Sunshine Boys were pure entertainment. They did not testify of Christ or give invitations. Richman told preachers, "We do not testify; we are an entertaining group. You pay us to sing these songs, and we'll sing 'em. But that's all." J.D. Sumner almost lost his marriage because of his moral recklessness. He went on to sing bass with the famous Blackwood Brothers, then with the Stamps Quartet. During the years in which Sumner and the Stamps were backing Elvis Presley at Las Vegas and elsewhere, Sumner's nephew, Donnie, who sang in the group, became a drug addict and was lured into the licentious pop music field. Laverne Tripp, who sang with the Sierra Quartet and the Blue Ridge Quartet, was well known for his carnality. The piano player with the Sierra Quartet was a known homosexual. At one Kingsmen Quartet concert a screaming, hair-pulling fight broke out between the bass singer's ex-wife and his current girlfriend. These sad facts could be multiplied.

We believe the worldly living produced the worldly music. Carnality produces spiritual blindness and powerlessness (1 Pet. 2:11; 1 Cor. 3:1-2; Heb. 5:12-14; Rev. 3:16-17).

> "Many Christians see some things, but because their hearts are still in a carnal state (in a sympathy for the world), their sight is distorted. ... A Christian, even if he is faithfully working in the vineyard for Christ, can possibly have a lukewarm life. According to Revelation 3:17, lukewarmness in a Christian's life (and it does not matter if he is a leader in the church or not) produces blindness. Some men who have been viewed as the authorities of music, who have led in the forefront years ago in the Christian circles, are now compromising the principles of God's word with their music. Dear reader, it is an evidence of either lukewarmness or backsliding. Their music has become eclectic and dialectic with sounds of this age" (Dr. H.T. Spence, *Confronting Contemporary Christian Music*, 1997, p. 8).

Dr. H.T. Spence, vice president of Foundations Bible College & Seminary, is a fundamentalist historian and teacher who has taught music, history, and theology for 25 years. He received part of his music training at Bob Jones University. In the late 1960s he sang with a gospel trio called The Seminaries. At the time he was a Pentecostal and was singing in Pentecostal churches. In his book on CCM he notes that popular Southern gospel quartets were singing in the same churches, and on three occasions his trio appeared with Laverne Tripp and the Sierra Quartet. He describes how Tripp attempted "to influence our young trio to change its style" by dressing in a contemporary manner and by adopting an entertaining stage presence. They refused to heed Tripp's counsel and on the third occasion they walked out of the program. The following is Dr. Spence's testimony:

> "I was born in a Pentecostal home in October 1948 at a time when my grandfather was bishop of the Pentecostal Holiness Church. ... I received a call from God for the ministry in my college freshman year (1966), and was chosen to sing in a male trio called The Seminaries; we traveled and ministered to churches on the weekends, representing the seminary I was attending at that time. Although the Pentecostal music was not the best even from the beginning, there were definite changes coming by the late 1960s. ... During the two years I was part of the group, we came in contact with the Southern gospel quartets who were making their appearance in the Pentecostal churches. At times, we were appointed to sing in the same services. One gospel music personality I remember was Laverne Tripp, who then had a reputation for his vacillation to backsliding, including his drinking, yet AN ABILITY TO SWAY A CROWD OF PEOPLE WITH HIS CRYING AND COUNTRY-SOUND SINGING. He was with the Sierra Quartet at that time (whose piano player was a known homosexual). He tried to influence our young trio to change its style, but his flair of clothing and aggressive presence on 'stage' was truly too much for us. During a third mutual service with him, we as a trio walked out. The Pastor met us out at the parking lot and inquired of our action. We told him in a most honorable way that we could not share the service with such a man as Mr. Tripp. The Pastor agreed with our appraisal of him, but he said, 'IT DRAWS THE CROWD.' With that remark, we left. Eventually, sad to state, our piano player married one of the sisters of Laverne and was sucked into the vortex of 'Southern Gospel Music.' Mr. Tripp went on to become lead singer for The Blue Ridge Quartet when Elmo Fagg left the group. During his years with that national quartet, he was given to heaven drinking and drugs. An invitation came to him during that time to go solo on the Las Vegas strip. Some years ago he supposedly came back to the Lord. He has become a permanent fixture with TBN along with his wife and children (who now have families of their own). His own personal recording studio is part of the lucrative business he has come to enjoy through the CCM medium" (Dr. H.T. Spence, *Confronting Contemporary Christian Music*, 1997, pp. x,xi).

This testimony opens a window into a large portion (though not all, by any means) of the ecumenical, entertainment-oriented Southern gospel scene of recent decades. New books on Southern gospel by Bill Gaither and others tend to ignore or gloss over its worldly facets, but the Bible loudly warns of the dangers of worldliness. "Ye adulterers and adulteresses, know ye not that the friendship of the world is enmity with God? whosoever therefore will be a friend of the world is the enemy of God" (James 4:4). Worldliness can be forgiven by repentance and confession, praise the Lord, but it must not be ignored or excused. Worldly ministers produce worldly fruit. "Be not deceived; God is not mocked: for whatsoever a man soweth, that shall he also reap" (Galatians 5:7).

This testimony also reminds us of pastoral responsibility in protecting churches. When Brother Spence and his trio protested against worldly music, the pastor, though admitting that the musicians were carnal, excused it because the people liked it. People-pleasing pastors will answer to God for their cowardly disobedience to the Scriptures.

The worldliness of many of the Southern gospel groups is reflected in their close and uncritical association with secular rockers. This is not only true today but has characterized many of the most popular groups for decades. The Jordanaires performed as background singers on Elvis Presley records and as session singers for many other raunchy rock and country recordings. Members of the Speer Family (Ben and Brock) also sang on Elvis recordings, including "I've Got a Woman" and "Heartbreak Hotel." The Jordanaires provided vocals for Elvis's 1956 megahit "Hound Dog." The Jordanaires toured with Eddy Arnold as well as with Elvis. They also performed on some of Elvis's indecent movies. J.D. Sumner and the Stamps toured with Elvis from 1969 until his death in 1977, performing backup for the King of Rock & Roll in sin-holes such as Las Vegas night clubs. Ed Hill, one of the singers with the Stamps, was Elvis's announcer for two years. It was Hill who concluded the Elvis concerts with, "Ladies and gentlemen, Elvis has left the building. Goodbye, and God bless you." The Imperials and the Oak Ridge Boys also performed as back up singers for Hollywood shows and Nashville recordings.

One of Elvis's favorite gospel singers was Hovie Lister, the leader of the Statesmen. This gospel group made large sums of money from their appearances. The Blackwood Brothers and the Statesmen would receive $1,000 to $1,500 per night for their music shows. Not content with this, the Statesmen sold their services to the Nabisco Company in the 1950s. Lister became their spokesman, emceeing for Nabisco commercials. At their peak they were making a half million dollars per year. That would be more like five million dollars per year in today's dollars. The group performed on the Nabisco television show. "In their personal appearances, the Statesmen participated in a complete merchandising campaign on behalf of their sponsor..." (Taylor, *Happy Rhythms*, p. 53). One photo in David Taylor's history of the Statesmen shows the group performing in front of a large wall mural of a woman dressed in a short skirt as "the Sweetheart of the South" for Nabisco Vanilla Wafers. This was part of Nabisco's advertising campaign surrounding the Statesmen. For their work with Nabisco the group recorded music with Wade Creager's dance orchestra at the Biltmore Hotel in Atlanta.

As already mentioned, the flamboyant Hovie Lister popularized an entertainment-oriented, jazzy gospel music presentation. He was characterized by 'flashy dress, oversized rings, and upbeat entertainment style" (*The Music Men*, p. 146). Lister and the Statesmen went so far beyond that which was traditionally acceptable in Christian music in the middle of this century that some Christian radio stations would not play their music. In fact, some stations broke their records in protest! This occurred in 1955 when they recorded some gospel songs with a "New Orleans jazz flavor." The instrumental group which backed the Statesmen on the album included country guitarist Chet Atkins, Ernie Newton on the stand-up bass guitar, and Farris Coursey on drums. This was essentially a country-rock band. (The Statesmen pioneered the CCM practice of using unsaved musicians on their recordings.) Hovie Lister played the boogie-woogie piano. One preacher protested by calling it "stripping music" (Taylor, p. 55). Some of the Statesmen Quartet's music was brought over from the swinging black spirituals. "So many of their early hits began to stray away some from the southern, singing convention style—the music that was coming out of Stamps-Baxter—and basically were coming out of the black tradition" (Taylor, p. 32). In one of their early hits, *Happy Rhythm* (1950), the Statesmen actually used the phrase rock and roll to describe what they were doing! "There's a happy rhythm keeps a-rockin' and a-rollin'." This was set to a "rollicking, boogie setting" (Taylor, p. 34). Their 1961 album contained the song "God Is God," "featuring a rockabilly Chet Atkins guitar solo which was similar to early Elvis Presley releases" (Taylor, p. 86).

Southern Gospel in Recent Years

In the last three decades, Southern gospel in general has become increasingly worldly, rocky, and ecumenical. Lee Roy Abernathy, originally with the Ranger Quartet, wrote "The Gospel Boogie," which became a million selling national hit as performed by Pat Boone. The Oak Ridge Boys and many other Southern gospel groups experimented with rock beats and long hair.

The extremely popular Gaithers exemplify of the direction of Southern gospel in recent years. They have increasingly used rock styles. During a concert tour in New England in 1986, Bill Gaither admitted that he had changed his musical style due to the influence of the "world's culture." He said he believed there was a place for Christian rock, and he expressed his philosophy of music in these words: "God speaks through all different kinds of art forms and musical styles and musical forms" and the "format itself is not necessarily spiritual or non-spiritual" (*FBF News Bulletin*, March-April 1986, p. 3). Gaither is promoting the Devil's lie that music is neutral and that any type of music can be used to glorify God.

During the disco craze in the late 1980s, the Gaither Trio recorded a disco album (*Calvary Contender*, August 15, 1989). They have a song titled "Singin' with the Saints" which is a boogie-woogie version of "He Keeps Me Singing." This is confusion.

Bill Gaither has mentored many of the popular CCM artists, including those who use very hard rock. Gaither mentors include Sandi Patty, Russ Taff, Michael English, Carman, and the members of Whiteheart (*CCM Magazine*, July 1998, p. 20).

The following is an eyewitness description of the Gaither's appearance at the Southern Baptist Convention in St. Louis in 1980: "The Bill Gaither Trio entertained 15,000 Southern Baptists on Sunday evening with a musical program worldly enough to make any true believer weep. The music was so loud that some people left and others put their hands to their ears to block the intense amplification of the music" (Robert S. Reynolds, "Southern Baptists on the Downgrade," Report on the 1980 SBC Convention in St. Louis, *Foundation*, Volume VI, Issue 1, 1985, p. 9).

The Gaithers provided the music one evening at Indianapolis '90, a large ecumenical charismatic gathering I attended with press credentials. One-half of the 25,000 participants were Roman Catholics. A Catholic mass was held each morning during this conference, and Catholic priest Tom Forrest from Rome brought the closing message. Roughly 40 other denominations were present. The Gaithers were perfectly at home in this unscriptural gathering, entertaining the mixed multitude with their lively music while turning a blind eye to the heresy all around them. They did not say one word about the abominable Catholic mass which was conducted each morning of the conference. They did not say one word about the demonic spirit slaying and spirit drunkenness which was being practiced. They did not lift their voice to warn of the cursed false gospels which were represented. They did not reprove priest Tom Forrest for preaching at the Indianapolis conference that he praised the Lord for purgatory and for Mary the Queen of Heaven.

The Gaithers represent the very heart and soul of Southern gospel music today. In recent years they have held "homecoming" specials which have brought together most of the well known Southern gospel groups. These include members of the Statesmen, the Blackwood Brothers, the Cathedrals, the Goodman's, the Speer Family, the Florida Boys, the Gatlin Brothers, and many others. Those who have attended these gatherings have put their stamp of approval upon the ecumenical-charismatic-rock music side of Southern gospel by not separating from those who are guilty of these things and by not lifting their voices to reprove them. The Bible instructs us to "have no fellowship with the unfruitful works of darkness, but rather reprove them" (Eph. 5:11). Revelation 18:4 warns God's people to come out from among the apostasy of the last hours "that ye be not partakers of her sins." COMPLICITY WITH DOCTRINAL AND SPIRITUAL ERROR MAKES ME A PARTAKER WITH THAT ERROR. 2 John warns that even to bid God speed to a false teacher makes me "partaker of his evil deeds" (2 John 11). I realize this is a very hard line and one that is completely foreign to the thinking of this ecumenical-crazed age, but this is what the Word of God says. I also realize that the Gaithers and the other groups we have mentioned have produced some lovely Christian music, such as "How Long Has It Been" (written by Mosie Lister, who wrote many songs for the Statesmen), "He Knows Just What I Need" (Mosie Lister), "Jesus" (Bill Gaither), "Great Is the Lord" (James Wetherington of the Statesmen), "What A Day that Will Be" (Jim

Hill of the Statesmen), and many others, but this is no excuse for disobedience to God's Word. When the Gaithers greet 12,000 Roman Catholics, including many priests and nuns, as brethren in Christ, as they did at Indianapolis '90, they are partakers of the evil deeds of Rome and God's people should protest. I don't believe it is wrong to use some of the music which groups like these have produced which is Christ-honoring and Bible-based, but I do believe it is wrong to associate with them and to support them with record sales and to bring their jazzed up music with its ecumenical philosophy into our churches and homes.

The Florida Boys represent the contemporary-ecumenical side to Southern gospel. Les Beasley, who has been with the group since its inception, says they never get past the basic plan of salvation in their songs "because when you do that you're getting past our basic reason for existence" which is entertainment (*The Music Men*, p. 286). He says, "When you start trying to sell them a particular religion, or your set of do's and don'ts, then I think we are stretching what we are trying to do." That statement demonstrates their ecumenical, non-dogmatic, non-doctrinal, entertainment-oriented approach to Christian music, which is precisely the approach which has been adopted by Contemporary Christian Music at large. The preachers in the early churches certainly did not draw back from preaching "a particular religion" and a dogmatic set of "do's and don'ts"!

The Imperials are another key example of the changes occurring within Southern gospel. They were formed in 1964 and during the past 35 years the group has undergone a metamorphous in style, from southern gospel, to contemporary, to rock. *Lighthouse Magazine*, which is rock oriented, has taken note that the music of the Imperials has changed radically. Their 1987 album, *This Year's Model*, "took a sharp turn to a youthful techno pop/rock sound that caused many long time Imperial fans to fall by the wayside" (Stephen Trickey, "The Imperials: Reaching the Church in the 90s with Music and Ministry," *The Lighthouse Electronic Magazine*, December 1996). In reality, the Imperials had become extremely jazzy long before 1987. Many of the songs on albums in the 1970s and early 1980s had a heavy boogie-woogie/disco dance rhythm.

The Imperials are also very ecumenical. In 1992, for example, they conducted concerts at the First Assembly of God in Virginia Beach, Virginia, and at the Lancaster Bible College the same month. They frequently appear on the radically ecumenical Trinity Broadcasting Network. TBN promotes Catholic priests and nuns as born again Christians and disregards their false sacramental gospel. On August 21, 1998, they appeared at Focus on the Family in Colorado Springs, Colorado.

The Statesmen are another prime example of how Southern gospel has changed. As already noted, they were quite jazzy and entertainment-oriented from their inception.

A *Time* magazine article about the Southern gospel quartets of the 1950s described their concerts as "swinging from rowdy boogie to fervent waltzes, all in praise of the Lord." Things got worse as time passed. In the 1970s the Statesmen, with many personnel changes but with Hovie Lister still at the helm, added more contemporary numbers to their already somewhat jazzed up traditional fare. For example, they recorded songs by Christian rockers Larry Norman ("Sweet Song of Salvation") and Mylon LeFevre ("You're on His Mind"). They even recorded Simon and Garfunkel's "Bridge over Troubled Water," Kris Kristoferson's "Why Me, Lord," and Gene MacLellan's "Put Your Hand in the Hand," even though none of these men are Christians. By 1973 two members of the Statesmen, Sherrill Nielsen and Tim Baty, sported shoulder length hair. The group had grown to six members with the addition of bass guitarist Baty. In the 1990s Hovie Lister has worked closely with ecumenist Bill Gaither. Gaither produced a "Bill Gaither Remembers The Statesmen" video in 1990. Three of the old Statesmen were present: Hovie Lister, Jake Hess, and Jim Hill. The show was telecast nationally on Pat Robertson's ecumenical-charismatic *700 Club*. Following this, Gaither organized a reunited Statesmen called the New Statesmen. In 1994 Gaither released a documentary entitled *Bill and Gloria Gaither Present Hovie Lister and the Sensational Statesmen, An American Classic*.

In 1997 Southern gospel legend Vestal Goodman joined Roman Catholic Kathy Troccoli and 40 other CCM artists to record *Love One Another*, a song with an ecumenical theme: "Christians from all denominations demonstrating their common love for Christ and each other." The song talks about tearing down the walls of denominational division. The broad range of participants who joined Kathy Troccoli in recording "Love One Another" demonstrates the ecumenical agenda of Contemporary Christian Music. The song witnessed Catholics, Pentecostals, Baptists, etc., yoked together to call for Christian unity. A representative of the Southern gospel world was right in the midst of this unscriptural alliance.

The Connection Between Southern Gospel and CCM

In case someone still has the impression that Southern gospel is separate from Contemporary Christian Music and Christian rock, let me hasten to note that all of the popular commercial Southern gospel groups are yoked together with CCM and Christian rock in the Gospel Music Association. In fact, it was some of the more famous Southern gospel performers who helped establish the Gospel Music Association (GMA) in 1964. The formation took place at the National Quartet Convention that year. Members of the original GMA Board of Directors included Urias and Meurice LeFevre of the famous LeFevre singing family, James Blackwood of the Blackwood Brothers, Hovie Lister and James Wetherington of the Statesmen, and J.D. Sumner of the Stamps. Don Butler, director of archives for the GMA, was the Statesmen's manager during the 1950s.

In was the GMA, in turn, which in 1969 began handing out the Dove Awards for outstanding achievement in the Christian music industry. The vice president of the GMA that year was Hovie Lister. The Dove Awards have honored Contemporary Christian Music artists of every stripe, including very hard rock groups such as Bride, the Newsboys, Petra, and dc Talk. Catholic singer Kathy Troccoli has been nominated as the Gospel Music Association's female vocalist of the year five times. The GMA has even extended its Dove Award to Amy Grant's *Behind the Eyes* album, which is not Christian in any sense.

Thus we see that the well-known Southern gospel groups are yoked together with and are supportive of the rock-oriented, ecumenical-charismatic CCM crowd. For the most part there is no separation from and no reproof of the error of CCM by the commercially-successful Southern gospel people. They are peas in one unscriptural pod.

In summary, we offer the following practical guidelines about **WHEN TO AVOID SOUTHERN GOSPEL MUSIC**.

(1) Avoid Southern gospel when it uses the world's sensual pop/rock/ragtime/boogie-woogie rhythms. Southern gospel has always been too quick to use boogie-woogie styles. The late Bruce Lackey, who was the Dean of Tennessee Temple Bible School in the 1970s, played the piano professionally in bars before he was saved. He often warned that much of the Southern gospel music would be at home in these licentious environments because the rhythm is the same. Boogie-woogie is boogie-woogie, regardless of the words which accompany it. It arose from the same sleazy side of 1920s and 1930s Negro juke joint culture as rhythm & blues. It is sensual dance music and is not fitting for the Gospel of Jesus Christ. Southern gospel today is being immersed in the larger CCM world and is adopting the pop and soft rock rhythms, the "Nashville sound," of popular commercial music today. You cannot serve the Spirit with fleshly music. Sensual music is very enticing to the flesh; thus it is extremely attractive and desirable. Like everything associated with the flesh, sensual music is addicting. It creates an appetite for more and more worldly music. God has called us to deny the flesh; to die to self (which refers to our old fleshly nature). Though it is not easy to know exactly where to draw the line with rhythms to Christian music, the best place to the draw the line is to draw it as far from the world as possible. If the music sounds worldly, it is worldly! Our goal as Christ-honoring Christians should not be to try to stay as close to the world as possible without becoming completely worldly, but to stay as separated from the world as possible. We are to avoid even the appearance of evil (1 Thess. 5:21). If a piece of music would be comfortable in a bar, then we should not use it in the church.

(2) Avoid Southern gospel when it is associated with the charismatic-ecumenical movement. The charismatic-ecumenical movement is at the very heart of end-times apostasy which is working to create a one-world "church." It is dangerous in the extreme and must be avoided in obedience to the Scriptures (Rom. 16:17). I don't care how pleasant the Gaithers and the Imperials and many other popular groups might be; I must reject them because they are openly disobeying and flaunting the Bible's command to separate from error. If I listen to them I am in grave danger of picking up their spirit of compromise. Not only is it wrong, but it is grossly hypocritical for a church that preaches against the ecumenical movement to turn around and use musicians who are associated with the same.

(3) Avoid Southern gospel when the performers are worldly. If a Southern gospel group is worldly, it is impossible for them to produce spiritual music. The Bible warns that like produces like. "Whatsoever a man soweth, that shall he also reap. For he that soweth to his flesh shall of the flesh reap corruption; but he that soweth to the Spirit shall of the Spirit reap life everlasting" (Gal. 6:7,8). A pastor who does not want his people to be worldly will not bring in worldly singing groups. The same is true for parents. If we want our homes to be spiritual we must fill them with that which is spiritual, not that which is carnal and worldly. Many of the Southern gospel groups, even in fundamental Baptist circles, are worldly. They dress like the world. They love the world's vile movies. They are sports-crazy like the world. Their lives are not saturated with the Word of God. They don't walk cautiously and holily in the fear of God. Worldly singing groups present themselves like the world. On many occasions I have been distracted by the manner in which a church singing group was dressed. My friends, I don't go to church to be distracted by the immodest appearance of some carnal woman pretending to be a gospel singer. What a wicked thing it is for women to pretend to be singing for the glory of a holy God even while drawing men's attention away from Christ to their carnal appearance! Godly women do not want to draw attention to themselves with worldly hairstyles (notice how many of them whack their hair off in accordance with the world's unisex fashions), gobs of makeup (we don't believe makeup is wrong in moderation but we also don't believe Christian women should look like painted hussies), and tight or revealing clothing. Godly women do not want men in the congregation to be enticed by their appearance. I praise the Lord for humble, Spirit-filled gospel groups which dress modestly and which draw attention to Christ instead of themselves, but I intend to avoid worldly singing groups.

(4) Avoid Southern gospel when it is entertainment instead of edification. The Bible says everything in the church is to be done to edification. "Let all things be done unto edifying" (1 Cor. 14:26). The entertainers will ask, "What is wrong with entertaining the saints?" The answer is that there is no authority in the Word of God for it. I like to laugh and have a good time, but I don't see any justification whatsoever in the Word of God for turning the church service into a dinner club. Where do we see the Apostles doing anything like that? The only thing even similar to this in the New Testament is when the carnal Corinthians turned the Lord's Supper into a party time. For this they were rebuked soundly by Paul (1 Cor. 11:20-22). He did not permit it, and I don't believe we should permit singing groups which want to turn the house of God into an entertainment platform today. Sure, lots of people like jazzed up gospel music. Sure, it can draw a big crowd. That does not mean it is right, though. Just the opposite. The flesh loves entertainment, but that which is flesh is not spiritual. "For the flesh lusteth against the Spirit, and the Spirit against the flesh: and these are contrary the one to the other: so that ye cannot do the things that ye would" (Gal. 6:17). I have heard pastors argue that their people like the jazzy music, but it is the pastor's job not to give people what *they* want but to give them what *God* wants. Carnal Christians, even unsaved religionists, love worldly gospel music. Observe the Southern gospel sings which attract large numbers of people who are not faithful to the house of God and who do not live faithfully for God in their daily lives. Even Elvis Presley, the king of rock & roll, loved jazzy Southern gospel the likes of the Statesmen and the Blackwood Brothers, but he did not love to honor and glorify Jesus Christ. "No man can serve two masters: for either he will hate the one, and love the other; or else he will hold to the one, and despise the other. Ye cannot serve God and mammon" (Matt. 6:24). Probably no other single man in this century has done more to destroy the moral and spiritual climate of this world than Elvis Presley. He lived to glorify himself and to serve the flesh and the devil, and the fact that he loved some of the Southern gospel music proves nothing except confusion.

We praise the Lord for every Southern gospel singer and music group which is not characterized by the above traits. Many humble Southern gospel singers refuse to participate in the ecumenical-charismatic movement. Not only do they separate from end-times apostasy but they publicly warn God's people of it. Their chief concern is faithfulness to the Word of God and they do not make a god out of music. They do not want to please apostate religious crowds. They only minister in faithful Bible-based churches. They refuse to use the world's pop and rock rhythms. They don't try to get the saints boogying in the aisles. They refuse to turn the music of a holy God into sensual dance music. They do not seek to entertain people; they sing and play strictly for the glory of Jesus Christ and the edification of the saints. They refuse to dress like the world or imitate the world's methods. They strive to live holy lives separated from the wickedness of this hell-bound world. They pay the price for their faithfulness to God's Word by not being popular with the CCM crowd or even with the commercially successful Southern gospel crowd. They do not sell millions of albums. They do not appear on Trinity Broadcasting Network. The large contemporary "seeker" churches won't invite them. You will not hear their music coming through the loudspeakers at most Christian bookstores. You *will* see them one day, though, before the Judgment Seat of Christ hearing "well done, thou good and faithful servant"!

See also Cathedrals, Gaithers, Imperials, Hovie Lister, and J.D. Sumner.

PART VI
CONTEMPORARY WORSHIP MUSIC AND THE LAUGHING REVIVAL

CONTEMPORARY WORSHIP MUSIC AT HOME IN LAUGHING REVIVAL CHURCHES

Michael W. Smith's *Worship* album, which was released on September 11, has sold over 500,000 copies to reach gold status. The album was recorded live at the Carpenter's Home Church in Lakeland, Florida. This is the Pentecostal church where the weird and dangerous laughing revival was born during extended meetings conducted by Rodney Howard-Browne in 1993.

Lakeland is my hometown, and I have known of this church since I was a boy. Formerly named the First Assembly of God, the church purchased the retirement center in the 1980s and built a massive 10,000-seat auditorium. It is on the shores of one of Lakeland's many picturesque lakes. My maternal grandfather was a retired carpenter and he died at the old Carpenter's Home. By the time I was saved in 1973, the center was closed and the buildings were vacant. When I was a new Christian, I moved back home for a year before going off to Bible school. During that year, I often drove to the old Carpenter's Home grounds and had my daily devotions. It was a joy to walk among the lovely oak trees and down by the lake and pray. Sometimes I would sit on an old dock that was still there at that time. This was about 10 years before the Assemblies of God established themselves on the property.

When Howard-Browne blew in to Lakeland in 1993, people started falling on the floor and laughing hysterically and staggering around like drunks. (This is why Howard-Browne calls himself the "Holy Ghost Bartender.") A pastor who drove over to the meetings from nearby Tampa fell on the floor laughing when he tried to give a testimony and was still lying there hours later. Within the following year, Howard-Browne was invited back to Lakeland three more times.

People began to flock to Lakeland with a desire to receive the "anointing." Many key Charismatic leaders made the journey, including Oral Roberts' son Richard, Marilyn Hickey, and Charles and Francis Hunter. Richard Roberts says he and his family ended up on the floor laughing at every Howard-Browne meeting. On the flight back to Tulsa from his trip to Lakeland, Richard laughed so uncontrollably that the flight attendant thought something was wrong with him. Perpetually in financial straits, Oral and Richard Roberts claimed that God is helping them laugh their way out of debt. Marilyn Hickey (author of *God's Seven Keys to Make You Rich*) also spent her time in Lakeland on the floor laughing. When Howard-Browne called this Pentecostal female preacher to the microphone, she laughed and fell down and could not speak (Charles and Frances Hunter, *Holy Laughter*, 1994, p. 35).

The experiences which were occurring in Lakeland through the Howard-Browne meetings began to occur in many parts of the world. In a video entitled *The Laugh Heard 'round the World* (Lakeland, FL: Spiritual Warfare Ministries, 1994), Ken and Nancy Curtis of Carpenter's Home Church record this strange phenomenon occurring in meetings they conducted in Eastern Europe, Africa, and Asia. The video depicts people being "slain with the Spirit" and falling on the floor where they writhe in uncontrollable laughter. When many of those so overcome attempt to speak, they are unable to do so. The people line up, and the Curtises move down the lines and touch them on the foreheads or throw their arms at them and shout, "Receive the Spirit, receive the Spirit, receive the Spirit..." When the lines of people have fallen to the floor, the Curtises move among them and touch many of them on their bellies. The common response is an increase in the laughter.

The Curtises were sent out from the Carpenter's Home Church to minister the laughing revivals worldwide.

In August of 1993 Rodney Howard-Browne took the Laughing Revival to another large center of the Charismatic Word-Faith movement when he spoke at Kenneth Hagin's Rhema Bible Training Center near Tulsa, Oklahoma. One of the visitors to the Howard-Browne Rhema meetings was a discouraged pastor on the verge of a breakdown named **RANDY CLARK**. At the time he pastored a congregation in St. Louis, Missouri, associated with the late John Wimber's Vineyard Christian Fellowship. Clark testifies that he was opposed to the doctrine and practices of Rhema, but in his discouragement he ignored the Bible's warnings about false doctrine and allowed himself to be led to the Howard-Browne Rhema meetings by a friend. When the "Holy Ghost Bartender" prayed for Clark, he fell down and was "pinned to the floor," where he began laughing. He became so drunk in the "spirit" that he was afraid he would be arrested on his way home from the meeting. Clark also testifies that he felt power in his hands, "like they were ice cold." Howard-Browne told him that "this is the fire of God in your hand--go home and pray for everybody in your church." The Laughing Revival anointing is passed on most commonly by the laying on of hands.

Pastor Randy Clark took the Laughing Revival back to his congregation in St. Louis. During Clark's first service after arriving back from Rhema, a woman on the worship team fell down and began to laugh uncontrollably throughout the 45 minute worship service. At the end of the service, many rushed forward for Clark to lay hands on them, and they, too, fell down. Clark claims that 95 percent of the people fell.

The Laughing Revival was on the verge of an explosion. Not only was this experience being furthered by the Rodney Howard-Browne crusades, but it was being multiplied by those who attended these crusades and who carried the Laughing Revival anointing back to their various places of ministry. It was also being multiplied by the Charismatic print and electronic media. The very influential *Charisma* magazine has published favorable articles on the Laughing Revival in many issues since 1993.

Large numbers of people have also been influenced by television. Paul and Jan Crouch, owners of the Trinity Broadcasting Network, have featured Rodney Howard-Browne on their program and have otherwise promoted this movement.

One of the Vineyard pastors who responded to the testimony of Randy Clark was **JOHN ARNOTT**, of the Toronto Airport Vineyard church, Toronto, Ontario, Canada. Prior to becoming a pastor, Arnott had been influenced by Kathryn Kuhlman's unscriptural ministry and also by Benny Hinn during the early days of his ministry, which began in Toronto before later relocating to Orlando, Florida. After his first few years in the ministry, Arnott joined himself with John Wimber and the Vineyard movement in 1987. Among other things, he was drawn by Wimber's false claim that believers today can perform the kingdom working miracles of the first century. We don't fault pastors for wanting to see "something real" in the ministry of God's Word, for desiring the power of God, but unscriptural wildfire is not the answer to the problem of spiritual powerlessness.

John Arnott and his wife, Carol, were earnestly seeking a special touch from God, but, sadly, they were following the unscriptural charismatic prophecies and methodologies instead of relying strictly on the Holy Scriptures. They claim that God had told them to "hang around people that have an anointing." Instead of defining the Holy Spirit anointing biblically, they defined it according to Pentecostal Word-Faith theology. In September 1992, they attended several of Benny Hinn's meetings at Mapleleaf Gardens in Toronto. After Hinn would pray for them, Carol Arnott would be so drunk that she had to be carried home and put to bed. In June 1993, Rodney Howard-Browne laid hands on Arnott during a meeting in Texas.

In November 1993, the Arnotts flew to Argentina to have the aforementioned Claudio Friedzon lay hands on them. This occurred during an Argentinean pastors' conference organized by Luis Palau's brother-in-law, Ed Silvoso. This event is described as follows by Guy Chevreau, who works with Arnott in Toronto. Chevreau co-pastored a Baptist church with his wife before being swallowed up in the Laughing Revival:

> "John was standing with his hands up, posturing his openness to the Lord, and Claudio looked at him and said, 'Do you want it?' He said, 'Yes. I really want it.' Then Claudio said, 'Then take it!' and he slapped John on both of his hands. John fell again. BUT THIS TIME HE DIALED DOWN A LOT OF THE ANALYSIS and said, 'I don't care, I'm just going to take what God has to

give.' Something clicked in his heart at that moment" (emphasis added) (Chevreau, *Catch the Fire*, p. 24).

This is a very significant testimony. Arnott had been unable to receive the "anointing" BECAUSE HE WAS ANALYZING IT BY THE BIBLE. When he finally broke down and stopped analyzing it, he began receiving the strange unscriptural experiences. In a message preached by Arnott entitled "Hard to Receive" (Shippensburg, PA: Holy Smoke Productions, 1997) he gives advice for those who find it hard to receive the manifestations of the Laughing Revival. He says that one of the chief reasons why many cannot "receive" the Holy Spirit's (alleged) ministrations (such as slaying or drunkenness or rolling on the floor or maniacal laughter) is the "fear of deception." Arnott claims that this fear is used by the devil to keep people from receiving all that the Holy Spirit has for them.

In light of the New Testament's continual warnings, this is absolute nonsense. The Bible commands us to "prove all things…" (1 Thess. 5:21). Proverbs 14:15 tells us it is the foolish person who believes every word, whereas the prudent man is very careful. When the Lord Jesus prophesied of conditions prior to His return, three times He warned that extreme caution would be required for protection from spiritual deception (Matt. 24:4,5,11,23,24). Eight times in the New Testament the Christian is solemnly warned to "be sober." This means to be in control of one's self, to be spiritually alert, to be on guard against deception. Why? Because there are great spiritual dangers. "Be sober, be vigilant; because your adversary the devil, as a roaring lion, walketh about, seeking whom he may devour" (1 Peter 5:8). This one verse alone would keep me away from the Laughing Revival, which demands that I do just the opposite of what the Word of God instructs me to do. The Laughing Revival tells people to stop analyzing, to let go of our minds and mouths, to be open to strange experiences even if they cannot be supported by the Bible, to be incautious about fleshly and demonic deceptions.

After hearing of the phenomenon occurring at Rhema and St. Louis, Arnott invited Randy Clark to minister in the Toronto Airport Vineyard church. The Clark meeting in Toronto was originally scheduled for four nights in January 1994. The first service was held on January 20, and a large percentage of the 120 in attendance fell to the floor. John Arnott says: "It was like an explosion. We saw people literally being knocked off their feet by the Spirit of God." People shook, jerked, laughed, danced, cried, shouted. Some lay on the floor for hours. The man operating the sound system got "drunk in the spirit," and the church receptionist could not speak for three days and after that, except in "tongues" (Hanegraaff, *Counterfeit Revival*, p. 49).

The Laughing Revival had broken out in all its strange fury at the Toronto Airport Church, and by the end of the Clark meetings the decision was made to continue holding services six nights a week as long as the crowds continued coming. Visitors began to flock to Toronto from around the world. By the end of that first year an estimated 200,000 people had visited the Toronto Airport Vineyard Church. Thousands of churches have attended the meetings in Toronto.

Since then, the strange Laughing Revival has swept throughout the world and has broken out in new centers such as the Brownsville Assembly of God in Pensacola, Florida, and Holy Trinity Brompton Anglican church in London.

Now we return to our original subject of Contemporary Christian Worship music. IT IS INSTRUCTIVE THAT THE MICHAEL W. SMITH *WORSHIP* ALBUM WAS RECORDED AT THE MOTHER CHURCH FOR ALL OF THIS UNSCRIPTURAL NONSENSE. The CCW (Contemporary Christian Worship or Contemporary Charismatic Worship) music is sweeping through all denominations of churches, including fundamental Baptist. Yet there is something inherently wrong with a music that is at home in the midst of the most wretched kind of heresy and apostasy and confusion. And that is exactly where Contemporary Christian Worship is at home. That is where it was birthed. It was birthed in the midst of Pentecostal confusion and error. It is content in the midst of the most radical kinds of ecumenical disobedience, such as the yoking together of Roman Catholics and Lutherans and Methodists and Baptists at conventions like New Orleans 1987 and Indianapolis 1990 and St. Louis 2000. I have been an eyewitness to many such conferences in order to report on them for *O Timothy* magazine, and such meetings represent gross disobedience to the Word of God. At some of those meetings Roman Catholic priests have glorified Mary as the Queen of Heaven and have said that no one can go to heaven except through purgatory. Yet CCW smiles broadly at everything and is comfortable there. CCW is perfectly at home at Laughing Revival meetings where people stagger around like drunks. CCW is completely at ease at the loudest, strangest, worldliest Christian rock concert.

Lord, please give Thy people wisdom in these evil last hours that they might discern truth from error and that they might not judge music by their fleshly appetites and feelings but by the blessed and holy Scriptures. I pray that the eyes of Michael W. Smith will be opened before it is too late and that he will publicly disavow Contemporary Christian Music and warn his followers to flee from ecumenism and charismaticism.

PART VII
RESOURCES AND BIBLIOGRAPHY

SUGGESTED RESOURCES ON MUSIC

The following materials offer biblical guidelines on music in an hour of confusion.

APOSTASY AND DECEPTION IN CHRISTIAN MUSIC by Gordon Sears. The six chapters are titled Apostasy in Music, Deception in Music, The Sin of Carnality, The Strange Silence, What Others Say, and Preparing for the Storm. 104 pages. Songfest, P.O. Box 182, Coldwater, MI 49036. 517-238-4877 (voice), songfest@cbpu.com (e-mail), www.songfest.org (web site).

THE BATTLE FOR CHRISTIAN MUSIC by Tim Fisher. This excellent book answers many of the questions which are raised pertaining to contemporary Christian music, including the alleged neutrality of music and the truth about Luther's use of secular songs. 211 pages. Sacred Music Services, P.O. Box 17072, Greenville, SC 29606. 800-767-4326 (orders), www.smsrecordings.com (web site).

BIBLICAL MUSIC IN A CONTEMPORARY WORLD by Ken Lynch. Evangelist Lynch is an accomplished musician, and his evangelistic ministry has carried him to 45 states and several foreign lands. He was a member of the Springfield Symphony Orchestra prior to entering college in preparation for the ministry. In addition to his studies at Bob Jones University, he has studied with such men as Jerome Wigler of the Philadelphia Orchestra, Edgar Ortenberg of the Settlement Music School in Philadelphia, and Alvin Rudnitsky, a concert violinist formerly from Ardmore, Penn. Ken's violin is an original Luigi Marconcini (a student of the famous Stradiveri) dating 1767. Ken Lynch's important book deals primarily with Contemporary Christian Music. Chapter titles include: The Place of Music, The Power of Music, the Problem with CCM vs. Separation, The Personnel of Music, and the Performance of Music. 129 pages. Ken Lynch, 1810 Edgmont Ave., Chester, PA 19013-5306. 610-876-1984 (voice), Evangelistkenlynch@juno.com (e-mail).

CONFRONTING CONTEMPORARY CHRISTIAN MUSIC: A PLAIN ACCOUNT OF ITS HISTORY, PHILOSOPHY, AND FUTURE by Dr. H.T. Spence. This is an exceptionally informative and thought-provoking book. Dr. Spence develops the philosophy of Christian music from the Bible and contrasts it with a worldly approach. He shows the importance of separation from the world. He traces the history of Gospel music. The chapter titled "The Fundamentalist and His Music" warns of the worldly music which is creeping into fundamental Bible-believing churches. 164 pages, 8.5X11. Foundations Press, P.O. Box 1166, Dunn, NC 28335. 910-892-8761 (voice).

CONTEMPORARY CHRISTIAN MUSIC UNDER THE SPOTLIGHT by David W. Cloud. This 1999 book is, to our knowledge, the most extensive examination of Contemporary Christian Music in print. It has the following features: A definition of Contemporary Christian Music. The spiteful anti-fundamentalist attitude which permeates CCM. The intimate connection between end-time apostasy and CCM. Southern gospel yesterday and today. The love affair between CCM musicians and secular rock music. The ecumenism of Contemporary Christian Music. The close association of CCM with Roman Catholicism. The intimate connection between CCM and the Charismatic Movement. An encyclopedia of 200 CCM musicians, containing profiles of their lives and ministries, church affiliations, philosophies, ecumenical associations, music, etc. Documentation proving that CCM is owned largely by secular corporations. Lyrics to CCM songs illustrating the vagueness and heresy of their message. Twenty-three key CCM arguments answered (we must use rock music to win young people, music is neutral, people are getting saved, God doesn't look on the outward appearance, Luther used tavern music, God created all music, Christians are not to judge, etc.). Careful documentation of every fact presented. How to keep Contemporary Christian Music out of churches. Where Christians should draw the line with music. The book contains a list of Suggested Resources on Music, listing sources for sound Christian music, hymnals, resources for song leading, and materials for further reading on the topic of Contemporary Christian Music. There is also an extensive bibliography on the subject of Christian music. 450 pages, 7X8, perfect bound. Way of Life Literature, P.O. Box 610368, Port Huron, MI 48061. 866-295-4143 (voice), fbns@wayoflife.org (e-mail), http://www.wayoflife.org (web site). See the Way of Life online catalog.

EVILS OF UNSPIRITUAL MUSIC by Steve Pigott. Sound Recordings, P.O. Box 128, Valdosta,, GA 31603-0128.

GOSPEL MUSIC: BLESSING OR BLIGHT? by Ken Lynch. See *Biblical Music in a Contemporary World* for information about the author. Ken Lynch's important book deals primarily with Contemporary Christian Music. Chapter titles include: Musical definitions, The morality of music, What about Gospel rock? CCM: Alternative or Conformity? The biblical purpose of Christian music, and Guidelines for Gospel Music. 44 pages. Ken Lynch, 1810 Edgmont Ave., Chester, PA 19013-5306. 610-876-1984 (voice).

HARMONY AT HOME by Tim Fisher. Though there are many good things in this new book by Tim Fisher, in my opinion it is not as strong as his first book, *The Battle for Christian Music*. It is a little vague and doesn't mention names or get specific enough about CCM in many cases to be practical enough, in my estimation, but it does contain much helpful information on the use of good music in the home. It would be a good addition to your library, especially in conjunction with *Contemporary Christian Music Under the Spotlight*, which is very specific and in depth on the subject of Contemporary Christian Music. Sacred Music Services, P.O. Box 17072, Greenville, SC 29606. 800-767-4326 (orders), www.smsrecordings.com (web site).

HOW TO TELL THE RIGHT KIND OF MUSIC by Alan Ives. This is an excellent video presentation on music. Alan Ives is a man of God and a Christian musician. Together with his wife Ellen he has produced some excellent music albums for God's people. Alan knows music. He is trained both in secular and Christian styles of music. Before conversion he played in a rock and roll band. The Ives spend much of their time traveling to churches, preaching the Word of God and ministering in music. They are based out of the Wyldewood Baptist Church (Box 3143, Oshkosh, WI 54903. 414-235-5400). The video was recorded during one of Brother Ives' presentations in which he masterfully uses the piano and guitar to illustrate good and bad music. Any church which could get a meeting with Brother Ives would greatly benefit. Very few Christians can properly identify the characteristics of spiritual and unspiritual music. A few years ago we transcribed this music presentation and published it under the title "The Difference Between Good and Bad Music." The article is under the Music section of the End Times Apostasy Database at the Way of Life web site. The great advantage of the video presentation over the booklet is that the viewer can hear the actual examples of music. We would urge every Christian family and every Bible-believing church to obtain the video and use it from time to time to reinforce the importance of good music. To our knowledge, there is no other single hour-long presentation which is as effective as "How to Tell the Right Kind of Music" by Brother Ives. Park Meadows Baptist Church, 800 Memorial Park Rd., Lincoln, IL 62656. 800-500-8853 (orders), http://www.wyldewood.org/cah/ (web site).

IS TODAY'S CHRISTIAN MUSIC "SACRED"? by Gordon Sears. "You may not have noticed that the word SACRED is no longer used in connection with gospel music. Perhaps this is because the word 'sacred' means 'holy, consecrated, opposed to profane and secular,' according to *Webster's* dictionary. ... Separation from the world in music is just as important as any other area of Bible separation." An excerpt from *Is Today's Christian Music "Sacred"?* 32 pages. Songfest, P.O. Box 182, Coldwater, MI 49036. 517-238-4877 (voice), songfest@cbpu.com (e-mail), www.songfest.org (web site).

MEASURING THE MUSIC: ANOTHER LOOK AT THE CONTEMPORARY CHRISTIAN MUSIC DEBATE by John Makujina. The author of this book moves in Evangelical rather than Fundamentalist circles, but he takes a discerning stand against CCM and brings out many important facts in this new book. Chapter titles include "Worldliness According to the New Testament," "Rock Music and Body Image," "The Language of

Clothing," "Toward the Meaning of Rock," "Rock Music and Psychological Studies," and "The History of Ecclesiastical Music and CCM." 303 pages. Schmul Publishing, P.O. Box 716, Salem, OH 44460. 800-772-6657 (orders), 330-222-0001 (fax).

MUSIC IN THE BALANCE by Frank Garlock and Kurt Woetzel. In our estimation, this 204-page book is one of the best books ever published on the subject of Christian music. The authors, both accomplished musicians, present a wealth of well-researched information as they delve into the complex subject of musical rhythms. Their thesis is that "order in music offers harmony in life." They show how melody, harmony, and rhythm combine together to form spiritual or unspiritual music. "If the body and physical things are a priority in one's life, that person is sensual. If the rhythm is the primary dominating part of any piece of music, then that music is sensual" (p. 65). 204 pages. Majesty Music, P.O. Box 6524, Greenville, SC 29606. 800-334-1071 (orders), info@majestymusic.com (e-mail), http://www.majestymusic.com/ (web site).

Dr. Garlock also has a six-part video series which deals with the nature of music. It is filled with helpful graphics and musical examples which illustrate the various points. It is titled the **LANGUAGE OF MUSIC**. Majesty Music, P.O. Box 6524, Greenville, SC 29606. 800-334-1071 (orders), info@majestymusic.com (e-mail), http://www.majestymusic.com/ (web site).

POP GOES THE GOSPEL: ROCK IN THE CHURCH by John Blanchard. This is an excellent book written from a British perspective. 203 pages. Evangelical Press, 12 Wooler St., Darlington, Co Durham DL1 IRQ, England.

ROCK MUSIC VS. THE GOD OF THE BIBLE by David Cloud. An extensive examination of rock music and its evil influence on society. Chapters include "My Experience with Rock Music" (the author's testimony), "The Roots of Rock" (focusing on the blues, jazz, black spirituals, and Southern Gospel), "The Pioneers of Rock" (the families and lives of pioneer rockers, the influence of 50s rock on society, etc.), "The Character of Rock Music," "Rock and the Occult," "Rock and Spirituality," "Rock and Violence," "Rock and Love," "Rock and Voodoo," "Rock and Drugs," "The Rock & Roll Deathstyle" (a list of more than 500 rockers who have died young due to the rock & roll lifestyle), "Rock and Rebellion," "Rock Music and Insanity," "Rock Musicians as Mediums," "Rock Music and Pagan Religion," "Death Metal Rock Music," and "How to Raise a Rock and Roll Rebel." 430 pages, 7X8, perfect bound. Way of Life Literature, P.O. Box 610368, Port Huron, MI 48061. 866-295-4143 (voice), fbns@wayoflife.org (e-mail), http://www.wayoflife.org (web site). See the Way of Life online catalog.

THEIR ROCK IS NOT AS OUR ROCK. An excellent look at Contemporary Christian

Music by Dr. Adrian Van Manen, music director and teacher. 162 pages. Windsor Hills Baptist Church, 5517 NW 23rd Street, Oklahoma City, OK 73127. 405-943-3326 (voice), avanmanen@aol.com (e-mail).

WHAT'S WRONG WITH CHRISTIAN ROCK? by Jeff Godwin. A hard hitting examination of Christian rock music. Evangelist Godwin names names and pulls no punches in exposing the worldliness of CCM. 287 pages. The Rock Ministries, P.O. Box 2181, Bloomington, IN 47401. Also order from Chick Publications, P.O. Box 662, Chino, CA 91708. 909-987-0771 (voice), 909-941-8128 (fax), info@chick.com (e-mail), www.chick.com/ (web site).

HYMNALS

BEEBE PUBLICATIONS. 166 Swan Lake Dr., Stockbridge, GA 30281-6107. 800-828-4595 (orders), 770-474-3636 (voice), 770-389-4833 (fax), beebe5@bellsouth.net (e-mail), http://www.beebepublications.com (web site). They carry 36 different hymnals and offer discounts to churches which order in quantity.

MAJESTY MUSIC, P.O. Box 6524, Greenville, SC 29606. 800-334-1071 (orders), 803-242-6722, info@majestymusic.com (e-mail). Order via the Internet from Worthwhile Company Online Mall — www.worthwhile.com/mall/storefront.asp (web site).

MATERIALS ON SONG LEADING

ALL ABOUT THE CHURCH MUSIC DIRECTOR by Wally & Winifred Beebe. This 1998 book deals song leading, accompanists, the invitation, choirs, specials, doctrine and standards, copyrights, even radio broadcasts. Sword of the Lord, P.O. Box 1099, Murfreesboro, TN 37133. 800-247-9673 (orders), 615-893-6700 (voice), 615-895-7447 (fax), booksales@swordofthelord.com (e-mail), www.swordofthelord.com (web site).

BEGINNING SONG LEADING TECHNIQUES by Steve Attaway. This video production is well done and the music used as samples is excellent. There is an introduction to musical notes, demonstrations for leading various types of music (2,3,4,6, and 9 beats), and various pointers for church song leading. At-A-Boy Productions, P.O. Box 62, Argyle, TX 76226. 817-464-3149 (voice). Please note that it is possible that Attaway has changed his musical styles since first producing this video, and we cannot guarantee that he currently promotes sound Christian music.

CHORAL DIRECTOR'S REHEARSAL AND PERFORMANCE GUIDE by Lewis Gordon (Parker Publishing Company, West Nyack, New York). This book was described by a reader as follows: "It is easy reading with excellent ideas about working with your group, building their vocal quality (breathing, warming up, etc.). It shows the basic directing patterns and conducting techniques. It also includes a brief description of Music history."

CHURCH MUSIC FOR THE GLORY OF GOD by Urang (Christian Service Foundation, Moline, Illinois). This book is currently out of print.

ESSENTIALS IN CONDUCTING by Gehrkens (Presser). This book is out of print, but it is possible to obtain archival copies for those willing to pay for it. Presser Company, 1 Presser Place, Bryn Mawr, Pennsylvania 19010. 610-525-3636 (voice), 610-527-7841 (fax), presser@presser.com (e-mail), http://www.presser.com (web site).

CORRESPONDENCE MUSIC COURSE by Bryan Dodson. This course includes a video by Christian musician/evangelist Alan Ives. Generations Baptist Mission, R.R. # 2, Box 424, Hunlock Creek, PA. 18621. 717-542-7442 (voice), 717-542-5882 (fax), gbm@mail.microserve.net (e-mail).

HOW TO DIRECT MUSIC. A course in church music direction. Swan Productions, 7122 Franklin Rd., Murfreesboro, TN 37128. 615-904-2156.

LINDSAY TERRY AND CHURCH MUSIC: A MANUAL FOR CHOIR MEMBERS, MUSIC DIRECTORS, AND PASTORS. This is an excellent book by a fundamental Baptist music director with many helpful suggestions for developing a spiritual church music program. Includes information on the concept of church music, various aspects of the choir, fundamentals of conducting, the relationship of the pastor to the music program, Christian music in the home, and effective congregational singing. 112 pages. Sword of the Lord, Box 1099, 224 Bridge Ave., Murfreesboro, TN 37130. 800-247-9673 (orders), 615-893-6700 (voice), 615-895-7447 (fax), booksales@swordofthelord.com (e-mail), www.swordofthelord.com (web site). I called Brother Lindsay at his home in Texas, and he told me that the book has been revised and is being republished. He can be contacted at Forward Leadership Resources, 3526 Lakeview Parkway, Suite B-230, Rowlett, TX 75088. 800-874-6359.

THE MINISTRY OF MUSIC by Kenneth W. Osbeck (Kregel Publications). This book covers the history of the development of sacred music, qualifications for a church music director, congregational singing, children's choirs, young people's choirs, senior's choirs, the instrumental program, and the worship service. The author was a teacher at Grand Rapids Baptist College and Seminary and at the Grand Rapids School of the Bible and Music. 192 pages. Kregel Bookstores, P.O. Box 2607, Grand Rapids, MI 49501-2607. 800-776-0988 (orders), 616-459-9444 (voice), 888-873-2665 (fax), http://

www.gospelcom.net/kregel/pub.html (web site).

SOFT (ACE) MUSIC COURSE by Accelerated Christian Music (ACE). This is described by a friend as follows: "This would probably be great for most church song leaders. It seems to be a very thorough course designed for a one semester upper level high school elective. Suggested retail price was about $49.90 which includes six PACEs, two score & test keys, and two cassette tapes that go with the course. Almost half of the cost is the tapes; of course, we only keep one or two sets at the school and reuse them for each student." School of Tomorrow, P.O. Box 299000, Lewisville, TX 75029-9000. 972-315-1776, comments@schooloftomorrow.com (e-mail), http://www.schooloftomorrow.com/ (web site).

SONG LEADERSHIP by Homer Rodeheaver (The Rodeheaver Company). Rodeheaver (1880-1955)was the famous music director and hymn writer who led music for Billy Sunday and William Biederwold, then founded the Summer School of Sacred Music at Winona Lake and the Rodeheaver Hall-Mack Company to publish gospel music. This book is currently out of print.

SONG LEADING AND CHURCH MUSIC by Don Scovill, c/o Ambassador Baptist College, P.O. Box 158, Lattimore, NC 28089. 704-434-0303 (voice). Dr. Scovill is the music at Ambassador Baptist College (founded by Ron Comfort), and this is a practical book on song leading and church music. It contains illustrations.

UPBEAT DOWNBEAT: BASIC CONDUCTING PATTERNS AND TECHNIQUES by Sandra Willetts. Professor of Choral Conducting at the University of Alabama School of Music. Abingdon Press, Nashville, Tennessee. 1993.

YOU CAN LEAD SINGING: A SONG LEADER'S MANUAL by Glenn Lehman. Order directly from Lehman at 850-477-8812. Or order via the web at Amazon Books, P.O. Box 80387, Seattle, WA 98108-0387. 800-201-7575, info@amazon.com (e-mail), http://www.amazon.com (web site).

VIDEO AND WORKBOOK by Don Woodard, Sr. 3248 India Hook Rd., Rock Hill, SC 29732. 803-329-4998.

WHAT SHALL WE SING by Christopher Idle. The Fellowship of Word and Spirit, P.O. Box 39, Buxton, Derbyshire England SK17 6PR, U.K.

SCORES FOR INSTRUMENTAL HYMNS

DAVID E. SMITH PUBLICATIONS, 4826 Shabbona Rd., Deckerville, MI 48427. 800-672-2733 (orders), 810-376-8429 (voice), despub@greatlakes.net (e-mail), www.despub.com (web site). Catalog consisting of over 2,500 items by over 50 writers. Includes graded solos and ensembles for woodwinds, brass, strings, piano, string orchestra and concert band. Featured are "Heritage," a band method supplement utilizing hymns and sacred songs sequenced to traditional band methods, and "Hymnsembles" and "Hymns for Multiple Instruments" which are designed to work with mix-and-match or unusual instrumentations. Distributor for C.T. Smith Publications, Curnow Press, Majestic Music (not to be confused with Majesty Music), and Salvation Army.

HOPE PUBLISHING COMPANY, Carol Stream, IL 60187.

LILLENAS PUBLISHING, 2923 Troost Ave., Kansas City, MO 64109. 800-877-0700 (orders), 800-849-9872 (fax), http://www.lillenas.com/ (web site). *500 Hymns for Instruments* (to go with the *Worship in Song* hymnal).

MAJESTIC MUSIC, GNMS Order Dept., 10415 Beardslee Blvd., Bothell, WA 98011-3271. 800-821-9207 (voice), 425-489-2883 (voice), 425-489-2887 (fax). Recordings and arrangements for voice and instruments by Gordon Schuster and other composers. See also David E. Smith Publications. www.gnms.com/majestic (web site).

SOUNDFORTH, Greenville, SC 29614. 800-258-7288 (orders), 864-298-0268 (fax), www.soundforth.com/ (web site), soundforth@bju.edu (e-mail).

TABERNACLE PUBLISHING, 380 S. Main Pl., Carol Stream, IL 60187.

CHORAL ARRANGEMENTS

IDEAL SACRED MUSIC. Ambassador Baptist College, P.O. Box 158, Lattimore, NC 28089. P.O. Box 158, Lattimore, NC 28089. 704-434-0303 (voice), 704-434-8331 (fax), www.ambassadors.edu (web site), ambassadorbaptistcollege@juno.com (e-mail). Choral and instrumental arrangements.

LOWERY, DOUG. Box 342, Sun Priarie, WI 53590. 920-478-4286 (voice). Has a tape/CD/songbook with vocal solos and duets and choral numbers.

MAJESTIC MUSIC, GNMS Order Dept., 10415 Beardslee Blvd., Bothell, WA 98011-3271. 800-821-9207 (voice), 425-489-2883 (voice), 425-489-2887 (fax). Recordings and arrangements for voice and instruments by Gordon Schuster and other composers. See also David E. Smith Publications. www.gnms.com/majestic (web site).

SOUNDFORTH, Greenville, SC 29614. 800-258-7288 (orders), 864-298-0268 (fax),

www.soundforth.com/ (web site), soundforth@bju.edu (e-mail).
SOURCES FOR SOUND MUSIC

Please note that we cannot guarantee that all of the music produced by the following organizations and ministries is sound. We publish this list because it is difficult to locate good Christian music and we desire to point the way to some of the music that we have found helpful. It is not possible for us to listen to every single thing which has been produced by the following sources, nor is it possible for us to keep up with every new recording which they publish. Ultimately it is the responsibility of each listener to prove the music by the Word of God and the guidance of the indwelling Holy Spirit. We encourage our readers to contact us if some of the music by any of the following sources is found to be particularly offensive. In such cases we will consider the feasibility of removing the name from the list or adding a word of warning.

AMBASSADOR BIBLE COLLEGE. See Ideal Sacred Music.

C & L PUBLICATIONS. 135 White Oak Dr., Greenville SC 29607. Piano and vocal.

CAMERATA TRIO. 915 Forrest Hill Dr., Clermont, FL 34711.

CHRISTIAN MELODY. Alan McGill, a noted Christian baritone, has 96 selections on eight cassettes. P.O. Box 292, Lutherville, MD 21094. We must warn that McGill is not a separatist and his associations are not all fundamentalist.

CHRISTIAN PURITIES FELLOWSHIP. Various conservative music titles from Foundations Bible College. P.O. Box 1166, Dunn, NC 28333. 800-849-8761 (orders), www.foundations.edu (web site).

CLARK, MIRIAN JARRELS. "While He Is Near." Lovely piano/vocal arrangements. P.O. Box 292, Penn Laird, VA 22846.

CLEARWATER CHRISTIAN COLLEGE. Various recordings by college groups. 3400 Gulf-to-Bay Blvd., Clearwater, FL 33759. 727-726-1153 ext. 603 (bookstore phone), http://www.clearwater.edu/ (web site).

COMFORTING MERCIES MUSIC, Box 207, Taylors, SC 29687.

CONCORD & HARMONY, 328 Rosalia Street, Oshkosh, WI 54901. 920-231-4807 (home), 920-235-5400 (Wyldewood Baptist Church), http://www.wyldewood.org/cah/ (web site).

THE CYBER HYMNAL. This is a large resource. It contains a collection of 2,100 hymns and gospel songs organized alphabetically. We would not recommend every hymn, but there are some good ones in this collection. The MIDI arrangements are tastefully done, at least the ones we have listened to. The MIDI files are accompanied by the lyrics and articles explaining the background information pertaining to the hymn. There are also biographies of 120 hymn writers. http://tch.simplenet.com/

DAVID E. SMITH PUBLICATIONS, 4826 Shabbona Rd., Deckerville, MI 48427. 800-672-2733 (orders), 810-376-8429 (voice), despub@greatlakes.net (e-mail), www.despub.com (web site). Catalog consisting of over 2,500 items by over 50 writers. Includes graded solos and ensembles for woodwinds, brass, strings, piano, string orchestra and concert band. Featured are "Heritage," a band method supplement utilizing hymns and sacred songs sequenced to traditional band methods, and "Hymnsembles" and "Hymns for Multiple Instruments" which are designed to work with mix-and-match or unusual instrumentations. Distributor for C.T. Smith Publications, Curnow Press, Majestic Music (not to be confused with Majesty Music), and Salvation Army.

DISCOVER CHRISTIAN MUSIC, 519 Piedmont Golf Course Rd., Piedmont, SC 29673. 800-767-4326) (orders), http://www.dcmrecordings.com/ (web site).

DRAMATIC DIFFERENCE PUBLICATIONS, RR #3, Box 3178, Farmington, ME 04938. 207-778-2766 (voice). ddp@exploremaine.com (e-mail), http://www.dramaticdifference.com (web site). This sound music ministry is operated by Mrs. Sandi Rebert, wife of Pastor Rebert of New Hope Baptist Church in Farmington, Maine. Selections include *Dramatic Hymn Stories*, *Bible Women of Virtue*, and *Christmas Memories*.

FAIRHAVEN BAPTIST COLLEGE, 86 E. Oak Hill Rd., Chesterton, IN 46304. 800-733-3422 (orders), 219-926-6636 (voice), Fairhaven@CleanInter.net (e-mail).

FAITH MUSIC MISSIONS, Boeke Road Baptist Church, P.O. Box 2463, Evansville, IN 47728. 800-867-0554 (orders), www.faithmusicmissions.com (web site). Faith Music Missions "does not tolerate CCM, modern Southern Gospel or any type of music with a rock beat, regardless of the words." In addition to a wealth of beautiful music, Faith Music Missions has many other helpful resources. They offer a line of conservative, drumless soundtracks. They produce Congregational Evangelistic style piano hymns on CDs "for the church or servant of God to use in lieu of a pianist or to assist their music program." They also have recording and duplication services, blank tapes, etc.

FAITHWAY BAPTIST COLLEGE OF CANADA, Faithway Baptist Church, 1964 Salem Rd., Ajax, Ontario L1S 4S7. 905-686-0951 (voice), 905-686-1450 (fax), faithway@faithway.org (e-mail), www.faithway.org (web site).

FISHER, TIM. See Sacred Music Services.

FOUNDATIONS BIBLE COLLEGE. See Christian Purities Fellowship.

GREER, GORDON AND JEAN, 605 Del Norte Rd., Greenville, SC 29615. 864-244-9152 (voice), Jgreer@bju.edu (e-mail). The Greers have two sacred music CDs (the latest of which is scheduled to be available by June 1st, 2000).

HEART PUBLICATIONS, P.O. Box 116, Pembine, WI 54156.

IDEAL SACRED MUSIC. Ambassador Baptist College, P.O. Box 158, Lattimore, NC 28089. P.O. Box 158, Lattimore, NC 28089. 704-434-0303 (voice), 704-434-8331 (fax), www.ambassadors.edu (web site), ambassadorbaptistcollege@juno.com (e-mail). Choral and instrumental arrangements.

JOYFUL NOISE MUSIC. Congregational and listening hymns on piano. Dale Dutridge, www.joyfulnoisemusic.com (web site).

KINGSWAY MUSIC, Lottbridge Drive, Eastbourne, East Sussex, BN23 6NT, United Kingdom. A series of 12 CDs called "The Hymns Makers."

LOWERY, DOUG. Box 342, Sun Prairie, WI 53590. 920-478-4286 (voice). Has a tape/CD/songbook with vocal solos and duets and choral numbers.

MAKKEDAH MUSIC, 10 Michael Dr., Greenville, SC 29611. 864-269-1771 (voice).

MAJESTIC MUSIC, GNMS Order Dept., 10415 Beardslee Blvd., Bothell, WA 98011-3271. 800-821-9207 (voice), 425-489-2883 (voice), 425-489-2887 (fax). Recordings and arrangements for voice and instruments by Gordon Schuster and other composers. See also David E. Smith Publications. www.gnms.com/majestic (web site).

MAJESTY MUSIC, P.O. Box 6524, Greenville, SC 29606. 800-334-1071 (orders), 803-242-6722 (voice). http://www.majestymusic.com/ (web site). While most of the music produced by Majesty Music is excellent, we must warn that some of the newer recordings are moving in a contemporary direction. This is particularly true of the newer *Patch the Pirate* children's tapes.

MARANATHA BAPTIST BIBLE COLLEGE, 745 W. Main St., Watertown, WI 53094. 920-261-9300 (voice), 920-261-9109 (fax), administration@mbbc.edu (e-mail), www.mbbc.edu (web site). As of 1998 Maranatha Baptist Bible College offered 20 tapes and CDs of music.

MARSHALL FAMILY, P.O. Box 5264, Astoria, NY 11105. 718-728-4410 (voice), jmarsh777@aol.com (e-mail), www.av1611.org/marshall (web site).

MUSIC FOR MINISTRY. Good selection of conservative piano soundtracks produced by Sharon Fields, a pastor's wife and accomplished pianist. 8431 W. Mission Lane, Peoria, AZ 85345. 623-412-7931 (voice), http://www.angelfire.com/az/musicforministry/ (web site), missionfields@integrityonline5.com (e-mail).

NORTHLAND BAPTIST BIBLE COLLEGE, W10085 Pike Plains Road, Dunbar, WI 54119. 715-324-6900 (voice), 715-324-6133 (fax), info@nbbc.edu (e-mail), www.nbbc.edu (web site).

OGLESBY, MINA. 632 North Moore Road, Chattanooga, TN 37411.

OKLAHOMA BAPTIST COLLEGE. 5517 NW 23rd St., Oklahoma City, OK 73127. 405-943-3326 (voice), 405-946-9150 (fax), jav9@juno.com (e-mail).

OUTREACH QUARTET, 419 S. Montgomery, Watertown, WI 53094.

PAYNE, GENE AND BARBARA. See Scripture Songs Publications.

PENSACOLA CHRISTIAN COLLEGE. 25 Brent Lane, Box 18000, Pensacola, FL 32523-9160. 877-787-4723 (voice), 850-479-6548 (fax), 850-478-8496 (voice), www.pcci.edu/pts (web site). Though I have not listened to much of Pensacola's music, that which I have heard is good. On their radio network (which has more than 50 satellite stations across the country) they are moving toward a more contemporary approach; so their music bears watching.

PETTIT, STEVE. See Heart Publications.

PINNER PUBLICATIONS, 800-884-6775. String solos, duets etc.

REJOICE PUBLICATIONS, Associate Pastor Mark Poorman, Woodcrest Baptist Church, 6875 University Ave. NE. Fridley, MN 55432. 763-571-6409 (church), 763-780-9835 (home). Cantatas, solos, duets, a wedding book, etc.

SACRED MUSIC SERVICES, P.O. Box 17072, Greenville, SC 29606. 800-767-4326 (orders), www.smsrecordings.com (web site).

SCRIPTURE SONGS PUBLICATIONS, 5510 Falls of Neuse Rd., Raleigh, NC 27609. 919-876-0585 (voice).

SEIDEL, LENNY. Grace Unlimited Ministries, 7124 Freshaire Dr., Springfield, VA 22153.

SHEPHERD'S STAFF MINISTRIES, 9426 Brookville Road, Indianapolis, IN 46239. 317-862-4908 (voice), ssm@tcon.net (e-mail), http://mem.tcon.net/ssm/ (web site).

SMITH, DAVID E. See David E. Smith Publications.

SONGFEST. Gordon Sears, P.O. Box 182, Coldwater, MI 49036. 517-238-4877 (voice), songfest@cbpu.com (e-mail), www.songfest.org (web site). Distribute music by the Old Fashioned Revival Hour as well as by the Sears family.

SOUNDFORTH, Greenville, SC 29614. 800-258-7288 (orders), 864-298-0268 (fax), www.soundforth.com/ (web site), soundforth@bju.edu (e-mail). Music tapes and arrangements, song books, choir and choral, children's music programs, dramas. Also "A Guide to Hymn Playing" by Rebecca Bonam and Duane Ream.

SWORD PUBLISHERS, P.O. Box 290, Redmond, WA 98073-0290. 425-391-7315 (voice). Several excellent music selections.

THE WILDS Christian Camp and Conference Center. Order their music via the Internet from Worthwhile Company Online Mall -- www.worthwhile.com/mall/storefront.asp (web site).

BIBLIOGRAPHY ON CHRISTIAN MUSIC

MISC. MATERIALS TOUCHING ON MUSIC

Apel, Willi. *Harvard Dictionary of Music*. Cambridge: Harvard University Press, 1946.
Barber, David W. *Bach, Beethoven and the Boys*. Toronto: Sound and Vision Publications, 1986.
Bernstein, Leonard (1918-1990). *The Infinite Variety of Music*. New York: Simon and Schuster, 1966.
———. *The Joy of Music*. New York: Simon and Schuster, 1959.
Blood, Allan. *The Closing of the American Mind*. New York: Simon and Schuster, 1987.
Brand, Oscar. *The Ballad Mongers the Rise of the Modern Folk Song*. New York: Funk and Wagnalls, 1967.
Byrnside, Ronald. *Music, Sound and Sense*. Dubuque, Iowa: William C. Brown Pub., 1985.
Campbel, Don, ed. *Music and Miracles*. Wheaton: Quest Books, 1992. 280 p.
Chasins, Abram (1903-). *Music at the Crossroads*. New York: Macmillan Co., 1972.
Copeland, Aaron (1900-). *Copeland on Music*. Doubleday, 1960.
———. *What to Listen for in Music*. New York: McGraw-Hill Book Company, 1957, 1999. 266 p.
Diamond, John. *The Life Energy in Music*. Valley Cottage, NY: Archaeous Press, 1981.
———. *Your Body Doesn't Lie*. New York: Warner Books, 1980.
Edgar, William. *Taking Note of Music*. London: SPCK, 1986. 146 p.
Elson, Arthur (1873-1940). *The Book of Musical Knowledge*: the history, technique, and appreciation of music, together with lives of the great composers. New York: Houghton Mifflin Co., 1927.
Fishman, Carol Merle, and Shelley Katsh. *The Music Within You*. New York: Simon & Schuster, 1985.
Forcucci, Samuel L. *Let There Be Music*. Boston: Allyn and Bacon, 1973. 280 p.
Franklin, Aretha (1942-), and David Bitz. *Aretha: From These Roots*. New York: Villard, 1999. 251 p.
Frith, Simon. *Sound Effects: Youth, Leisure, and the Politics of Rock 'n' Roll*. New York: Pantheon Books, 1978, 1981.
Gaston, E. Thayer, ed. *Music in Therapy*. New York: Macmillan, 1968.
Green, Joseph F. *Biblical Foundations for Church Music*. Nashville: Convention Press, 1967. 144 p.
Grout, Donald Jay. *A History of Western Music*. New York: W.W. Norton and Co., 1960 (3rd ed., 1980).
Halpern, Steven. *Tuning the Human Instrument*. Belmont, Calif.: Spectrum Research Institute, 1978.
Hanson, Howard. "A Musician's Point of View Toward Emotional Expression," *American Journal of Psychiatry*, Vol. 99, p. 317; Dr. Hanson was an American composer, conductor, and teacher, Director of the Eastman School of Music at the University of Rochester.
Harrison, Luther A., and B.B. McKinney. *Practical Music Lessons*. Nashville: Broadman Press, 1950. 184 p.
Hart, Micky, and Fredric Lieberman. *Spirit into Sound: the Magic of Music*. Petaluma, CA: Grateful Dead Books, 1999. 208 p.

Henderson, William James (1855-1937). *What Is Good Music? Suggestions to persons desiring to cultivate a taste in musical art*. New York: C. Scribner's Sons, 1935.

Hindemith, Paul (1895-). *A Composer's World*. Cambridge: Harvard University Press, 1952.

Hoffer, Charles R. *The Understanding of Music*. Belmont, Calif.: Wadsworth Publishing, 1976. 455 p.

Hutchinson, Enoch (1810-1885). *Music of the Bible; or, Explanatory notes upon those passages in the Sacred Scriptures which relate to music, including a brief view of Hebrew poetry*. Boston: Gould and Lincoln, 1864. [513 p.]

Institute in Basic Life Principles. *Ten Scriptural Reasons Why the "Rock Beat" Is Evil in Any Form*. Oak Brook, IL: Institute in Basic Life Principles, 1990. 19 p.

Jones, Robert L. *The Junior Choir Leadership Manual*. Nashville: Convention Press, 1967. 143 p.

Keith, Edmond D. *Christian Hymnody*. Nashville: Convention Press, 1956. 147 p.

Krehbiel, Henry Edward (1854-1976). *How to Listen to Music*. New York: Charles Scribner's Sons, 1922.

Lingerman, Hal A. *The Healing Energies of Music*. Wheaton: Theosophical Publishing House, 1983.

McCommon, Paul. *Music in the Church*. Nashville: Convention Press, 1956. 111 p.

Machlis, Joseph (1906-). *The Enjoyment of Music*. New York: W.W. Norton and Co., 1963.

Merle-Fishman, Carol, and Shelley Katsh. *The Music Within You*. New York: Simon Schuster, 1985.

Meyer, Leonard B. *Emotion and Meaning in Music*. Chicago: University of Chicago Press, 1956.

Mussulman, Joseph Agee. *The Uses of Music*. Englewood Cliffs, NJ: Prentice-Hall, 1974.

Nininger, Ruth. *Growing a Musical Church*. Nashville: Broadman Press, 1947. 157 p.

Pattison, Robert. *The Triumph of Vulgarity*, 1987.

Peyser, Joan. *Bernstein a Biography*. New York: Beech Tree Books, 1987. 481 p.

Portnoy, Julius (1910-). *Music in the Life of Man*. New York: Holt, Rinehart and Winston, 1963.

Riddle, Blanche Lee. *Gospel Song and Hymn Playing*. Nashville: Broadman Press, 1950. 116 p.

Rouget, Gilbert. *Music and Trance*. Chicago: University of Chicago Press, 1985.

Sachs, Curt (1881-1959). *Our Musical Heritage*. Englewood Cliffs: Prentice Hall, 1941.

Sample, Tex. *White Soul: Country Music, the Church, and Working Americans*. Nashville: Abingdon Press, 1996.

Schoen, Max (1888-). *The Psychology of Music: A survey for teacher and musician*. New York: The Ronald Press Co., 1940.

Scott, Cyril (1879-). *Music, Its Secret Influence Throughout the Ages*. London: Rider & Co., 1934.

Seashore, Carl Emil (1866-1949). *Psychology of Music*. New York and London: McGraw-Hill Book Co., 1938.

Sims, W. Hines. *Church Music Manual*. Nashville: Convention Press, 1957. 152 p.

Smith, Jane Stuart, and Betty Carlson. *The Gift of Music: Great Composers and Their Influence*. Wheaton: Crossway Books, 1995. 317 p.

Spaeth, Sigmund Gottfried (1885-1965). *The Common Sense of Music*. Garden City, NY: Garden City Publishing Co., 1924.

———. *Stories Behind the World's Great Music*. New York: Garden City Publishing Co., 1940.

Tame, David. *The Secret Power of Music*. Rochester, Vermont: Destiny Books, 1984. 304 p.

Tooze, Ruth, Korne, Beatrice. *Literature and Music*. Englewood Cliffs: Prentice Hall, 1955.

Wilhoit, Bert H. *Rody: Memories of Homer Rodeheaver*. Greenville: Bob Jones University Press, 2000. 126 p.

Young, Robert H. *The History of Baptist Hymnody in England from 1612 to 1800*. Ann Arbor: University Microfilms, 1959. D.M. Thesis. from the University of Southern California, 1959.

CONTEMPORARY CHRISTIAN MUSIC (SEE ALSO SOUTHERN GOSPEL)

Alford, Delton L. *Music in the Pentecostal Church*. Cleveland, TN: Pathway Press, 1967. 120 p.
Atkins, Tim and Patty. *Music Worth Talking About: A Guide for Youth Leaders*. Grand Rapids: Baker Books, 1995. 216 p.
Baker, Paul. *Contemporary Christian Music*. Westchester, IL.: Crossway Books, 1985.
———*Why Should the Devil Have All the Good Music*. Waco: Word Books, 1979. 235 p.
Bergerson, Charles. *The New Church Music*. Regular Baptist Press.
Best. *Music Through the Eyes of Faith*.
Blanchard, John (1932-), with Peter Anderson and Derek Cleave. *Pop Goes the Gospel: Rock in the Church*. Durham: Evangelical Press, 2nd ed. 1989. 203 p.
Boa, Kenneth, and Kerry Livgren. *Seeds of Change: The spiritual quest of Kerry Livgren, writer, guitarist, and keyboard player with Kansas*. Westchester, IL: Crossway Books, 1983. 189 p.
Briner, Bob. *Roaring Lambs: A gentle plan to radically change your world*. Grand Rapids: Zondervan, 1993. 202 p.
Broughton, Viv. *Black Gospel*. New York: Blandford Press, 1985.
Brown, Scott Wesley. *Keeping the Gospel in Gospel Music: A Guide for Success and Survival in Contemporary Christian Music*. Phoenix: ACW Press, 1998. 165 p.
Carmichael Ralph. *He's Everything to Me*. Waco, TX: Word Books, 1986. 189 p.
Campbell, Glen (1936-), with Tom Carter. Rhinestone Cowboy. New York: Villard Books, 1994. 253 p.
Card, Michael. "Can't Buy Me Ministry," *Christianity Today*, May 20, 1996.
Cash, Johnny. *Man in Black*. Grand Rapids: Zondervan, 1975. 244 p.
Christensen, Pete. *Musical Chairs: Bandstand Exposed*. 1996. 248 p.
Cloud, David Wayne (1949-). *Contemporary Christian Music Under the Spotlight*. Oak Harbor, WA: Way of Life Literature, 1998. 450 p.
Cooley, Lindell (1963-). *A Touch of Glory*. Shippensburg, PA: Revival Press, 1997. 165 p.
Coppernoll, Christopher L. (1963-). *Soul 2 Soul*. Nashville: Word Publishing, 1998. 233 p.
Crouch, Andrae, with Nina Ball. *Through It All*. Word Books.
Cusic, Don. *Sandi Patti: The Voice of the Gospel*. New York: Doubleday, 1988. 226 p.
———. *The Sound of Light: A History of Gospel Music*. Bowling Green, OH: Bowling Green State University Popular Press, 1990. 267 p.
Ellsworth, Donald Paul. *Christian Music in Contemporary Witness*. Grand Rapids: Baker Book House, 1979.
Fisher, Tim. *The Battle for Christian Music*. Greenville, SC: Sacred Music Services, 1992. 211 p.
———. *Harmony at Home*. Greenville, SC: Sacred Music Services, 1999. 203 p.
Frame, John M. (1939-). *Contemporary Worship Music: A Biblical Defense*. Phillipsburg, NJ: P&R Publishing, 1997. 212 p.
Franklin, Kirk. *Church Boy: My Music and My Life*. Nashville: Word Publishing, 1998. 232 p.
Garlock, Frank. *The Big Beat*. Greenville, SC: Bob Jones University Press, 1971. 54 p.
———. *Jesus Christ Superstar: Blessing or Blasphemy?* Greenville, SC: Bob Jones University Press, 1972.
———. *The Language of Music*. Greenville, SC: Majesty Music.
———, and Kurt Woetzel. *Music in the Balance*. Greenville, SC: Majesty Music, 1992. 204 p.

———. *The Symphony of Life Seminar*. Greenville, SC: Majesty Music, 1973.
Godwin, Jeff. *What's Wrong with Christian Rock?* Chino, CA: Chick Publications, 1990. 287 p.
Green, Keith. *Can God Use Rock Music?* Linsdale, TX: Last Days Ministries, 1982.
Green, Melody, and David Hazard. *No Compromise: The Life Story of Keith Green*. Chatsworth, CA: Sparrow Press, 1989. 290 p.
Hart, Lowell. *Satan's Music Exposed*. Chattanooga, TN: AMG Publishers, 1981. 187 p.
Hooper, William Lloyd (1931-). *Church Music in Transition*. Nashville: Broadman Press, 1963.
Ives, Alan. *The Difference Between Good and Bad Music*. Oak Harbor, WA: Way of Life Literature, 1993. 23 p.
Johansson, Carl. *Music and Ministry: A Biblical Counterpoint*.
Joseph, Mark (1968-). *The Rock & Roll Rebellion: Why people of faith abandoned rock music and why they're coming back*. Nashville: Broadman & Holman Publishers, 1999. 316 p.
Kaiser, Glenn. *The Responsibility of the Christian Musician*. Chicago: Cornerstone Press, 1994. 74 p.
Kartsoniakis, Dino, with Jeanette Lockerbie. *The Dino Story*. Foreword by Kathryn Kuhlman. Old Tappan, NJ: Fleming H. Revell, 1975. 128 p.
Key, Dana, with Steve Rabey. *Don't Stop the Music*. Grand Rapids: Zondervan, 1989. 155 p.
Larson, Bob (1944-). *Rock and the Church*. Carol Stream, IL: Creation House, 1971. 90 p.
Leggett, Carol. *Amy Grant*. New York, 1987.
Licciardello, Carman. *Absolute Best Videos: Satan: Bite the Dust, A Witch's Invitation, Who's in the House, Revival in the Land, Sunday School Rock, Great God, Addicted to Jesus, America Again*. Brentwood, TN: Sparrow Communications Group, 1998.
Liesch, Barry Wayne (1943-). *The New Worship: Straight talk on music and the church*. Grand Rapids: Baker Books, 1996.
Lynch, Ken. *Biblical Music in a Contemporary World*. Chester, PA: Key Lynch, 1999. 129 p.
———. *Gospel Music: Blessing or Blight?* Chester, PA: Ken Lynch, 4th ed. 1992. 44 p.
Makujina, John. *Measuring the Music: Another Look at the Contemporary Christian Music Debate*. Salem, OH: Schmul Publishing Co., 2000. 303 p.
Menconi, with Dave Hart. *Staying in Tune: A sane response to your child's music*. Cincinatti, OH: Standard Publishing, 1996. 212 p.
Millard, Bob. *Amy Grant*. New York: St. Martin's Griffin, 1986, 1996. 218 p.
Miller, Steve (1957-). *The Contemporary Christian Music Debate: Worldly Compromise or Agent of Renewal?* Waynesboro, GA: OM Literature, 1993. 261 p.
Morrison, Alan. *Open Thou our Lips! The Great Hymn Controversy*. Diakrisis International, 1999. 50 p.
Moser, Stan. , "We Have Created a Monster", *Christianity Today*, May 20, 1996.
Noebel, David A. *Christian Rock: A Strategem of Mephistopheles*. Manitou Springs, CO: Summit Youth Ministries, nd. 31 p.
O'Neill, Dan. *Troubadour for the Lord: The Story of John Michael Talbot*. New York: Crossroad, 1983. 148 p.
Parker, David G. *Music in Our Contemporary Christian Culture*. Greenville, SC: Dimensions in Music, 1997. Audio.
Parks, Bob. *Music: Does It Make Any Difference?* Grand Rapids, MI: Grand Rapids School of the Bible and Music, 1970. 64 p.
Peck, Richard (1934-). *Rock: Making Musical Choices*. Greenville, SC: Bob Jones University, 1985. 164 p.
Peters, Dan, and Steve Peters and Cher Merrill. *What About Christian Rock*. Minneapolis: Bethany House Publishing, 1986.

Peterson, Patrick, and Jane Hertenstein. *More Like the Master: A Christian Musician's Reader.* Chicago: Cornerstone Press, 1996. 140 p.

Pickering, Ernest D. *The Kind of Music that Honors God.* Decatur, AL: Baptist World Mission, nd. 12 p.

Robbins, Larry. *Music: Why We Do It This Way.* Westminster, CO: Tri-City Baptist Church, 1992. 45 p.

Sears, Gordon E. (1922-) *Apostasy and Deception in Christian Music.* Coldwater, MI: Gordon Sears, 1998. 104 p.

———. *Is Today's Christian Music Sacred?* Coldwater, MI: Gordon Sears, nd. 32 p.

Seay, Davin. *Point of Grace: Life love and other mysteries.* New York: Pocket Books, 1996. 222 p.

Seidel, Leonard J. *Face the Music: Contemporary Church Music on Trial.* Foreword by Warren W. Wiersbe. Springfield, VA: Grace Unlimited Productions, 1988. 163 p.

Shea, George Beverly, with Fred Bauer. *Then Sings My Soul.* Old Tappan, NJ: Fleming H. Revell, 1968. 176 p.

Smith, Kimberly. *Let Those Who Have Ears to Hear: If They Took the Music Away...Would You Still Follow Jesus?* Enumclaw, WA: WinePress Publishing, 2001. 202 p.

———, with Lee Smith. *Oh, Be Careful Little Ears: Contemporary Christian Music... Is That in the Bible?* Mukilteo, WA: WinePress Publishing, 1997. 143 p.

Spence, Hubert Talmadge II (1948-). *Confronting Contemporary Christian Music: A Plain Account of Its History, Philosophy, and Future.* Dunn, NC: Companion Press, 1997. 164 p.

Spence, O. Talmadge. *The Lord's Song in a Timely Music Primer.* Dunn, NC: Foundations Bible College, 1997.

Spencer, Ron. *Christian Music in the Light of God's Word.* Richton, MS: Committee for the Preservation of Truth, 1998. 24 p.

Styll, John, ed. *The Best of CCM.* Nashville: Star Song Communications, 1991. 152 p.

Sweatt, Danny M. (1944-). *Church Music: Sense and Nonsense.* Greenville, SC: Bob Jones University Press, 1981. 33 p.

Talbot, John Michael. *The Music of Creation.* New York: Penguin Putnam, 1999. 235 p.

Tripp, LaVerne. *An Offer I Couldn't Refuse: The LaVerne Tripp Story*, as told to Carl Morris. Riverside, CA: LaVerne Tripp Ministries, 1990.

Van Manen, Adrian (1950-). *Their Rock Is Not as Our Rock.* Oklahoma City, OK: Windsor Hills Baptist Church, 1989. 162 p.

Walsh, Sheila (1956-). *Holding on to Heaven with Hell on Your Back.* London: Hodder & Stoughton, 1990. 222 p.

———. *Never Give It Up.* Old Tappan, NJ: Fleming H. Revell, 1986. 141 p.

Woetzel, Kurt. "Is Music Neutral? An Interview with Robert Shaw." *FrontLine*, September-October 1998, pp. 11-12.

Wohlgemuth, Paul W. *Rethinking Church Music.* Carol Stream, Ill.: Hope Pub. Co., 1981.

SACRED MUSIC

Appleby, David. *History of Church Music.* Chicago: Moody Press, 1965.

Austin, Mike. *Liberty Bible Course on Music.* Greenville, MI: Liberty Baptist Church, 1997. 29 p.

Beattie, David J. *The Romance of Sacred Song.* London and Edinburgh: Marshall, Morgan & Scott, 1931.

Berglund, Robert (1930-). *A Philosophy of Church Music.* Chicago: Moody Press, 1985

Best, Harold M. *Music through the Eyes of Faith.* San Francisco: HarperSanFrancisco, 1993.

Blume, Friedrich. *Protestant Church Music*. New York: W.W. Norton, 1974.

Breed, David R. *The History and Use of Hymns and Hymn Tunes*. Tarrytown, NY: Revell, 1903.

Brown, Theron, and Hezekiah Butterworth. *The Story of the Hymns and Tunes*. New York: American Tract Society, 1906. 564 p.

Burrage, Henry Sweetser (1837-1926). *Baptist Hymn Writers and Their Hymns*. Portland, Maine: Brown Thurston & Co., 1888. 682p.

Cusic, Don. *The Sound of Light: A History of Gospel Music*. Bowling Green, OH: Bowling Green State University Popular Press, 1990. 267 p.

Davidson, Archibald T. *Church Music, Illusion and Reality*. Cambridge: Harvard University Press, 1952.

Davies, Walford (1869-1941). *Music and Worship*. London: Eyre and Spottiswoode, 1948.

Delamont, Vic. *The Ministry of Music in the Church*. Chicago: Moody Press, 1980.

Demaray, Donald E. *The Innovation of John Newton: Synergism of word and music in eighteenth century evangelism*. Lewiston: Edwin Mellen Press, 1988.

Etherington, Charles L. *Protestant Worship Music: Its history and practice*. Westport, Conn.: Greenwood Press, 1978.

Foote, Henry Wilder (1875-). *Three Centuries of American Hymnody*. Cambridge, Mass: Harvard University Press, 1940.

Free Church of Scotland. *The Scottish Psalmody*. Inverness: Eccleslitho, 1970.

Gaither Music Company. *The Statesmen with Rosie Rozell*. Alexandria, IN: Gaither Music Company, 1996. Video.

Garlock, Frank. *The Language of Music*. Greenville, SC: Majesty Music.

———, and Kurt Woetzel. *Music in the Balance*. Greenville, SC: Majesty Music, 1992. 204 p.

———. *The Symphony of Life Seminar*. Greenville, SC: Majesty Music, 1973.

Gillman, Frederick J. *The Songs and Singers of Christendom*. London: Headley Brothers, c. 1907. 144 p.

Girardeau, John Lafayette (1825-1898). *Instrumental Music in the Public Worship of the Church*. Still Waters Revivals Books, 1992, reprint of 1888 Whittet & Shepperson edition.

Harrell, Robert Lomas. "A Comparison of Secular Elements in the Chorales of Martin Luther with Rock Elements in Church Music of the 1960's and 1970's." M.A. Thesis, Bob Jones University, 1975.

———. *Martin Luther: His Music, His Message*. Greenville, S.C.: Musical Ministries, 1980.

Hart, D.G. *The Regulative Principle of Worship: Scripture, Tradition, and Culture*. Glenside, PA: Westminster Campus Bookstore, nd. 64 p.

Houghton, Elsie. *Classic Christian Hymn-writers*. Fort Washington, PA: Christian Literature Crusade, 1982, 1992. 348 p.

Hustad, Donald P. *Jubilate: Church music in the evangelical tradition*. Carol Stream: Hope Pub. Co., 1981.

Jefferson, H.A.L. *Hymns in Christian Worship*. New York: The Macmillian Co., 1950.

Johansson, Calvin M. *Music and Ministry*. Peabody, Mass.: Hendrickson Publishers, 1984.

Julian, John. *A Dictionary of Hymnology*. London: John Murray, 1908. 1768 p.

Kerr, Phil. *Music in Evangelism and Stories of Famous Christian Songs*. Grand Rapids: Singspiration, 1962. 216 p.

Kettring, Donald D. *Steps Toward a Singing Church*. Philadelphia: Westminster Press, 1958.

Lovelace, Austin Cole, and William C. Rice. *Music and Worship in the Church*. Nashville: Abingdon Press, 1960.

Maus, Cynthia Pearl (1880-). *Christ and the Fine Arts*. New York, Evanston: Harper & Row, 1938, 1959. 813 p.

Miller, Ross James (1934-). *John Calvin and the Reformation of Church Music in the Sixteenth Century.* Ph.D. thesis. Claremont Graduate School, 1970.

Montell, William Lynwood. *Singing the Glory Down: Amateur Gospel Music in South Central Kentucky 1900-1990.* Lexington, KY: University Press of Kentucky. 248 p.

Morsch, Vivian Sharp. *The Use of Music in Christian Education.* Philadelphia: Westminster Press, 1956.

Ninde, Edward S. *The Story of the American Hymn.* Nashville, TN: Abingdon, 1921.

Osbeck, Kenneth W. *The Ministry of Music.* Grand Rapids: Kregel Publications, 1961. 192 p.

Patrick, Millar. *The Story of the Church's Song.* Richmond, VA: John Knox Press, 1972.

Pickering, Ernest D. *The Kind of Music that Honors God.* Decatur, AL: Baptist World Mission, nd. 12 p.

Quasten, Johannes (1900-). *Music and Worship in Pagan and Christian Antiquity.* Washington D.C.: National Association of Pastoral Musicians, 1983.

Reeves, Francis Brewster (1836-). *The Evolution of Our Christian Hymnology.* Philadelphia: John C. Winston Co., 1912.

Rodeheaver, Homer Alvan (1880-). *Awakening Songs: for the church, Sunday school and evangelistic services.* Chicago: Rodeheaver Co., nd.

Rookmaaker, Hendrik Roelof (1922-1977). *Jazz, Blues, Spirituals.* Wageningen: Zomer & Keuning, 1960.

Rothwell, Helen. *Sankey: The Singer and His Song.* Belfast, Ireland: Ambassador Productions, 1946,1996. 61 p.

Routley, Erik (1917-). *Church Music and the Christian Faith.* Carol Stream: Agape Publishers, 1978.

———. *Church Music and Theology.* London: SMC Press, 1959.

———. *The Music of Christian Hymnody: A study of the development of the hymn tune since the Reformation.* London: Independent Press, 1957.

———. *Twentieth Century Church Music.* New York: Oxford University Press, 1966.

Ryden, Ernest Edwin. *The Story of Christian Hymnody.* Philadelphia: Fortress Press, 1959. 670 p.

Sallee, James. *A History of Evangelistic Hymnody.* Grand Rapids: Baker Book House, 1978.

Smith, Henry Augustine (1874-1952). *Lyric Religion: The Romance of Immortal Hymns.* New York: The Century Co., 1931. 517 p.

Squire, Russell Nelson (1908-). *Church Music: Musical and hymnological developments in Western Christianity.* St. Louis: Bethany Press, 1962.

Stevenson, Arthur Linwood (1891-). *The Story of Southern Hymnology.* New York: AMS Press, 1931.

Stevenson, Robert Murrell. *Protestant Church Music in America.* New York: W.W. Norton, 1966.

Sweatt, Danny M. (1944-). *Church Music: Sense and Nonsense.* Greenville, SC: Bob Jones University Press, 1981. 33 p.

Sydnor, James Rawlings. *The Hymn and Congregational Singing.* Richmond: John Knox Press, 1960.

Taylor, Richard M. *The Disciplined Lifestyle.* Minneapolis: Bethany Fellowship, 1973.

Terry, Lindsay. *Lindsay Terry and Church Music.* Murfreesboro, TN: Sword of the Lord, 1979. 112 p.

Urang, Gunnar. *Church Music for the Glory of God.* Moline: Christian Service Foundation, 1956.

Westermeyer, Paul (1940-). *Te Deum: The Church and Music.* Minneapolis: Fortress Press, 1988. 412 p.

Wilson, John F. *An Introduction to Church Music*. Chicago: Moody Press, 1965.
Wilson-Dickson, Andrew. *The Story of Christian Music*. Minneapolis: Fortress Press, 1996. 256 p.
Wohlgemuth, Paul W. *Rethinking Church Music*. Carol Stream, Ill.: Hope Pub. Co., 1981.

SONG LEADING

Attaway, Steve. *Beginning Song Leading Techniques*. Argyle, TX: At-A-Boy Productions.
Beebe, Wally & Winifred. *All about the Church Music Director*. Murfreesboro, TN: Sword of the Lord Publishers, 1998. 109 p.
Carnett, E.L. *Technique of Conducting*. Nashville: Broadman Press, 1948. 88 p.
Dodson, Bryan. *Correspondence Music Course*. Hunlock Creek, PA: Generations Baptist Mission.
Gehrkens. *Essentials in Conducting*. Bryn Mawr, PA: Presser Company.
Gordon, Lewis. *Choral Director's Rehearsal and Performance Guide*. West Nyack, NY: Parker Publishing Co.
Lehman, Glenn. *You Can Lead Singing: A Song Leader's Manual*. Seattle, WA: Amazon Books.
Lindsay, Terry. *Lindsay Terry and Church Music: A Manual for Choir Members, Music Directors and Pastors*. Rowlett, TX: Forward Leadership Resources.
Osbeck, Kenneth W. *The Ministry of Music*. Grand Rapids: Kregel Publications.
Rodeheaver, Homer. *Song Leadership*.
School of Tomorrow. *Soft ACE Music Course*. Lewisville, TX: School of Tomorrow.
Scovill, Don. *Song Leading and Church Music*. Lattimore, NC: Ambassador Baptist College.
Swan Productions. *How to Direct Music*. Murfreesboro, TN: Swan Productions.
Urang. *Church Music for the Glory of God*. Moline, IL: Christian Service Foundation.
Willetts, Sandra (1943-). Upbeat Downbeat: Basic Conducting Patterns and Techniques. Nashville: Abingdon Press, 1993. 78 p.
Woodard, Don. *Song Leading Video and Workbook*. Rock Hill, SC: Don Woodard.

SOUTHERN GOSPEL

Cloud, David Wayne (1949-). *Contemporary Christian Music under the Spotlight*. Oak Harbor, WA: Way of Life Literature, 1998. 450 p.
Collins, Ace. *Turn Your Radio On: The stories behind gospel music's all-time greatest songs*. Grand Rapids: Zondervan, 1999. 269 p.
Cusic, Don. *The Sound of Light: A History of Gospel Music*. Bowling Green, OH: Bowling Green State University Popular Press, 1990. 267 p.
Davis, Paul. *The Legacy of the Blackwood Brothers: Authorized Biographies of Cecil and James Blackwood*. Greenville, SC: Blue Ridge Publishing, 2000. 200 p.
Dennis, Allen, ed. *James Blackwood Memories*. Memphis: Quail Ridge Press, 1997. 192 p.
Gaither, William J., with Jerry Jenkins. *I Almost Missed the Sunset: My Perspectives on Life and Music*. Nashville: Thomas Nelson, 1992. 214 p.
———. *Homecoming: The Story of Southern Gospel Music through the Eyes of Its Best-Loved Performers*. Grand Rapids: Zondervan, 1997. 217 p.
Gaither, Gloria. *Because He Lives*. Grand Rapids: Zondervan 1997. 224 p.
Goodman, Vestal, with Ken Abraham. *Vestal*. Colorado Springs, CO: Waterbrook Press, 1998. 290 p.

Heilbut, Tony. *The Gospel Sound: Good News and Bad Times*. New York: Simon and Schuster, 1971.

Hess, Jake, with Richard Hyatt. *Nothin' But Fine: The Music and the Gospel According to Jake Hess*. Columbus, GA: Buckland Press, 1996. 256 p.

Lane, Christy. *One Day at a Time*. Madison, TN: LS Records, 1983. 288 p.

Morris, Carl. *An Offer I Couldn't Refuse: The LaVerne Tripp Story*. Publisher unknown.

Widner, Ellis, and Walter Carter. *The Oak Ridge Boys: Our Story*. Chicago, New York: Contemporary Books, 1987. 212 p.

Oldham, Doug, with Fred Bauer. *I Don't Live There Anymore*. Nashville: Impact Books, 1973. 192 p.

Oldham, Laura Lee and Doug. *There Is Hope*. Grand Rapids: Fleming H. Revell, 1996. 192 p.

Payne, Glen, and George Younce. *The Cathedrals: The Story of America's Best-Loved Gospel Quartet*. Grand Rapids: Zondervan, 1998. 211 p.

Rambo, Buck, as told to Bob Terrell. *The Legacy of Buck and Dottie Rambo*. Nashville: Star Song, 1992. 192 p.

Spence, Hubert Talmadge II (1948-). *Confronting Contemporary Christian Music: A Plain Account of Its History, Philosophy, and Future*. Dunn, NC: Companion Press, 1997. 164 p.

Sumner, J.D., with Bob Terrell. *Gospel Music Is My Life*. See Terrell, *The Life and Times of J.D. Sumner*.

Taylor, David L. (1952-). *Happy Rhythm: A Biography of Hovie Lister & the Statesmen Quartet*. Lexington, IN: TaylorMade Write, 1994. 145 p.

Terrell, Bob. *The Life and Times of J.D. Sumner*. Nashville: J.D. Sumner, 1994. 269 p.

———. *The Music Men: The Story of Professional Gospel Quartet Singing*. Boone, NC: Bob Terrell Publisher, 1990. 332 p.

———. *What A Wonderful Time: The Story of the Inspirations*. Alexander, NC: Mountain Church, 2000. 335 p.

Tripp, LaVerne. *An Offer I Couldn't Refuse: The LaVerne Tripp Story as Told to Carl Morris*. Riverside, CA: LaVerne Tripp, 1990. 138 p.